VOLUME TWO

BIBLICAL THEOLOGY

NEW TESTAMENT

BIBLICAL THEOLOGY

VOLUME TWO
NEW TESTAMENT

By Chester K. Lehman

HERALD PRESS, SCOTTDALE, PENNSYLVANIA

BIBLICAL THEOLOGY: NEW TESTAMENT
Copyright © 1974 by Herald Press, Scottdale, Pa. 15683
Library of Congress Catalog Card Number: 74-141829
International Standard Book Number: 0-8361-1725-5
Printed in the United States

To my students of
Theology of the New Testament
Who through the past years have inspired me with
Their interest and enthusiasm in this course.

PREFACE

The preface in the first volume stated in a general way the fundamental viewpoint, method of approach, and purpose, which also underlie this volume. Just as the Old Testament revealed a structure of God's progressive revelation, so the New Testament discloses an unfolding of divine truth which serves as a foundation for a culminating presentation of God's revelation to mankind. Even though the time element of this new era of revelation is less than a century, as compared with the three or more millenniums of Old Testament revelation, a progress of unfolding truth is clearly evident. While the chronological order of the New Testament books does not have great significance, the grouping of these writings as to authorship and subject matter does give a clear structure of this new body of God's revelation. Note the life and teachings of Jesus as presented in the four Gospels; the account in Acts of the origin and early history of the church; the letters to the churches by James, Peter, Paul, the author of Hebrews, Jude, and John; and finally, the Revelation to John.

The order of presentations of these teachings in a biblical theology structure presents some real problems. First, we need to see the order of events such as the teachings of Jesus viewed in their historical setting, the evangelizing activities of the apostolic church leaders, and the rise of the new body of writings — the New Testament. Second, the doctrinal content of the teachings of Jesus and the apostles needs to be grasped. Third, the structuring of these teachings as they set forth God's unfolding revelation and mark the final disclosure of truth to mankind, difficult as it is, manifests the distinctive nature and values of New Testament biblical theology.

I have structured the contents of this volume so that it will serve as a guide to the reader in grasping the mode of approach to this discipline. We also need to become aware of such factors as the distinctive message of each gospel writer (Part One, Chapter III), methods of approach to Pauline theology (Part Three, Chapter I), Paul's teachings on the Holy Scriptures (Part Three, Chapter IX), the use of the Old Testament by the author of Hebrews (Part Four, Chapter I, No. 7), John's use of the Scriptures (Part Four, Chapter II, No. 13), and other components.

It is in order at this point that we understand the special values of biblical theology as a way of approach to the study of the New Testament. First, the matchless accounts of the early life and ministry of Jesus Christ our Lord. Each Gospel record possesses distinctive values. Second, Jesus' teachings and miracles interpret for us His incarnation, suffering, death, resurrection, and ascension. Third, the fulfillment of Old Testament predictions, centering in the person and work of our Lord and the outpouring of the Holy Spirit, give untold meaning to the nature and content of the New Testament. Fourth, the eschatological viewpoint of the New Testament leads to a true understanding of world affairs and of how God is directing the course of world history.

As in the first volume I have arranged the contents in such a way as to present the structural pattern of the book. This should serve as a guide to the reader in understanding the distinctive nature of biblical theology as a theological discipline. At the close of each chapter I have appended a limited bibliography for additional reading and reference, by which the reader can broaden his approach to the chapter contents. Also at the close of the volume I have appended selected bibliographies under ten headings. These should enable the reader to gain access to additional treatments of this theological discipline.

The reader may desire to read the Preface to Volume One for some additional suggestions, ideas, and convictions which served as a guide to my thinking in the preparation of this volume also.

I desire to express special appreciation and thanks to Dr. J. C. Wenger for the contribution he made to this work by way of detailed corrections, comments, and suggestions which he made on the manuscript. I shall not forget his red pencil markings, which could not escape my attention or be erased.

To my wife I am indebted for her untiring labor in typing the manuscript. She made many corrections in style and grammar and also gave many helpful suggestions for improvement.

Conscious of the Holy Spirit's guidance and direction I am praying that this volume may be of value to all who are seeking to know of God's unfolding revelation in the New Testament. As I said in Volume One, "I have sought to prepare it for as wide as possible use. It should be sufficiently comprehensive and deep for seminary students and graduates. Technical problems of literary criticism, linguist inquiries, and philosophical approaches have been held to a minimum so that the book should be serviceable to upper-level students in colleges and Bible schools. Ministers who have not had the opportunity of securing advanced biblical training, and others who are devoting themselves to serious Bible study should also be able to use the book with profit."

INTRODUCTION

The New Testament, or new covenant, stands as the full Word of God in Jesus Christ. Dr. Chester K. Lehman in his second volume of *Biblical Theology* writes with a high view of Scripture, a high Christological theology, and a Christocentric hermeneutic. True to his Anabaptist faith, seeing the whole Bible as the Word of God written, he sees the New Testament on a higher level than the Old Testament as God's full Word in Christ.

This approach to the Scripture, seeing two levels between the Testaments, is to affirm that all the way through the Old Testament God had something more to say until He said it finally in Jesus Christ. It is the conviction that Jesus Christ is God in the flesh which affirms that the full Word of God is known in Christ. Contrary to some Bible students, Dr. Lehman does not believe that the high Christology of St. Paul and St. John was superimposed upon a simple humanitarian message of Jesus of Nazareth. Dr. Lehman regards the revelation of Christ to be the revelation of His total life, what He said, what He did, and what He was, all expressing the Word of God.

The quest for the historical Jesus has moved from seeking His historical character in the Gospels as biographical data to a new quest in which His person and character is sought in the Gospels as kerygma or proclamation. We now see the four Gospels as examples of early church preaching or announcing the good news of the life and meaning of Jesus Christ. The differences between the accounts in the Gospels are to be understood as different facets of the story of Christ, of announcing of the kerygma. This does not minimize the historicity of Jesus Christ, but it says that the larger meanings of the Christo-event are expressed in the story. Dr. Lehman's approach is valid when he interprets the Gospels by their themes of biblical theology and seeing them in their highest expression in Jesus Christ.

While regarding the New Testament Scripture as fully inspired and as the Word of God written, Dr. Lehman does not see the four Gospels at a higher level than the epistles. The nature of the kerygma and the full development of the theological understandings of the person of Christ is both confirmed and expanded by such great passages as Philippians 2, Colossians 1, the Epistles to the Romans and to the Hebrews. The author's treatment of the Book of Acts and the epistles indicates the continuing work of the Holy Spirit to interpret Jesus Christ as risen Lord, verifying the resurrection power and authority of Jesus Christ in the transformation of lives and in the building of the church.

This volume is the result of years of study and of significant scholarship evidenced in classroom teaching at Eastern Mennonite College and Seminary, Harrisonburg, Virginia. Dr. Lehman is a theologian of distinction, and a scholar whose writings carefully express his theological interpretation of the Scripture, revealing a deep conviction of the grand unity of the whole. Having retired from basic classroom assignments he continues his interaction with faculty and students at Eastern Mennonite College and Seminary, a relationship deeply appreciated. We are especially grateful for his diligence in completing this volume, sharing his theological insights and his deep commitment to Jesus Christ as Lord.

It is most fitting that a Mennonite/Anabaptist theologian should prepare a biblical theology as a scholarly expression of the nature of Mennonite biblicism. Under the anointing of the Spirit this work can and will be a blessing to both church leaders and laymen who want to hear God's Word for our time. Jesus is Lord, the Lord of Scripture, the Lord of history, and the Lord for all who will believe.

Myron S. Augsburger
President, Eastern Mennonite College
and Eastern Mennonite Seminary

CONTENTS

CHAPTER I

THE STRUCTURE OF NEW TESTAMENT REVELATION

1. Introduction

A theology of the New Testament encounters first of all a problem of structure. Some elements of this problem appear (1) in the character of this body of writings as composed of records of the life and teachings of Christ, the record of apostolic history, the letters of the apostles and others, and the apocalypse of John (2) in the time element of the appearance of these books, arising chiefly during the two decades from about AD 50 to AD 68, together with the Johannine books from the tenth decade; and (3) in the source of these writings, the living church.

All these factors need to be recognized if a structure is to arise from an inductive approach to this literature. Already in the Old Testament we receive intimations or basic ideas relating to the structure of the revelation in the age to come, that of the New Testament. Let us examine briefly what may be gained already from the Old Testament as to the structure of the new body of revelation.

2. The Structure of New Testament Revelation as Forecast in the Old Testament

One of the leading characteristics of the Old Testament is its eschatological outlook. As early as in the account of Creation, writers pointed to something better to take place in the future. Implicit in the absence of a statement such as, "And there was evening and there was morning, a seventh day," which would be expected after Genesis 2:3, is the idea that God's work of creation had not ceased. In the future He would again create. This took form in the definite prediction, "Behold, I create new heavens and a new earth; and the former things shall not be remembered" (Is. 65:17).

Another sample of this forward look in the Old Testament is found in Genesis 3:15, when God said, "I will put enmity between you and the woman, and between your seed and her seed; he shall bruise your head, and you shall bruise his heel." He would have Eve look forward to some future time when this would be accomplished. In a very real way the entire Old Testament is a revelation dealing with this forward look expressed in the promise to Eve.

The eschatological aspect of God's promises to Abraham was plainly evident (Gen. 12:1-3; 15:5; 17:6-8). These promises led Abraham and his descendants to look forward to the time when his people would become a great nation, and when all families of the earth would be blessed. They became a determining factor throughout Israel's history and gave the pattern for the structure of New Testament revelation.

This forward look was unfolded further in God's covenant with Israel at Mt. Sinai (Ex. 19:4-6; 24:3-11). In this God revealed Himself as the covenant-making God. He was carrying forward the covenant made with Abraham by way of a new covenant to be made with the people of Israel. It is quite certain that God's chosen people did not see the limitations in their covenant relationship with God. It would seem that the devout Israelites would naturally long for a covenant relationship with God that would do away with repeated bloody sacrifices. It is not surprising, then, that the prophet Jeremiah near the close of Old Testament history looked forward to a new era. He was privileged to quote God as saying: "I will make a new covenant with the house of Israel and the house of Judah" (Jer. 31:31). Elements of the superiority of this new covenant are found in the spiritual character of its laws being written upon the hearts of the people rather than on tables of stone and that God would forgive their iniquity and no more remember their sins. Other prophets declared that this new covenant would be an everlasting covenant and also a covenant of peace (Is. 55:3; 61:8; Ezek. 16:60; 34:25).

The most remarkable characteristic of the coming new era centered in a person. One strand of predictions concerning this Person portrayed His *kingly* work, the earliest traces of which are found in Jacob's promise to Judah concerning a Descendant who would wield a scepter and of Balaam's predictions of a kingly Descendant in Israel, advancing to an anointed One of the Lord (Ps. 2), who would reign forever. [1] Undoubtedly the author of Psalm 2 picked up these isolated strands of a kingly One to come and spoke of Him as the anointed of the Lord, the Messiah. Later prophets laid hold of this prophecy and centered in Him all the predictions of the future age. Another strand of this forward look centered in the Prophet whom God would raise up like unto Moses (Deut. 18:15, 18). The preeminence of this coming Prophet lay in the fact that He would be like Moses, whom the Lord knew face-to-face.

A third prophetic strand concerning the One to come centered in the

Servant of the Lord (Is. 40 — 66). This most extraordinary Person, spoken of in Isaiah 40 — 66 bore the characteristics of a priest, in fact, more than a priest. The sublime language of Isaiah 52:13 — 53:12 featured Him as the suffering Servant, the sacrifice provided by God for man's sin. In a very special way, the Spirit of the Lord God would rest upon Him. He would have the special task of bringing good tidings to mankind and of proclaiming the year of the Lord's favor (Is. 61:1-3). The Old Testament did not identify this Servant of the Lord with the King and Prophet whom God would raise up. Nevertheless, the prediction is clear that in the coming era this Servant of the Lord would appear; the Spirit of the Lord God would be upon Him; He would proclaim the gospel; and He would announce the acceptable year of the Lord. Above all, He would make Himself an offering for sin.

Another great theme centering in Old Testament predictions of the coming era related to the outpouring of God's Spirit upon all flesh. It is significant that the prophet Joel located this act of God in an era following the day of the Lord. Peter spoke of this time as *the last days*. Thus the prophets clearly marked off a coming age having its beginning after the imminent day of the Lord, in which God would overthrow Jerusalem extending to a future age which came to be known as the *days of the Messiah*. Peter's expression *the last days* suggested that this is the culminating age of the world (2 Pet. 3:3). All previous history looks forward to this era. According to Joel, the pouring out of God's Spirit upon all flesh earmarks the age. Isaiah identified the time when the Spirit is poured upon his people as that in which a King will reign in righteousness (Is. 32:1, 15; cf. 59:20, 21). In similar contexts the prophet Ezekiel quoted God as saying, "I will put my Spirit within you" (Ezek. 36:25-27; 37:11-14; 39:29). Note how he pointed up the inner spiritual change which will take place in those in whom God puts His Spirit.

The significant use of the word *new* in these Scriptures can hardly escape our attention. In the language of Vos, "The term *new* emerges in a semiconscious manner, as it were, to give expression to the contrast to what is and what shall be." [2]

With these forward-looking Scriptures in view, the Old Testament predictions of the coming age become quite clear and distinct. The finality and organic unity of this impending era of revelation are evident. It is a period of time which lies beyond the imminent day of the Lord. It is defined as *the last days*, or *the latter days*, and will be the culminating age of the world. Structurally, this coming age is monolithic. Its unifying factor is the coming anointed One, who is at once Prophet, Priest, and King, the incomparable Son of God. Since God knows Him face-to-face, He will speak the words of God. He will institute a new covenant in His own blood. He will take His seat on the restored throne of David, even at the right hand of God.

3. The New Testament Structural Pattern Revealed by Jesus

According to the Gospel of Mark, Jesus opened His ministry with the words, "The time is fulfilled, and the kingdom of God is at hand; repent, and believe in the gospel" (Mk. 1:15). This expression, "the time is fulfilled," referred to the period between the predicted judgment of the day of the Lord and the beginning of *the last days*. The kingdom of God being at hand marked the beginning of the new era, and the preaching of the gospel was witness to this fact. In another context (Mt. 11:12-14; Lk. 7:28, 29) Jesus made a very significant distinction between the Old and the New by sayng, "The law and the prophets were until John; since then the good news of the kingdom of God is preached" (Lk. 16:16). He identified this new era by declaring that John is the messenger preceding the Lord, and also the Elijah who was to come (Mal. 3:1; 4:5).

Another structural pattern revealed by Jesus is found in His bisection of the ages of the world. He spoke of this age and of the age to come.[3] From these Scriptures we learn that the present age is temporal and the age to come is eternal. The present age is the time of Christ's kingdom, and the age to come, that of the Father. The dividing line between the two is the time when "The Son of man will send his angels, and they will gather out of his kingdom all causes of sin and all evildoers" (Mt. 13:41). This will be the judgment which will take place at Christ's return, when He will sit on His glorious throne to judge all mankind (Mt. 16:28; 25:31-46).

Jesus made another significant statement when He said, "In the new world, when the Son of man shall sit on his glorious throne, you who have followed me will also sit on twelve thrones, judging the twelve tribes of Israel" (Mt. 19:28). The Greek work *palingenesia,* translated *new age,* carries the meanings *renewal, restoration,* and *regeneration.* According to Cremer, "The word may also be taken in a still deeper, more comprehensive sense, noting the restoration of all things to their former state."[4] Cremer holds that this word is equivalent to *apokatastasis* (*restoration*), the verb form of which was used by the disciples in their question, "Lord, will you at this time *restore* the kingdom to Israel?" (Acts 1:6). Speaking about Jesus, Peter said, "Whom heaven must receive until the time for *establishing [apokatastasis]* all that God spoke by the mouth of his holy prophets from of old" (Acts 3:21). If Cremer is correct in identifying *palingenesia* with *apokatastasis,* then Christ and Peter were speaking of the same era of time, which in Peter's message refers to the times of refreshing which come from the presence of the

Lord. This is a clear reference to Christ's return, showing how Christ made a distinction between *the present age* and *the age to come.*

The last incident in which Jesus gave a structural pattern of New Testament revelation centered in the institution of the Lord's Supper. "This cup," Jesus said, "is the new covenant in my blood" (Lk. 22:20). This statement, seen in the light of Jeremiah's prediction, marks the beginning of the new age, that of the Messiah. As the old covenant instituted the theocracy, the rule of God, so the new covenant instituted the Christocracy, the rule of Christ. Christ then declared, "I will not drink henceforth of this fruit of the vine, until that day when I drink it new with you in my Father's kingdom" (Mt. 26:29, KJV). With these words Jesus was spanning the time from the institution of the new covenant, which marked the beginning of His reign, on to the time of His Father's kingdom, which, according to Jesus' interpretation of the parable of the wheat and the tares, would begin at the end of this age.

The structural pattern of New Testament revelation as given by Jesus should now be clear. The Old Testament order of things as found in the law and the prophets terminated with John the Baptist. Since then the good news of the kingdom of God is preached. Jesus mapped out the future in two ages: the present age, temporal in character, and the age to come, which is eternal. The making of the new covenant inaugurated the present age. It marked the beginning of His messianic reign, which will continue until the end of this age, when He shall return to consummate His kingdom in the judgment and to hand all things over to the Father.

4. The Structural Pattern of New Testament Revelation as Found in Christ's Exaltation to Messianic Kingship

Jesus' last words spoken to the disciples before His ascension were significant in preparing them for the meaning of the Pentecost experience. He spoke to them concerning the kingdom of God; and in connection with this, He said that they were soon to be baptized with the Holy Spirit. But the disciples were still looking for a literal restoration of the kingdom to Israel. In response to their question on this matter Jesus said, "It is not for you to know times or seasons which the Father has fixed by his own authority. But you shall receive power when the Holy Spirit has come upon you; and you shall be my witnesses in Jerusalem and in all Judea and Samaria and to the end of the earth" (Acts 1:7, 8). This conversation was very significant for our purpose. While we do not know specifically the content of Jesus' words concerning the kingdom of God, undoubtedly it was climactic in leading the disciples to see the meaning of the kingdom of God in the light of His resurrection and in the coming of the Holy Spirit. Jesus brushed aside the disciples' hope for a literal restoration of Israel's kingdom. Instead, He pointed to the coming of the Holy Spirit and of the disciples' worldwide mission as Christ's witnesses. From the standpoint of the structure of New Testament theology, we are thus prepared to think of the life and teachings of Jesus as a separate division from that which followed His resurrection and ascension. We are led to anticipate an explanation of Christ's work by the apostles in the light of the coming experience of the pouring out of the Holy Spirit.

The spectacular experience of the pouring out of the Holy Spirit at Pentecost required explanation. As might be expected, Peter became the interpreter of this very extraordinary event. He at once identified this experience as the fulfillment of Joel's prediction. Peter declared that they were then in *the last days* spoken of by Joel, the prophet. He accounted for the outpouring of the Holy Spirit as the work of the risen and glorified Jesus. Exalted at the right hand of God and being given all power and authority, Jesus had begun His mediatorial kingship. His first work as the reigning Messiah was the pouring out of the Holy Spirit upon all flesh. By this act all Israel could know that God had made Him both Lord and Christ. This act, then, marked a new era in the work of Christ.

On the occasion of the healing of the lame man (Acts 3), Peter spoke further on the work of Christ: "God glorified his servant Jesus" (v. 13). In this expression Peter identified Jesus with the Servant of the Lord. The new era in the life of the Servant of the Lord was His glorification. By way of explanation, Peter noted that Christ's suffering was foretold by the prophets. He exhorted the Jews to repent so that times of refreshing might come from the presence of the Lord. There is an evident connection between this context and that of Jesus when He spoke of the new world when He would sit on His glorious throne (Mt. 19:28). Peter brought his message to a fitting close by noting that all the prophets had spoken of these days (Acts 3:24). The promise made to Abraham that in his posterity all families of the earth would be blessed had been fulfilled (v. 25).

Peter gave another very significant summary of the work of Christ in his conversation with Cornelius and his companions. In this encounter the structural pattern of New Testament revelation again becomes clear. God had anointed Jesus of Nazareth with the Holy Spirit and with power. He went about doing good and healed all that were oppressed of the devil, for God was with Him. The Jews had put Christ to death but God raised Him on the third day and made Him manifest. God ordained this One to be Judge of the living and the dead (Acts

10:38-42). In these words Peter again pointed to the grand bisection between our Lord's earthly ministry and His messianic glory.

5. Paul's Explication of the Structural Pattern of New Testament Revelation

Paul's first reference to a structural pattern of New Testament revelation is found in his sermon at Antioch of Pisidia (Acts 13:23-29). After tracing Israel's history to the time of David, Paul declared that God had brought to Israel a Savior, Jesus, as He had promised. He declared further that to them, as sons of Abraham, had been sent the message of this salvation. The Jews who lived at the time of Jesus did not recognize Him nor understand the utterances of the prophets which they fulfilled in the condemnation of Jesus. This Jesus whom they crucified God raised from the dead. These events were the foundation for the good news which God had promised to the fathers and had fulfilled in raising Jesus from the dead. Paul clinched his point by quoting from Psalm 2; Isaiah 55:3; and Psalm 16:10. In his defense before Agrippa (Acts 26:16-18, 22, 23), Paul referred to Jesus' words to him at the time of his conversion in which the Lord commissioned him in the language of Isaiah 42:7, 16. Thus in fulfillment of a Servant of the Lord passage Paul was commissioned "to open their eyes, that they may turn from darkness to light and from the power of Satan to God" (Acts 26:18). On this basis Paul was making clear that he was saying nothing but what the prophets and Moses said would come to pass in the death and resurrection of Christ, which laid the foundation for his proclaiming light both to the people and to the Gentiles. In this manner Paul built the time of the preaching of the gospel directly on what had been foretold by Moses and the prophets.

Repeatedly in the Letter to the Romans, Paul structured New Testament revelation as the fulfillment of Old Testament predictions. Thus Paul stated that Hosea had in mind both Jews and Gentiles when he wrote, "Those who were not my people I will call 'my people,' and her who was not beloved I will call 'my beloved' " (Rom. 9:25). See Rom. 9:22-26; Hos. 2:23; 1:10. In this quotation from Hosea it is evident that the prophet was looking forward to a new era, in which apostate Israel would again become God's people and His beloved. Later in the book, Paul indicated that the prophets Isaiah and Jeremiah had predicted the extension of salvation to Jews and Gentiles.[5] The Deliverer had come to Zion and was banishing ungodliness from Jacob. The new covenant had been made. Still another chain of Old Testament quotations occurs in Romans 15:7-13,[6] in which predictions were given concerning the offer of salvation to the Gentiles. Most climactic is the statement,

"The root of Jesse shall come, he who rises to rule the Gentiles; in him shall the Gentiles hope" (Rom. 15:12). Thus Paul showed that the era of salvation for the Gentiles would come when "the root of Jesse" would ascend to His throne.

Paul enlarged on the structure of the New Testament revelation when he showed the vast superiority of the new covenant over the old. The new is written in the Spirit. The Spirit gives life, while the old covenant showed splendor symbolized by the brightness of Moses' face. But the dispensation of the Spirit is attended with greater splendor, that of the glory of the Lord (2 Cor. 3:4-18). In a similar way Paul developed the contrast between the law and the prophets. God had promised Abraham that in his offspring all nations of the earth would be blessed. The law coming 430 years afterward did not annul the covenant promise. It merely served as a custodian until the offspring, Christ, should come. In this manner Paul showed that the promise fulfilled in Christ had its origin in God's word to Abraham. Structurally, New Testament revelation had its roots in this promise.

Paul followed Christ in viewing Old Testament revelation as looking forward to, and giving the pattern of, the coming revelation in Christ. He also built his revelational structure on Old Testament revelation and elaborated his views of revelation on the foundation already laid by Christ. Observe Paul's references to the making of the new covenant, to the worldwide mission of the gospel, to the work of the Holy Spirit, to the exaltation of Christ to messianic kingship, to the church as the body of Christ, to the division of the last days into the present age and the age to come, and to the Lord's return to raise the dead and to judge the world.

6. The Structure of Revelation According to Hebrews

The author of Hebrews showed his deep insight into the structural pattern of divine revelation. In the opening verses of his letter he wrote, "In many and various ways God spoke of old to our fathers by the prophets; but in these last days he has spoken to us by a Son, whom he appointed the heir of all things, through whom also he created the world" (Heb. 1:1, 2). The words, "God spoke," set forth the character of divine revelation. God's revelation has two major divisions: first that which was spoken by God through the prophets; and second, that which was spoken through His Son. These determine the great time eras of human history. The first is marked by the expression, "of old," and the second by the words, "in these last days." By this language the author of Hebrews identified the era of God's speaking in His Son, as initiating the "last days" spoken of by the prophets. He referred also to the appearing of Christ, "at the end [*sunteleia*] of the age" (9:26). All the ages prior to Christ's appearing prepared for and looked forward to this age which marks the consummation of all ages. In the same context the writer declared that Christ "will appear a second time . . . to save those who are eagerly waiting for him" (9:28).

Fundamental to our understanding of the structure of New Testament revelation is the author's presentation of the work of Jesus in terms of the Old Testament revelation. Jesus became a high priest after the order of Melchizedek (6:20). On this account He became "the surety of a better covenant" (7:22). In fulfillment of Psalm 110:1 this Jesus is now "seated at the right hand of the throne of the Majesty in heaven, a minister in the sanctuary and the true tent which is set up not by man but by the Lord" (8:1, 2). For this reason the tabernacle served as a copy and shadow of the heavenly sanctuary (v. 5). The climax to this structural pattern appears in 10:1-18. Having offered for all time a single sacrifice for sins, Christ sat down at the right hand of God. The Holy Spirit through the prophet Jeremiah had already borne witness to this finished work of Christ which is evident in God's words, "I will remember their sins and their misdeeds no more" (Heb. 10:17).

In a very appropriate closing exhortation and warning the author of Hebrews looked forward to the ultimate cataclysm foretold by God when He promised, "Yet once more I will shake not only the earth but also the heaven" (12:26). The author exhorted his readers in the words, "Let us be grateful for receiving a kingdom that cannot be shaken" (12:28). The author's benediction looks to "the God of peace who brought again from the dead our Lord Jesus, the great shepherd of the sheep, by the blood of the eternal covenant" (13:20). These words capture the great prophetic truths given by the prophets Isaiah, Zechariah, and Ezekiel, evidence again of the New Testament's fulfillment of Old Testament predictions and of the structure of the new revelation.

7. The Structure of Revelation According to 1 and 2 Peter

Peter also gave witness to the structure of the New Testament revelation. He put his finger on the problem encountered by the prophets concerning the sufferings of Christ and the subsequent glory. The prophets seemed to be unable to gain the perspective of the suffering Christ alongside the glorified Christ. With the events of Christ's life culminating in His exaltation, Peter was in position to grasp the true perspective in the light of fulfillment and of later revelation. Peter set forth his understanding of Christ's work by saying, "He was destined before the foundation of the world but was made manifest at the end of the times for your sake" (1 Pet. 1:20). Here then is a structural pattern of divine revelation which had its beginning before the foundation of the world. The manifestation of Christ took place at the *end of the times.* By this language Peter gave further attestation to the eschatological aspect of Old Testament revelation. He viewed Christ's manifestation as the climax of divine revelation because there are no times succeeding the end of the times. But Peter did look forward and declared that Christ "is ready to judge the living and the dead. . . . The end of all things is at hand" (1 Pet. 4:5, 7). He expanded this idea in his second letter by framing his message under the eschatological thesis, the day of the Lord (2 Pet. 3:8-13).

This prophetic theme had already gained tremendous significance among the Old Testament prophets as they foretold the imminent judgment to be brought upon Israel and Judah. Peter's use of the expression in this setting suggests that this theme was not exhausted in these judgments, but they were the beginning of God's judgments which were deeply eschatological in their character and forecast a culminating aspect of the day of the Lord. The destruction of the present world order in Peter's viewpoint precedes the fulfillment of God's promise to create "new heavens and a new earth in which righteousness dwells" (2 Pet. 3:13). Here again Peter built his eschatology on Old Testament predictions, this time on Isaiah 65:17.

8. Summary of New Testament Structural Pattern

The total structural pattern of New Testament revelation should now be apparent. It is exceedingly significant that there is a grand unity among New Testament speakers and writers concerning the structure of this revelation. Needless to say, if such unity did not exist, a systematic treatment of New Testament biblical theology would be impossible.

In the first place we should note that New Testament speakers and writers purposely built their revelation on Old Testament revelation. They structured their messages as the fulfillment of the Old, the culmination of divine revelation. The new revelation confirmed the eschatological outlook of the old. The evidence stands as follows: (1) The *latter days* have begun. (2) These *last days* constitute the age of the Messiah. The teaching ministry of Christ fulfilled the prophetic work of the coming Messiah. The suffering Servant of the Lord fulfilled the priestly aspect of the coming Messiah's work. Christ's exaltation to the throne of David and His sitting at the right hand of God fulfilled the kingly aspect of the coming Messiah. (3) The making of the new covenant climaxed the covenant structure of Old Testament revelation and became the focal point of New Testament revelation. (4) The outpouring of the Holy Spirit structured as taking place in the *latter days* came to fulfillment. It marked the first work of the exalted and reigning Messiah. (5) The acceptable time, the day of salvation, had come. This pointed up the universalism of the offer of salvation in the days of the Messiah. (6) The church constitutes the people of the reigning Christ under the new covenant.

In the second place, the new structural pattern centering in the new covenant has emerged. (1) The law and the prophets terminated with John the Baptist and were succeeded by the kingdom of God in which God spoke in His Son. (2) The work of Christ falls into two divisions: first, His earthly ministry centering in His life, teachings, suffering, death, and resurrection; and second, His work as the reigning Messiah beginning with His exaltation to the right hand of God. The line of cleavage between the two was the institution of the new covenant. (3) The *latter days* fall into two ages: *the present age,* which will be succeeded by the *age to come.* The first is temporal in character, and the second is eternal. A catastrophism will mark the close of this age. Christ will return to raise the dead and to judge the world. The closing act of this consummation will be Christ's delivery of His kingdom over to the Father.

9. Divisions of New Testament Theology

The structural pattern of New Testament revelation has a very definite bearing on the plan of developing a theology of the New Testament. A definite line of cleavage separates the revelation given directly through Christ during His earthly ministry from that mediated by Christ through the apostles. The former examines the life and teachings of Christ culminating in His death and resurrection, while the latter includes the preaching of the Gospel and the teachings of the apostles and other New Testament writers. The Gospel records furnish the material for the former, and the remainder of the New Testament for the latter.

I accept the Gospels as authentic records of the life and teachings of Christ. While they arose out of the church some thirty years after the ascension of Christ, they purport to be historical in character, and we should accept these Gospels as to what they claim to be. I shall deal with this matter more fully in a later chapter.

We will need to observe also that each Gospel writer prepared his record under different situations in the church, and for this reason each Gospel possesses a distinctive theological viewpoint. This too calls for some elaboration in a later chapter.

The revelation mediated by Christ through the apostles also divides itself quite naturally into several parts, such as: the early preaching of the apostles found in Acts 1 to 10; the theology of Paul, based on his preaching and letters; the theology of Peter, James, and Jude, based on their letters; the theology of Hebrews; and finally, the theology of John, based on his writings. The author recognizes a fundamental unity in all this literature and the breakdown of treatment of these parts does not nullify this unity. This division of subject matter seeks to capture the revelation of the New Testament in its unfolding process. Even though the New Testament period of revelation is limited to less than a century in time and the writing of the books is limited to a few decades the unfolding process is very instructive.

For Additional Reading and Reference:

Barr, *Old and New in Interpretation,* pp. 65-102.
Bernard, *The Progress of Doctrine in the New Testament,* pp. 1-29.
Bowman, *Prophetic Realism and the Gospel,* pp. 20-47.
Bruce, F. F., *New Testament Development of Old Testament Themes,* pp. 11-21.
Bultmann, *Theology of the New Testament,* Vol. II, pp. 237-251.
Filson, *Jesus Christ, the Risen Lord,* pp. 9-30.
Hunter, *Introducing New Testament Theology* (scan entire work).
Van Osterzee, *The Theology of the New Testament,* pp. 19-24.
Vos, *Biblical Theology,* pp. 321-327.
Weidner, *Biblical Theology of the New Testament,* Vol. I, pp. 13-27.
Weiss, *Biblical Theology of the New Testament,* Vol. I, pp. 1-42.

1. Gen. 49:10; Num. 23:21; 24:7, 17; 2 Sam. 7:13.
2. Geerhardus Vos, *Biblical Theology — Old and New Testaments* (Grand Rapids: Wm. B. Eerdmans Publishing Co., 1948), p. 321. See Is. 65:17; 66:22; Jer. 31:31; Ezek. 11:19; 36:26.
3. Mt. 12:32; 13:37-43, 49, 50; 19:28, 29; Mk. 10:30; Lk. 18:29, 30.
4. *Biblical-Theological Lexicon of New Testament Greek* (Edinburgh: T. & T. Clark, 1954), p. 151.
5. Rom. 11:20-32; Is. 27:9; 59:20, 21; Jer. 31:33.
6. Ps. 18:49; Deut. 32:43; Ps. 117:1; Is. 11:10.

CHAPTER II

THE SOURCES OF GOSPEL HISTORY

1. Introduction: The Reasons for This Inquiry

A study of the sources of gospel history lies outside the realm of biblical theology, but an examination of these sources soon reveals far-reaching consequences with regard to our understanding of the unfolding process of divine revelation. Questions such as the following need to be considered.

a. Do the New Testament records present an authentic account of the life and teachings of Jesus?

b. What were the purposes of the Gospel writers? Did they seek to present events in the life of Christ with historical accuracy? May we accept the details of their accounts? If we hold that each Gospel writer did not produce a "life of Christ" in the modern concept of historical presentation, does it then follow that the incidents of Jesus' life and His teachings cannot any longer be accepted as historical?

We can become more aware of the nature of the task before us by listing some of the centers of this problem: (a) The nature of the infancy narratives, including the birth of Jesus. (b) The ministry of John the Baptist and of his witness to Jesus. (c) Such crucial events in Jesus' life as His baptism and the voice from heaven, the temptation, the transfiguration, the Last Supper, Gethsemane, the crucifixion, the resurrection, and the ascension. (d) The working of miracles, such as healing the sick, cleansing the lepers, giving sight to the blind, feeding the multitudes, and raising the dead. (e) The teachings of Jesus, including the longer discourses such as the Sermon on the Mount, the kingdom parables, the Olivet discourse and the Upper Room discourses, together with the teaching given incidentally throughout His ministry.

c. What is the bearing of the stated purposes, as well as the implied objectives of the Gospel writers, upon the historicity of their narratives? While the writers of the Gospels of Matthew and Mark did not give stated purposes for their writing, it is clear that each had some well-defined objective in view. Matthew, on the one hand, undoubtedly had a Jewish audience in view and sought to show that Jesus is the Messiah. Mark, on the other hand, having in view, perhaps, Gentile Christians of the Roman world, sought to present Jesus as the Servant of the Lord as proved by the mighty demonstrations of miracle-working, and the great space given to Christ's Passion. Luke wrote very pointedly of his purpose in the opening words of both his Gospel and the Acts. Reserving for a later discussion the details of Luke's testimony, we should note here that Luke was seeking to give a historically accurate account of the facts underlying the Gospel message as given by eyewitnesses. This account had to do with what Jesus had done and taught. This expressed purpose on the part of Luke was not nullified by some of the other significant thrusts of his Gospel, chief of which was undoubtedly the presentation of Jesus as the Son of God and the Savior of the world. The note of universalism of the Gospel is paramount in his writing.

In similar fashion John expressed his purpose in the words, "These are written that you may believe that Jesus is the Christ, the Son of God, and that believing you may have life in his name" (Jn. 20:31). John had devoted much space to presenting the signs which Jesus did in the presence of the disciples. This at once points to the historical character of all that John wrote. The manner in which he opened his first letter confirms this interpretation. It underscores the nature of eyewitness testimony as having to do with things which were heard, which were seen with the eyes, which were looked upon, and which were touched with the hands, "concerning the word of life" (1 Jn. 1:1). Here again John's purpose went beyond the mere relating of historical facts. His ultimate purpose was to lead his readers to believe that Jesus is the Christ, the Son of God, and that believing they may have life in His name.

In his first letter he gave a slightly different slant to his purpose. Here he was concerned with the resulting fellowship that his readers should have with himself and with the Father. Again these ultimate purposes on the part of John do not in the least destroy the historicity of what he wrote concerning the works and teachings of Christ. Rather, they lie at the very foundation of Christian faith.

2. The Bearing of Biblical Criticism upon the Historical Character of the Gospel Record

This criticism has taken on several forms: the first, centering in the literary character of the Gospel records; the second, having to do directly with their historical character; and the third, focusing on the form of these records. Each of these approaches possesses definite values for the study of biblical theology. At the same time, certain scholars in each of these areas have wrought great havoc by reason of the skeptical presuppositions and conclusions reached. This points to the rigid necessity of dealing with the Gospel records with openness of mind, without philosophical presuppositions, and with utmost honesty in dealing with both the internal evidence as to their historicity, as well as such external evidences which point to authorship and the acceptance of the Gospel records in the early church. Obviously, a full treatment of all this material lies beyond this discipline, but we cannot escape the implications of biblical criticism for this study.

Literary criticism has shown that there are stylistic peculiarities of each of the Gospels. After due consideration is given to the distinctive character of unnamed sources common to two or more of the Gospels the overall conclusion still remains: each Gospel possesses a distinctive unity in style and character. This overall characteristic persists after due recognition is given to other literary characteristics common to two or more of the Gospels. Recognizing on one hand the material common to Mark and to one or both of the other synoptic Gospels, which consists mainly of narratives, and on the other hand the material common to Matthew and Luke, which is not found in Mark, commonly called "Q," the fact remains that the several Gospel writers were not mere collectors of data which they threw together in an unorganized manner of which each Gospel is now the finished product. The author maintains that each Gospel stands in its own right as a literary whole in which each writer presented the life and teachings of Jesus in such a manner as to set forth his own respective purpose in writing his Gospel.

Historical criticism has sought to approach the Gospel narrative in the same manner as the historian deals with the data of history. This approach is entirely legitimate. The difficulties here require careful study. This first comes to light in an effort to draw up a harmony of the Gospels. Among the problems encountered are the differences among the Gospels in the order of presenting events, conflicting data among the events, and variations in the order, form, and content of Jesus' teachings. So great are the problems encountered that some scholars have turned away from the Gospel narrative and hold that there is little or no historical basis to the Gospel record. They hold that there may be sufficient historical evidence to believe that Jesus lived in the land of Palestine so many years ago, but that the Gospel records furnish no historical basis for our knowing what He did and what He taught. Perhaps the most significant aspect of the whole matter rests in the element of the miraculous in the Gospel records. On this account, according to some historical scholars, there is little or no basis of comparison of the Gospel records with secular history. Secular history, they hold, gives no support to the occurrence of miracles in human history. Consequently, to them, the Gospel records are unhistorical.

Part of the approach to this matter is the philosophical and theological presupposition that miracles are impossible. As a result, the

Gospel records cannot be accepted as giving a true account of historical events. Let me ask, Who knows enough to say that miracles are impossible? Recognizing that secular history has not recorded miraculous events, this fact does not exclude the possibility of miracles.

At this point one of the most distinctive characteristics of biblical history comes to the fore. It is a record of God's divine interventions in human history for the purpose of revealing Himself to mankind. The Bible represents miracles as the divine credential of a divine Messenger for His message. The Bible is not extravagant in its presentation of the miraculous. A little study will show how very restrictive their occurrence really was.

Biblical miracles are limited in the large to four periods of biblical history. Each was in its own way a crisis in God's dealing with man. The first period centered in God's deliverance of Israel out of Egypt. The second was the crisis of the true religion with that of the worship of Baal in the days of Elijah and Elisha. The third was the conflict of the true religion with pagan worship in a Gentile kingdom in the days of Daniel. The fourth was the proof of Jesus as the Messiah, the Son of God, and the Savior of the world. Thus the grounds for the occurrence of miracles in the Bible are adequate and satisfying. Certainly, no one would contend that if God would perform miracles in the world, His world would be capsized.

The task that remains to satisfy properly the legitimate requirements of the historical inquiry is to examine the biblical records. Our present concern is those of the New Testament, to determine whether or not these records on the basis of internal claims actually assert giving sight to the blind, the cleansing of the lepers, the raising of the dead, the resurrection of Jesus, as actual happenings in the land of Palestine, over 1900 years ago. This problem, the performance of miracles in the Bible, imposes upon the biblical records the severest conceivable test: Do the biblical records give such weighty evidence for their historical character that we, in whose experience such miracles do not take place, have sufficient grounds for believing that these signs, wonders, and mighty works did occur in Bible history? Putting the question in a different way: Are we moved to believe the eyewitness testimony of competent and trustworthy witnesses to such miraculous events which lie entirely outside our experience?

Some modern scholars have yet another way of approach to this problem closely related to that of historical criticism. According to their view, the early preaching of the church built up the faith on the part of the early Christians in the supernatural happenings of Christ's life, the resurrection in particular, and that this faith precedes the records of these miracles. Therefore, the miracles have their bases only in the faith of the church and not in the authentic records of the Gospels. This sort of argument gives a show of learning but is hardly worth serious consideration. How ridiculous it is to say that faith precedes the fact, becomes exceedingly clear when the sole basis for discussion is the New Testament record. There is no other source of information. Our only source presents the evidence for miracles in the language of eyewitnesses who were competent and trustworthy. If these sources of information are rejected, we have absolutely no basis for believing anything that happened outside our own personal experience.

The most recent development of biblical criticism is known as form criticism. The names Martin Dibelius, Rudolph Bultmann, Vincent Taylor, and Norman Perrin are the great exponents of form criticism. Brevity of treatment must rule here. Form criticism pays much attention to the period of oral tradition out of which the written Gospels arose. It seeks to discover the forms or structure in which the earliest preaching of the apostles was given. The labels used to describe these forms are sayings, paradigms, wonder tales, legends, and myths. The materials of the Gospels are classified according to these respective forms. In the hands of Bultmann and Perrin form criticism becomes a tool by which they judge the historical character of the Gospels. They see in these forms of oral tradition a definite lack of historical reference. They find it almost impossible to go from the Jesus who was preached to the Jesus of actual history. In other words, the Gospel records are not authentic historical accounts of the life and teachings of Jesus.

Vincent Taylor, on the other hand, draws away from the radicalism of Bultmann and would limit form criticism to the history of the material and its use in the church. Among present-day form critics there appears to be a healthy return to believing that the testimony of eyewitnesses to the life and teachings of Christ gave rise to oral tradition.

Like other forms of biblical criticism, form criticism has rendered a definite service to exegesis. The Gospel writers had theological and kerygmatic objectives in writing. But this service need not be interpreted so as to lower the historical value of the Gospel records. In fact, the Gospel writers built the preaching values of the Gospel on the facts of history found in the life of Jesus.

In his article, "The Growth of the Gospel," [1] Alfred M. Perry gives a very commendable presentation of form criticism. He holds, "Form criticism has made an undoubted contribution to the study of the Gospels. It has emphasized the independence and completeness of the individual portions of tradition, which is a real service to interpretation. It has called attention to the vital relationship between tradition and the life of the church." He notes that some of the forms are real literary types and that the existence of form had much to do in the perpetuation of tradition.

Perry also notes some limitations of form criticism. Among these he notes, "The assumption, tacit or open, that the form created the tradition is subject to doubt. Communities in general do not create; they shape and conserve. And the material of the Gospel tradition bears marks of authenticity quite apart from the forms into which it has been shaped." To this he adds, "This failure to distinguish sharply between the history of the subject matter and the history of the form has introduced a subjective element into many of the critic's historical and literary judgments — of legends and miracles, for example." Still further he says, "The form critics have concentrated too narrowly on the forms in the construction of history. Their picture of early church life is often one-sided and inadequate, ignoring the great variety which the records describe, and taking little account of the factors which would control the growth of tradition, other than the forms." He very wisely adds a concluding limitation. "As a historical tool, then, we should limit form criticism to the history of the material and its use in the church; it will hardly provide us with primary evidence for the history of the church or the historical accuracy of the tradition."

To these limitations the author would add that form criticism has failed to recognize the individuality of each author of the four Gospels. While they drew from a common oral tradition they had a more direct connection with the actual events of the life of Christ than form criticism would allow. Matthew and John were official witnesses, apostles chosen by Christ. Perhaps even Mark was an eyewitness to many of the events of Christ's ministry (Mk. 14:51), and Luke was far more than a mere collector and assembler of oral tradition (Lk. 1:1-4).

Dr. Perry does another very commendable thing in drawing attention to "controls of the tradition." He says, "We may also note that tradition did not run wild in the church. There were several forces at work to control it and maintain its authenticity.

"1. Actual memory of Jesus was always the historic basis of the faith; He was not a mere myth, like the redeemers of the mystery religions.

"2. The leaders of the community, and many others, were themselves eyewitnesses of the events (cf. Lk. 1:1), competent to correct errors in the tradition, and such eyewitness testimony was prized as late as the time of Papias (ca. 135).

"3. There were eyewitnesses too among the opponents of Christianity, before whom it was necessary to justify the case for the gospel preaching.

"4. The analogy of folklore is not entirely adequate, for there were educated people in the church from the outset. It is a mistake to assume that all unwritten 'literature' is illiterate; the literature of Judaism offers striking confutations of such a supposition."

I would add that the apostles chosen by Christ as the official witnesses of His ministry culminating in the resurrection and the ascension (Acts 1:21-25) undoubtedly functioned as authoritative guides and controls of the tradition. Christian faith rested directly on the life and work of Christ and this would naturally serve to correct any false traditions that might arise.

Two concluding observations of Dr. Perry are very pertinent:

"1. In the liberal direction the pregospel tradition can no longer be regarded as a static deposit, directly delivered by Peter or another, but as a living testimony, organic to the experience of the church.

"2. Yet in harmony with an older judgment, it again becomes apparent that the concern of this tradition is not with mere history, but with the salvation announced in the kerygma; it is oriented not to a memory from the past, but to a present experience, which we believe to have perpetual relevance."

Let us bear in mind, by way of conclusion, that the Gospels became a deposit in the living church. Their acceptance by the church and their incorporation into the New Testament canon give final attestation to the historical character of the Gospel records.

While form criticism would attract our attention to the human aspects relating to the origin of the Gospels and would tend to weaken or even destroy their historical trustworthiness, we need to assert that there is also the divine side to the origin of the written Word. While none of the Gospel writers claim inspiration, the grounds for believing that "all Scripture is inspired by God" remain. While obviously there are serious intellectual problems that men wrote (keeping in mind all their human limitations) and that these "men moved by the Holy Spirit, spoke from God," Christian faith glories in the fact that these human productions, nevertheless, speak the very words of God.

3. A Positive Approach to the Historical Character of the Gospels

a. The Call and Special Mission of the Apostles

The most natural starting point to a study of the historical character of the Gospels lies in the special mission of the apostles. Mark wrote, "And he appointed twelve, to be with him, and to be sent out to preach and have authority to cast out demons" (Mk. 3:14, 15). Jesus enlarged on this mission when He gave the Great Commission, "All authority in heaven and on earth has been given to me. Go therefore and make disciples of all nations, baptizing them in the name of the Father and of the Son and of the Holy Spirit, teaching them to observe all that I have commanded you; and lo, I am with you always, to the close of the age" (Mt. 28:18-20). Jesus repeated this command in slightly different words when He said, "But you shall receive power when the Holy Spirit has come upon you; and you shall be my witnesses in Jerusalem and in all Judea and Samaria and to the end of the earth" (Acts 1:8).

Peter recognized most clearly the official character of the apostolic office when he said, "So one of the men who have accompanied us during all of the time that the Lord Jesus went in and out among us, beginning from the baptism of John until the day that he was taken up from us — one of these men must become with us a witness to his resurrection" (Acts 1:21, 22). The appointment of the Twelve as official witnesses to the life and ministry of Christ possesses tremendous significance. Thus the preaching of the apostles throughout the apostolic age was not by casual observers of some of the things Jesus said and did, but rather it was that of men chosen beforehand with a full realization of their responsibility as eyewitnesses to the most extraordinary event of human history, namely, that of the earthly life of the Son of God.

In courts of law two witnesses to an event are accepted as sufficient to establish its authenticity. Many times such witnesses are only casual observers. What more could we wish for than to have twelve specially chosen and appointed witnesses who knew their special mission while all the events were taking place? It is to be held with sacred regard that our Lord in the appointment of the apostles recognized that only on the basis of eyewitnesses can we bridge the gap between our personal experience and the events which lie beyond our experience. In fact, this characterizes all the testimony which the apostles gave. It is to this testimony that I shall now address myself.

b. Peter, the Spokesman of the Apostles

At Pentecost and afterward Peter was the first to speak concerning his Lord. Special interest attaches to the manner of his presentation. The multiplicity of his references to this is of deep interest and profound meaning for us. [2]

When speaking of Christ's resurrection, Peter's distinctive way of confirming his message was "to this we are witnesses." (Acts 3:15;

cf. 4:20; 5:32; 10:39-41.) This kind of claim could not be gainsaid. There is a definite value for us to observe the details of the life and ministry of Christ to which Peter refers in his preaching and in his letters. Among these, note the following, "Men of Israel, hear these words: Jesus of Nazareth, a man attested to you by God with mighty works and wonders and signs which God did through him in your midst, as you yourselves know — this Jesus . . . you crucified and killed by the hands of lawless men. But God raised him up, having loosed the pangs of death" (Acts 2:22-24). Later, when Peter was addressing the Jews, he said, "The God of our fathers, glorified his servant Jesus, whom you delivered up and denied in the presence of Pilate, when he had decided to release him. But you denied the Holy and Righteous One, and asked for a murderer to be granted to you, and killed the Author of life, whom God raised from the dead. To this we are witnesses" (3:13-15). Observe closely the details of Jesus' life which he gave to Cornelius and his Gentile friends, "You know the word which he sent to Israel, preaching good news of peace by Jesus Christ (he is Lord of all), the word which was proclaimed throughout all Judea, beginning from Galilee after the baptism which John preached: how God anointed Jesus of Nazareth with the Holy Spirit and with power; how he went about doing good and healing all that were oppressed by the devil, for God was with him. And we are witnesses to all that he did both in the country of the Jews and in Jerusalem. They put him to death by hanging him on a tree; but God raised him on the third day and made him manifest; not to all the people but to us who were chosen by God as witnesses, who ate and drank with him after he rose from the dead. And he commanded us to preach to the people, and to testify that he is the one ordained by God to be judge of the living and the dead" (10: 36-42).

Peter, in his letters, made some very significant references to the earthly life of Christ. Note the following: "For to this you have been called, because Christ also suffered for you, leaving you an example, that you should follow in his steps. He committed no sin; no guile was found on his lips. When he was reviled, he did not revile in return; when he suffered, he did not threaten; but he trusted to him who judges justly. He himself bore our sins in his body on the tree" (1 Pet. 2:21-24). Observe yet another reference which Peter made to a significant event in Christ's life: "We were eyewitnesses of his majesty. For when he received honor and glory from God the Father and the voice was borne to him by the Majestic Glory, 'This is my beloved Son, with whom I am well pleased,' we heard this voice borne from heaven, for we were with him in the holy mountain" (2 Pet. 1:16-18). By way of conclusion, Peter's witness confirms some of the most crucial and important events in Christ's earthly ministry as recorded in the Gospels.

c. The Witness of Paul

The number of details in the life of Christ to which Paul refers is also significant. His sermon at Antioch of Pisidia is an illustration of what Paul may have said repeatedly in his preaching. Quoting from his message, "Of this man's posterity God has brought to Israel a Savior, Jesus, as he promised. Before his coming John had preached a baptism of repentance to all the people of Israel. And as John was finishing his course, he said, 'What do you suppose that I am? I am not he. No, but after me one is coming, the sandals of whose feet I am not worthy to untie.' . . . For those who live in Jerusalem and their rulers, because they did not recognize him nor understand the utterances of the prophets which are read every sabbath, fulfilled these by condemning him. Though they could charge him with nothing deserving death, yet they asked Pilate to have him killed. And when they had fulfilled all that was written of him, they took him down from the tree, and laid him in a tomb. But God raised him from the dead; and for many days he appeared to those who came up with him from Galilee to Jerusalem, who are now his witnesses to the people" (Acts 13:23-31).

In Paul's teaching concerning the Lord's Supper, observe how many details concerning this incident confirm what the Gospels records relate. He wrote, "The cup of blessing which we bless, is it not a participation in the blood of Christ? The bread which we break, is it not a participation in the body of Christ?" (1 Cor. 10:16). In chapter 11 he added, "For I received from the Lord what I also delivered to you, that the Lord Jesus on the night when he was betrayed took bread, and when he had given thanks, he broke it, and said, 'This is my body which is for you. Do this in remembrance of me.' In the same way also the cup, after supper, saying, 'This cup is the new covenant in my blood. Do this, as often as you drink it, in remembrance of me.' For as often as you eat this bread and drink the cup, you proclaim the Lord's death until he comes" (1 Cor. 11:23-26).

A number of details concerning Christ's resurrection also deserves attention. Paul wrote, "Christ died for our sins in accordance with the scriptures, that he was buried, that he was raised on the third day in accordance with the scriptures, and that he appeared to Cephas, then to the twelve. Then he appeared to more than five hundred brethren at one time, most of whom are still alive, though some have fallen asleep. Then he appeared to James, then to all the apostles" (1 Cor.

15:3-7). With this language Paul built up the strongest case possible for belief in Christ's resurrection. In accord with all the others who wrote or spoke of Christ's resurrection Paul enumerated the witnesses to this great event.

In the letter to the Philippians when Paul challenged his readers to have the mind of Christ, he described Christ's humiliation in the words, "He . . . did not count equality with God a thing to be grasped, but emptied himself, taking the form of a servant, being born in the likeness of men. And being found in human form he humbled himself and became obedient unto death, even death on a cross" (2:6-8). Here again are details of the life of Christ which stand as additional confirmation of the Gospel records.

A final observation of Paul's witness to the life of Christ is that his testimony stands as an independent verification to the historical character of the Gospels. The number of details of Christ's life to which he referred rivals in number those which Peter gave, and interestingly includes some details to which Peter made no reference.

d. The Witness of the Synoptic Writers

Turning now to the central source of Gospel history, the synoptic Gospels, we should note first the bearing of the date of these Gospels upon their historical character. Written within thirty or forty years after the time of Christ, these records are unsurpassed in their forthright presentation of the most wonderful events of human history. The unassuming character of the authors and their respective unlabored presentations of Jesus who is represented as the *Son of David* and *Son of God* commend these writings to us for acceptance without any misgivings or hesitance. How different these records are from the apocryphal writings! The inclusion of these Gospels into the New Testament canon speaks very strongly for their acceptance as being historical in character.

Recognizing the problems connected with the authorship of the Gospel according to Matthew, I believe that this Gospel stands forth in its own right as an accurate presentation of Jesus as the Messiah. Whether the traditional view of Matthew's having written the entire Gospel or the more recent one that he wrote those portions which are common to both his Gospel and that of Luke, commonly called the "Q" source, or whether he did not write any of this work is of small consequence in dealing with the historical character of this book. Elements of its historical character appear on almost every page of this book. Among other details chosen almost at random, note the genealogies from Abraham to Christ, the date of the birth of Jesus in the days of Herod the king, the flight of Joseph and Mary with Jesus into Egypt and their return to Nazareth, Jesus going about all Galilee teaching in the synagogues, the teaching of Jesus as One who had authority, His entering Capernaum and being met by the centurion, crossing the Sea of Galilee in a boat, the Pharisees accusing the disciples of breaking the Sabbath, Christ's teaching beside the sea, Jesus going from Galilee to the region of Judea, Jesus going up to Jerusalem and coming to Bethphage to the Mount of Olives, eating the Passover with His disciples, His trial before Caiaphas and before Pilate, Pilate's efforts to give Jesus a fair trial in the face of the Jewish mob, and the crucifixion. What should be noticed in these incidents, many of which are relatively trivial, is the historical setting in which they are given. From a historian's point of view, all this commends the narrative as being historically accurate.

Taking a brief look at the Gospel according to Mark, we are impressed with the author's effort to present Jesus as the mighty Worker of miracles. It would seem as though Mark had in his mind the image of the Servant of the Lord as set forth in Isaiah and seeks to show how Jesus fulfilled this image. His interest is not that of a modern historian. He is not attempting to relate all the events of Christ's life in consecutive order, as a historian would likely do, but rather he is gleaning from the active ministry of Jesus those elements that best fulfill the Old Testament predictions of the coming Messiah who is the Son of Man, the Son of God, and the Servant of the Lord. This method of precedure does not weaken the historical character of the events described, but rather builds on them a structure that would be very insecure if the foundation were not historically accurate.

In the case of the Gospel according to Luke the opening verses naturally call for careful consideration. Here Luke gave an explicit statement of his purpose and method. His claims call for acceptance until it can be shown wherein he failed to fulfill them. In the first place, Luke is asserting that he gained his material from eyewitnesses and by stating this he is claiming that he is not such himself. This appeal to what eyewitnesses say shows Luke's recognition of a historian's viewpoint. Second, the personal research on the part of Luke stands forth. His statement, "having followed all things closely for some time past," carries the idea of his having traced the events in a historian's style so as to satisfy himself of their historical accuracy. Third, Luke declares explicitly his purpose. It was that Theophilus may know the truth concerning the things of which he had been informed. This carries with it the idea of the certitude of what Luke had told Theophilus.

Fourth, the historical connection with secular history with which the author related the events of Jesus' life is very significant. Thus, it was in the days of Herod the king of Judea that the birth of the Baptist took place. The date of the birth of Jesus is definitely linked with the decree from Caesar Augustus that all the world should be enrolled. Specifically, this was the first enrollment, when Quirinius was governor of Syria. The time in which the Word of God came to John the Baptist is still more explicitly dated "in the fifteenth year of the reign of Tiberius Caesar, Pontius Pilate being governor of Judea, and Herod being tetrarch of Galilee, his brother Philip tetrarch of Ituraea and Trachonitis, and Lysanias tetrarch of Abilene, in the high-priesthood of Annas and Caiaphas" (Lk. 3:1, 2).

Thus the entire ministry of Christ took place when Pontius Pilate was governor of Judea. With a historian's sense of historical values Luke wove the events of our Lord's earthly life into the course of secular history. Luke's interest in depicting Jesus as the Son of God and as the Savior of the world does not in the least lower the historical character of his Gospel. On the contrary, the historical foundation of what Luke wrote constitutes the solid ground for setting forth Him whose ancestry could be traced to Adam and who was in the most real way the Son of God and the Savior of the world.

e. The Witness of John

John's witness is perhaps the most unique. This becomes evident when we discover the profound teachings of this Gospel rooted and grounded in the historic career of Jesus, the Son of the living God. On this account we should examine this Gospel with great scrutiny to discover whether or not its doctrinal content is congruent with an acceptance of the historical character of the events described. We may take our beginning at 1:14, "And the Word became flesh and dwelt among us, full of grace and truth; we have beheld his glory, glory as of the only Son from the Father." In these words the writer stated the most wonderful fact of world history, namely, that the Word became flesh. He hastens to add that this One dwelt among us and that they saw His glory such as belongs to the only Son from the Father. Here he described the unspeakable mystery of the incarnation. Yet with all clarity John and his fellow disciples had a clear-cut, experiential confrontation with the only Son from the Father. Throughout the book this grand truth repeatedly shines upon us. The incidents, many of them, are from common life, such as a marriage feast, a nighttime conversation, a conversation with the woman at Jacob's well, Jesus' attendance at several Jewish feasts, His visits in the home of Mary, Martha, and Lazarus, and the like. But in each of these stories, which from the human side, are entirely real, even commonplace, there is the presence of Him who is none less than the Son of God. John's stated purpose in writing his Gospel shows the profound double purpose of the book (20:30, 31). The first is that of the signs which Jesus did in the presence of the disciples; the second expresses the purpose of these signs, that of leading men to believe that Jesus is the Christ, the Son of God, and that in believing they may have life in His name.

f. Factual Data from Geography and History

Note the geographical data which give confirmation to the accuracy and authenticity of these records: Bethlehem of Judea (Mt. 2:1), Egypt (v. 13), Nazareth in the district of Galilee (v. 22), wilderness of Judea (3:1), Jordan River (v. 6), the holy city and the temple (4:5), Capernaum by the sea, in the territory of Zebulun and Naphtali (v. 12), the place called The Skull (Lk. 23:32), Jewish town of Arimathea (v. 50), village named Emmaus about seven miles from Jerusalem (24:13), Bethany (v. 50), the Passover in Jerusalem (Jn. 2:13, 23), Jews' Feast of Tabernacles (7:2), Akeldama — the Field of Blood (Acts 1:19), synagogues at Damascus (9:2), left Athens and went to Corinth (18:1), arrived at Rhegium . . . came to Puteoli . . . came to Rome (28:13, 14), etc.

With the same confidence we may accept the historical references such as: Herod the king (Mt. 2:2); his death (v. 19); Archelaus' reign in place of his father; Herod (v. 22); Pharisees and Sadducees (3:7); Pilate and Herod (Lk. 23:1-24); the centurion (v. 47); the band of soldiers, their captain, and the officers of the Jews (Jn. 18:12); Annas, the father-in-law of Caiaphas, who was the high priest that year (v. 12); written in Hebrew, in Latin, and in Greek (19:20); Parthians and Medes . . . Arabians (Acts 2:9-11); Epicurean and Stoic philosophers (17:18); Artemis of the Ephesians (19:28); Agrippa, the king, and Bernice arrived at Caesarea to welcome Festus (25:13), etc.

g. Summary of the Evidence

To what conclusions do these accounts of Gospel history sources lead? It is my uppermost desire to evaluate these evidences with absolute fairness and with a keen consciousness of one's responsibility in treating matters of such high importance. The recognition by Gospel writers and speakers of eyewitness testimony shows their understanding of what supports authentic history. For this reason the testimonies of Peter and Paul were most significant. (1) It is evident that the only way in which we can learn of things lying outside our personal experience is through the testimony of those who had actual experience with the matters in question. All mankind living after the time of Christ must depend on eyewitness testimony for a knowledge of these stupendous events. There is no question that eyewitness testimony of those who are competent and trustworthy is entirely valid. There is no other way of bridging the gap between our experience and that of the apostles.

(2) The adequacy of this witness to the most extraordinary events of human history is most certainly established. Without question the life of the sinless Jesus, the miracles He performed, the teachings which He gave, His crucifixion, resurrection, and ascension are the most wonderful events of world history. Accordingly, the grounds for our believing such events which lie entirely outside our experience lead us to examine most carefully the nature and character of the eyewitness testimony to these events. To begin with there is the testimony of the twelve official witnesses, the disciples. They were chosen for this very purpose at the beginning of Christ's ministry. They knew their task and manifested a consciousness of their personal responsibility in this matter. Add to this the confirming testimonies of Paul who also *saw* the risen Lord. Then there is the witness of the five hundred who *saw* the risen Lord. This sort of testimony is irrefutable.

We need to observe also that the writing of the three Gospels took place during the lifetime of most of these witnesses. If there were historical inaccuracies in these Gospel records, there were many people, both friend and foe, who would have risen up to expose the errors. The nature of Luke's investigation calls for special notice. As one who was not an eyewitness, he learned from those who had firsthand information of the whole story. The final confirmation, that of John's testimony, is the capsheaf to this witness of the most extraordinary events of human history.

(3) The similarities and differences among the synoptic Gospels do not pose unsolvable problems. With all consistency we may say that we do not know enough about the existing problems to hold that there are errors in the narratives. We do not close our eyes to the existence of minor differences in the narratives, but with all frankness we may state that after we have given full recognition to the grand harmony found in all the witnesses of the life of Christ, these trivial apparent conflicts shrink to insignificance. We can regard Peter as the first spokesman who gave the pattern for presenting the life and teachings of Christ. Undoubtedly he was not the only spokesman who gave form to the preaching of the good news. The oral tradition of the Gospel stories was rich and meaningful and perhaps not entirely free from some historical inaccuracies. But the Gospel records did not merely spring from this oral tradition. Their roots go back directly to the eyewitnesses of Christ's earthly ministry.

(4) There is a total absence of any evidence that disproves the authenticity of the records. This leaves the Gospel records unchallenged

as representing faithful accounts of our Lord's ministry.

With full confidence in the validity of these conclusions I shall proceed with the task of seeking to unfold the revelation of God in Christ, building on the records of the entire New Testament.

For Additional Reading and Reference:

Baker's *Dictionary of Theology*, pp. 227-228.
Bernard, *The Progress of Doctrine in the New Testament*, pp. 30-54.
Bowman, *Prophetic Realism and the Gospel*, pp. 51-78.
Bruce, F. F., *The New Testament Documents, Are They Reliable?*
Conzelmann, *An Outline of the Theology of the New Testament*, pp. 1-93.
Interpreter's Bible, Vol. I, pp. 136 ff.
Interpreter's Bible, Vol. VIII, pp. 69-74.
Interpreter's Bible Dictionary, E-J, pp. 320-321.
Jeremias, *New Testament Theology*, pp. 1-41.
New Bible Dictionary, p. 153.
Taylor, *The Formation of the Gospel Tradition*, pp. 22-189.
Weidner, *Biblical Theology of the New Testament*, Vol. I, pp. 31-39.
Weiss, *Biblical Theology of the New Testament*, Vol. I, pp. 283-310.

1. Alfred M. Perry in article, "The Growth of the Gospel," *The Interpreter's Bible* (New York: Abingdon-Cokesbury Press, 1951), Vol. III, pp. 68 ff.

2. See Acts 2:14, 22, 32; 3:6, 12, 15; 4:8, 13, 20; 5:30, 32, 42; 10:36-43; 11:16; 1 Pet. 1:1, 3, 11, 19, 21; 2:21-24; 3:18, 21, 22; 4:1, 13; 5:1; 2 Pet. 1:16-18; 3:2.

CHAPTER III

THE DISTINCTIVE MESSAGE OF EACH EVANGELIST

1. Introduction

It became evident in the preceding chapter that each Gospel writer had a distinctive message and purpose. The common details of the synoptic Gospels do not overshadow the distinctive character of each. This fact is all the more instructive by reason of the synoptic view of these Gospels. A study of the distinctive message of each of the four Gospels possesses at least three significant values. First, it becomes an essential prelude to the study of the unfolding revelation common to all the Gospels. It contributes to gaining an accurate perspective of the total revelation. Second, it helps us to understand better the distinctive emphases on the part of each writer. To follow a pattern based solely on a harmony of the Gospels can result in failing to discover the individuality of each writer together with his distinctive viewpoint and purpose. Third, this should strengthen the impact of the teachings given by two or more of these authors on the same theme.

2. The Distinctive Message of the Gospel According to Matthew

Search for the central message of the first Gospel reveals two great themes which serve as the foci of his message. Matthew seeks first to show that Jesus is the Messiah. His second objective is to disclose the nature of the Messiah's kingdom. Let us seek to discover how these two themes become the main thrusts of this Gospel.

a. Jesus Is the Messiah

The first thing in this Gospel with which Matthew confronts us is the genealogy of Jesus Christ, the son of David, the son of Abraham. By this genealogy Matthew brought to the reader's attention two things: first, what descendant of David living at the time of Jesus was the rightful heir to David's throne; and second, this genealogy establishes the fact that Jesus could rightfully be regarded as the seed of Abraham in whom all nations of the world would be blessed.

Jesus also bore the name, Immanuel. On these grounds, Matthew proceeded to present Jesus, the Messiah, and as God with us. Matthew sought to give evidence of Jesus' messiahship. This he did by setting forth the fulfillment and realization of the messianic predictions concerning Him as found in the prophetic writings of Micah, Jeremiah, Isaiah, and Zechariah. [1] These references to Old Testament predictions, about forty in number, show that Matthew was addressing Jewish readers who regarded the Old Testament as the Scriptures. For Matthew to make this use of the prophetic Scriptures indicated his recognition of the messianic character of the Old Testament.

Matthew sought also to show the character of the King. He is in a real way the King of love. He is humble, gentle, compassionate, and tender. What could be more expressive of the character of the King than Jesus' own words, "Come to me, all who labor and are heavy laden, and I will give you rest. Take my yoke upon you, and learn from me; for I am gentle and lowly in heart, and you will find rest for your souls. For my yoke is easy, and my burden is light" (Mt. 11:28-30). Repeatedly Matthew referred to Jesus' compassion for those in need (9:36; 14:14; 15: 32; 20:34).

He felt that it was imperative to make clear the distinctive nature of Jesus' kingship. This he did by quoting Jesus' words, "All things have been delivered to me by my Father; and no one knows the Son except the Father, and no one knows the Father except the Son and any one to whom the Son chooses to reveal him" (11:27). Matthew also noted Jesus' claim to kingly authority just prior to His ascension, when Jesus said, "All authority in heaven and on earth is given to me" (28:18). Exercising this kingly authority Jesus then gave the Great Commission.

Matthew focused attention on the nature of Jesus' kingship in several of the parables (13:1-50). For instance, in the parable of the weeds of the field, Jesus pointed to His present kingship which is spiritual in character. The good seed means the sons of the kingdom; the harvest is the close of the age. At that time the Son of Man will send His angels and they will gather out of His kingdom all causes of sin and all evil doers. Then the righteous will shine like the sun in the kingdom of their Father. With this language Jesus showed that His kingdom is the same in character as that of the Father's. It is a spiritual reality (13: 37-43). As a further indication of the nature of Jesus' kingship, Matthew wrote of Jesus "preaching of the gospel of the kingdom and healing every disease and every infirmity among the people" (4:23; 9:35). What we should observe in these instances is Matthew's bringing together the Gospel preaching and the kingdom, thus showing that the Gospel centered in the kingdom. The kingship of Jesus was, therefore, bringing to realization the good tidings predicted by the prophet Isaiah (Is. 52:7-10).

The miracles of healing associated with this preaching of the kingdom served to show that the King had all power. He manifests His power both in the natural realm of healing and in the spiritual realm of delivering souls from the bondage of Satan. This is why Jesus said on an occasion, "If it is by the Spirit of God that I cast out demons, then the kingdom of God has come upon you" (Mt. 12:28). The most climactic way in which Matthew depicted the nature of Jesus' kingship is found in the Olivet Discourse. Jesus said, "When the Son of man comes in his glory, and all the angels with him, then he will sit on his glorious throne. Before him will be gathered all the nations, and he will separate them one from another as a shepherd separates the sheep from the goats. . . . Then the King will say to those at his right hand, 'Come, O blessed of my Father, inherit the kingdom prepared for you from the foundation of the world' " (25:31, 32, 34). How majestic is this messianic kingship of Jesus! It was Matthew's supreme purpose to show that the messianic kingship would not follow the pattern of an earthly kingdom. The measure of the majesty of messianic kingship is found in Christ's return in glory and in His sitting on His glorious throne for the final judgment of all mankind.

b. The Kingdom

The sublime majesty of Jesus' kingship should prepare us for understanding the nature of the Messiah's kingdom. The wealth of the material presented by Matthew helps us to see how central the kingdom is to his Gospel. Matthew's reference to Jesus' preaching the gospel of the kingdom noted above almost immediately precedes the Sermon on the Mount. Can it be that the Sermon on the Mount constitutes the Magna Charta of the kingdom! To begin with, Jesus gave new dimensions to the kingdom concept: it includes the poor in spirit, those who mourn, the meek, those who hunger and thirst for righteousness, the merciful, the pure in heart, the peacemakers, those who are persecuted for righteousness' sake, and those who are reviled and persecuted. All are blessed. This is true because theirs is the kingdom of heaven; they shall see God; and they shall be called the sons of God. With these Beatitudes Jesus completely overturned the commonly accepted standards of blessedness. We become aware of a new level of morality. The ethical standards of the kingdom far surpass the pharisaical perversions of the Mosaic law. Jesus was introducing a new order of things in which love is supreme. Anger, lustful thinking, marital unfaithfulness, oaths, retaliation — all are condemned. Jesus said, "You, therefore, must be perfect, as your heavenly Father is perfect" (5:48). Thus, the Messiah's kingdom upholds new standards measured by such divine attributes as righteousness, perfection, and love.

The practice of true piety must extend even to the motives of worship. We dare not engage in almsgiving, praying, and fasting to be seen of men. The practice of piety is not meritorious; it is a gracious privilege which, when exercised in the true spirit, will bring to us the Father's reward. There are only two masters, God and mammon. We cannot serve them both. On this account Jesus said, "Seek first his kingdom and his righteousness, and all these things shall be yours as well" (6:33). God's righteousness will rule out the spirit of censoriousness. It will hold forth the practice of the Golden Rule. It will recognize that the way to life is by way of a narrow gate. Only those who do the will of the Father shall enter the kingdom of heaven. There dare be no disparity between hearing and doing.

Matthew, more than any of the other Gospel writers, sought to show the nature of the kingdom through the parables given by Jesus. Jesus vividly portrayed the spiritual character of His kingdom. The word of the kingdom must be received in the heart and nurtured so that it bears fruit. The cares of the world and the delight in riches tend to choke out this word. The kingdom is a growing reality, both externally and internally. Its value is measured in being like a treasure being hidden in a field, or a merchant who finds a pearl of great value. (13:1-51). In another parable Jesus described the forgiving spirit of God and showed the necessity of our having a similar spirit of forgiveness (18:23-35). There are no greater or lesser rewards in this spiritual kingdom. All will share alike in the reward given by God (20:1-16). Jesus taught that the gross sinners of His day, the tax collectors, and the harlots would go into the kingdom because they repented of their sins. The unbelieving Jews, even though they claimed to be loyal to Moses, will not go into the kingdom of God (21:28-32).

Jesus pointed up the spiritual issues concerning the kingdom in the parable of the household. He asserted to the unbelieving Jews that they were the builders who were rejecting the very stone which would become the head of the corner. Therefore, the kingdom of God would be taken from them and given to a nation producing the fruits of it. This should certainly have convinced the Jews of the spiritual nature of God's kingdom (21:33-44). In another parable Jesus declared to the Jews their personal responsibility to respond to God's call to salvation. Jesus declared that their invitation to the marriage feast carried with it serious responsibilities on the part of the Jews. They had been called, but only those who from the heart responded were chosen.

In these kingdom parables, Matthew noted certain time aspects concerning the kingdom which Jesus had disclosed. There is a present aspect of the kingdom, temporal in nature, which is the kingdom of the Son of Man. This present age will be brought to a close by the return of the Son of Man, at which time His angels will gather out of His kingdom all causes of sin and all evil doers. Then the righteous will shine like the sun in the kingdom of their Father. This is the eternal aspect of the kingdom. In the parable of the dragnet Jesus taught that at the close of the age the angels will come forth and separate the evil from the righteous. In the Olivet Discourse Jesus made it clear that the coming of the Son of Man in His glory will terminate the present age. It is the time in which He will sit on His glorious throne and judge all mankind. The righteous will be invited by the King to inherit the kingdom of the Father which was prepared for them from the foundation of the world. The ungodly will go away into eternal punishment but the righteous into eternal life.

Matthew also recorded Jesus' teachings which showed the perspective of the church in relation to the kingdom. Peter's noble confession that Jesus is the Christ, the Son of the living God, led Jesus to express its meaning when He said, "On this rock I will build my church, and the powers of death shall not prevail against it. I will give you the keys of the kingdom of heaven, and whatever you bind on earth shall be bound in heaven, and whatever you loose on earth shall be loosed in heaven" (Mt. 16:18, 19). This connection of Christ's church with the kingdom of heaven bore a close relationship to the Old Testament structure of the theocracy, the rule of God with Israel as the people of God. Under this rule the congregation (*qahal*) of Israel became known in the Greek Septuagint as the *ekklesia.* Christ picked up this word and spoke of His *ekklesia* (church). Thus the church constitutes the people of Christ, under His rule.

Jesus spoke of the church also as a local assembly in which a brotherhood relationship would be found (18:15-20). This brotherhood would maintain a discipline among themselves. To this teaching of the church must be added all that Jesus had to say on the matter of its perpetuation in the world, notably, as set forth in the Great Commission. Jesus commanded His disciples to go and "make disciples of all nations, baptizing them in the name of the Father and of the Son and of the Holy Spirit, teaching them to observe all that I have commanded you; and lo, I am with you always, to the close of the age" (28:18-20). This means that under the absolute authority of the glorified Lord, the church shall reach out to all mankind to lead them to discipleship.

Matthew recorded a final aspect of the kingdom by noting its basis in the new covenant made by Jesus Christ. In his record of the institution of the Lord's Supper he quoted Jesus as saying, "This is my blood of the covenant, which is poured out for many for the forgiveness of sins" (26:28). Jesus added that He would not drink again of the fruit of the vine until the day when He would drink it new in the Father's kingdom. With these words Jesus was teaching that the making of the new covenant established His rule as the Messiah, and the blood of this covenant was His own blood. This shows us that Christ's kingdom had its basis in His redemptive work. In a very real way, the kingdom is a product of Christ's shed blood. In Jesus' own words, He gave "his life as a ransom for many" (20:28). Finally, it was to the risen Christ that all authority in heaven and on earth was given (28:18).

3. The Distinctive Message of the Gospel According to Mark

Mark began his story with the words "The beginning of the gospel of Jesus Christ, the Son of God." Many scholars regard these words as the heading of the book. If this is correct, it gives a meaningful perspective to the content and purpose of this Gospel. Mark introduced the ministry of Jesus by saying that He came into Galilee, "preaching the gospel of God." He continued with Jesus' own words, "The time is fulfilled, and the kingdom of God is at hand; repent, and believe in the gospel" (1:14, 15). Mark used the title *Son of God* which is definitive of Jesus' deity. Mark immediately gave the roots of this Gospel by quoting from the prophets Malachi and Isaiah. In both contexts the prophets foretold the work of the Baptist as preparing the way of the Lord. Mark would have us understand that Jesus is the Lord. Jesus' initial declaration asserted that He also grounded His work in the predictions of the prophet concerning the coming age of the Messiah. When the Messiah comes, the kingdom of God is at hand. The center of Mark's message becomes still clearer when we observe the threefold uses of the word "Gospel" in these opening verses (1, 14, 15). It would suggest that his Gospel centers particularly in a disclosure of the gospel of Jesus Christ. Jesus had come preaching the gospel of God. He was declaring, "Repent, and believe in the gospel."

As Mark proceeds with the unfolding of his story, it becomes increasingly clear that his interest does not lie in giving a biography of Jesus. It is far more significant than this. Mark's purpose becomes clear as he pursues the narrative of Jesus' intense activity throughout His ministry. At least two great purposes lie at the center of Mark's Gospel. The first of these becomes evident when Mark states that Jesus fulfilled the mission of Isaiah's Servant of the Lord (1:2, 3). The development of this truth led to a second emphasis in which he showed that the life of Jesus, the Servant of the Lord, led inevitably to His Passion. Around these two foci, in reality one great truth, all the details of the Gospel find their true significance. Thus the Gospel of Mark stands in its own right as portraying in most graphic fashion the fulfillment of Isaiah's great prediction concerning the Servant of the Lord.

a. The Disclosure of Jesus as the Servant of the Lord

The nature of this disclosure is more implicit than explicit. If we had only one echo of the Servant of the Lord passages in Isaiah, the case might be different. There are no less than eight clear reflections which are sufficient to confirm this central message of Mark's Gospel.[2] Thus the voice from heaven declaring Jesus to be God's beloved Son, in whom He is well pleased, reflects the picture of the Servant as God's chosen One in whom His soul delighted.

When Jesus referred to the Old Testament predictions that He should suffer many things and be treated with contempt, we think of the Redeemer of Israel as the One who was despised and rejected by men, a Man of sorrows and acquainted with grief. When Jesus described His conflict with Satan in casting out demons, we see the prey taken from the mighty, the captives of the tyrant rescued, and the victorious note of the Servant dividing a portion with the great, and the spoil with the strong. Jesus' extended announcement of His suffering, death, and resurrection clearly brings to mind the Suffering Servant of Isaiah 53. In giving His life as a ransom for many, Jesus identified Himself as the offering for sin. When Jesus instituted the Lord's Supper, He referred to His blood as being that of the covenant, which is poured out for many, a clear reference to Isaiah 53. When Jesus made no further answer to Pilate in the face of all the accusations of the chief priests, we are drawn to the picture of the Servant who "like a sheep that before its shearers is dumb, so he opened not his mouth" (v. 7).

All these references testify that Mark's Gospel is not a pointless narrative of the events of Jesus' life, but rather that they are a most forceful presentation of Jesus as the Servant of the Lord. We need to note further that in a number of these contexts, Jesus used the title Son of Man in referring to Himself.[3] In this manner Jesus established the identity of the Son of Man and the Servant of the Lord. On the lips of Jesus the title *Son of Man* is the most significant declaration of Jesus' messiahship that He used. The impact which this must have had on Jesus' hearers should have been great. It served to show that all the predictions of the Old Testament concerning the coming of the Son of Man, the Servant of the Lord, and the Messiah, converge in one person, Jesus, the Son of God.

The activity of Jesus thus had profound significance. His preaching, His healing of the sick, and His casting out of demons — all declared the actual realization of the Servant of the Lord. While Mark did not give us much of the content of Jesus' teaching, he did refer repeatedly to His teaching ministry. It lay at the very heart of the gospel of God.

b. The Passion-Centered Pattern of Development

Mark's narration of the events of Jesus' life included a number of references to the developing opposition to Jesus which culminated in His suffering and death.[4] Mark stressed the real nature of this opposition. The scribes and Pharisees were very quick to accuse Jesus of blasphemy, of eating with tax collectors and sinners, of breaking the Sabbath, and of other transgressions of the law. It was this kind of opposition which led them to demand that Jesus be crucified. These oppositions to Jesus lay back of His repeated references to His coming sufferings (8:31; 9:31; 10:32-34, 38, 39). While the other synoptists also mentioned the oppositions on the part of the Jews to Christ, as well as His announcements of coming suffering and death, Mark seems to possess a more definitely Passion-centered purpose. This is all the more apparent when we observe the repeated references to the suffering Servant of the Lord.

In view of the time in which Mark was writing, it is likely that he had a practical purpose in developing this Passion motif in his Gospel. It was a time of crisis brought on by the Neronian persecution. His readers were soon to experience sufferings similar to that of their Lord. On this account a section such as 8:31 to 9:1 may have had great practical significance. It begins with Jesus' announcement of His coming sufferings and then He adds, "If any man would come after me, let him deny himself and take up his cross and follow me. For whoever would save his life will lose it; and whoever loses his life for my sake and the gospel's will save it. . . . For whoever is ashamed of me and of my words in this adulterous and sinful generation, of him will the Son of man also be ashamed, when he comes in the glory of his Father with the holy angels" (8:34, 35, 38).

Mark undoubtedly desired to tell his readers that Jesus foresaw a cross for each of His followers similar to His own cross. No one should be ashamed of Jesus and His words in this wicked world. In Mark's account of the Olivet Discourse he quoted such portions of Jesus' words which centered in the coming trouble upon His followers. One of Jesus' warnings was, "But take heed to yourselves; for they will deliver you up to councils; and you will be beaten in synagogues; and you will stand before governors and kings for my sake, to bear testimony before them" (13:9). Mark continued to quote, "For in those days there will be such tribulation as has not been from the beginning of the creation which God created until now, and never will be" (v. 19). Through these announcements of coming tribulation, Mark would have his readers know that just as the Servant of the Lord suffered and died, in like manner they also may need to suffer and die.

4. The Distinctive Message of the Gospel According to Luke

a. The Historical Foundation of Christian Faith

Luke opened his Gospel by stating in forthright manner his purpose of writing. He had the concern that Theophilus, probably a Greek friend of his, might know the truth or certainty of the things underlying the Christian faith. It was written likely in the seventh decade, and Luke's approach to a believer's problem was natural. For more than thirty years the Gospel of Jesus Christ had been preached. To the Greek mind the alleged basis of the Christian faith might seem unreasonable and impossible. Luke sensed the nature of this problem and addressed himself to the task of giving a satisfying answer. Not having had the privilege of witnessing the facts underlying the Christian faith, he followed the method of a true historian, namely, to trace the course of all things accurately from the first, based on the testimony of eyewitnesses and ministers of the Word. By such a procedure alone could Theophilus be led to the certainty of the foundations of Christian faith.

Luke proceeded then to write of these things. He began with the prophetic witness to Christ given by the men and women of God at the time of Jesus' birth. He proceeded to depict the life of Jesus who was baptized with the Holy Spirit. Much of the life of this One had to do with the many intimate contacts with people, in which Jesus' human touch, His interest in people, His compassion upon the poor and needy, His word of counsel to the rich and to those in high stations in life speak for themselves as to the character of Him who was the Son of God and the Savior of the world. Luke used these commonplace human experiences as stepping-stones to presenting the profound truths coming from Jesus' lips concerning the kingdom of God, His own work as Savior of the world, and the universal mission of the gospel.

It was pertinent to this historical purpose for Theophilus to know that the events of the life of this Jesus formed a definite part of, and had a vital connection with world history. Thus Luke dated the birth of Jesus in the days of Caesar Augustus when Quirinus was governor of Syria. He dated the beginning of the Baptist's ministry with still greater details, linking this event with the time of Tiberius Caesar, Pilate, Herod, Philip, Lysanius, Annas, and Caiaphas. The trial of Jesus took place under Pilate and these Jewish leaders.

b. Jesus, the Heir to the Throne of His Father David

Luke found in the prophetic announcements given at the time of Jesus' birth the great themes which set forth the gospel of the kingdom.

The angel declared to Mary that Jesus "will be called the Son of the Most High; and the Lord God will give to him the throne of his father David, and he will reign over the house of Jacob for ever; and of his kingdom there will be no end" (Lk. 1:32, 33). The kingly work of Jesus became central to His mission. This accounts for the large place which Luke gave to the kingdom of God in his Gospel. Early in His preaching ministry Jesus said, "I must preach the good news of the kingdom of God to the other cities also; for I was sent for this purpose" (4:43). From this we gather that the kingdom of God lies at the heart of the gospel.

Jesus brought together closely the preaching of the kingdom of God and a healing ministry (9:2; 10:9). This close relationship led people to see that Jesus was the great Physician. He saved people through bodily healing, as well as through spiritual healing. The former led to a larger understanding of the latter. The supreme demand of proclaiming the kingdom of God had its basis in Jesus' claim, "All things have been delivered to me by my Father" (10:22). Jesus gave a new perspective to the common anxieties of life when He said, "Seek his kingdom . . . Fear not, little flock, for it is your Father's good pleasure to give you the kingdom" (12:31, 32).

Anticipating a question that would naturally arise in the minds of His hearers, Jesus asked, "What is the kingdom of God like? And to what shall I compare it?" (13:18). He gave His answer in two parables, the former of the grain of mustard seed and the latter of the leaven (13:18-21). In these simple stories Jesus revealed two great truths; the first, that of the external growth of the kingdom and of its providing spiritual privileges to those under the rule of God; and the second, to the personal spiritual permeation of the kingdom. It is a reality that pertains to the heart. There are stringent spiritual requirements for entering this kingdom. Jesus said, "Strive to enter by the narrow door; for many, I tell you, will seek to enter and will not be able" (13:24). On a later occasion Jesus said, "Whoever does not receive the kingdom of God like a child shall not enter it" (18:17). To the rich ruler who was unwilling to part with his wealth Jesus exclaimed, "How hard it is for those who have riches to enter the kingdom of God! For it is easier for a camel to go through the eye of a needle than for a rich man to enter the kingdom of God" (18:24, 25). Seeing that His hearers were dismayed at this statement Jesus said further, "Truly, I say to you, there is no man who has left house or wife or brothers or parents or children, for the sake of the kingdom of God, who will not receive manifold more in this time, and in the age to come eternal life" (18:29, 30).

Jesus made it clear to His hearers that the kingdom of God was not a mere addition to the law and the prophets. There is a great bisection in God's revelation to man: "The law and the prophets were until John; since then the good news of the kingdom of God is preached" (16:16). By this language Jesus showed that the good news of the kingdom of God marks the beginning of a new era in God's dealing with man. The One who brought the good news was not only a Prophet, He was more than a Prophet, He was the Son of God.

As Jesus was coming near to Jerusalem, people were supposing that the kingdom of God was to appear immediately. By way of a parable Jesus pointed to a more pertinent matter. It was not whether the kingdom of God was to appear immediately, but rather their willingness to have Christ reign over them. To each would-be citizen of His kingdom, the King has entrusted specific responsibility. There will be varying results in assuming this responsibility, but the King will not judge according to the achievements of His servants, but rather on the basis of their faithfulness to that entrusted to each. Those who refuse to yield to the rule of Christ bring upon themselves bitter condemnation and judgment (19:11-27). This parable had a definite bearing on the meaning of Jesus' presentation of Himself to Israel as their King (vv. 28-40). Jesus fulfilled in a literal way Zechariah's prediction (Zech. 9:9). His enthusiastic followers cried, "Blessed be the king who comes in the name of the Lord." This was Jesus' official call to Israel to receive Him as their Messiah and King. The time of their visitation had come, but they rejected their King. This brought upon them the awful judgment of the destruction of Jerusalem. Their Holy City, the symbol of Israel's kingdom, was to be cut down by the Gentiles and to remain so until the times of the Gentiles are fulfilled.

The messianic kingdom was established in spite of Israel's rejection of their King. This will become evident to all mankind when they "will see the Son of man coming in a cloud with power and great glory" (Lk. 21:27). Christ's return as King will bring redemption to all who have received Him. When all the terrible things spoken of by Christ will have taken place, Israel will know "that the kingdom of God is near" (v. 31).

Luke disclosed his perspective of Jesus' messiahship still more clearly when he noted how Jesus revealed the relation of the kingdom of God to the keeping of the Passover. The Passover came to its full realization in the kingdom of God. Jesus would not drink of the fruit of the vine until the kingdom of God comes. The Passover was the type of Jesus' suffering and death (22:15-18). It is not entirely clear whether Jesus was here referring to His drinking of the fruit of the vine after His resurrection, or whether He has in view the eschatological aspect of the kingdom of God which will have its beginning at His return. In view of Matthew's account of this saying, "When I drink it new with you in my Father's kingdom" (Mt. 26:29), we may conclude that Jesus here referred to the eternal state of the kingdom which will be the Father's kingdom. Before the assembly of the elders, Jesus said, "From now on the Son of man shall be seated at the right hand of the power of God" (Lk. 22:69). By this He declared His entrance upon His messianic kingship in fulfillment of Psalm 110:1.

The good and righteous Joseph of Arimathea had made enough progress in his understanding of Christ that Luke could make the comment, "He was looking for the kingdom of God" (23:51). Luke concluded his Gospel by giving a summary of Jesus' words to His disciples as He was about to ascend to heaven. For our present purpose these words are significant. Jesus told the disciples, "Everything written about me in the law of Moses and the prophets and the psalms must be fulfilled. . . . Thus it is written, that the Christ should suffer and on the third day rise from the dead, and that repentance and forgiveness of sins should be preached in his name to all nations, beginning from Jerusalem" (24:44, 46, 47). The disciples were to remain in Jerusalem until they should be clothed with power from on high. This power would come from their ascended, glorified, and enthroned Lord. Thus the kingdom of God as established by Christ was certainly the most distinctive theme of Luke's Cospel.

c. *The Son of God Baptized with the Holy Spirit*

One of the first impressions gained from reading Luke's Gospel is the manner and frequency of references to the Holy Spirit.[5] Thus one of the distinctive purposes of Luke's message is to magnify the work of Jesus, the Son of God, who was baptized with the Holy Spirit. This impression is heightened when we observe the manner in which Luke set forth the outpouring of the Holy Spirit and His work in the apostolic church (more than fifty references). This is a major point of unity between Luke's Gospel and the Acts. The meaning of this aspect of Luke's message stands out in bold relief when a survey is made of his references to Holy Spirit activity in the life and ministry of Christ. The story takes its beginning in the angel's announcement to Zechariah that the son to be born will be filled with the Holy Spirit even from birth, and he will go before the Lord "in the spirit and power of Elijah" (1:17). The angel also announced to Mary that her child will be conceived of the Holy Spirit and, "therefore the child to be born will be called holy, the Son of God" (1:35). Luke stated specifically that Elizabeth, Zechariah, and Simeon were all filled with the Holy Spirit.

Undoubtedly, both John and Jesus experienced great blessings from these Spirit-filled people. Through the power of the Spirit they spoke the great prophetic messages with reference to the work of the Baptist and of Jesus. The most significant aspect of the Baptist's work was to identify Jesus as the One who "will baptize you with the Holy Spirit and with fire" (3:16). It was John's unspeakable privilege to witness the descent of the Holy Spirit upon Jesus at His baptism and to hear the voice from heaven, "Thou art my beloved Son; with thee I am well pleased" (v. 22). Thus Jesus' baptism with the Holy Spirit became the occasion for Luke's presenting Jesus as the Savior of the world, which work He accomplished through the power of the Holy Spirit.

Let us follow this record of the Holy Spirit's work in Christ. Luke began his account by saying, "And Jesus, full of the Holy Spirit returned from the Jordan, and was led by the Spirit for forty days in the wilderness, tempted by the devil" (4:1, 2). By this Luke made it clear that the temptation was not an insignificant incident in the life of Jesus, but one into which the Spirit had led Him. Jesus' encounter with Satan was necessary for Him to be the Savior of the world. After overcoming Satan's temptation, "Jesus returned in the power of the Spirit into Galilee" (4:14). The message of the Gospel thus became the story of how the Holy Spirit empowered Jesus for His work. In the synagogue in Nazareth, Jesus appropriately read from the prophet Isaiah those very significant predictions concerning the Servant of the Lord: "The Spirit of the Lord is upon me, because he has anointed me to preach good news to the poor. He has sent me to proclaim release to the captives and recovering of sight to the blind, to set at liberty those who are oppressed, to proclaim the acceptable year of the Lord" (4:18, 19). This manner of introducing Christ's ministry permits us to believe that all of Jesus' teachings and works were done through the power of the Holy Spirit. When the seventy returned from their preaching mission and reported how even the demons were subject to them in Christ's name, Jesus declared, "I saw Satan fall like lightning from heaven" (10:18). Luke then added, "In that same hour he rejoiced in the Holy Spirit" (v. 21). This rejoicing in the Holy Spirit was possible because Christ could say, "All things have been delivered to me by my Father; and no one knows who the Son is except the Father, or who the Father is except the Son and any one to whom the Son chooses to reveal him" (v. 22). In the context of Jesus teaching His disciples how to pray, He assured them that the heavenly Father will give the Holy Spirit to those who ask Him (11:13).

While we do not know why Luke did not make specific reference to the Holy Spirit in casting out demons, it is significant to note His words, "If it is by the finger of God that I cast out demons, then the kingdom of God has come upon you" (v. 20). Matthew's specific reference to the Holy Spirit in his parallel account (Mt. 12:28) may justify our believing that Luke's expression "The finger of God" referred to the Holy Spirit.

Luke's references to the Holy Spirit reached a climax when he quoted Jesus, "He who blasphemes against the Holy Spirit will not be forgiven. And when they bring you before the synagogues and the rulers and the authorities, do not be anxious how or what you are to answer or what you are to say; for the Holy Spirit will teach you in that very hour what you ought to say" (12:10-12). Luke placed the capsheaf on his references to the Holy Spirit when he quoted Jesus' parting words to His disciples, "Behold, I send the promise of my Father upon you; but stay in the city, until you are clothed with power from on high" (24:49). Here was Jesus' promise of Pentecost. When Luke picked up this story in the Acts of the Apostles he repeated Jesus' promise, "Before many days you shall be baptized with the Holy Spirit" (Acts 1:5), to which He added, "But you shall receive power when the Holy Spirit has come upon you; and you shall be my witnesses in Jerusalem and in all Judea and Samaria and to the end of the earth" (v. 8). By way of conclusion it would appear that Luke intended his readers to know that just as the Holy Spirit had empowered Christ to carry on His work as the Lord and Savior of the world, in the same manner the Holy Spirit would empower His disciples to bring this gospel to the lost world in order that they too might be saved.

d. Jesus, the Savior of the World

This theme becomes evident in the opening words of Mary's song, "My soul magnifies the Lord, and my spirit rejoices in God my Savior" (Lk. 1:46, 47). It is significant that Mary thinks first of God as her Savior. Having received through the angel the announcement of Jesus' birth, she believed that her child, who would be called the Son of the most High and to whom God would give the throne of his father David, would Himself become the Savior of the world. In like manner Zechariah, in prophetic spirit, said, "Blessed be the Lord God of Israel, for he has visited and redeemed his people, and has raised up a horn of salvation for us in the house of his servant David" (vv. 67, 68). So Zechariah could address his child as the one to go before the Lord, "to prepare his ways, to give knowledge of salvation to his people in the forgiveness of their sins, through the tender mercy of our God" (vv. 76-78). This salvation-centered work of Jesus is struck again in the message of the angel to the shepherds when he announced, "For to you is born this day in the city of David a Savior, who is Christ the Lord" (2:11). The Spirit revealed to Simeon the same truth concerning the child Jesus when he said, "Mine eyes have seen thy salvation which thou hast prepared in the presence of all peoples, a light for revelation to the Gentiles, and for glory to thy people Israel" (vv. 30-32). Even the aged prophetess Anna "gave thanks to God, and spoke of him to all who were looking for the redemption of Jerusalem" (v. 38).

Luke carried forward this salvation theme when he noted the beginning of the Baptist's preaching centered in the baptism of repentance for the forgiveness of sin. He based his message on the words of Isaiah and concluded his quotation by saying, "All flesh shall see the salvation of God" (3:6). From a Servant of the Lord passage Jesus read in the synagogue, "He has anointed me to preach good news to the poor. He has sent me to proclaim release to the captives and recovering of sight to the blind, to set at liberty those who are oppressed, to proclaim the acceptable year of the Lord" (4:18, 19). Obviously, *the acceptable year of the Lord* is the very time that "all flesh shall see the salvation of God" (3:6). With this official announcement on the part of Jesus of His mission as the Servant of the Lord whose good news is the salvation of God, Luke unfolded the life of this Savior of the world.

The saving work of Jesus took on various forms, one of which was His healing ministry, samples of which were the healing of the man who was paralyzed, the healing of the centurion's son, and the raising of the son of the widow of Nain. Luke also presented significant teachings of Jesus which had to do with His saving work. Note the parable of the sower and observe in Jesus' explanation that there are those in whose hearts the Word was sown, but that the devil took away "the word from their hearts, that they may not believe and be saved" (8:12). But there were those who, "hearing the word, hold it fast in an honest and good heart, and bring forth fruit with patience" (v. 15). As Jesus was journeying toward Jerusalem, someone asked, "Lord, will those who are saved be few?" (13:23). We do not know what lay back of this question, but it is significant that Luke recorded the question and gave Jesus' answer. In response Jesus showed that they who are saved are those who enter by the narrow door (v. 24). Abraham, Isaac, Jacob, and the prophets had entered the kingdom of God, and "men will come from east and west, and from north and south, and sit at table in the kingdom of God" (v. 29). But those who refuse to enter will not be saved.

When the tax collectors and sinners were all drawing near to hear Jesus, the Pharisees and scribes murmured saying, "This man receives sinners and eats with them" (Lk. 15:2). In reply Jesus gave three matchless stories which pictured the saving of lost sinners. Thus the parables of the lost sheep, the lost coin, the lost son, given only by Luke, are understood best as picturing Jesus the Savior of the world. When Jesus confronted the rich ruler with the challenge to sell all that he had and to distribute to the poor, by which he would have treasure in heaven, the latter became sad. He was not willing to part with his wealth, and follow Jesus. When Jesus spoke of how hard it is for those who have riches to enter the kingdom of God, and that it is easier for a camel to go through the eye of a needle than for a rich man to enter the kingdom of God, His hearers were troubled and asked, "Then who can be saved?" (Lk. 18:26). The evident answer is that Christ can save only those who yield their all to Him and follow Him. But the reward is plain, "There is no man who has left house or wife or brothers or parents or children, for the sake of the kingdom of God, who will not receive manifold more in this time, and in the age to come eternal life" (vv. 29, 30). Eternal life is the richest synonym of salvation.

Zacchaeus, the rich tax collector, grasped this point of self-surrender when he told Jesus, "Behold, Lord, the half of my goods I give to the poor; and if I have defrauded any one of anything, I restore it fourfold" (19:8). To this Jesus answered, "Today salvation has come to this house, since he also is a son of Abraham. For the Son of man came to seek and to save the lost" (v. 10). This is another of the incidents recorded by Luke because it expressed clearly and explicitly Jesus' mission as Savior of the world. The cumulative significance to all these incidents gives the perspective of this theme in Luke's Gospel.

e. The Universal Mission of the Gospel

The preceding section has also made it clear that the gospel was for all mankind. This perspective, the universal mission of the gospel, becomes evident in Luke's Gospel. Simeon had observed that this salvation had been "prepared in the presence of all peoples, a light for revelation to the Gentiles, and for glory to thy people Israel" (2:31, 32). This universalism had already been predicted by Isaiah when he declared, "All flesh shall see the salvation of God" (3:6). It is not mere conjecture that Luke had the universal mission of the gospel in mind when he traced Jesus' ancestry back not only to Abraham, but to Adam, even to God (3:23-28). In Luke's mind this Jesus would be the Savior not merely of the descendants of Abraham, but of all mankind.

In Jesus' conversation with His audience in the synagogue (4:16-28) He noted that already in Old Testament times Elijah had brought a great spiritual blessing to the widow woman and that Elisha had cleansed Naaman, the Syrian. At this word all those in the synagogue were filled with wrath because they could not accept the idea that God's blessings through Christ would reach beyond Israel. With the faithful Abraham, Isaac, and Jacob, and the prophets shall be seated men who "will come from east and west, and from north and south, and sit at table in the kingdom of God" (13:29). This is a sublime picture of the company of the saved in the eternal kingdom of God.

When one who sat at the table with Jesus made the comment, "Blessed is he who shall eat bread in the kingdom of God!" (14:15), Jesus vividly portrayed in parable form the rejection on the part of Israel of God's invitation to the *banquet.* Jesus added in parabolic language that the servants were to go out to the streets and lanes of the city, to the highways and hedges, and to compel people to come in that His house may be filled. This pictures Gentiles sitting at this banquet table in the kingdom of God, while the unbelieving Jews, the invited guests, were excluded. It was most fitting then for Luke to quote Christ's Great Commission in the language, "that the Christ should suffer . . . and that repentance and forgiveness of sins should be preached in his name to all nations" (24:47). Thus Luke linked the historic events of his Gospel with world history. This Gospel had its origin not in a small isolated part of the world, but in the great Roman world under the rule of the Caesars. The reader could naturally conclude that this Gospel would reach out to all mankind in this Roman world. This constituted the final thrust of Luke's message.

5. The Distinctive Message of the Gospel According to John

The distinctive message of John's Gospel becomes evident in his expressed purpose in writing the words, "These are written that you may believe that Jesus is the Christ, the Son of God, and that believing you may have life in his name" (Jn. 20:31). The twofold purpose in writing this Gospel had at least three distinctive aspects: first, was his witness that Jesus is the Christ, the Son of God; second, was his disclosure of Jesus as the Revealer of Himself, the Revealer of the Father and of the Holy Spirit; and third, was the explication of the meaning of faith. In support of this John presented its basis in the signs and wonders performed by Jesus and also in the testimony of eyewitnesses. He also testified that faith centers in Christ. It was John's purpose also to declare the issue of faith, namely, life.

a. Jesus Is the Christ, the Son of God

The prologue of the Gospel leads us at once into the heart of John's message. Here he declares the profound mystery: "In the beginning was the Word, and the Word was with God, and the Word was God" (1:1). All that Jesus did had its foundation in this declaration concerning the Word. John hastened to add that "the Word became flesh and dwelt among us . . . we have beheld his glory, glory as of the only Son from the Father" (v. 14). This declaration prepared the reader to look for the glory that shone forth from the Word who became flesh. John would lead his readers to discover for themselves that this glory was that of the only Son from the Father. He concluded his prologue with the declaration: "No one has ever seen God; the only Son, who is in the bosom of the Father, he has made him known" (v. 18). This prepared the reader to anticipate Jesus' own disclosure of the Father.

John began to unfold this distinctive message by introducing the prophetic witness of John the Baptist. The Baptist declared that he was preparing the way of the Lord. His distinctive message was, "Behold, the Lamb of God, who takes away the sin of the world!" (1:29). The redemptive mission lay at the very heart of Jesus' work and proved Jesus to be the Messiah. John set forth the major purpose of the Baptist's mission by quoting his declaration, "He who sent me to baptize with water said to me, 'He on whom you see the Spirit descend and remain, this is he who baptizes with the Holy Spirit.' And I have seen and have borne witness that this is the Son of God" (vv. 33, 34).

This bringing together of the truths that Jesus was the Lamb of God together with the descent of the Spirit upon Him and of His baptizing with the Holy Spirit, constituted a significant unfolding of this part of John's distinctive message. When Jesus appeared on the scene of John's preaching, Andrew's contact with Him led the group to believe that they had found the Messiah. From this point on John allowed the witnesses of Jesus to give their own testimonies. Occasionally along the way, John added his own evaluation of an incident, typical of which is: "This, the first of his signs, Jesus did at Cana in Galilee, and manifested his glory; and his disciples believed in him" (2:11). [6]

Along with John's distinctive message that Jesus is the Son of God was the accusation on the part of the Jews that Jesus blasphemed because He said, "I am the Son of God" (10:36). This lay at the basis of their charge against Jesus before Pilate. They declared, "He ought to die, because he has made himself the Son of God" (19:7). In this way John showed that his distinctive message concerning Jesus as the Son of God was the real issue in the charges made by the Jews against Christ. John's purpose, nevertheless, was to show that in spite of the Jews' rejection of Jesus as the Son of God, he had presented ample evidence to show clearly that Jesus was the Son of God.

b. Jesus, the Revealer of Himself

John was also supremely concerned to present Jesus as the Revealer of Himself. This becomes evident in Jesus' repeated references to Himself as the Son of Man.[7] In each of these instances Jesus had given some significant teaching which had supreme significance in view of His being the Son of Man. In Jesus' conversation with Nathanael He was building up his faith which led him to exclaim: "You are the Son of God." Jesus put the capsheaf on His conversation in the words: "Truly, truly, I say to you, you will see heaven opened, and the angels of God ascending and descending upon the Son of man" (1:51). Jesus concluded His conversation with Nicodemus by saying, "No one has ascended into heaven but he who descended from heaven, the Son of man. And as Moses lifted up the serpent in the wilderness, so must the Son of man be lifted up, that whoever believes in him may have eternal life" (3:13-15). Through this claim, Jesus would have Nicodemus recognize the dignity of the One speaking to him.

On the occasion of healing the man at the pool, Bethzatha, Jesus declared that His Father is working and so also He is working. Later Jesus said that the Father had "given him authority to execute judgment, because he is the Son of man" (5:27). It is significant that Jesus explicitly made this claim to being the Messiah (4:26) to the woman of Samaria. To Pilate, Jesus said: "My kingship is not of this world; if my kingship were of this world, my servants would fight, that I might not be handed over to the Jews; but my kingship is not from the world" (18:36). With these words Jesus confirmed His claim of being the Messiah.

John continued to present Jesus' revelation of Himself through the great self-assertions, each given on a momentous occasion. At the feeding of the five thousand Jesus said, "I am the bread of life" (6:35). Thus in Christ everyone finds his deepest spiritual hunger and thirst entirely satisfied. Jesus said also, "I am the light of the world; he who follows me . . . will have the light of life." In other contexts Jesus said: "I am the door of the sheep"; . . . "I am the good shepherd" (10:7, 14). "I am the resurrection and the life" (11:25). "I am the way, and the truth, and the life" (14:6). "I am the true vine" (15:1). "If you abide in me, and my words abide in you, ask whatever you will, and it shall be done for you" (v. 7). These self-assertions represent many facets of Christ's nature as they relate to His people. They become an essential part of John's distinctive message in presenting Jesus as the Revealer of Himself.

c. Jesus, the Revealer of the Father-Son Relationship

Quite climactic in Jesus' self-revelation were His frequent references to God as His Father. Undoubtedly, John brought in these Father-Son references to show Jesus' relationship to the Father. They declared most certainly that He was the Son of God. It was Jesus' ultimate desire to reveal the Father. Let us take a rapid glance at some of these contexts. In the pool of Bethzatha incident Jesus said, "My Father is working still, and I am working" (5:17). Jesus carried the truth still further by declaring: "For as the Father raises the dead and gives them life, so also the Son gives life to whom he will" (v. 21). Jesus added: "For as the Father has life in himself, so he has granted the Son also to have life in himself, and has given him authority to execute judgment, because he is the Son of man" (vv. 26, 27). Later Jesus said: "My Father gives you the true bread from heaven. For the bread of God is that which comes down from heaven, and gives life to the world" (6:32, 33). In Jesus' last public presentation of Himself, He brought to a climax the meaning of the Father-Son relationship: believing in Christ means believing in Him who sent Jesus. Christ will not sit in judgment on those who will not receive His words. The words which He spoke will be their judge on the last day. The reason for this is that Jesus had not spoken on His own authority. He had spoken what the Father had commanded Him to speak. His final word then is, "What I say, therefore, I say as the Father has bidden me" (12:50). In the intimacy of Jesus' conversations with His disciples we have Jesus' final testimony concerning the Father. He declared: "I am in the Father and the Father in me" (14:11; cf. vv. 13, 16). He who loves Christ will be loved by the Father. Christ is going to the Father. The Father is greater than He. Prayer to the Father is efficacious if we abide in Christ and His Word abides in us. If we have asked anything of the Father, He will give it to us in Christ's name. The Lord's Prayer of John 17 gives final confirmation of the Father-Son relationship.

d. Jesus, the Revealer of the Holy Spirit

Since Jesus came forth from the Father, it is most natural to expect that He would reveal the Holy Spirit who would proceed from the Father. The Baptist had declared that Jesus on whom the Spirit descended would baptize with the Holy Spirit (1:33). Jesus had spoken to Nicodemus concerning his need of being born of the Spirit. He needed to be baptized with the Spirit in the same way that Jesus was baptized with the Spirit. Entrance into the kingdom of God required an inward change by the Spirit. It is a supernatural working of God.

To the disciples alone Jesus disclosed the person and work of the Spirit. He said: "I will pray the Father, and he will give you another Counselor . . . the Spirit of truth (14:16, 17). "He will convince the world of sin and of righteousness and of judgment" (16:8). He will guide Jesus' followers into all the truth. He will glorify Christ. By way of conclusion, John's testimony showed clearly that Jesus was the Revealer of Himself, of the Father, and of the Holy Spirit. He had come from the Holy of Holies of heaven to reveal to us the nature of God who is at once the Father and the Son and the Holy Spirit.

e. The Meaning of Faith

John's stated purpose of writing his Gospel declares yet another distinctive message. It is the meaning of faith. When John wrote: "These are written that you may believe that Jesus is the Christ, the Son of God, and that believing you may have life in his name," he set forth three aspects of faith: first, the grounds or basis of faith; second, its center, Christ, the Son of God; and third, the issue of faith, life. We do not go far in this Gospel until we discover that the ground of faith has two aspects. The first centers in the personal experiences of individuals with Christ, and the second has to do with the signs performed by Jesus whereby He manifested His glory. John focused thought on the first of these in his prologue, where he made a very inclusive statement concerning the Word who became flesh and dwelt among us (1:14, 15). This made possible the most personal and intimate contacts with the Word.

Growing out of this experience John said: "We have beheld his glory, glory as of the only Son from the Father" (v. 14). It was not merely John who beheld His glory but all who witnessed the Word made flesh. Quite specifically this referred to the twelve disciples, but it included the multitudes who heard His words, saw His mighty deeds, and had a personal relationship with Him. This total experience lay at the basis of belief in Jesus as the only Son from the Father. By way of confirmation, John brought in also the witness of the Baptist. This witness centered in the deity of Jesus by reason of His eternal preexistence. To this he added the significant experiential note, "And, from his fulness have we all received, grace upon grace" (v. 16). Thus in these initial statements centering in the grounds of faith we learn that faith has its center in a personal experience with another. It was this personal experience with Jesus that led the disciples of the Baptist to place their faith in Jesus as the Messiah.

It is this experientially centered aspect of the leading incidents depicted in this Gospel which proves the unquestionable sufficiency of the ground of Christian faith. Examine closely this aspect of Jesus' encounters with Nicodemus, with the woman of Samaria, with the blind man who received his sight, with Mary and Martha at the raising of Lazarus, with the disciples in the upper room, and with many others. It is this kind of experience which led the Samaritans to say to the woman who had been at the well, "It is no longer because of your words that we believe, for we have heard for ourselves, and we know that this is indeed the Savior of the world" (4:42). The author presented a similar picture of the occasion when Jesus went across the Jordan to the place where John had first baptized. John noted: "And many came to him; and they said, 'John did no sign, but everything that John said about this man was true.' And many believed in him there" (10:41, 42). Through these personal experiences with Jesus they came to believe in Him.

f. The Grounds of Faith

In a number of instances John noted the signs and wonders that lay at the basis of faith. John brought this into focus in his closing observation concerning Jesus' miracle at the marriage feast at Cana in Galilee. John made the observation: "This, the first of his signs, Jesus did at Cana in Galilee, and manifested his glory; and his disciples believed in him" (2:11). This word "sign" (semeion) is a definitive word with regard to the meaning of miracles. They were signs of divine authority and had meaning.[8] In specific cases they were attestations to Christ's deity and glory. By them He manifested His glory. On this foundation then the disciples grounded their faith in Christ.

The validity of faith having its foundation in a sign came under the severest test in the case of the healing of the man born blind (chapter 9). The man who received his sight could most confidently believe that the miracle took place. The devices used by the Pharisees to repudiate the meaning of this sign became utterly ridiculous. They could not gainsay his conclusion: "If this man were not from God, he could do nothing" (v. 33). All they could do was cast him out. But in doing this they did not disprove the miracle nor did they invalidate the basis for the man's faith. In Jesus' closing words with the Pharisees a final aspect of the adequacy of faith as being based on signs wrought by Jesus comes sharply into view. Of such sufficiency was the sign the basis of faith that to refuse to believe the sign brought upon the individual the judgment of spiritual blindness (v. 39). True indeed, the witnessing of the performing of a sign does not compel belief, but this does not in the least weaken the validity of signs as the ground of faith. Here we become aware of the spiritual aspect of faith and unbelief. Jesus pointed to this spiritual aspect when He concluded, "If you were blind, you would have no guilt; but now that you say, 'We see,' your guilt remains" (v. 41).

The scene of raising Lazarus brings the two-sidedness of the grounds of faith into clearest perspective. Here was a home where a love relationship existed among Jesus, Martha, Mary, and Lazarus. This was a close experiential relationship. In this setting the raising of Lazarus took place. Mary and Martha did not need this miracle in order to establish their faith in Jesus. Their association with Him was sufficient ground for believing in Him. Most assuredly the raising of Lazarus confirmed this faith. But the tomb of Lazarus was scarcely two miles from Jerusalem and many Jews had come to the home of Mary and Martha to comfort them. This miracle, taking place so near to the center of Jewish opposition to Christ, served as the most crucial test as to whether or not the supernatural work of Christ constituted sufficient ground for reposing faith in Him. John observed, "Many of the Jews therefore, who had come with Mary and had seen what he did, believed in him; but some of them went to the Pharisees and told them what Jesus had done" (11:45, 46). The reaction of the chief priests and Pharisees was significant. They said, "What are we to do? For this man performs many signs. If we let him go on thus, everyone will believe in him" (vv. 47, 48). Here was a secret admission of the actuality of these signs, but with it a stubborn resistance to believe what the signs meant.

John closed his account of the public work of Jesus with these prophetic words: "Though he had done so many signs before them, yet they did not believe in him" (12:37). He proceeded to quote the words of Isaiah as descriptive of the spiritual implications of unbelief: "He has blinded their eyes and hardened their heart, lest they should see with their eyes and perceive with their heart, and turn for me to heal them" (v. 40). In conclusion, observe that the rejection of the meaning of signs did not weaken in the least their validity. In a positive way the signs performed by Jesus which were supported by intimate personal association with Him gave complete assurance that the basis of their faith was sure and steadfast.

John gave some of Jesus' own presentations of witness to Himself (Jn. 5:30-47). These were climactic in showing the grounds of faith. The first was the witness of the Baptist. Jesus recognized that John was only human but added: "He was a burning and shining lamp." Jesus then advanced to the testimony that was greater than that of John. It was His own works which the Father granted Him to accomplish. In this language Jesus gave the true significance of His miracles. Jesus then referred to the witness borne by the Father to Himself. He was likely referring to the voice of the Father at His baptism and at the transfiguration. The fourth witness was the Scriptures. In these Scriptures His hearers thought they had eternal life. By reason of this, Jesus could very properly claim that they bore witness to Him. Finally, Jesus claimed that Moses wrote of Him. The conclusiveness of Jesus' appeal to these testimonies as the bases for believing in Him was evident.

g. Christ, the Center of Faith

This Gospel shows most clearly the center of faith, Christ. Faith has to do with a person. It is not nebulous or vacuous. The references already given make this clear. If Jesus had not built up close personal ties with the people of His day, especially His disciples, they would never have believed in Him. This is the essence of Peter's noble confession when he said: " 'Lord, to whom shall we go? You have the words of eternal life; and we have believed, and have come to know, that you are the Holy One of God' " (6:68, 69). Note Jesus' tender words: "Let not your hearts be troubled; believe in God, believe also in me" (14:1). In this manner Jesus held before the disciples the person-centered character of faith.

h. The Issues of Faith and Unbelief

We need to examine the issues of faith and its opposite, unbelief; namely, life and death. Returning yet once more to John's prologue we read: "In him was life, and the life was the light of men" (1:4). These words prepare us to see the issue of believing Jesus or rejecting Him. This becomes clearer as we read further: "To all who received him, who believed in his name, he gave power to become children of God; who were born, not of blood nor of the will of the flesh nor of the will of man, but of God" (vv. 12, 13). This thought is carried forward in those matchless words: "For God so loved the world that he gave his only Son, that whoever believes in him should not perish but have eternal life" (3:16). Here are the issues of eternal life and its opposite that of perishing. John brought this section to a fitting climax with the words: "He who believes in the Son has eternal life; he who does not obey the Son shall not see life, but the wrath of God rests upon him" (3:36). Jesus Himself spoke these identical words in the midst of His bread of life discourse, "Truly, truly, I say to you, he who believes has eternal life. I am the bread of life" (6:47, 48).

This issue of life and its opposite death came to the fore in Jesus' message on the good shepherd. Keeping in mind the background of this discussion, that of the Pharisees' stubborn resistance to Christ, we can see the deep significance of Jesus' words as a good shepherd when He said, "I came that they may have life, and have it abundantly" (10:10). Near the end of this message Jesus added: "My sheep hear my voice, and I know them, and they follow me; and I give them eternal life, and they shall never perish" (vv. 27, 28).

On the occasion of Lazarus' death Jesus challenged Martha with the most sublime issue of faith, in the words, "I am the resurrection and the life; he who believes in me, though he die, yet shall he live, and whoever lives and believes in me shall never die" (11:25, 26).

With this brief presentation of the meaning of faith including its grounds, its center, and its issues, John's purposive words mount to highest significance, "These are written that you may believe that Jesus is the Christ, the Son of God, and that believing you may have life in his name" (20:31).

For Additional Reading and Reference:

Conzelmann, *An Outline of the Theology of the New Testament,* pp. 140-152.
Klassen and Snyder, *Current Issues in New Testament Interpretation,* pp. 79-90.
Weidner, *Biblical Theology of the New Testament,* Vol. I, pp. 220-226.
See articles on the several Gospels in Bible dictionaries and encyclopedias.

1. See quotations in Mt. 2:6, 15, 18; 4:15, 16; 8:17; 12:18-21; 21:4, 5.
2. Mk. 1:11 (an echo of Is. 42:1); 2:20 (53:8 LXX); 3:23-27 (49:24 f.; 53:12); 8:31 (52:13 — 53:12); 9:12 (49:7; 53:3); 10:45 (53:10, 11); 14:24 (53:12); 15:5 (53:7).
3. Mk. 2:10; 8:31; 9:9, 12; 10:33; 14:62.
4. Mk. 2:5, 16, 24; 3:2; 7:5; 8:11; 10:2; 11:15-19, 28; 12:12, 13.
5. Lk. 1:15, 35, 41, 67; 2:25-27; 3:16, 22; 4:1, 14, 18; 10:21; 11:13; 12:10, 12.
6. Cf. Jn. 2:23; 4:54; 6:68, 69; 8:30; 10:41, 42; 11:45; etc.
7. Jn. 1:51; 3:13, 14; 5:27; 6:27, 53, 62; 8:28; 9:36, 37; 13:31.
8. See Jn. 2:11, 18, 19, 23; 3:2; 4:54; 6:2, 14, 26; 7:31; 9:16; 10:41; 11:47; 12:17, 18, 37; 20:30.

CHAPTER IV

JESUS' BIRTH: THE BEGINNING OF THE NEW COVENANT REVELATION

1. Introduction

Even a casual examination of the opening chapters of Matthew and Luke will show the unique character of their contents. Among other things observe the genealogies, the angel appearances, the deep spirituality of the devout God-fearing Jews, the Holy Spirit activity, and, most of all, the nature of Jesus' birth. The prophetic voices of Zechariah, of Simeon, of Anna, and of Mary reveal their profound comprehension of Israel's prophetic Scriptures. They had grasped their meaningful spiritual content. These scenes formed the most appropriate environment for the birth of Jesus.

2. The Messianic Era Heralded by Angelic Annunciation and Actualized by the Holy Spirit

The appearance of an angel of the Lord and also of the angel Gabriel served as the credentials to these holy people that God was beginning a new era of divine revelation. Angelic appearances were one of the evidences to Old Testament saints of a divine revelation being given to them. In the cases of Zechariah, Mary, and Joseph, God revealed the meaning of the extraordinary events about to take place. God had again begun to act in history.

The activity of the Holy Spirit also came clearly into view. The Baptist would be filled with the Holy Spirit. The Holy Spirit brought about the conception of Jesus. Through being filled with the Holy Spirit both Elizabeth and Zechariah prophesied. The Holy Spirit was upon Simeon and revealed to him "that he should not see death before he had seen the Lord's Christ" (Lk. 2:26). He gave predictions concerning the messianic work of Jesus. This activity of the Holy Spirit in relation to the birth of Jesus prepares us to anticipate that the Holy Spirit would be active throughout the life and ministry of Jesus.

3. The Predicted Mission of the Baptist

By reason of the great work which the Baptist was chosen to fulfill, he was to be brought up under the strict discipline of a Nazarite. In brief, his mission was to turn many of the children of Israel unto the Lord their God. The angel declared that John would go before the

Lord "in the spirit and power of Elijah" (Lk. 1:17). This indicated that Malachi's prediction was fulfilled in the Baptist. From this we should learn that the era of time about which Malachi prophesied was beginning to come to its fulfillment in the Baptist. This is an important link between this new era of revelation and Old Testament prophecy. The angel also declared that John was "to make ready for the Lord a people prepared" (v. 17). It may be that these words reflect the predictions of Isaiah 40:3; 57:14; and 62:10. The first of these clearly foretold the work of the Baptist. The last two have a more general reference to the preparation for the coming of the Lord. From this angelic annunciation we may gather that John's work would compare with that of Elijah and that he had the specific task of making ready for the Lord a people prepared. No prophet ever had a greater mission than this.

Zechariah himself gave prediction of John's mission. Speaking to John, he said, "You . . . will be called the prophet of the Most High; for you will go before the Lord to prepare his ways, to give knowledge of salvation to his people in the forgiveness of their sins" (Lk. 1:76, 77). Here again several Old Testament Scriptures seem to find expression, such as Isaiah 40:3 and Malachi 3:1; 4:5. Being a prophet of the Most High he had the great task of preparing the way for the coming of the Lord. This forecast indicated most clearly the spiritual nature of John's work.

4. The Nature of Jesus' Birth and Its Significance for Theology

a. The Historical Character of the Virgin Birth Narratives

Both Matthew and Luke unquestionably assert that Jesus was without human father. He was conceived of the Holy Spirit. The details supplied by each writer cannot escape attention. In Matthew's account we have Joseph's side of the story. On learning that Mary was with child, Joseph resolved to divorce her quietly. As he was considering this, an angel of the Lord appeared to him and gave the explanation that what was conceived in her was of the Holy Spirit. On this account Joseph took Mary for his wife but did not know her until she had borne her child. Undoubtedly Matthew would not have presented these details of so private a matter if he had not known of their historical accuracy.

The same may be said for Luke's narrative. In this case the conception of Jesus was described against a background of the conception of John. Elizabeth was barren and was advanced in years. The angel promised Zechariah that Elizabeth would bear him a son and that he would be filled with the Holy Spirit from his mother's womb. Mary, on the other hand, was a virgin. The angel Gabriel declared to her that she would have a son and that this would come to pass through the power of the Holy Spirit. Luke added the detail in which Mary asked the angel the question: "How can this be, since I have no husband?" (Lk. 1:34). This account tells the story from Mary's viewpoint and safeguards her integrity of character. It should be evident that Luke would not have supplied the details of a matter as personal as this without having had sufficient grounds for doing so. In both narratives the integrity of the writers is at stake.

John's Gospel may also make reference to the virgin birth. It appears, as we would expect, in the prologue. Irenaeus, Tertullian, and Augustine gave witness to the reading of 1:13 as found in the old Latin *b* which reads *qui natus est* (who was born). The Sinaitic Syriac reads, "Who (plural) was born (singular) . . . of God." According to Tertullian, the gnostic Valentinians, ca. AD 140, changed the original singular verb to the plural. The Occidentals, however, held to the singular until the third or possibly the fourth century. None of the oldest Greek manuscripts has the singular form. On this account an evaluation of the textual problem differs radically from the usual method of comparing the readings of the Greek codices. While most modern scholars reject the reading, "Who was born . . . of God," Fr. Blass, Theodore Zahn, Geerhardus Vos, and R. C. H. Lenski support it. The textual evidence supporting this reading antedates the earliest Greek codices B, Aleph, A, and C.

Furthermore, since *He* (the Word) is the subject of each sentence in verses 9-12, 14, the singular form *who was born . . . of God* is entirely congruent with the context both grammatically and in thought content. It was the most fitting way for John to present the meaningful data preparatory to the climactic declaration of verse 14, "And the Word became flesh." In this context it was most natural, indeed essential, for John to give his testimony to the virgin birth of Christ. John set forth two facts which are involved in the virgin birth: first, the absence of reference to the male parenthood of the *Logos;* and second, the clear affirmation that God was His Father. This interpretation of John 1:13 undoubtedly runs counter to almost all modern scholars. At the same time many expositors of John's Gospel give passing notice to it. [1]

Though a discussion on the historicity of the virgin birth does not belong to the discipline of biblical theology, yet the denials of its historical character are so persistent that some attention should be given to it. In Chapter II I drew attention to the various forms of biblical criticism which have bearing on the historical character of the Gospels. I proceeded to give a positive approach to their historical character. All that I gave with reference to the Gospel records in general applies specifically to the accounts of Jesus' birth.

Let us examine some of the arguments raised against the historical character of these virgin birth accounts.

(1) Mark knows nothing about the virgin birth. This is an argument from silence. Unless it can be shown why Mark did not include this in his Gospel, his failure to mention it has no significance. A careful study of the distinctive message of Mark, as I attempted to show in the foregoing chapter, will give grounds for believing that the record of Jesus' birth did not relate to his purpose. Since he did not include this account in his Gospel, its absence does not in any way weaken the testimony of the two Gospel records which do present it.

(2) There is nothing in the body of Matthew and Luke to confirm the accounts of the virgin birth. This again is an argument from silence. We might ask, Why should we expect additional references to Jesus' birth in these Gospels? We cannot so easily detach the narratives from the remainder of these respective records. From the angle of textual criticism all the oldest manuscripts of these Gospels contain these accounts. Hence the deletion of them from the Gospel records has its sole basis in subjective criticism. On this account it is an utterly unscholarly procedure.

(3) The genealogies are only through Joseph. While this is true, there is no ground for the conclusion that therefore Jesus was the Son of Joseph. Genealogically, He was the Son of Joseph, but not so in actual fact. Both Matthew and Luke explicitly state that Joseph did not bring about the conception of Jesus. Both declared that Jesus was conceived of the Holy Spirit.

(4) No other New Testament writers who refer to Jesus in the flesh make any mention of the virgin birth. This is again an argument from silence. It is true that we might expect Paul in some context, such as Philippians 2:1-11, to have included this detail. The author of Hebrews could also have made mention of it in 2:14-18. In view of what John wrote in the prologue to his Gospel, the reader may even be surprised that he made no mention of it in that context. But in none of these cases can we say that their failure to make any mention of the virgin birth constitutes an argument against its historicity. In order to appreciate how fallacious this kind of argument is, why didn't Paul or the author of Hebrews or James or even John make any reference to the transfiguration? Why didn't these same writers make any reference to the Sermon on the Mount, the kingdom parables, or to the Olivet Discourse? Is it not possible to say that the multiple testimony to the incarnation as found in Philippians, Hebrews, the Gospel and First Letter of John all give indirect support to the accounts of

the virgin birth? The mysteries which these writers reveal concerning the incarnation are entirely compatible with the mystery of the virgin birth.

(5) The virgin birth has its parallels in pagan myths of polytheistic promiscuity and therefore it is also a myth without any historical basis. On this point it is sufficient to quote the very well-written words of Dale Moody, "The yawning chasm between these pagan myths of polytheistic promiscuity and the lofty monotheism of the virgin birth of Jesus is too wide for careful research to cross."[2] This is a brief but scholarly article in support of the virgin birth of Jesus. [3]

(6) The virgin birth interpreted as a myth. Space forbids a detailed grammatico-historical approach to the records. Manifestly, the problem is not one of exegetical interpretation because the denials of the historicity and actuality of the virgin birth have their bases in literary criticism and philosophical prepossessions. Nevertheless, the interpretation of the biblical records requires an honest approach and inquiry into the thoughts which the writers intended to express. Assuming the moral integrity of the authors, our task is to reproduce in our minds the thoughts which they sought to convey. First, both writers presented their narratives in simple forthright language with a solid basis in contemporary history and in an accurate geographical setting. Second, the divine communications given to Joseph and to Mary harmonized perfectly with other revelations of God to His people throughout biblical history. Third, the verbal messages to both Joseph and Mary were stated in simple intelligible language and were entirely free from enigmatic, obscure, ambiguous, fictitious, or legendary connotations. Fourth, the respective statements of the account in Matthew and Luke stand in complete harmony with each other. Both clearly state that the Holy Spirit effected the child's conception. Both assert that there had been no marital relations before the child was conceived. Fifth, the two records are clearly independent from each other.

b. The Doctrinal Significance of the Virgin Birth

Neither Matthew nor Luke gave a formal doctrinal presentation of the virgin birth. The words which accompany the formal announcements of the nature of Jesus' birth are, nevertheless, very rich in suggesting the doctrinal significance of this event.

(1) It accounts for the dignity of the person Jesus as divine and human. Clearly the one to be born would be genuinely human. He was born of a human mother. It is equally clear that the conception for His birth came about through the power of the Holy Spirit. This would suggest that the human Jesus was also genuinely divine. This is exactly

what the angel declared to Mary when he said, "He will be great, and will be called the Son of the Most High; and the Lord God will give to him the throne of his father David" (Lk. 1:32). This announcement at once declared the deity and humanity of Jesus. Matthew's account expressed the same truth. Mary will bear a Son. Pointing up the dignity of the One to be born Matthew quoted the significant Isaiah 7:14 passage which reads, " 'Behold, a virgin shall conceive and bear a son, and his name shall be called Emmanuel' (which means, God with us)" (Mt. 1:23). The manner in which this quotation is brought in by Matthew is such that the name, Emmanuel, carried its strict meaning. It is no wonder then that the wise men from the East fell down and worshiped the child of Mary. In further proof that the name "Emmanuel" carried a sense of deity is found in the quotation from Hosea 11:1, "Out of Egypt have I called my son" (Mt. 2:15). In this quotation the Lord is the speaker.

(2) The virgin birth also accounts for the sinless nature of Jesus. This is the most natural connotation of the word *holy* by which Jesus was to be called. He is the Son of God, therefore, sinless. Sinlessness is the most natural connotation of Emmanuel. Recognizing full well the unexplainable mystery revealed in Jesus, it requires only a cursory reading of the Gospel records to satisfy oneself that Jesus was genuinely human, as well as genuinely divine. Being true Deity He was without sin in His nature.

(3) The virgin birth accounts for the aspect of preexistence bound up in His titles: the Son of God, and Son of the Most High. Neither Matthew nor Luke referred to Jesus' preexistence but the record of the virgin birth at once removes an almost insuperable difficulty concerning Jesus. John's prologue and Paul's account of the humiliation of Jesus (Phil. 2) would be almost unexplainable without the account of the virgin birth.

(4) The virgin birth accounts most satisfactorily for the divine-human nature of Jesus. The Gospel records present Him as at once human and divine. John wrote of how "the Word became flesh and dwelt among us"; and Paul, that He, who "was in the form of God" took "the form of a servant, being born in the likeness of men."

By way of conclusion, in an effort to state the meaning of the virgin birth, we should state that it was left for all the writers of the New Testament to unfold the meaning of this greatest event of world history. All that these New Testament writers gave concerning the divine-human nature of Jesus ultimately had their basis in the historic fact that Jesus was conceived of the Holy Spirit and born of the Virgin Mary.

5. Forecasts of the Mission of Jesus

In a most remarkable way the infancy narratives of Matthew and Luke gave predictions of the work of Jesus. These forecasts may be grouped under five headings, each of which is a designation of Jesus as found in the Old Testament. This fact shows again the close connection between the new revelation of Christ with the Old Testament predictions of His work. They all grow out of the fact of the virgin birth of Jesus and show that His supernatural birth "is the sign of the inauguration of the Last Things."[4] These narratives present Jesus as (1) the Savior, (2) the Lord, (3) the Messiah, (4) the Servant of the Lord, and (5) the Branch. Let us discover the profound manner in which the mission of Jesus as predicted by God's spokesmen shines forth in all its glory.

a. Jesus, the Savior

This came definitely to the forefront when the angel told Joseph: "You shall call his name Jesus, for he will save his people from their sins" (Mt. 1:21). Thus Jesus' work was comprehensively the task of saving His people from their sins. Zechariah had already given predictions centering in the saving work which God would bring about in the days of the Messiah. In the magnificent prophetic words of Luke 1:68-79, he spoke of God as having "raised up a horn of salvation for us" (v. 69). As noted earlier, John's mission was to prepare the way of the coming Lord. This preparation centered in giving knowledge of salvation to God's people in the forgiveness of their sins (v. 77). In the announcement of the angels to the shepherds of Jesus' birth they declared that "a Savior, who is Christ the Lord" (2:11), was born. These three references to the saving work of Jesus were the fulfillment of a number of significant Old Testament Scriptures which looked to Israel's God as the One who would bring salvation to all mankind.[5]

There is a great buildup of thought in the Old Testament on this salvation theme. It had its beginning in the deliverance of Israel out of Egypt. When Israel was bidden to stand still and see the salvation of the Lord, they experienced a great physical deliverance from Egypt by the power of God. We need to observe, also, that this liberation was in a larger way a spiritual one. The sacrifice of the Passover lamb, as well as the bloody sacrifices which instituted the covenant at Mt. Sinai, shows that this salvation was at heart a saving from sin. These Old Testament references show how the prophets of Israel led God's people to grasp the spiritual character of salvation and of God as their Savior. The significance of this reaches its highest point when it becomes predictive of the work of the Coming One. The announcing angel who gave the name "Jesus" to the baby born in Bethlehem adds final certification to this point.

Let us note also that the salvation to be brought by Jesus would extend to all people. The salvation prepared by God took place in the presence of all peoples. He would be "a light for revelation to the Gentiles, and for glory to thy people Israel" (Lk. 2:10, 30-32).

b. Jesus, the Lord

The angel announced to Zechariah that the son to be born to Elizabeth "will turn many of the sons of Israel to the Lord their God" (Lk. 1:16). In this message the angel was reflecting on the prediction of Malachi with reference to the coming of Elijah (Mal. 4:5, 6). The Baptist fulfilled this prediction by turning many of Israel to the Lord, their God. In this manner Jesus received the title "Lord." Elizabeth spoke to Mary as the one who would become the mother of her Lord (Lk. 1:41-43). This title came to Zechariah's lips as he himself predicted concerning the work of his own son that he would go before the Lord to prepare His ways. (1:76). These words reflected the prophecies of Isaiah 40:3-5; Malachi 3:1, 2.

In this manner the Old Testament predictions of the coming of the Lord had their fulfillment in Jesus. This gives added meaning to the words of the angel who spoke to the shepherds saying that there was born "in the city of David a Savior, who is Christ the Lord" (Lk. 2:11). The mission of Jesus, then, had to do with the exercise of this lordship. It is likely that the psalmist who wrote: "But thou, O Lord, art enthroned for ever; thy name endures to all generations. Thou wilt arise and have pity on Zion; it is the time to favor her; the appointed time has come" (Ps. 102:12, 13) was identifying the exercise of Jesus' lordship as a kingship. The coming Lord would be enthroned forever. The frequency of the use of this title "Lord," both by Jesus Himself and His followers indicates how fully and completely this prediction of Jesus as Lord came to fulfillment.

c. Jesus, the Messiah

In both Luke and Matthew the messianic significance of the predictions centering in Jesus is clear. It becomes evident first in the annunciation to Mary of Jesus' birth. The angel said, "He will be great, and will be called the Son of the Most High; and the Lord God will give to him the throne of his father David, and he will reign over the house of Jacob for ever; and of his kingdom there will be no end" (Lk. 1:32, 33). In this announcement there seems to be a clear reference to Nathan's words to David concerning the birth of a son who would reign in his stead. Clearly, the fulfillment of this was in the person of Solomon, but the prediction carried a potential of fulfillment in One who is greater than Solomon. This becomes evident in Psalms 2; 45; 110. While Solomon was an anointed one, the prophetic note in these psalms looks to One who in the most real way would be the *anointed one*. Concerning this One, God addressing the One to come says, "Therefore God, your God, has anointed you with the oil of gladness above your fellows" (Ps. 45:7).

In similar manner David's Psalm 110 begins, "The Lord says to my lord: 'Sit at my right hand, till I make your enemies your footstool.' " The One addressed as Lord in this psalm was also spoken of as "a priest for ever after the order of Melchizedek." From this we should learn that Jesus, the Messiah, was also the "priest for ever after the order of Melchizedek." Just as Melchizedek combined in himself the offices of king and priest, so the Christ would also exercise the same offices. Observe also that the Holy Spirit revealed to Simeon that he would see the Lord's Christ (Lk. 2:26). This was the basis for his confidence in "looking for the consolation of Israel" (v. 25). In this context Simeon saw the salvation aspect of the Messiah's work. The salvation which God had "prepared in the presence of all peoples" centered in the Lord's Christ. In Simeon's reflection on the *Servant of the Lord* passage from Isaiah, he was identifying the Messiah with the Servant of the Lord. Whether or not the author of the Servant of the Lord passages had already made this identification, we do not know. If Simeon was the first to identify the two, it marks an important forward step in the unfolding of divine revelation centering in Jesus (Lk 2:30-32).

Let us now observe how Matthew portrayed the Messiah in the opening chapters of his Gospel. At least two things become clear in Matthew's genealogy, both being apparent in the first verse of the book. It reads, "The book of the genealogy of Jesus Christ, the son of David, the son of Abraham." Matthew's first concern was to declare the descent of Jesus from David; and second, to show Jesus' descent from Abraham. Each carried a point of great significance. The former becomes evident when we realize that Jesus was the heir to David's throne, should it be reestablished. The messianic import of this is clear. Matthew sought to present the life and ministry of Jesus as the heir to David's throne. He climaxed his Gospel with Jesus' own claim to messianic kingship in the words, "All authority in heaven and on earth has been given to me" (Mt. 28:18). When Matthew began his genealogy with Abraham, he evidently saw some connection between Jesus' work and the promises given to Abraham. God had said, "By you all the families of the earth will bless themselves" (Gen. 12:3). Note the alternate reading, "In you all the families of the earth will be blessed." It would appear that Matthew saw in Jesus the fulfillment of this promise. This note of universalism becomes apparent throughout the Gospel and reaches its climax in the Great Commission, "Go therefore and make disciples of all nations" (Mt. 28:19). In a word, Jesus, the Messiah, will bring to fulfillment the universal mission of the gospel.

Under the discussion of Jesus, the Savior, I noted that the angel spoke of the work of Jesus Christ as being a Savior. Matthew performed another service by identifying Jesus Christ as the Emmanuel. Most scholars would hold that Isaiah had already identified the Emmanuel with the promised child of Isaiah 9 and also with the Branch that would grow out of the stump of Jesse (Is. 11). The angel's word to Joseph simply confirmed this identification. Matthew's story of the wise men was also clearly messianically oriented in the Messiah. They inquired, "Where is he who has been born king of the Jews?" (Mt. 2:2). The answer given to the wise men was naturally messianic in its character. They quoted the prophet Micah, who had predicted that out of Bethlehem a Ruler would come who would be Ruler in Israel (5:2). The wise men on coming to Bethlehem gave Jesus gifts that were appropriate for a king. Matthew, accordingly, had set the stage for the presentation of Jesus, the Messiah.

d. Jesus, the Servant of the Lord

At the expense of a bit of repetition let us observe again how Simeon reflected the Servant of the Lord passages of Isaiah. A study of these references (Is. 42:1-7; 49:1-6; 50:4-9; 52:13 — 53:12; 61:1-3) shows that the prophet's concept of the Servant of the Lord depicted the Servant as a towering figure and most naturally to be identified with the Messiah. In this fashion Luke used this story to forecast the mission of Jesus.

e. Jesus, the Branch

We should also observe that the question of the wise men reflected two of the great *Branch* passages from Jeremiah and Zechariah (Jer. 23:5; Zech. 9:9). Thus the wise men were identifying the One that was born and the righteous Branch predicted by God through Jeremiah. Matthew's including this wise men story in his Gospel confirmed the fulfillment of the Branch prophecy in Jesus. It means that all the predicted work concerning the Branch centering in His kingly work was fulfilled in Jesus.

f. Jesus, the Son of God

The message of the angel to Mary came to its climax in the prediction: "Therefore the child to be born will be called holy, the Son of

God" (Lk. 1:35). This may have its background in Nathan's prophetic message to David concerning the birth of Solomon: "I will be his father, and he shall be my son . . . your throne shall be established for ever (2 Sam. 7:14-16). When Jesus was baptized by John the Baptist, a voice from heaven said, "This is my beloved Son" (Mt. 3:17). This quite certainly reflects Ps. 2:7: "You are my son, today I have begotten you."

By way of conclusion let us note how significant these forecasts of the mission of Jesus really are. When we see the total picture of Jesus as the Savior, the Lord, the Servant of the Lord, the Branch, and the Son of God, we have for all practical purposes the total Old Testament prediction concerning the mission of Jesus. They prepare us in a most significant way for pursuing our study of the life and teachings of Jesus as depicted in all four of the Gospels.

For Additional Reading and Reference:

Bruce, F. F., *New Testament Development of Old Testament Themes*, pp. 68-82.
Interpreter's Dictionary of the Bible, "Jesus Christ."
Lindars, *New Testament Apologetic*, pp. 189-221.
Richardson, *An Introduction to the Theology of the New Testament*, pp. 169-178.
Ryrie, *Biblical Theology of the New Testament*, pp. 38-45.
Sheldon, *New Testament Theology*, pp. 56-59.
Vos, *Biblical Theology*, pp. 328-334.

1. Works which make reference to the content of verse 13 follow: (1) *Commentaries on the Gospel of John*, Plummer (*Cambridge Greek Testament for Schools and Colleges)* Godet, Westcott, Maccgregor, Robertson (*Word Pictures in the New Testament*), Lenski, Howard (*The Interpreter's Bible*), Hendrikson, Richardson (Torch Bible Commentaries), Tasker (*Tyndale Bible Commentaries*); (2) *Textual Criticism:* Robertson; (3) *The Virgin Birth.* Orr, pp. 111, 112; Machen, pp. 255-258; (4) *The Self-Disclosure of Jesus*, Vos, pp. 208-212; (5) *The Jerusalem Bible.*

2. *The Interpreter's Dictionary of the Bible* (New York and Nashville: Abingdon Press, 1962), Vol. R-Z; article, "Virgin Birth," p. 791.

3. A sample of how an author can utterly disregard the most natural sense of language is found in the article by F. C. Grant in *The Interpreter's Dictionary of the Bible*, Vol. E-J, pp. 879,880.

4. Allan Richardson, *An Introduction to the Theology of the New Testament* (New York: Harper and Brothers, 1958), p. 174.

5. See Ps. 3:8; 27:1; 62:2; 68:19; 118:14, 21; Is. 12:2, 3; 33:2; 52:7, 10 — all of which deal with the salvation theme. See also 45:15, 21; 49:26; 60:16; 63:8, which center in the coming Savior.

CHAPTER V

THE REVELATION THROUGH JOHN THE BAPTIST

1. John's Place in the Organism of Revelation

The prophetic announcements given concerning John the Baptist by the angel and by Zechariah prepare us for pursuing further a study of him who came in the spirit and power of Elijah. Perhaps the best way of pursuing this inquiry is to examine: first, John's place as given by the synoptists; second, John's own claims; and third, the place Jesus ascribed to John.

a. John's Place as Given by the Synoptists

In the synoptic accounts (Mt. 3:1-6; Mk. 1:1-3; Lk. 3:1-6) John is suddenly brought on the scene "preaching a baptism of repentance for the forgiveness of sins" (Mk. 1:3). His text was: "Repent, for the kingdom of heaven is at hand" (Mt. 3:2). All three of the synoptists identified the Baptist as fulfilling what was spoken by the prophet Isaiah. Interestingly enough, Mark began his Isaiah quotation with the words of Malachi 3:1 and Luke gave the longest quotation from Isaiah (40:3-5). By identifying John with the *messenger*, Mark linked the Baptist with the great messianic prophecy from Malachi, the last of the writing prophets. The messenger's work was to prepare the way for the Lord (Mal. 1:1-3). The size of John's task got its dimensions from the greatness of the work of the Lord, who was the messenger of the covenant. He would sit as a refiner and purifier of silver. He would purify the sons of Levi till they present the right offerings to the Lord.

Translated into the language of fulfillment, John's task was a momentous spiritual one that had to do with a very much needed cleansing of Israel from their sin. Since it is very clear that this messenger would be the same as the "Elijah who is to come" (Mal. 4:5, 6), we may properly conclude that this also lay in Mark's mind in his identifying John with the messenger.

The quotation from Isaiah 40:3-5 is equally significant. It begins with the words of comfort that God would speak to Jerusalem. Jerusalem's warfare is ended and her iniquity is pardoned. In a simple figure the prophet pictured the coming one who would prepare the way of the Lord. Through desert, mountain, and valley he would prepare a highway for his God. As a result of this spiritual road-building, the glory of the Lord would be revealed and all flesh would see it together (v. 5). From these two contexts it becomes clear that to John was given a task of tremendous significance, to which he had to give himself. This responsibility was greater than that of any prophet before his time. The prophetic perspective of both Isaiah and Malachi placed John at the inauguration of the great messianic era spoken of by all the Old Testament prophets. In the unfolding of God's plan for the world this was to be the greatest era of human history, that to which all eschatological predictions looked and served as a preparation.

b. John's Own Claims

John himself had a clear understanding of the greatness of his mission. According to the synoptic record (Mt. 3:11, 12; Mk. 1:7, 8; Lk. 3:15-18) John made it clear that his baptizing with water was unto repentance and that the One coming after him would baptize with the Holy Spirit and with fire. By this language John showed that his work was one of preparation for the greater work of the Messiah, which centered in Holy Spirit baptism. John plainly enlarged on the greatness of the One to come and of his own lower rank to Him when he said, "After me comes he who is mightier than I, the thong of whose sandals I am not worthy to stoop down and untie" (Mk. 1:7). In vivid language John described the nature of the work of the Christ. Said John, "He will baptize you with the Holy Spirit and with fire. His winnowing fork is in his hand, to clear his threshing floor, and to gather the wheat into his granary, but the chaff he will burn with unquenchable fire" (Lk. 3:16, 17; Mt. 3:12). Only those who repented would be baptized with the Holy Spirit. The coming Messiah would perform a thorough work of cleansing which would terminate in fiery judgment upon those who refused to be cleansed. John made it clear to his Jewish hearers that the work of the coming Christ would not allow any careless attitudes toward, or disregard of, this spiritual revival.

Some problem exists as to the meaning of the language "with the Holy Spirit and with fire." Some students feel that John referred to two baptisms, one with the Holy Spirit and the other with fire. We may gain a clue as to the correct interpretation by observing that the Greek preposition *en* ("in," "by," "with") controls both the words, Holy Spirit and fire. This may suggest that the two are virtually one. Thus, baptism with the Holy Spirit by its nature is a baptism with fire. It may suggest the strongest kind of purging work which takes place in the individual who is baptized with the Holy Spirit. The words which follow this expression in both Matthew and Luke would suggest this interpretation. Luke helps us to gain their true meaning when he adds:

"With many other exhortations, he preached good news to the people" (Lk. 3:18). Certainly the heart-searching words of John were exhortations to Israel, but in all of them he was preaching good news to the people.

The Apostle John was concerned to present the testimony of the Baptist to the priests and Levites who came from Jerusalem to ask him who he was (Jn. 1:19-34). In response to their question, the Baptist spoke pointedly that he was not the Christ nor the prophet, but he did say: "I am the voice of one crying in the wilderness, 'Make straight the way of the Lord,' as the prophet Isaiah said" (Jn. 1:23). Thus John himself claimed to be "the voice" of Isaiah (Is. 40:3). John understood his mission in terms of this Isaianic prediction. He carried the meaning of his mission further when he said: "He who sent me to baptize with water said to me, 'He on whom you see the Spirit descend and remain, this is he who baptizes with the Holy Spirit.' And I have seen and have borne witness that this is the Son of God" (Jn. 1:33, 34). In this experience two profound truths were made clear to him: first, that this Jesus is He who baptizes with the Holy Spirit; and second, that He is the Son of God.

In this manner John claimed to be the official witness sent by God to identify Jesus as the Messiah. John's final word with respect to his mission appears in the words, "He who has the bride is the bridegroom; the friend of the bridegroom, who stands and hears him, rejoices greatly at the bridegroom's voice; therefore this joy of mine is now full. He must increase, but I must decrease" (Jn. 3:29, 30). This is a beautiful picture of the genuine humility of John, even though "there has risen no one greater than he" (Mt. 11:11).

c. The Place Jesus Ascribed to John

We should naturally expect that Jesus would speak in still clearer language of the place that John would fill in this new era of divine revelation. The first incident (Mt. 11:2-19; Mk. 9:11-13; Lk. 7:18-35) in which Jesus spoke of John was during his imprisonment when he sent his disciples to Jesus with the question, "Are you he who is to come, or shall we look for another?" (Mt. 11:3).

A word of explanation concerning the significance of John's question may be in order at this point. It would appear that John was unable to interpret the unfolding of events in the ministry of Jesus. Another look at the preaching of John would lead us to believe that after Jesus' call to Israel to repent, judgment would immediately follow. John said, "His winnowing fork is in his hand, and he will clear his threshing floor and gather his wheat into the granary, but the chaff he will burn with unquenchable fire" (Mt. 3:12). However, instead of Jesus bringing immediate judgment upon unbelieving Israel, His preaching was marked by the offer of continued mercy and grace. In fact, a new era of salvation appeared to be dawning in Israel. John apparently did not understand this. Jesus' reply, nevertheless, took hold of John's problem in a direct manner. John's disciples were commanded to report: "The blind receive their sight and the lame walk, lepers are cleansed and the deaf hear, and the dead are raised up, and the poor have good news preached to them" (Mt. 11:5). Jesus would have John understand that there was another element in the message of the Old Testament prophets. True indeed the prophets had predicted God's judgment upon His people, but there was also a message of salvation such as predicted in Isaiah 35:5, 6 and 61:1. In other words, if John had had the privilege of being in close contact with Jesus through the intervening time from Jesus' baptism to John's imprisonment, he would have gained this new perspective in the fulfillment of Old Testament predictions in this new era.

This gave Jesus the occasion for pointing up the greatness of John. John was not to be thought of as one being affected by all the cross-currents of the religious thought of his time. He was not a reed shaken by the wind. He was a prophet and, in fact, "more than a prophet" (Mt. 11:9). In this statement Jesus raised John above the level of the great Old Testament prophets. He was the messenger predicted by Malachi with the important task of preparing the way before the Lord. This responsibility placed John above all mankind. There is no one greater than John the Baptist, but in the same breath Jesus added, "Yet he who is least in the kingdom of heaven is greater than he" (v. 11). By this Jesus appears to be saying that the spiritual privileges of those in the kingdom of heaven are greater than those of John who still belonged in the Old Testament order of things. Jesus continued by saying, "All the prophets and the law prophesied until John; and if you are willing to accept it, he is Elijah who is to come" (vv. 13, 14).

Jesus was thus drawing a clear line between two ages: that of the prophets and the law until and including John; and that of the new era, the kingdom of God, in which the good news is preached (Lk. 16: 16). Thus in the words of F. F. Bruce, "He stood on the threshold of a new order as its herald (as Moses viewed the promised land from Pisgah) without entering in."[1] Jesus was also identifying John with Elijah as given in Malachi's prediction, thus to be the forerunner of the Messiah. Having come in the spirit and power of Elijah and being the announcer of the dawning new age, that of the kingdom of God, John's supreme greatness becomes entirely evident.

In the setting of Jesus' conversation with the disciples as they were coming down from the mountain on the occasion of the transfiguration, Jesus added another significant explanation of the place of John. The disciples were perplexed by the claims of the scribes that first Elijah must come (Mt. 17:10-13; Mk. 9:11-13). In reply Jesus said, "Elijah does come, and he is to restore all things; but I tell you that Elijah has already come, and they did not know him, but did to him whatever they pleased" (Mt. 17:11, 12). In this language Jesus fitted John into the new order of things which He as the Messiah was establishing. John's place was to restore all things. He stood at the threshold of the messianic era. His work was that of preparing for the Messiah.

On still another occasion, that of the inquiry of John's disciples with reference to fasting when at the same time Jesus' disciples were not fasting (Mt. 9:14-17; Mk. 2:18-22; Lk. 5:33, 38), Jesus answered their question in the language of a parable. He asked, "Can the wedding guests fast while the bridegroom is with them? As long as they have the bridegroom with them, they cannot fast. The days will come, when the bridegroom is taken away from them, and then they will fast in that day" (Mk. 2:19, 20). By this Jesus was saying that it was entirely "appropriate for John's disciples to fast, because they had not arrived at that wedding feast of joy in which Jesus' disciples are guests." [2]

Jesus proceeded to describe the meaning of His own mission in parabolic language by stating that no man puts a piece of unshrunk cloth on an old garment; no one puts new wine into old wineskins. By this Jesus meant that His work was not a mere continuation of Old Testament revelation but rather that His was a new movement, a new era. These two parables give a distinctive meaning to the word *new*. It is that which gives unique meaning to the new covenant as compared to the old covenant. The new is, qualitatively, vastly superior to the old. Hence the disciples were made to see that their master, John, great as he was, still belonged to the old order of things, even though he was on the threshold of the new.

2. John's Testimony to Jesus as the Messiah

a. The Synoptic Account of John's Testimony

We have already noted the witness that these accounts gave to John's testimony concerning himself. Let us now examine what John said about Jesus. He first pointed up the dignity of the coming One. John said, "He who is coming after me is mightier than I, whose sandals I am not worthy to carry" (Mt. 3:11). In genuine humility the Baptist led his disciples to look to Jesus rather than to himself. The difference between Jesus' greatness and his own is found in the fact that John baptized with water, while the coming One would baptize with the Holy Spirit and with fire. His water baptism was merely preparatory to and symbolic of the Holy Spirit baptism of Jesus. It is altogether possible that John's disciples thought at once of the Old Testament prophetic announcement of God's pouring out His Spirit upon all flesh in the days of the Messiah. These days were evidently at hand. The One who would do this Holy Spirit baptizing would soon appear on the scene. As noted above, John indicated that this Holy Spirit baptism would involve a thorough cleansing of the people. Thus the Baptist brought to focus the total Old Testament foreview of the greatness and mission of the coming Messiah.

b. The Meaning of John's Baptism

In view of Jesus' appearing on the scene to be baptized by John, it is necessary to interpret John's baptism in general. Since he did not relate his baptism to any existing ceremonial act involving water, nor did he refer to any Old Testament ablution with water, his act of baptizing was distinctive. As the records stand, John practiced his water baptism as standing in its own right without following any precedent. The synoptic records (Mt. 3:1-12; Mk. 1:1-8; Lk. 3:1-18) represent John as preaching the baptism of repentance for the forgiveness of sins. He baptized those who repented. Through being baptized by John people gained assurance that God pardons those who sincerely repent. In the words of Norval Geldenhuys, "So the baptism is the outward sign and seal that God has forgiven their sins." [3]

John's baptism needs to be seen also in the light of the prophetic words of Malachi and Isaiah concerning the meaning of the Baptist's work. These predictions make it clear that John was not baptizing on his own initiative or authority. But he was doing so in carrying out his mission as the forerunner of the Christ. By reason of the kingdom of heaven being at hand John's baptism symbolized the blessings to be received in the coming of this kingdom.

Confession of sins also accompanied the act of being baptized. In blunt language John warned the Pharisees and the Sadducees of their hypocrisy. He declared: "Bear fruits that befit repentance" (Lk. 3:8). John contended that they could not depend on blood-descent from Abraham as grounds for God's special blessings. Rather he pointed to the urgency of immediate repentance. John said: "Even now the axe is laid to the root of the trees; every tree therefore that does not bear good fruit is cut down and thrown into the fire" (v. 9).

Some students think of John as coming from the Essenes and that his baptism thus bore a close relationship to the beliefs of this group.

We have no proof of any such connection between John and the Essenes. Neither John nor the Gospel writers make any such reference. Characteristic of baptism among the Essenes was that the individual baptized himself. This places John's baptism into a different category. On the other hand there appears to be no evidence that John did not have any connection with the Essenes. As I see the problem, such connection would not lower the value of John's work. My concern is to show that John's work had its origin in the call of God, and that its distinctiveness arose from the nature of God's commission to him. According to the Gospel records John's mission is to be interpreted in the light of the Old Testament prophets as understood by John and concerning which he made definite claims.

There are some possible Old Testament precedents or analogies with which John's baptism may have some relationship. One of these may be the washing preparatory to the making of the old covenant (Ex. 19:10, 14), when God announced to Moses that He was about to make a covenant with Israel by virtue of which they would be to God a kingdom of priests and a holy nation (vv. 5, 6). He told Moses: "Go to the people and consecrate them today and tomorrow, and let them wash their garments" (19:10). This act of washing the garments may have carried a symbolism of making the people ceremonially clean and of their consecration to God.

Another possible precedent may be found in the language of washing as found in several of the prophets (Is. 1:16; 4:4; Ezek. 36:25-33; Zech. 13:1). Thus as Isaiah presented God's case against Israel he says: "Wash yourselves; make yourselves clean; remove the evil of your doings from before my eyes; cease to do evil, learn to do good; seek justice, correct oppression" (1:16). In such severe language God called Israel to repentance. In another context Isaiah wrote of the time "when the Lord shall have washed away the filth of the daughters of Zion and cleansed the bloodstains of Jerusalem" (4:4). This would be accomplished "by a spirit of judgment and by a spirit of burning" (v. 4). A bit of reflection on these stern words may lead us to see some similarity between John's work and that predicted by the prophet. Later God spoke through Ezekiel, saying: "I will sprinkle clean water upon you, and you shall be clean from all your uncleannesses, and from all your idols I will cleanse you" (Ezek. 36:25). In connection with this sprinkling God added: "A new heart I will give you, and a new spirit I will put within you" (v. 26). By this God meant that He would put His Holy Spirit within His people. This language in its context also bears similarity to that used to describe John's work. In slightly different language God spoke through Zechariah: "On that day there shall be a fountain opened for the house of David and the inhabitants of Jerusalem to cleanse them from sin and uncleanness" (Zech. 13:1). All these contexts have in view the coming age of the Messiah and are descriptive of the spiritual character of this era.

In a *Servant of the Lord* passage occurs the significant words, "I will pour water on the thirsty land, and streams on the dry ground; I will pour my spirit upon your descendants, and my blessing on your offspring" (Is. 44:3). Even some of the words of David's great penitential psalm may suggest a possible source of the ideas given concerning the meaning of John's baptism, for instance: "Wash me thoroughly from my iniquity, and cleanse me from my sin! . . . Purge me with hyssop, and I shall be clean; wash me, and I shall be whiter than snow" (Ps. 51:2, 7). In passing we might note that there is danger of reading into these Old Testament references more than their writers intended. On the other hand we are constantly reminded that there was a conscious eschatological outlook on the part of the prophets, as well as an equally conscious effort on the part of New Testament writers, to show its fulfillment through the use of similar picturesque language.

By way of conclusion to this effort of giving the meaning of John's baptism, let us observe three aspects as noted by Vos.[4] The first is the symbolic aspect. Clearly the baptism with water carries a symbolism of something spiritual. It had as its precedent the Old Testament ablution with water which was the symbol of repentance and forgiveness of sins. Perhaps Jesus made reference to this symbolism when He told Nicodemus, "Truly, truly, I say to you, unless one is born of water and the Spirit, he cannot enter the kingdom of God" (Jn. 3:5).

The second is the typical aspect of which we become aware when the eschatological background to John's baptism is grasped. Even the people were conscious of this, as noted by Luke: "As the people were in expectation, and all men questioned in their hearts concerning John, whether perhaps he were the Christ" (Lk. 3:15). John had described his baptism as indicating the imminent judgment of God (v. 17). His baptism served as the preparation of the people for this imminent judgment. In the larger picture of the Old Testament prophetic outlook with reference to the coming Messiah, John's baptism bore significant eschatological meaning. The coming of Jesus did not exhaust this prophetic outlook. It was only the beginning of the agelong work of the Messiah which would culminate in the judgment at the end of the messianic era.

The third is the sacramental aspect. God sent John to prepare the nation of Israel, His people, for their Messiah. John's baptism sealed them with reference to the imminent eschatological crisis. The day of

Israel's salvation had come, and with it Israel's judgment if they refused to repent.

John's baptism sealed the people of Israel with reference to the coming of the Messiah in the same manner as Paul wrote of Christian baptism, "In him you also, who have heard the word of truth, the gospel of your salvation, and have believed in him, were sealed with the promised Holy Spirit, which is the guarantee of our inheritance until we acquire possession of it" (Eph. 1:13, 14). From this it would appear that Paul framed his language concerning the sacramental aspect of Christian baptism according to that already done by John.

c. The Significance of Jesus' Baptism by John

We gain a perspective of the significance of Jesus' baptism when we observe that on this occasion, as well as at the transfiguration and at the visit of the Greeks, a voice came from heaven giving witness to the Father-Son relationship of the One speaking from heaven and Jesus. In each case there was a real need for this witness. On this occasion Jesus needed this testimony as He entered upon His messianic work.

(1) Reasons for Jesus' submitting to baptism. In the conversation of John with Jesus it becomes evident that both of them recognized that Jesus had no personal need for baptism because His life was without sin. As the promised Messiah, the sinless One, He had no need for repentance. Yet Jesus said, "It is fitting for us to fulfill all righteousness" (Mt. 3:15). Jesus understood that John's baptism was a call to Israel, both individually and corporately, to repentance. No Israelite was free from responding to this call. John was addressing Israel as the people of God. To be baptized, then, was "to fulfill all righteousness." As a true Israelite Jesus submitted to this commandment. The reason for Jesus' being circumcised was likely the same as for His being baptized.

Richardson finds a close relationship between Jesus' baptism and His crucifixion. He believes, "It is a reasonable inference that He had already accepted His vocation as the Servant-Messiah when He went with the crowds to be baptized by John. He had already accepted the role of the Suffering Servant who 'was stricken for the transgression of his people, although he had done no violence, neither was any deceit in his mouth' (Is. 53:8). He was the Servant . . . who would justify many and bear their iniquities (Is. 53:11), and this is why He was baptized. The sinless One is baptized with John's 'baptism of repentance unto remission of sins' (Mk. 1:4) for the same reason that He died: 'the Lord hath laid on him the iniquity of us all' (Is. 53:6). As the representative Man He bears the sins of the world to the baptism of repentance, as later He would bear them to the baptism of the cross."[5]

In this manner we may see in Jesus' baptism the larger aspect of the ushering in of the messianic era and of John's relation to it. As the Messiah, Jesus needed to yield to everything that was required of those over whom He would rule.

(2) The descent of the Spirit of God (the Holy Spirit). It is most significant that the Holy Spirit descended upon Christ in bodily form as a dove. This was an objective experience for both Jesus and John. What meaning we may gain from the bodily form of a dove is not easy to determine. Tasker finds in it "a symbol of gentleness and meekness." [6] Geldenhuys says, "In the Scriptures a dove symbolizes purity, innocence, and loveliness. So when the Holy Ghost here descends upon Jesus in the shape of a dove, this symbolizes the nature of that holy and lovely Spirit and the everlastingness and completeness of His descent upon Him."[7]

The descent of the Spirit upon Jesus was the anointing for His work as the Messiah. Thus kings were anointed with oil, and, as in the case of David, "The Spirit of the Lord came mightily upon David." [8] Priests were also anointed for their work. [9] God commanded Elijah to anoint Elisha as prophet in his place (1 Kings 19:16). All this shows how significant were the prophetic announcements of Isaiah concerning the anointing of the coming One (Is. 11:2; 42:1; 44:3; 61:1; see other Old Testament predictions concerning the outpouring of the Holy Spirit in the latter days). Through this anointing with the Holy Spirit, Jesus knew that He was the One predicted by Isaiah as having the Spirit of the Lord resting upon Him and that He was the Servant upon whom God had put His Spirit. He could say as He did say later: "The Spirit of the Lord is upon me, because he has anointed me to preach good news to the poor" (Lk. 4:18). By this Jesus knew that He was the Servant of the Lord in whom were united the offices of prophet, priest, and king.

The descent of the Spirit upon Jesus showed also that through the power of the Holy Spirit He would be enabled to perform His work as the Messiah. We need to understand the interrelation of the divine and the human in Jesus' nature. On the one hand, Jesus' powers were limited by His finite human nature; on the other, He — the Son of God — was empowered by the Holy Spirit to perform the works of Deity. While this fact lies beyond human comprehension, the Gospel records clearly depict genuine humanity in Jesus, as well as genuine Deity. Let us believe this great mystery even though it lies beyond human comprehension. From this time onward Jesus was led and empowered by the Spirit (Lk. 4:1, 14). By the Spirit of God Jesus cast out demons (Mt. 12:28). It is well to note how Peter at a later time set forth the work of the Holy Spirit in Jesus when he declared: "How God anointed Jesus of Nazareth with the Holy

Spirit and with power; how he went about doing good and healing all that were oppressed by the devil, for God was with him" (Acts 10:38). Observe also that when Matthew accounted for Jesus' power of healing, he spoke of it as the fulfillment of Isaiah's prediction concerning the Servant (Mt. 12:18-21). In Jesus' reply to the Pharisees when they charged Him of casting out demons by Beelzebul, the prince of demons, He made it clear that Satan and his demons were arrayed against Him and that His power to cast out demons was alone through the Spirit of God (vv. 24-28).

The Gospel of John also presents the Baptist's witness concerning this baptism scene of the Holy Spirit descending upon Jesus. Among other things the Baptist noted that the Spirit descended as a dove upon Jesus and remained on Him (Jn. 1:32, 33). This gave affirmation to the abiding presence of the Holy Spirit in Jesus throughout His entire earthly ministry. It would appear that the Apostle John referred to still another testimony of the Baptist concerning Jesus. Whether John 3:31-36 represent the words of the Baptist or the words of the apostle makes little difference. Either way the words reflect the Baptist's thought. Speaking of Jesus, the writer said: "For he whom God has sent utters the words of God, for it is not by measure that he gives the Spirit" (v. 34). By this we should understand that Jesus received the Spirit in His fullness. It amplifies the obvious sense of the Spirit's appearance in bodily form as a dove which expressed the totality and undividedness with which the Spirit came upon Christ.

(3) The Voice from heaven (Mt. 3:17; Mk. 1:11; Lk. 3:22). The Voice from heaven said, "This is my beloved Son, with whom I am well pleased." These words reflected such passages as Psalm 2:7, "You are my son, today I have begotten you," and Isaiah 42:1 in which God spoke of the Servant as "my chosen, in whom my soul delights." Identified as the Servant of the Lord, that great person of Isaiah 40 — 66, Jesus in loving obedience would seek to perform the entire Servant role, including His work as the Suffering Servant (Is. 52:13 — 53:12). Thus Jesus as the Servant of the Lord was already standing in the shadow of the cross.

d. John's Record of the Baptist's Testimony to Jesus

The author, John, wrote: "There was a man sent from God, whose name was John. He came for testimony, to bear witness to the light, that all might believe through him. He was not the light, but came to bear witness to the light" (Jn. 1:6-8). John conceived of the Baptist's mission as being a testimony. Officially appointed by God, he bore witness to *the* light. His message had an evangelical ring, namely, that all might believe through him. In an exclusive manner, Jesus was *the* light. The author, John, gave further explanation of Jesus as the light by saying: "The true light that enlightens every man was coming into the world" (v. 9). This also appears to be the Baptist's conception of Jesus as the light. The word "light" carries the usual spiritual significance given to it elsewhere in the Bible. The author, John, gave it specific dimensions by saying: "In him was life, and the life was the light of men" (v. 4). The Baptist very aptly described the greatness of the Word which became flesh in the words, "He who comes after me ranks before me, for he was before me" (v. 15). By this John meant, "He comes after me, but takes rank before me; for before I was born he already was" (NEB). That is, the unique dignity of the Word lay in His eternal preexistence so that even though John was born before Jesus, the Word was already existing. This understanding of the nature of the person, the Word, obviously came by the direct revelation of God to him. This revelation of the Word not only heightened the importance of the work of the Baptist, but gave much more clarity to the eternal existence of the Word.

The next significant witness John gave concerning Jesus found expression in the words: "Behold, the Lamb of God, who takes away the sin of the world!" (Jn. 1:29, 36). We do not know what flashed through the minds of John's hearers when he made this declaration. Perhaps they thought first of the Servant of the Lord concerning whom it was said: "Like a lamb that is led to the slaughter, and like a sheep that before its shearers is dumb, so he opened not his mouth" (Is. 53:7). If this was the case, John's hearers were being led to identify the One whom they saw as the Servant of the Lord and to associate with Him all that the author wrote concerning this Servant. It could be that their minds went back to the Passover lamb (Ex. 12) or to the lambs offered at the morning and evening sacrifices (Ex. 29:38-42; Num. 28:3-10). In both of those sacrifices certain elements were very significant. Perhaps the most important was that of *expiation,* the lamb dying in the place of another. It also involved the idea of consecration, the setting apart of the individual wholly to God. Since these sacrifices were perpetuated in Israel's history, they were significant to John's hearers. Richardson would have us go back to Abraham's sacrifice of the ram in place of his son Isaac.[10] He finds the expression, "your only son," of 22:12, expressed in the Septuagint translation "your beloved Son," the expression used by God Himself at the baptism of Jesus. I believe that all three of these Old Testament references were in the mind of the Baptist when he pointed out Christ as the Lamb of God. This is simply to assert the meaning of common themes and their cumulative value in the unfolding of divine truth. The Lamb of God had its beginning in the lamb provided for sacrifice in the place of Isaac. It grew in dimensions in the offering of the Passover Lamb, in the morning and evening sacrifices, and finally its greatest significance in the sufferings of the Servant of the Lord who is "like a lamb that is led to the slaughter" (Is. 53:7).

A few details as to the meaning of the clause "takes away the sin of the world" call for study. First, observe the present participle which looks at the taking away of the sin of the world as a present or continuing act. The verb itself carries the idea of what the scapegoat did in carrying away into the wilderness the sins of the people. The meaning of the word grew to greatest meaning when, in Isaiah 53, the idea was expanded to His bearing our griefs and carrying our sorrows; of the Lord laying on Him the iniquity of us all; and finally, of His bearing the sin of many. The singular *sin*, rather than *sins*, looks at the totality of sin, as well as the oneness of the common corruption of humanity. It is the sum total of the sins of all mankind. The word "world" looks at the creation including all humanity, potentially extending to all mankind.

The Baptist's last witness to Christ (Jn. 3:25-30) pictured his own relationship to the Christ as that of the friend of the bridegroom. The importance of Christ is seen in this that He, the Bridegroom, has the bride. John's humble place, though of ineffable joy to him, was that of being "the friend of the bridegroom, who stands and hears him, rejoices greatly at the bridegroom's voice; therefore this joy of mine is now full. He must increase, but I must decrease" (vv. 29, 30). Vos rightly observed "that this figure of 'the bridegroom' reminds of Jehovah's relation to Israel."[11]

Inasmuch as John 3:31-36 likely gives some of the reflections of John, the author, on the words of the Baptist, we should note their significance in the witness they give to Christ. Christ is the One who comes from above and is above all. This points to Deity as over against the humanity of Him who is of the earth. Jesus alone could bear wit ness to what He has seen and heard in the realm that is above; therefore, he who receives the witness of Christ sets his seal to this, namely, "that God is true" (v. 33). Christ honored the words of God. Even in His incarnation His utterances were of God because He did not receive the Spirit by measure. Since the Father loves the Son, He has given all things into His hand. We should understand this in the totality of Christ's work as Prophet, Priest, and King. Jesus supported the same idea (Mt. 11:27; Jn. 13:3).

On this account, "He who believes in the Son has eternal life; he who does not obey the Son shall not see life, but the wrath of God rests upon him" (Jn. 3:36). The element of faith becomes essential in our relationship to the Son. The one who thus believes in the Son has eternal life as a present possession. Those who refuse to obey the Son shall not see life. What more terrible language could be used than to say: "The wrath of God rests upon him"?

In summary we need to realize how foundational to our understanding of the entire ministry of Christ is this revelation through John. He considered this witness to be essential to his general purpose expressed at the close of the Gospel when he wrote, "These are written that you may believe that Jesus is the Christ, the Son of God, and that believing you may have life in his name" (Jn. 20:31).

For Additional Reading and Reference:

Jeremias, *New Testament Theology,* pp. 43-56.
Richardson, *An Introduction to the Theology of the New Testament,* pp. 178-181.
Ryrie, *Biblical Theology of the New Testament,* pp. 45-46.
Stagg, *New Testament Theology,* pp. 212-217.
Stauffer, *New Testament Theology,* pp. 21-25.
Van Oosterzee, *The Theology of the New Testament,* pp. 50-52.
Vos, *Biblical Theology,* pp. 335-354.

1. *The New Bible Dictionary,* J. D. Douglas, Ed. (Grand Rapids: Wm. B. Eerdmans Publishing Co., 1962), article, "John the Baptist," p. 642.
2. Vos, *op. cit.,* p. 338.
3. *Commentary on the Gospel of Luke (The New International Commentary on the New Testament)* (Grand Rapids: Wm. B. Eerdmans Publishing Co., 1954), p. 136.
4. Vos, *op. cit.,* p. 342.
5. Richardson, *op. cit.,* pp. 179, 180.
6. R. P. G. Tasker, *The Gospel According to Saint Matthew, Tyndale Bible Commentaries, New Testament Series* (Grand Rapids: Wm. B. Eerdmans Publishing Co., 1961) Vol. I, p. 50.
7. *Commentary on the Gospel of Luke, The New International Commentary on the New Testament* (Grand Rapids: Wm. B. Eerdmans Publishing Co., 1954), p. 146.
8. See also 1 Sam. 10:1, 6, 10; Ps. 89:20; 2 Kings 9:3.
9. Ex. 29:7; 40:13-15; Lev. 8:1-13; Ps. 133:2.
10. Richardson, *op. cit.,* p. 180.
11. Vos, *op. cit.,* p. 352.

CHAPTER VI

THE FAITH OF JESUS REVEALED IN HIS PROBATION

1. Introduction

There is evident purpose on the part of the synoptic writers to recount the story of Jesus' temptation as immediately following His unique experience of being baptized with the Holy Spirit and of hearing the voice from heaven declaring Him to be the Son of God. This is one of the few if not the only incident in the life of Christ in which Jesus is the only source of our information. Undoubtedly, He told His disciples about this experience, and in this way it became a part of the Gospel tradition.

The Gospel writers present the story as an objective experience of temptation. Satan encountered Christ in a threefold attack. We are not told nor do we need to know in what precise manner Satan tempted Jesus. Suffice it to say that it was not merely a subjective experience on the part of Jesus. There was an objective approach of Satan to Christ, whether visible or invisible. On a later occasion (Mt. 12:24-30; Mk. 3:22-27; Lk. 11:15-23) Jesus told of an encounter with Satan in which He made a specific reference to His temptation. After Jesus had healed a deaf and blind demoniac the Pharisees retorted, "It is only by Beelzebul, the prince of demons, that this man casts out demons" (Mt. 12:24). In reply, Jesus declared, "If Satan casts out Satan, he is divided against himself" (v. 26). He added, "If it is by the Spirit of God that I cast out demons, then the kingdom of God has come upon you. Or how can one enter a strong man's house and plunder his goods, unless he first binds the strong man?" (vv. 28, 29). In this statement Jesus definitely referred to a previous encounter with Satan, the strong man of the house. The result of the encounter was the binding of the strong man. This made possible the casting out of demons, for in the words of Jesus He was plundering his house. This incident showed that Satan had encountered Christ and that Jesus had overcome Satan. It was an attack made by Satan against the incarnate Son of God. Hence it was entirely real.

Some students of the temptation scene are concerned on several matters such as: How could Jesus be tempted? How could Satan appeal to Jesus? How could he find a point of contact? How could he induce a choice? Was it possible for Jesus to sin? It seems to me that we can quickly dispose of these questions. From the standpoint of the narratives we learn that the temptation was real. It implied the possibility of Jesus yielding to Satan. All these questions belong to a still larger inquiry, that of understanding the mystery of the person of Christ who was at once divine and human — God manifest in flesh. We need to believe the mystery even though we are not able to explain it. This is a valid application of the element of faith in the life of the Christian.

2. Led by the Spirit to Be Tempted by the Devil

God manifested a divine purpose in the Spirit's leading of Jesus into the wilderness. Satan's tempting of Jesus presupposed Jesus' being under a test or probation. God does not tempt His children but He does put them under tests. We may find an instructive analogy in the test of Adam and Eve in the garden. Our first parents were permitted to eat freely of every tree of the garden. There was one prohibition. They were forbidden to eat of the tree of the knowledge of good and evil. Undoubtedly, there was nothing sinful in itself in the eating of the fruit of this tree. God had a wise purpose in making the prohibition. God would lead our first parents from a state of untested innocence to that of tested innocence. He would lead them to moral maturity by which they would know the difference and antagonism between right and wrong through enduring the test without experiencing sin. In their yielding to Satan's temptation they learned the difference between good and evil, right and wrong, by the way of disobedience and its accompanying guilt. Jesus, the second Adam, the new Head of the race, was being subjected to the same kind of test as that experienced by Adam and Eve. His messianic work depended on His being free from all sin. Being sinless by nature, Jesus was proved by God through the tests which centered in His human nature. In a word, God was testing the faith of Jesus through His human nature. Would He exercise the obedience, trust, and patience which belonged to a man who had faith in God?

As in the Garden of Eden, Satan used the test and probation of Jesus as the occasion for tempting Him to disobey God. A careful study of each encounter will show that Satan sought to tempt the Son of God by way of His human nature.

In our approach to the interpretation of the temptation we need to give careful thought to the nature of Satan's approach to Christ and much more to the manner in which Jesus answered Satan. We will discover that the Deuteronomy quotations given by Jesus lead to the very heart of the meaning of each of Satan's encounters. I shall follow the order of temptations as given in the Gospel of Matthew as being in all probability the order of the temptations. The forty-day period was spent in fasting in which Jesus was undoubtedly involved in deep meditation concerning His work as the Messiah and in prayer to God. Why Mark did not give the details of the temptation we are not able to say. However, he did give a detail not mentioned by Matthew or Luke. It was that Jesus was with the wild beasts. What Mark intended by giving this detail is a mere guess. Perhaps he intended to show the loneliness of Jesus in the wilderness and gave the occasion for angels to minister to Him.

3. The First Temptation

Satan said, "If you are the Son of God, command these stones to become loaves of bread" (Mt. 4:3). The form of the conditional clause used by Satan assumes the truth of the condition. It is practically equivalent to saying, "Since you are the Son of God." This makes it clear that the point of Satan's statement was not designed to cast doubt in the mind of Jesus of His being the Son of God. Rather, Satan was using the fact of Jesus being the Son of God as the basis for His exercising divine power to turn stones into loaves of bread. Why should Jesus suffer hunger if He had the power to provide food for Himself? There was nothing ethically wrong in turning stones into loaves of bread, just as there was nothing sinful in eating of the fruit of the tree of the knowledge of good and evil, the test Adam and Eve faced. Jesus' answer, however, gave a different view of this matter. His reply began with the words, "It is written," by which appeal Jesus recognized the authority of the written Word, in this case the Book of Deuteronomy. The verse quoted comes from a very significant context of that book. The words "Man shall not live by bread alone, but by every word that proceeds from the mouth of God" captured the outstanding admonition of Deuteronomy 8:1-10. As Moses was rehearsing the experiences of Israel in the wilderness, he explained that the leading of God through those forty years had a profound purpose expressed in the words: "That he might humble you, testing you to know what was in your heart, whether you would keep his commandments, or not. And he humbled you and let you hunger and fed you with manna, which you did not know, nor did your fathers know" (Deut. 8:2, 3); the next words were the ones that Jesus quoted. Israel's trying circumstances had the purpose of testing what was in the hearts of the people. Their experiences centered in the matter of obedience to God's commandments. This gave a profound meaning to God's providential dealings with His people. Jesus was saying to Satan that His experience was similar in purpose to that of Israel's. Jesus, who possessed divine power as the Son of God, needed to learn obedience such as is necessary for man to give to God. As Israel's wilderness experience was a walk of faith, so Jesus' incarnate life was a walk of faith. In a word, this temptation was a test of the *obedience* of faith.

4. The Second Temptation

Taking Jesus to the Holy City and setting Him on the pinnacle of the temple, Satan said, "If you are the Son of God, throw yourself down; for it is written, 'He will give his angels charge of you,' and, 'On their hands they will bear you up, lest you strike your foot against a stone' " (Mt. 4:6). This precious psalm (91) gives a beautiful picture of the charge God gave to angels to guard His people in all their ways. Jesus' temptation was really this. Within the preceding forty days He had had the most extraordinary experience of hearing the voice from heaven saying, "This is my beloved Son, with whom I am well pleased." Should He not have repeated miraculous experiences which would confirm His being the beloved Son? To have cast Himself down from the pinnacle of the temple would be asking of God of a repetition of His manifestation in Jesus' behalf. Jesus saw at once the real meaning of this temptation. To respond to Satan's challenge would be to tempt the Lord, His God.

Again, the significant experience showed the real character of Satan's temptation. It was the incident to which Moses referred when he said, "You shall not put the Lord your God to the test." This had taken place at Massah (Ex. 17:1-7) on Israel's journey from the wilderness of Sin toward Sinai when they camped at Rephidim, but there was no water for the people to drink. The people at once found fault with Moses and asked why he had brought them out of Egypt to kill them and their cattle with thirst. Moses interpreted these complaints as testing the Lord. Didn't God know that they would need water? Why didn't God give them at all times a plenteous supply of water for themselves and their flocks? But God had higher purposes in this experience. Israel had to learn that the way of faith is that of dependence upon God. God would test Israel by allowing them to thirst for water. In their dependence upon Him He sought to develop an implicit trust in Him. He, their God, who had so marvelously delivered His people out of Egypt as manifested in the ten plagues and in the dividing of the Red Sea, was certainly mindful of their needs. He would not let His people die of thirst in the wilderness. Israel needed such an experience to develop their trust in God.

Jesus saw in this test something very near to His own. God who had manifested Himself to Jesus in such a marvelous way would not need to demonstrate repeatedly His power to save Jesus from death. Jesus had to learn that faith involves trust. It would have been tempting God to ask for repeated miraculous demonstrations of His power throughout life. In a word, this temptation was a test of the *trust* of faith.

5. The Third Temptation

Once more Satan encountered Jesus. This time it was the severest and most subtle temptation of the three. Taking Jesus to a very high mountain, Satan showed Him all the kingdoms of the world and the glory of them. He said, "All these I will give you, if you will fall down and worship me" (Mt. 4:9). The severity of this temptation lay in the fact that the kingdoms were rightfully Christ's. But in the plan of God, Jesus' humiliation, suffering, and death would precede His exaltation and enthronement over all the kingdoms of the world. But Satan was offering immediate power and glory. Satan's offer was exceedingly subtle. In the first place the glory of the kingdom under Satan would not begin to compare with the glory of the kingdom under God, the Father. To be a second Caesar or a Nebuchadnezzar had the glory only of the political kingdoms, but to be the Lord's Messiah would involve His exaltation above all principalities and powers. All things would be put under His feet. The most serious aspect of Satan's sublety involved Jesus' escaping the suffering and death on the cross in which case God's plan of salvation for all mankind would have been defeated.

A third time Jesus found an appropriate Scripture drawn from Israel's history which answered Satan. The words, "You shall worship the Lord your God and him only shall you serve" (Mt. 4:10), also come from Moses' exhortations to Israel on the eve of their entrance into the land of Canaan. There they would find great and goodly cities, houses full of good things, cisterns hewed out, vineyards and olive trees, all of which could lead Israel to believe (albeit erroneously), that the gods of the Canaanites were real gods and that by worshiping them, they would gain all these good things. The God whom they were worshiping had not supplied them with such great riches and plenty. They had suffered the hardships of Egyptian bondage and in their wanderings in the wilderness. As Israel thus stood at the crossroads as to whom they should worship, Moses commanded them, "You shall fear the Lord your God; you shall serve him, and swear by his name" (Deut. 6:13). Israel needed the patience to see that the blessings God had in store for them would be given to them in God's own time.

The lesson of patience had to be learned through a long period of want and hardships, but the blessings that God would bestow upon them would far exceed all the wealth of the nations of Canaan. God's supreme blessing would be spiritual in nature and not merely temporal. Jesus saw in Israel's experience a parallel to His own. He needed to learn also that the man of faith will patiently endure all things until God's time of giving him honor and glory. Jesus saw that the valley of humiliation leading to the cross would make possible the salvation of all mankind. The exaltation and glory gained through His death would lead all the redeemed to honor Him as Lord and King. For this reason Jesus could worship only the Lord, His God, even though the realization of His faith called for the patient endurance of suffering and death. In a word, this temptation was the test of the *patience* of faith.

The bearing of all this on Christ's entrance upon His messianic work now becomes clear. In the inseparable union of the divine and the human in Jesus His work as the Messiah could alone be accomplished. Through these temptations Jesus maintained His integrity in the most important aspect of faith, that of dependence upon God. This faith involved implicit obedience, absolute trust, and enduring patience. Through this threefold victory against Satan, Jesus, in terms of the parable, bound the strong man of the house, and therefore, He could plunder his goods. The meaning of all this for the unfolding of the work of Jesus should be apparent. In this conflict against Satan with all of his demons arrayed against Jesus, He would now be victor. In speaking to God's people of the kingdom of God, Jesus was now in position to expound the rule of God and to be enthroned at the right hand of the Father after the accomplishment of His saving work on the cross. By proving Himself sinless He qualified Himself to be a fit offering for sin, when He as God's Lamb would take away the sin of the world.

The concept of discipleship taught later by Jesus (Mt. 16:24-26; Mk. 8:34-38; Lk. 9:23-26; 14:25-35) would show us that the disciple taking up his cross and following Jesus would experience the same encounters with Satan as Jesus did, and thus it is proper for us to see the relation between Jesus' temptations and those of His disciples. Even though a fundamental difference between His temptation and that of His disciples lies in His sinless nature as compared with the sinful nature of His disciples, yet a great similarity does exist. As the faith of Jesus was tested in the respective areas of *obedience, trust,* and *patience,* His disciples came to realize that their faith was also tested in these three areas. In fact, hardly any temptation to which Jesus' disciples were subject lay outside of these three kinds of encounter by Satan. Jesus' disciples needed to learn also that the overcoming of Satan in his attacks in these several areas made possible the continued overthrowing of Satan through the power of God.

For Additional Reading and Reference:

Barclay, *The Mind of Jesus*, pp. 31-39.
Hunter, *The Work and Words of Jesus*, pp. 37-40.
Ryrie, *Biblical Theology of the New Testament*, pp. 47-48.
Vos, *Biblical Theology*, pp. 355-367.
I.S.B.E., Vol. V, pp. 2943-2944b.

CHAPTER VII

THE PUBLIC MINISTRY OF JESUS

This chapter seeks to look at Jesus' public ministry to gain a true perspective for a study of the major approaches to Christ's earthly ministry including His messianic consciousness, the good news of the kingdom of God, the eschatological aspect of His teaching, and the meaning of His death and resurrection. These major inquiries will be treated in chapters VIII through XI. The more immediate purpose of this chapter has to do with some of the aspects of Jesus' public ministry which have a vital bearing on the meaning of God's revelation through Jesus. Factors to receive consideration include the meaning and purpose of Jesus' miracles, the special significance of His healing ministry, the objective development of His teaching ministry, the method and mode of Jesus' teaching, noting especially His parables, His use of the Old Testament, and His teaching on the nature of God. These and other inquiries possess great significance for New Testament theology. Let us continue to appropriate the vital contributions which the life and teachings of Jesus make to biblical theology.

1. The Beginning of Jesus' Public Ministry

a. Jesus Revealed to Israel as the Son of God

When John the Baptist bore witness to his disciples of Jesus' being the Lamb of God and the Son of God, two of his disciples immediately followed Jesus. In their conversation with Him they soon became convinced that Jesus was the Messiah. To Philip Jesus gave the significant command, "Follow me" (Jn. 1:43). The present imperative used by Jesus carried the meaning of their becoming His lifelong followers. They became His disciples. The term "disciple" (*mathetes)* carries the meanings of *learner, pupil, disciple, apprentice,* and *adherent.* Naturally, then, a follower of Jesus was His disciple. This concept of following Jesus and of being His disciple carried great significance with reference to Jesus' comprehension of His person and work. This became all the more evident at a later time when He chose twelve followers to be His disciples, whom He named apostles (Lk. 6:13). This inauguration of Jesus' public ministry came to a climax when He told these first followers, "You will see heaven opened, and the angels of God ascending and descending upon the Son of man" (Jn. 1:51). In this statement Jesus brought all the

Son of Man predictions to a focus upon Himself. The meaning of this title and the use which Jesus made of it will receive consideration in the following chapter.

b. Jesus' Sinlessness

The ministry of Jesus gains a new dimension in that He demonstrated a life free from sin. In a positive way, He showed perfection of character through His holiness, righteousness, and love. His perfect example raised ethics to the highest level of importance for human attainment. This becomes essential to a true evaluation of His person, ministry, and teaching. These factors obtain highest importance for the discipline of biblical theology, for in Christ we have the fullest revelation of perfection. Obviously, this gives new meaning to Jesus' public ministry, for the Teacher exemplified perfectly His teaching.

Satan's temptation of Jesus brought His sinlessness to a focal point. As noted in the preceding chapter, Satan's encounter tested Jesus with respect to three aspects of His faith in God: obedience, trust, and patience. The writer of Hebrews wrote of Jesus' steadfastness of faith as the One "who in every respect has been tempted as we are, yet without sinning" (Heb. 4:15).

Jesus' perfection and righteousness were evident in the Sermon on the Mount. These standards had complete fulfillment in His own life. He exemplified heavenly Father perfection and righteousness. All the virtues of life which have come to be known as Christian graces were fully realized in Christ. Note especially His *love* (Mk. 10:21; Jn. 11:5; 13:1, 23, 34), *compassion* (Mt. 9:36; 14:14; 15:32; Lk. 7:13), *humility* (Mt. 21:5; Phil. 2:8), *forgiving spirit* (Mt. 6:14, 15; Lk. 23:34) and *knowledge of man's sinful heart* (Mk. 7:18-23), and so on.

Paul stressed most forcefully Christ's sinlessness when he wrote, "For our sake he made him to be sin who knew no sin, so that in him we might become the righteousness of God" (2 Cor. 5:21). Paul's most extensive witness to Christ's perfect life stands forth in his exhortation to the Philippians (Phil. 2:1-11), where he held forth Jesus as the perfect example of *love, affection, sympathy, humility,* and *obedience.* Repeatedly, the author of Hebrews in settings of Jesus' uprightness of character as our High Priest spoke of His sinlessness (Heb. 3:1-6; 4:15; 7:26; 9:14; 12:2, 3). To be God's sacrifice for sin Jesus needed to be *without blemish.* He was *holy, blameless, unstained, separated from sinners,* and *without sin.*

As one would expect, Peter also gave strong witness to Jesus' blameless life (1 Pet. 1:19; 2:21-24). Addressing servants who many times were suffering unjustly, Peter directed their attention to Christ's sufferings and exhorted them to follow in His steps. He added the significant words, "He committed no sin; no guile was found on his lips. When he was reviled, he did not revile in return; when he suffered, he did not threaten; but he trusted to him who judges justly. He himself bore our sins in his body on the tree, that we might die to sin and live to righteousness" (1 Pet. 2:22-24).

It remained for John to complete the witness to Jesus as *the righteous, the pure, the One without sin,* and *the One full of grace and truth* (Jn. 1:14, 17; 1 Jn. 2:1; 3:2, 3, 4, 7, 24). These testimonies to Jesus' perfect righteousness place the public ministry of Jesus into its true perspective. His personal life, His ministry, and His teachings proved conclusively that He was God manifest in the flesh. Therefore what Jesus exemplified in His entire life possessed divine authority. Let us allow these facts to bring upon us the true impact of Jesus' public ministry.

c. Two Early Incidents of Great Significance

It is noteworthy that the first incident on record of Jesus' public ministry was His attendance at the marriage in Cana of Galilee, where He turned the water into wine (Jn. 2:1-11). John's observation draws attention to its significance. "This, the first of his signs, Jesus did at Cana in Galilee, and manifested his glory; and his disciples believed in him." The word *semeion* carries the meanings *sign, mark,* or *token* (cf. 4:54). John's use of this word in this context gave it this distinctive meaning by its reference to a miracle or wonder through which God authenticated Jesus as having divine power. In this way He manifested His glory. The performing of this sign gave His disciples adequate grounds for believing in Him. This step of faith on their part was possible alone through this manifestation of supernatural power. All this leads us to a clearer understanding of Jesus' first public act in His ministry.

Jesus' cleansing the temple marks the second recorded incident of His ministry and calls for careful study (Jn. 2:13-22). Since the observance of the Passover brought many Jews to the temple, Jesus' cleansing the temple was a spectacular act. He broke up the moneymaking business of the Jews by driving all the sheep and oxen out of the temple. He gave the stern command, "You shall not make my Father's house a house of trade" (v. 16). Without a doubt Jesus' calling the temple His Father's house aroused the indignation of the Jews. At once the disciples remembered the words of the psalmist who wrote, "Zeal for thy house will consume me" (Ps. 69:9). Unwilling to admit their sin the Jews required of Jesus a sign for having broken up their business. But why should they ask for a sign when they knew full well that they had been desecrating their holy temple?

This demand for a sign was equivalent, it would seem, to their requiring of Jesus proof that God was His Father. It is this aspect of the scene which made clear the crucial significance of Christ's claim to deity. This strange Jew called God His Father. Since they were far from being willing to acknowledge their gross sin of desecrating God's holy temple, Jesus added to their guilt-consciousness the words, "Destroy this temple, and in three days I will raise it up" (v. 19). While they knew that Jesus was referring to the temple of His body, they did their utmost to dodge the issue by interpreting His words as referring to the temple.

The impact of this episode becomes clear when we observe that, from the very beginning of Jesus' public ministry, He was confronted with such intense opposition on the part of the Jews. This antagonism to Jesus on the part of the Jews forecast His own suffering and death. To the disciples this incident obtained special meaning when Jesus was raised from the dead. It led them to believe the Scripture and the word which Jesus had spoken (Jn. 2:22). There were, nevertheless, many at this Passover feast who believed in His name when they saw His signs. In passing, let us observe that John drew attention in both of these incidents to the fact that the signs which Jesus wrought before the people led many to believe in Him (v. 23).

d. Jesus and Nicodemus

John added two incidents which also possess profound meaning for our understanding of Jesus' public ministry. The former of these was His conversation with Nicodemus. Here we meet Jesus' first reference to the kingdom of God. This theme is of such importance that I shall devote Chapter IX to an exposition of its meaning. But let us observe that Jesus' description of the kingdom of God in this context becomes indicative of its strategic importance in all His teachings. The spiritual character of this kingdom is at once apparent. Nicodemus needed to learn that the kingdom of God is a spiritual reality, the appropriation of which required a spiritual renewal, his being born anew. It is a spiritual experience wrought by the Holy Spirit, having its analogy in human life — natural birth. The being born anew is a spiritual experience wrought by the supernatural power of the Holy Spirit.

Nicodemus' bewilderment led Jesus to expose the limitations of his thinking. To begin with, Nicodemus was not comprehending Jesus' words. On this account Jesus proceeded to show this ruler of the Jews that what He had spoken with reference to the Holy Spirit's work of spiritual birth was the prerequisite for entering the kingdom of God. His refusal to believe these spiritual truths showed his inability to believe heavenly things. The heavenly things constituted a category of reality immeasurably superior to earthly things, even though the latter were spiritual in nature. Only the One who descended from heaven, the Son of Man, could disclose the heavenly things. Thus Nicodemus, the Jew trained in the Jewish law, was unable to grasp the spiritual meaning of Jesus' teachings and, consequently, would be unable to lay hold of the vastly superior character of the heavenly things.

We do not know at what point Nicodemus drops out of this narrative, or specifically, where John passes from the words of Jesus to his own message. It would appear that verses 13-15 were Jesus' closing words to Nicodemus, and that from this point on John proceeds with the narrative. If this is correct, then we should note how Jesus confronted Nicodemus with the overwhelming truth that He, the Son of Man, had descended from heaven, and that, like the serpent being lifted up in the wilderness, He, Himself, would be lifted up. But Nicodemus should learn that the saving power of the Son of Man was infinitely superior to that of the brazen serpent. Whoever believes in the Son of Man has eternal life. While this may have been a new truth for Nicodemus, he could have drawn from the Old Testament some statements which were basic to it. Among these are the words of David, "In thy presence there is fulness of joy, in thy right hand are pleasures for evermore" (Ps. 16:11). Note also the words of Daniel, "And many of those who sleep in the dust of the earth shall awake, some to everlasting life, and some to shame and everlasting contempt" (Dan. 12:2).

Since the concept — eternal life — becomes such an absorbing theme in the New Testament, we should note well the great buildup of thought expressed by these words in this context (Jn. 3:15-21). Only those who believe in the uplifted Son of Man have eternal life. The efficacy of His suffering and death underlies this possession of eternal life. But this sacrifice of the Son had its origin and source in God's love for the world. Two destinies confront man: eternal life or eternal damnation. Only through the saving act, the death of the Son, can man receive eternal life. This salvation can be received only through faith. Herein is the heart of salvation.

A stern truth blazes forth from the closing words of this message. It is that those who do not believe in the Son are condemned already (3:18). Herein is the grievous sin of unbelief. Its heinousness becomes still clearer when we are told that "men loved darkness rather than light, because their deeds were evil" (v. 19). They refused to come to the light lest their deeds should be exposed. In sharp contrast with those who hate the light are those who in doing what is true come to the light.

Through this, it is clearly seen that their deeds have been wrought in God. The word "truth" (*aletheia)* and its adjective forms are John's key words and will receive more attention later in the chapter. Here we should observe that the deeds which have been wrought in God possess the quality of truth.

In a different setting John gave several additional ideas which bear a close relation to the preceding comments (vv. 31-36). Expanding the contrast of the earthly things and the heavenly, John declared that Jesus who came from heaven is above all. This gives supreme value to Jesus' witness, relating "to what he had seen and heard." The One whom God had sent spoke the words of God. This was made possible through His Spirit given to the Son in His fullness. On this account: "The Father loves the Son and has given all things into his hands." For this reason the ministry of Jesus possessed deity quality and authority. At a later time Jesus expressed this truth in the words, "All things have been delivered to me by my Father" (Mt. 11:27).

e. Jesus and the Samaritan Woman

The story of the Samaritan woman also furnishes some valuable insights to the beginning of Jesus' public ministry. Consider how Jesus entered into conversation with the woman which soon led to a spiritual encounter with her. This way of approach became typical of Jesus' ministry, whether in private or public. It is a splendid illustration of how He could pass from natural things to spiritual parallels. Moving from the value of natural water to that of spiritual water welling up to eternal life led to a profound truth. It illustrates an effective pattern which became dominant in Jesus' teaching. When the disciples returned to Jesus, He answered their question by using another simple, but effective metaphor drawn from the fields already white for harvest. Through this comparison Jesus showed that spiritual things lie in close relationship with natural things. The readiness for natural harvest has a spiritual likeness to bringing sinners to salvation.

Jesus' claim to being the Messiah and the people's conclusion that He was the Savior of the world illustrate the central foci of Jesus' ministry. It clarified the spiritual nature of His work as compared to the political interpretation which even the disciples ascribed to Jesus' messiahship. Associated with this was another truth which possesses larger dimensions than we ordinarily recognize. Jesus told the woman that salvation is from the Jews, and that the true worshipers worship the Father in spirit and truth. This expressed the eschatological purpose of the Jews' religion bound up in their Scriptures. Jesus followed with a definitive statement which expressed one of the profoundest truths of divine revelation. He said, "God is spirit, and those who worship him must worship in spirit and truth" (Jn. 4:24).

2. The Galilean Ministry of Jesus

a. Jesus' Teaching Ministry

In the contents and purpose of the three following chapters my approach here continues to be chiefly historical. I am endeavoring to draw attention to the several incidents and aspects of Jesus' ministry which furnish the perspective of Jesus' unfolding service. Let us note how Mark introduced Jesus' ministry, that He came "preaching the Gospel of God" (1:14). He quoted Jesus' words, "The time is fulfilled, and the kingdom of God is at hand; repent, and believe in the gospel" (v. 15). These words "The time is fulfilled," at once tied in the kingdom of God with the eschatological unfolding of events. Without question, this eschatological perspective had its origin and development in the Old Testament, and on this account the era being inaugurated was predicted in the Old Testament. In Chapter IX I shall endeavor to explore the Old Testament foundations of this new era. Jesus spoke of this prophetic period as being that of the kingdom of God or the rule of God. While this designation does not occur in the Old Testament, the idea was certainly advanced in the predictive messages of the prophets. Undoubtedly, this announcement by Jesus conveyed immeasurable meaning to His hearers. The Nazarene was preaching the good news of God. Through His preaching, the kingdom of God would be established. Without a doubt His audience was not able to fathom the meaning of what was taking place in their experience.

The message of the gospel of God had two focal points: repentance and belief in the gospel. The verb "repent" *(metanoeo)* was used in the Septuagint to translate the Hebrew verb *nacham* and carried the meaning *be sorry, suffer grief, repent, comfort one's self,* and *ease one's self.* The Greek word carried the literal sense of *change one's mind* or *purpose,* hence *to repent.* Jesus' use of this verb in this setting led undoubtedly to its becoming the most frequently used verb for *repentance* in the New Testament.

The verb "believe" *(pisteuo)* had the literal sense, *to have faith* (in), *to believe.* The noun form in its active sense carried the meanings *faith, belief, trust,* and *confidence.* The verb form occurred in the Septuagint chiefly for *aman* which in the hiphil form meant *stand firm, trust,* and *believe.* Thus Jesus' command was deeply rooted in Old Testament thought. The present imperative use of both verbs carried the distinctive idea of continuous or repeated acts of repenting and of believing. This idea became significant in the New Testament occurrences of these verbs.

The word "gospel" (*euaggelion*) also perpetuated an important Old Testament idea expressed by *basar* carrying the meaning *bear tidings, gladden with good tidings, herald as glad tidings*. This verb in the Hebrew was the word used for *good news* in general, but especially of messianic blessings as predicted in Isaiah 49; 52:7; 60:6; 61:1. With this background to the word "gospel," it was entirely natural that the noun and verb forms of this word should occur so frequently throughout the New Testament.

b. Jesus' Healing Ministry

Coincident with the preaching ministry of Jesus was His work of healing. The Gospel records vary from giving detailed accounts of special cases[1] to that of giving some general statements such as: "And he went about all Galilee, teaching in their synagogues and preaching the gospel of the kingdom and healing every disease and every infirmity among the people. So his fame spread throughout all Syria, and they brought him all the sick, those afflicted with various diseases and pains, demoniacs, epileptics, and paralytics, and he healed them" (Mt. 4:23, 24). In this quotation Matthew brought into view the two aspects of Jesus' ministry: preaching the gospel of the kingdom and healing the sick. In this way Matthew set forth the fundamental relationship between our Lord's preaching and healing ministries. Luke became more specific when he noted that Jesus' "word was with authority," and that after casting out a demon from a man the multitude observed, "For with authority and power he commands the unclean spirits, and they come out" (4:36). In the same context Luke recorded the healing of Simon's mother-in-law from her high fever. Luke then added, "When the sun was setting, all those who had any that were sick with various diseases brought them to him; and he laid his hands on every one of them and healed them. And demons also came out of many" (vv. 40, 41). From these and other instances we may gain the insight that His healing ministry was an act in the physical realm which symbolized the spiritual healing through His preaching ministry. Faith in Jesus as the physical Healer led to faith in Him as the Savior from sin.

This observation becomes explicitly clear in the account of Jesus' healing of the paralytic (Mk. 2:1-12). In this case Jesus first declared that the paralytic's sins were forgiven, and when some of those present charged Jesus with blasphemy, He healed the paralytic. In this way Jesus showed that the Son of Man had authority on earth to forgive sins. Another facet of Jesus' healing ministry becomes evident when on the Sabbath He healed a man who had been ill for thirty-eight years (Jn. 5:2-18). For this reason the Jews persecuted Him. To this, Jesus replied, "My Father is working still, and I am working" (v. 17). By this statement Jesus showed that His healing work was similar in nature to that of the Father. It was very obvious that in calling God His Father He was making Himself equal with God.

Jesus' healing ministry also fulfilled the predictions of Isaiah (Mt. 8:16, 17; 12:17-21). In the first reference Matthew noted that Jesus' healing ministry fulfilled Isaiah's words, "He took our infirmities and bore our diseases" (Is. 53:4). This reference to Isaiah disclosed the potential meaning bound up in the prophet's declaration. This quotation also illustrates how Jesus' healing ministry most significantly portrayed the manner in which the Servant of the Lord actually bore our griefs and carried our sorrows. In the second illustration Matthew referred to Jesus' healing ministry as fulfilling the Servant of the Lord passage of Isaiah 42:1-4. Here again there does not appear to be an explicit prediction of the Servant's healing ministry, but what is significant is that God had put His Spirit upon the Servant, thus enabling Him to proclaim justice to the Gentiles. This would continue "till he brings justice to victory" (Mt. 12:20). We may conclude that Matthew's quotation of this Servant of the Lord passage shows that it implicitly predicted the work of the Servant in the way of healing the sick, through which means He brought justice to victory.

c. *The Choosing of the Twelve Apostles*

The choosing of the twelve apostles constituted yet another important step in Jesus' ministry. [2] This call to apostleship was marked by two stages: first, the call to discipleship; and second, their being named apostles. This procedure suggests that from the large number of disciples or followers of Jesus twelve of the most dedicated and qualified were chosen for the special responsibility of apostleship. While the term "apostle" was used before the time of Jesus, it always connoted a person who had been entrusted with a special task or responsibility. Jesus' use of this title gave it a distinctive connotation which became cumulative in its distinctive meaning. The special authority given to them with respect to casting out unclean spirits and to healing diseases and infirmities suggests a permanent office as apostles. Jesus restricted their mission to the lost sheep of the house of Israel. The keynote of their message was "The kingdom of heaven is at hand." Jesus endowed them with the gift of the Holy Spirit so that the Spirit of the Father spoke through them. The extensive instruction given to them in their first mission (Mt. 10) shows the strategic importance of their task in this stage of Jesus' ministry.

As we follow the ministry of Jesus, the unfolding of their mission becomes evident. By way of anticipation these twelve apostles heard the teachings of Jesus and witnessed all His wonders and signs. They shared in the Lord's Supper and followed Christ to Gethsemane. Jesus gave to them the Great Commission (Mt. 28:18 20). In a different setting Luke recorded Christ's Commission in the words "You shall receive power when the Holy Spirit has come upon you; and you shall be my witnesses in Jerusalem and in all Judea and Samaria and to the end of the earth" (Acts 1:8). At the ordination of Matthias, Peter expressed explicitly the most distinctive pronouncement of the apostle's mission, "One of the men who have accompanied us during all the time that the Lord Jesus went in and out among us, beginning from the baptism of John until the day when he was taken up from us — one of these men must become with us a witness to his resurrection" (Acts 1:21, 22). From this we may properly conclude that Jesus chose the Twelve to be the official witnesses of His earthly ministry, including His death and resurrection. As I stated in an earlier context and will make further reference to it later, we have positive evidence for the authenticity of the New Testament records dealing with Jesus' earthly ministry, of which the most important event was His resurrection.

3. The Objective Development of Jesus' Ministry

Another step in gaining a true perspective of Jesus' teaching has to do with the objective development of His ministry. This should contribute vitally to our grasping the unfolding revelation through Christ. Let us consider some of the guiding factors in the unfolding of Jesus' teaching. Note the problem confronting the disciples relating to the meaning of His earthly ministry. It becomes evident that the disciples thought that the Messiah would establish a political kingdom after the pattern of David's kingdom. All through the ministry of Jesus the disciples were failing to grasp the real spiritual nature of the Messiah's kingdom. Even after the Lord's resurrection they were still entertaining the idea that Jesus would restore the kingdom to Israel (Acts 1:6). This need for a radical revision of their understanding of the kingdom may account for Jesus' extended teachings on this theme. As a result, the Gospel records constitute a veritable storehouse of precious and sublime teachings pertaining to the kingdom of God.

The rising opposition to Jesus constitutes another factor which determined the course of His teaching ministry. This led Him to predict His suffering and death, and to structure His teachings accordingly. A significant example of this occurs in Mt. 16:21-28, where Jesus announced

His coming suffering, and then added the meaningful statement, "If any man would come after me, let him deny himself and take up his cross and follow me" (v. 24). The remainder of the paragraph expands this thought more fully, thus showing the close relationship between His cross and that of His followers. A third guiding factor in the unfolding of Jesus' teaching becomes evident in His messianic mission which determined the nature of His entire ministry. Thus every act and word of Jesus had messianic import.

While the Gospel records do not mention any specific events which determine stages in Jesus' ministry, there were a number of events which lead us to believe that the Caesarea-Philippi incident (Mt. 16:13-20) does mark a watershed in this development. John's Gospel indicates a crisis at the close of Jesus' discourse on the bread of life (Jn. 6:22 — 7:1). Many of the disciples turned back from following Jesus, and He left Judea because the Jews sought to kill Him. Another indication of a crisis becomes evident when Jesus condemned the pharisaic traditions and hypocrisy (Mk. 7:1-23). The crisis aspect of the Caesarea-Philippi incident becomes still clearer when we note Jesus' words, "On this rock I will build my church, and the powers of death shall not prevail against it." It was on this occasion that Jesus began to show His disciples that He must go to Jerusalem to suffer and die. If anyone would come after Him he would need to deny himself and take up his cross and follow Jesus. The most climactic event which also marks the turning point in Jesus' ministry was the transfiguration (Mt. 17:1-8).

Let us take note of some of the incidents which were distinctive in Jesus' ministry before the crisis at Caesarea-Philippi. Two of His greatest discourses — the Sermon on the Mount and the kingdom parables — reveal the dominant character of His ministry before Caesarea-Philippi. The former discourse set forth the pattern of living which should mark the lives of those who are seeking His kingdom and His righteousness. They must be perfect as their heavenly Father is perfect.

The kingdom parables portray likenesses between the natural world and the kingdom of heaven. The honest seeker for spiritual truth would come to see that God created the universe in such a manner that the natural world reflects the spiritual law. When the disciples heard Jesus' parables of the sower, the grain of mustard seed, treasure hidden in a field, and the other parables, they were gaining a knowledge of the kingdom of heaven. We can hardly imagine a more effective way of depicting this great truth than that used by Jesus. The explication of the kingdom of heaven was certainly the very heart of His teaching during this stage of His ministry. As I noted earlier Jesus' sending the twelve apostles on their preaching mission to Israel also gave expression to the central purpose of His ministry at this time. Their message centered in the glad tidings concerning the kingdom of heaven. In this manner Jesus was seeking to lead Israel to become sharers in the kingdom of heaven which God had promised His people through Moses and the prophets.

A third incident which characterized this period of Jesus' ministry was the great miracle of feeding of the five thousand, followed by His discourse on the bread of life. The importance of this miracle becomes apparent by the fact that all four Gospels record the incident. The impact of this miracle was very significant. There were those who said, "This is indeed the prophet who is to come into the world!" (Jn. 6:14).

The popularity of Jesus reached its highest point when He perceived that the people were about to come to take Him by force to make Him king. He sought to correct this misdirected enthusiasm by telling them that they should labor for the food which endures to eternal life. It is the kind of food which the Son of Man would give to them and they would need to believe in Him whom the Father had sent. The Father gives the true bread from heaven. As a climax Jesus said, "I am the living bread which came down from heaven; if any one eats of this bread he will live for ever; and the bread which I shall give for the life of the world is my flesh" (Jn. 6:51). In spite of the spectacular miracle of feeding the five thousand, many of His disciples drew back and no longer went about with Him. This was the first evidence of an impending crisis.

The attitude toward Jesus took another turn for the worse when some Pharisees and scribes charged His disciples with eating with unwashed hands. They insisted that His disciples should live according to the tradition of the elders. Jesus countered this charge with a very appropriate quotation from Isaiah in the words " 'This people honors me with their lips, but their heart is far from me; in vain do they worship me, teaching as doctrines the precepts of men.' You leave the commandment of God, and hold fast the tradition of men" (Mk. 7:6-8; Is. 29:13). Jesus rebuked them still more severely in the words, "You have a fine way of rejecting the commandment of God, in order to keep your tradition!" (Mk. 7:9). Also He proceeded to show to them how tragic it was for them to attach more authority to their tradition than to the Word of God. In a very apt illustration He showed that nothing that a person eats causes defilement but rather that which comes out of a person defiles him. He added, "For from within, out of the heart of man, come evil thoughts, fornication, theft, murder, adultery, coveting, wickedness, deceit, licentiousness, envy, slander, pride, foolishness. All these evil things come from within, and they defile a man" (vv. 21-23). These words most clearly exposed the utter lack of ethical perception on the part of the Pharisees, which fact lay at the basis of their rejection of Jesus and led to their plans for killing Him.

Let us now observe the turn of events which took place after Caesarea-Philippi when Peter declared to Jesus, "You are the Christ, the Son of the living God" (Mt. 16:16). The crisis character of this confession becomes evident when we search for the implication of Jesus' words "On this rock I will build my church, and the powers of death shall not prevail against it. I will give you the keys of the kingdom of heaven, and whatever you bind on earth shall be bound in heaven, and whatever you loose on earth shall be loosed in heaven" (Mt. 16:18, 19). Through these words Jesus was saying that His mission in the world was not merely to add to the structure of Judaism, but that He would build a new spiritual structure, the *church (ekklesia).* This at once identified Christ's work as being comparable to the Old Testament *qahal* (*congregation, assembly*) which was established under the Sinaitic covenant. Under the theocracy, the rule of God, the people of Israel constituted the *qahal.* What Jesus was saying then was as God built His *qahal* under the old covenant He Himself would build a new congregation, the church under a new covenant. This implied the passing away of the old covenant together with its *qahal.* All this gave new dimension to Jesus' ministry. It was on this occasion that He foretold His death and resurrection. From this point onward these predictions determined the pattern and focus of His ministry.

Jesus then informed His disciples that this course of events in His own life would change the pattern of discipleship. He explained this change in the words, "If any man would come after me, let him deny himself and take up his cross and follow me" (Mt. 16:24).

The transfiguration scene (Lk. 9:28-36) unfolded still further the changed pattern of Jesus' ministry. As a forecast of His glorification He was transfigured before three of His disciples. Present with Him were Moses and Elijah who "spoke of his departure, which he was to accomplish at Jerusalem" (v. 31). The scene came to a climax when they heard the voice from the cloud saying, "This is my beloved Son, with whom I am well pleased; listen to him" (Mt. 17:5).

A number of additional words and acts of Jesus also illustrate the dominance of the messianic idea after the Caesarea-Philippi event. Among these are the following: discipline in the church (Mt. 18:1-35), Jesus' promise of the Spirit to those who believe in Him (Jn. 7:37-39), and some of Jesus' distinctive discourses during this period (Mt. 19, 20; Lk. 10 — 19; Jn. 7 — 10). All of these Gospel facts give a clear perspective for interpreting Jesus' acts and teachings.

4. The Method and Mode of Jesus' Teaching

A study of the teachings of Jesus soon reveals a distinctive way in which He presented His ideas. In His conversation with Nicodemus (Jn.3:3, 8) He said, "Unless one is born anew, he cannot see the kingdom of God." And again, "The wind blows where it wills, and you hear the sound of it, but you do not know whence it comes or whither it goes; so it is with every one who is born of the Spirit." Here it is evident that two kinds of birth are compared, natural birth and spiritual birth. The unknown elements of the blowing of the wind are comparable with the mystery of being born of the Spirit. In this manner Jesus was leading Nicodemus to grasp the great spiritual mystery in terms of happenings in the natural realm. In the same manner He led the woman of Samaria (Jn. 4:7-15) to pass from the life-giving elements of natural water to that of water welling up to eternal life. In His conversation with the disciples in this same setting, Jesus passed in thought from natural food to spiritual food, as well as from the natural harvest to the spiritual harvest.

In the Sermon on the Mount He used more than a dozen figures of speech in order to make His teaching more vivid and expressive. Among these note the metaphors; salt and light. Further, if one's eye or hand causes one to sin He gave the severe remedy of removing these members by which He most vividly taught that the sins committed through their lustful use must be removed. A comparison which was almost ironical in nature becomes evident in the speck in one person's eye and the log in another's eye. Jesus' hypocritical hearers could not escape the lesson being taught. With equal vividness Jesus presented a great spiritual truth by comparing the narrow gate with the wide one. Climactically, He concluded this sermon with the similitude of a storm's effect upon a house built upon a rock and of one built upon the sand compared with one who hears Jesus' words and does them in relation to one who hears these words and does not do them.

These figures of speech chosen almost at random serve to show the manner in which Jesus revealed truth. The chief point of concern is to discover the bearing of these methods of teaching on the unfolding of divine truth. This is the genius of biblical theology. Note the several examples of each figure of speech in the following references: *simile* (Mt. 11:16; 13:52; Lk. 6:47-49; 7:31, 32; 12:36), *metaphor* (Lk. 13:32; Jn. 4:35-38; 6:48, 51; 10:7, 11; 14:6), *similitude* (Mt. 24:32, 33, 37-44), *parable* (Mt. 13:1-52), and *allegory* (Lk. 15:11-32; Jn. 15:1-11).

This outline of the several figures of speech used by Jesus together with the great number of their occurrences leads us to see that there was almost an entire absence of systematizing in Jesus' teaching. We might expect that Jesus would give systematic presentations on such themes as the kingdom of God, ethics, or eschatology. Obviously the parables of Matthew 13 relate to the kingdom of heaven; the Sermon on the Mount possesses a great concern for ethics; and the Olivet Discourse relates to future things. But in none of these cases do we have a logical, formal, or systematic presentation. This characteristic of our Lord's teaching does not in any way weaken the effectiveness of His messages. Rather, the mode of His teaching was dynamic to the superlative degree.

A fundamental problem, nevertheless, does confront us at this point. It pertains to the method or guidelines to understanding the meaning of Jesus' mode of teaching. It is at once evident that these various figures of speech make the truth plain; that is, they illustrate the picture, they dramatize the truth. Further, in view of the opposition shown by many of the Jews, it becomes clear that this way of teaching often disarmed prejudice. Those who may have been inclined to reject the truths which Jesus would present gave their assent to the clear meaning of a parable before they realized the full impact of what Jesus was saying. However, we need to note Jesus' own answer as to why He spoke in parables (Mt. 13:10-17). A parable veiled the truth. Jesus explained to the disciples that because of their open-mindedness to truth, it was being given to them to know the secrets of the kingdom of heaven, but those whose minds were closed to the truth were seeing and yet not seeing, and hearing yet not hearing or understanding. Isaiah had already described their spiritual deafness and blindness, and attributed the cause of it to their willful rejection of God's words and to their unwillingness to turn from sin to God. They refused to repent and acknowledge their sins.

This leads us to explore the spiritual meaning of parables. Vos, to whose discussion I am deeply indebted, speaks of parables as being "spiritual discoveries, because they are based on a certain parallelism between the two strata of creation, the natural and the spiritual (redemptive) one, because the universe has been thus constructed. On the principle of 'Spiritual law in the natural world,' the nature-things and processes reflect as in a mirror the super nature-things, and it was not necessary for Jesus to invent illustrations."[3] In this connection Jesus claimed that His speaking in parables fulfilled what was spoken by the prophet. "I will open my mouth in parables, I will utter what has been hidden since the foundation of the world" (Mt. 13:35; Ps. 78:2). Vos continued; "The marvelous acquaintance of Jesus' mind with the entire compass of natural and economic life, observable in His parables, may be explained from this, that He had been the divine Mediator in bringing this world with all its furnishings into being, and again was the divine Mediator for producing and establishing the order of redemption."[4] Dr. Walter Russell Bowie, in his discussion of the parables of Jesus,[5] goes to some length in enumerating data from Jesus' parables which show His knowledge of nature and the everyday experiences of life. By way of illustration Bowie enumerates such details from "the pageant of human life," the leaven, the lost coin, the lilies of the field, the hen gathering the chickens under her wing, and many others. All this gives testimony to the supreme human interest on the part of Jesus. His knowledge of the world was so great because it was His Father's world. This also gives witness to Jesus' deity, for He was Lord of Creation. Still further, all this throws light on our Lord's supernaturalism. His miraculous works served as evidences that this world was His creation.

While John did not use the word, "parable," he did record a number of Jesus' stories which set forth the duplex nature of the universe according to which they could very properly be called parables.[6] Jesus' story about the shepherd (Jn. 10:1-6) is called *paroimia* meaning *figure, parable, allegory,* or *dark saying.* This is the figure which Jesus used to illustrate the attitude toward Him on the part of the blind man who had received his sight as compared with the Jews who refused to believe in Jesus. The latter were not entering the sheepfold by the door, but were trying to climb in another way. Those of genuine faith would not follow a stranger but only the real shepherd. Jesus used another illustration, in the words, "Unless a grain of wheat falls into the earth and dies, it remains alone; but if it dies, it bears much fruit" (Jn. 12: 24). Through these words Jesus was showing the necessity of His death in order to fulfill His mission of providing salvation for all mankind. He applied this truth also to His disciples, "He who loves his life loses it, and he who hates his life in this world will keep it for eternal life" (v. 25). The duplex element in Jesus' teaching is very apparent in His teaching on the vine and the branches. So many details of this illustration possess a spiritual meaning that this might very properly be called an allegory. These illustrations are sufficient to show that John understood these modes of Jesus' teaching in which He passed from things in the natural realm to the spiritual and in this way presented most grand and profound spiritual truths. It is this characteristic of Jesus' teaching that marks one of the outstanding contributions made by John in his Gospel.

There are several expressions in the Gospel of John (Jn. 3:31; 8:23; 15:19; 17:14) which account for this duplex nature in Jesus' teaching. He was able to speak of heavenly things because He "comes from above and is above all." He is not of this world. Since He, the Son of Man, descended from heaven, He is able to speak of heavenly things. This accounts for the distinctive ideas bound up in the words, *truth* and *true,* in this Gospel. His use of them in the prologue at once arrests our attention. He regarded the *logos* (Word) as the true light. The incarnate Word was full of grace and truth. In sharp contrast with the law given to Moses, "grace and truth came through Jesus Christ" (1:17).

A search for the distinctive meaning which John attached to *aletheia* leads to the Hebrew word *emeth,* which it translates in the Septuagint. Significant uses of *emeth* (Gen. 32:10; Mic. 7:20) show that it is heavily weighted with meaning which in English bears the sense of *firmness, stability, faithfulness, fidelity,* and *truth.* When John brought together the words *grace* and *truth,* he was showing their close relationship in meaning in which each contributes profound meaning to the other. In Jesus' conversation with the woman of Samaria He noted: "The true worshipers will worship the Father in spirit and truth" (Jn. 4:23). He added the explanatory words, "God is Spirit, and those who worship him must worship in spirit and in truth" (v. 24). Since God is spirit, it becomes clear that God is also the embodiment of truth.

Jesus' conversation with the Pharisees (Jn. 8:12-47) unfolded further the content of these words. Jesus' claim, "I am the light of the world," led the Pharisees to rebut His affirmation. They insisted that since He was bearing witness to Himself, His testimony was not *true (alethes).* Jesus answered their charge by stating that His testimony is true because He had come from heaven and would be going there. His judgment is true also because the One who had sent Him judges also. To the Jews who believed Jesus' words, He said, "If you continue in my word, you are truly [*alethos*] my disciples, and you will know the truth, and the truth will make you free" (vv. 31, 32). But to the Jews who refused to believe in Jesus, He declared that He had told them the truth which He had heard from God. He repeated the claim that He had proceeded and came forth from God (v. 40). The father of the unbelieving Jews, Jesus declared, was the devil in whom there was no truth. Again He asserted, "Because I tell the truth, you do not believe me. . . . If I tell the truth, why do you not believe me? He who is of God hears the words of God; the reason why you do not hear them is that you are not of God" (vv. 45-47). In this conversation Jesus was declaring the heavenly character of the truth. The prerequisite for knowing the truth was to continue in His words. Then the truth would make them free. On this account the acquiring of the truth is not an intellectual attainment. Implicit obedience to Jesus' words would alone result in knowing the truth. The truth alone makes one free.

Let us observe some of Jesus' claims which assert and intensify the identification of Himself with the truth. Referring to Himself Jesus said, "My Father gives you the true bread from heaven" (Jn. 6:32). To Thomas' question Jesus answered, "I am the way, and the truth, and the life; no one comes to the Father, but by me" (14:6). Here the words *way, truth,* and *life* are brought into close relationship and in this way the meaning of the word *truth* is intensified. In this discourse Jesus promised to give the disciples another Counselor, even the Spirit of truth. Later He added, "When the Spirit of truth comes, he will guide you into all the truth; for he will not speak on his own authority, but whatever he hears he will speak, and he will declare to you the things that are to come" (16:13). Jesus gave some additional facets of meaning to these words in His prayer (17:3, 17, 19). Here He asserted that eternal life is to know God as the only true God and Jesus Christ whom God had sent. On this account Jesus petitioned the Father, "Sanctify them in the truth; thy word is truth. . . . And for their sake I consecrate myself, that they may also be consecrated in truth" (16:17, 19). Let us observe that not only the Father and the Son are the truth, but the Counselor is the Spirit of truth (15:26). Thus the triune God is the highest embodiment of the truth. With this supreme meaning given to this word we are enabled to understand Jesus' teaching that the Father is the only true God.

We should yet observe that truth is not a self-contained idea, for God is the very embodiment of truth, and this fact underlies Jesus' prayer that God should sanctify (*hagiazo*), that is *dedicate, separate, set apart, purify, treat as holy,* His disciples in the truth. This is possible because God's Word is truth. Jesus used this verb twice in the following verse when He spoke of consecrating Himself in order that His disciples might "be consecrated in truth." There appears to be an intensification of meaning in these usages, having its beginning in being set apart for God, and advancing to being made conformable in character to God. This involved an internal purifying work effecting a complete inner renewal of life. This gives *truth* a real dynamic.

5. Jesus' Attitude Toward the Old Testament

A survey of Jesus' public ministry as it relates to biblical theology very naturally includes a study of His attitude toward the Old Testament. It is not my purpose to explore all the teachings which He based on the Old Testament, but rather to gain an understanding as to how He regarded the Scriptures. We should note first that He built His teachings on the fulfillment of the Scriptures. John, as well as Peter, made reference to the fulfillment of the Scriptures, independent of Jesus' words.[7] All but one of these references speak of the fulfillment of Old Testament predictions and almost uniformly they note that the events took place for the purpose of fulfilling the prediction. This shows their understanding of the Old Testament. Since the Scriptures were to be fulfilled, these writings possessed divine authority. In other words, since God spoke through the prophets, He brought about the fulfillment of the predictions.

Jesus held the same view of Scripture fulfillment.[8] This selected group of Jesus' references to the fulfillment of Old Testament predictions is instructive. Mark quoted the opening words of Jesus' teaching ministry as follows: "The time is fulfilled, and the kingdom of God is at hand; repent, and believe in the gospel" (1:15). While Jesus did not refer to a written prediction, this is nevertheless clearly implied. In the synagogue service at Nazareth, He read from Isaiah and then commented, "Today this scripture has been fulfilled in your hearing" (Lk. 4:21). In this manner He testified to its prophetic character, and identified Himself as fulfilling the prediction. As Jesus was speaking with the disciples in the upper room, He quoted from Isaiah 53, prefacing the quotation with the words, "This Scripture must be fulfilled in me" (Lk. 22:37). Here the emphatic language expressing the necessity of Scripture fulfillment shows His attitude toward the prophetic Word. A summary statement on the part of Jesus possesses immeasurable significance. He said, "Everything written about me in the law of Moses and the prophets and the psalms must be fulfilled" (Lk. 24:44). This blanket statement which referred to all the messianic predictions constitutes so much evidence that He recognized the accuracy and the infallible authority of the Old Testament. Jesus allowed no exceptions to His all-inclusive statement. He concluded this conversation by showing that the Old Testament foretold His suffering, death, and resurrection, and also the preaching of the gospel in His name to all nations, beginning at Jerusalem (vv. 46, 47).

Jesus' attitude toward the Old Testament gains breadth of meaning when we examine His frequent quotations from the Old Testament. First, these quotations occur in meaningful and strategic teaching situations such as the Sermon on the Mount, the kingdom parables, the good shepherd message, the Olivet Discourse, and others. In the Sermon on the Mount, Jesus was undoubtedly encountering a common charge that He had come to abolish the law and the prophets. In reply He referred to six Old Testament teachings, in each of which He was fulfilling its specific intent (Mt. 5:17-48). In justification of His teaching by parables He quoted two Scriptures: Is. 6:9, 10; Ps. 78:2. In the Olivet Discourse, as Jesus was unfolding the future, He supported this teaching with about a dozen Old Testament predictions (Mt. 24, 25)

Second, through frequent quotations Jesus showed that He regarded the Old Testament as the rule of faith and life. This becomes evident in His replies to Satan during His temptation. In each encounter Jesus quoted from the Old Testament introducing each quotation with the formal expression, "It is written" (Mt. 4:3-11). Since the Pharisees supported their traditions by their direct appeal to the law, Jesus rebuked their hypocrisy by quoting Old Testament Scriptures which directly exposed their departure from the law (Mt. 12:2-8; 15:2-9). Jesus' fidelity to the law became evident also in His reply to the Pharisees on the matter of divorce (Mt. 19:3-9). Here again He asserted the authoritative character of the Old Testament and showed that Moses had allowed divorce by reason of their hardness of heart and then added, "But from the beginning it was not so." A borderline case occurs in the incident where the Jews accused Jesus of blasphemy (Jn. 10:31-39) in which He quoted the Old Testament as refuting their charge and then added, "And scripture cannot be broken." This attests yet again that Jesus regarded this body of writing as the infallible standard for holy living.

Another aspect of Jesus' attitude toward the Old Testament becomes evident in His reply to the inquiry made by the disciples of John with reference to fasting. He gave two similitudes: the former, that of putting a piece of unshrunk cloth on an old garment; and the latter, that of putting new wine into old wineskins. Through these illustrations He showed that a new era of divine revelation had begun. The revelation of God in the Old Testament was not God's final word to mankind. The new revelation through Christ was not a mere addition to the old but advanced beyond it in a further unfolding of divine truth. God's revelation was progressive. Jesus expanded this idea when He showed that what a person eats does not defile him, but rather that which comes from within, out of the heart of man, these defile him (Mk. 7:14-23). The tradition-bound Pharisees were not able to grasp the increasingly spiritual content of God's progressive revelation. This aspect of divine revelation became still more evident when Jesus spoke of the Passover as being fulfilled in the kingdom of God. Thus in one decisive expression Jesus showed that the ceremonial law had served its function and was being replaced by the vastly superior character of worship under the new covenant. However, this progressive character of divine revelation did not destroy the continuity between the old and the new covenants.

6. Jesus' Teaching on the Nature of God

A survey of the public ministry of Jesus naturally involves consideration of the distinctive elements of God's nature as taught by Jesus. Since the attributes of God will be brought into view in Chapter IX, let us note here Christ's exalted views of God as His Father. On various occasions Jesus' words concerning God have their source in the Old Testament. In His encounter with Satan (Mt. 4:1-11) each of His responses to Satan made reference to the God of the Old Testament. Quoting Deuteronomy 6:13, Jesus' most emphatic reply to Satan was, "You shall worship the Lord your God and him only shall you serve" (Mt. 4:10). This makes it entirely clear that Jesus was not introducing a new or different idea of God from that found in the Old Testament, but rather He was giving witness to the same God as revealed therein. When Nicodemus, the ruler of the Jews, addressed Jesus with the words, "We know that you are a teacher come from God," the conversation which followed centered in the God of the Jews (Jn. 3:1-15). In the synagogue at Nazareth, reading from Isaiah, Jesus said, "The Spirit of the Lord is upon me" (Lk. 4:16). Jesus' declaration that this Scripture was then fulfilled stands as evidence that the Lord referred to by the prophet was Himself, the Lord. The following Scriptures confirmed this conclusion: Matthew 15:3, 4; 22:17; 20:37-44.

Jesus spoke a great deal on the fatherhood of God. This truth was already taught in the Old Testament.[9] The expressive language of these Scriptures formed the solid foundation on which Jesus could build. This became evident in the Sermon on the Mount, where Jesus made fourteen references to God, the Father. John recorded about 120 of Jesus' references to God, the Father. The familiarity of these teachings should not lead us to neglect their profound content. Our conduct should lead others to give glory to the heavenly Father. Perfection of character is one of the most comprehensive ways of describing the central attribute of the Father. The outreaching expression of the Father's perfection is love for all mankind.

In the Lord's Prayer Jesus disclosed the Father's nature very profoundly in the words, "Hallowed be thy name" (Mt. 6:9). This bears a close relation to that of being perfect. The rule of God is supreme. On this account His will should be done on earth as it is in heaven. God's holiness requires repentance on the part of sinners before they can be forgiven. He alone can deliver us from the forces of evil.

Alongside the perfection and holiness of God stands His righteousness. While each of these words possesses a distinctive meaning, there is a most profound common meaning in all three. There is need for our associating these transcendent attributes of God, the Father, with their immanent relation to mankind. Jesus made this very clear when He told His disciples not to be anxious about the things of this life. Since God provides for the birds of the air and the lilies of the field, how much more will He take care of His people's needs? In a similar setting Luke recorded Jesus' promise that the heavenly Father would give the Holy Spirit to those who asked Him (Lk. 11:13). Luke also noted Jesus' promise that it was the Father's good pleasure to give His followers the kingdom (12:32).

John's Gospel is filled to overflowing with references to the intimate relationship between the Father and Jesus Christ. While this theme will receive special consideration in Part III, Chapter II, "The Theology of John," let us note briefly a few significant teachings. Jesus told the woman of Samaria that the true worshipers worship the Father in spirit and truth. This adds the deepest meaning to the believer's personal relationship to the Father. This relationship gains additional meaning in view of Jesus' words, "No one comes to the Father, but by me" (Jn. 14:6). Exceedingly precious is the truth that the Father and the Son will come to the one who loves them and will make their home with Him (v. 23). Jesus also disclosed the promise of the Counselor, the Holy Spirit, whom the Father would send in His name (v. 26). He spoke further of His return to the Father and gave the testimony that "the Father is greater than I" (v. 28). Jesus said, "Whatsoever ye shall ask of the Father in my name, he may give it to you" (15:16). He promised also to intercede with the Father in behalf of those who pray to the Father. The Father loves the disciples because they have loved Christ and believed that He came from the Father (16:23-28).

When Jesus instituted the Lord's Supper, He declared the Father's relation to the kingdom of God in the words, "I shall not drink again of this fruit of the vine until that day when I drink it new with you in my Father's kingdom" (Mt. 26:29). These words confirm yet again the supremacy of the Father with particular reference to the kingdom of God. Moving on to the scene in Gethsemane we hear Jesus' prayer, "Father, if thou art willing, remove this cup from me; nevertheless not my will, but thine, be done" (Lk. 22:42). Matthew quoted Jesus' second prayer, "My Father, if this cannot pass unless I drink it, thy will be done" (Mt. 26:42). This submission of Christ's will to that of the Father is witness again that Jesus was subject to the Father. This truth should always be evident in a study of the Father-Son relationship.

Jesus' teaching on the nature of God includes about every conceivable attribute revealed in the Bible. His statements are brief but clear in meaning. A full exposition of these teachings hardly seems necessary, for there is no theological implication in any of His words which require elucidation. I shall refer very briefly to a number of these outstanding references. He spoke of the Father's transcendence and almighty power: Mt. 5:45; 6:10; 11:25, 27; 19:26; Mk. 10:27; 14:36; Lk. 10:

21, 22; the Father's love and mercy: Mt. 5:45; 6:14, 15, 25-32; 11:25, 26; Mk. 11:25; Lk. 8:39; Jn. 3:16, 17; 14:21, 23; 16:27; of the Father as being holy and righteous: Mt. 5:48; 6:9, 33; Lk. 4:26; Jn. 17:11, 25; that man should worship God, the Father: Mt. 4:10; 5:16; Jn. 4:23, 24; 9:31; Jesus' relation to the Father and the Spirit: Mt. 11:27; 28:19; Jn. 5:23; 7:39; 14: 1, 16; 15:26; 16:7-15; 17:3; and finally, of God as the Judge of all mankind: Mt. 8:11, 12; 10:15, 28; 11:22, 24; 12:36, 37, 41, 42; 15:13; 18:8, 9; 22:13, 14; 25:30, 41-46; Lk. 10:12-15; 13:28, 29; 19:27; Jn. 5:27-30; 8:16; 16:8-11.

7. Some Concluding Thoughts

This survey of Jesus' public ministry should serve to show how it stands without parallel in human history. Among other things, Jesus' manifest interest and concern for mankind are most instructive. He saw man with his many and varied needs: physical, social, psychological, and spiritual. Jesus alone was able to probe into these aspects of humanity. No other human being possessed these insights. For these reasons Jesus alone was able to furnish the cure, the renewal, and the dynamic needed for man's salvation. In the largest sense Jesus' miraculous deeds possessed unfathomable meaning. When we consider the scope of His supernatural works, such as feeding the multitudes, healing the sick, raising the dead, walking on the waters, turning water into wine, together with the transformation of human lives, we begin to grasp the ultimate purpose of His ministry. In the largest sense it forecast Paradise regained, the restoration of what was lost in the Garden of Eden. God, through Christ, was undoing the work of Satan. When we listen to Jesus' teachings and begin to comprehend their nature, scope, and content, all of which reveal His insights, understanding, and comprehension of the truth, we must conclude, "No man ever spoke like this man!" (Jn. 7:46). No teacher ever revealed with such uncompromising reality man's sinful nature, his spiritual needs, the way of salvation, and the Christian way of life. Jesus' unfolding of the kingdom of God and of man under God's rule was divine revelation in the most real sense. This revelation reached its highest point when He unfolded the nature of Deity, in the person of God, the Father; of Himself, the Son of God; and the Holy Spirit. Certainly the Old Testament gave foregleams of this truth, and the apostolic writings unfolded further their meaning for the church. But it was Jesus who disclosed in most meaningful language the nature of Deity, the truth expressed most compactly in His baptismal formula when He said, "Baptizing them in the name of the Father and of the Son and of the Holy Spirit . . ." (Mt. 28:19).

For Additional Reading and Reference:

Beyschlag, *New Testament Theology,* Vol. II, pp. 88-132.
Bruce, *The Parabolic Teaching of Christ,* pp. 1-9.
Filson, *The New Testament Against Its Environment,* pp. 58-92.
Hunter, *Introducing New Testament Theology,* pp. 12-24.
Hunter, *The Work and Words of Jesus,* pp. 41-67.
Hunter, *Interpreting the Parables.*
Klassen and Snyder, *Current Issues in New Testament Interpretation,* pp. 91-110.
Lindars, *New Testament Apologetic,* pp. 138-188.
Morgan, *The Parables and Metaphors of Our Lord,* pp. 13-45.
Newman, *The Meaning of the New Testament,* pp. 62-131.
Sheldon, *New Testament Theology,* pp. 68-87.
Vos, *Biblical Theology,* pp. 368-396.

1. Mk. 1:21-28, 40-44; 2:3-12; 3:1-6; Jn. 4:46-54; 5:2-9; etc.
2. Mt. 4:18-22; 10:2-42; Lk. 5:1-11, 27, 28; 6:12-16.
3. Vos, *op. cit.*, p. 380.
4. *Ibid.*
5. *The Interpreter's Bible* (New York, Abingdon-Cokesbury Press, 1951), Vol. 7, article, "The Parables," pp. 169, 170.
6. Jn. 3:8; 10:1-6, 7-18; 11:7-10; 12:24; 13:10; 15:1-6; 16:21.
7. Mt. 1:22; 2:15, 17, 23; 8:17; 12:17; 21:4; Jn. 18:9, 32; 19:24, 36; Acts 1:16; 3:18.
8. Mt. 26:54, 56; Mk. 1:15; 14:49; Lk. 4:21; 21:22; 22:37; 24:44; Jn. 13:18; 15:25; 17:12.
9. Ex. 4:22; Deut. 1:31; 8:5; 32:6; Is. 1:2; 63:16; Jer. 3:19; 31:9; Hos. 11:1; Mal. 1:6.

CHAPTER VIII
THE MESSIANIC CONSCIOUSNESS OF JESUS

1. Introduction

"I who speak to you am he" (Jn. 4:26). This is the answer Jesus gave to the woman of Samaria when she said, "I know that Messiah is coming (he who is called Christ); when he comes, he will show us all things" (v. 25). Here we have the earliest recorded direct claim made by Jesus that He is the Messiah. By reason of the tremendous significance which must be given to this claim, it is in order to present the Gospel evidence for Jesus' consciousness of being the Messiah. Interwoven with this evidence will be an account of Jesus' fulfillment of His messianic mission. This truth is of greatest meaning and consequence in the study of New Testament biblical theology.

I am keenly aware of the views of Bultmann on this subject. On this account it is necessary to move forward on the most tested principles of interpretation. Our supreme task is: Did Jesus actually consider Himself to be the Messiah? Did He fulfill the messianic mission as foretold in the Old Testament? In answer to these questions Bultmann says, "This opinion is burdened with serious difficulties. It does agree with the evangelist's point of view, but the question is whether they themselves have not superimposed upon the traditional material their own belief in the Messiahship of Jesus. . . . The acknowledgment of Jesus as the one in whom God's word decisively encounters man, whatever title be given to Him — 'Messiah' (Christ). 'Son of man,' 'Lord' — is a pure act of faith independent of the answer to the historical question whether or not Jesus considered Himself the Messiah.

" . . . . It is just as possible that belief in the Messiahship of Jesus arose with and out of belief in His resurrection. The scene of *Peter's confession* (Mk. 8:27-30) is no counter evidence — on the contrary! For it is an Easter story projected backward into Jesus' life-time, just like the story of the transfiguration (Mk. 9:2-8). The account of Jesus' baptism (Mk. 1:9-11) is a legend, certain though it is that the legend started from the historical fact of Jesus' baptism by John. It is told in the interest not of geography but of faith, and it reports Jesus' consecration as Messiah. It originated in the time when Jesus' life was already regarded as having been Messianic, whereas the transfiguration story, originally a resurrection account dates His messiahship from the resurrection onward. The temptation story (Mk. 1:12 f. or Mt. 4:1-11 par.) which involves reflection about what kind of Messiah Jesus was or what kind of Messiah the Christian believes in, is legend. The story of Jesus' entry into Jerusalem has been colored by legend, and the passion narrative is also to a considerable degree overspread with legend, for the Church had venerated the crucified as the Messiah. It was soon perfectly certain that it was as Messiah that He had been crucified." [1]

In this fashion Bultmann proceeds to deal with the question of the messianic consciousness of Jesus. It seems to me that Bultmann has imposed on the Gospel narratives his own philosophical prepossessions which rejects the internal evidence of the Gospel records. His procedure is entirely subjective without any foundation in the Gospel narratives, the other New Testament writings, or secular history. It will suffice to give Richardson's evaluation of this matter as follows: "Bultmann's view that Jesus never thought of Himself as being in any way identified with the eschatological Son of man follows naturally from his desire to show that Jesus had no messianic consciousness at all, in order that faith in Christ might be liberated from all historical questions, such as whether Jesus considered Himself to be the Messiah. It is based on modern existenialist philosophy, rather than on a scholarly consideration of historical evidence, and we need not pursue it here." [2]

Vincent Taylor is dissatisfied with the conventional labeling of this inquiry "the messianic consciousness of Jesus," feeling that Jesus had little esteem for the current messianic idea and was never happy with the name Christ. Taylor says, "I propose, therefore, to abandon the phrase 'messianic consciousness,' except insofar as it is included in the bolder and more comprehensive expression 'the divine consciousness of Jesus.' By this phrase I mean the sense in which He was conscious of being more than a man, of sharing during His earthly existence in the life of Deity itself. This putting of the question has the advantage of raising the central issue." [3]

There is a great deal to commend Vincent's adoption of the title "The Divine Consciousness of Jesus." It is true that with this heading he is able to bring together the several strands of thought, such as the titles Son of Man and Son of God, Jesus' use of the Old Testament, His conception of the meaning of His suffering and death as the suffering Servant of the Lord, as well as His claim of being the Messiah. With due appreciation of Taylor's effort to sum all things under the heading "The Divine Consciousness of Jesus" and with little interest in being critical of it, I believe that we sense more accurately the central thrust of all the evidence as converging in Jesus' messiahship rather than His divine consciousness. Jesus' use of several of the divine titles, together with all His words on His relationship to the Father, have their orientation in the Old Testament concept of the Messiah, which in the light of New Testament interpretation, associates the coming of the Lord, the coming of the Servant of the Lord, with the greater Son of David, the coming Anointed One, the Messiah. Psalm 110 confirms this conclusion. This psalm directs attention to Him who sits at the right hand of God. This is strictly messianic in viewpoint, but in this very context the One who sits at the right hand of God is also Lord.

How crucial the importance of understanding Jesus' own consciousness of Himself comes to the fore when Jesus asks His disciples while they were in Caesarea Philippi, "Who do men say that the Son of man is?" (Mt. 16:13). Mark and Luke report Jesus' question in a more personal way, "Who do men say that I am?" (Mk. 7:27; Lk. 9:18). The several answers given by the people indicate some of the confusion in their minds, but Peter's witness was clear-cut and accurate. He said, "You are the Christ, the Son of the living God" (Mt. 16:16). Definitely, Jesus declared that Peter's confession was a revelation of the Father to him. The vast amount of evidence given in the Gospel records of Jesus' messianic consciousness and of His fulfillment of this mission confirms the greatness of this inquiry. How to treat this adequately in view of space limitations presents a real problem. Let us enter into the investigation of this evidence with due recognition of the strategic place it occupies in the whole discipline of biblical theology. Without any claim to accuracy in the chronological order of events, I am following a harmony of the Gospels in this study, and in order to gain the proper perspective of the evidence, I am grouping the material under the several periods of Christ's earthly ministry.

2. The Earliest Evidences of Jesus' Messianic Consciousness

We take our beginning with the answer Jesus, at the age of 12, gave to His parents in the words, "Did you not know that I must be in my Father's house?" (Lk. 2:49). This revealed Jesus' consciousness that God was His Father, and it may have the implication of His messianic consciousness.

The entire incident of Jesus' baptism by John gave Jesus positive evidence for believing that He was the Messiah. Jesus had responded to the baptism which was imposed upon Israel as a people. He experienced the baptism of the Holy Spirit. He heard the voice from heaven which declared that He was God's beloved Son. In this manner God verified to Jesus that this baptism with the Spirit was His anointing as the Messiah, for it had fufilled the prediction, "And the Spirit of the Lord shall rest upon him" (Is. 11:2). This, then, was the factual and experiential basis for Jesus' messianic consciousness. The temptation scene which followed shows that Satan was tempting Jesus as the Messiah. The messianic concept involved both deity and humanity. Satan would have Jesus the Son of God sin as a human being. To do so would have made Jesus unfit to be the Messiah. Jesus' replies to Satan voiced His understanding of this implication.

Jesus' conversation with His first disciples (Jn. 1:35-51) was messianically centered. The Baptist had pointed out Jesus as the Lamb of God who takes away the sin of the world. Their first touch with Jesus led them to feel that they had found the Messiah. Nathanael exclaimed, "Rabbi, you are the Son of God! You are the King of Israel! (Jn. 1:49). Jesus closed the scene with the words, "You will see heaven opened, and the angels of God ascending and descending upon the Son of man" (v. 51). This incident brought together the idea of Jesus being at once the Son of God and the King of Israel; the former asserting deity and the latter messiahship. Jesus' words asserted the intimate relation and communication between Himself and God.

Jesus chose the title Son of Man as descriptive of His own position. While Jesus did not give the source of this title, the setting in which He used it would lead us to believe that He was here claiming to be the Son of Man whom Daniel saw in the night vision, "And behold, with the clouds of heaven there came one like a son of man, and he came to the Ancient of Days and was presented before him. And to him was given dominion and glory and kingdom, that all peoples, nations, and languages should serve him; his dominion is an everlasting dominion, which shall not pass away, and his kingdom one that shall not be destroyed" (Dan. 7:13, 14). Devout Jews associated the "son of man" of Daniel's vision with the whole Messiah concept of the Old Testament prophets. For this reason the title *Son of Man* becomes one of the evidences of Jesus' consciousness that He was the Messiah.

In the light of other messianic passages, the story of the marriage at Cana in Galilee contributed to the evidence. Here Jesus asserted that His hour had not yet come, but John closes the account of the performing of the sign with the words that Jesus "manifested his glory; and his disciples believed in him" (Jn. 2:1-11). The *hour* to which Jesus refers is evidently the time of His engaging in messianic activity. The *glory* He manifested was the glory of His messiahship, and the faith of the disciples was their belief in His messiahship. Even the cleansing of the temple (Jn. 2:13-22) revealed definite messianic consciousness. Jesus' action was well nigh spectacular. His Father's house had been made a house of trade. Being the incarnate Son of the Father, the cleansing of the temple was His responsibility as the Messiah.

The conversation of Jesus with Nicodemus (Jn. 3:1-15) yields significant meaning when understood as the heart-searching words of the Messiah to a ruler of the Jews. He who possessed the insight that unless one is born of water and the Spirit, he cannot enter the kingdom of God and who distinguished between earthly things and heavenly things, was speaking from clear messianic insight. He who called Himself the Son of Man who descended from heaven and who also must be lifted up to die, with the result that whoever believes in Him may have eternal life, this One could be none less than the Messiah.

The heart-searching words of Jesus to the Samaritan woman are such that only the Messiah could be the speaker. And still further we have the indisputable right to believe that John was honest when he reported Jesus' words to the woman, "I who speak to you am he."

Matthew and Mark reported (Mt. 4:17; Mk. 1:15) the opening words of Jesus' preaching in Galilee which unmistakably come from Him who is indeed the Messiah. Jesus said, "The time is fulfilled, and the kingdom of God is at hand; repent, and believe in the gospel." Only He who believed Himself to be the Messiah could use the eschatological expression, "the time is fulfilled," which marked the beginning of the predicted messianic era. Corollary to this was the fact that the kingdom of God was at hand. The call to repentance coincided with the spiritual requirement associated with the kingdom of God. In this manner Jesus began to fulfill His messianic work. Jesus labeled the message concerning the kingdom of God as the gospel. This confirms still further the messianic consciousness of the Speaker (Mk. 1:15).

From a study of these earliest evidences of Jesus' messianic consciousness, we may conclude that it was not a consciousness that developed gradually and after a long period of time became clear to Him, but rather that from the time He heard the voice from heaven at His baptism, Jesus was fully aware that He was the Messiah. In order that this thesis may be fully established, let us proceed to examine some of the evidences which characterize Jesus' public ministry.

3. Jesus' Messianic Consciousness Revealed in His Public Ministry

In the synagogue at Nazareth, Jesus read the familiar words of Isaiah 61:1, 2. He then made the statement, "Today this Scripture has been fulfilled in your hearing" (Lk. 4:21). By identifying Himself with the speaker of Isaiah 61 Jesus was asserting the indwelling of the Holy Spirit through which He was performing the messianic task of proclaiming the good news, and most definitively of proclaiming the acceptable year of the Lord.

a. Jesus' Messianic Consciousness Revealed in His Healing Ministry

The healing ministry of Jesus was the occasion for repeated witness to His consciously engaging in messianic activity. When Jesus healed the mother-in-law of Peter and then cast out demons and healed others who were sick, Matthew made the observation, "This was to fulfill what was spoken by the prophet Isaiah, 'He took our infirmities and bore our diseases' " (Mt. 8:14-17). In this manner he identified Jesus as the *Servant of the Lord*. Matthew was certainly interpreting Jesus as performing these mighty works in the consciousness of being the Messiah. Luke noted that the demons cried out saying, "You are the Son of God." In response to this Luke noted that Jesus "rebuked them, and would not allow them to speak, because they knew that he was the Christ" (Lk. 4:41). On another occasion of healing (Mt. 12:15, 21; Mk. 3:7-12) Matthew observed that His healing work fulfilled another Servant of the Lord passage, this time Isaiah 42:1-4. It seems legitimate to conclude that Matthew's second observation of the fulfillment of a Servant of the Lord passage in Christ's healing ministry is evidence that he was thereby giving witness to Jesus' consciousness of being the Messiah.

The healing of a demon-possessed man (Mt. 12:22-29; Mk. 3:20-27; Lk. 11:14-22) brings to us in graphic fashion the consciousness lying back of Jesus' casting out of demons. In a positive manner Jesus said, "If it is by the Spirit of God that I cast out demons, then the kingdom of God has come upon you" (Mt. 12:28). Jesus had bound the strong man of the house and was thus able to plunder Satan's house. Thus by casting out demons through the power of the Spirit, Jesus was acting in His capacity as the Messiah. These several incidents of Jesus' casting out demons are cumulative in their bearing on Jesus' consciousness of being the Messiah. The repeated connection of Jesus with the Servant of the Lord and of His being the Son of Man served to bring this conclusion to a focus.

b. Jesus' Messianic Consciousness Revealed in the Choosing of the Twelve Apostles

Several of John's disciples, who later became Jesus' disciples through their contact with Jesus, were convinced that He was the Christ. Another preparatory step toward the appointment of the Twelve was Jesus' call to the four fishermen, "Follow me, and I will make you fishers of men" (Mt. 4:18). Already conscious of Jesus' messiahship these four fisherman undoubtedly sensed that this call to follow Jesus had definite messianic implications. On a later occasion Jesus "called his disciples, and chose from them twelve, whom he named apostles" (Lk. 6:13). To them He gave power and authority over all demons and to cure diseases, and He sent them out to preach the kingdom of God and to heal (Mk. 3: 14). The nature of the instruction which Jesus gave to the Twelve would show the real significance of their mission (Mt. 10). They were sent specifically to the lost sheep of the house of Israel. Their message was, "The kingdom of heaven is at hand" (10:7). This command gained still larger meaning when Jesus gave the Great Commission to the apostles before His ascension (28:18-20). Speaking of the "all authority" which He then possessed, Jesus said, "Go therefore and make disciples of all nations, baptizing them in the name of the Father and of the Son and of the Holy Spirit, teaching them to observe all that I have commanded you; and lo, I am with you always, to the close of the age." From these incidents we gather that the appointment of the Twelve had first reference to the twelve tribes of Israel, but it was expanded to their making disciples of all nations. Only the Messiah could give such power and authority.

c. Jesus' Messianic Consciousness Revealed in the Sermon on the Mount and in the Kingdom Parables

The Sermon on the Mount (Mt. 5 — 7; Luke 6:20-49) also disclosed the mind of Jesus. In the Beatitudes He revealed a profound comprehension of the kingdom. Only the Messiah through whom the blessedness of the kingdom would be achieved could speak these words. Jesus clearly showed His relation to the law and the prophets when He said, "Think not that I have come to abolish the law and the prophets; I have come not to abolish them but to fulfil them" (Mt. 5:17). In the six illustrations that followed this statement, Jesus asserted the oneness of His teaching with that of the law and the prophets.

As God revealed Himself through the Old Testament writings, so He was then revealing Himself through Jesus. This revelation reached its climax through Him who could say, "You, therefore, must be perfect, as your heavenly Father is perfect" (Mt. 5:48). We naturally wonder who is He who could tell His people not to be anxious about life with all of its cares and troubles; but in a positive way could say, "Seek first his kingdom and his righteousness, and all these things shall be yours as well" (6:33). Only the Messiah could say, "Not every one who says to me, 'Lord,' 'Lord,' shall enter the kingdom of heaven, but he who does the will of my Father who is in heaven" (7:21). He concluded this thought with a look at His work as final Judge who will need to condemn those who did not do the will of the Father. Who other than the Messiah could be the final Judge of all mankind?

The closing words of this sermon (vv. 24-27) reveal an authoritativeness which was appropriate only on the lips of the Messiah. Matthew's closing words confirm this conclusion: "When Jesus finished these sayings, the crowds were astonished at his teaching, for he taught them as one who had authority, and not as their scribes" (Mt. 7:28, 29).

The kingdom parables (Mt. 13:1-53; Mk. 4:1-34; Lk. 8:4-18) also revealed Jesus' consciousness of being the Messiah. Jesus used parables through which He made known the secrets of the kingdom of heaven, and expounded the nature of the kingdom of God. In doing this He revealed His own relation to the kingdom, which is best understood in the light of His being the Messiah. When Jesus spoke of Himself as the Son of Man, the One who sows the good seed, this title definitely possessed messianic significance. This gives us a very accurate perspective of all the kingdom parables. In a word, the Son of Man is the Ruler of the kingdom. Hence He is the Messiah.

This parable also gave a very important eschatological note which is so essential in understanding the Messiah's relation to the kingdom. The kingdom of the Son of Man, the Messiah, belongs to this age. In the consummation of this kingdom the righteous will shine like the sun in the kingdom of their Father. Such an exposition of the kingdom arises from Jesus' consciousness of being the Messiah. The parables spoken by Jesus near the close of His ministry are equally significant in revealing Jesus' attitude toward Himself. Perhaps the most explicit case is the parable of the householder (Mt. 21:33-44; Mk. 12:1-11; Lk. 20:9-18). The main point of this parable becomes clear when we note that the householder finally sent his son to get the fruit from the tenants.

The slight differences among the Gospels with reference to the son may suggest something of messianic import. It is possible that Jesus' exact words were those given by Luke, "my beloved son." God had sent His beloved Son into the world, entrusted with the responsibility of leading Israel back to God. But the builders rejected the stone which God had made the Head of the corner (Ps. 18:20-23). In prophetic terms the psalmist was predicting the Jews' rejection of their Messiah. This and other parables given during the closing week of our Lord's ministry reflected the coming crisis of the Messiah's death in the most vivid manner possible. Jesus was not only conscious of being the Messiah who soon would be killed, but He also carried forward His messianic work by explaining His imminent death.

d. Jesus' Use of the Messianic Title, "the Son of Man"

Through this title Jesus most clearly expressed His messianic consciousness. This becomes increasingly clear in a study of the most significant cases where Jesus used this title. While the generally accepted source of this title is one of the dream visions of Daniel (Dan. 7:13, 14), some students would trace it to the Book of Ezekiel, where it occurs more than ninety times as a designation of the prophet himself. Jesus' use of the title proves conclusively that He is giving it the meaning that it had in the vision of Daniel. It reads, "I saw in the night visions, and behold, with the clouds of heaven there came one like a son of man, and he came to the Ancient of Days and was presented before him. And to him was given dominion and glory and kingdom, that all peoples, nations, and languages should serve him; his dominion is an everlasting dominion, which shall not pass away, and his kingdom one that shall not be destroyed" (Dan. 7:13, 14).

In the case of the healing of the paralytic (Mt. 9:1-8; Mk. 2:1-12; Lk. 5:17-26) Jesus' claim to being the Son of Man was made in response to the criticism of the scribes and Pharisees with reference to His act of forgiving sins. At this point Jesus said, "But that you may know that the Son of man has authority on earth to forgive sins." He then said to the paralytic, "Rise, take up your bed and go home." Through Jesus' use of this title in this incident, the human Jesus forgave sins and also exercised messianic power in healing the paralytic. When Jesus replied to John's inquiry (Mt. 11:12-19; Lk. 7:18-35), He not only identified John's place in preparing for the coming Messiah but also gave a significant comparison between Himself and John in which He used the title Son of Man. Jesus' comment answered the confusion of the people in His being able to understand John's life as a Nazarite expressed in the words, "Eating no bread and drinking no wine," as compared with that of "the Son of man has come eating and drinking." In this setting Jesus showed that He, the Messiah, was genuinely human.

The meaning of Jesus' consciousness of being the Messiah comes sharply into focus on the occasion of His being charged with the casting out of demons by Beelzebul, the prince of demons (Mt. 12:22-45; Mk. 3:19-30; Lk. 11:14-36). Jesus severely condemned this blasphemous charge against Him and claimed that it is by the Spirit of God that He cast out demons. As the conversation continued, Jesus showed that blasphemy against the Spirit would not be forgiven, and over against this He said, "And whoever says a word against the Son of man will be forgiven." The meaning of this distinction is a bit difficult to state. It may be that Jesus was conveying to His hearers that by reason of His being in human form, it was pardonable for them to blaspheme the Son of Man. The mystery of the divine and human in Jesus was a problem solved alone by faith. If this interprets correctly this problem, it reveals again Jesus' clear insight of being the Messiah.

On the occasion of the scribes and Pharisees coming to Jesus and asking to see a sign from Him (Mt. 12:38-42; Lk. 11:28-32), He replied, "As Jonah was three days and three nights in the belly of the whale, so will the Son of man be three days and three nights in the heart of the earth" (Mt. 12:40). He condemned their impenitent attitude by saying that the queen of the South will arise at the judgment and condemn them, "For she came from the ends of the earth to hear the wisdom of Solomon, and behold, something greater than Solomon is here" (v. 42). Contrary to the messianic concept of the scribes and Pharisees, Jesus spoke of the death of the Son of Man. He spoke also of Himself as being greater than Solomon, and by doing so, Jesus placed the Son of Man title into the same class as the kingship of Solomon, thus giving it clear messianic import.

In this recounting of the Son of Man passages, let us note again Jesus' confrontation of the disciples with this crucial question as to who the Son of Man is. Peter answered forthrightly, "You are the Christ, the Son of the living God" (Mt. 16:13-20; Mk. 8:27-30; Lk. 9:18-21). Jesus then assured Peter that this answer came by revelation from the Father to him. Jesus further declared that on this rock He would build His church and that the powers of death would not prevail against it. Just as the people of Israel were God's church under the theocracy, so those who believe that Jesus is the Christ, the Son of the living God, will constitute Christ's church under the Christocracy. Accordingly, He, the messianic King, will give the keys of the kingdom of heaven to His disciples. It is in order to evaluate this incident as being the most strategic of all the Son of Man passages as revealing Jesus' consciousness of being the Messiah.

Confirmation of this view becomes evident when Jesus proceeded to forecast His suffering and death (Mt. 16:21, 28; Mk. 8:31 — 9:1; Lk. 9:22-27). Undoubtedly, it was beyond the disciples' comprehension to be told, "The Son of man must suffer many things . . . and be killed, and after three days rise again" (Mk. 8:31). That the Son of Man, the Messiah, must suffer and die seemed to be utterly impossible from their understanding of the messianic predictions. They had not yet come to see that the messianic King was also the suffering Servant. This fact made Jesus' claim all the more astounding and unbelievable. Jesus made the problem still more difficult for the disciples when He declared, "If any man would come after me, let him deny himself and take up his cross and follow me" (Mt. 16:24). Only through such self-denial could they hope to share in the glory promised by the Son of Man when He said, "For the Son of man is to come with his angels in the glory of his Father, and then he will repay every man for what he has done" (v. 27). In this way Jesus resolved the apparent contradiction between the ideas: on the one hand, the Son of Man suffering and dying; and on the other hand, His coming with the angels in the glory of the Father.

Jesus expanded the messianic connotation of the title Son of Man in the words, "In the new world, when the Son of man shall sit on his glorious throne, you who have followed me will also sit on twelve thrones, judging the twelve tribes of Israel" (Mt. 19:28). Thus the Son of Man is the messianic King. This fact lay at the very center of Jesus' consciousness.

Yet one more incident deserves attention (Mt. 20:20-28; Mk. 10:35-40). The mother of the sons of Zebedee had the ambition that her two sons have the positions of honor in sitting one on His right hand and one on His left hand in Christ's kingdom. To this Jesus replied, "To sit at my right hand and at my left is not mine to grant" (Mt. 20:23; Mk. 10:40). To this Jesus added another dimension to the nature of His work when He concluded, "The Son of man came not to be served but to serve, and to give his life as a ransom for many" (Mt. 20:28).

Thus Jesus again brought together the apparently irreconcilable facts of the reigning Son of Man and of the suffering Son of Man. This study of Jesus' use of the title Son of Man leads us to conclude that Jesus most expressly set forth His consciousness of His being the Messiah.

e. Jesus' Use of the Title "Son of God"

With unfathomable depths of meaning Jesus used the title Son of God to express His consciousness of being the Messiah. In the words of Vos, "The title, Son of God, opens up to us a new perspective from which to view the Messiahship." He added that in Jesus' use of this title, He declared, "The relation of God to the Messiah, and of the Messiah to God . . . here lie those lines of revelation which connect the soteric function and work of Jesus with the great transcendental verities of our faith concerning Him. Here we see the Messiahship, though existing in time, yet solidly resting upon the eternal things of the Godhead. Here the profoundest Christology of the New Testament shows its ultimate roots." [4] Reflecting on the baptismal scene of Jesus we are prepared to anticipate that the voice from heaven saying, "This is my beloved Son," not only identified the person of Jesus but also asserted the greatness of Jesus' work in the world. In other words, Jesus' work as the beloved Son of God would have the dimensions of Deity activity.

While the expression, the Son of God, did not directly assert messianic activity, we have occasion to study closely Jesus' use of this title to discover the messianic connotations that it did carry. Let us examine first Jesus' words, "All things have been delivered to me by my Father; and no one knows the Son except the Father, and no one knows the

Father except the Son and any one to whom the Son chooses to reveal him" (Mt. 11:27; Lk. 10:22). These words lead us to an understanding of sonship to the Father in terms of what the Father delivered to the Son. It is the "all things." This unlimited power and authority is conceivable only in terms of the Father's unique relation to the Son. Clearly this deliverance of "all things" to the Son had to do with the carrying forward of God's purposes in the world to its consummation.

Jesus used almost identical language in John 3:35, which reads, "The Father loves the Son, and has given all things into his hands." The context of this affirmation points up the dignity of Jesus as compared with that of John the Baptist. The Baptist had predicted that Jesus must increase but that he himself must decrease. This was possible because Jesus had come from above and is above all. From this context we should gather that all that Jesus performed in His earthly ministry was accomplished through the "all things" given into His hand. John made another observation, "Jesus, knowing that the Father had given all things into his hands, and that he had come from God and was going to God" (Jn. 13:3). This comment shows that the "all things" included all that pertained to Jesus' messianic work, the total earthly ministry of our Lord.

Further light as to the meaning of the "all things" shines forth from the Old Testament. Even a casual reading of the messianic psalms, the Servant of the Lord passages, the promise of the making of a new covenant, and Daniel's vision centering in the coming of "one like a son of man," will show what lay back of Jesus' words that God had given all things into His hands.[5] By this statement He was expressing most profoundly His consciousness of being the Messiah.

Looking at the parable of the householder (Mt. 21:33-44; Mk. 12:1-11; Lk. 20:9-18), we see that the son in the parable is none other than the Son of God. The larger meaning of the parable has in view God's dealings with His people, Israel. He has finally sent His Son to harvest the spiritual fruit which should come to God. But the spiritual leaders of Israel would not receive the Son but put Him to death. Thus in most vivid parabolic language Jesus, as the Son, spoke of the "all things" (Jn. 13:3) delivered to Him to accomplish in this world. Later Jesus asked the Pharisees, "What do you think of the Christ? Whose son is he?" They answered very correctly, "The son of David." Jesus then confronted them with the staggering question as to how David called his son, Lord, as he did in Psalm 110, " 'The Lord said to my Lord, sit at my right hand, until I put thy enemies under thy feet'? If David thus calls him Lord, how is he his son" (Mt. 22:44, 45)? Our inquiry centers here in what Jesus thought of Himself in this conversation.

Beyond question, Jesus was conscious of His being the Lord who was addressed with the words " 'sit at my right hand, till I put thy enemies under thy feet'?" This psalm definitely identified the son of David with the Lord who shall sit on the right hand of the Lord God. This confirms the messianic consciousness of Jesus as He used the title Son of God.

There are a number of passages in the Gospels of Matthew and of Luke in which Jesus spoke of God as being His Father. [6] All these reflect, more or less clearly, Jesus' messianic consciousness. Used in these Gospels in which Jesus represented Himself as the Son of God, they serve to confirm the main thrust of this entire discussion.

4. Jesus' Messianic Consciousness Revealed During Passion Week

As Jesus' earthly ministry led to His suffering and death, His statements concerning His messiahship became still more pointed. Let us begin with Jesus' entry into Jerusalem. [7] In this scene Jesus fulfilled literally the prediction of Zechariah 9:9 through which He laid claim to being Israel's King. When the disciples and the multitudes who were also on the way to Jerusalem, saw Jesus riding upon the ass, they gave the joyful expression of "Hosanna" to the son of David and shouted, "Blessed is the King who comes in the name of the Lord!" (Lk. 19: 38). The tragedy of the entire incident was voiced by Jesus in the words, "You did not know the time of your visitation" (v. 44). According to the prediction, Jesus, their King, had publicly presented Himself to His people but they rejected their King.

In the parable of the wicked husbandman Jesus gave His interpretation of it in the words: " 'The very stone which the builders rejected has become the head of the corner; this was the Lord's doing, and it is marvelous in our eyes' " (Mt. 21:42; Ps. 118:22, 23). This psalm is clearly messianic and Jesus' use of it indicated His consciousness of being the stone which the builders rejected.

Coming to the Olivet Discourse we meet again the most emphatic uses of the title Son of Man on the part of Jesus. Jesus found it necessary to warn the disciples of many who would come in His name claiming to be the Christ. Through this warning Jesus was saying in an indirect manner that He, Himself, was the Christ. The discourse mounted to the height of Jesus' picturing His return in the language, "Then will appear the sign of the Son of man in heaven, and then all the tribes of the earth will mourn, and they will see the Son of man coming on the clouds of heaven with power and great glory" (Mt. 24:30). After giving appropriate exhortations, Jesus concluded His discourse with the words, "When the Son of man comes in his glory, and all the angels with him, then he will sit on his glorious throne" (Mt. 25:31). In this way Jesus showed that Daniel's prediction would have its culminating fulfillment when He, the Son of Man, will sit on His glorious throne in messianic splendor judging the world. For this reason Jesus' use of the title Son of Man proves to be His most emphatic claim to His being the Messiah.

When Jesus was eating the Passover meal with the disciples, He told them: "The Son of man goes as it is written of him, but woe to that man by whom the Son of man is betrayed!" (Mt. 26:24). Thus Jesus interpreted Psalm 41:9 as a prediction of Judas' betrayal and of its having definite messianic reference. After Judas left the group, Jesus gave further explanation of Judas' actions in the words, "Now is the Son of man glorified, and in him God is glorified; if God is glorified in him, God will also glorify him in himself, and glorify him at once" (Jn. 13:31, 32). The intimate relation between the Son of Man and God possessed such deep meaning by reason of Jesus' being the Messiah.

It belonged to the "all things" delivered by the Father to the Son that He, the Messiah, should institute the new covenant. For its ratification blood was required and the only blood which would avail was that of the God-Man, Jesus, the Messiah. For this reason Jesus added, "I tell you I shall not drink again of this fruit of the vine until that day when I drink it new with you in my Father's kingdom" (Mt. 26:29). Only the Messiah could speak these words.

The "all things" delivered by the Father to the Son did not terminate with Jesus' earthly ministry. It would continue with His exaltation to the right hand of the Father. In anticipation of this, Jesus promised the disciples, "I will pray the Father, and he will give you another Counselor, to be with you for ever, even the Spirit of truth . . . he dwells with you, and will be in you" (Jn. 14:16, 17). This promise, along with the other teachings given by Jesus in this upper room discourse, showed that in the future Jesus would carry on His work in the world through the Holy Spirit. He would be continuing this work as the reigning Messiah (Jn. 14:25; 15:26; 16:12-15).

As Jesus moved forward to the events of His arrest and trial, He confronted Judas with the question, "Would you betray the Son of man with a kiss?" (Lk. 22:48). His rebuke of Peter in the latter's effort to defend Jesus expressed the same messianic consciousness. He asked Peter, "Do you think that I cannot appeal to my Father, and he will at once send me more than twelve legions of angels? But how then should the scriptures be fulfilled, that it must be so?" (Mt. 26:53, 54). In the midst of Jesus' trial "the high priest asked him, 'Are you the Christ, the Son of the Blessed?' And Jesus said, 'I am; and you will see the

Son of man seated at the right hand of Power, and coming with the clouds of heaven' " (Mk. 14:61, 62). In this language Christ most climactically expressed the identity of the Christ: the Son of God and the Son of Man. To Pilate's question, "Are you the King of the Jews?" Jesus gave an affirmative reply (Mt. 27:11).

Jesus explained further the nature of His kingly office when He said, "My kingship is not of this world; if my kingship were of this world, my servants would fight" (Jn. 18:36). We gather from this part of the trial that Jesus not only affirmed His messiahship to Pilate but also that His kingship is not of this world. This was a different interpretation of messianic kingship from that held by the Jews. Most touching of all are Christ's words on the cross when He twice addressed God as Father. The prayer, "Father, forgive them," and His final words, "Father, into thy hands I commit my spirit!" certainly came from One who recognized God as His Father in the most real sense.

Jesus gave further witness to His messianic consciousness after His resurrection. This testimony possesses supreme importance by reason of His being raised from the dead. To Mary He said, "I have not yet ascended to the Father . . . I am ascending to my Father and your Father, to my God and your God" (Jn. 20:17). In like manner He addressed the disciples, saying, "As the Father has sent me, even so I send you" (v. 21). Then "he breathed on them, and said to them, Receive the Holy Spirit. If you forgive the sins of any, they are forgiven; if you retain the sins of any, they are retained" (vv. 22, 23). In this manner Jesus exercised His messianic authority. It belonged to the enthroned Messiah to pour out the Holy Spirit upon His disciples.

In Jesus' conversation with the two disciples on their way to Emmaus, He sought to solve for them the most perplexing problem of the suffering Messiah. Jesus asked them, "Was it not necessary that the Christ should suffer these things and enter into his glory?" (Lk. 24: 26). He then proceeded to interpret to them all the Scriptures which predicted His work. This interpretation was possible alone to Jesus who had suffered death and had entered into His glory, and by so doing, gave the final proof of His being the Messiah. In line with this conversation, the Great Commission expressed Jesus' final testimony to His being the Messiah. These familiar words read, "All authority in heaven and on earth has been given to me. Go therefore and make disciples of all nations, baptizing them in the name of the Father and of the Son and of the Holy Spirit, teaching them to observe all that I have commanded you; and lo, I am with you always, to the close of the age" (Mt. 28:18-20). Add to this Commission an almost identical command, "But you shall receive power when the Holy Spirit has come upon you; and you shall be my witnesses in Jerusalem and in all Judea and Samaria and to the end of the earth (Acts 1:8). Only He, the enthroned Messiah, could pour out the Holy Spirit as promised by the prophet Joel. The expressed purpose of the Apostle John in writing his Gospel gives a fitting evaluation of all the Gospel records as they related to Jesus' consciousness of being the Messiah. John wrote, "These are written that you may believe that Jesus is the Christ, the Son of God, and that believing you may have life in his name" (Jn. 20:31).

5. Conclusion

The crucial importance of the subject matter considered in this chapter justifies this detailed treatment. The untold number of instances which prove so conclusively that Jesus regarded Himself as the Messiah shows the importance of this idea as it lay in the minds of the Gospel writers. Along with this we have observed the fullness and completeness of Jesus' fulfillment of His mission as the Messiah. Some important aspects of His messianic work remain to be considered but in the large we have seen Christ's fulfillment of all that was predicted of Him to accomplish as the Messiah. The discussion of this theme served also to present the Gospel evidence of the deity of Jesus. This became clear in Jesus' use of the several titles: Son of Man, Son of God, Lord, and Messiah. All these revealed Jesus in the fullness of His divine and human natures. They all served as a marvelous self-disclosure of Jesus to the world.

This discussion has also led us to explore the meaning of the several titles used by Jesus. The biblical orientation and use of these titles served as the basis for gaining their true meaning as used by Jesus. As such, these titles constitute the most important content of unfolding divine revelation.

For Additional Reading and Reference:

Beyschlag, *New Testament Theology,* Vol. I, pp. 56-79.
Bruce, F. F., *New Testament Development of Old Testament Themes,* pp. 83-99.
Bultmann, *Theology of the New Testament,* Vol. I, pp. 26-32.
Conzelmann, *An Outline of the Theology of the New Testament* (1968), pp. 72-86, 127-140.
Filson, *The New Testament Against Its Environment,* pp. 58-77, 111-132.
Hunter, *The Works and Words of Jesus,* pp. 80-100.
Richardson, *An Introduction to the Theology of the New Testament,* pp. 125-126.
Ryrie, *Biblical Theology of the New Testament,* pp. 38-71.

Sheldon, *New Testament Theology*, pp. 59-67.
Stauffer, *New Testament Theology*, pp. 103-152.
Stevens, *The Theology of the New Testament*, pp. 41-64.
Stonehause, *The Witness of Matthew and Mark*, pp. 50-85.
Taylor, *The Person of Christ*, pp. 155-189.
Vos, *The Self-Disclosure of Jesus*, pp. 13-36, 105-302.
Weidner, *Biblical Theology of the New Testament*, Vol. I, pp. 48-59.
Weiss, *Biblical Theology of the New Testament*, Vol. I, pp. 73-92.

1. Rudolf Bultmann, *Theology of the New Testament* (New York: Charles Scribner's Sons, 1951), Vol. I, pp. 26, 27.

2. Richardson, *op. cit.*, pp. 134, 135.

3. Vincent Taylor, *The Person of Christ in New Testament Teaching* (New York: St. Martin's Press, Macmillan & Co., Ltd., 1958), p. 156.

4. Geerhardus Vos, *The Self-Disclosure of Jesus* (Grand Rapids: Wm. B. Eerdmans Publishing Co., 1954), p. 141.

5. Ps. 2; 72; 110; Is. 9:6-8; 11:1-10; 42:1-7; 49:1-7; 52:13 — 53:12; Jer. 31:31-34; Dan. 7:13, 14.

6. Mt. 7:21; 10:32, 33; 11:27; 12:50; 15:13; 16:17; 18:10, 14, 19, 35; 20:23; 25:34; 26:29, 39, 42, 53; Lk. 2:49; 22:29; 24:49.

7. Mt. 21:1-11; Mk. 11:1-11; Lk. 19:29-44; Jn. 12:12-19.

CHAPTER IX

THE GOOD NEWS OF THE KINGDOM OF GOD

1. Introduction

Mark introduced the preaching ministry of Jesus with the words, "Jesus came into Galilee, preaching the gospel of God, and saying, 'The time is fulfilled, and the kingdom of God is at hand; repent, and believe in the gospel' " (Mk. 1:14, 15). When He began His first circuit through Galilee Jesus said, "I must preach the good news of the kingdom of God to the other cities also; for I was sent for this purpose" (Lk. 4:43). This chapter seeks to deal with the content of Jesus' preaching mission. In a word, His mission had to do with the good news of the kingdom of God. The content of the good news, or the gospel, was the kingdom of God. That the gospel should center in the kingdom of God constituted the focal point of Jesus' preaching. All four Gospels have this theme as their central message, the setting forth of the kingdom of God. For this reason the books of Matthew, Mark, Luke, and John are called the Gospels.

° ° °

Since the subject matter of this chapter is so extensive it may prove helpful to give a breakdown of its contents at this point.

1. *The Time Is Fulfilled*

In this section the Old Testament predictions of the coming kingdom will receive attention. Since Jesus unfolded the kingdom of God in the light of the Old Testament this subdivision will also serve as giving Jesus' view of the Old Testament. It also gives the opportunity for presenting Jesus' view of the grand unity of divine revelation and of the fundamental harmony between the New and the Old.

2. *The Concept of the Kingdom Held by Jesus*

3. *The Essence of the Kingdom as Revealed by Jesus*

In this section my thought has to do with that which belongs to the very nature of God's rule. I desire again to give recognition to Vos's explication of the essence of the kingdom. The framework of this discussion follows that of Vos.[1] I have expanded this structure according to the following pattern. The wide spread of subject matter dealing with the essence of the kingdom includes at least eight areas of God's supremacy in the kingdom of God. With each of these one may associate a respective counterpart in man's response to the respective area of God's supremacy. While there is some overlapping of these eight spheres of God's supremacy, as well as their respective counterparts in man's response, their study should lead to an understanding of their supremacy, as well as to their ultimate unity in the kingdom of God.

The Essence of the Kingdom

Spheres of God's Supremacy

1. Fatherhood of God
2. Righteousness
3. Power
4. Blessedness
5. Life
6. Love
7. Authority — Lordship
8. Revelation

The Counterpart in Man's Response

1. Sonship, Worship, Perfection
   (The Ethics of Jesus)
2. Repentance
3. Faith
4. Salvation
5. New Birth (Regeneration)
6. Obedience
7. Discipleship
8. Belief, Knowledge

4. *The Kingdom in Relation to Jesus' Death, the New Covenant, the Church, and the Great Commission*

The aim of this section will be to give the meaning of Jesus' death as set forth in the Gospels and to show the relation that it bore to the making of the new covenant, the establishment of the church and the command to worldwide evangelization — all this in the perspective of the kingdom of God.

5. The Kingdom in Relation to Time

The purpose of this section is to treat the eschatological aspect of the present age and of the age to come, and to show its relation to the kingdom of God.

° ° °

2. The Time Is Fulfilled

Jesus' expression, "The time is fulfilled" (Mk. 1:15), plainly looked back to the Old Testament for a prophetic structuring of future events. Jesus was evidently interpreting the prophets as foretelling a lapse of time between their predictions and the beginning of a new era. This new age, as Mark understood it, was that of the kingdom of God. Let us take a brief look at the Old Testament Scriptures which undoubtedly supported Mark's statement.

a. The Old Testament Foreview of the Latter Days[2]

According to the prophets, the day of the Lord centered in the judgment which God was about to bring on the nations of Israel and Judah. In view of the dreadfulness of this coming judgment the prophets challenged the faith of Israel's faithful remnant in a coming era of time in which the Lord would again bestow blessings upon His people. This future period became known as the latter days or the last days. This future period would be unparalleled in the outpouring of God's blessings on Israel. In these latter days the Messiah, the Anointed One, would come[3] and the Servant of the Lord would appear.[4] It does not appear that any of the Old Testament prophets identified the coming Servant of the Lord with the Anointed One. It remained for Jesus to show that He embodied in Himself both the messianic and Servant of the Lord predictions. The devout people of Israel laid hold of these predictions in genuine faith. Their religion was predominantly eschatological in character. Throughout all Old Testament revelation God would have His people put their confidence and trust in a hope to be realized through His ever continuing acts among His people. These predictions set forth a most sublime hope.

b. Jesus and the Gospel Writers Built on Old Testament Revelation

Since the Gospel writers, Mark in particular, had observed Jesus' significant words, "The time is fulfilled, and the kingdom of God is at hand," it is natural to expect that Jesus would base His preaching on the Old Testament predictions concerning the coming age. The Gospel writers captured this element in Jesus' teaching and preserved for us its content as well as their own interpretation of this new era. This fact is one of the most outstanding characteristics of the Gospel records, not only of the Synoptic Gospels but also of that of John.

First, let us observe how Jesus authenticated His messianic mission by Old Testament predictions. On entering the synagogue in His hometown, Nazareth, He read from Isaiah 61:1, 2 and then He said, "Today this scripture has been fulfilled in your hearing" (Lk. 4:21). Through this prophetic message Jesus made the explicit claim to being the One spoken of in this passage. Its messianic aspect is evident. Having been baptized with the Holy Spirit, Jesus could properly say, "The Spirit of the Lord is upon me." Through this anointing with the Holy Spirit Jesus was empowered to preach good news to the poor — this in fulfillment of the prediction, "How beautiful upon the mountains are the feet of him who brings good tidings, who publishes peace, who brings good tidings of good, who publishes salvation, who says to Zion, 'Your God reigns' " (Is. 52:7). It would appear that the expressions *good news* or *good tidings* had their origin in these two passages from Isaiah. For Jesus to say that He had been anointed to preach these good tidings was to authenticate His mission as the Servant of the Lord and the Messiah.

When Jesus left Nazareth to dwell in Capernaum, Matthew observed that this fulfilled Isaiah's prediction (Is. 9:1, 2). This fact underlay Jesus' first messianic preaching when He said, "Repent, for the kingdom of heaven is at hand" (Mt. 4:12-17). Matthew made a similar observation on the occasion of Jesus' healing ministry in Peter's house when he wrote, "This was to fulfill what was spoken by the prophet, Isaiah, 'He took our infirmities and bore our diseases' " (Mt. 8:14-17; Is. 53:4). A third time Matthew observed that Jesus' healing ministry fulfilled a Servant of the Lord passage (12:15-21; Is. 42:1-4). Most certainly Matthew interpreted Jesus' earthly ministry as being the fulfillment of both messianic and Servant of the Lord predictions.

Second, let us examine some of Jesus' own words which authenticated His messianic mission. At one of the feasts in Jerusalem Jesus concluded a very significant claim for Himself by saying, "If you believed Moses, you would believe me, for he wrote of me. But if you do not believe his writings, how will you believe my words?" (Jn. 5:46, 47). Jesus was evidently referring to Moses' prediction that God would raise up a prophet like himself (Deut. 18:18). Both Peter and Stephen held that Jesus fulfilled this prediction (Acts 3:22, 23; 7:37). Mark quoted Jesus' words, "Elijah does come first to restore all things; and how is it written of the Son of man, that he should suffer many things and be treated with contempt?" (Mk. 9:12). In this context Jesus referred to the treatment that the Baptist had received, which treatment was indicative of what He, Himself, would suffer in due time (Mt. 17:11-13). Evidently, Jesus was referring to the suffering Servant of Isaiah 53, and by so doing, identified Himself as the Servant of the Lord.

In conversation with the chief priests and the elders Jesus put the question, "Have you never read the scriptures: 'The very stone which the builders rejected has become the head of the corner; this was the Lord's doing, and it is marvelous in our eyes'?" (Mt. 21:42; Mk. 12: 10, 11; Lk. 20:17). Here Jesus quoted Psalm 118:22, 23, which had clear messianic connotation. At the Last Supper, Jesus said to the twelve disciples. "The Son of man goes as it is written of him, but woe to that man by whom the Son of man is betrayed!" (Mt. 26:24; Mk. 14: 21; Lk. 22:22). That same night Jesus said to them, "You will all fall away because of me this night; for it is written, 'I will strike the shepherd, and the sheep of the flock will be scattered' " (Mt. 26:31; Mk. 14:27). Yet once more during that night Jesus said, "For I tell you that this scripture must be fulfilled in me, 'And he was reckoned with the transgressors'; for what is written about me has its fulfillment" (Lk. 22:37). For my present purpose, these three cases of Jesus' looking to the fulfillment of the Scriptures which had to do with His sufferings show plainly the manner in which Jesus was authenticating to His disciples His messianic mission.

In the garden after Peter struck the slave of the high priest, Jesus rebuked him for the act and concluded His words by saying, "But how then should the scriptures be fulfilled, that it must be so?" (Mt. 26:54). To the crowd that had gathered Jesus said further, "But all this has taken place, that the scriptures of the prophets might be fulfilled" (v. 56). Even by the details of His arrest Jesus authenticated His messianic mission through the fulfillment of the Scriptures.

Finally, and in a most comprehensive manner, Jesus authenticated His messianic mission on the basis of Old Testament predictions as He conversed with the two disciples on the way to Emmaus after His resurrection. Jesus said, " 'O foolish men, and slow of heart to believe all that the prophets have spoken! Was it not necessary that the Christ should suffer these things and enter into his glory?' And beginning with Moses and all the prophets, he interpreted to them in all the scriptures the things concerning himself" (Lk. 24:25-27). Later Jesus said, " 'These are my words which I spoke to you, while I was still with you, that everything written about me in the law of Moses and the prophets and the psalms must be fulfilled.' Then he opened their minds to understand the scriptures, and said to them, 'Thus it is written, that the Christ should suffer and on the third day rise from the dead, and that repentance and forgiveness of sins should be preached in his name to all nations, beginning from Jerusalem' " (vv. 44-47).

In conclusion, the frequency with which Jesus authenticated His messianic mission on the grounds of the fulfillment of Old Testament predictions is of utmost significance. All through His ministry, Jesus, as well as the Gospel writers, referred to the manner in which the Scriptures were being fulfilled. All this builds an irrefutable argument that Jesus and the Gospel writers were building the new revelation on the firm foundation of the Old Testament Scriptures. All this confirms Mark's meaningful statement that the time is fulfilled and that the kingdom of heaven is at hand.

Third, Jesus upheld in His own practice the Old Testament way of life. By way of illustration, Jesus encountered Satan's threefold temptations with the Old Testament Scriptures by which He was guided. Three times He quoted from the Book of Deuteronomy introducing each quotation with the words "It is written," and in this way showed that His manner of life was subject to the Old Testament Scriptures (Mt. 4:1-11). When the Pharisees criticized Jesus' disciples for plucking ears of grain on the Sabbath, Jesus answered, "Have you not read what David did?" Later He asked, "Have you not read in the law how on the sabbath the priests in the temple profane the sabbath, and are guiltless? . . . And if you had known what this means, 'I desire mercy, and not sacrifice,' you would not have condemned the guiltless" (Mt. 12:1-8). Thus the charge of the Pharisees had no foundation because Christ could prove from the Scriptures that He was obeying Old Testament law.

On another occasion the Pharisees brought a charge against the disciples to the effect that they ate with hands defiled. To this Jesus answered, "Well did Isaiah prophesy of you hypocrites, as it is written, 'This people honors me with their lips, but their heart is far from me; in vain do they worship me, teaching as doctrines the precepts of men.' You leave the commandment of God, and hold fast the tradition of men." Jesus continued, "You have a fine way of rejecting the commandment of God, in order to keep your tradition!" (Mk. 7:6-9). In this sharp encounter with the Pharisees, Jesus was upholding the Old Testament way of life as against their traditions (Mk. 7:1-13).

The Pharisees tested Jesus further on the matter of divorce. By way of reply Jesus asked them, "Have you not read that he who made them from the beginning made them male and female?" Jesus then referred to the words of Genesis 1:27 and 2:24 as giving the standard by which man should live. He even went so far as to say that by reason of their hardness of heart Moses allowed men to divorce their wives; but He added, "From the beginning it was not so" (Mt. 19:1-9). These several illustrations cover a relatively wide spread of Old Testament standards of living. In each case Jesus looked to the Old Testament as being authoritative with reference to man's way of life. All this shows again Jesus' attitude toward the Old Testament.

Fourth, Jesus said, "Think not that I have come to abolish the law and the prophets; I have come not to abolish them but to fulfill them" (Mt. 5:17). It is evident that Jesus gave this statement in response to some charges made against Him to the effect that His teachings were abolishing the law and the prophets. Jesus' answer was a forthright denial of such a charge. Even in the Beatitudes Jesus reflected several Old Testament Scriptures.[5] Thus when Jesus upheld these beautiful standards in the Beatitudes, He was, in this manner, basing His teaching on the Old Testament.

Jesus' statement in Matthew 5:17 presents some problems as to its meaning. They center chiefly in the words *abolish* and *fulfill.* The literal meaning of these two words is simple enough, but when they are brought together as opposites in meaning, and in this peculiar setting, their sense is not grasped so easily. The former word translated *abolish* (Greek, *kataluo*) carries the literal meaning *destroy, cast down,* while its metaphorical sense is to *overthrow, annul, abrogate.* The word translated *fulfill* (Greek, *pleroo)* has the literal meaning *fill to the full;* and then slightly removed from the literal rendering, it means *complete, fulfill, accomplish, carry out to the full;* and still further removed from its literal sense is *bring to pass.*

Our task then is to gain the sense of these two words as they are used in antithesis in this particular setting. First, let us seek to discover what thinking on the part of the people served as the occasion for Jesus' making these statements (vv. 17-20). Apparently the Jews were interpreting Jesus' words as doing away with the law as though He were introducing some new teaching foreign to the law and the prophets. Second, six illustrations used by Jesus in the remainder of this chapter lead to the idea that the antagonism did not lie between Jesus' teachings and the law, but rather with the pharisaical perversions of the law and the prophets. If this interprets correctly the overall meaning of the passage, we may conclude that the expression to abolish the law and the prophets carried the meaning *overthrow, annul,* or *abrogate;* and the verb *fulfill* had the connotation *carry out to the full, realize its full meaning,* or *put into practice,* what the law and the prophets taught. Some have interpreted *fulfill* as *complete;* that is, *give further develop-*

ment, in the perfecting of the Old Testament law. The verb certainly has this connotation as a number of its uses in the New Testament would justify. (Jn. 3:29; 15:11; 2 Cor. 10:6; etc.) It would seem that the meaning of this verb in this setting is similar to that which it carries in Mt. 3:15, "It is fitting for us to fulfill all righteousness"; Rom. 8:4, "In order that the just requirement of the law might be fulfilled in us"; and Gal. 5:14, "for the whole law is fulfilled in one word, 'You shall love your neighbor as yourself.' " McNeile expressed the meaning in these words, "He came to fill the law, to reveal the full depth of meaning that it was intended to hold."[6]

Matthew 5:18 also presents a problem of interpretation, bound up in the verb *is accomplished* (Greek, *ginomai*). The translations of this verb vary among the several versions from *fulfill, has taken place, purpose is complete, is finished,* and *take place.* What Jesus was saying in this verse appears to be that the law will continue until all that it was intended to accomplish is fulfilled. He may be referring to His own perfect fulfillment of the law's requirements. At this point the tragic failure of the scribes and Pharisees became glaringly apparent. They had pared down or perverted its meaning so that their lives would appear perfectly righteous. Herein lay their hypocrisy. They appeared to be loyal adherents to the law but inwardly they were failing to keep its precepts.

Let us examine briefly the six illustrations given by Christ to show how the scribes and Pharisees were perverting the law while He was giving its true intent. In 5:21-26 Christ showed how the Pharisees distorted the meaning of the law against murder. Accordingly, the Pharisees believed that they did not break this commandment regardless of how angry they might become with their brothers. Jesus declared that the commandment "You shall not kill" forbade the heart condition of anger which leads to murder. Jesus showed that the command "You shall not commit adultery" (vv. 27-30) also condemned lustful thoughts that lead to this sin. In other words the Pharisees were condoning sins of the mind and heart, and regarded only the outward acts as breaking the law and as sin. Jesus held to the integrity of the marriage relation, whereas the Pharisees had found any number of occasions in which a man could divorce his wife and marry again (vv. 31, 32), basing this liberty on the one ground on which Moses allowed a man to put away his wife. In another context, Jesus asserted that Moses had allowed divorce by reason of the hardness of heart on the part of the people (Mt. 19:1-9). Jesus made it clear that the law of marriage established at the creation set forth its inviolability.

The next illustration leads into another area of life, namely, that of personal integrity (vv. 33-37). Under the law God allowed men to swear by His name in order to set forth man's responsibility to give honest testimony. The Jews had gotten around this provision through swearing by heaven, or by the earth, or by Jerusalem and by this device made it appear that they were performing to the Lord their oaths. On this ground they could swear falsely with the appearance of giving honest testimony through their alleged swearing by the Lord. Christ showed the sinfulness of this practice by declaring the personal responsibility of man's honesty before God without the cover of any oaths. Jesus said, "Let what you say be simply 'Yes' or 'No'; anything more than this comes from evil."

Matthew 5:38-42 appears on the surface to present a radical change between what Jesus taught and what the law said. Closer study may show that the law, "An eye for an eye and a tooth for a tooth," instead of actually sanctioning retaliation served instead as a radical restraint to those who had been wronged by another. The law forbade retaliation beyond that of the injury received. Jesus' words suggest that lying back of the severe restraint with regard to retaliation was, in all reality, the law of love. On this account Jesus said, "But if anyone strikes you on the right cheek, turn to him the other also." The same principle obtains with reference to being sued, and with compulsion imposed upon a person, as well as responding to those who are begging for help.

This interpretation is carried further in verses 43 to 48. Here the pharisaical perversion of the law became still more evident. The law did not say, "You shall hate your enemy"; that is, the law did not distinguish between neighbor and enemy. Without any limitation it read, "You shall love your neighbor as yourself" (Lev. 19:18). In fact, the Proverbs gave a very positive command in the words, "If your enemy is hungry, give him bread to eat; and if he is thirsty, gave him water to drink; for you will heap coals of fire on his head, and the Lord will reward you" (Prov. 25:21, 22). Jesus added a most significant motivation for love of enemies when He said, "Love your enemies and pray for those who persecute you, so that you may be sons of your Father who is in heaven" (Mt. 5:44, 45).

This leads to the highest goal of ethical attainment, expressed explicitly in Jesus' closing words, "You, therefore, must be perfect, as your heavenly Father is perfect" (5:48). His audience could hardly escape thinking of similar commands as "You shall be holy; for I the Lord your God am holy" (Lev. 19:2) and "You shall be blameless before the Lord your God" (Deut. 18:13), which are almost identical with those of Christ. The word *blameless* is the great Old Testament word which points to moral integrity of character, in the same manner as the word *perfect* expresses the New Testament ethical goal explicitly set forth as likeness to our heavenly Father. With these six illustrations we see clearly how Jesus came not to abolish the law and the prophets but to fulfill them, and that in Him alone was the perfection as found in His heavenly Father.

Some later teachings of Jesus should not be interpreted as being contradictory to those just considered. A sample occurs in Jesus' words, "No one puts a piece of unshrunk cloth on an old garment, for the patch tears away from the garment, and a worse tear is made. Neither is new wine put into old wineskins; if it is, the skins burst, and the wine is spilled, and the skins are destroyed; but new wine is put into fresh wineskins" (Mt. 9:16, 17; Mk. 2:21, 22; Lk. 5:36-38). In these words Jesus asserted that His place in God's relations with His people was not that of being merely an addition or supplement to Moses and the prophets, but that He was instituting a new law, a new order of things centering in the kingdom of God.

Another case where Jesus was apparently giving teaching contrary to the law, was that having to do with eating things unclean (Mt. 15: 10-18; Mk. 7:14-19). On the surface it may have appeared as though Jesus was nullifying the law, but in reality He was going beyond the law to a higher moral level. He made it clear that the eating of unclean meat does not defile one, and by this statement He declared all foods clean. It is rather, "What comes out of a man is what defiles a man. For from within, out of the heart of man, come evil thoughts, fornication, theft, murder, adultery, coveting, wickedness, deceit, licentiousness, envy, slander, pride, foolishness. All these evil things come from within, and they defile a man" (Mk. 7:20-23). Jesus expressed this principle explicitly in another setting when He said, "The law and the prophets were until John; since then the good news of the kingdom of God is preached" (Lk. 16:16; Mt. 11:13). In this manner Jesus was saying that the law and the prophets did not constitute God's final revelation. It was an era of divine revelation which closed with John. Jesus Himself was inaugurating the new era of divine revelation centering in the good news of the kingdom of God.

3. The Concept of the Kingdom of God as Held by Jesus

a. The Old Testament Basis for Jesus' Concept of the Kingdom

While Jesus did not make any specific reference to God's rule established at Mt. Sinai (Ex. 19 and 24), it is evident from His preaching the gospel of the kingdom and His institution of the Lord's Supper that He was setting up His kingdom on the pattern and foundation of that established at Mt. Sinai. Just as the institution of the old covenant inaugurated God's rule over His people Israel, so Christ's institution of the new covenant, symbolized by the Lord's Supper, established His rule over the new people of God, the church. It is in this relationship that we gain the true meaning of the word *kingdom*. The old covenant did not establish an earthly political kingdom, but rather the rule of God. In the same way, through the institution of the new covenant Jesus did not set up a temporal worldly kingdom; but on the contrary, a spiritual rule. Thus the kingdom of God and the kingdom of Christ constitute, respectively, the rule of God and the rule of Christ. The Old Testament gives a broader concept of kingdom as shown in Psalm 103:19, "The Lord has established his throne in the heavens, and his kingdom rules over all." (See also Ps. 47:2; Dan. 4:25, 34, 35.) Thus the rule of God has its seat in the heavens. Add to this the frequent expression, "The Lord reigns." [7]

b. The Old Testament Prophetic Disclosure of the Messianic Kingdom Fulfilled in the Kingdom of God

While the subject matter of this section almost duplicates that of an earlier one, the crucial nature of the present topic seems to justify a separate presentation. I am seeking to gain Jesus' concept of the kingdom by way of observing the manner in which He described the kingdom of God as the fulfillment of the Old Testament disclosure of this kingdom. Throughout His earthly ministry, Jesus repeatedly referred to some prediction of the messianic kingdom as being fulfilled in a particular incident of His ministry. We have already noted an interpretation given by Jesus of His experience in the Nazareth synagogue, His identification of John the Baptist with Elijah, as well as the manner in which Matthew explained Jesus' going to dwell in Capernaum as it fulfilled Isaiah's prediction. In each of these cases Jesus was giving His concept of the kingdom of God in terms of the respective Old Testament predictions of the messianic kingdom.

Matthew noted that Jesus' entry into Jerusalem was the fulfillment of Zechariah's prediction (Mt. 21:4, 5; Zech. 9:9). In this way Jesus revealed His concept of the kingdom. He, the Messiah of Israel, was presenting Himself as Israel's Messiah. This called for their voluntary acceptance of Him since the time of the setting up of the messianic kingdom was then present. Jesus showed further His concept of the kingdom through the words "This gospel of the kingdom will be preached throughout the whole world, as a testimony to all nations" (Mt. 24:14). Add to this Jesus' command in the Great Commission, "Go therefore and make disciples of all nations" (28:19). Most certainly Jesus grasped the universal character of the kingdom of God in accordance with the message of universalism as given in the Old Testament prophets.[8] According to these Scriptures, the rule of the Servant of the Lord, the Messiah, would bring salvation to the end of the earth. Thus the kingdom foretold by the prophets was spiritual in nature, and Jesus interpreted it as such.

When Jesus commanded His disciples to remain in Jerusalem until they would be "clothed with power from on high" (Lk. 24:49), which was fulfilled in the outpouring of the Holy Spirit at Pentecost, He revealed His concept of the kingdom as one in which the Holy Spirit would be poured out on all flesh. According to the prophets this would take place in the days of the Messiah and would be a definite confirmation of the messianic kingdom.[9] These predictions showed still more fully the spiritual character of the Messiah's rule. Finally, let us observe Jesus' claim, "All authority in heaven and on earth has been given to me" (Mt. 28:18). Earlier Jesus had said, "All things have been delivered to me by my Father" (11:27). Isaiah had said, "The government will be upon his shoulders" and "The spirit of counsel and might would rest upon him" (Is. 9:6; 11:2). In similar strain such messianic psalms as 2, 72, and 110 spoke of the *all-authority* to be exercised by the Messiah. These and other Gospel references show how fully and completely Jesus' concept of the kingdom rested upon the Old Testament predictions of the messianic kingdom.

4. The Essence of the Kingdom as Revealed by Jesus

a. The Fatherhood of God and Its Correlates: Sonship, Worship and Perfection

The first and most significant sphere of supremacy in the kingdom of God is very naturally, the Fatherhood of God.

(1) The Concept of Fatherhood as Taught by Jesus. In the most natural way possible, Jesus brought God's supremacy into clear view when He taught the disciples how to pray, saying, "Our Father who art in heaven, hallowed be thy name" (Mt. 6:9). Prayer to God as our Father naturally places the sphere of fatherhood at the top-most point of supremacy in the kingdom. Let us observe how Father-centered Jesus' teaching actually was. Jesus had already said, "Love your enemies and pray for those who persecute you, so that you may be sons of your Father who is in heaven" (5:44). Jesus brought this trend of thought to a climax in the words, "You, therefore, must be perfect, as your heavenly Father is perfect" (v. 48). Then Jesus warned them, "Beware of prac-

ticing your piety before men in order to be seen by them; for then you will have no reward from your Father who is in heaven" (Mt. 6:1). It is the Father alone who should see us give alms, pray, and fast. It is He, the Father, who will reward His worshipers. There is no need for anxiety for the temporal affairs of life because the heavenly Father knows all human needs. Later in this message Jesus added, "If you then, who are evil, know how to give good gifts to your children, how much more will your Father who is in heaven give good things to those who ask him?" (Mt. 7:11; Lk. 11:13). Jesus brought this sphere of fatherhood to a climax in the words, "Fear not, little flock, for it is the Father's good pleasure to give you the kingdom" (Lk. 12:32).

(2) The Fatherhood Concept in the Old Testament. Jesus' teaching on the fatherhood of God had its basis in the Old Testament. Already in the song of Moses the question is raised, "Do you thus requite the Lord, you foolish and senseless people? Is not he your father, who created you, who made you and established you?" (Deut. 32:6). A psalmist quoted the Lord who spoke concerning David, "He shall cry to me, 'Thou art my Father, my God, and the Rock of my salvation' " (Ps. 89:26). In another psalm David wrote, "As a father pities his children, so the Lord pities those who fear him. For he knows our frame; he remembers that we are dust" (Ps. 103:13, 14). Hosea quoted God as saying, "When Israel was a child, I loved him, and out of Egypt I called my son" (Hos. 11:1). The author of Isaiah 63:16 wrote, "For thou art our Father, though Abraham does not know us and Israel does not acknowledge us; thou, O Lord, art our Father, our Redeemer from of old is thy name." He wrote also, "O Lord, thou art our Father; we are the clay, and thou art our potter; we are all the work of thy hand" (64:8).

This sampling of Old Testament Scriptures shows what a rich heritage Israel had received from their God. All of their relationships with God found their deepest meaning in that of son to father. The nation of Israel looked to their God as Father. In this kingdom setting, Jesus spoke of God as our Father. Embedded in these Scriptures lie at least three correlates or counterparts which show man's proper response to God as his Father. I shall consider these counterparts in order of their logical sequence. Naturally, *sonship* comes first. This lies at the basis of worship and leads to this experience. The final impact of God's fatherhood upon man is that of the ethical requirement of perfection and likeness to God. Their close relationship one to another serves to show that they are properly the kind of responses that man should make to God, his Father. The ethics of Jesus belongs to this section and will be given brief treatment.

(3) The Correlate of Sonship. When Jesus exhorted the disciples, "Love your enemies and pray for those who persecute you, so that you may be sons of your Father who is in heaven," sonship as a correlate to fatherhood becomes plainly evident. Sons need to demonstrate the same kind of love that the Father shows. The parable of the prodigal son (Lk. 15:11-32) illustrates further the kind of conduct that a son should exemplify. When the younger son left home, he was disregarding the moral standards of sonship. When he finally came to himself, he was ready to say, "Father, I have sinned against heaven and before you; I am no longer worthy to be called your son; treat me as one of your hired servants" (vv. 18, 19). By this he was recognizing that his life needed to be conformed to that of his father; otherwise, he could not be a son. In this parable Jesus was teaching that in the heavenly family the lives of the sons must conform to that of the Father. Otherwise, they are not sons. This truth becomes clear when we note Jesus' conversation with Nicodemus. Jesus told Nicodemus, "Unless one is born anew, he cannot see the kingdom of God. . . That which is born of the flesh is flesh, and that which is born of the Spirit is spirit" (Jn. 3:4-6). In this language Jesus was showing Nicodemus that sonship is a spiritual relationship gained through being born of the Spirit. The sons partake of the spiritual nature of the Father. The Jews failed to grasp the nature of this relationship to the Father. It was necessary for Jesus to say that because they did not love Him, God was not their Father. They were of their father, the devil. Their lives did not conform to that required by their heavenly Father. Thus in the kingdom of God, sonship is the counterpart to the fatherhood of God.

(4) The Correlate of Worship. The most intimate relationship of son to the Father finds expression in worship. Jesus set this forth very clearly in His teaching on alms giving, praying, and fasting (Mt. 6:1-18). He closed each word of counsel with the promise, "Your Father who sees in secret will reward you" (vv. 4, 6, 18). The Lord's Prayer brought this teaching into clear focus. The supremacy of God as Father becomes evident in the form of address in the words, "Our Father who art in heaven." By reason of the Father's being supreme, the son's approach to Him is that of hallowing His name. In the time of Moses, God had already said, "You shall keep my commandments and do them: I am the Lord. And you shall not profane my holy name, but I will be hallowed among the people of Israel; I am the Lord who sanctify you, who brought you out of the land of Egypt to be your God: I am the Lord" (Lev. 22:31-33). This commandment goes deeper than mere outward obedience. In the words of Filson it "means to respond to God

with reverent worship, grateful faith, and humble acceptance of his claim and promise."[10]

The kingdom-centered nature of this prayer becomes evident in the petition, "Thy kingdom come, thy will be done, on earth as it is in heaven." This gives support to the idea of the Father's supremacy in the kingdom of God. Naturally, then, a son will pray that the Father's will be done on earth as it is in heaven. Just as Israel, God's son, was dependent on the manna given daily in the wilderness, so the sons of the Father are now dependent on Him for their daily bread. Further, sons can be forgiven of their debts only as they themselves forgive their debtors. Sons recognize that they are living in a world in which they are beset with temptations and need deliverance from evil. Only the Father is able to answer this petition. While the doxology does not seem to have adequate textual support, its message is, nevertheless, true to fact. "For thine is the kingdom and the power and the glory, for ever. Amen." These closing words thoroughly affirm the Father's supremacy in the kingdom. It is His kingdom and by reason of this the power and the glory of it are also His. This is a prayer which can be uttered alone by a son. Jesus framed this prayer purposefully to show worship as it stands in correlation to God's supremacy as Father.

Effective prayer has an involvement which gives still deeper meaning to worship as it relates to the fatherhood of God. Jesus stressed this element when He told the people a parable "to the effect that they ought always to pray and not lose heart" (Lk. 18:1). A great preacher paraphrased this statement as follows. He said that prayer is a collapse forward on God, while fainting is a collapse backward on self. The importunate widow by her insistent plea to the judge illustrated this collapse forward on God. She did not lose heart in setting her case before the judge. Lifted to the high plane of the experiential relation of man to God, prayer illustrates the warm family relationship of son to father. For reasons unknown to the son, the father may delay in giving ear to the requests of the son. But even so, he does not want the son to depart from the warmth of family relationships. So it is with our heavenly Father. There is that in which the child of God may be "importunate." But the heavenly Father would have us preserve the warmth of Father-son relationship. For this reason men "ought always to pray and not lose heart."

Jesus moved into still another aspect of the relation of prayer to worship through telling the parable of the Pharisee and the tax collector who went up into the temple to pray. The Pharisee's prayer was really with himself. He thanked God that he was so much better than other people, including the tax collector who had also come to pray. In utter self-condemnation the latter cried, "God, be merciful to me a sinner!" Jesus added, "This man went down to his house justified rather than the other; for everyone who exalts himself will be humbled, but he who humbles himself will be exalted" (Lk. 18:9-14). The Pharisee's fault lay in that he trusted in himself that he was righteous, and he despised the tax collector. On the other hand, the tax collector was aware of his undone condition and pleaded for the mercy of God. All this shows that prayer, which lies at the very heart of worship, constitutes an essential correlate to the fatherhood of God. God, the Father, is righteous and when man worships God through prayer, he must recognize himself as a sinner who must plead for the mercy of God.

Worship as a correlate to the fatherhood of God gains its deepest meaning in the high priestly prayer of Jesus (Jn. 17). The first thing to be observed is the intimacy of the Father-Son relationship in this prayer. This prayer serves to show how both sonship and worship constitute counterparts in man of the Father's supremacy. Repeatedly, Jesus addressed God as His Father. The intimate relation between Father and Son finds expression in this prayer. The Son had accomplished the work which the Father had given Him to do. Rightfully He could pray, "Father, glorify thou me in thy own presence with the glory which I had with thee before the world was made" (v. 5). Here we find intercession and petition. He had a deep burden that His followers might be kept from the evil one. He prayed further, "Sanctify them in the truth; thy word is truth. As thou didst send me into the world, so I have sent them into the world. And for their sake I consecrate myself, that they also may be consecrated in truth" (vv. 17-19). Jesus, the Son, identified Himself with all of God's sons in the words, "I in them and thou in me, that they may become perfectly one, so that the world may know that thou hast sent me and hast loved them even as thou hast loved me" (v. 23). From this prayer we see that, as a part of worship, Jesus exemplified in the most meaningful way possible the believer's response to the fatherhood of God.

As we go with Jesus to the garden, we see Him suffering the severest tension that comes to man (Mt. 26:39-46; Mk. 14:36-42; Lk. 22: 42-46). Jesus prayed, "Father, if thou art willing, remove this cup from me; nevertheless not my will, but thine, be done." In this prayer we see the struggle of the Son to yield His will to that of His Father. It stands forever as the perfect example of full and complete submission of the Son to the Father.

(5) The Perfection Correlate. The supremacy of the fatherhood of

God finds yet another correlate, that of perfection or likeness to God. As noted earlier this becomes apparent in Jesus' words, "You, therefore, must be perfect, as your heavenly Father is perfect" (Mt. 5:48), or as the Gospel of Luke expresses it, "Be merciful, even as your Father is merciful" (Lk. 6:36). These statements show that in the Father-Son relationship, the Son needs to exemplify in his own life the perfection and mercifulness found in the Father.

The Old Testament background to Jesus' words gives support to their overwhelming meaning. The statement which is nearest in structure and meaning to Jesus' words is God's command, "You shall be holy; for I the Lord your God am holy" (Lev. 19:2). The word *holy* is the most significant word used in the Bible to describe the inner nature of God. Its literal meaning is that of *being separate* or *aloof.* Even though God dwelt with His people as symbolized by His presence in the holy of holies of the tabernacle, yet He was separate from Israel in that only the high priest could come into His presence only once a year and only with a bloody sacrifice. Why was the Lord so aloof from His people? It was because of Israel's sinfulness. The Lord was teaching Israel that in order to have fellowship with Him, their sins must be removed. This literal connotation of the word *holy* easily led to that of the inner nature of God marked by personal purity and moral excellence. We seem to lack definitive vocabulary for expressing the positive meaning of this word — *holy.*

Another Old Testament statement which may lie at the basis of Jesus' words leads us nearer to the positive content of the word *holy.* The Lord said to Israel, "You shall be blameless [*tamim*] before the Lord your God" (Deut. 18:13). The Hebrew word *tamim* carries the meanings: *complete, whole, free from defect,* and *blameless.* It is the word used with *tsaddiq* (righteous) to describe the character of Noah. It is these words, *holy, blameless,* and *righteous,* which are most descriptive of the inner nature of God. The word *perfect* translates the Greek word *teleios,* the word used in the Septuagint to translate the Hebrew word *tamim.* This may give grounds for believing that Jesus' command reflected Deuteronomy 18:13, as well as Leviticus 19:2.

The word *teleios* gives some new dimensions to the Old Testament idea of *blamelessness.* It carries the positive meaning of having achieved the objective of being *mature, complete* or *perfect.* The word lends itself to an ethical sense of complete goodness as used in Matthew 5:48.[11] Paul described this goal in somewhat similar language in the words, "And we all, with unveiled face, beholding the glory of the Lord, are being changed into his likeness from one degree of glory to another" (2 Cor. 3:18).

Thus the inner nature of the Father which Jesus would have His followers appropriate for their own inner life are *holiness, blamelessness, perfection,* and *likeness to the glory of the Lord.* These become the goals of Christian ethics. For this reason it seems in order to give at this place a general survey of the ethics of Jesus.

(6) The Ethics of Jesus. The ethical teachings of the Sermon on the Mount will serve as the basis and point of departure for this survey. It should become apparent at once that Jesus' teachings in the sphere of ethics revealed most clearly the ethical import of *perfection* or *likeness to God* as the counterpart of God's supremacy as the Father in the followers of Christ.

(a) The Beatitudes (Mt. 5:1-12; Lk. 6:20-23). Jesus gave a new perspective to blessedness. It overturned the commonly accepted Jewish ideas of ethics. Thus the supposed negative experiences of life, such as being poor in spirit, mourning, being meek, hungering and thirsting for righteousness, which are negative from the angle of the perverted judgments of the Pharisees, are immeasurably offset or nullified by the great plus signs which lay at the basis of kingdom blessedness. Immeasurable values are the possession of the kingdom of heaven, the comfort that comes from God, the inheritance of the earth, the satisfying of the hunger and thirst for righteousness, the obtaining of mercy, the seeing God, and of being called sons of God.

These values mark the character of true blessedness. They give a new approach to the whole matter of ethics. On this account the followers of Jesus will not shrink from enduring the negative experiences of life which undoubtedly take place, but they will suffer them, knowing that the unspeakable privileges which come to them lead to true blessedness. The ethical quality of these negative experiences is readily apparent. Being poor in spirit reveals the inner nature of humility. Many of the occasions of mourning arise as a disciple of Jesus witnesses the apparent triumphs of wickedness. The spirit of meekness, so beautifully illustrated in Moses, shows the grace of being able to keep silent when falsely accused. The hunger and thirst for righteousness reveal an attitude of self-condemnation by reason of one's sin, and express the longing of the soul for likeness to God who is righteous. The grace of mercy is most transparent in those who have suffered wrong at the hands of others. Being pure in heart expresses the burden of David when, after indulging in his grievous sin, he prayed, "Create in me a clean heart, O God, and put a new and right spirit within me" (Ps. 51:10). Peacemakers are fully conscious of the sins of quarreling, fighting, and waging war. They seek to bring about peace in the same manner as God strives to establish peaceful relations, as well as peace in the soul. They who are persecuted for righteousness sake, being reviled, persecuted, and suffering all kinds of evil charges brought against them, most assuredly are experiencing the inner peace and quietness of soul which belong to the innocent. This kind of experience illustrates the severity of the antagonism between right and wrong, good and evil, God and Satan, which the child of God endures as he seeks to achieve likeness to the glory of the Lord.

(b) The Ethical Principles of the Law Upheld by Jesus. Having already noted how Jesus came not to abolish the law and the prophets but to fulfill them, let us observe the ethical character of this law as upheld by Jesus. Jesus taught that the command "You shall not kill" involved more than a prohibition of actual murder. He made it clear that anger is "the stuff out of which murder is made." By tracing murder back to the heart condition which leads to this act He revealed a profound insight as to the nature of right and wrong. The ethics He upheld was that which recognized the inner nature of both sin and righteousness. The sin of committing adultery possesses the same inner aspect. Lustful looking and thinking precede the act of adultery. In quite graphic language Jesus spoke of plucking out the eye and of cutting off the hand as the means of curbing or preventing lustful conduct. This language symbolizes the inner character of sin. When God instituted marriage, He spoke of man and woman as becoming one flesh. Jesus pointed up the sinful perversion of this fundamental law by saying, "Whoever divorces his wife and marries another, commits adultery against her" (Mk. 10:11). While a textual problem centers in a so-called exceptive clause (except on the ground of unchastity) (Mt. 5:32), the ethical principle involved is fundamentally the same. Whether or not Jesus allowed one ground, that of unchastity, for rupturing the marriage bond is difficult to decide. From one point of view, the act of adultery destroys the marriage bond and would thus permit remarriage on the part of the innocent party. From another point of view, love is able to overrule even in the case of adultery, and this opens the way for the innocent party to forgive and to receive back the penitent offender.

Jesus probed into the ethical character of a very important Old Testament command having to do with swearing. This command read, "You shall not swear falsely, but shall perform to the Lord what you have sworn."[12] God had commanded Israel to perform to the Lord what they had sworn. The evident purpose of this was to impress upon the people of Israel the need for giving honest testimony. They needed to know that their swearing was in the presence of God who knew whether or not they were telling the truth. Undoubtedly, this command left a deep impact upon the people of Israel, and they gained the reputation of being truthful. There were those, however, who sought to find loopholes in this law whereby they could make it appear that they were swearing unto the Lord but by an ingenious device such as swearing by the temple, or by the altar in the temple they could escape giving an honest testimony, at least in their own thinking. Jesus brought the ethics of this form of false testimony into view by prohibiting entirely the use of oaths, so that one giving a testimony needed to realize that the responsibility for giving a true witness rested solely upon himself. This exposed the grievous sin on the part of many of the Jews and showed most emphatically the ethical involvements of sheer honesty in giving testimony. Jesus' concluding statement spoke directly to this point when He said, "Let what you say be simply 'Yes' or 'No'; anything more than this comes from evil" (Mt. 5:33-37).

(c) The Principle of Love and Mercy. Jesus gave a considerable body of teaching in the area of love and mercy. When the Pharisees of Christ's day read the law, "An eye for an eye and a tooth for a tooth," they failed to see that this law served as a restraint to retaliation rather than a license to carry out vengeance to the degree of the offense. A study of human nature will clearly show that few individuals are content to retaliate with such precision. The spirit of retaliation goes beyond the offense. Jesus taught that a vital ethical principle became involved in this law. This principle, expressed in Jesus' words, was: "Do not resist one who is evil. But if anyone strikes you on the right cheek, turn to him the other also" (5:39). In this teaching Jesus showed that the principle of love must operate under the most difficult circumstances, even when one might desire to retaliate. Love is seen at its best when it is under test.

Jesus spoke of another principle which the Pharisees had sorely perverted (Mt. 5:43-48). The law had said, "Love your neighbor," but the Pharisees made a distinction between neighbor and enemy and argued, "You shall love your neighbor and hate your enemy." But the law had not made this distinction between neighbor and enemy. All those who are in need are our neighbors, whether they be friend or foe. Jesus continued with the words, "Love your enemies and pray for those who persecute you, so that you may be sons of your Father who is in heaven" (vv. 44, 45). Such is the character of love. It makes no distinction between friend or foe. Jesus bound this law of love of enemies to that of being sons of the Father. Thus the principle of love and mercy is God-centered.

Jesus proceeded to expand the ethical character of love in the words, "If you love those who love you, what credit is that to you? For even sinners love those who love them. And if you do good to those who do good to you, what credit is that to you? For even sinners do the same. And if you lend to those from whom you hope to receive, what credit is that to you? Even sinners lend to sinners, to receive as much again. But love your enemies, and do good, and lend, expecting nothing in return; and your reward will be great, and you will be sons of the Most High; for he is kind to the ungrateful and the selfish. Be merciful, even as your Father is merciful" (Lk. 6:32-36). This explanation needs no further elucidation. It spoke to the very nature of genuine love.

The application of the principle of love came to the fore in Jesus' conversation with the lawyer (Lk. 10:25-37). The lawyer recognized the two fundamental commands of the law: love to the Lord, and love to neighbor. That he had not sensed the full implication of neighbor love, became clear in Jesus' story of the good Samaritan. Undoubtedly the man going down from Jerusalem to Jericho was a Jew who would think most assuredly that the priest and the Levite, who were Israel's spiritual leaders, would certainly have sensed his need. But they passed by on the other side. Then came the Samaritan, a man whom the Jews despised and mistreated. He saw the man's need and most graciously took care of him. The Samaritan might have argued with himself that this Jew is his enemy and why should he show compassion on him. But the Samaritan loved his neighbor-enemy.

When Jesus was speaking to His disciples in the upper room, He stressed again this love principle in the words, "A new commandment I give to you, that you love one another; even as I have loved you, that you also love one another. By this all men will know that you are my disciples, if you have love for one another" (Jn. 13:34, 35). With these significant words Jesus showed His disciples that love lay at the very center of their relationship one to another, as well as to Christ. This love became the earmark of a disciple of Jesus. So characteristic was this love-relationship among the followers of Christ that later a Roman official of Asia Minor wrote to the Roman Emperor that he marveled how these Christians love one another. Jesus spoke further of this love-relationship in the words, "As the Father has loved me, so have I loved you; abide in my love. If you keep my commandments, you will abide in my love, just as I have kept my Father's commandments and abide in his love. These things I have spoken to you, that my joy may be in you, and that your joy may be full. This is my commandment, that you love one another as I have loved you. Greater love has no man than this, that a man lay down his life for his friends. You are my friends if you do what I command you" (Jn. 15:

9-14). Jesus soon exemplified in His own life the extent of His love even for enemies in His suffering and death on the cross.

Apparently Jesus' words on love had failed to register with Peter. In the garden when the soldiers, chief priests, and Pharisees came to arrest Jesus, Peter stood up in defense of his Lord, but Jesus said to Peter, "Put your sword into its sheath; shall I not drink the cup which the Father has given me?" (Jn. 18:11). In this setting Jesus was teaching Peter that love does not resist evil. Under trial before Pilate Jesus spoke most emphatically of how love operates under test. "My kingship is not of this world; if my kingship were of this world, my servants would fight, that I might not be handed over to the Jews; but my kingship is not from the world" (v. 36). In this language Jesus brought the ethical principle of love into relationship with His kingship. The most fundamental ethical principle of His kingship was love.

Late in Peter's life he wrote of this love as follows, "For one is approved if, mindful of God, he endures pain while suffering unjustly. For what credit is it, if when you do wrong and are beaten for it you take it patiently? But if when you do right and suffer for it you take it patiently, you have God's approval. For to this you have been called, because Christ also suffered for you, leaving you an example, that you should follow in his steps. He committed no sin; no guile was found on his lips. When he was reviled, he did not revile in return; when he suffered, he did not threaten; but he trusted to him who judges justly" (1 Pet. 2:19-23). These words from Peter may well serve as a commentary on Jesus' teaching on love both in principle and practice.

While Paul had never heard Jesus' teaching in person, yet he interpreted Christian love in the words, "Love is patient and kind; love is not jealous or boastful; it is not arrogant or rude. Love does not insist on its own way; it is not irritable or resentful; it does not rejoice at wrong, but rejoices in the right. Love bears all things, believes all things, hopes all things, endures all things" (1 Cor. 13:4-7). Further confirmation of the manner in which Paul grasped the love-principle of Christ's teaching appears in Romans 12:9-21. Among other things Paul wrote, "Let love be genuine. . . . Bless those who persecute you. . . Repay no one evil for evil . . . never avenge yourselves. . . . Do not be overcome by evil, but overcome evil with good." These words of the apostles Peter and Paul show how accurately they interpreted the teachings of Jesus, and by so doing, gave support to the central place of love in the ethics of Jesus.

(d) Sin Centered in Man's Inner Being. Jesus' teaching on the ethical principles of the law (Mt. 5) brings to the surface yet another crucial idea. All six of the pharisaical perversions of the law show that sin is not merely an outward act. As stated earlier, Jesus traced murder to the inner spirit of anger, adultery to inner lust, swearing falsely to inner dishonesty, retaliation and fighting to lack of love. This aspect of the nature of sin was the occasion for additional teaching on the part of Jesus. When the Pharisees accused the disciples of breaking the tradition of the elders, Jesus showed that it is not what goes into a man from the outside that defiles him but rather that which comes from the man, out of his heart. He said. "What comes out of a man is what defiles a man. For from within, out of the heart of man, come evil thoughts, fornication, theft, murder, adultery, coveting, wickedness, deceit, licentiousness, envy, slander, pride, foolishness. All these evil things come from within, and they defile a man" (Mk. 7:20-23). In confirmation of Jesus' rebuke of the Pharisees He spoke further in the words, "So, for the sake of your tradition, you have made void the word of God. You hypocrites! Well did Isaiah prophesy of you, when he said: 'This people honors me with their lips, but their heart is far from me; in vain do they worship me, teaching as doctrine the precepts of men' " (Mt. 15:6-9). The real trouble of the Pharisees was that their heart was far from God. Their sin lodged in their hearts.

(e) Motives of Thought and Conduct Tested by Jesus' Principles of Ethics. In an earlier section I examined Jesus' teachings in Matthew 6:1-18 from the angle of worship. Studied more closely this portion gives an insight into another principle of ethics. This centers in one's motives, both in thought and in conduct. They who practice their piety in the forms of giving alms, praying, and fasting, in order to be seen of men, were blameworthy, not because of any sinfulness involved in these acts of piety, but on account of their reason for doing them. To practice piety in order to receive praise from men revealed human pride. The reason why we think or act as we do comes under the searching test of Christian ethics. The sin that Jesus exposed in this setting is most glaring because all these acts in themselves are good. The subtlety of this sin traces to the fact that no one but God knew why they were giving alms, praying, or fasting. By concealing their motives, they were acting the lie before those who observed their worship. This form of sin lay at the heart of Jesus' condemnation of the Pharisees (Mt. 23:1-36). Among the charges which Jesus brought against them was: "They preach, but do not practice. . . . They do all their deeds to be seen by men; for they make their phylacteries broad and their fringes long, and they love the place of honor at feasts and the best seats in the synagogues, and salutations in the market places, and being called rabbi by men" (vv. 3-7). Jesus could tell His disciples that they should "practice and observe whatever they tell you, but not what they do" (v. 3). Jesus exposed their hypocrisy by showing that their motives were wrong. There was complete absence of genuine piety on the part of the Pharisees, but to the people they gave the impression of deep personal piety. Herein lay their grievous sin. He said further, "Woe to you, scribes and Pharisees, hypocrites! for you tithe mint and dill and cummin, and have neglected the weightier matters of the law, justice and mercy and faith; these you ought to have done, without neglecting the others. You blind guides, straining out a gnat and swallowing a camel!" (vv. 23, 24). Through their tithing these insignificant garden products, such as mint, and cummin, they gave the impression of observing the smallest detail of the law, but in reality they failed to fulfill the most important matters of the law. They wore masks of being devout obedient Jews, but back of the masks were their true selves which neglected justice, mercy, and faith. Their sin centered in their hypocritical motives. Outwardly they appeared righteous to men but within they were full of hypocrisy and iniquity. Outwardly they built the tombs of the prophets and adorned the monuments of the righteous but in reality they were the sons of those who murdered the prophets. So grievous was their guilt that upon them came all the righteous blood shed on earth, from the blood of innocent Abel to the blood of Zechariah. Such is the heinousness of wrong motives in thought and conduct.

(f) Seeking First His Kingdom and His Righteousness. This heading gives the focal point of Jesus' teaching in Matthew 6:19-33. When I considered perfection as the correlate to the fatherhood of God, I observed how fundamental to God's nature were *holiness, blamelessness,* and *perfection*. In this section Christ used the word *righteousness* to express the inner glory of God. Reserving for a later section a discussion of this word, let us look at the ethical principles involved which led Jesus to declare, "Seek first his kingdom and his righteousness, and all these things shall be yours as well" (v. 33). In verses 19-33 Jesus exposed several areas of life in which severe tensions may exist. There is the desire to lay up treasure on earth which stands opposed to the laying up of treasures in heaven. It is the tension between a lust for an abundance of things that pertain to this life and the opposing desire for treasures of a spiritual nature in heaven. The two kinds of treasures stand in antagonism, the one to the other. For as Jesus says, "Where your treasure is, there will your heart be also" (Lk. 12:34). Jesus' discussion led to the conclusion that the laying up of treasures for one's self on earth stands opposed to seeking first the kingdom of God and His righteousness. The failure to see this antagonism shows that the eye is not sound. As a result the whole body is full of darkness. This antagonism became more vivid when Jesus said, "No one can serve two masters; for either he will hate the one and love the other, or he will be devoted to the one and despise the other. You cannot serve God and mammon" (Mt. 6:24). The effort to serve these two masters leads inevitably to the most serious anxiety about this life. They who seek to serve both God and mammon are, in all reality, not placing their trust in the heavenly Father. They are men of little faith. There is no need for anxiety if we trust our heavenly Father. He will supply all our needs.

The ethical scope involved in seeking first His kingdom and His righteousness includes the entire gamut of life. Lack of trust in God resolves itself in a rejection of God's righteousness. How sinful it is not to seek first His kingdom and His righteousness! In the language of the parable of the sower they who fail to seek first His kingdom and His righteousness are such who hear the word, "but the cares of the world and the delight in riches choke the word, and it proves unfruitful" (Mt. 13:22). The ruler who asked Jesus, "What shall I do to inherit eternal life?" came to face the same kind of tension. Jesus told him, "Sell all that you have and distribute to the poor, and you will have treasure in heaven; and come, follow me" (Lk. 18:18-30). On hearing this he became sad because he was very rich. On this response Jesus said, "How hard it is for those who have riches to enter the kingdom of God!" (v. 24). Jesus brought this encounter to a close by showing the relationship between the material things of life and the spiritual, in the words, "Truly, I say to you, there is no man who has left house or wife or brothers or parents or children, for the sake of the kingdom of God, who will not receive manifold more in this time, and in the age to come eternal life" (Lk. 18:29). These words gave the true perspective by seeking the kingdom of God and His righteousness as it relates to every other area of life. God's righteousness is the standard by which we should judge all things pertaining to this life.

(g) The Golden Rule. Jesus concluded another section of the Sermon on the Mount (Mt. 7:1-12) with the words, "So whatever you wish that men would do to you, do so to them; for this is the law and the prophets." These words have gained the recognition of being called the "Golden Rule." This caption recognizes the high value of this exhortation in the sphere of ethics. Jesus introduced this part of His sermon with the exhortation, "Judge not, that you be not judged" (v. 1). In this manner Jesus condemned the spirit of censoriousness. He gave the warning, "With the judgment you pronounce you will be judged, and the measure you give will be the measure you get" (v. 2). The critic sees the speck in his brother's eye but does not notice the log in his own eye. There is a bit of humor, even irony, in Jesus' words. It becomes apparent in the contrast between the dimensions of the speck and those of the log. This exposed the hypocrisy of the censorious. If the critic first removes the massive piece of timber out of his own eye, he will then be able to see clearly to take the microscopic speck out of his brother's eye. This condemnation of censoriousness presented the golden rule in negative form.

Jesus made a similar approach to the golden rule when He said, "Do not give dogs what is holy; and do not throw your pearls before swine, lest they trample them underfoot and turn to attack you" (7:6). By this Jesus was saying that in human relations some people act like dogs and do not receive the things of precious value from others. The sin lying back of this unusual teaching is that of personal conceit. Some people are too proud to receive good counsel, advice, and direction, let alone rebuke, from a brother. On this account it is profitless to share spiritual treasures with them. We should accept most graciously the pearls, the holy things given to us.

Jesus prepared the way for His next point by inspiring faith and confidence in prayer. Without expressed limitation Jesus said, "Ask, and it will be given you; seek, and you will find; knock, and it will be opened to you" (Mt. 7:7). This expresses God's response to our petitions and gives us a pattern of what man's response to the requests of others should be. He made His advice practical through the words, "If you then, who are evil, know how to give good gifts to your children, how much more will your Father who is in heaven give good things to those who ask him?" (v. 11). Through these several illustrations Jesus set forth the high place which we should give to the golden rule. Its application extends to all areas of human relations. On this account this rule occupies such a large place in the ethics of Jesus.

The parable of the rich man and Lazarus (Lk. 16:19-31) may serve as an illustration of the failure on the part of a person to recognize the golden rule. The rich man had no concern for the poor man, Lazarus, who lay at his gate. He could not imagine himself as exchanging places with the poor man. If he had recognized the ethical principle of the golden rule, he would have shared most liberally with Lazarus. There would not have been the great gulf between his wealth and luxury, and the poverty of Lazarus. The complete reversal of the positions of the rich man and Lazarus after leaving this world made this principle still clearer. The rich man was entirely unable to reconcile his anguish in the fiery flames of hell with the comfort Lazarus received in Abraham's bosom. It was impossible for the rich man to accept this radical change of conditions between himself and Lazarus. If he had treated Lazarus in his lifetime like he wanted Lazarus to treat him in his punishment, both could have enjoyed the legitimate pleasures of this world, as well as the glories of the world to come.

(h) Entering by the Narrow Gate. In this brief section (Mt. 7:13, 14) Jesus compressed to a few words teaching of tremendous significance. Jesus' language was pictorial and graphic. At once we visualize the narrow gate and the hard way that leads to life; and alongside it, the wide gate and the easy way that leads to destruction. The former has only a few traveling on it, while the latter has many. In this manner Jesus held in contrast the way to life as over against the way to destruction. It would appear that He was saying that the road which leads to life is one of restraint and self-discipline. There is need for the curbing of all our sinful desires and lusts. The old sinful self must be crucified. The two ways exemplify two opposite and opposing ways of life. Those on the narrow way seek to do the will of God, while those on the broad way reject their responsibility to God and follow their own sinful desires. This teaching of Jesus asserts the sharp antagonism between the righteousness of God and the sinfulness of man. These words take us to the very heart of Christian ethics. This discipline draws a sharp line between right and wrong, good and evil, holiness and unholiness, righteousness and unrighteousness, perfection and imperfection, and light and darkness. Our sinful nature places us in the center of this conflict. Jesus made it clear that the only way that leads to life is by entering the narrow gate and traveling the hard way.

(i) Hearing and Doing. This section, Matthew 7:21-29, serves as a fitting close to the Sermon on the Mount, as well as to this general survey of the ethics of Jesus. It brings to completion also this study of the perfection-correlate to the supremacy of the fatherhood of God. Jesus confronted His hearers with the necessity of doing the will of the Father who is in heaven. There dare be no schism between profession and being, and between hearing and doing. A sin of most serious consequences exists when a person fails to live as he professes. If the confession of Jesus as Lord is not accompanied by doing the will of the Father, it is empty and meaningless.

At a later time, when Paul wrote his letters to the Galatians and to the Romans, he structured them according to this pattern. In Galatians 1-4 and in Romans 1-5, he described the nature of faith which leads to justification before God. The remaining sections of these two letters have to do with the manner of life which should accompany saving faith. Paul clearly taught that faith and life are inseparable. There dare be no schism between theology and ethics. This is precisely the point to which Jesus is speaking in this section. He drove the point home in His description of the two builders, the wise man who built his house upon the rock and the foolish man who built his house upon the sand. Through this illustration He taught the outcome of the failure to do as we have heard. The ethical aspect of this condition of heart becomes very evident. Obviously, those who do not do the will of the heavenly Father are consciously refusing to conform their lives to the righteousness of God. This was the flagrant sin of the Pharisees. Later in Jesus' ministry He exposed all this hypocrisy (Mt. 23:1-36; Lk. 11:37-52). It centered in the disparity between their profession and their manner of life. As Jesus said, "They preach, but do not practice" (Mt. 23:3). The deep-seated nature of this sin lay in their open dishonesty before God. It belongs to the integrity of character to be honest. All the subtle forms of hypocrisy, as exposed in this discourse against the Pharisees, confirm the heinousness of the breach between faith and life.

b. The Righteousness of God and Its Correlate: Repentance

The ethical nature of righteousness became evident in the survey of the ethics of Jesus. The deep ethical import of this word prepares us to grasp the second sphere of God's supremacy, righteousness. One need not pursue this inquiry very far until he begins to recognize the broad gamut and profound significance of God's supremacy in this area.

(1) The Concept of God's Righteousness Revealed in the Old Testament. It becomes very evident in Jesus' teaching of God's righteousness that its foundation and basic content are found in the Old Testament. Genesis 6:9 reads, "Noah was a righteous man, blameless in his generation; Noah walked with God." In other words Noah was godlike. Abraham learned that God was the Almighty One and righteous (Gen. 17:1; 18:19). When the Lord revealed to him the coming destruction of Sodom and Gomorrah by reason of their wickedness, Abraham was greatly concerned about the welfare of the very few righteous, Lot and his family living in Sodom. Abraham raised the question, "Wilt thou indeed destroy the righteous with the wicked? . . . Shall not the Judge of all the earth do right?" (Gen. 18:23-25). In these questions Abraham voiced the conviction that to destroy the righteous with the wicked was contrary to the inner nature of the Judge of all the earth.

Most instructive for our purpose are the words of Moses, "The Rock, his work is perfect; for all his ways are justice. A God of faithfulness and without iniquity, just and right is he" (Deut. 32:4). Six very important words for my present purpose occur in this statement. They are *perfect (tamim), justice (mishpat), faithfulness (emunah), iniquity (awel), just (saddiq),* and *right (yashar).* Moses' statement moves from a characterization of God's work as being *perfect,* on to the word *justice* as being descriptive of His ways, culminating in language descriptive of God's very nature, stated positively in the word *faithfulness* and negatively, *without iniquity,* and finally, in the forthright statement, "just and right is he." There is a tremendous buildup of meaning in these six words which by their association with *saddiq* (just) leads to the proper understanding of the word, *righteousness.* Richardson has given a very valuable study of this word.[13] From these studies we gain the idea that righteousness is the fundamental attribute of God. His judgments issue from His inner nature of righteousness. Consequently, whatever God wills, is right. In His covenant relations with His people, the Lord remains faithful because He is righteous. In Isaiah (40 — 66) the prophet associated righteousness and salvation, "A righteous God and a Savior; there is none beside me" (Is. 45:21).[14]

(2) The Righteousness of God as Upheld by Jesus. With this Old Testament concept of God's righteousness in view, it is entirely to be expected that Jesus would address God in the language, "O righteous Father" (Jn. 17:25). So completely did Jesus build on the Old Testament concept of God's righteousness that He at no place gave a specific exposition of this great theme. Looking at the Sermon on the Mount, Jesus did not introduce the concept of God's righteousness with an explanation of its meaning. On the contrary He brought to a grand climax one of the major teachings of this sermon with the words, "But seek first his kingdom and his righteousness" (Mt. 6:33). Undoubtedly His audience was well aware of the true meaning of the righteousness of God.

When Jesus gave the Beatitudes, He had no occasion to explain what He meant by "hunger and thirst for righteousness" or of being "persecuted for righteousness' sake" (5:6, 10). Without defining the word He could say, "Unless your righteousness exceeds that of the scribes and Pharisees, you will never enter the kingdom of heaven" (v. 20). In His lengthy pronouncement of woe upon the scribes and Pharisees Jesus was able to expose their hypocrisy in the pointed language, "You also outwardly appear righteous to men, but within you are full of hypocrisy and inquity" (23:28). By reason of this hypocrisy, "All the righteous blood shed on earth, from the blood of innocent Abel to the blood of Zechariah" (v. 35) came upon these scribes and Pharisees. The Godcenteredness of the righteousness characteristic of God's children stands out in Jesus' words, "Then the righteous will shine like the sun in the kingdom of their Father" (13:43). Those who shall hear the joyful words of the King, "Come, O blessed of my Father," are the righteous, and these righteous shall go away into eternal life (25:34-46).

As reflecting still further the righteousness of God, Jesus spoke concerning the coming Holy Spirit, "He will convince the world of sin and of righteousness and of judgment: of sin, because they do not believe in me; of righteousness, because I go to the Father . . . of judgment, because the ruler of this world is judged" (Jn. 16:8-11). The words *sin, righteousness,* and *judgment* bear a close relationship to one another. Sin stands as the antithesis of righteousness. Judgment is that which comes upon the ruler of this world through the righteous Father.

These teachings of Jesus, found chiefly in contexts which describe the righteousness to which man should attain, ultimately declare the righteousness which is found in the Father. Most certainly *righteousness* lies in the sphere of God's supremacy.

(3) Repentance the Counterpart to Righteousness. In Jesus' words, "I have not come to call the righteous, but sinners to repentance" (Lk. 5:32), the word *repentance* stands as the counterpart to the righteousness of God. Jesus' parable of the two sons, whose father commanded them to work in his vineyard, confirms this conclusion. Here Jesus showed that John's coming in the way of righteousness, to whom the tax collectors and the harlots responded, stood as a rebuke to others who did not afterward repent and believe John (Mt. 21:28-32). Both the Baptist and Jesus preached the baptism of repentance for the forgiveness of sin. The reason for this kind of preaching lay in the fact that the kingdom of God was at hand. God's holy and righteous nature called for repentance on the part of man in order to become a sharer in this kingdom. This note of repentance also has deep roots in the Old Testament.[15]

On another occasion, when folks were troubled about Pilate's unjust treatment of certain Galileans, Jesus gave a similar teaching in the words: "Unless you repent you shall also likewise perish" (Lk. 13:5). Jesus drew attention to the seriousness of His command by adding the parable of the man who planted a fig tree in his vineyard. When it failed to produce fruit, he commanded the vinedresser to cut it down. The vinedresser pleaded, "Let it alone, sir, this year also, till I dig about it and put on manure. And if it bears fruit next year, well and good; but if not, you can cut it down" (vv. 8, 9). Through this language Jesus was teaching the necessity of repentance on the part of His hearers. In another encounter with the Pharisees and scribes Jesus gave the parables of the lost sheep, the lost coin, and the lost son, in which He showed the joy in heaven over one sinner who repents (15:3-32). On still another occasion Jesus related a parable "to some who trusted in themselves that they were righteous and despised others" (18:9). The story had to do with the Pharisee and the publican who had gone up to the temple to pray. The Pharisee found no room for repentance and was telling God all that he was doing in the way of obeying the law. The tax collector, on the other hand, in deep penitence beat his breast saying, "God, be merciful to me a sinner!" (v. 13). This man went down justified rather than the other for as Jesus said, "Every one who exalts himself shall be humbled, but he who humbles himself will be exalted" (v. 14).

All these incidents illustrate how deeply the idea of repentance was imbedded in Jesus' teaching. In order to get a clearer idea of this experience of repentance, let us make a brief study of the three great words *(metanoeo, metamelomai,* and *epistrepho)* which underlie the idea of repentance.

(a) The Vocabulary of Repentance. The most common word for repentance is *metanoeo.* It has the literal sense *to change one's mind* or *purpose.* This word was used frequently in the Septuagint to translate the Hebrew word *naham,* which has the literal sense to *pant, sigh, groan.* These two words as used in the Old Testament frequently signify *a change of mind* or *a sighing in a nonmoral sense,* but a moral sense does obtain in such passages as Jeremiah 6:8; 31:19 and Job 42:6. The Lord portrayed Ephraim's repentance in vivid language as follows, "For after I had turned away I repented; and after I was instructed, I smote upon my thigh; I was ashamed, and I was confounded, because I bore the disgrace of my youth" (Jer. 31:19). Here we see the elements of genuine repentance as expressed by *naham* and its Greek equivalent *metanoeo.* This meaning underlies the frequent usage of *metanoeo* and *metanoia* in the New Testament.[16]

The verb *metamelomai* is a passive deponent verb meaning *to regret, repent oneself, be sorry afterward.* This is the word used by Jesus when He spoke of the man who had two sons. He told one of them to go and work in his vineyard. At first he refused to go but afterward he *repented* and went (Mt. 21:28-32). Jesus explained, "The tax collectors and the harlots go into the kingdom of God before you. For John came to you in the way of righteousness, and you did not believe him, but the tax collectors and the harlots believed him; and even when you saw it, you did not afterward repent and believe him" (Mt. 21:31, 32). Matthew used this verb to describe Judas' experience when he *repented* and brought back the thirty pieces of silver. It expressed the emotional element of regret and remorse, literally, "the backbiting of the soul upon herself."[17]

Paul helps us to understand the similar but yet different meanings attached to *metamelomai* and *metanoeo* in 2 Corinthians 7:8-10: "For even if I made you sorry with my letter, I do not regret [*metamelomai*] it (though I did regret [*metamelomai*] it), for I see that that letter grieved you . . . into repenting [*metanoian*]. . . . For godly grief produces a repentance [*metanoian*] that leads to salvation and brings no regret [*ametameletos*]." In these uses the emotional aspect has its basis in the word *metamelomai,* whereas the complete change of mind and purpose are expressed in the word *metanoeo.* This similarity and difference of senses in these two words become more apparent when we observe that *metamelomai* is also used in the Septuagint to translate the Hebrew *naham.* In these cases where *metamelomai* is used to translate *naham*, it carries the nonmoral sense of regret or repent, whether on the part of people or of God.[18] Even though the New Testament use of *metamelomai* with a moral sense is so infrequent, its occurrence is significant because it translates the Hebrew *naham* and also because it enters into the broad gamut of what we commonly call *repentance.* Paul's use of the word as noted above confirms this idea.

The third Greek verb used to express the idea of *repentance* is *epistrepho.* Its literal meaning is *to turn about, around,* or *toward* (Mt. 9:22; 12:44). This literal usage easily lends itself to a metaphorical sense of *turning to* God or *causing to return* to God. Already in the angelic announcement to Zechariah concerning the birth of John we find the words, "And he will turn many of the sons of Israel to the Lord their God, and he will go before him in the spirit and power of Elijah, to turn the hearts of the fathers to the children" (Lk. 1:16, 17). These two uses of *epistrepho* reflect the Septuagint translation of Malachi 4:6, but interestingly the Septuagint uses the verb *apokathistemi,* which carries the sense of *restore* or *bring back. Epistrepho* is the verb usually used to translate the Hebrew *shub.* This verb gives distinctive meaning to the several uses of the verb *epistrepho* in the New Testament, especially since several of its significant occurrences in the New Testament[19] are quotations of Isaiah 6:10, where the Septuagint uses *epistrepho* to translate the Hebrew *shub.* The frequent uses of the verb *shub*[20] give a tremendous buildup in meaning of this word. Especially significant are the words: "Let the wicked forsake his way, and the unrighteous man his thoughts; let him *return* to the Lord, that he may have mercy on him, and to our God, for he will abundantly pardon" (Is. 55:7). Here the return to the Lord must be preceded by the wicked forsaking his way and the unrighteous man his thoughts. Still more emphatic are the words of the Lord to Joel, "*Return* to me with all your heart, with fasting, with weeping, and with mourning; and rend your hearts and not your garments," to which Joel added, "Return to the Lord, your God, for he is gracious and merciful, slow to anger, and abounding in steadfast love, and repents of evil." Here the return to the Lord must be accompanied with fasting, weeping, mourning, rending of hearts. (Joel 2:12,13.)

This prepares us to understand the heart-searching meaning of Jesus' use of the verb *epistrepho*. Thus when Jesus explained His teaching in parables, He quoted the Isaiah 6:9, 10 passage in order to show that this kind of teaching was used on account of the hardness of hearts of many of the people (Mt. 13:10-15). Their spiritual dullness prevented them from seeing with their eyes, hearing with their ears, understanding with their hearts, and turning to God to heal them. A return to God required all this. The Apostle John made his appeal through the same words from Isaiah in bringing the severe indictment against the people at the close of Christ's earthly ministry (Jn. 12:38-40). It showed again the serious nature of Israel's sin at the time of Christ and the kind of internal change necessary in order to be healed by God.

Jesus used this same verb in giving His warning to Peter before his denial of his Lord. Its use here helps us understand the kind of change necessary in the heart of Peter in turning back to Jesus. Jesus said, "Satan demanded to have you, that he might sift you like wheat, but I have prayed for you that your faith may not fail; and when you have turned again, strengthen your brethren" (Lk. 22:31-34). It is noteworthy that in Peter's early preaching he made his appeal in the words, "Repent [*metanoeo*] therefore, and turn again [*epistrepho*], that your sins may be blotted out" (Acts 3:19). Here the verbs *metanoeo* and *epistrepho* are used in close relationship, thus suggesting their close similarity in meaning. Paul used the same two verbs in his defense before Agrippa, when he explained his mission to Jews and Gentiles in the words, "They should *repent* and *turn to* God and perform deeds worthy of their repentance" (Acts 26:20). Observe that Paul added words by which genuine *repentance* and *turning to* God are tested, namely, "Perform deeds worthy of their repentance." With this study of the three great words of repentance, including their foundations in the Old Testament, we are now in a position to analyze more fully the nature of repentance.

(b) The Nature and Character of Repentance. With little effort toward systematic presentation, let us observe how both John and Jesus unfolded the concept of repentance. First, the responsibility for repentance rests with man. This was plainly taught in the Old Testament.[21] Repeatedly, God called on Israel to repent from their sins. Both the Baptist and Jesus used the same language as the prophets. This underscored human responsibility for turning away from sin and back to God.

Second, repentance bears a close relation to faith and forgiveness of sin. Mark presented John as "preaching a baptism of repentance for the remission of sins" (1:4). He quoted Jesus as saying, "The time is fulfilled, and the kingdom of God is at hand; repent, and believe in the Gospel" (v. 15). This leads us to understand that the *turning away from sin* naturally included the *turning to belief* in the gospel. God would forgive sins only when man repented from his sins. Jesus enlarged on this truth in the story of the prodigal son. He concluded His earthly ministry by giving the pattern of world evangelism in the words, "That repentance and the forgiveness of sins should be preached in his name to all nations" (Lk. 24:47).

Third, John the Baptist, in particular, demanded of the hypocritical Pharisees and Sadducees that they "bear fruit that befits repentance" (Mt. 3:8). Genuine repentance lay much deeper than mere lip profession. He emphasized his warning with the words, "Even now the axe is laid to the root of the tree; every tree therefore that does not bear good fruit is cut down and thrown into the fire" (v. 10). Speaking of Jesus, the Baptist added the severe words, "His winnowing fork is in his hand, and he will clear his threshing floor and gather his wheat into the granary, but the chaff he will burn with unquenchable fire" (v. 12). No superficial notion of repentance could stand against such piercing language.

Fourth, repentance is required of all men. No one is excepted. Both the Baptist and Jesus expressed this most explicitly. Neither one used a conditional clause to the effect that if you are sinners, you should repent. This pattern of preaching gave witness to the universal sinfulness of mankind. No man can stand before God in his own righteousness. This note characterized the preaching of Peter and Paul in their proclamation of the gospel (Acts 2:38; 13:24, 38, 39).

Fifth, repentance is God-centered. While the expression, "Repentance to God" (Acts 20:21) belongs to Paul, the idea is implicit in all of Jesus' teaching. It is most dramatically pictured in the story of the prodigal son. When he came to himself, he decided to return to his father, to whom he said, "Father, I have sinned against heaven and before you; I am no longer worthy to be called your son; treat me as one of your hired servants" (Lk. 15:18, 19). The prodigal's return to his natural father dramatizes the sinner's return to God. It is against God, the heavenly Father, against whom all have sinned.

Sixth, repentance involves an absoluteness of self-renunciation. It is that which is involved in following some of Jesus' pointed sayings. Note the following: "No one can serve two masters; for either he will hate the one and love the other, or he will be devoted to the one and despise the other. You cannot serve God and mammon" (Mt. 6:24). Jesus commanded that if your hand or your foot or your eye causes you to sin, each respective member must be removed (Mk. 9:43-47). Jesus said, "If any man would come after me, let him deny himself and take up his cross daily and follow me" (Lk. 9:23). Jesus spoke in still more incisive language in the words, "If anyone comes to me and does not hate his own father and mother and wife and children and brothers and sisters, yes, and even his own life, he cannot be my disciple. . . . Whoever of you does not renounce all that he has cannot be my disciple"(Lk. 14:26-33). In this forceful manner Jesus showed clearly that man cannot divest himself of his responsibilities to God. He cannot be unreligious. In reality a profession of being unreligious is clearly that of being irreligious. In order for one to be religious he must renounce self with all of its sinfulness.

c. The Power of God and Its Correlate: Faith

(1) Jesus' Presentation of the Power of God. The closing words of the Lord's Prayer, though not textually supported, present, nevertheless, an unquestioned truth. The words, "For thine is the kingdom, and the power, and the glory, for ever. Amen" (Mt. 6:13, KJV) express the infinite power of God. The structure of the language is such as to express the centrality of God's power and glory in the kingdom of God. It is a meaningful expression setting forth the supremacy of God in the sphere of power. The nature of this supremacy becomes very apparent in Jesus' reply to the charge that He was casting out demons by Beelzebul. Jesus cast out demons by the Spirit of God. This indicated that God's supremacy in power was spiritual and not political (Mt. 12:28; Lk. 11:20). In this answer Jesus also asserted the source of kingdom power. It is through the Spirit of God that this power is manifested.

Repeatedly, Luke focused attention on the Holy Spirit as the one through whom kingdom power manifested itself.[22] He noted that after Jesus was baptized with the Holy Spirit, He was led by the Spirit and entered into His ministry in the power of the Spirit. In the context of an individual's importunity, Jesus taught His disciples to ask, seek, and knock, and then He promised that the heavenly Father would give the Holy Spirit to those who ask Him (11:13). Luke brought his Gospel to a close with Jesus' promise, "I send the promise of my Father upon you; but stay in the city, until you are clothed with power from on high" (24:49). Luke also captured the very significant words of Peter in his sermon to Cornelius when he said, "God anointed Jesus of Nazareth with the Holy Spirit and with power . . . he went about doing good and healing all that were oppressed by the devil, for God was with him" (Acts 10:38). Through these instances we should gather that Jesus was manifesting this power through the Holy Spirit.

Just before His transfiguration Jesus told His disciples, "There are some standing here who will not taste death before they see the kingdom of God come with power" (Mk. 9:1). The transfiguration scene had for its supreme purpose, so far as the disciples were concerned, to manifest kingdom power in the glorified Christ. When Jesus was in conversation with the Sadducees on the subject of the resurrection, He had another grand occasion to present the power of God in relation to the resurrection. Jesus told them, "You are wrong, because you know neither the scriptures nor the power of God. . . . And as for the resurrection of the dead, have you not read what was said to you by God, 'I am the God of Abraham, and the God of Isaac, and the God of Jacob'? He is not God of the dead, but of the living" (Mt. 22:29-32; Mk. 12:24-27; Lk. 20:33-38). In this language Jesus predicted the supreme manifestation of God's power to be revealed at the consummation of the kingdom.

In the Olivet Discourse Jesus gave further teaching on the power to be revealed at the consummation. Note His words, "But in those days, after that tribulation, the sun will be darkened, and the moon will not give its light, and the stars will be falling from heaven, and the powers in the heavens will be shaken. And then they will see the Son of man coming in clouds with great power and glory. And then he will send out the angels, and gather his elect from the four winds, from the ends of the earth to the ends of heaven" (Mk. 13:24-27; Mt. 24:29-31; Lk. 21:25-28). When Jesus was on trial before the Sanhedrin, He said, "You will see the Son of man sitting at the right hand of Power, and coming with the clouds of heaven" (Mk. 14:62; Mt. 26:64; Lk. 22:69). It should be noted that these references to the power of God in relation to the kingdom of God center in His extraordinary activities whether in the past, present, or future: such as the casting out of demons, Jesus' transfiguration, the return of the Lord, the resurrection, and the final judgment. Events such as these require deity power, and Jesus manifested this infinite power of God in these aspects of His messianic activity.

(2) Jesus' Teaching of the Power of God Rooted in the Old Testament. Jesus was not announcing a new understanding of God's power; rather, He was building directly on the Old Testament. Repeatedly throughout the Old Testament, God revealed Himself as the omnipotent One. This became evident in God's work of creation (Gen. 1 and 2; Ps. 136:4-9; Jer. 10:12; 51:15). While the author of Genesis 1 and 2 did not draw attention to the greatness of God's creative work, later writers

did set forth this truth, a sample of which is Psalm 136, which centers in the power and majesty of God as shown in the creation, as well as in Israel's early history. Add one sample from the writing prophets, the words of Jeremiah, when he wrote, "It is he who made the earth by his power, who established the world by his wisdom, and by his understanding stretched out the heavens" (Jer. 10:12; 51:15). The Lord revealed Himself to Abraham as God Almighty. This revelation made a deep impression on the Hebrews. God manifested Himself in His deliverance of Israel from Egypt through many signs and wonders (Ex. 15; Ps. 106:8-12; 136:10-16). The psalmist took delight in magnifying the power and might of God. A couple samples follow: "Who by thy strength hast established the mountains, being girded with might" (65:6) and "He has shown his people the power of his works, in giving them the heritage of the nations" (111:6).[23] Daniel pictured the majesty and power of the Son of Man in this language, "And to him was given dominion and glory and kingdom, that all peoples, nations and languages should serve him; his dominion is an everlasting dominion, which shall not pass away, and his kingdom one that shall not be destroyed" (Dan. 7:14).

(3) The Miracles of Jesus as Demonstrations of the Power of God. The vocabulary for miracles, both in the New Testament and the Old, is rich and expressive. Since the New Testament words for miracles are the same as those used in the Septuagint, it will be advantageous to examine each of the Greek words in the settings of their Old Testament Hebrew equivalents.

(a) *Dunamis — power, might, strength, ability.* The Septuagint translators used this word to translate *chayil — force, valor* (Ps. 59:11; 103); *tsaba — host, warfare, service* (Gen. 2:1; Ex. 12:41; Deut. 4:19); *geburah — might* (1 Chron. 29:11; Judg. 5:31; Job 12:13; Ps. 54:1); *oz — strength, hardness* (Ps. 59:16; 63:2; 66:3; 150:1). With these uses of *dunamis* in the Septuagint, it becomes clear why this word should occur so frequently to describe the mighty works of Jesus. Thus Jesus upbraided the cities where most of His *mighty works* had been done "because they did not repent" (Mt. 11:20-23; Lk. 10:13). When Jesus came to His own country and taught in their synagogues, the people were astonished on seeing His *mighty works.* These powers at work in Jesus made Herod think that He was the Baptist raised from the dead (Mt. 14:1, 2). Luke recorded an incident of Jesus' healing ministry in the presence of the Pharisees and teachers of the law. They had come from every village of Galilee to Cana and even from Jerusalem. With such witnesses at hand Luke wrote, "The power of the Lord was with him to heal" (Lk. 5: 17-26). The scene became tense when men brought to Jesus a man who was paralyzed, and Jesus responded by saying to the man that his sins were forgiven. Accused of blasphemy, Jesus healed the paralyzed man and thus demonstrated that His *power* to heal was proof of His authority to forgive sins. Luke also recounted Jesus calling the Twelve together and of giving them *power* and authority over all demons and to cure diseases.

In this commission Luke brought together the two closely related words, *power* and *authority*. This adds another dimension to the idea of *power*. To perform these mighty works required a corresponding authority from the One who gives miraculous power. Only with divine authority could the infinite power of God be manifested so that, on the occasion of Jesus' entry into Jerusalem, the whole multitude of disciples accompanying Jesus "began to rejoice and praise God with a loud voice for all the mighty works that they had seen" (Lk. 19:37). With these samples of the use of the word *dunamis* we may observe the emphasis which this word gave to the *power* manifested in the miracle. This power infinitely transcends human power. That kind of power alone could give attestation to Jesus as being the Messiah, the Anointed One of the Lord. It was these mighty works wrought through Jesus which demonstrated the supremacy of God in the sphere of power.

(b) *Semeion — sign, mark, token*. The distinctive use of this word in the New Testament is with reference to wonders or miracles which are contrary to the course of nature. The Septuagint translators used this word to convey the thought expressed by the Hebrew *oth — sign, mark, token*, a word used with particular reference to miraculous signs.[24] When the Lord chose Moses to deliver Israel from the land of Egypt, He gave him power to perform certain *signs*, miraculous in nature, through which he would show to the people that God had actually commissioned him as Israel's leader. The plagues brought upon the land of Egypt constituted *signs* to Pharaoh and his people that the Lord of heaven and earth was the God of Israel. All through Israel's history they looked back to the deliverance from Egypt as the arch example of God's manifestation of miraculous power to serve as signs both to the Egyptians and to Israel that the Lord was their God.

It was entirely natural that in the days of Jesus' earthly ministry the people should expect the performance of signs in order to validate His claims as Messiah. Tragically, the scribes and Pharisees did not grasp the meaning of Jesus' healing ministry, especially in the manifestations of power shown in the casting out of demons. They demanded of Jesus to show them a *sign (semeion)*. By reason of their refusal to attach to Jesus' miracles the meaning which they most conclusively demonstrated, Jesus replied that no sign would be given to that generation except the sign of the prophet, Jonah (Mt. 12:38-42; Lk. 11:29-32). The three days and three nights spent by Jonah in the belly of the whale typified the three days and three nights that the Son of Man would spend in the heart of the earth. Thus the miracle of miracles, the resurrection of our Lord, would stand as the most conclusive sign that Jesus was the Christ.

It is in the Gospel of John that the word *sign* is used most frequently and significantly, both by the author and by Jesus. John described the turning of water into wine at the marriage feast of Cana as the first of Jesus' *signs*. It was a most significant example of all the miracles recorded in this Gospel to demonstrate the purpose of these manifestations of supernatural power during the earthly ministry of our Lord. The miracle was a *sign* which showed in the most effective way possible, the supernatural working of divine power which lies beyond all human power and is possible alone to God. By no other means could the revelation of God through His Son Jesus Christ be authenticated to man than through these miraculous signs.

A hurried glance at some of the other signs recorded by John serve to support this conclusion. Witness the case of the official whose son was ill when he came to Jesus requesting Him to come down and heal his son. Jesus tested him by saying, "Unless you see *signs* and wonders you will not believe" (Jn. 4:48). The official broke through the apparent barrier of this test by repeating his request that Jesus should heal his son. Jesus' reply, "Go, your son will live," was a genuine challenge to the man's faith. He believed the word of Jesus and experienced the fulfillment of Jesus' promise. The writer John called this the second *sign* performed by Jesus. The healing of the man born blind (9:1-12) is another graphic illustration of the meaning of Jesus' miracles. Everyone knew that this man had been blind from his birth. The disciples had only two alternatives for the man's blindness: either this man or his parents had sinned. They seemed unable to anticipate a third alternative, namely, "that the works of God might be made manifest in him" (v. 3). This healing which took place on the Sabbath day was utterly baffling to the Pharisees who could not understand how Jesus could be a man from God and yet not keep the Sabbath. But others pushed the question, "How can a man who is a sinner do such *signs*?" (v. 16). This pointed question made the issue clear. The giving of sight to the blind man was an irrefutable *sign* that this man Jesus came from God. The conversation with the man who had received his sight showed conclusively into what a most ridiculous position one is placed who refuses to believe a *sign*.

Of still greater meaning was the raising of Lazarus. Since Lazarus' home in Bethany was so near to Jerusalem, many of the Jews had known him and had attended his funeral. It was these Jews who witnessed the man, Lazarus, coming forth from his tomb. All that they could do was to plot to put Lazarus to death, apparently unaware that if Jesus had raised Lazarus once, He could do it a second time. This whole incident illustrates the fact that while miracles could not compel belief, their evidential value as *signs* that Jesus was the Son of God was irrefutable. John accounted for the great multitude following Christ in the words, "The reason why the crowd went to meet him was that they heard he had done this sign" (12:18). John put his finger on the tragedy of unbelief in these *signs* when he wrote, "Though he had done so many *signs* before them, yet they did not believe in him" (v. 37). John brought his Gospel to a climactic close in the words, "Now Jesus did many other signs in the presence of the disciples, which are not written in this book; but these are written that you may believe that Jesus is the Christ, the Son of God, and that believing you may have life in his name" (Jn. 20:30, 31). In this expressive language John stated the positive meaning of all Jesus' miracles. This experiential act of believing in Jesus issues in having life in His name. In all these uses of the word *sign*, we observe the stress laid on the teleological significance of miracles.

(c) *Teras — wonder, marvel, portent.* The Septuagint translators used this word to express the meaning of *mopheth*. This is a forceful word carrying the meaning of *miracle, wonder, sign, portent.* It expressed a special display of God's power, especially in the case of the wonders performed before Pharaoh by Moses and Aaron (Ex. 4:21; 11:9, 10). It is instructive to note the frequent combination of *oth (sign)* and *mopheth (wonder)* throughout the Old Testament.[25] The combining of these two words in the Hebrew suggests their similarity in meaning. *Mopheth* complements *oth* in the way of showing that a *sign* also possessed the character of a *wonder* or *portent,* thus indicating a special display of God's power.

The word *teras* was used frequently in the New Testament, and in the Gospels always with *signs*. We have already noted one of these cases with reference to the healing of the official's son (Jn. 4:48). Jesus predicted, "False Christs and false prophets will arise and show great signs and wonders, so as to lead astray, if possible, even the elect" (Mt. 24:23, 24). On the day of Pentecost, Peter gave witness to Jesus' miracles in the language, "Jesus of Nazareth, a man attested to you by God with mighty *works* and *wonders* and *signs*, which God did through him in your midst, as you yourselves know" (Acts 2:22). This use of the three words for miracles shows how Peter could refer to them as being their attestation to the people of Jesus' messiahship. It is the evidential value of miracles which Peter so forthrightly presented on this occasion.

These three words are definitely cumulative in their significance.

(d) *Ergon — work, task, employment, deed, action, that which is wrought or made.* This word was used in the Septuagint to translate two significant Hebrew words, both of which add meaning to the New Testament use of *ergon.* The first of these is *melakah — work, ministry, service.* This word is used frequently (Gen. 2:2; Ps. 73:28; Jer. 50:25) to express the work of God, particularly in the act of creation. The second Hebrew word *maaseh — work, labor, deed, act*[26] also sets forth God's creation. Thus the heavens are the work of God's fingers. They are the work of His hands. With this language the psalmist viewed God as the divine Artificer of the universe. The use of *ergon* in the New Testament with reference to the works of Christ builds on the cumulative meaning of these two Hebrew words.[27] Jesus used this word to compare His mighty deeds with those of the Father. He was doing the *works* which His Father granted Him to accomplish for the purpose of bearing witness that the Father had sent Him. For the very reason that Jesus claimed to be doing the same kind of works as His Father performed, the Jews interpreted His claim as being blasphemy. But Jesus testified that His performance of these works showed that He and the Father are one.

(e) *Thaumasios* (neuter plural as substantive): *wonders, marvels, miracles, wonderful things.* In the Septuagint this word translates the verb *pala — be surpassing, be extraordinary, work wonders* (Ex. 3:20; Josh. 3:5; Judg. 6:13), and *pele — wonder* (Ex. 15:11; Ps. 89:5, 6). While the substantive use of *thaumasios* occurs only once in the New Testament, its use is quite significant. Matthew noted (21:14-16) that when the blind and the lame came to Jesus in the temple, He healed them. He labeled these miracles *wonderful things.* The miraculous connotation of *thaumasios* becomes more significant when we observe that the verb form *thaumazo — to wonder, to marvel —* is used to express the impact upon the people who witnessed the miracles performed by Jesus (Mt. 9:8, 33; 15:31; 21:20; Jn. 5:20, 28).

By way of conclusion we should observe that this vocabulary for miracles is meaningful and significant. The buildup of vocabulary of Old Testament and New Testament words affords a sound basis for understanding the miracles of the Bible. Studied in their contexts these words yield a decisive meaning, thus making it possible to give a definition of this word. Davis-Gehman wrote, "In the narrowest Biblical sense, miracles are events in the external world, wrought by the immediate power of God and intended as a sign or attestation. They are possible because God sustains, controls, and guides all things, and is personal and omnipotent."[28] These authors noted further, "Miracles are not to be credulously received, but their genuineness must be tested. The tests are:

1. They exhibit the character of God and teach truths concerning God. 2. They are in harmony with the established truths of religion. . . . 3. There is an adequate occasion for them. God does not work them except for great cause and for a religious purpose. They belong to the history of redemption, and there is no genuine miracle without an adequate occasion for it in God's redemptive revelation of Himself. 4. They are established, not by the number of witnesses, but by the character and qualification of the witnesses."

(4) The Historicity of Miracles. One of the perplexing problems encountered in the study of miracles centers in the question as to whether or not they actually occurred. After reading such modern authorities as Bultmann, Richardson, and McCasland, it is almost impossible to determine whether these scholars actually believe that Jesus did heal the sick, open the eyes of the blind, and raise the dead.[29] Both Richardson and McCasland dwell at great lengths on the spiritual significance of miracles, giving them, for all practical purposes, parabolic or mythical meaning. Undoubtedly, miracles, such as healing the sick, involved more than the physical cure of the disease; the giving of sight to the blind undoubtedly led to the gaining of spiritual sight; the raising of the dead revealed Christ to be the Giver of spiritual life or the One who will raise the dead — all these physical miracles most vividly expressed the spiritual aspect involved. One's viewpoint is certainly suffering severe limitations if he fails to recognize the spiritual meaning involved in each literal miracle. With this background of thought, let us note the internal evidence in support of miracles in accordance with the definition given above.

The present discussion builds on the materials of Chapter II, where I discussed the historical character of the Gospel records. Let us begin with Peter's testimony (Acts 2:22, 24; 3:13-16; 4:10-12). In genuine law court procedure he said, "Jesus of Nazareth, a man attested to you by God with mighty works and wonders and signs which God did through him in your midst, as you yourselves know." The verb *apodeiknumi* has the meanings: *to prove, to declare, to attest.* The grounds for this proof lay in the threefold vocabulary for miracles considered above. There is here the augmented support to the attestation: the miracles viewed from the angles of the mighty power manifested, their terrifying wonder, and their being signs or tokens of divine authority. Peter testified that the apostles were witnesses of the suffering, death, and resurrection of Christ. The word *martus (witness)* is used in a legal sense. While Peter was not in a courtroom giving his witness, nevertheless, the setting of his testimony for all practical purposes leads to its forensic sense.

Undoubtedly, Christ's resurrection was the miracle of miracles of all human history. Let us observe again the detailed evidence given by the New Testament in support of this miracle. As I noted in an earlier discussion, all the Gospel writers, Peter, and Paul gave definite attestation to this miracle. It bears repeating to note how Paul built up his testimony to Christ's resurrection (1 Cor. 15:3-8). He saw fit to mention specifically the several appearances of Jesus to the disciples and finally to himself. In this way Paul followed the strict rules of giving legal testimony. John's witness to the miracles of Jesus stands out with great clarity (Jn. 20:30, 31). In this familiar passage John was referring to the many signs recorded in his Gospel and alluding to many others performed in the presence of His disciples. This is proof again of the special calling of the disciples to be the official witnesses to Christ's ministry. John concluded his testimony by asserting that these signs gave adequate grounds for his readers to believe that Jesus is the Christ, the Son of God.

The author of Hebrews followed the same method of giving official testimony as used by Peter, Paul, and John (Heb. 2:1-4). In this context the author was exhorting his readers to pay closer attention to what they had heard. He noted how the message of angels was valid *(bebaios: reliable, dependable, certain, sure* (in the sense of legally guaranteed security). "It was declared at first by the Lord, and it was attested *(bebaioo)* to us by those who heard him, while God also bore witness by signs and wonders and various miracles and by gifts of the Holy Spirit" (Heb. 2:3, 4). We should observe that the Lord's testimony was supported by the signs, wonders, various miracles, and by the gifts of the Holy Spirit. We should note also that the only way in which God could vouchsafe to us His message was through these supernatural manifestations.

This is the impact which a reading of the Gospel narratives should make upon us. In answer to the Baptist's searching question to Jesus, "Are you he who is to come, or shall we look for another?" Jesus said, "Go and tell John what you hear and see: the blind receive their sight and the lame walk, lepers are cleansed and the deaf hear, and the dead are raised up" (Mt. 11:2-5). Each of these was specifically a miracle requiring supernatural power for its being performed. There was no more effective way in which Jesus could show to John that He was the Christ. The testimony of Luke bears repetition (Lk. 1:1-4). His Gospel had its basis in the eyewitness testimony which he received from those who accompanied Jesus throughout His ministry. With reference to Christ's resurrection Luke noted that Jesus presented Himself alive to the apostles after His Passion by many proofs (Acts 1:3). The word *tekmerion* is a word with a precise connotation meaning: *a sure sign, a proof which is positive, convincing, and decisive.* A final word has to do with the integrity of these witnesses: Matthew, Mark, Luke, John, Peter, and Paul. They were able to interweave nonmiraculous incidents with the miraculous, with the result that both bear the marks of authentic history. When we interweave the teachings of Jesus with His words relating to miracles, both of these most conclusively attest the integrity of His witness. It is beyond human understanding that Jesus who preached His incomparable messages should have been dishonest in referring to His miracles.

There is little need to deal with the problem of defining miracles. It is regrettable that many modern scholars wrangle over this problem and do not allow the Bible to speak for itself. It is utter folly to declare that miracles are impossible. Advocates of such claims are showing the influence of their philosophical prepossessions. They have closed minds to believing the testimony of eyewitnesses who were both competent and trustworthy. Christ's words quoted above are quite definitive as to the scope of miracles. Note again His words, "The blind receive their sight and the lame walk, lepers are cleansed and the deaf hear, and the dead are raised up" (Mt. 11:5). If Christ had claimed the power to make two plus two equals five, or the sum of the angles of a triangle to be equal to three right angles, or a crooked line to be the shortest distance between two points, and other equally ridiculous claims, then it would be entirely in order to say that miracles are impossible. Most certainly, Christ our Lord possesses power over His creation, such as stilling the tempest; power over disease, such as His healing ministry; power over life, such as the raising of Lazarus, or His own resurrection.

(5) The Messianic Import of Miracles. Peter's words at Pentecost gave solid affirmation to this interpretation in most compact language. He declared, "Men of Israel, hear these words: Jesus of Nazareth, a man attested to you by God with mighty works and wonders and signs which God did through him in your midst, as you yourselves know — this Jesus, delivered up according to the definite plan and foreknowledge of God, you crucified and killed by the hands of lawless men. But God raised him up, having loosed the pangs of death, because it was not possible for him to be held by it" (Acts 2:22-24). What we should observe at this point is that the miracles gave conclusive attestation to Jesus as being the Messiah. As noted earlier, Peter brought together the three great words for miracles, each with its distinctive connotation, and combined they assert the cumulative import of these words. Continuing with this messianic message Peter testified that all the apostles and others were witnesses to Christ's resurrection (v. 32). He closed his message with the glorious truth that God had made the exalted Jesus both

Lord and Christ (v. 36). This sermon spoken so directly to the house of Israel adds all the more weight to its messianic import.

Looking again at Jesus' response to the Baptist's question, observe that He answered John by quoting the messianic predictions of Isaiah 35:5, 6 and 61:1 (Mt. 11:5). A similar example, this time the observation made by Matthew (Mt. 12:15-21), is the note that Jesus' healing ministry was to fulfill what was spoken by Isaiah (42:1-4). This passage obtains all the greater meaning for our present inquiry, when we note that its use by Matthew confirmed the identity of Jesus, the Messiah, and the Servant of the Lord.

The next incident in Matthew's Gospel, the healing of the blind and dumb demoniac (12:22-32), leads to further confirmation of Jesus' messiahship. The people were all amazed and exclaimed, "Can this be the son of David?" (v. 23). The context suggests their belief that the Healer of the young man was the Messiah. But this was too much for the Pharisees. In a pointed manner, Jesus exposed their unbelief and asserted that through His casting out demons by the Spirit of God, the kingdom of God had come upon them (v. 28). Since Jesus had bound the strong man of the house, He was able to plunder his goods. Jesus made it clear that they were blaspheming the Son of Man. By so doing He was identifying Himself with the Messiah. This rebuke took a severer turn when He said that He cast out demons by the Spirit of God, and later added that "whoever speaks against the Holy Spirit will not be forgiven" (v. 32). Thus the entire incident constituted a most conclusive proof that Jesus was the Messiah as attested by His casting out of demons.

The healing of the paralytic (Mk. 2:1-12) carries us a step further in this inquiry. When Jesus saw the faith of those who brought the paralytic to Him, His first statement was, "My son, your sins are forgiven." When those who were present were questioning within themselves about Jesus' forgiving sins, Jesus added, " 'But that you may know that the Son of man has authority on earth to forgive sins' — he said to the paralytic — 'I say to you, rise, take up your pallet and go home' " (vv. 10, 11). Purposefully, Jesus brought together His declaration of forgiveness of sins and His act of healing. His healing power confirmed His right to forgive sins — both proving His messiahship.

By way of conclusion let us note again that the various kinds of miracles carried corresponding spiritual values to those who experienced them. Thus the giving of sight to the blind had its correlate in a spiritual experience of seeing; the feeding of the five thousand led people to believe that Jesus was the bread of life; the casting out of demons revealed the regenerating power of the Holy Spirit within us; the healing of the sick symbolized the spiritual cures of the many spiritual ailments of life; the raising of the dead foreshadowed the resurrection and our transformation into the likeness of Christ's glorified body.

(6) Faith the Subjective Counterpart to the Power of God. Obviously, God's supremacy in the sphere of power had its counterpart in faith to believe. The manifestation of power in the kingdom of God implied faith on the part of the one who witnessed God's power. Every miracle performed by Jesus had the design of stimulating the faith of those who experienced the working of the miracle, as well as of those who beheld it. A few striking examples of this close relationship will clarify this point. The two blind men who followed Jesus crying, "Have mercy on us, Son of David," were confronted with Jesus' question, "Do you believe that I am able to do this?" To this they replied, "Yes, Lord." Touching their eyes, Jesus said, "According to your faith be it done to you." At once their eyes were opened (Mt. 9:27-31). In the same graphic manner, Mark related the healing of the epileptic boy (Mk. 9:14-29). The father said, "If you can do anything, have pity on us and help us." While some authorities interpret Jesus' reply as a retort to the father, I believe that the syntactical structure of verse 23 leads, rather, to the idea that Jesus was leading the despairing father to a commitment of faith in His power to heal. In response to Jesus' words, "All things are possible to him who believes," the father said, "I believe; help my unbelief!"

In a setting which involved the disciples, the story of the withered fig tree, faith, as the counterpart to God's omnipotence, again becomes the focal point. Peter's amazement at the withered fig tree led Jesus to say, "Have faith in God. Truly, I say to you, whoever says to this mountain, 'Be taken up and cast into the sea,' and does not doubt in his heart, but believes that what he says will come to pass, it will be done for him. Therefore I tell you, whatever you ask in prayer, believe that you have received it, and it will be yours" (Mk. 11:22-24). Many Christians have stumbled at such a promise but Jesus meant exactly what He said. These miraculous incidents are but a sampling of many similar ones wrought by Christ, through which He led the people to believe in His messiahship. The meaning of faith should now be clear. Nevertheless, for the purposes of this study, there are values to probe more deeply into its various connotations.

The word *pistis* means *faith, belief, trust, confidence*. The verb form in the Septuagint is used to translate *aman*. This verb in its cognate forms occurs frequently in the Old Testament.[30] The verb form carries the meaning: *to be true, to remain faithful, to believe, to be firm, to be stable,* etc. This buildup of meaning throughout the Old Testament gave tremendous meaning to the word *pistis* and its cognates. Used in such incidents as Abraham's response to God's promises, Israel's deliverance from Egypt, and other great crises in Israel's history, these words became the natural response of New Testament believers to the miraculous signs performed by Jesus. It shows how the word *oligopistos: short of faith, little faith or trust* (Mt. 6:30; 8:26; 14:31; 16:8) was so forceful in rebuking those who refused to believe in God's miraculous power. The prepositions *eis* (Mt. 18:6; Jn. 3:15, 16, 18, 36) and *epi* (Mt. 27:42, 43) frequently used with *pistis* give the meaningful dimension of movement toward someone in the act of believing. This linguistic phenomenon adds stress to the relation between the believer and Christ.

It is also essential to lay hold of the ingredients of faith. With this quest in mind a rapid review of the miracles of Jesus will disclose at least two essential components: *knowledge* and *trust*. Jesus did not expect His followers to believe in His being the Messiah without adequate grounds. On this account, in every encounter with people in need He made Himself known to them through personal conversation; through sharing in their joys, sorrows, and inner conflicts; through His messages; and through His miracles. In other words, the first ingredient of faith is *knowledge*. They could not believe without adequate grounds on which to build their faith. This assumes the capability and willingness to understand the evidences upon which faith rests. The second element, *trust*, grows out of this knowledge. With open-mindedness to this knowledge of Jesus gained through His words, acts, and miracles, people were inspired to place their trust in Jesus. This becomes plain in the more detailed incidents such as His conversation with His earliest followers, His interchange of words with the woman of Samaria, the heart-to-heart words with Mary and Martha, and the faith-building words to the blind man. This trust, which became manifest among the believers, was not an act of momentary duration, but of an abiding nature. As Jesus spoke to the woman who had suffered from a hemorrhage, He said, "Take heart, daughter; your faith has made you well [has saved you]" (Mt. 9:22). The verb *save* is in the perfect tense and expressed the abiding nature of faith. Perhaps most climactic are the words of Peter's confession when he said, "We have believed, and have come to know, that you are the Holy One of God" (Jn. 6:69). These words are matched by Jesus' testimony, "The Father himself loves you, because you have loved me and have believed that I came from the Father" (Jn. 16:27).

This examination of faith's ingredients stands in sharp contrast with the component elements of unbelief. A few thoughts on the makeup of unbelief will contribute to a positive understanding of faith. When Jesus was teaching in the synagogue of His own country, many people were astonished at His words. They asked, "Where did this man get all this? What is the wisdom given to him? What mighty works are wrought by his hands!" (Mk. 6:2). Because He was of their own town and they knew all of His relatives, they could not accept Jesus as a prophet. On this account "he could do no mighty work there, except that he laid his hands upon a few sick people and healed them" (Mk. 6:5). Their trouble was *unbelief.* The Greek word used here is *apistia* meaning: *faithlessness, unbelief, lack of belief, want of faith and trust,* etc. The minds of the people were closed to the idea that one of their number could be a prophet. On the occasion of the disciples' inability to heal the epileptic boy, Jesus exclaimed, "O faithless and perverse generation" (Mt. 17:17). The two descriptive adjectives used here are very forceful. The adjective *apistos* means *without faith or trust.* In this setting it referred specifically to their being *without trust in God.* The second adjective intensified the idea of *faithlessness* by the use of a participial form *diastrepho.* Jesus labeled them as *being perverted, corrupted, distorted* — in a word, *wicked.*

Thus faithlessness went deeper than merely a lack of faith. There was an inward corruption and perversity which expressed itself in a refusal to believe. Jesus used yet another descriptive term, *hardness of heart,* when He explained why Moses had allowed divorce among the people. This is an expressive figurative term which describes a spiritual condition of a wide scope. The uses of the word *heart (kardia)* denotes the seat and center of all physical and spiritual life. In the latter sense it looks to "the soul or mind, as it is the fountain and seat of the thoughts, passions, desires, appetites, affections, purposes, endeavors."[31] The bearing of all this upon the meaning of faith in its correlate relation to God's supremacy in the sphere of power should now be evident. When man refuses to believe in God's omnipotence, there is inevitably the most serious spiritual defection. It is not a mere absence or lack of faith, putting it as mildly as possible, but rather a refusal to believe, having its basis in inward corruption and perversity due to stubbornness, obstinancy, and hardness of heart.

The Gospel of John presents quite distinctive teaching on the subject of faith and on this account deserves a separate treatment. A book-study approach to this Gospel leads us to observe that the dominant structure of thought in this book has to do with the issues of faith and unbelief. The prologue (1:1-18) gives a forecast of these issues. John presented the issues in 1:19 — 4:54; chapters 5 to 12 deal with these issues; and chapters 13 to 20 show their culmination. The clue to this structure appears in 20:31: "These are written that you may believe that Jesus is the Christ, the Son of God, and that believing you may have life in his name." His approach was by way of presenting testimony in support of this purpose and finally by showing that this faith in Christ leads to eternal life.[32]

It was John's central purpose to show how faith is based on personal witness and testimony, and that it centers in Christ. One of the most striking phenomena is the aspect of faith expressed by the language "believed in him."[33] As noted earlier, this construction represents a movement toward or a commitment to someone. Among the pertinent ideas expressed in these references, note that they who believe in Him have eternal life. They receive the Holy Spirit. They shall never die but shall see the glory of God.

Another distinctive teaching on faith found in this Gospel is the intimate relation between believing and knowing. As Peter expressed it, "We have believed, and have come to know, that you are the Holy One of God" (Jn. 6:69). In the good shepherd passage Jesus said, "I am the good shepherd; I know my own and my own know me, as the Father knows me and I know the Father; and I lay down my life for the sheep" (10:14, 15). Observe that the same intimate relationship which exists between the Father and the Son expresses the relationship between us and Christ. Jesus stated this truth in a negative fashion when He replied to the unbelieving Pharisees: "You know neither me nor my Father; if you knew me, you would know my Father also" (8:19). The Pharisees, through their refusal to believe in Jesus, were thus unable to know Him, neither did they know the Father even though they professed to be loyal to the law and to God.

Jesus expressed this same truth in a positive way to the disciples in the upper room. Among other things Jesus said, "No one comes to the Father, but by me. If you had known me, you would have known my Father also; henceforth you know him and have seen him. . . . He who has seen me has seen the Father. . . . The Father who dwells in me does his works. Believe me that I am in the Father and the Father in me" (14:6-11). Through this language Jesus was leading His disciples to comprehend the great truth that believing in Him leads to their knowledge of both Himself and the Father. Later in the upper room discourse (16:2, 3) Jesus said that the unbelieving Jews would put His disciples out of the synagogue because they did not know the Father or Himself.

John also recorded the source of unbelief, as well as of faith (Jn. 3:19-21). He wrote, "And this is the judgment, that the light has come into the world, and men loved darkness rather than light, because their deeds were evil. For every one who does evil hates the light, and does not come to the light, lest his deeds should be exposed. But he who does what is true comes to the light, that it may be clearly seen that his deeds have been wrought in God." The stern truth revealed in these words is that unbelief is not due to a lack of knowledge but rather to a love of darkness rather than light, to a love of sin rather than righteousness. A guilty conscience revolts against the exposure of sin. The source of faith is the individual's love for the light. He comes to the light that he may gain the assurance that his deeds have been wrought in God. Thus the source of faith is the inner desire to gain the approval of God.

Worthy of stress is the truth that the believer in Christ already has eternal life.[34] One of the most pointed statements are the words: "He who believes in the Son has eternal life; he who does not obey the Son shall not see life, but the wrath of God rests upon him" (3:36). The present tenses in this verse express continuous action in present time. Thus, believing in the Son and not obeying the Son do not refer to single acts as the aorist tense would express. The same idea applies to the present possession of eternal life as well as the present reality of God's wrath resting upon an unbeliever. In slightly different language, Jesus said, "He who hears my word and believes him who sent me, has eternal life; he does not come into judgment, but has passed from death to life" (5:24). Here the perfect tense (has passed) expresses a present state resulting from a past act.

d. The Blessedness of God and Its Correlate: Salvation

The grounds for recognizing blessedness as a sphere of God's supremacy may not be as explicit as some of the other aspects, but I trust that in this presentation this sphere of supremacy will become entirely clear and full of meaning. The words of Jesus which suggest this idea come from His Olivet Discourse. "Well done, good and faithful servant; you have been faithful over a little, I will set you over much; enter into the *joy* [*chara*] of your master" (Mt. 25:21). "Then the King will say to those at his right hand, 'Come, O *blessed [eulogeo]* of my Father, inherit the kingdom prepared for you from the foundation of the world" (v. 34). At the close of this judgment scene the righteous will go away into eternal life. On the occasion of the triumphal entry the people cried out saying, "Hosanna! *Blessed [eulogeo]* be he who comes in the name of the Lord!" (Mk. 11:9). When Jesus was being tried before the chief priests and the elders, the high priest asked Him, "Are you the Christ, the Son of the *Blessed [eulogetos]*?" To this Jesus replied, "I am; and you will see the Son of man seated at the right hand of Power, and coming with the clouds of heaven" (Mk. 14:61, 62). Since the righteous enter into a state of blessedness in heaven we may properly conclude that in this sphere of blessedness God is supreme.

(1) The Old Testament Background of Jesus' Teaching on Blessedness. The earliest references to blessedness in relation to God occur in Genesis (Gen. 9:26; 14:19, 20; 26:29; 49:25). In the prophetic blessing given by Noah to Shem he said, "Blessed by the Lord my God be Shem" (9:26). From this we may gather that only a God of blessedness could bless Shem. Melchizedek pronounced a prophetic blessing upon Abraham, in the words, "Blessed be Abram by God Most High, maker of heaven and earth; and blessed be God Most High" (14:19, 20).

Significant for our purpose are the words of the psalmist, "Thou dost show me the path of life; in thy presence there is fulness of joy, in thy right hand are pleasures for evermore" (Ps. 16:11). While Jesus did not quote this verse, the thought contained herein certainly constitutes the substratum of all that He spoke about the joys of heaven. Along with this there are a number of psalms which speak of the present joy and felicity of the godly, of those who fear God, of those who are forgiven, of those who put their trust in Him.[35] A study of these precious gems would certainly lead to the conclusion that these righteous ones do not have joy and happiness only in this life but that at God's right hand they will enjoy pleasures for evermore.

(2) Jesus' Teaching of Blessedness Centered in Kingdom Eschatology

(a) Blessedness Taught in the Sermon on the Mount. Jesus opened this great message by using the word *makarios (blessed)* which is used frequently in the Septuagint to translate the Hebrew word *ashere*, which has the meaning: *happy, blessed.* Its frequent use in the Old Testament, especially in the Psalms listed in note 35, shows that the word in its adjective and verb forms was very familiar to those who read their Scriptures. It is evident that Jesus regarded *makarios* and *ashere* as synonyms.

The most remarkable phenomena in the Beatitudes is the fact that He calls those blessed who are experiencing suffering in life. Thus the poor in spirit, those who mourn, those who hunger and thirst for righteousness, and especially those who are persecuted for righteousness' sake, are blessed and happy. In each case the sad and painful experiences of life are offset by those of superlative value which far outweigh the negative experiences of life. Thus to be a possessor of the kingdom of heaven, to be comforted, to inherit the earth, to see God, to be called sons of God, etc., possess values which lead to unmistakable happiness and joy. Thus while many experiences of life are most heartrending, the spiritual values to all who are suffering through these experiences are so immeasurable great that they are truly happy.

In view of all these circumstances Jesus could very properly say, "Rejoice and be glad, for your reward is great in heaven" (Mt. 5:12).

Later in this sermon Jesus encouraged His disciples not to be anxious about the temporal needs of life in the framework of thought of an Oriental king who is a dispenser of gifts to his subjects. He concluded His advice with the words, "But seek first his kingdom and his righteousness, and all these things shall be yours as well" (6:33). It is possible that Jesus continued His message with the words, "Fear not, little flock, for it is your Father's good pleasure to give you the kingdom" (Lk. 12:32). These words give the promised blessedness a real eschatological connotation in relation to the kingdom. To be a sharer in the kingdom means to experience fullness of joy.

In parable form, Jesus showed how the kingdom of heaven may be compared to a king who gave a marriage feast for his son (Mt. 22:1-14). When the invited guests did not come to the feast, he invited others of lower status to share the feast. When the king discovered that one of these did not have a wedding garment, he was cast into outer darkness. Jesus closed the parable with the words, "For many are called, but few are chosen." This again sets forth the blessedness of those who shall share in the kingdom of heaven. Jesus' closing words present a truth which adds another perspective to this theme of kingdom blessedness. In the parable, only those who wear the wedding garment will be permitted to share in the blessedness of the marriage feast. Luke recorded a similar story (Lk. 14:12-24), evidently not a parallel to Matthew's parable. One of those who sat at a table with Jesus commented: "Blessed is he who shall eat bread in the kingdom of God!" (v. 15). In response to this Jesus gave the story similar to Matthew's parable. The point to be observed is the blessedness of those who shall eat bread in the kingdom of God. It suggests the eternal joys of the redeemed in heaven.

(b) Kingdom Blessedness as Taught in the Parables. The parables of the hidden treasure and of the pearl of great price (Mt. 13:44-46) speak of kingdom blessedness from a slightly different angle. On discovering these treasures the individuals sell all that they have to purchase them. In the former, the note of joy is sounded, but this is also implied in the latter. Both of these parables undoubtedly have first reference to the present reality of the kingdom of heaven. However, the eternal aspect of the kingdom is undoubtedly also held in view. The earthly joys of acquiring these treasures undoubtedly have their spiritual counterpart in the future, eternal kingdom of heaven.

In the parable of the talents (Mt. 25:14-30) those who had used their talents as their master had designed hear the joyful commendation, "Well done, good and faithful servant; you have been faithful over a little, I will set you over much; enter into the joy of your master" (v. 21). This graphic manner of picturing the kingdom of heaven again sets forth the blessedness of the future. As I noted earlier this is one of the key verses which support the idea of God's supremacy in this sphere of blessedness. In the presence of God is supreme blessedness. Jesus passed from this parable to His message on the last judgment (vv. 25:31-46). In this scene "the King will say to those at his right hand, 'Come, O blessed of my Father, inherit the kingdom prepared for you from the foundation of the world' " (v. 34). The perfect participle form of *eulogeo* (blessed) expresses God's pronouncement of praise and blessedness upon those who shall inherit the heavenly kingdom. They shall enter into eternal life. Such commendation given by the King by its very content expresses the blessedness of the Father which will be shared by those at His right hand. Luke recorded the parables of the lost sheep and of the lost coin in which he said, "There will be more joy in heaven over one sinner who repents than over ninety-nine righteous persons who need no repentance" (Lk. 15:7, 10).

The closing thought given in the parable of the prodigal son expresses a similar note of joy. It reads, "It was fitting to make merry and be glad, for this your brother was dead, and is alive; he was lost, and is found" (Lk. 15:11-32). Moving to the spiritual significance of this parable, we see the note of joy on the part of the heavenly Father. There is restoration to sonship both in this life and in the next.

(c) Nature of Kingdom Blessedness. Here are Jesus' gracious words: "Come to me, all who labor and are heavy-laden, and I will give you rest. Take my yoke upon you, and learn from me; for I am gentle and lowly in heart, and you will find rest for your souls" (Mt. 11:28, 29). Jesus drew a comparison between the rest from physical labor and the carrying of heavy burdens, and that of a spiritual relief from the cares and perplexities of life. There are the spiritual burdens of defeat, severe trials, unsolvable problems, and conflicts with sin for which God, through Christ, alone can give rest. Thus one aspect of God's blessedness is the rest which He can bestow upon His children. The nature of kingdom blessedness becomes apparent again in Jesus' discourse on humility (Mt. 18:3-14; Mk. 9:42-50). Here kingdom blessedness becomes evident in the language of entering into life and of entering into the kingdom of God. The angels are always beholding the face of the Father who is in heaven. In parable language the shepherd rejoices more over the recovery of the lost sheep than of those which never had gone astray. So it is with the heavenly Father. In sharp contrast with those doomed to the outer darkness is the immeasurable glory of the scene picturing Abraham, Isaac, and Jacob and all the prophets, together with the men who will come from the east and west and from the north and the south who will sit at table in the kingdom of God (Lk. 13:28-30). Those sitting at this table will be sharing in the blessedness of the Father. One of those who sat at the table with Jesus at the house of the Pharisee said, "Blessed is he who shall eat bread in the kingdom of God!" (Lk. 14:15). One more illustration comes in Jesus' response to the ruler who asked, "What shall I do to inherit eternal life?" Jesus' closing words in His reply were, "In the new world when the Son of man shall sit on his glorious throne, you who have followed me will also sit on twelve thrones, judging the twelve tribes of Israel. And everyone who has left houses or brothers or sisters or father or mother or children or lands, for my name's sake, will receive a hundredfold, and inherit eternal life" (Mt. 19:28, 29; Mk. 10:28-31; Lk. 18:18-30). Such is the descriptive language of the new world, that which pictures the blessedness of being in the presence of the heavenly Father.

By way of a brief summary: (1) Where God is, is blessedness. This asserts the heaven-centered character of blessedness. (2) Blessedness needs to be viewed in its eschatological aspect. While blessedness is experienced already in this life, the culmination of blessedness will be realized in the new world, where the heavenly Father who is supreme in blessedness rules in glorious majesty.

(3) Salvation, the Correlate to Blessedness

(a) The Basis of This Correlate. This point becomes evident when we observe Jesus' words to the twelve disciples on the occasion of their being sent out on a preaching mission (Mt. 10:5-23). He warned them that they were being sent out as sheep in the midst of wolves and of their being hated by their fellow countrymen. Nevertheless, He encouraged them with the words, "He who endures to the end will be saved" (v. 22). This looks to a future experience having its beginning after this life. When Jesus told the disciples that it is the Father's good pleasure to give them the kingdom, He added the words, "Blessed are those servants whom the master finds awake when he comes" (Lk. 12:32-38). This counterpart, salvation, gains larger meaning through the following expressions: (1) Blessedness (Mt. 5:3-12; Lk. 14:14, 15). (2) Life (Mt. 19:29; 25:46; Mk. 9:42-50; Jn. 3:16). (3) Joy (Mt. 25:21). (4) Rest (Mt. 11:28, 29). (5) Salvation (Mt. 10:22; 24:13; Lk. 1:68; 8:12; 19:10).

(b) The Old Testament Concept of Salvation. Frequent nonreligious uses of the verb *save* in its various forms furnish the mold for their spiritual meaning (Gen. 47:25; Num. 10:9; Josh. 6:25; 1 Sam. 10:19; 2 Sam. 19:5). The formative idea in these uses of the verb *save* is that a person is not able to save himself. He is saved by another. Throughout Israel's history the Lord sent saviors and deliverers to His people (Gen. 45:7; Judg. 3:9, 15; 2 Kings 13:5; Neh. 9:27). Significant in these instances is that God had provided these saviors. It was entirely natural that the idea of salvation should gain a spiritual connotation. Accordingly herein lies the foundation of Hoffmann's *Heilsgeschichte* (salvation history) which interpreted Old Testament history as being an account of God's saving acts. He saw in this sacred history an organic and progressive unfolding of God's plan of salvation. The core-idea of this salvation became apparent in Moses' words to Israel at the Red Sea when he said, "Fear not, stand firm, and see the salvation of the Lord, which he will work for you today" (Ex. 14:13). Israel needed to put their trust in the Lord who would deliver them by His divine power in dividing the Red Sea.

Throughout the Old Testament the words *salvation, deliverance, Redeemer,* and *Savior* gained a spiritual significance which was definitely foundational to the New Testament meaning of these several terms.[36] Among the most expressive with regard to the spiritual meaning of these words are the following, "Let the words of my mouth and the meditation of my heart be acceptable in thy sight, O Lord, my rock and my redeemer" (Ps. 19:14). "The Lord is my light and my salvation; whom shall I fear? The Lord is the stronghold of my life; of whom shall I be afraid?" (Ps. 27:1). "Was it not I, the Lord? . . . a righteous God and a Savior. . . . Turn to me and be saved, all the ends of the earth! For I am God, and there is no other" (Is. 45:21, 22).

The great Servant of the Lord passage (Is. 52:7 — 53:12) is the *summum bonum* of the Old Testament teachings on salvation. It centers in the good tidings which announce the salvation to be wrought by the Servant of the Lord. This salvation is made possible through His suffering and death. This is the cost of removing our transgression and iniquities. The Lord laid on Him the iniquity of us all. The Servant was an offering for sin. Through knowledge of His redemptive work this righteous Servant will make many to be accounted righteous. This, in brief, was the prophet's forecast of the salvation made possible through the Servant of the Lord. Jesus and the apostles interpreted this Servant of the Lord passage as being fulfilled in Christ.

(c) Jesus Heralded as the Savior. In further pursuit of this study of salvation as the correlate to blessedness it is essential to observe that the infancy narratives of Jesus announced Him as being the Savior. An angel of the Lord told Joseph that Mary would bear a son who should be named Jesus, "For he will save his people from their sins" (Mt. 1:20, 21). Before the birth of Jesus, Zechariah prophesied, "Blessed be the Lord God of Israel, for he has visited and redeemed his people, and has raised up a horn of salvation for us in the house of his servant David" (Lk. 1:68). Referring to his newborn son Zechariah added, "You will go before the Lord to prepare his ways, to give knowledge of salvation to his people in forgiveness of their sins, through the tender mercy of our God" (vv. 76-78). To the shepherds the angel said, "I bring you good news of a great joy which will come to all the people; for to you is born this day in the city of David a Savior, who is Christ the Lord" (2:10, 11).

When Simeon saw the baby Jesus he said, "Mine eyes have seen thy salvation which thou hast prepared in the presence of all peoples, a light for revelation to the Gentiles, and for glory to thy people Israel" (vv. 30-32). When the Baptist preached a baptism of repentance for the forgiveness of sins, he quoted Isaiah's words, "All flesh shall see the salvation of God" (3:3-6). The heart of these words concerning Jesus centered in His being the Savior who would bring salvation to mankind. Jesus embodied all the Old Testament predictions concerning the salvation promised by God.

(d) The Concept of Salvation Revealed in Jesus' Teaching. This discussion centers in the word *soteria* (*salvation, deliverance, preservation, safety*) and its correlate forms. These words were frequently used in the Septuagint to translate the Hebrew word *Yeshuah* and its correlates. In this linguistic manner the New Testament teaching on salvation built directly on the Old Testament. The spiritual connotation of the word *salvation* soon becomes evident in Jesus' teaching. To the woman of Samaria Jesus said, "Salvation is from the Jews" (Jn. 4:22). And after the Samaritans heard the woman's testimony they said, "We know that this is indeed the Savior of the world" (v. 42). In order to gain a more accurate understanding of this word, let us examine some of its different usages. The verb *sozo* carries the literal meaning *to heal, to cure*.[37] These uses vary from a medical connotation to that of being healed of demon-possession to the raising of one from the dead. In these cases the English translation of *sozo* varies from heal to make well. The element of faith on the part of those who were being healed added significance to Christ's miraculous acts of healing. These expressions of faith suggest a spiritual aspect of these healings, and this becomes a meaningful stepping-stone to the spiritual uses of the verb *sozo*. This verb is used also to express a being saved from death (Mt. 8:25; 14:30; 16:25). On the stormy sea of Galilee the disciples said to Jesus, "Save, Lord; we are perishing" (8:25). These incidents of being saved from physical death bear a close relationship to the definitely spiritual acts of being saved from spiritual death.[38] The spiritual aspect of *sozo* is plainly evident when it is equated with entrance into the kingdom of God. Those who believe in the Son of God will not perish but have eternal life. The purpose of the Son's coming into the world was to save the world. Those who do not believe in the Son are condemned. In the thought framework of Jesus' being the door of the sheep, they who enter the sheepfold through Jesus will be saved. Jesus enriched this idea still more by saying, "I came that they may have life, and have it abundantly" (Jn. 10:10). The price of this salvation is the life of the shepherd. In another context Jesus said, "I did not come to judge the world but to save the world" (12:47). This being saved is the receiving of eternal life.

Another approach to the meaning of *sozo* is by the way of its antonym *apollumi* (*to destroy, lose utterly, perish, to be lost, lose eternal life*). Many of the occurrences of this verb are in close proximity to the uses of *sozo*.[39] These examples of saving one's life and of perishing teach that man in his natural state is lost and can be saved only through the redemptive act of Jesus the Savior — this appropriated by faith. The connotations of being condemned and being subject to judgment speak expressly of the awfulness of perishing and of being lost. Other uses of *apollumi* intensify the special meaning of this verb as it stands in opposition to being saved.[40] The most significant among these is Jesus' warning, "Fear him who can destroy both soul and body in hell" (Mt. 10:28). This leads us to understand that the idea expressed by perishing is not merely the negative one of not gaining eternal life but rather that of suffering eternal punishment.

By way of summarizing the concept of salvation in Jesus' teachings let us note the following. First, Christ through His death became the Savior of the world. Second, by nature all men are lost. They are saved alone through repentance from sin. Third, salvation looks both to the present and also to the future. This eschatological factor broadens and intensifies the concept of salvation. The present aspect of salvation has its basis in the experience of being born of the Spirit. It includes the forgiveness of sins and the deliverance from the bondage and power of sin. The future aspect of salvation looks to its eternal character. The expression *eternal life* is most descriptive of this future aspect. Fourth, to be saved means to gain entrance to the kingdom of God. Fifth, there is need for the one who has been born anew to remain faithful and to endure to the end of life in order to gain eternal life. Sixth, those who gain eternal life enter into the blessedness of God.

(*e*) The Life of God and Its Counterpart, New Birth

(1) The Old Testament Background of God's Supremacy in the Sphere of Life. This becomes apparent in the Genesis accounts of Creation, according to which God created all the living creatures on the earth — the climax of which was the creation of man. Created in the image of God, man was a living being. God "breathed into his nostrils

the breath of life; and man became a living being" (Gen. 2:7). God made the *tree of life*, the fruit of which He designed man to eat after he had been obedient to the test of not eating from the *tree of the knowledge of good and evil*. By reason of his disobedience God drove him from the garden, lest he should take also of the *tree of life*, and eat, and live forever (3:22). So early did the Lord reveal two aspects of life, temporal and eternal. To Israel, God made clear two distinctions: on the one side, *life and good*, and on the other, *death and evil* (Deut. 30:15). The way of obedience to the commandments of the Lord would bring life, while disobedience, manifested by turning their hearts away from the Lord and of worshiping other gods, would cause them to perish. While these words do not explicitly set forth the idea of eternal life, this becomes implicit by reason of its being the opposite of death. Life and length of days in the promised land became the symbol of entering into the heavenly rest as described by the author of Hebrews (Heb. 3:7—4:13). Israel came to realize that "the word of God is living and active" (Heb. 4:12). Moses could properly conclude this admonition by saying, "Therefore choose life, that you and your descendants may live, loving the Lord your God, obeying his voice, and cleaving to him; for that means life to you and length of days" (Deut. 30:19, 20). David wrote the sublime words, "Thou dost show me the path of life; in thy presence there is fulness of joy, in thy right hand are pleasures for evermore!" (Ps. 16:11). He wrote also, "For with thee is the fountain of life; in thy light do we see light" (36:9). Most reverently another psalmist wrote "My soul thirsts for God, for the living God. When shall I come and behold the face of God?" To this he added, "By day the Lord commands his steadfast love; and at night his song is with me, a prayer to the God of my life" (42:2, 8). It was the special and unique joy of these godly Old Testament saints to speak or write of their living God.

(2) Jesus' Unfolding of God's Supremacy in the Sphere of Life. For purposes of clarity and greater accuracy the great number of references which set forth Jesus' unfolding of God's supremacy in the sphere of life may be grouped in three sections: the direct assertions of Christ concerning this supremacy of God, the manifestations of this supremacy in Christ, and indirect statements which quite clearly assume God's supremacy in the sphere of life.

When Peter made his noble confession, "You are the Christ, the Son of the living God," Jesus replied that the Father had revealed this truth to him (Mt. 16:16, 17). In a setting where Jesus was speaking of the resurrection He said, "He is not God of the dead, but of the living; for all live to him" (Lk. 20:38). Caiaphas accused Jesus, "I adjure you by the living God," to which Jesus gave no rebuttal (Mt. 26:63). Jesus' view of God was in perfect harmony with the Hebrew Scriptures.

We look to John's Gospel for the fullest testimony to Jesus' unfolding of God's supremacy in the sphere of life. When John recorded Jesus' testimony concerning Himself, he quoted the words, "For as the Father raises the dead and gives them life, so also the Son gives life to whom he will. . . . The hour is coming, and now is, when the dead will hear the voice of the Son of God, and those who hear will live. For as the Father has life in himself, so he has granted to the Son also to have life in himself" (Jn. 5:21-26). This profound truth will become evident when "all who are in the tombs will hear his voice and come forth, those who have done good, to the resurrection of life, and those who have done evil, to the resurrection of judgment" (vv. 28, 29). Jesus closed His bread of life discourse with the words, "As the living Father sent me, and I live because of the Father, so he who eats me will live because of me. . . . He who eats this bread will live for ever" (6:57, 58).

Most certainly God's supremacy in the sphere of life was also manifested in Christ the Son. From the very beginning of his Gospel John attributed life to Christ. Concerning the *logos* John wrote, "In him was life, and the life was the light of men" (Jn. 1:4). The greatest verse of the Holy Writ included the words, "Whoever believes in him should not perish but have eternal life" (3:15, 16, 36). To the woman of Samaria Jesus said, "The water that I shall give him will become in him a spring of living water welling up to eternal life" (4:14). To Martha, Jesus spoke the comforting words, "I am the resurrection and the life; he who believes in me, though he die, yet shall he live, and whoever lives and believes in me shall never die" (11:25, 26). Jesus told Thomas, "I am the way, and the truth, and the life; no one comes to the Father, but by me" (14:6). In Jesus' prayer to the Father, we read, "Glorify thy Son that the Son may glorify thee, since thou hast given him power over all flesh, to give eternal life to all whom thou hast given him. And this is eternal life, that they know thee the only true God, and Jesus Christ whom thou hast sent" (17:1-3). The keynote to John's Gospel is expressed in the words "These are written that you may believe that Jesus is the Christ, the Son of God, and that believing you may have life in his name" (20:31).

So crucial are these references to the supremacy of God and of Christ in the sphere of life that a number of indirect statements deserve notice.[41] Among others, note the following in their respective contexts: "The gate is narrow and the way is hard, that leads to life" (Mt. 7:14). "It is better for you to enter life maimed or lame than with two hands or two feet to be thrown into the eternal fire" (18:8). "If you would enter life, keep the commandments" (19:17). "And everyone who has left houses or brothers . . . for my name's sake, will receive a hundredfold, and inherit eternal life" (v. 29). "And they will go away into eternal punishment, but the righteous into eternal life" (25:46). This sampling of indirect statements opens up a grand vista of the life which the only true and living God imparts to those who believe.

(3) Being Born Anew, the Subjective Counterpart of Life. This heading based on the words of Jesus to Nicodemus (Jn. 3:1-15) leads to the thought that this Gospel reveals most fully the nature of the experience of being born anew. Jesus clearly explained to Nicodemus that a spiritual experience like that of natural birth was necessary for entrance into God's kingdom. This new-birth experience was one brought about through the Holy Spirit. This analogy with natural birth prepares one to understand spiritual birth. Being born anew is being born from above. God's power through the Holy Spirit brings about this birth. Entrance into the kingdom of God is accomplished through this inner working of the Holy Spirit. This conversation clearly sets forth the counterpart in human experience of God's supremacy in the sphere of life.

Throughout the Gospel of John this truth becomes evident in other settings of Jesus' teaching. Jesus revealed Himself as the Life-Giver. He makes possible this new experience of receiving life from above. The climax of Jesus' words with Nicodemus expressed this idea most fully. The grand truth is that whoever believes in the Son has eternal life. To the woman of Samaria Jesus said, "The water that I shall give him will become in him a spring of water welling up to eternal life" (Jn. 4: 14). To the Jews in Jerusalem Jesus said, "The Son gives life to whom he will. . . . he who hears my word and believes him who sent me, has eternal life" (5:21-24). In the bread of life discourse (6:26-51) Jesus told His followers to labor "for the food which endures to eternal life, which the Son of man will give to you" and concluded with the words, "I am the living bread which came down from heaven; if any one eats of this bread, he will live for ever; and the bread which I shall give for the life of the world is my flesh" (v. 51).

To the Pharisees at the Feast of Tabernacles Jesus said, "If any one thirst, let him come to me and drink. He who believes in me, as the scripture has said, 'Out of his heart shall flow rivers of living water.' " John interpreted these words as referring to the Holy Spirit which those who believed in Him were to receive (7:37-39). In His good shepherd message Jesus said, "I came that they may have life, and have it abundantly" (10:10). Near the close of this message He added, "I give them eternal life, and they shall never perish" (v. 28). Centered in the work of the Holy Spirit are Jesus' words, "Because

I live, you will live also" (14:19). In His prayer Jesus spoke of Himself as the Life-Giver in the words, "Glorify thy Son that the Son may glorify thee, since thou hast given him power over all flesh, to give eternal life to all whom thou hast given him. And this is eternal life, that they know thee the only true God, and Jesus Christ whom thou hast sent" (17:1-3). John had certainly grasped the great purpose of Jesus' ministry and in a unique way set forth the main purpose of his Gospel (20:30, 31).

It is essential to observe further the conditions or requirements for receiving life as taught by Jesus. Several of the passages quoted above give an explicit answer to this inquiry. Briefly stated, "He who hears my word and believes him who sent me, has eternal life."[42]

The other Gospel records also unfold the ethical conditions for receiving life. Thus the Sermon on the Mount holds forth perfection as found in the Father, together with His righteousness, as the standard of life for the believer. It involves a life of self-discipline which necessitates entering by the narrow gate and going forward on the hard way. It requires implicit obedience to the words taught by Jesus. This self-discipline comes forcefully into the foreground when Jesus said, "If your hand or your foot causes you to sin, cut it off and throw it from you; it is better for you to enter life maimed or lame than with two hands or two feet to be thrown into eternal fire." The same is true of the offending eye (Mt. 18:8, 9; Mk. 9:43-50). The lawyer who asked Jesus what he should do to inherit eternal life, himself gave the correct answer, "You shall love the Lord your God with all your heart, and with all your soul, and with all your strength, and with all your mind; and your neighbor as yourself." In response Jesus said, "Do this, and you will live" (Lk. 10:25-28). This incident presents in a positive manner the condition for receiving life. In sharp contrast with this requirement for receiving life, Jesus spoke of all the evil things which come from the heart and defile the man. The practice of these sins causes one to lose life. The thirteen evil things listed by Jesus expose so many ways of failing to meet the conditions for receiving life. Tragically, these evil things come from the heart (Mk. 7:18-23).

Being born anew as the subjective counterpart of life possesses another dimension of inexpressible meaning. It is the eschatological perspective bound up in the present and future aspects of life. A number of the Johannine passages already noted set forth this truth.[43] At least two truths should be gained from these references: first, the present possession of eternal life experienced by those who believe; and second, the future experience bound up in the words "the resurrection of life." The present stage of life leads to the inexpressibly most glorious resurrection life. Jesus described this future stage of life in the words, "In the new world, when the Son of man shall sit on his glorious throne, you who have followed me will also sit on twelve thrones, judging the twelve tribes of Israel. And every one who has left houses or brothers or sisters or father or mother or children or lands, for my name's sake, will receive a hundredfold, and inherit eternal life" (Mt. 19:28-30). Mark's reference to these words makes it clear that the hundredfold blessings are experienced now in this time, and the blessedness of eternal life in the age to come (Mk. 10:29-31).

In Chapter X I will discuss more fully Jesus' division of time between the present age and the age to come. This has its bearing on the kingdom of God. First, there is the temporal aspect of this kingdom; and second, is the eternal aspect or facet. The return of Christ will terminate the temporal stage of the kingdom. This becomes evident in Jesus' explanation of the weeds of the field parable. The harvest marks the close of the age when "the Son of man will send his angels, and they will gather out of his kingdom all causes of sin and all evildoers. . . . Then the righteous will shine like the sun in the kingdom of their Father" (Mt. 13:37-43). In this parable Jesus declared that His rule in the kingdom continues until His return, which marks the close of this age. At the consummation of this age the Father begins His rule. In the present kingdom both righteous and unrighteous are found, but in the Father's kingdom only the righteous will share its glory.

Jesus expanded this eschatological aspect of the kingdom most fully in His Olivet Discourse (Mt. 24, 25). Building on the story of the Flood Jesus spoke of the imminency of His return. Just as the Flood in the days of Noah destroyed all things on the earth, so the return of our Lord will terminate this age, marked by the passing away of heaven and earth. The judgment scene of Matthew 25:31-46 leads to the righteous inheriting the kingdom prepared for them from the foundation of the world. The inheritance of this kingdom is their entrance into eternal life. This judgment scene stands as the climax in the way of distinguishing the present and future aspects of life. Taking a final look at the supremacy of God in the sphere of life, let us observe the most glorious truth, that the counterpart in human experience to this sphere of life is the new birth. This new-birth experience leads to the present possession of eternal life and advances to the eternal stage of this life brought about by our Lord in the resurrection.

f. The Love of God and Man's Response in Love and Obedience

Since each of these spheres of God's supremacy possesses overwhelming meaning to a child of God, the order of their discussion possesses little significance. Further, since each sphere of God's supremacy sets forth some attribute of His nature, all of them possess Deity significance. By reason of man's sinfulness God's love comes the closest to human need. On this account we may feel that the love of God stands first among His attributes. Moreover, since all of these spheres of God's supremacy constitute one grand unity in God's nature, there are no grounds for compartmentalizing them. This truth becomes evident when we observe the overlapping of the multitude of Scripture references which support these several spheres of supremacy. The sole purpose of my giving separate treatment of each sphere of God's supremacy is to magnify the greatness of God's glory.

The Old Testament background of God's love and of man's response in love and obedience is instructive.[44] In the Ten Commandments, God made the declaration that He shows steadfast love to thousands of those who love Him and keep His commandments (Ex. 20:6). A portion like Deuteronomy 7:6-13 brings together God's love for His chosen people and of Israel's response of love and obedience to Him. It also brings to the fore the covenant basis for God's love. Significant in this connection is the repetition of the statement just quoted from Exodus, but in this passage this love of God for His people is bound up with the covenant (vv. 9, 12). Israel was a people holy to the Lord and chosen for His own possession. On this account the faithful God keeps covenant and steadfast love with those who love Him and keep His commandments.

John 3:16 is the *summum bonum* New Testament disclosure of God's love for the world. This became most manifest in the suffering, death, and resurrection of our Lord. It was John's supreme mission to magnify God's love for Jesus and Jesus' love for the world. Interwoven with these great statements is the counterpart of man's response in love and obedience to God. Jesus said, "A new commandment I give to you, that you love one another; even as I have loved you, that you also love one another. By this all men will know that you are my disciples, if you have love for one another" (Jn. 13:34, 35). Other rich statements from the lips of Jesus occur in John 14:15, 21, 23, 24; 15:12, 17; 17:24, 26.

The synoptic Gospels record a number of significant teachings dealing with man's response of love and obedience to God. In the Sermon on the Mount, Jesus established a new standard in human relations which expresses the way of love which rises above the Old Testament teaching of "an eye for an eye and a tooth for a tooth." Jesus taught the turning of the other cheek and the going of the second mile. He said, "Love your enemies and pray for those who persecute you." Near the close of His sermon He declared that they who shall enter the kingdom of heaven are those who do the will of the heavenly Father (Mt. 5:38-46; 7:21). When Jesus sat down opposite the treasury He observed how many rich people put in large sums of money into the treasury, but the poor widow who put in her whole living received His special commendation. This was a graphic illustration of the difference between halfhearted obedience and truehearted obedience (Mk. 12:41-44).

In response to the lawyer's question as to which was the great commandment of the law, Jesus replied, "You shall love the Lord your God with all your heart, and with all your soul, and with all your mind, and with all your strength. . . . You shall love your neighbor as yourself" (Mk. 12:30, 31). Such a love response to God certainly involves implicit obedience. Jesus' Gethsemane prayer revealed the supreme test of obedience of the Son of God to the Father. He yielded to the will of the Father. So significant was this response of obedience on the part of Jesus that Paul used it in his letter to the Philippians in which he gave the pattern for Christian living. He encouraged the Philippians to have the mind of Christ who emptied Himself of His glory and took upon Himself the form of a servant. He humbled Himself and became obedient unto death, even death on the cross. This was the supreme response of the Man, Jesus, to the Father's love. Jesus would have us take up our cross and follow Him (Mt. 10:38; 16:24).

The author of Hebrews also laid hold of Jesus' obedience to the Father when he wrote, "Although he was a Son, he learned obedience through what he suffered" (Heb. 5:8). All this should lead us to recognize the supremacy of God in the sphere of love and man's response to God in love and obedience.

g. *The Authority (Lordship) of God and Man's Response in Discipleship*

(1) Old Testament Teaching on God's Authority. A vast array of passages in the Old Testament give support to the supremacy of God in the sphere of authority. As man's Creator, God gave authoritative commandments to Adam and Eve in the garden. He forbade them to eat of the tree of the knowledge of good and evil warning them of the death penalty if they would not be obedient. When man's wickedness degenerated to the point "that every imagination of the thoughts of his heart was only evil continually," God "determined to make an end of all flesh" (Gen. 6:5, 13). After the Flood the Lord declared that He would never again destroy every living creature.

Abraham recognized the supreme authority of the Lord when he left his homeland to go to the land of promise. When the Lord commanded Moses to lead Israel out of Egypt, he was deeply concerned about the way in which the people would challenge the authority of this command. God said to Moses, "Say this to the people of Israel 'I AM has sent me to you' " (Ex. 3:14). Incidents such as these could be drawn from all the rest of Old Testament history. They all have their basis in the authority set forth in the words, "The Lord is God in heaven above and on the earth beneath; there is no other" (Deut. 4:39). God's supreme authority shines forth in many of the psalms (19, 24, 33, 47, 93, 96, 97, 99).

(2) Jesus' Teaching on the Supremacy of God's Authority. To this authority Jesus gave witness when He declared that the Father had given all things into His hand (Jn. 3:35). Later in His ministry Jesus said, "All things have been delivered to me by my Father" (Mt. 11:27). John expressed his awareness of this fact when he wrote that Jesus knew that the Father had given all things into His hands (Jn. 13:3). Jesus' final testimony stood forth in the words, "All authority in heaven and on earth has been given to me" (Mt. 28:18). Peter's closing words in the sermon at Pentecost stand as a grand climax to this fact. He said, "Let all the house of Israel therefore know assuredly that God has made him both Lord and Christ, this Jesus whom you crucified" (Acts 2:36). From these Scriptures we may conclude that God's supremacy was manifested in His authority and that this authority was given to Jesus, the Messiah.

Jesus exercised this authority in a number of ways throughout His ministry. At the close of the Sermon of the Mount, Matthew noted, "the crowds were astonished at his teaching, for he taught them as one who had authority, and not as their scribes" (Mt. 7:28, 29). Jesus manifested His authority again in the choice of the twelve disciples whom He named apostles. To them He gave "authority over unclean spirits, to cast them out, and to heal every disease and every infirmity" (Mt. 10:1-4; Lk. 6: 13-16). The special responsibility given to the apostles of being witnesses of Jesus' ministry and of His resurrection as voiced by Peter gave added dimensions to the authority exercised by Him (Acts 1:21, 22). Jesus Himself voiced this in the Great Commission given to the apostles just before His ascension (Mt. 28:18-20).

Noting briefly the meaning of this Commission, Jesus gave attestation to the "all authority" which He was exercising. To the apostles He gave the charge of their making disciples of all nations. As I shall note later, the term *disciple* carried the connotation of being a committed follower of Jesus, a task that involved a cross as well. Those who were to become disciples were to be initiated into the body of Christ through water baptism, this to be done "in the name of the Father and of the Son and of the Holy Spirit." The apostles performed the initiatory rite of baptism under the authority of the triune God. This Commission included a teaching ministry through which all of Jesus' teaching would be brought to the entire human race. He to whom all authority had been given would be with them, "always to the close of the age." This is the manner in which Jesus was fulfilling the supreme authority given to Him and was giving direction to His declaration centering in the building of His church (Mt. 16:16-19). To the apostles Jesus gave the keys of the kingdom of heaven which indicated the authority entrusted to them of binding and loosing on earth. Heaven would validate the proper exercise of this delegated authority to the apostles.

(3) Discipleship, the Correlate to God's Supreme Authority. The counterpart in human experience to the supremacy of God in the sphere of authority is the response of discipleship. We have already noted that Jesus had a multitude of followers called disciples (Jn. 4:1; 6:60). Undoubtedly, many of Jesus' followers did not realize the meaning of being a disciple. On the occasion of Peter's great confession Jesus told His disciples of His coming suffering and death. Then He said, "If any man would come after me, let him deny himself and take up his cross daily and follow me" (Lk. 9:18-23). In this manner Jesus confronted His followers with the staggering truth that discipleship involved a cross. He declared further, "For whoever would save his life will lose it; and whoever loses his life for my sake, he will save it. For what does it profit a man if he gains the whole world and loses or forfeits himself? (vv. 24, 25). As Jesus and His disciples were on their way to Jerusalem, a man came to Him and said, "I will follow you wherever you go" (Lk. 9:57).

This gave Jesus the opportunity of explaining further the meaning of being a follower of Christ (vv. 58-62). Thus a disciple will need to suffer the human needs experienced by his Lord. When Jesus asked another person to follow Him, this one thought his first responsibility was that of fulfilling a son's responsibility to his father but Jesus told him that proclaiming the kingdom of God had first priority in his life, even above that of burying his father. A third man desired to become a follower of Christ but his affections were still set on those at his home. Jesus interpreted his attitude with the words, "No one who puts his hand to the plow and looks back is fit for the kingdom of God" (v. 62). These three incidents disclosed so many facets centering in the cross of discipleship.

Jesus gave yet another explication of the cross involved in discipleship (Lk. 14:25-35). On an occasion when great multitudes accompanied Jesus, He turned and spoke to them most forthrightly in heartrending language. "If any one comes to me and does not hate his own father and mother and wife and children and brothers and sisters, yes, and even his own life, he cannot be my disciple" (v. 26). It required language such as this for Jesus to show the multitudes, "Whoever does not bear his own cross and come after me, cannot be my disciple" (v. 27). Christian discipleship involves a fidelity to Christ which has dimensions far exceeding the fidelity of human family relationships. Nothing dare stand in the way of becoming a disciple of Christ. True indeed, it may involve a cross. By way of two illustrations, that of building a tower, and that of a king encountering another king in war, Jesus illustrated the far-reaching implications of counting the cost of discipleship (vv. 28-33). He closed this message with a fitting illustration drawn from a property of salt. He said, "Salt is good; but if salt has lost its taste, how shall its saltness be restored?" (vv. 34, 35). On the significance of this metaphor, Geldenhuys says, "Salt is valuable only when it possesses its special quality of saltness. So a follower of Jesus is of use and a blessing only when he possesses the particular character natural to a true disciple, and from the foregoing it is clear that the characteristic attribute of the true followers of Jesus is absolute unselfishness and self-sacrificing loyalty towards Him. He who does not renounce everything and is not willing to sacrifice for His sake is, as a disciple, just as valueless as salt that has gone stale and is consequently thrown away as useless."[45] Therefore, let us recognize God's supremacy in the sphere of authority by taking up our crosses and following Christ.

h. God's Revelation and Its Correlates: Belief and Knowledge

(1) God's Revelation in the Old Testament. The author of Hebrews sets forth this sphere of God's supremacy in the words, "In many and various ways God spoke of old to our fathers by the prophets; but in these last days he has spoken to us by a Son" (Heb. 1:1, 2). The frequent occurrences of such expressions as: "The Lord said . . ." "The Word of the Lord came to. . . ," and similar ones possess great meaning with reference to God's revelation to man. In a word, Deity was disclosing Himself to man. While the occurrences of the word *galah* translated *reveal* are limited, yet their significance is most meaningful. On Jacob's return to Canaan, "He built an altar, and called the place El-bethel, because there God had revealed himself to him" (Gen. 35:7). This revelation had taken place in the form of a dream in which he had seen angels of God ascending and descending on a ladder. The Lord spoke to Jacob and assured him that He would fulfill His promises made to him on the occasion of receiving his father's blessing. This experience portrayed the central truth of divine revelation. It is an unfolding, a disclosing, a manifesting act of God possible alone to the almighty God. A similar disclosure becomes evident in Pharaoh's dream concerning

which Joseph said, "God has revealed to Pharaoh what he is about to do" (41:25). In this case God's revealing work was one of making known or of showing Pharaoh what He was about to do. Moses' closing words to his covenant message were, "The secret things belong to the Lord our God; but the things that are revealed belong to us and to our children for ever, that we may do all the words of this law" (Deut. 29:29).

Another significant illustration comes to the fore in the case of Samuel. "Samuel was established as a prophet of the Lord. And the Lord appeared again at Shiloh, for the Lord revealed himself to Samuel at Shiloh by the word of the Lord" (1 Sam. 3:20, 21). This passage gives a buildup of the ideas associated with *revealed,* such as *prophet of the Lord, appear,* and *the word of the Lord.* These expressions give breadth and depth of meaning to the revealing word of the Lord.

Daniel's involvement in the interpretation of Nebuchadnezzar's dream disclosed still more fully the meaning of God's revealing activity (Dan. 2:19, 22, 28-30, 47). Nebuchadnezzar's dream confronted Daniel and his companions with a humanly unexplainable mystery. But this mystery was revealed to Daniel in a vision. It is God who "reveals deep and mysterious things; he knows what is in the darkness, and the light dwells with him" (v. 22). God revealed to Daniel not only the content of Nebuchadnezzar's dream but also its interpretation. The prophet Amos stressed still another aspect of God's revealing work by showing that God revealed His secrets to His servants, the prophets (Amos 3:7). Since the prophets were set apart to be the spokesmen of the Lord to His people, it was entirely natural that God should make His revelations to the prophets. This fact stresses both the importance and the authority of God's revelations to His people.

(2) God's Revelation in Christ. God's revelation to man ascended to its highest point in the person of Jesus our Lord. In the synagogue at Nazareth, Jesus read from Isaiah 61:1, 2 and commented that this Scripture was fulfilled in Him (Lk. 4:16-21). On another occasion Jesus said, "I thank thee, Father, Lord of heaven and earth, that thou hast hidden these things from the wise and understanding and revealed them to babes. . . . All things have been delivered to me by my Father; and no one knows the Son except the Father, and no one knows the Father except the Son and any one to whom the Son chooses to reveal him" (Mt. 11:25-27). It was this truth which led the crowds of people to recognize the authority of His teaching (7:28, 29). When the disciples asked Jesus why He spoke to them in parables, His answer revealed the real foundation of His teaching. Jesus said, "To you it has been given to know the secrets of the kingdom of heaven, but to them it has not been given. . . . Because seeing they do not see, and hearing they do not

hear, nor do they understand" (13:11-13). By this Jesus was saying that those who were willing to see and hear were granted the gift of knowing the secrets of the kingdom of heaven. My present interest in these words of Jesus centers in His making known to His disciples the secrets of the kingdom of heaven through His parables. This was clearly a disclosure through revelation. At Caesarea Philippi when Peter made his noble confession, "You are the Christ, the Son of the living God," Jesus answered, "Flesh and blood has not revealed this to you, but my Father who is in heaven" (16:16, 17). From this we would conclude that Peter's confession was not an intellectual appraisal of Jesus but rather that of a revelation to him by the Father. It was a spiritual comprehension gained through the Father's disclosure of this truth to him.

The Apostle John expanded most fully God's revelation through the Son. In the prologue he wrote, "The Word became flesh and dwelt among us, full of grace and truth; we have beheld his glory, glory as of the only Son from the Father." A few verses further on he wrote, "Grace and truth came through Jesus Christ. No one has ever seen God; the only Son, who is in the bosom of the Father, he has made him known" (Jn. 1:14, 17, 18). These declarations lay at the very heart of the entire Gospel. The Baptist sensed God's revealing work through Christ when he said, "I came baptizing with water, that he might be revealed to Israel" (v. 31). One of Jesus' earliest statements concerning Himself expressed this revelation which would come through Him. "You will see heaven opened, and the angels of God ascending and descending upon the Son of man" (v. 51). Jesus challenged Nicodemus with the words, "If I have told you earthly things and you do not believe, how can you believe if I tell you heavenly things?" (3:12). When the Jews challenged Jesus for healing the lame man He gave the fitting answer, "My Father is working still, and I am working" (5:17). Jesus underscored His answer by adding, "For as the Father raises the dead and gives them life, so also the Son gives life to whom he will" (v. 21). Jesus made it clear that the Father was revealing Himself in His Son. He explained this truth further in the words, "The works which the Father has granted me to accomplish, these very works which I am doing, bear me witness that the Father has sent me. And the Father who sent me has himself borne witness to me" (vv. 36, 37).

Jesus' discourse on the bread of life stated very clearly that the Father was revealing Himself through the Son (6:25-59). Note the statements, "My Father gives you the true bread from heaven" (v. 32); "I have come down from heaven, not to do my own will, but the will of him who sent me" (v. 38); and "As the living Father sent me, and I live because of the Father, so he who eats me will live because of me" (v. 57).

In another context, where Jesus was speaking of His mission in the world (8:12-59), He said, "I speak of what I have seen with my Father" (v. 38). And also, "I proceeded and came forth from God; I came not of my own accord, but he sent me" (v. 42). The contention which rose out of Jesus' good shepherd message led Him to say, "The works that I do in my Father's name, they bear witness to me" (10:25). And further on, "The Father is in me and I am in the Father" (v. 38). Most explicit are Jesus' words, "For I have not spoken on my own authority; the Father who sent me has himself given me commandment what to say and what to speak. . . . What I say, therefore, I say as the Father has bidden me" (12:49, 50). According to John's Gospel these were the last words spoken by Jesus in His public ministry. On this account they are exceedingly strategic in giving support to Jesus' claims that God was revealing Himself through the Son. With still greater clarity Jesus expressed His claims at the close of His upper room discourse (17:6-26). Note some of His outstanding expressions: "Now they know that everything that thou hast given me is from thee; for I have given them the words which thou gavest me, and they have received them and know in truth that I came from thee; and they have believed that thou hast sent me" (vv. 7, 8). "I made known to them thy name, and I will make it known, that the love with which thou hast loved me may be in them, and I in them" (v. 26).

(3) Belief and Knowledge, the Correlates of God's Revelation. The line of thought just presented leads us to see most clearly its bearing on the whole discipline of biblical theology. The core of this study is God's revelation. The climax of this revelation was in Jesus Christ. This grand truth helps us gain the proper understanding of the sphere of God's supremacy. The correlates, belief and knowledge, became evident in the Scriptures just presented. Looking again at the bread of life discourse note Jesus' words, "He who comes to me shall not hunger, and he who believes in me shall never thirst" (Jn. 6:35). These words were directed to some who refused to believe. This established the truth that God's revelation does not compel belief.

The response of belief and its accompanying knowledge is a voluntary act and is spiritual in nature. Most expressive are the words of Peter at the close of this scene when he said, "We have believed, and have come to know, that you are the Holy One of God" (v. 69). Peter was here testifying that Jesus had the words of eternal life. This evaluation of Jesus' teaching was about as compact and forthright as any recorded statement of His teaching. Jesus revealed the words of eternal life.

Jesus asked the man who had just received his sight, "Do you believe in the Son of man?" (Jn. 9:35). When he responded "Lord, I believe"

(v. 38), Jesus gave the spiritual significance of belief and unbelief. He said, "For judgment I came into this world, that those who do not see may see, and that those who see may become blind" (v. 39). Some of the Pharisees who heard this conversation refused to believe and therefore remained spiritually blind. They were aware of God's revelation through the miracle wrought by Jesus but refused to believe. In sharp contrast to this, the man born blind witnessed the same revelation but responded in faith and thereby came to know the Son of Man.

Looking again at Jesus' conversation during the Feast of Dedication (Jn. 10:22-42), He said, "The works that I do in my Father's name, they bear witness to me; but you do not believe" (v. 25). As the Jews were about to stone Him Jesus added, "If I am not doing the works of my Father, then do not believe me; but if I do them, even though you do not believe me, believe the works, that you may know and understand that the Father is in me and I am in the Father" (vv. 37, 38). This is another sample of how the Jews, who witnessed Jesus' revelation of God by word and deed, refused to believe. On this account they did not know and understand that the Father was in Christ and Christ was in the Father.

In sharp contrast to this attitude of unbelief was the response of faith on the part of others who came to Him and observed that everything spoken by the Baptist concerning Jesus was true. On this account many believed on Him (10:41, 42). The story of the raising of Lazarus disclosed again how Christ's revelation of Himself to Martha led to her response of belief and knowledge. Jesus said, "I am the resurrection and the life . . . and whoever lives and believes in me shall never die" (11:25, 26). To this she responded, "Lord; I believe that you are the Christ, the Son of God, he who is coming into the world" (v. 27). This response of belief and knowledge stands as a parallel to Peter's great confession. It would appear that John purposely presented this narrative as the climax of God's revelation through Christ with the accompanying response of belief and knowledge.

John's closing paragraph of Jesus' public ministry (12:44-50) may be regarded as Jesus' own summary of God's revelation through Him and of the intended response of belief and knowledge on the part of His hearers. Note His words, "He who believes in me, believes not in me but in him who sent me. . . . I have come as light to the world, that whoever believes in me may not remain in darkness. . . . I have not spoken on my own authority; the Father who sent me has himself given me commandment what to say and what to speak" (vv. 44-49). In Jesus' prayer to the Father He expressed yet again these same truths, this time in the context of prayer (Jn. 17). He prayed, "This is eternal life, that they know thee the only true God, and Jesus Christ whom thou hast sent" (v. 3). Later He said, "Now they know that everything thou hast given me is from thee; for I have given them the words which thou gavest me, and they have received them and know in truth that I came from thee; and they have believed that thou hast sent me" (vv. 7, 8). These words are a fitting climax to Jesus' teaching that knowledge and belief are the correlates to God's revelation in Christ.

Jesus' explanation of why He taught in parables expressed the same truth. He said, "To you it has been given to know the secrets of the kingdom of heaven, but to them it has not been given" (Mt. 13:11). Through parables He was revealing the secrets of the kingdom of heaven. But these secrets were understood only by those who were willing to "perceive with their eyes, and hear with their ears, and understand with their heart, and turn for me to heal them" (v. 15). Thus in the language of Isaiah, Jesus showed the spiritual requisite for believing and knowing God's revelation.

In closing let me note briefly the trend of thought which I have endeavored to set forth. I have sought to present the central truth of the good news as it sets forth the kingdom of God. Jesus had unfolded the concept of this kingdom. Throughout His teaching He revealed its essence. The pattern of my presentation has been to set forth the several spheres of God's supremacy as taught by Jesus and then to relate the respective responses or counterparts on the part of man. These human responses should lead us to understand more fully God's supremacy. Just as God is supreme in every aspect of His being, so man's response to God involves his total being.

For Additional Reading and Reference:

Bernard, *The Progress of Doctrine in the New Testament,* pp. 55-79.
Beyschlag, *New Testament Theology,* Vol. I, pp. 41-56.
Bowman, *Prophetic Realism and the Gospel,* pp. 190-234.
Bruce, A. B., *The Kingdom of God.*
Bruce, F. F., *New Testament Development of Old Testament Themes,* pp. 22-39.
Bultmann, *Theology of the New Testament,* Vol. I, pp. 3-11.
Conzelmann, *An Outline of the Theology of the New Testament,* pp. 106-127.
Filson, *The New Testament Against Its Environment,* pp. 93-110.
Hunter, *The Works and Words of Jesus,* pp. 68-79.
Jeremias, *New Testament Theology,* pp. 76-121.
Ladd, *Jesus and the Kingdom,* Chaps. 2, 3, 5, 9-12, 14.
Lundstrom, *The Kingdom of God in the Teaching of Jesus,* note, pp. 232-238.

Morgan, *The Teaching of Christ,* pp. 197-227.
Newman, *The Meaning of the New Testament,* pp. 132-163.
Richardson, *An Introduction to the Theology of the New Testament,* pp. 84-102.
Ryrie, *Biblical Theology of the New Testament,* pp. 72-95.
Sheldon, *New Testament Theology,* pp. 73-87, 107-122.
Stevens, *The Theology of the New Testament,* pp. 27-40.
Van Oosterzee, *The Theology of the New Testament,* Vol. I, pp. 71-131.
Weidner, *Biblical Theology of the New Testament,* Vol. I, pp. 41-47, 60-76.
Weiss, *Biblical Theology of the New Testament,* Vol. I, pp. 62-73, 92-120.
Vos, *Biblical Theology,* pp. 397-429.
Vos, *The Kingdom and the Church.*
Vos, *The Self-Disclosure of Jesus,* pp. 273-302.

1. Vos, *The Self-Disclosure, op. cit.,* pp. 411-426.
2. Joel 2:28-32; Hos. 14:4-7; Amos 9:11-15; Mic. 4:1-7; Is. 4:2-6; 35:5-10; Jer. 31; etc.
3. Is. 4:2-8; 7:14, 15; 9:1-7, 11; Jer. 23:5-8; 33:14-26; Zech. 6:12, 13; etc.
4. Is. 42:1-9; 49:6, 7; 50:4-9; 52:13 — 53:12; 61:1-4.
5. Mt. 5:4 (Is. 61:2); 5:5 (Ps. 37:11); 5:6 (Is. 55:1, 2); 5:8 (Ps. 24:4); 5:12 (2 Chron. 36:16).
6. Quotation by A. T. Robertson, *Word Pictures of the New Testament* (New York: Richard R. Smith, Inc., 1930), Vol. I, p. 43.
7. Ps. 93:1; 96:10; 97:1; 99:1; 4; Is. 24:23; 52:7; Obad. 21; Zech. 14:9.
8. Acts 15:17; Is. 49:6; 52:7, 10; 60:1-3; Amos 9:11, 12.
9, Joel 2:28; Is. 11:2; 32:15; 42:1; 44:3; 59:21; Ezek. 36:27; 37:14; 39:21; Zech. 12:10.
10. Floyd V. Filson, *The Gospel According to Matthew, Harper's New Testament Commentaries* (New York: Harper and Bros., 1960), p. 95.
11. See G. Abbott Smith, *A Manual Greek Lexicon of the New Testament* (Edinburgh: T. & T. Clark, 1937), p. 442.
12. Mt. 5:33; Lev. 19:12; Num. 30:2; Deut. 23:21.
13. Richardson, *op. cit.,* pp. 79-83. See also A *Theological Word Book of the Bible,* edited by Richardson; article, "Righteous, Righteousness," by Snaith; Kittel's *Bible Key Words* (New York, Harper Bros., 1951), Vol. I, Book IV, "Righteousness" by Quell and Schrenk; and the general works in Old Testament biblical theology such as those of Eichrodt, Jacob, von Rad, Snaith, Vriezen, etc.
14. For other significant references to the righteousness of God, see Ps. 7:8-11; 11:7; 71:2, 15, 16, 19, 24; 103:6-18; Is. 51:4, 5; Jer. 12:1-3.
15. 1 Sam. 15:29; 1 Kings 8:47, 48; 2 Chron. 6:37, 38; Job. 42:6; Is. 1:27; Jer. 5:3; Ezek. 14:6; 18: 30; etc.
16. Mt. 3:2, 8, 11; 4:17; 11:20, 21; Mk. 1:4, 15; 6:12; Lk. 3:3; 5:32; 11:32; 13:3, 5; 15:7, 10; 16:30; 17: 3, 4.
17. Vos, *op. cit.,* p. 423.
18. Ex. 13:17; 1 Sam. 15:35; 1 Chron. 21:15; Ps. 106:45; 110:4; Jer. 20:16; Ezek. 14:22.
19. Mt. 13:14, 15; Mk. 8:18; Jn. 12:39-41; Acts 28:26-27.
20. Deut. 4:30; 30:10; 2 Kings 23:25; 2 Chron. 6:26, 37; 15:4; 36:13; Neh. 1:9; Is. 31:6; 55:7; 59:20; Jer. 3:14; 18:8; Ezek. 14:6; 18:21, 30: Hos. 12:6; 14:2; Joel 2:12, 13; Zech. 1:3.
21. Is. 1:16; 55:6; Jer. 3:12; Ezek. 18:30; Hos. 6:1; Joel 2:12; Amos 5:4.
22. Lk. 1:17, 35; 4:1, 14; 11:13; 24:49; Acts 10:38.
23. See also 21:13; 66:7; 79:11; 106:8; 110:2; 145:11; 147:5.
24. Ex. 4:8, 9, 17, 28, 30; 7:3; 10:1, 2; 13:9; Num. 14:11; 16:38; Deut. 7:19; 13:2, 3.
25. Ex. 7:3; Deut. 4:34; 6:22; 7:19; 13:1; 26:8; 28:46; 29:3; 34:11; Neh. 9:3; Ps. 105:27; Is. 8:18; Jer. 32:20.
26. Ps. 8:3, 6; 33:4; 66:3; 86:8; 92:4, 5; 102:25; 103:22; 104:13, 24, 31; 107:22, 24; 111:2, 6, 7; 118: 17; 138:8; 139:14; 145:4, 9, 10, 17.
27. Mt. 11:2; Lk. 24:19; Jn. 5:20, 36; 9:3, 4; 10:25, 32, 37, 38; 14:10,11, 12; 15:24.
28. John D. Davis and Henry Snyder Gehman, *The Westminster Dictionary of the Bible,* rev. ed. (Philadelphia: Westminster Press, 1944), p. 399.

29. Bultmann, *op. cit.*, Vol. II, pp. 44 ff. Richardson, *op. cit.*, pp. 95-102, 192-196. See also S. V. McCasland in his article, "Miracle," in *The Interpreter's Dictionary of the Bible*, Vol. K-Q, pp. 392-402.

30. Gen. 15:6; Ex. 4:1, 5, 8, 9, 31; Deut. 7:9; 32:4; Ps. 19:7; 36:5; 40:10; 80:11; 119:75; Is. 11:5; etc.

31. Joseph Henry Thayer, *A Greek-English Lexicon of the New Testament* (New York: American Book Company, 1889), p. 325. See also Bible dictionaries and encyclopedias for extended articles on the "Heart."

32. Chester K. Lehman, *New Testament Studies: The Gospels and the Acts* (Scottdale: Mennonite Publishing House, 1956), rev. by C. Norman Kraus, pp. 49-59.

33. Jn. 2:11; 3:16; 4:39; 7:38, 39; 9:35, 36; 11:45, 48; 12:44; 14:1, 12; etc.

34. Jn. 3:14, 15, 36; 5:24; 6:27, 40, 47; 7:38; 11:25; 15:7, 16; 16:23, 24.

35. Ps. 1:1; 2:12; 21:4; 32:1, 2; 33:12; 44:8; 40:4; 41:1, 112:1, 2; 119:1, 2; 128:1; 144:15; 146:5; etc.

36. Note the following references to these ideas: Ex. 14:13; 15:2; Deut. 32:4, 15, 30, 31; Ps. 3:7, 8; 18:1, 2; 19:14; 27:1; 34:6, 7; 62:2, 6, 7; 68:19, 20; 79:8, 9; 85:4-7; 95:1; 118:14, 21; Is. 12:2, 3; 43:3, 11; 44:6; 45:15, 21, 22; 46:13; 49:26; 60:16.

37. Mt. 9:21, 22; Mk. 5:23-28, 34; 6:56; 10:52; Lk. 8:36; 17:19; 18:42.

38. Mt. 10:22; 18:11; 24:13; Mk. 10:26; Lk. 7:47-50; 19:10; Jn. 3:16, 17; 5:34; 10:9; 12:47.

39. Mt. 8:25; Mk. 8:35; Lk. 19:10; Jn. 3:16-18, 36; 10:28.

40. Mt. 10:28; Lk. 13:3-5; 19:10; Jn. 10:28; 17:12.

41. Mt. 7:14; 18:8, 9; 19:17, 29; 25:46; Mk. 10:30; Lk. 18:18-30; Jn. 4:36.

42. Jn. 5:24; 6:29, 35-40, 47; 7:38, 39; 11:25-27; 12:44-48; 20:31.

43. Jn. 3:36; 4:14, 36; 5:21-29; 6:39, 40, 54; 11:25, 39-44.

44. Ex. 26; Lev. 19:17, 18; Deut. 6:5; 7:6-13; 11:1, 13, 22; Jer. 31:3; Hos. 11:1-4; 14:4; Mal. 1:2.

45. Norval Geldenhuys, *Commentary on the Gospel of Luke, The New International Commentary on the New Testament*, N. B. Stonehouse, Gen. Ed. (Grand Rapids: Wm. B. Eerdmans Publishing Co., 1954), p. 399.

CHAPTER X

THE ESCHATOLOGICAL ASPECT OF THE KINGDOM OF GOD

1. The Great Bisection of Human History

Jesus set forth this great bisection in the words, "The law and the prophets were until John; since then the good news of the kingdom of God is preached" (Lk. 16:16; Mt. 11:11-14). By this statement Jesus was building on the Old Testament eschatological view of the ages to come.[1] The prophets in their forward look saw a future age which they called the Latter Days. In their viewpoint an imminent judgment would come upon Israel and Judah which they called the day of the Lord, but the prophets looked to a future age, the age of the Messiah. This gave most significant meaning to the Latter Days.

This prophetic viewpoint was the source and foundation of the time eras expressed by Jesus. The former era was that of the law and the prophets, which extended to and included John. The new era was marked by the preaching of the good news of God's kingdom. On another occasion Jesus identified the work of the Baptist with another Old Testament prediction, that given by Malachi. Speaking through the prophet, the Lord said, "I will send you Elijah the prophet before the great and terrible day of the Lord comes" (4:5, 6). Jesus interpreted this prediction by saying, "Elijah does come, and he is to restore all things; but I tell you that Elijah has already come, and they did not know him, but did to him whatever they pleased" (Mt. 17:11, 12). The disciples understood that Jesus was speaking to them of John the Baptist. In the perspectives of Malachi's prediction and Jesus' testimony concerning the Baptist, we can understand the eschatological significance of the Baptist's work followed by the preaching of the good news. This great bisection of human history became basic to Jesus' eschatological unfolding of the future.

2. Jesus' Foreview of This Age and the Age to Come

Jesus disclosed this division of time on the occasion of a serious argument with the Pharisees, in which He declared, "Whoever speaks against the Holy Spirit will not be forgiven, either in this age or in the age to come" (Mt. 12:32). Mark recorded the last part of Jesus' words by saying, "Whoever blasphemes against the Holy Spirit never has forgiveness, but is guilty of an eternal sin" (3:29). This leads us to understand that Jesus' expression *this age* and *the age to come* has its beginning in the present time and extends throughout eternity. It suggests that this age is temporal in character and is followed by an eternal age. This distinction becomes still clearer in the parable of the weeds of the field (Mt. 13:36-43), in which the kingdom of the present age is that of the Son of Man. On His return this age will come to a close. It will be marked by a judgment in which the wicked will be thrown in a furnace of fire and the righteous will shine like the sun in the kingdom of their Father. This parable discloses a number of very important truths among which are the present messianic reign of Christ, His return for judgment, the eternal destinies of the righteous and of the wicked, and the eternal nature of the Father's kingdom. The harvest at the end of the age sets forth the close of the aeon of salvation. For the wicked, the age to come is that of eternal damnation, while for the righteous it marks their entrance into the eternal glory of heaven. On another occasion Jesus declared that those who had left their homes for His sake and for the gospel will receive a hundredfold now in this time, and in the age to come, eternal life (Mk. 10:29, 30). Here is the contrast between the almost immeasurable temporal blessings of the present age and the eternal life of the age to come. The context of this conversation leads us to understand that one enters the kingdom of God at the beginning of the age to come. In still another setting where the Sadducees were raising questions relating to the resurrection, Jesus replied, "The sons of this age marry and are given in marriage; but those who are accounted worthy to attain to that age and to the resurrection from the dead neither marry nor are given in marriage, for they cannot die any more, because they are equal to angels and are sons of God, being sons of the resurrection" (Lk. 20:34-36). From this we learn that human relationships obtain only in this age, and that the resurrection from the dead marks the beginning of the blessed state of being sons of God.

3. The Nature of the Present Age

a. The Age of Preaching the Good Tidings

Perhaps the most descriptive language of the present age was set forth by Jesus in the synagogue service, when He read from Isaiah 61:1, 2 as follows, "The Spirit of the Lord is upon me, because he has anointed me to preach good news to the poor. He has sent me to proclaim release to the captives and recovering of sight to the blind, to set at liberty those who are oppressed, to proclaim the acceptable year of the

Lord" (Lk. 4:18, 19). These prophetic words from this part of Isaiah serve as the introduction to a larger context which most beautifully predicts the real content of the good tidings relating to the year of the Lord's favor. It is the time when "the Lord God will cause righteousness and praise to spring forth before all the nations" (Is. 61:11). Another prophetic statement from this part of Isaiah reads, "Behold, the former things have come to pass, and new things I now declare; before they spring forth I tell you of them" (42:9). These prophetic words also appear to be descriptive of the present age. Coming from a Servant of the Lord passage, this verse expresses clearly the nature of the Servant's work. Both literally and spiritually He will open the eyes of the blind. He will bring out the prisoners from the dungeon and enable them to sing to the Lord a new song. Another Servant of the Lord prediction, centering in the character of the present age reads, "The ransomed of the Lord shall return, and come with singing to Zion; everlasting joy shall be upon their heads; they shall obtain joy and gladness, and sorrow and sighing shall flee away" (51:11). Yet another prediction of this present age reads, "How beautiful upon the mountains are the feet of him who brings good tidings, who publishes peace, who brings good tidings of good, who publishes salvation, who says to Zion, 'Your God reigns' " (52:7).

b. The Age of Healing the Sick and Casting Out of Demons

The Gospel records give witness to the central place which Jesus' healing work occupied in His earthly ministry (Mt. 4:23, 25; 9:35; Mk. 1:39; Lk. 6:17-19; etc.). Mark drew special attention to Jesus casting out demons. The special significance of these acts was stated by Jesus when He said, "If it is by the Spirit of God that I cast out demons, then the kingdom of God has come upon you" (Mt. 12:22-29; Lk. 11:19, 20). Note the meaningful language in which the present aspect of the kingdom was expressed. The kingdom of God had come upon them. In response to the question of the Pharisees as to when the kingdom of God was coming, Jesus gave the forthright answer, "The kingdom of God is in the midst of you" (Lk. 17:20, 21). The Greek preposition *entos* used here may carry the sense *within* or *among*. In whichever way this preposition is understood, Jesus' statement expressed the present reality of the kingdom. Thus the casting out of demons bore witness to the power of God manifest in the kingdom.

c. The Present Reality of the Kingdom as Taught by the Parables (Mt. 13)

The parable of the sower illustrated the varied responses to the word of the kingdom. The good news of the kingdom does not compel acceptance. When those who have received the word experience tribulation or persecution or when they are enticed by the cares of the world and the delight in riches, many do not bear fruit. But some are fruitful even to the extent of a hundredfold. Thus the kingdom of heaven encounters in a very direct way all the evils of this world. The parables of the mustard seed and of the leaven disclose the growth of the kingdom in the respective aspects of its worldwide expansion and of the permeation of the gospel within man. The parable of the weeds shows the coexistence of the sons of the kingdom and the sons of the evil one. The arch-antagonist of the kingdom is the devil who is seeking to bring all men under his control. The present aspect of the kingdom will come to a close at the end of this age at which time the ungodly will be separated from the godly and doomed to eternal punishment. The kingdom of the Father, on the other hand, stands in sharp contrast with the present aspect of the kingdom in that only the righteous enter into its glory and that it is eternal. The appeal of the gospel of the kingdom has its likeness to a treasure hidden in a field and the pearl of great value. Thus there are those who hear the gospel and do all in their power to appropriate its immeasurable value. In a very real way the kingdom parables taught with utmost clarity the evangelizing power of the gospel.

d. The Nature of the Present Kingdom as Disclosed in the Olivet Discourse (Mt. 24, 25)

While this discourse is predominantly eschatological in nature, it discloses some characteristics of the present age. Jesus' portrayal of this age was dark and filled with gloom. All these conditions would have a most serious impact upon the present kingdom. He predicted wars, famines, earthquakes, and the increase of wickedness in the world. As a result many believers will be delivered up to tribulation and put to death. They will be hated by all nations for Christ's sake. As a result many will fall away, betray one another, and hate one another. This gruesome picture of world conditions gives a different perspective to the present aspect of God's kingdom. The kingdom of heaven must encounter all the wickedness of this world. Nevertheless, the gospel of the kingdom will be preached throughout the whole world as a testimony to all nations. When all these things are fulfilled, and in God's own time, the end will come. The parables of the wise and foolish maidens and of the talents also contribute to our understanding of God's kingdom in the present age. The wise maidens always lived in readiness for the coming of the bridegroom while the foolish maidens made no preparation for his coming. Thus our manner of life as subjects of God's kingdom requires faithful service so as to be ready for Christ's return. The parable of the talents declares that in the present kingdom God entrusts us with varying numbers of gifts, and each of us carries the responsibility for faithfully using these gifts whether great or small for the advancement of His kingdom. Even the one-talent person should strive to be worthy of receiving God's commendation, "Well done, good and faithful servant; you have been faithful over a little, I will set you over much; enter into the joy of your master" (Mt. 25:21). These two parables served to teach still more explicitly man's responsibility to God in this present stage of His kingdom.

e. The Character of the Present Age as Depicted in the Upper Room Discourses (Mt. 26; Jn. 13-16)

In the institution of the Lord's Supper, Jesus gave the symbol of the institution of the new covenant. Thus the Mosaic covenant was superseded by the new covenant which will continue throughout His kingdom. The explication of this new covenant as set forth by Paul and the author of Hebrews made it clear that it is the most significant and dominant aspect of the present age (1 Cor. 11:23-26; 2 Cor. 3:4-18; Heb. 7: 15 — 12:24). The Christian church has its foundation in this covenant. It is the continuing body of Christ's disciples under His messianic kingship. Throughout this age the Holy Spirit sent by the Father and the Son is the everpresent Counselor who dwells with His people and is in them. Throughout this age the Holy Spirit will "convince the world of sin and of righteousness and of judgment" (Jn. 16:8). Jesus declared that His followers will experience tribulation throughout this age (v. 33).

f. Jesus' Closing Messages with Regard to the Present Age (Mt. 28:18-20; Lk. 24:45-49; Acts 1:3-11)

Jesus spoke of this present age at the eve of His ascension. Bound up with the Great Commission given to the disciples, Jesus declared that all authority had been given to Him in heaven and on earth. On the basis of this authority He commanded His disciples to go and make disciples of all nations. He repeated His promise with reference to the coming of the Holy Spirit upon them and declared that they should be His witnesses in Jerusalem and outward to the end of the earth. These commands express the character of the present age. Briefly stated, it is marked by worldwide evangelization under our Lord's authority through the power of the Holy Spirit.

The character of this present age should now be clearly understood. Much of Jesus' teaching dealt with its nature, especially as it related to the overthrow of evil in this world. The eschatological emphasis in Jesus' teaching concerning the present age was most predominant, and as noted above, many of His parables held in view the close of the present age. the words *telos* (*end*) and *sunteleia* (consummation, close) gained a new significance through Jesus' teaching as it focused on the consummation of this age (Mt. 13:39, 40; 24:3, 6, 13, 14; 28:20). A great tribulation will be evidence of the imminent close of the age. World conditions at the end of the age will bear a close resemblance to the days of Noah. From this great body of Jesus' teachings we have grounds for believing in the imminency of His return, which event will terminate the present age.

4. The Coming of the Son of Man (Mt. 24:27 — 25:47; Mk. 13:24-37; Lk. 21:25-36)

It is essential for my purpose to take a direct look at the return of our Lord. First in importance is His personal return. Beyond all question Jesus Himself will return to this earth. The verbs *erxomai (come)* and *apokalupto* (reveal) and the noun *parousia* (coming) give adequate substantiation to this assertion. Each of these words expresses a separate aspect of His return. Second is the imminency of His return. In none of the references to His coming is there any reference to an intervening time era before His coming. Jesus said, "Watch therefore, for you know neither the day nor the hour" (Mt. 25:13). Careful study of these references shows that the imminence of His return stands forth as a warning for all mankind to be ready for this event. Third, the *parousia* marks the close of this age and of the day of grace. Just as the opportunity for being saved from the Flood closed when Noah entered the ark, so it will be at the coming of the Son of Man. The prediction of the judgment to take place at our Lord's return confirms this most sobering truth. Finally our Lord's *parousia* will be in His glory. This stands in sharp contrast with His coming as a babe born in Bethlehem. True indeed, "The Word became flesh and dwelt among us, full of grace and truth; we have beheld his glory, glory as of the only Son from the Father" (Jn. 1:14). But Jesus declared repeatedly that "the Son of man is to come with his angels in the glory of his Father" (Mt. 16:27; 24:30; 25:31; Lk. 21:27; Jn. 17:24). This shows how appropriate it was for Christ, Paul, and Peter to use the verb *apokalupto* (reveal), to portray the Lord's return. It will be a revelation, a disclosure or manifestation of His glory.

5. The Resurrection

Perhaps the most expressive of Jesus' teachings on the resurrection is recorded in John 5:19-29 in a context where Jesus was speaking of His work in relation to that of the Father. He said, "For as the Father raises the dead and gives them life, so also the Son gives life to whom he will" (v. 21). Jesus also declared that the Father had given all judgment to Him and then He added, "He who hears my word and believes him who sent me, has eternal life; he does not come into judgment, but has passed from death to life" (v. 24). On these foundational truths Jesus built His teaching on the resurrection. He spoke first of a spiritual experience cast in resurrection language when He said, "The hour is coming, and now is, when the dead will hear the voice of the Son of God, and those who hear will live. For as the Father has life in himself, so he has granted the Son also to have life in himself, and has given him authority to execute judgment, because he is the Son of man" (vv. 25-27). From this Jesus advanced to a disclosure of the bodily resurrection, "The hour is coming when all who are in the tombs will hear his voice and come forth, those who have done good, to the resurrection of life, and those who have done evil, to the resurrection of judgment" (vv. 28, 29).

The Father has given to the Son work on the level of Deity. Prior to the earthly ministry of Christ the resurrection and the judgment were ascribed to God the Father. The possession of eternal life rests on believing in the Son. The spiritual dead who hear the voice of the Son will live. Analogous to this is the bodily resurrection. Comparable to what Jesus had said with reference to the spiritual resurrection, He distinguished between the resurrection of life and the resurrection of judgment. The line of division between the two turns on the manner of life which the resurrected had lived before death. Those who had done good attained to the former, and those who had done evil, to the latter. This forthright language raises the teaching concerning the resurrection to greater significance.

Jesus did not speak of two resurrections with an intervening thousand-year reign of the Messiah, but rather of one resurrection leading to two destinies. This unfigurative language leaves no room for injecting the messianic reign of Christ between the resurrection of life and the resurrection of judgment. In another discourse Jesus declared "All things have been delivered to me by my Father" (Mt. 11:27), and just before His ascension He said, "All authority in heaven and on earth has been given to me" (28:18). On the basis of this language, as well as on Psalms 16, 110, and 132, Peter could state, "Let all the house of Israel therefore know assuredly that God has made him both Lord and Christ, this Jesus whom you crucified" (Acts 2:36).

Late in Jesus' ministry the Sadducces encountered Him with a seemingly inexplicable problem (Mt. 22:23-33; Mk. 12:18-27; Lk. 20:27-40). In brief the question was "In the resurrection, therefore, to which of the seven will she be wife?" Jesus exposed their ignorance by declaring that they knew neither the Scriptures nor the power of God. He added, "The sons of this age marry and are given in marriage; but those who are accounted worthy to attain to that age and to the resurrection from the dead neither marry nor are given in marriage, for they cannot die any more, because they are equal to angels and are sons of God, being sons of the resurrection" (Lk. 20:34-36). In this reply Jesus distinguished clearly between this age and the age to come. Natural affairs of life, such as marriage, belong to this age. The experience of the resurrection from the dead leads to a quality of life equal to that of angels according to which they are sons of God. This is an exceedingly rich portrayal of the resurrection. It stands at the very foundation of Christian hope to be realized in the age to come.

It is the source of genuine comfort to those of this age who know that in the world to come they cannot die any more. Jesus added another instructive note when He declared that the idea of the resurrection was already portrayed through Moses. Recording God's words Moses wrote, "I am the God of your father, the God of Abraham, the God of Isaac, and the God of Jacob" (Ex. 3:6). On this account Jesus could properly add, "He is not God of the dead, but of the living; for all live to him" (Lk. 20:38). Thus as early as the time of Moses the fundamental truth underlying the resurrection had been disclosed. This is not beyond human comprehension because man by creation is the son of God.

6. The Judgment

Predictions of the judgment have already received incidental attention. Let us now direct our thought to this most solemn act of God to take place in the imminent future. Jesus did not introduce the judgment as a new unfolding of a future event, for already in the Old Testament there were many predictions of coming judgment, some of which may refer to the final judgment of all mankind.[2] In view of these Old Testament references to coming judgment, Jesus had a solid foundation on which to build His teachings. The frequency of His casual, as well as more lengthy references to coming judgment leads us to grasp the supreme importance of this teaching. Jesus often spoke of His present work of judging people, but the climax of these teachings centers in the final judgment at His return.

Let us note first Jesus' references to those who shall be judged. In the Sermon on the Mount Jesus corrected an erroneous idea of the Pharisees by showing that not only those who kill will be liable to judgment, but: "Every one who is angry with his brother shall be liable to judgment; whoever insults his brother shall be liable to the council, and whoever says, 'You fool!' shall be liable to the hell of fire" (Mt. 5:22). Later in this sermon Jesus said, "Judge not, that you be not judged. For with the judgment you pronounce you will be judged, and the measure you give will be the measure you get" (7:1, 2). These statements are quite significant because our depraved human nature might bypass the seriousness of these transgressions and decide that such offenders would not be judged.

Jesus taught His disciples that those who would reject their preaching would receive severer condemnation on the day of judgment than the wicked cities of Sodom, Gomorrah, Tyre, and Sidon. Thus the gospel message preached by the disciples, together with the miracles that they performed, laid upon the people the responsibility for responding to the message, and by reason of all this teaching it would be more tolerable on the day of judgment for the people of those wicked cities than for those who heard this gospel message (Mt. 10:14-16; 11:22-24). Nevertheless, all shall be judged, the peoples who had the least knowledge of God's righteousness, as well as those who had received the full truth of the gospel. Obviously this includes all mankind, but Jesus did declare, "He who hears my word and believes him who sent me, has eternal life; he does not come into judgment, but has passed from death to life" (Jn. 5:24). This reference to judgment seems to center upon those who do not believe. In the context where Jesus was speaking of the Holy Spirit's work He said, "When he comes, he will convince the world of sin and of righteousness and of judgment . . . of judgment, because the ruler of this world is judged" (16:8-11). This statement was especially important because God's judgment will extend to all created beings whether men or fallen angels including Satan himself.

This prepares us for grasping the nature of the judgment. Jesus said, "I tell you, on the day of judgment men will render account for every careless word they utter; for by your words you will be justified, and by your words you will be condemned" (Mt. 12:36, 37). This statement makes it clear that the final judgment has its likeness to a human court where those being tried must give an account of their deeds. Some people may feel that man should not be accountable for careless words which they have spoken. But Jesus had shown that these words come from the heart and that "out of the abundance of the heart the mouth speaks" (Mt. 12:34). Thus the judgment will deal with the wickedness that springs from a sinful heart. A slightly different aspect of the judgment becomes evident when Jesus answered the Pharisees who were seeking a sign from Him. The Ninevites who repented at the preaching of Jonah and also the queen of the south who came to hear the wisdom of Solomon will arise at the judgment and condemn those who refuse to repent after witnessing the mighty works of Jesus which proved His messiahship. In another context Jesus said, "He who believes in him is not condemned; he who does not believe is condemned already, because he has not believed in the name of the only Son of God. And this is the judgment, that the light has come into the world, and men loved darkness rather than light, because their deeds were evil" (Jn. 3:18, 19).

Several of Jesus' parables set forth the nature of the judgment. Looking again at the parables of the weeds of the field and of the net which was thrown into the sea, we see that just as the weeds are gathered and burned with fire and the bad fish are thrown away, so at the coming of the Son of Man the angels will gather out of His kingdom all causes of sin and all evildoers, thus separating the evil from the righteous. The wicked shall be thrown into the furnace of fire where men will weep and gnash their teeth. The righteous, on the other hand, will shine like the sun in the kingdom of their Father. Even the parable of the ten maidens presents a stern reality in that the five foolish maidens, because of no oil in their lamps, were denied entrance to the marriage feast. In spiritual language this parable teaches the constant need of being ready for the Lord's return. Undoubtedly this involved a genuine experience of being saved from a life of sin and of pursuing a life of holiness before God. The parables of the talents and pounds present a similar warning concerning the nature of the judgment. Those who used their pounds and talents as real stewards received similar commendation in the words, "Well done, good and faithful servant . . . enter into the joy of your master" (Mt. 25:21). Similar stern condemnation was pronounced on the unfaithful servants when their masters said, "You wicked and slothful servant!" and then gave the command to cast him "into the outer darkness; there men will weep and gnash their teeth" (vv. 26, 30).

The issues of the judgment stand forth most clearly in Jesus' climactic presentation of His return for final judgment (Mt. 25:31-46). Seated on His glorious throne, Jesus the King will say to those at His right hand, "Come, O blessed of my Father, inherit the kingdom prepared for you from the foundation of the world" (v. 34). But to those on His left hand He will declare, "Depart from me, you cursed, into the eternal fire prepared for the devil and his angels" (v. 41). The judgment scene closes with the words, "And they will go away into eternal punishment, but the righteous into eternal life" (v. 46). Thus the issues of the judgment stand forth as the most serious and solemn warning to all mankind. In homiletic language this biblical teaching has been most tragically neglected by many professed Christians. Christ commissioned His disciples to declare the gospel of salvation to all mankind. Inseparable from these glad tidings is this message of eternal punishment to be suffered by those who reject the good news of salvation.

Furthermore, this scene of the last judgment also revealed who the Judge will be. He is the enthroned Son of Man who will exercise His kingly authority as the final Judge. Jesus had declared, "All things have been delivered to me by my Father" (Mt. 11:27). It is quite significant that John recorded several of Jesus' declarations that the Father had given all judgment to Him as the Son (Jn. 5:22-29; 8:16; 9:39; 12:48-50). This adds profound meaning to Jesus' mission as the Messiah. His work as Judge stands as the most solemn expression of His work as Prophet, Priest, and King. Thus as we behold Him as the mighty Prophet of prophets, the Servant of the Lord who in His priestly work suffered and died for all mankind, the Messiah, and King of kings, His work as final Judge gains proper perspective.

7. The Character of the Age to Come

In the contexts of the Scriptures noted so far in this chapter, the character of the age to come becomes quite clear. The destinies, respectively, of the righteous and of the unrighteous, become definite. "The righteous will shine like the sun in the kingdom of their Father" (Mt. 13:43). They will inherit the kingdom prepared for them from the foundation of the world (25:34). They will go away into eternal life. Many will come from the east and west, and from north and south, and sit at the table in the kingdom of God together with Abraham, Isaac, and Jacob and all the prophets (8:11; Lk. 13:29). They will be equal to the angels and will in the richest conceivable sense be sons of God. Their resurrection experience will impart to them eternal life and raise them up to this high level of existence. The wicked, on the other hand, will be cast into eternal fire where men will weep and gnash their teeth. This eternal torment was prepared for the devil and his angels, and the ungodly will share with them the eternal punishment throughout eternity (Mt. 8:12; Lk. 13:27, 28). The Father will sit on His throne in His kingdom.

8. The Kingdom of God in Relation to Israel

Since the nation of Israel was God's chosen people, it is essential to give careful consideration to the relation of the kingdom of God to His people. Beginning with the ministry of John the Baptist, we should note that he preached in the wilderness of Judea, and that "there went out to him all the country of Judea, and all the people of Jerusalem" (Mk. 1:5). Jesus began His ministry by the Sea of Galilee. This led Matthew to observe that Jesus' coming to dwell in Capernaum by the sea was the fulfillment of Isaiah's prediction, "The land of Zebulun and the land of Naphtali, toward the sea, across the Jordan, Galilee of the Gentiles — the people who sat in darkness have seen a great light, and for those who sat in the region and shadow of death light has dawned" (Mt. 4:15, 16). Matthew's quotation from Isaiah (9:1, 2) carried great significance. As Isaiah looked forward to the coming of the Messiah, he naturally related the Messiah's work to God's chosen people. Matthew expanded this idea further in the words, "And Jesus went about all the cities and villages, teaching in their synagogues and preaching the gospel of the kingdom, and healing every disease and every infirmity (9: 35). This preaching of the gospel to the Jews became still clearer when Jesus sent the twelve disciples on a preaching mission giving them the charge,"Go nowhere among the Gentiles, and enter no town of the Samaritans, but go rather to the lost sheep of the house of Israel. And preach as you go, saying, 'The kingdom of heaven is at hand' " (10: 5-7).

When the Jews began to realize the spiritual nature of Christ's messiahship and His kingdom, they were unwilling to meet the requirements for entering into this kingdom. The Pharisees looked for a political messianic kingdom in which their legalistic interpretation of the law would find support. Jesus proceeded to rebuke the people saying they were "like children sitting in the market places and calling to their playmates, 'We piped to you, and you did not dance; we wailed, and you did not mourn.' For John came neither eating nor drinking, and they say, 'He has a demon'; the Son of man came eating and drinking, and they say, 'Behold, a glutton and a drunkard, a friend of tax collectors and sinners!' " (Mt. 11:16-19). Jesus proceeded "to upbraid the cities where most of his mighty works had been done, because they did not repent. 'Woe to you, Chorazin! woe to you, Bethsaida! for if the mighty works done in you had been done in Tyre and Sidon, they would have repented long ago in sackcloth and ashes' " (vv. 20, 21). This rejection of Jesus became still clearer when He expounded the real meaning of His miracle in feeding the five thousand. The Jews murmured when they heard Jesus' claim, "I am the bread which came down from heaven" (Jn. 6:41). Even though Jesus had performed the wonderful miracle of feeding the multitude, the Jews were unwilling to believe that He was the Son of the Father and had come down from heaven.

Jesus gave the real meaning of His rejection by the Jews on the occasion of His coming back to Jerusalem. He said, "Would that even today you knew the things that make for peace! But now they are hid from your eyes. For the day shall come upon you, when your enemies will cast up a bank about you and surround you, and hem you in on every side, and dash you to the ground, you and your children within you, and they will not leave one stone upon another in you; because you did not know the time of your visitation" (Lk. 19:42-44).

The real meaning of this rejection of Jesus and its bearing on Israel's share in the kingdom of God stood forth in a later declaration of Jesus in the words, "Have you never read in the scriptures: 'The very stone which the builders rejected has become the head of the corner; this was the Lord's doing, and it is marvelous in our eyes'? Therefore I tell you, the kingdom of God will be taken away from you and given to a nation producing the fruits of it" (Mt. 21:42, 43). This declared that the people of Israel would suffer the loss of the kingdom through their refusal to repent from sin and to believe in the spiritual mission of their Messiah. On this account Jesus went further and told His disciples, "Fear not, little flock, for it is your Father's good pleasure to give you the kingdom" (Lk. 12:32). This was a remarkable promise because this small band of believers became the recipients of all the treasures of the Father's kingdom.

The outcome of this issue becomes clear in a setting where Jesus is pronouncing woes upon the scribes and Pharisees (Mt. 23:13-39). Jesus spoke sternly that because of all of their sins they were filling up the measure of their fathers, and on this account there would come upon them all the righteous blood shed on earth, from the blood of innocent Abel to the blood of Zechariah, the son of Barachiah. This would come in their generation. Jesus expanded this prediction in His Olivet discourse (Mt. 24; 25; Lk. 21:20-36). Jesus' teaching on the character of this present age in this discourse included some important predictions relating to the nation of Israel. To the disciples Jesus spoke of their being delivered up to tribulation, of being put to death, and of being hated by all nations for His name's sake. But they who would endure to the end would be saved. He then declared that this gospel of the kingdom will be preached throughout the whole world as a testimony to all nations. These words served as an orientation to the remainder of this discourse.

Jesus then spoke of the desolating sacrilege predicted by the prophet Daniel (Mt. 24:15 ff.; Lk. 21:20 ff.). Luke appears to interpret these words as making reference to the city of Jerusalem being surrounded by armies which would bring desolation to the Holy City. The course of history during the next half century showed that this was a grim picture of Rome's destruction of Jerusalem. Those who immediately left the city when it came under attack, escaped while those who remained there suffered the most horrible bloody death reported in human history. So severe would be this tribulation that unless those days would be shortened no human being would be saved. But God's act of judgment would follow the same pattern as those which He brought upon

His people all through Old Testament history; that is, for the sake of the elect these days of great tribulation would be shortened. In this context it would appear that the elect are the faithful disciples of Christ. It is conceivable that Jesus may have been referring to all the Jews who lived in Jerusalem. Jesus gave no hope that Jerusalem would ever gain its political independence. He declared, "Jerusalem will be trodden down by the Gentiles, until the times of the Gentiles are fulfilled" (Lk. 21:24). All this would take place because Israel did not know the time of their visitation (19:44). Jesus gave no prediction of a second visitation. There remained the problem of determining what would happen after the times of the Gentiles are fulfilled. The Lukan context gives grounds for believing that the times of the Gentiles extends to the return of Christ. (21:25-28).

Bringing together the several strands of thought dealing with the kingdom of God in relation to Israel, we see Israel's rejection of Jesus as the Messiah brought to an end God's dealing with Israel as His chosen people. According to the Great Commission the apostles were sent out into the world to make disciples of all nations. Christ would build His church as a spiritual structure composed of those who believe in Him as Christ and Lord. It would not be limited to the Hebrew race but would include all true believers from the entire human race. After Jesus was raised from the dead, He continued to speak concerning the kingdom of God. He said to His disciples, "You shall be my witnesses in Jerusalem and in all Judea and Samaria and to the end of the earth" (Acts 1:8). Accordingly the apostles began their preaching in Jerusalem and Judea, and later, Paul in particular, proclaimed the gospel to Jews and Gentiles throughout the Roman world. In his letter to the Romans, Paul dealt specifically with the problem of Israel's unbelief. He made it clear that if Israel did not persist in their unbelief they would be grafted in again. He concluded his explanation with the significant statement, "A hardening has come upon part of Israel, until the full number of the Gentiles come in, and so all Israel will be saved" (Rom. 11:25, 26). In this manner Paul made clear the future of Israel in relation to the church of Jesus Christ and the kingdom of God.

For Additional Reading and Reference:

Bright, *The Kingdom of God,* pp. 187-274.
Bruce, A. B., *The Kingdom of God.* pp. 273-328.
Cullmann, *Christ and Time;* see Contents.
Filson, *Jesus Christ the Risen Lord,* pp. 259 ff.; see Index.
Hunter, *The Work and Words of Jesus,* pp. 101-111.
Jeremias, *New Testament Theology,* pp. 122-158.
Ladd, *Crucial Questions About the Kingdom of God.*
Ladd, *Jesus and the Kingdom,* Chaps. 1, 4, 6, 7, 8, 13.
Perrin, *The Kingdom of God in the Teaching of Jesus,* pp. 79-89, 130-147.
Ridderbos, *The Coming of the Kingdom,* pp. 36-56.
Ryrie, *Biblical Theology of the New Testament,* pp. 72-95.
Stagg, *New Testament Theology,* pp. 305-338.
Stauffer, *New Testament Theology,* pp. 205-231.
Sheldon, *New Testament Theology,* pp. 107-122.
Stevens, *The Theology of the New Testament,* pp. 150-166, 234-244.
Strawson, *Jesus and the Future Life,* pp. 16-236.
Vos, *Biblical Theology,* pp. 397-411.
Vos, *The Kingdom and the Church,* pp. 27-40.
Weidner, *Biblical Theology of the New Testament,* Vol. I, pp. 91-123.
Weiss, *Biblical Theology of the New Testament,* Vol. I, pp. 143-158.

1. Gen. 49:1; Num. 24:14-17; Deut. 4:30; Is. 2:2; 4:2; 9:1; 11:10; Jer. 31:31; Joel 2:28-32; 3:18-21; Amos 9:11; etc.
2. Ps. 1:5; 7:11; 50:4-6; 75:7; 76:8; 96:10-13; Is. 33:22; 66:16; etc.

CHAPTER XI

THE KINGDOM OF GOD VIEWED IN THE PERSPECTIVE OF CHRIST'S COMPLETED WORK

1. Introduction

This chapter examines the messianic work of Christ viewed in the perspective of His completed earthly ministry. This should bring into focus the various aspects of Jesus' work including (1) His preaching of the kingdom (Mt. 9:35); (2) the declaration that all things had been delivered to Him by His Father (Mt. 11:27; 28:18; Jn. 13:3); (3) the announcement of building His church (Mt. 16:18); (4) the institution of the new covenant (Mt. 26:28; Lk. 22:20); (5) His death and resurrection (Mt. 27:32 — 28:20); and (6) the Great Commission (Mt. 28:18-20; Lk. 24:46 -49).

2. The Institution of the New Covenant

Most central in our Lord's earthly ministry was His act of instituting the new covenant (Mt. 26:26-29). In Matthew's setting of Jesus eating the Last Supper with the disciples, this meal obtained great significance because it stood as a symbol of His suffering and death. He said that the bread was His body and the wine was His blood. So forceful was this language that the Christian church has for centuries wrestled with its meaning. The interpretations of Jesus' words vary all the way from understanding the bread and the wine as being the actual body and blood of Christ over to the idea that Jesus was in, with, and under the elements of the bread and wine, and also the view that regards these elements as being the most expressive symbols of the broken body and shed blood of Christ. From an exegetical point of view the statements "This is my body" and "This is my blood" express the identity of the respective predicate nouns with its subject. Since this is clearly expressed according to the clear-cut syntax of the Greek language, adequate grounds must be found for accepting either of the other two interpretations. Since Jesus Himself made these declarations being present with them in bodily form, the idea of symbolism appears to express the real meaning of Jesus' words. This interpretation gains support when we observe other pictorial expressions used by Jesus, the most vivid of which are His commands to pluck out one's offending eye and to cut off one's offending hand or foot. With this explanation in mind we should see that Jesus was establishing an ordinance to be perpetuated in His church. Thus the Lord's Supper and water baptism as Christian ordinances related directly to the believer's covenant relationship with Christ.

Jesus' explanation of the bread and the wine expressed most clearly the meaning of His death. His broken body and shed blood in the language of Old Testament sacrifices was at once a blood offering symbolizing expiation for sin, commitment to God, and the resulting fellowship with Him. Jesus had said earlier that He had come "to give his life as a ransom for many" (Mt. 20:28). These words add to the meaning of His declaration, "This is my blood of the covenant" (26: 28). When the disciples heard these words, most undoubtedly they thought of the burnt and peace offerings through which the Lord had made His covenant with Israel at Mount Sinai. The disciples came to realize the stupendous fact which possessed unfathomable meaning, namely, that their Lord and Christ was instituting the new covenant, which had been predicted by the prophet Jeremiah (Jer. 31:31). Jesus was declaring that His blood would be poured out for the forgiveness of their sins. Through this new covenant they would realize unspeakable peace and fellowship with Jesus their Lord. It is conceivable that the disciples began to realize that this new covenant fulfilled and displaced the old covenant. In due time the Apostle Paul and the author of Hebrews gave to the church a full account of these new covenant privileges and fellowship (1 Cor. 10:14-22; 11:23-34; Heb. 8-10).

3. Jesus as Messianic King

Implicit in Jesus' institution of the new covenant was His enthronement as the messianic King. As the institution of the old covenant established God's rule over His people Israel, the theocracy, so Jesus' institution of the new covenant established His rule, the Christocracy. The disciples may have recalled an earlier declaration of Jesus, "All things have been delivered to me by my Father" (Mt. 11:27). John had also become aware of this when in connection with the Last Supper he noted, "Jesus, knowing that the Father had given all things into his hands" (Jn. 13:3). Jesus Himself declared His sovereignty in the words, "All authority in heaven and on earth has been given to me" (Mt. 28: 18). Peter confirmed this testimony in his message at Pentecost when he declared that Jesus had been exalted at the right hand of God and that the Father had made Him both Lord and Christ (Acts 2:33-36). It is essential for our understanding of the kingdom of God to note the integral relation of Christ's messianic kingship and the institution of the new covenant.

4. "My Church"

Following Peter's noble confession, "You are the Christ, the Son of the living God," Jesus said, "On this rock I will build my church, and the powers of death shall not prevail against it" (Mt. 16:16-18). The words *my church* undoubtedly arrested the attention of the disciples because they were aware of God's *church (qahal)* in the wilderness (Acts 7:37, 38). Undoubtedly the disciples on hearing these words from Jesus thought of the Old Testament church in precisely the same manner as Stephen later spoke of it. As God instituted the theocracy through the setting up of the Sinaitic covenant under which the people of Israel constituted His *qahal,* so Christ established the Christocracy under which all believers constitute His church.

Concerning this church Jesus declared, "The power of death shall not prevail against it" (Mt. 16:18). This gave the new body of believers grounds for believing that their ruling Lord was all-powerful and that the forces of Satan could not overthrow them. To Peter, Jesus said, "I will give you the keys of the kingdom of heaven, and whatever you bind on earth shall be bound in heaven, and whatever you loose on earth shall be loosed in heaven" (v. 19). While this charge to Peter presents some problems for interpretation, it may declare that Jesus was giving to Peter the responsibility of being the chief steward in His kingdom. In the exercise of this stewardship, whatever he shall bind or loose on earth shall be bound or loosed in heaven. The future perfect passive tense used here means that Jesus as Lord and Christ will recognize and honor the work of the faithful steward in the exercise of the responsibilities entrusted to him. Thus when Peter and all the stewards of Christ's kingdom are faithful to the trust committed to them and are obedient to their Lord, Christ will recognize their faithful exercise of stewardship and will deal accordingly with those serving under stewards.

In Matthew 18:15-35 Jesus spoke further of the exercise of this stewardship. A practical problem of how to deal with a brother who has sinned against another received consideration. It begins with the effort of one brother to show the other brother how he has sinned against him. If this fails, the harmed brother confronts the offender with one or two brethren; if this effort is not successful, the problem is brought to the church. If the one who had sinned against his brother refused to listen to the church he is deprived from sharing this brotherhood. To paraphrase Jesus' repeated statement of what He had told Peter: whatever the brotherhood of believers, the church, does in the sphere of discipline, will be approved by Christ the Lord. Jesus added these words, "If two of you agree on earth about anything they ask, it will be done for them by my Father in heaven. For where two or three are gathered in my name, there am I in the midst of them" (Mt. 18:19, 20). In this same general category Peter raised a pertinent question in the words, "Lord, how often shall my brother sin against me, and I forgive him? As many as seven times?" (v. 21). In the language of the parable Jesus likened our debt to God to that of ten thousand talents and the debt of the fellow believer to a hundred denarii. By this Jesus showed that unless we are willing to forgive one another a small debt from the heart, we cannot hope to be forgiven such a great debt by the Father.

This picture of the church as a brotherhood finds expression elsewhere in Jesus' teaching. In the context of the Sermon on the Mount He declared that we should not judge lest we be judged. And then He added, "Why do you see the speck that is in your brother's eye, but do not notice the log that is in your own eye?" (Mt. 7:3). By this Jesus showed the hypocrisy of attempting to remove the speck from the brother's eye and failing to remove the log from one's own eye. In a setting where Jesus' mother and His brothers desired to speak to Him while He was involved in some earnest conversation, Jesus asked, "Who is my mother, and who are my brothers?" Then stretching out His hand toward His disciples He said, "Here are my mother and my brothers! For whoever does the will of my Father in heaven is my brother, and sister, and mother" (12:48-50). In this manner Jesus enriched the idea of brotherhood by including all of the disciples as brothers and sisters. Jesus brought yet another facet of brotherhood into view when He said, "Every one who is angry with his brother shall be liable to judgment; whoever insults his brother shall be liable to the council, and whoever says, 'You fool!' shall be liable to the hell of fire" (5:22). Certain problems are resolved when the offender becomes reconciled to the innocent person. The exercise of genuine friendship and love quickly resolves such problems.

Our understanding of Christ's lordship of the church becomes still clearer when we grasp the meaning of discipleship. In a forthright manner Jesus brought this truth to His disciples in the words, "If any man would come after me, let him deny himself and take up his cross daily and follow me" (Lk. 9:23). Jesus had just told the disciples that He must suffer many things and be rejected by the Jewish leaders. He revealed to the disciples that their being followers of Christ involved a similar cross. No compromise position is possible as Jesus said, "For whoever would save his life will lose it; and whoever loses his life for my sake, he will save it" (v. 24). Jesus made it clear that those who were unwilling to suffer reproaches such as Christ did in this world cannot hope to be honored by Christ when He comes in His glory.

In a later setting Luke recorded the words of three would-be disciples to each of whom Jesus gave a fitting reply which makes still clearer the real meaning of discipleship (Lk. 9:57-62). Apparently the first would-be disciple did not want to part with his wealth, to which Jesus replied, "The Son of man has nowhere to lay his head" (v. 58). To the second man who felt that his first responsibility was to take care of home duties, Jesus replied, "Go and proclaim the kingdom of God" (v. 60). The third inquirer evidently had divided interests in life. Jesus blasted his inadequate view of discipleship by saying, "No one who puts his hand to the plow and looks back is fit for the kingdom of God" (v. 62). In this manner Jesus expressed the rigid and unequivocal requirement of discipleship.

In a third setting Jesus spoke still more forcefully of the absolute demands of discipleship (Lk. 14:25-32). Bluntly He said, "If any one comes to me and does not hate his own father and mother and wife and children and brothers and sisters, yes, and even his own life, he cannot be my disciple" (v. 26). Jesus proceeded to show the need of counting the cost in committing one's self to discipleship. No one would build a tower without figuring its cost. No one would go out to battle without a full determination to fight until victory is gained. Jesus concluded these illustrations by saying, "Whoever of you does not renounce all that he has cannot be my disciple" (v. 33).

Jesus imposed this unrelenting and uncompromising concept of discipleship upon His disciples when He commanded them, "Go therefore and make disciples of all nations. . . . teaching them to observe all that I have commanded you" (Mt. 28:19, 20). This willingness of the disciples to take up their crosses and to follow Jesus had its ultimate basis in His authority, for He is Lord of lords and King of kings.

5. The Death of Christ

Most crucial to the institution of the Lord's Supper and the new covenant was Jesus' reference to the pouring out of His blood as being symbolized by the drinking of the wine and as establishing or ratifying this new covenant. The meaning of this becomes clear when we note the significance of the burnt and peace offerings which instituted the covenant at Mount Sinai. All the bloody sacrifices symbolized the expiation of sin. The burnt offering was a symbol of the offerer's personal commitment to God, and the peace offering expressed the resulting fellowship between God and Israel. This furnishes adequate grounds for believing that Jesus' shed blood made expiation for the sins of all mankind, through which He offered Himself in complete consecration to God and thus established fellowship between God and man.

In confirmation of this interpretation note that Jesus declared that His blood was "poured out for many for the forgiveness of sins" (Mt. 26: 28). All this gives profoundest meaning to the death of Jesus.

After Jesus' resurrection He reminded the disciples that the prophets had spoken of His death, and on this account "was it not necessary that the Christ should suffer these things and enter into his glory?" (Lk. 24: 26). By this question Jesus was reminding His followers of the Suffering Servant prediction of Isaiah 53, and by so doing He declared the vicarious and efficacious aspect of His death. On an earlier occasion Jesus had already declared that He had come "to give his life as a ransom for many" (Mt. 20:28). The expression *a ransom for many* (*lutron anti)* possessed the meaning *price of release* and often referred to the ransom money paid for liberating a slave from his bondage. The preposition *anti (instead of, in place of, in behalf of)* gives support to the vicariousness of Jesus' death. He died as man's substitute. These explanations gave explicit meaning to the familiar words of Jesus found in John 3:14-16. Prior to His ascension Jesus said, "Thus it is written, that the Christ should suffer and on the third day rise from the dead, and that repentance and forgiveness of sins should be preached in his name to all nations" (Lk. 24:46, 47). These words gave final confirmation to the meaning of His death in accordance with His statement given prior to His crucifixion. They constitute the foundation for the preaching of repentance and forgiveness of sins throughout the world.

6. The Resurrection and Ascension of Jesus

Matthew, who wrote his Gospel with the definite purpose of showing that Jesus was the promised Messiah, fittingly concluded his book with Jesus' Great Commission in which we have the words, "All authority in heaven and on earth has been given to me" (Mt. 28:18). These words expressed the glorious truth that Jesus' resurrection constituted His exaltation and enthronement as the Messiah (Jn. 20:17). The aorist tense of the verb *edothe* (*has been given)* directs attention to God's act of giving authority to Jesus by raising Him from the dead. Significantly Jesus' resurrection declared His exaltation and enthronement. This act of God intensifies the meaning of His resurrection. He was not merely raised from the dead, but this coming to life declared His enthronement.

While most scholars do not recognize Mark 16:9-20 as having been written by Mark, there are no grounds for denying its historical character. In verse 19 we read, "So then the Lord Jesus, after he had spoken to them, was taken up into heaven, and sat down at the right hand of God." These words are peculiar to Mark; in fact, neither Matthew nor

John refer to our Lord's ascension, although Luke wrote, "He parted from them" (Lk. 24:51). He amplified this statement in the Acts and added Peter's words in which he said, "Being therefore exalted at the right hand of God, and having received from the Father the promise of the Holy Spirit, he has poured out this which you see and hear. For David did not ascend into the heavens; but he himself says, 'The Lord said to my Lord, Sit at my right hand, till I make thy enemies a stool for thy feet.' Let all the house of Israel therefore know assuredly that God has made him both Lord and Christ, this Jesus whom you crucified" (Acts 2:33-36). The meaning of Christ's ascension may be expressed in this way: His being lifted up to heaven as seen by the disciples served as external witness to His being enthroned. His throne was not in Jerusalem but at the right hand of the Father. Thus His ascension gave His disciples adequate proof of their Lord's exaltation and enthronement in heaven itself. In this manner we see the glorious nature of the kingdom of God in the perspective of the enthronement of Him who instituted the new covenant.

7. The Great Commission

The messianic kingly authority just noted served as the fitting introduction to the Great Commission given by Jesus. His command, "Go therefore and make disciples of all nations," possessed supreme authority. This command gains a new significance when it is compared with Jesus' words, "If any man would come after me, let him deny himself and take up his cross daily and follow me" (Lk. 9:23). This becomes evident when we recall Jesus' words to His earliest disciples, "Follow me." This would make clear the imperative demand of taking up one's cross and following Jesus. One of the Great Commission requirements was to make disciples of all nations. It naturally followed that He gave the invitation, "Follow me." Thus He would have all mankind to follow Him, that is, be His disciples, On another occasion Jesus said, "As the Father has sent me, even so I send you" (Jn. 20:21). With this commandment Jesus showed His followers that their being sent out into the world was a mission similar to that given by the Father to Him, and as the Holy Spirit came upon Jesus when He was baptized, so Jesus breathed on the disciples and said, "Receive the Holy Spirit." In this manner Jesus exercised the authority of His kingship. Peter in his sermon at Pentecost declared that the outpouring of the Holy Spirit upon the multitudes was the first kingly work of the enthroned Messiah.

In bringing this chapter to a close let us gain the full impact of the interrelations among the new covenant, the church, Christ's death.

His resurrection and ascension, and the Great Commission. In this perspective the ministry of Jesus most certainly centered in the kingdom of God.

For Additional Reading and Reference:

Bruce, A. B., *The Kingdom of God,* pp. 231-272.
Bruce, F. F., *New Testament Development of Old Testament Themes,* pp. 100-114.
Filson, *Jesus and the Risen Lord,* pp. 111-132, 181-223.
Hunter, *The Work and Words of Jesus,* pp. 91-100, 112-122.
Hunter, *The Message of the New Testament,* pp. 52-66, 96-117.
Jeremias, *New Testament Theology,* pp. 159-311.
Kunneth, *The Theology of the Resurrection.*
Ladd, *Jesus and the Kingdom,* pp. 258-273.
Lindars, *New Testament Apologetic,* pp. 32-137.
Morris, *The Cross and the New Testament,* pp. 13-106.
Richardson, *An Introduction to the Theology of the New Testament,* pp. 181-240, 307-321.
Ridderbos, *The Coming of the Kingdom,* pp. 185-284, 334-433.
Stagg, *New Testament Theology,* pp. 122-148, 170-249.
Stauffer, *New Testament Theology,* pp. 129-139.
Stevens, *The Theology of the New Testament,* pp. 119-149.
Weiss, *Biblical Theology of the New Testament,* Vol. I, pp. 125-142.

PART TWO:
THE BEGINNING OF JESUS' RULE AS THE ENTHRONED LORD AND CHRIST

CHAPTER I

THE EMERGING CHURCH AND THE LETTER OF JAMES

1. Introduction

The biblical materials which will receive consideration in this chapter are Acts 1 to 12 and the Book of James. We should expect that Luke would pursue the same general objectives and maintain the same viewpoint as found in his Gospel record. In Chapter III I discussed the distinctive message of Luke's Gospel record under the headings: (a) the historical basis of the Christian religion; (b) Jesus, the Heir to the throne of His father David; (c) the Son of God, baptized with Holy Spirit; (d) Jesus, the Savior of the world; and (e) the universal mission of the Gospel.

I drew attention to the significant words found in the opening verses of his Gospel in which he claimed to have gained from eyewitnesses and ministers of the Word the historical facts presented in his Gospel, and his desire to give an orderly account of the events so that Theophilus might know the truth concerning all the things of which he had been informed. This sets forth the procedure of a trained historian. It gives us adequate ground for believing that Luke followed the same purpose in writing his second book. He reminded Theophilus that in the Gospel record he had dealt with all that Jesus began to do and teach. He then noted that Jesus had presented Himself alive after His Passion by many proofs. The structure of this approach shows that the author would be pursuing the same historical approach in this book as he did in the Gospel. Luke thus proceeds to present an accurate historical record of the apostolic age. It is deeply to be regretted how some reputedly outstanding scholars can in a childish and unscholarly manner reject the historical nature of this book. On this account

I shall endeavor to show the manner in which Luke, as an accurate and unbiased historian, set forth the events of the apostolic age, particularly, the resurrection of Christ. In a word, he presented the testimony of eyewitnesses who were competent and trustworthy in giving witness to the most important event of human history, namely, the resurrection of Jesus.

2. Luke's Presentation of Jesus' Post-Resurrection Ministry

Luke's introduction to the Book of Acts revealed the same perspective that he gave in the introduction to his Gospel. He noted that his first book dealt with all that Jesus began to do and teach. This suggested that the forthcoming book would be a continuation of what Jesus did and taught. It asserted that the risen and enthroned Jesus would continue this activity through the Holy Spirit who would come upon the apostles.

Luke presented his testimony with regard to the historicity of Christ's resurrection by stating that Jesus presented Himself alive after His Passion by many proofs through appearances to the apostles during a forty-day period. The noun *tekmerion*, translated *proofs*, declared the indubitable evidence — the positive, convincing, and decisive proof of Christ's resurrection. Luke, the historian, knew well that this most important event of world history required adequate and trustworthy evidence in its support. This accounts for the historical procedure in which Luke gave support for the historicity of Christ's being raised from the dead.

Luke noted further that Christ continued to speak on the same momentous theme, the kingdom of God, which was His central message prior to His death. This shows again the true perspective which Jesus set forth concerning the kingdom of God. Jesus then charged His disciples to remain in Jerusalem until they would be baptized with the Holy Spirit. Jesus' reference to John's water baptism in relation to Holy Spirit baptism suggests a significant interrelation between the two. It suggests that water baptism symbolizes Holy Spirit baptism. John had prepared the way for Jesus, the Messiah, by baptizing with water those who repented from their sins. The transition of thought from water baptism to Holy Spirit baptism thus became easily understood, especially when Jesus, the Messiah, made the comparison.

The expectation on the part of the disciples of Jesus' restoring the kingdom to Israel shows again their failure to grasp the nature of the kingdom as taught by Jesus throughout His ministry. It proves how deeply ingrained in their thinking was the Jewish expectation of the restoration of a political kingdom to Israel. Jesus' response to their misconception of the kingdom led Him to tell the disciples, "It is not for you to know times or seasons which the Father has fixed by his own authority" (Acts 1:7). This declaration gave a new perspective to His earlier teaching when He said, "The kingdom of God will be taken away from you and given to a nation producing the fruits of it" (Mt. 21:43). Also, "Fear not, little flock, for it is your Father's good pleasure to give you the kingdom" (Lk. 12:32). He was guiding the course of history to its intended goal.

This led to Jesus' final commission to His disciples before He ascended to glory. They would receive power when the Holy Spirit would come upon them, and by reason of this power, He gave them the commission to be His witnesses in Jerusalem. Judea, Samaria, and to the end of the earth. The expression, my *witnesses,* stated "their direct personal relationship."[1] That is, the disciples were official witnesses of Jesus' life, death, and resurrection. The mission of the apostles was far greater than that of preaching concerning their Lord's earthly ministry. Supremely they shared in a personal relationship with their risen Lord. This extended throughout the entire ministry of Jesus, beginning from the baptism of John until the day when He was taken up to glory. Their having witnessed Christ's resurrection entrusted them with the responsibility of bearing witness to others of their experiences with Jesus. Repeatedly throughout Peter's ministry he gave testimony to what he had seen and heard (Acts 2:32; 3:15; 5:32; 10:39-41). Paul added his confirmation of the apostolic witness to Christ's resurrection in his sermon at Antioch (Acts 13:30-32). Undoubtedly the angelic message to the eleven disciples, giving the promise that Jesus would come in the same way that they had seen Him go into heaven, resolved their major problems.

3. The Company of the Believers

The author, Luke, demonstrated again his keen insight to the events which introduced the acts of the apostles. He recorded a significant meeting in the upper room made up of the eleven disciples, a group of women associated with Mary, the mother of Jesus, and also Jesus' brothers. This small company included those who were most closely associated with Jesus throughout His ministry and had fellowshiped with the risen Lord. Luke added the significant note, "All these with one accord devoted themselves to prayer." This is the first reference to the gathered assembly later to be called the church. At least two characteristics were distinctive of this meeting: first, the oneness of mind and purpose of those assembled; and second, that they were steadfastly continuing in prayer. This assembly was laying the pattern for worship in the Christian church.

Luke proceeded to relate a significant action taken by the 120 believers under the direction of Peter. This apostle began to exercise a leadership in this newborn church, possibly in response to Christ's special charge at Caesarea Philippi (Mt. 16:13-20). It is also possible that he moved forward by reason of his inborn leadership among the Twelve. Luke gave no hint that Peter overstepped his apostolic authority. On this account his leadership in choosing a successor to Judas may be regarded as directed by the Holy Spirit. Peter noted that Judas' betrayal of Jesus fulfilled what the Holy Spirit had spoken beforehand by the mouth of David (Ps. 65:25; 109:8). Peter saw in these predictions the authorization for choosing the successor to Judas as an apostle. Peter confirmed the qualifications for an apostle in the words, "So one of the men who have accompanied us during all the time that the Lord Jesus went in and out among us, beginning from the baptism of John until the day when he was taken up from us — one of these men must become with us a witness to his resurrection" (Acts 1:21, 22). In this manner Peter defined the office of an apostle in harmony with Jesus' appointment of the Twelve as recorded in the synoptic Gospels (Mt. 10: 1-4; Mk. 3:13-19; Lk. 6:12-16).

The manner of choosing the successor to Judas, namely by lot, shows that he was not the choice of the eleven apostles, but rather of Christ, Himself. Thus Matthias possessed the right to apostleship on the same basis as the eleven. Peter's leadership in the calling of Matthias was the legitimate exercise of his own authority as an apostle. He was thus laying the mold for the exercise of apostolic authority as entrusted to the Twelve by Christ. Peter added the responsibility of ministry or service (*diakonia*) to that of apostleship (Acts 1:25). This broadened view of apostolic responsibility shows that while the apostles were supremely the official witnesses to the earthly ministry of Christ climaxed in His death, resurrection, and ascension their mission also included "religious administration, and the exercise of ministerial function in the Church." [2]

4. Pentecost and Peter's Exposition of Jesus' Messiahship

a. The Outpouring of the Holy Spirit and Peter's Explanation of the Event

In vivid language Luke depicted the Pentecostal experience. The punctiliar coming of the Holy Spirit upon the group of believers was accompanied by miraculous phenomena such as the sound of the rush of a mighty wind, the appearance to the group of tongues as of fire, and their speaking in other tongues. These supernatural manifestations accompanying the outpouring of the Holy Spirit served as the proofs of the Spirit's coming upon the believers. They served the same purpose as the miracles performed by Jesus gave proof of His being the Messiah. If there had been no outward manifestation of the Spirit's coming upon the believers, they would not have had grounds for believing that they had received the Holy Spirit. This in a fundamental way gave further confirmation to the purpose of miracles in biblical history.

Since all were amazed and perplexed by this manifestation, Peter proceeded to explain what had taken place. He at once declared that the prediction of the prophet Joel had been fulfilled. This quotation from Joel 2:28-32 revealed several great truths which deserve careful study. First, Peter identified the outpouring of the Holy Spirit with Joel's prediction. His language, "This is what was spoken by the prophet Joel," was clear and decisive. From a certain point of view this declaration by Peter required prophetic insight. It was not always easy to identify a fulfillment with the prediction. Second, Joel identified the time of the coming of the Spirit as being "in *the last days*." This *aeon, the last days,* was the greatest theme of the Old Testament prophets. Several of the pre-exilic prophets predicted a coming judgment to take place in the day of the Lord. Their foreview of the future extended to a later era of time which they called the latter days or the last days. The central theme of these latter-day predictions centered in the coming Messiah.

Part of this great messianic future was the coming of the Holy Spirit as predicted by Joel and other prophets. Suddenly it dawned upon the company of believers at Pentecost that these last days had come. They were the recipients of the great blessings which would come upon the people of God through the Messiah and the Holy Spirit whom He would pour out upon the body of believers. Joel had predicted that when the Spirit would come upon God's people, they would prophesy. In the Old Testament the Holy Spirit came upon prophets, priests, kings, and others entrusted with special responsibilities. It appears that Joel was predicting a marked advance from that of the Old Testament in that God would pour out His Spirit upon all flesh. This factor makes the Pentecost experience distinctive because the Holy Spirit came upon every one present in this gathering.

There is need for holding in proper perspective the larger aspect of the progress in God's unfolding of Himself in both the Old and the New Testaments. On the one side there is a great similarity between the Old and the New Testaments in the manner in which the Holy Spirit encountered God's people. "These encounters were personal, ethical, inward, continuous, and supernatural. Through His Spirit, God entered intimately into the life of man. No part of man's being lay beyond the Spirit's touch."[3] On the other side we should observe the intimacy of the Holy Spirit's work in the believer as portrayed throughout the New Testament, especially as noted in the Book of Acts, Romans 8, and Galatians 5.

Joel had also predicted that God would show wonders and signs in the world which would inaugurate the last days. These were fulfilled in the miraculous events which took place at the close of Christ's earthly ministry and came to a climax in His resurrection. The most glorious aspect of these last days was expressed in the words, "It shall be that whoever calls on the name of the Lord shall be saved" (Acts 2:21). This became the focal point in the preaching of the apostles and marked the real content of the gospel message. All these things were to be fulfilled before the day of the Lord comes. From the standpoint of New Testament eschatology this declaration carries tremendous significance. These last days, the great era of salvation to all mankind, will terminate in the day of the Lord, the great day of God's judgment upon the world.

b. Peter's Pentecostal Sermon

Peter's first concern was to declare that God had attested the messiahship of Jesus of Nazareth through mighty works, wonders, and signs. He employed three of the great words used in the Bible for miracles, each possessing a distinctive significance. The *mighty works (dunamis)* set forth the power, the dynamic which the miracles manifested. The word *wonders (teras)* viewed the miracles from the angle of their impact upon those who beheld them. The word *sign (semeion)* interprets the miracles from the angle of their significance, including their meaning and purpose. Peter sought to show that God had given adequate grounds and proofs for believing that Jesus was the Christ.

Peter proceeded to show that Jesus' crucifixion was not merely an act of lawless men but that He was "delivered up according to the definite plan and foreknowledge of God" (Acts 2:23). This language disclosed a profound insight on the part of Peter with regard to the basis of God's acts in history. The word *boule* carries the meaning: *plan, purpose,* and *counsel,* while the word *prognosis* has the connotation: *foreknowledge, forethought,* and *prearrangement.* Both of these words are modified by the perfect passive participle of *horizo* which means *determined, appointed,* and *designated.* This participle intensifies the idea of God's personal involvement in all the events of Christ's earthly ministry. Since the plan and foreknowledge of God are bound to the same article, the distinctive meanings of these words merge quite closely.

Peter's words, "definite plan and foreknowledge of God," have a doctrinal significance independent of their use in this context. From the theological point of view this statement contributes a great deal to our understanding of the doctrine of God. His attributes ever remain before us as profound mysteries. Some students have great difficulty to reconcile these expressions, believing that the definite plan of God and His foreknowledge are irreconcilable. While I recognize the grand mystery bound up in these two attributes, I believe, nevertheless, that these expressions are not irreconcilable when properly interpreted. Most clearly, the divine person of God possesses the personal attribute of counsel and purpose. At the same time His infinite knowledge includes foreknowledge and forethought. Thus when these two ideas are held in proper focus we as finite beings should have no trouble in believing that these attributes involve predetermination as well as prearrangement. This interpretation should not jeopardize in any way man's free moral agency with which he was endowed by God the Creator. God's creation of man in His own image stands in perfect harmony with God's nature and personality.

Peter proceeded to show that God raised Jesus from the dead, declaring that this death experience did not lie beyond the power of God to loose the pangs of death. On this account Peter could properly call David a prophet and then he added his own testimony that he and the gathered assembly before him were all witnesses to Christ's resurrection. Peter also drew in three messianic psalms (132, 16, 110), which predicted Christ's exaltation at the right hand of God. In this manner the coming of the Holy Spirit upon these believers was proof positive that the exalted Christ in the exercise of His regal authority had poured out His Spirit upon them. In view of this, Peter could most triumphantly conclude, "Let all the house of Israel therefore know assuredly that God has made him both Lord and Christ, this Jesus whom you crucified" (Acts 2:36).

Luke presented the impact of Peter's message on his audience. Incidently, we should observe what materials Luke included in his narrative so that we may grasp more fully the structure of this book. In genuine historical procedure Luke saw fit to present the effect of Peter's sermon upon his hearers. Being cut to the heart they asked Peter and the rest of the apostles what they should do. Peter fulfilled Christ's command when he said, "Repent, and be baptized every one of you in the name of Jesus Christ for the forgiveness of your sins; and you shall receive the gift of the Holy Spirit" (Acts 2:38). Thus Peter was perpetuating water baptism as the seal of repentance and the initiatory rite for admission to the body of believers in Christ. Water baptism, which had its origin in the ministry of John the Baptist, was used by Christ throughout His ministry and was incorporated in His commission to the apostles in the words, "Make disciples of all nations, baptizing them in the name of the Father and of the Son and of the Holy Spirit, teaching them to observe all that I have commanded you" (Mt. 28:19, 20).

The prerequisite for baptism was repentance. This involved a complete change of mind and purpose with regard to sin. Involved in this was *a turning about and return* to God expressed by the verb *epistrepho,* used later by Peter alongside *metanoeo (repent)* (Acts 3:19). The experience of repentance also included faith. The penitent sinner needed to believe that his sins would be forgiven and that he would receive the gift of the Holy Spirit. All this was involved in discipleship.

Peter's use of the expression, "in the name of Jesus Christ," was in accord with Christ's words in the Great Commission. The exact meaning of this phrase is difficult to determine.[4] Bruce suggests, "Probably in the sense that the person being baptized confessed or invoked Jesus as Messiah." Being baptized in the name of Jesus Christ is inseparably bound up with the purposive phrase, "for the forgiveness of your sins." The entire sentence so far was the condition for receiving the gift of the Holy Spirit. Those who were baptized became disciples of Jesus and became members of Christ's church (Mt. 16:16-18). Those who were baptized were to receive the Holy Spirit in the same manner as the body of believers shared in the Pentecostal experience of the outpouring of the Holy Spirit. In other words, everyone who repents and is baptized in the name of Jesus Christ for the forgiveness of sins experiences a Pentecost.

In Luke's pursuit of his major objective in writing this book he gave another glimpse of the body of believers, then numbering about three thousand souls. They were devoting themselves "to the apostles' teaching and fellowship, to the breaking of bread and the prayers" (Acts 2:42). This worship experience was similar to that described in 1:14. Here Luke introduced a new word *koinonia (fellowship, communion),* which became quite definitive of the spiritual sharing experienced by this body of believers. While the breaking of bread may refer to their sharing together in meals, the unusual form of the expression in the Greek in which both nouns have the article may suggest that it refers to the breaking of bread in the Lord's Supper. In either case, the fellowship enjoyed together was a distinctive experience of those committed disciples of Christ. Their sharing in the prayers marked the climax of their experience.

Luke added another dimension of their fellowship together, namely that of having all things in common. They did this in order to make as large a distribution as possible to those who had physical needs. This was a practical outworking of their newborn Christian fellowship. Their sharing together included that of attending the temple together and of breaking bread together in their homes. They did this with glad and generous hearts and praising God. It led to their having favor with all the people. Luke concluded this description by adding, "And the Lord added to their number day by day those who were being saved" (Acts 2:47). Note that the Lord added to their number. It was not merely the result of human effort.

c. Peter's Later Declarations Concerning Jesus the Messiah

Perhaps the most significant contribution made by Peter to the unfolding revelation of Jesus, the Son of God, was the names and titles which he assigned to Him. The first two were *Lord* and *Christ* (Acts 2:36; see also 3:18; 5:42; 10:36). The title *Kurios (Lord)* was used in the Septuagint to translate *Yahweh,* and in this way ascribes to Jesus the most significant title of Deity. The title *Xristos (Christ)* was used to translate the Hebrew *Mashiach (Anointed).* In the Old Testament this title was given to Abraham, Isaac, and Cyrus. By reason of the promise made by the Lord to David that He would establish his throne forever, a number of the psalms focus on One to come known as the Anointed One.[5] Consequently all the messianic predictions of the Old Testament had their fulfillment in Jesus. To the three thousand souls who heard Peter's declaration in his sermon at Pentecost, this identification of Jesus as the Christ carried immeasurable meaning.

In later messages Peter spoke of Jesus as God's Servant (Acts 3:13, 26; 4:27, 31). Undoubtedly, Peter was identifying Jesus with the Servant of the Lord as foretold in the Book of Isaiah (Is. 42:1-7; 49:1-6; 50:4-9; 52:13 — 53:12). On the occasion of Peter's healing the lame man, He addressed the multitude using the meaningful expression, "men of Israel," and then declared that God had glorified His Servant Jesus. To this audience this reference to Jesus as God's Servant must have made a tremendous impact, especially so since Peter was implicitly identifying God's Servant and Jesus, the Christ (Acts 3:6, 13). To the devout men of Israel who heard Peter's words it was inevitable that they should become aware of the greatness of this Jesus whom they had delivered up to be killed. In this same message Peter called Jesus the holy and righteous One. Peter had already quoted the Septuagint version of Psalm 16:8-11, which he declared was David's prediction concerning Jesus. In calling Jesus the righteous One he may have had in mind 2 Samuel 23:3 and Isaiah 32:1 and 53:11. In the same sentence Peter called Jesus the Author of life. Quite paradoxically, Peter accused the Jews of killing the Author of life, and then intensified his point by saying that God had raised Him from the dead.

When Peter gave his defense to the Jewish council he declared among other things that God had exalted Christ at His right hand as Leader and Savior (Acts 5:31). The word *arxegos,* translated *Author* in the preceding passage, has the meaning of Leader or Prince in this reference, especially since Peter was referring to Christ in His exaltation. Undoubtedly, Peter had heard the Samaritan testify that Jesus is the Savior of the world, as well as Jesus' own words, "The Son of man came to seek and to save the lost" (Jn. 4:42; Lk. 19:10).

To Cornelius Peter declared that Jesus was "ordained by God to be judge of the living and the dead" (Acts 10:42). In this case Peter had heard Jesus say, "The Father judges no one, but has given all judgment to the Son" (Jn. 5:22). Undoubtedly, he recalled Jesus' prediction of the judgment scene which would take place at His return (Mt. 25:31-46). The cumulative meaning of all these titles reveals Peter's profound understanding of the person and work of Jesus the Messiah.

Interwoven with these declarations of Jesus' messiahship a number of significant statements by Peter gave the meaning of Christ's redemptive work. The efficacy of Christ's work became apparent in His command to the people to repent and be baptized in the name of Jesus through which they would gain forgiveness of sins and receive the gift of the Holy Spirit (Acts 2:38). In his second message Peter declared that the prophets had foretold Christ's sufferings and death. Through repentance and turning to God they could appropriate the efficacy of Christ's death by having their sins blotted out (Acts 3:18, 19). When Israel's spiritual leaders confronted Peter, asking him by what power or by what name he had done this, Peter replied that it was through the name of Jesus Christ, whom they had crucified and whom God had raised from the dead. He concluded his answer with the words, "There is salvation in no one else, for there is no other name under heaven given among men by which we must be saved" (Acts 4:10-12). In a word, Christ's death and resurrection bring salvation to mankind. There is no other way of being saved. To the Jewish council Peter concluded his testimony with the words, "God exalted him at his right hand as Leader and Savior, to give repentance to Israel and forgiveness of sins" (Acts 5:31). Here again Peter was declaring that Jesus through His death became the Savior of mankind. On this account man is able to repent and receive forgiveness of sins. In the following chapter I shall present Peter's explicit teachings on Christ's redemptive work.

d. The Emergence of the Church

I have already noted the small company of believers, made up of the eleven disciples, the women accompanying Mary, the mother of Jesus, and His brothers. This was in all truth the infant church. The second picture of an assembled body of believers numbered three thousand souls and "they devoted themselves to the apostles' teaching and fellowship, to the breaking of bread and the prayers" (Acts 2:42). Day by day "those who were being saved" (2:47) were added to their number.

Not until the incident of Ananias and Sapphira did Luke introduce the word *church* (Acts 5:11). However, his manner of introducing it suggests that it was already the recognized name of the gathered assembly of believers. Why Luke did not present in his Gospel parallels to Matthew's two references (16:18; 18:17), we do not know; nevertheless, he learned of this name, evidently through apostolic witness, likely Peter himself. Luke's free use of this term throughout the Acts shows his genuine comprehension of its meaning. It is impressive to note the rapid growth in numbers of the believers from three thousand to five thousand, plus the multitudes added later (Acts 2:42; 4:4; 5:14; 6:7). This growth gives evidence of the spiritual vitality and dynamic found in the early church.

It is essential to note also that this body of believers held closely to the apostles' *teaching (didache).* In time this *didache* became a fixed body of doctrine and thus lost much of its vitality. Nevertheless, the *didache* was essential to Christian belief and distinguished the believers from those of other religions. It is significant to observe what importance was attached to Christian doctrine by Paul, the author of Hebrews, and John.[6] This body of *didache* served to crystallize Christian thought and prepared the way for the creeds and confessions of the Christian church.

In contrast with the legalized form of Jewish worship this first group of Christian believers set forth the earliest pattern of Christian worship (Acts 1:14). The devotion to the apostles' teaching and fellowship, to the breaking of bread and the prayers, developed further the distinctive nature of Christian worship. Their being of one heart and soul, and of holding everything in common marked their spiritual unity in worship. The misconduct of Ananias and Sapphira underscored the necessity for holy living required of those engaged in worship.

The incident just mentioned opens another facet of the emerging church, namely that of it being a disciplined group. Peter assumed the responsibility of confronting this couple with regard to their dishonesty. Underlying this encounter was Peter's evident understanding of the church's responsibility to deal with misconduct among the body of believers.

Another need arose in the church, that of providing for the poor widows who lacked support. To meet this situation the apostles called together the body of disciples and laid the problem before them. The apostles felt that they should not give up preaching the Word of God in order to serve tables. They then took the initiative to appoint seven men to fill this need. There appears to have been no problem as to the church's responsibility in providing for the poor and needy in the church. This action shows the broadening horizon of the church's understanding of its mission in society. The apostles' method of procedure showed how a company of Christian believers should function. The body of the disciples chose "seven men of good repute, full of the Spirit and of wisdom," and brought these seven before the apostles who then entered into prayer and laid their hands upon them. It should be observed that while the apostles took the initiative for this appointment of the seven, the entire body of disciples were involved in choosing them. The laying of hands upon the seven on the part of the apostles likely carried a similar meaning to that found in the Old Testament. In some cases this fact symbolized the bestowing of a blessing upon another. Perhaps the nearest parallel is that of Moses laying hands on Joshua and by this act commissioning him to be Moses' successor (Num. 27:22, 23).

In this context of a broadening responsibility of the church we should note the activity of the church in Antioch when they learned of the famine in Judea. Here again the body of disciples took action to send relief to the brethren who lived there. Everyone gave according to his ability. Barnabas and Saul were delegated to take the relief to the elders of the Judean churches. This is the first information we have with reference to responsible brethren known as elders *(presbuteros).* These elders likely had a responsibility similar to those in the Jewish synagogue. Since the relief was sent to them, their responsibilities included this kind of service. At a later point I shall note the enlarged responsibilities of the elders as it developed in apostolic history.

5. The Church, the Goal of Hebrew History

Luke disclosed his understanding of apostolic history by apportioning a long chapter of sixty verses to the ministry of Stephen, including his lengthy defense. One's first impression of Stephen's defense may be that he was giving a wearisome recital of trivial details in Israel's history. But when we learn of the enraging impact that this recital of Hebrew history made upon his audience, we are compelled to make a closer study of his discourse. Briefly stated, Stephen was showing that the church was the goal of Hebrew history. This is why Luke saw fit to give such a full presentation of Stephen's witness to the gospel. For Luke's purpose it was central in apostolic history that the church should come to understand that all Hebrew history led forward and prepared the way for Christ and His church. From the point of view of biblical theology, this grasp of Hebrew history possesses highest priority.

The false charges brought by the Jews against Stephen may suggest the content of his preaching. They accused him of speaking blasphemous words against Moses and God. They also charged him of speaking against the holy temple and the law. They accused him of saying that Jesus would destroy the temple and change the customs delivered to them by Moses. Stephen in a masterful way exploded these false charges by giving a true perspective of Hebrew history. Three points deserve study in Stephen's defense. First, Stephen set forth God's gracious saving and merciful acts in Hebrew history (Acts 7:2-8, 9-16, 17-22, 23-34, 35-38, 44-50). Second, he exposed the disobedience and rebellious attitude of Israel toward God (vv. 39-43, 51-53). But most significantly, Stephen wove into his narrative predictions given by God centering in Christ and the indwelling of the Most High in heaven (vv. 37, 38, 48-50). In this manner Stephen was declaring to his Jewish audience the resistance of Israel to their God, the One who was acting all through their history from Abraham onward. In spite of Israel's repeated acts of stubbornness and resistance to God, showing themselves to be uncircumcised in heart and ears, and of persistent resistance to the Holy Spirit, God promised Israel to raise up a prophet among them like unto Moses. In place of the glorious temple which Solomon had built, Stephen directed their minds to God.

In this discourse Stephen made no less than seventy allusions or quotations from the Old Testament. To him the Old Testament constituted the Holy Scriptures. He was able not merely to quote copiously from these Sacred Writings, but to interpret them as authentic history and as God's very Word. He had some insights which not even Peter had yet grasped (Acts 10:12-16, 28, 29). Likewise, many Judean Christians, the circumcision party, held to radical views on this matter (Acts 11:2, 3; 15:1-7; 21:20-29). All these facts lead us to conclude that under the leadership of Stephen the church was in the process of grasping its universal mission. This gives supreme significance to Luke's historical perspective of apostolic history. Whether or not Stephen knew any of Jesus' teachings about the church and its task of worldwide evangelization, Luke had learned all these facts as shown in his Gospel, and was giving further recognition of this here by way of Stephen's defense.

6. The Beginning of the Church Universal

The ministry of Philip in Samaria marked a significant step in the church's realization of its universal mission. By reason of Stephen's defense of the gospel, which led to his martyrdom, a great persecution arose against the church in Jerusalem. Luke specifically stated that "they were all scattered throughout the region of Judea and Samaria, except the apostles" (Acts 8:1). Luke frankly stated that Saul (Paul) was laying waste the church. He wrote, "Those who were scattered went about preaching the word" (Acts 8:4). This was an especially commendable observation made concerning the scattered church, especially in view of the awful opposition imposed upon the membership by their fellow countrymen, the Jews in Jerusalem. Undoubtedly these scattered Christians had been thoroughly challenged through Stephen's witness.

The Jews of Jerusalem were so ingrown in their legalistic interpretation of the Old Testament that they would hardly share their Jewish faith with these half-Jews. But Philip, one of the seven, went down to Samaria where, "he preached good news about the kingdom of God and the name of Jesus Christ" (Acts 8:12). Multitudes of the Samaritans repented through his preaching and were baptized. When the apostles at Jerusalem heard that these people had received the Word of God, they sent to them Peter and John, who prayed for them that they might receive the Holy Spirit. While they had been baptized in the name of the Lord Jesus, the Holy Spirit had not yet fallen on any of them. But when the apostles laid their hands on these people, they received the Holy Spirit.

This entire incident carried great significance. Most important for our purpose was the fact that through their receiving the Holy Spirit when the apostles laid their hands on them, this body of believers, half-Jews, became members of the same body as the Jerusalem church. They did not compose another church. The participation of the apostles in this extension of the church was an expression of their apostolic authority in their major task of building the church. Philip continued his preaching mission in his witness to the Ethiopian eunuch. While a eunuch could worship in Jerusalem, he was denied the full rights of a Jew. Philip ignored this barrier and told the eunuch the good news of Jesus. Philip allowed nothing to stand in the way of his being baptized. This became a second important step toward the realization of the gospel being preached to all mankind. Undoubtedly, this fact led Luke to include this incident in his book.

The story of Cornelius stands as the major step toward achieving the goal of the universal gospel. Pertinent to this story were the visions both to Cornelius and to Peter with reference to the gospel's bridging the chasm between Jews and Gentiles. The command to Peter in his vision, to kill and eat the unclean animals shown to him, confronted him in an overwhelming manner. Through his life he had recognized the absolute authority of the Old Testament law. Being a loyal Jew he felt unable to heed the voice demanding him to kill and eat. He was inwardly perplexed as to what the vision meant. Even though Cornelius was an upright and God-fearing man, Peter up to this time would have been unable to fellowship with him as a Christian brother. Nevertheless, when Peter met Cornelius and learned of his vision, the whole issue became clear to the apostle. Peter then shared a real gospel message with Cornelius. While he was still speaking, the Holy Spirit fell on all who heard the Word. When this occurred, the believers among the circumcised were amazed because these Gentiles experienced the outpouring of the Holy Spirit upon them. These Gentiles also were speaking in tongues and extolling God. Peter then commanded them to be baptized in the name of Jesus Christ.

When Peter returned to Jerusalem, the circumcision party criticized him for eating with uncircumcised men. This gave him the opportunity of relating to them all that had happened in his relations with Cornelius. He concluded by saying, "If then God gave the same gift to them as he gave to us when we believed in the Lord Jesus Christ, who was I that I could withstand God?" (Acts 11:17). The church glorified God recognizing that to the Gentiles also God had granted repentance unto life.

A somewhat similar incident happened also at Antioch where some of those who were scattered from Jerusalem had gone. They also preached the Lord Jesus to the Greeks, and in response a great number believed and turned to the Lord. The church at Jerusalem then sent Barnabas to the city to give these new Gentile believers further spiritual guidance. Barnabas was the best qualified representative to be sent to Antioch because, "he was a good man, full of the Holy Spirit and of faith" (Acts 11:24). Since the company of believers continued to become much larger, Barnabas wisely went to Tarsus to secure the help of Saul in this new church at Antioch.

These two remarkable incidents of Gentile conversions showed how the Lord through the Holy Spirit was leading the church, especially through the witness of Peter, Barnabas, and Saul, to bring the gospel to the Gentiles. Through Luke's giving so much attention to the extension of the gospel to the Gentiles, he was demonstrating again his understanding of apostolic history and was recording these events for the enlightenment of the entire church. All this shows that Luke grasped the theological significance of apostolic history. He provided the church with an authentic record of how the Christian church with its beginnings in Jerusalem was reaching outward to include the Gentiles — all this according to the Lord's leading through the Holy Spirit.

The capsheaf to this extension of the gospel, to Gentiles as well as Jews, came in the Jerusalem council. This council was occasioned by the Judaizers who went down to Antioch and were declaring that unless the Gentile Christians were circumcised according to the custom of Moses they could not be saved. By reason of the discussion and debate which followed, the church appointed Paul and Barnabas to go to Jerusalem where the apostles and elders were gathered together in order to consider this problem. In this conference Peter testified that the Lord had given the Holy Spirit to the Gentiles in the same manner as to the Jews. God had made no distinction between them. He cleansed the hearts of the Gentiles by faith. Barnabas and Paul also added their testimony to the same effect.

James the moderator of the conference declared that Peter's testimony, that God had visited the Gentiles and had taken out a people for them for His name, was in agreement with what the prophet Amos had declared. This great prophet who had forecast the downfall of Judah concluded his forceful prophetic message with the note of hope that God would rebuild the dwelling of David — "that the rest of men may seek the Lord, and all the Gentiles who are called by my name" (Acts 15:17). On the basis of this prophetic message James gave his judgment that they "should not trouble those of the Gentiles who turn to God" (v. 19). This scripturally based judgment of James met the approval of the apostles, the elders, and the whole church (v. 22). This body was conscious of the Holy Spirit's direction in this decision. From this time onward the church was made free from its national barriers. The church was now in position to fulfill Christ's Great Commission of making disciples of all nations.

7. The Letter of James -- The First New Testament Book

a. Date, Authorship, and Destination of James' Letter

The opening verse states plainly that the author was James "a servant of God and of the Lord Jesus Christ." This internal claim to authorship continues to stand as irrefutable evidence that James, the brother of Jesus, was the author of this letter. No external evidence exists for rejecting this internal claim. The letter does not declare definitely when it was written. According to the late A. T. Robertson, "The sins condemned are those characteristic of early Jewish Christians. The book itself is more like the Sermon on the Mount than the epistles. The discussion of faith and works in chapter 2 reveals an absence of the issues faced by Paul in Romans 4 and Galatians 3 after the Jerusalem conference AD 49."[7] On this account Robertson dates it about AD 48. James addressed his letter to the twelve tribes in the dispersion. A careful study of its contents justifies this conclusion. It would appear that his readers had not yet grasped the full dimensions of the gospel. Since the pharisaical, legalistic view of the law had so thoroughly permeated Jewish thought, many of those who had become Christians continued to think in terms of this legalism. What James did was to present the truth of the gospel in the framework of the Old Testament law. He gave a spiritual interpretation of the law in the perspective of its fulfillment in the gospel.

When this is understood, the value of this book as the earliest New Testament document becomes clear. James met his readers on the level of their thinking but interpreted the Old Testament law in the light of the gospel. From the point of view of biblical theology, this is essential for gaining its contribution to the unfolding revelation of God. In my search for the leading theme of this letter, I have come to think of its message as setting forth the intertwining of true wisdom and genuine faith. It seems quite evident that faith and wisdom are the key words to this letter.

b. The Marks of Christian Wisdom

The opening verses of this letter bring the words *faith* and *wisdom* into focus and show also their close interrelation. The dispersed Christian Jews were experiencing many kinds of trials. James at once encourages them by interpreting these trials as the testing of their faith. It is conceivable that these dispersed tribes were so ingrown in their legalistic interpretation of the law that they were unable to understand the place of testings and trials in their religious experience. James unfolded the spiritual aspect of faith by showing that the testing of faith produces steadfastness and results in their being perfect and complete. By reason of Solomon's great book, the Proverbs, the people of Israel had come to interpret the way of life in terms of wisdom. By so doing they failed to relate wisdom and faith. Since the spiritual problems of these Christian Jews seemed to relate to this lack of understanding on their part, James probed into these practical problems which at heart centered in the relation of wisdom and faith.

He began by showing that wisdom is a gift from God and that God gives it to all men generously and without reproach. There was one requirement, nevertheless, and that was the need of faith on the part of one who is asking God for wisdom. It would appear that the readers of this letter did not regard wisdom as a gift from God or that a request for wisdom required faith. James' statement, nevertheless, placed wisdom into a new category. Wisdom was not a mere intellectual achievement, but it was a gift from God. This gift was received through the expression of a living faith. In 1:9 to 3:12 James proceeded to show the real nature of living faith. After making this point clear, he returned to the explanation of real wisdom and declared that the wise and understanding among them would show by their good life their works in the meekness of wisdom. This was a stern rebuttal of pharisaic pride in keeping the law. The Pharisees had failed to see that obedience to the law was no ground for personal pride. This pharisaical understanding of wisdom was earthly, unspiritual, devilish, "But the wisdom from above is first pure, then peaceable, gentle, open to reason, full of mercy and good fruits, without uncertainty or insincerity" (Jas. 3:17).

The Pharisees had failed to note that even Solomon had declared, "The fear of the Lord is the beginning of knowledge" (Prov. 1:7). The spiritual aspects of wisdom expressed by James gave a new understanding to the outworking of genuine faith. James had shown clearly that "faith apart from works is dead" (Jas. 2:26). This disclosure of the wisdom that comes from above gave a spiritual dimension to wisdom, the real nature of which is related to Christian living. James was concerned to make this clear to his readers. He was seeking to show them the spiritual content of the law. It was his concern to have these dispersed Jews see that their law rightly understood was genuinely spiritual in meaning and not a set of external rules for living. Let us observe how James sets forth the spiritual content of the law.

c. The Spiritual Content of the Law

The first point made by James was that life should not be measured by the gaining of wealth. There are real reasons for a rich person to actually boast in his humiliation. The loss of wealth properly understood was a trial, not necessarily a judgment of God. He who stands such a test will receive a crown of life. On this account temptations should not be regarded as coming from God. While it is true that God tests His people, James probed into their real nature by showing that through them a person is tempted by reason of his own sinful desires to yield to sin. The awful consequence is death. It is possible that James' readers had failed to grasp this aspect of Christian experience. The legalism of the Pharisees had practically choked out any thought of man's inner sinful nature through which he is tempted. They thought only of keeping the numberless rules and regulations set up by their leaders.

James advanced a step further by showing that there is such a reality as spiritual gifts which come from the Father. God's children have been brought forth by the Word of truth. God's purpose in His life-giving was, "We should be a kind of first fruits of his creatures" (1:18). James pressed his point further by showing that God's children need to manifest the righteousness of God in their lives. This affects every aspect of life, including the control of anger and the putting away of all forms of wickedness. In turn they needed to receive with meekness the implanted Word which was able to save their souls. In this manner the author was seeking to raise their spiritual insights from the cold legalism to that of the real spiritual nature of Christian living.

James pressed home his concern still further by showing the problem of being merely hearers of the Word and not doers of it. A spiritually minded person looks into the perfect law of liberty and then seeks to fulfill this law in his own life. A sample of failure to do this is found in the person who does not bridle his tongue. This person's religion is vain. Genuine religion will find expression in fulfilling one's social responsibility and also in an ethical way in keeping oneself unstained from the world. James carried his point still further by exhorting his readers to show no partiality to the rich as against the poor. Pharisaical legalism utterly failed to lay hold of this aspect of practical ethics. They did not see that those who are poor in this world may be rich in faith and heirs of the kingdom. James pushed his point still further by drawing attention to the ethical principles involved in the royal law, "You shall love your neighbor as yourself" (2:18). The cold and formal legalists among the Pharisees had lost the profound spiritual meaning bound up in this command. They failed to see that when a person justifies himself for disobeying one detail of the law, he becomes guilty of breaking all the law. These illustrations prepared the way for James' presentation of the real character of faith which was fundamental both in Old Testament times and in the Christian church.

d. The Moral Energy and Dynamic of Faith

One of the saddest tragedies of the Pharisees' religion was their failure to discern the ethical aspect of faith. Without any qualm of conscience they could ignore the outworking of one's faith in good works. It is likely that this erroneous idea still persisted among the Christian Jews addressed by James. On this account James confronted them with the grave fallacy in their thinking. He declared that a professed faith which sees no responsibility in caring for those in need is dead. At this juncture he confronted a supposed objector who maintained that the writer himself had faith and he himself had works, to which James responded that genuine good deeds constitute irrefutable evidence of real faith. In this way James exposed the error among some of his readers who were boasting about their good works. He dealt the crushing blow by referring to the case of Abraham who through his offering Isaac upon the altar proved that his faith was active along with his works, in fact, it was completed by his works. In this manner the Scripture was fulfilled, "Abraham believed God, and it was reckoned to him as righteousness" (Jas. 2:23; Gen. 15:6). Here was the unquestionable truth that real faith possesses a dynamic manifested in works. It is significant that James also referred to the faith manifested by works in the case of Rahab. In this manner he showed conclusively that "faith apart from works is dead" (2:26).

James advanced to another phase of life, the control of the tongue, which tests severely the moral energy and dynamic of faith. He noted that one who "makes no mistakes in what he says he is a perfect man, able to bridle the whole body also" (3:2). With most graphic figures he set forth what is perhaps man's most grievous sin and yet he assumes that genuine faith can bridle the tongue. This brings the author again to the second key word of his letter, *wisdom* (3:13). He proceeds to show that heavenly wisdom possesses the power to deal successfully with man's most formidable foe. He led his readers to realize that this wisdom from above, as mentioned earlier, is pure, peaceable, gentle, open to reason, full of mercy and good fruits, without uncertainty or insincerity (v. 17). Most confidently James could assert, "The harvest of righteousness is sown in peace by those who make peace" (v. 18). As James probed into another area of life, that of wars and fighting, he expressed in still clearer language the manner in which man can be victorious in this agonizing struggle. He declared, "God opposes the proud, but gives grace to the humble" (4:6). He admonished his readers to submit themselves to God and also to resist the devil. In this manner the real dynamic of faith operates in the children of God.

James scarcely bypassed any sphere of life in which the dynamic of faith was so necessary to achieve the Christian standard of living. He drew into the picture the practice of speaking evil of one another, failure to do what one knows is right, the oppressions of the rich upon the poor, grumbling, and other sins (4:11 — 5:9). Yet once more James drew attention to the dynamic of faith with respect to prayer for the sick. He noted that the prayer of faith will bring healing, thus intensifying the idea that "the prayer of a righteous man has great power in its effects" (5:16).

By way of conclusion I desire to reaffirm my understanding of the general purpose of this letter. James was seeking to lead these dispersed

Christian Jews who were still holding to the rigid legalism of the Pharisees by showing them that the Old Testament, their Scriptures, was not a mere code of external regulations, the keeping of which earned for them righteousness but rather that these Scriptures were definitely spiritual in nature and embodied the ethical principles bound up in the gospel. He set forth clearly the real spiritual content of the Old Testament laws. From the biblical theology approach we should gather that James most ably set forth the content of the gospel message in terms of the Mosaic law. In a word, he showed the grand harmony of both the Old Testament and the gospel. This book constituted a most formidable refutation of pharisaical legalism. It is conceivable that if James had been writing to Gentile Christians, his presentation would have followed an entirely different pattern. In a most fundamental way his message followed the pattern and content of his brother, the Lord Jesus Christ.

For Additional Reading and Reference:

Acts, Chapters **1 — 12:**

Bernard, *The Progress of Doctrine in the New Testament,* pp. 80-129.
Beyschlag, *New Testament Theology,* Vol. I, pp. 300-336; Vol. II, pp. 474-499.
Bultmann, *Theology of the New Testament,* Vol. I, pp. 33-62.
Conzelmann, *Theology of St. Luke,* pp. 29-93.
————, *An Outline of the Theology of the New Testament,* pp. 87-93.
Filson, *A New Testament History,* pp. 153-187.
Hunter, *Introducing New Testament Theology,* pp. 66-85.
Klassen and Snyder, *Current Issues in New Testament Interpretation,* pp. 178-209.
Lindars, *New Testament Apologetic,* pp. 251-286.
Morris, *The Cross in the New Testament,* pp. 107-143.
Newman, *The Meaning of the New Testament,* pp. 164-177.
Richardson, *An Introduction to the Theology of the New Testament,* pp. 321-325.
Ryrie, *Biblical Theology of the New Testament,* pp. 99-108.
Sheldon, *New Testament Theology,* pp. 140-153.
Stevens, *The Theology of the New Testament,* pp. 258-275.
Taylor, *The Person of Christ,* pp. 190-222.
Weidner, *Biblical Theology of the New Testament,* Vol. I, pp. 156-164.
Weiss, *Biblical Theology of the New Testament,* Vol. I, pp. 159-163, 181-197.
See Commentaries on Acts 1 — 10.

Letter of James:

Beyschlag, *New Testament Theology,* Vol. I, pp. 337-377.
Morris, *The Cross in the New Testament,* pp. 309-316.

Newman, *The Meaning of the New Testament*, pp. 269-274.
Richardson, *An Introduction to the Theology of the New Testament*, pp. 240-241.
Ryrie, *Biblical Theology of the New Testament*, pp. 131-147.
Sheldon, *New Testament Theology*, pp. 153-158.
Stevens, *The Theology of the New Testament*, pp. 276-292.
Taylor, *The Atonement in New Testament Teaching*, p. 43.
———, *The Person of Christ*, p. 134.
Weidner, *Biblical Theology of the New Testament*, Vol. I, pp. 202-213.
Weiss, *Biblical Theology of the New Testament*, Vol. I, pp. 168-172, 248-273.
See Articles on *The Letter of James* in Bible dictionaries and encyclopedias.

1. Knowling, quoted by A. T. Robertson from *Word Pictures in the New Testament*, Vol. III, *The Acts of the Apostles* by A. T. Robertson (New York: Richard R. Smith, Inc., 1930), p. 11.
2. G. Abbott Smith, *op. cit.*, p. 107.
3. Chester K. Lehman, *op. cit.*, p. 33.
4. See F. F. Bruce, *The Book of Acts, The New International Commentary on the New Testament* (Grand Rapids: Wm. B. Eerdmans Publishing Co., 1956) pp. 75-77.
5. Ps. 2:2; 18:50; 84:9; 89:38, 51; 132:10, 17.
6. Rom. 6:17; 16:17; Tit. 1:9; Heb. 13:9; 2 Jn. 9.
7. A. T. Robertson, *Word Pictures in the New Testament* (New York: Harper and Brothers, 1933), Vol. VI, p. 4.

CHAPTER II

THE THEOLOGY OF PETER AND OF JUDE

1. Introduction

a. Peter's Early Ministry — The Background to His Theology

It seems appropriate to present the theological viewpoint of Peter's early ministry in its Lukan setting as found in the Book of Acts. In a real way, Peter's early preaching was foundational to the birth of the church through the rule of the enthroned Lord and Christ. Significant in this preaching ministry were his witness to the resurrection, his exposition of the Pentecostal experiences, his first proclamations of the gospel, his vision, and his most significant mission of extending the gospel to the Gentiles.

b. Reasons for Presenting the Theology of Peter Before That of Paul

First of all there is a fundamental unity in the doctrinal content of his letters with that of his early preaching. Second, Peter addressed his letters to the exiles of the dispersion and so his message was oriented to the Christian Jews. Third, his two letters were written before the last of Paul's letters. This does not ignore the fact that a number of Paul's letters were written before those of Peter.

c. Problems Relating to the Authorship of 1 and 2 Peter

It lies beyond my purpose to probe deeply into this matter of literary criticism. There are good grounds for believing that the first letter of Peter was written by an amanuensis, likely Sylvanus (1 Pet. 5:12). This accounts for the high literary quality of this letter as compared with the crude and rugged Greek of the second letter which likely came directly from Peter's writing.

The doctrinal content of the first letter almost defies systematizing. Peter brought together a great number of doctrinal truths in the scope of a single sentence or paragraph (1 Pet. 1:2, 3-9). I have come to believe that the controlling idea of the first letter is the doctrine of Christian hope. Peter bound together this great truth and its foundation faith (1 Pet. 1:21). His treatment of Christ's sacrificial work, Christian suffering, the nature of the Christian life, and eternal salvation, all have their bases in faith and hope. Of almost equal significance is Peter's teaching on God and His people. The frequency of his references to the Old Testament shows his recognition of the Old Testament as the authoritative written Word (1 Pet. 1:16; 2:6). The dominant ideas of Christian ethics show clearly the purpose of Peter's writing. His evident purpose was to lead the dispersed Christian Jews to a genuine understanding of the Christian life in the setting of a pagan world.

2. Peter's Teaching on Faith, Hope, and Salvation

a. The Nature and Content of These Words[1]

Already in the great doxology (1:3-9) Peter used these expressions in a meaningful manner. Hope is a living thing gained through being born anew and made possible through the resurrection of Christ. His people are guarded by God's power which is appropriated through faith for the salvation which will be revealed in the last time. But this faith needs to be genuine, and on this account God allows His people to suffer various trials so that their faith may redound to praise, glory, and honor at Christ's revelation. The outcome of the Christian's faith is the obtaining of salvation.

In the setting of Christian sufferings Peter admonished his readers to set their hope fully upon the grace that would come to them at Christ's revelation. By reason of Christ's completed work, the believer's faith and hope are in God. On this account Peter continued his admonition that they should purify their souls through obedience to the truth and in love for one another.

Later in his letter Peter noted that the holy women of old hoped in God and gave expression of this hope through a gentle and quiet spirit and by submission to their husbands (3:1, 5). Being aware that his readers would be confronted by inquiries with regard to their Christian faith, Peter admonished his readers to be prepared to make a defense to those who would call upon them to give an account for their hope (v. 15). Evidently many of the Jewish exiles had lost the element of hope in their religion, and so Peter admonished the Christians among these exiles to give careful thought to the hope content of their newly gained Christian faith, which looked forward to the life beyond this world to the glories of heaven. The closing paragraph of Peter's letter sets forth a concluding admonition with regard to the place of faith, hope, and salvation in the lives of these dispersed Christian Jews who were constantly being encountered by the devil. He exhorted his readers, "Resist him, firm in your faith, knowing that the same experience of suffering is required of your brotherhood throughout the world. And after you have suffered a little while, the God of all grace, who has called you to his eternal glory in Christ, will himself restore, establish, and strengthen you" (1 Pet. 5:9, 10). Thus in a world of suffering and persecution, Peter sought to strengthen his readers in their Christian faith and hope (1:21; 3:15). These references give us grounds for believing that faith, hope, and salvation constitute the dominant thought and purpose of this letter. All the detailed theological references are brought to a focus in this great theme.

b. The Foundations of Christian Hope

The ultimate and absolute foundation of Christian hope was expressed by Peter when he addressed his readers as the "chosen and destined by God the Father." God foreknew their response to the preaching of the gospel and had chosen them to be His people. This was a sure foundation for Christian hope. Through God's great mercy these exiles had been born anew to a living hope which was a genuine spiritual experience, existential to its very core. What could be more assuring and real than a hope gained through the spiritual experience of being born anew! Peter saw fit to express their adequate grounds for this experience through the resurrection of Christ. Through the sprinkling with Christ's blood in His sacrificial death and His resurrection, these exiles had confidence in God. Their faith and hope were in God (1 Pet. 1:18-21). In this same context Peter challenged his readers with the realization of this hope in the words, "Set your hope fully upon the grace that is coming to you at the revelation of Jesus Christ" (v. 13). It is clear that Peter gave the strongest support to the foundations of Christian hope found in the New Testament.

3. The Sacrificial Work of Christ

Peter did not give an extensive exposition of Christ's sacrificial work in the opening chapters of Acts.[2] He had made it clear, nevertheless, that "everyone who believes in him receives forgiveness of sins through his name" (10:43). In this first letter Peter made frequent references to Christ's suffering and death not with the purpose of setting forth the theological meaning of Christ's work, but rather as the basis for his exhortations given to stimulate the faith and hope of his readers. It becomes very significant that Peter used meaningful and expressive language to set forth the sacrificial work of Christ. I shall note these references in the order of their occurrence in the letter.

The Trinitarian reference of 1:2 mentions the sprinkling with Christ's blood. This evidently reflected the use of the blood by Moses in the sacrifices which established the Sinaitic covenant (Ex. 24:3-8). In this way Peter related the shed blood of Christ to the institution of the new covenant. Later in the chapter Peter noted that his readers were ransomed with the precious blood of Christ (vv. 18, 19). With the

Passover lamb likely in mind Peter noted that Christ's sacrifice bore similarity to that of the lamb without blemish or spot. Undoubtedly, Peter recalled the words of Jesus that He had come to "give his life as a ransom for many" (Mt. 20:28). It is evident that both Peter and Jesus laid hold of the ransom passage of Isaiah 52:3. In this manner Peter was building on the solid structure of the Old Testament references to Israel's redemption from Egypt. The frequent occurrences of *gaal* and *padah* both translated *redeem* and *ransom* show clearly the doctrinal significance which Peter associated with the word ransom.[3]

Writing to Christians who were suffering unjustly, Peter encouraged his readers by noting that Christ had suffered *for* (*huper*) them. He added, "He himself bore our sins in his body on the tree. . . . By his wounds you have been healed" (2:23, 24). These words written in a context of Jesus' sinless life and also which reflected the suffering Servant of Isaiah 53 showed clearly the redemptive nature of Christ's suffering and death.

In a similar context Peter wrote, "Christ also died *for [peri]* sins *once for all [hapax]*, the righteous *for [huper]* the unrighteous, that he might bring us to God, being put to death in the flesh but made alive in the spirit" (3:18). It seems entirely clear that Peter intended these prepositions, as well as the adverb, to portray the substitutionary aspect of Christ's death. Through His death Christ brings sinners to God. The expiatory aspect of Christ's death also shines forth in the words, "Rejoice in so far as you share Christ's sufferings, that you may also rejoice and be glad when his glory is revealed" (4:13). Peter has shown clearly the relation of Christ's sacrifice to man's salvation. His death was vicarious and in our behalf. The dignity and glory of Christ formed the basis for the efficacy of His sacrifice.

4. Christian Suffering Presented in the Perspective of Christ's Sufferings

In the two contexts just noted let us observe how Peter links human suffering with that of Christ. Peter wrote that by taking suffering patiently Christians have God's approval. Christ through His sufferings left us an example that we should follow in His steps. It is better to suffer for doing right than for doing wrong (2:20, 21). Peter would have his readers observe that since Christ by reason of His perfect life needed to endure suffering, so His followers also suffer for righteousness' sake (vv. 22-24). In this way the sufferings of Christians gain far greater significance when seen in the perspective of Christ's suffering and death.

From the point of view of biblical theology this comparison possesses great meaning when we come to grasp the fact that God's people from the beginning through the entire scope of history have experienced suffering and death for righteousness' sake. On this account the way of redemption becomes possible alone through the suffering and death of Him who committed no sin. In this way only do we who enjoy salvation come to realize its price. This, in a word, is the theology of Christian suffering. The concluding paragraph of Peter's letter (5:6-11) gives final confirmation to this truth. Peter wrote, "Humble yourselves therefore under the mighty hand of God, that in due time he may exalt you. . . . The same experience of suffering is required of your brotherhood throughout the world. And after you have suffered a little while, the God of all grace, who has called you to his eternal glory in Christ, will himself restore, establish, and strengthen you."

5. Present and Future Salvation, the Outcome of Faith and Hope

Peter's teaching on *salvation* confirms and also adds to the meaning of this word. First and foremost is the future aspect of salvation (1:5). The realization of this hope will be by revelation. This disclosure will take place in the eschatological era known as *the last time,* an expression which builds on Christ's teaching with reference to *the age to come* (Mt. 12:32; 13:39, 40; Mk. 10:30; etc.). The event of supreme importance in the future is the revelation of Jesus Christ. It is then that the redeemed will obtain the salvation of their souls. This coming salvation will be the climactic expression of the grace that shall be manifested at His revelation.

In a setting of exhortation Peter admonished his readers in the words, "Like newborn babes, long for the pure spiritual milk, that by it you may grow up to salvation" (1 Pet. 2:2). Peter was apparently stressing a present stage of salvation which is nourished by spiritual food such as tasting the kindness of the Lord. Likely Peter's thought of salvation in this context included also its future and eternal aspects. Further, it was entirely natural that Peter should build a bridge between God's saving act in the days of Noah and the spiritual salvation symbolized by water baptism. He added a word of explanation according to which salvation is God's response to the penitent sinner's appeal for a clear conscience made possible through the resurrection of Christ. This clearly establishes the experiential aspect of salvation. As he encouraged his readers to share in Christ's sufferings, he also gave the warning to refrain from the wickedness of this world, making it clear that the righteous are scarcely saved (4:13-18; Prov. 11:31, Septuagint). Peter gave a final reflection on the future aspect of salvation when he noted that the God of all grace was calling them to His eternal glory in Christ (5:10).

In a different structure of thought Peter wrote of God's forbearance to mankind, "Not wishing that any should perish, but that all should reach repentance," and then added, "count the forbearance of our Lord as salvation" (2 Pet. 3:9, 15). From this we may rightly conclude that God has delayed the day of the Lord so that all men might come to repentance.

In somewhat similar vein Jude expressed his eagerness to write of the salvation experienced by all believers, earnestly exhorting his readers "to contend for the faith which was once for all delivered to the saints" (Jude 3). In view of the apostatizing of many believers he sought to draw a lesson from Israel's history: God, "who saved a people out of the land of Egypt, afterward destroyed those who did not believe" (Jude 5). In view of the return to wickedness of those whom God had saved, Jude gave a final exhortation, "Build yourselves up on your most holy faith; pray in the Holy Spirit; keep yourselves in the love of God; wait for the mercy of our Lord Jesus Christ unto eternal life. And convince some, who doubt; save some, by snatching them out of the fire; on some have mercy with fear" (Jude 20-23). In this manner Jude was seeking to salvage many of the believers who were on the brink of destruction. His benedictory prayer by which he concluded his letter gives the most sublime picture of God's saving work through Christ. He wrote, "Now to him who is able to keep you from falling and to present you without blemish before the presence of his glory with rejoicing, to the only God, our Savior through Jesus Christ our Lord, be glory, majesty, dominion, and authority, before all time and now for ever. Amen" (vv. 24, 25). This gives supreme meaning to eternal salvation which is the outcome of faith and hope.

6. The Eschatology of Peter and Jude

Both Peter and Jude added to the New Testament unfolding of eschatology. Peter wrote of Christ's manifestation, "at the end of the times" (1 Pet. 1:20). This expression reflects the Old Testament prophetic viewpoint known as *the latter days.*[4] From the Old Testament prophetic viewpoint *the latter days* would be the times of the Messiah. Peter divided this era into two ages: the former, that of the sufferings of Christ, and the latter, that of His subsequent glory (1 Pet. 1:11, 21; 3:22). Peter's forward look centered in the *revelation (apokalupsis)* of Christ (1 Pet. 1:7, 13; 4:13; 5:1). This is perhaps the most expressive word used in the New Testament with reference to Christ's return. This revelation of Christ would mark "the end of all things," and was to be viewed as being "at hand" (1 Pet. 4:7). Peter anticipated being "a partaker in the glory that is to be revealed." In the same context he expanded his thought "when the chief Shepherd is manifested (*phaneroo*), you will obtain the unfading crown of glory" (1 Pet. 5:1, 4). This verb carries the meaning *reveal, make known, show*, and *appear* and is synonymous with *(apokalupto)*, used in verse 1. These two verbs are the most expressive words used to set forth the disclosure of Christ in all of His glory. This *revelation* and *manifestation* of Christ will mark the greatest event of world history. On this account Peter could speak of it as the *end of all things*.

He also observed the imminency of this revelation by noting that "the end of all things is at hand" (1 Pet. 4:7). He also used the word *parousia (presence, arrival, advent)*. Reflecting on the transfiguration scene, Peter looked to the future, anticipating both the power and coming of the Lord (2 Pet. 1:16). This association of power with the Lord's return anticipates the coming day of the Lord in which the present creation will be superseded by the new heavens and the new earth in which righteousness dwells (2 Pet. 3:12). This new creation will be the outcome of the day of the Lord. Thus Peter picked up an Old Testament expression used by the prophets in their messages of imminent judgment upon God's people. This came to fulfillment in the Assyrian and Babylonian captivities.

The apostle is now predicting the culminating day of the Lord, the final day of judgment, which is now imminent. But God is "not wishing that any should perish, but that all should reach repentance." So then whether this day is near or thousands of years in the future, God is showing forbearance toward all mankind. The day of the Lord will mark the time of final judgment for the entire human race. "They will give account to him who is ready to judge the living and the dead" (1 Pet. 4:5). For this reason Peter gave the earnest exhortation, "For the time has come for judgment to begin with the household of God; and if it begins with us, what will be the end of those who do not obey the gospel of God?" (v. 17).

Jude gave a similar warning by quoting Enoch in the words, "Behold, the Lord came with his holy myriads, to execute judgment on all" (Jude 14, 15). He then specified different groups of ungodly people, such as grumblers and malcontents, people who follow their own passions, loudmouthed boasters who flatter people to gain advantage (v. 16).

The final judgment leads to two destinies. On the one hand there are those who perish and on the other those who enter the new heavens and new earth in which righteousness dwells. The two similar contexts (2 Pet. 2:4-10 and Jude 5-7), give a veiled description of the eternal punishment which the wicked will suffer. The doom of the angels who had sinned, the ancient world which perished in the Flood, and the destruction of Sodom and Gomorrah stand as symbols which forecast the eternal punishment of the wicked. These portions gave no support to the view that the wicked would be annihilated. Jude stated that the destruction of Sodom and Gomorrah and the surrounding cities "serve as an example by undergoing a punishment of eternal fire" (Jude 7). This interpretation agrees with the words of our Lord given on various occasions (Mt. 5:22; 13:42, 50; 18:8, 9; 25:41).

7. Christian Ethics in an Age of Persecution and Apostasy

Living in the era of Neronian persecution when many were departing from the faith, Peter and Jude were in a unique position for giving the Christian perspective of ethics under such circumstances. On this account their writings possess special value for Christians who live under similar situations. It is quite important for a biblical theology approach to the theology of Peter and Jude to lay hold of the pattern of Christian living as set forth by the apostles to the primitive church. Peter and likely Jude also had heard the teachings of Jesus as given to the multitudes before the founding of the Christian church (Mt. 5:1; 13:2; Jn. 6:5; etc.). It became the task of the apostles, Peter in particular, to give guidance to the early church as to their manner of life in the sinful world, especially in a time of persecution. Peter's involvement in this responsibility became evident in the salutation of his first letter where he, an apostle of Jesus Christ, addressed the exiles as "chosen and destined by God the Father and sanctified by the Spirit for obedience to Jesus Christ and for sprinkling with his blood" (1 Pet. 1:2). This revealed the priority Peter attached to the believer's obedience to Christ.

In a simple and straightforward manner he gave many practical exhortations, such as showing genuineness of faith; girding up their minds; being holy in all their conduct; purifying their souls by obedience to the truth; loving one another; putting away malice, guile, insincerity, envy, and slander; abstaining from passions of the flesh; maintaining good conduct among the Gentiles; being subject to every human institution; giving practical counsel to servants, wives, and husbands; having unity of spirit, sympathy, and love for the brethren; living together with a tender heart and humble mind; giving an account of their hope; showing gentleness and reverence; keeping their conscience clear; keeping sane and sober for their prayers; holding unfailing love for one another; practicing hospitality ungrudgingly; humbling themselves under the mighty hand of God; casting all their anxieties on Him; and other words of encouragement to right living. These exhortations were down to earth and practical in everyday life. They illustrate how significantly Peter was applying the Christian faith to the manner of life to these

Christian Jewish exiles. He did not approach these practical matters of Christian living in a legalistic fashion.

Peter also presented the pattern of the Christian life by way of a different but yet effective approach (2 Pet. 1:3-11). He declared to his readers that God's "divine power has granted to us all things that pertain to life and godliness, through the knowledge of him who called us to his own glory and excellence" (v. 3). He included a list of Christian graces which supplement one another in the personal experience of believers such as faith, virtue, knowledge, self-control, steadfastness, godliness, brotherly affection, and love. When these abound in us they make us effective and fruitful in the knowledge of Christ. This language assumed the greater spiritual maturity on the part of his readers than those who had access to his first letter. When we probe into the meaning of these Christian graces, it soon becomes clear how fundamental and all-pervasive they are. Peter assumed that his readers would be able to find expression of these graces in their daily walk and conduct. In view of the apostasy and the imminent return of Christ, Peter stressed the elements of holiness and godliness which are fundamental to Christian living (2 Pet. 3:11). His final exhortation reads, "Grow in the grace and knowledge of our Lord and Savior Jesus Christ" (v. 18).

In similar fashion Jude wrote, "Build yourselves up on your most holy faith; pray in the Holy Spirit; keep yourselves in the love of God; wait for the mercy of our Lord Jesus Christ unto eternal life" (Jude 20, 21). Jude challenged the faith of his readers by showing them that Christ was able to keep them from falling and to present them without blemish before the presence of His glory with rejoicing (v. 24).

Alongside of these significant presentations relating to the pattern of Christian living, many specific sins are mentioned by these writers. Since they were addressing fellow Christians, the sins named were those to which their readers were most susceptible. Observe the following: malice, guile, insincerity, envy, slander, passions, licentiousness, drunkenness, revelings, carousing, lawless idolatry, profligacy, pride, greed, adultery, wrongdoing, boasts of folly, deliberately ignoring facts, and instability. They mentioned also thieves, wrongdoers, mischief-makers, grumblers, malcontents, boasters, flatterers, and scoffers. While many of these sins characterized awful wickedness, it is possible that many of the others named were such that immature Christians would need to learn that they belong in the class of sin and evil.

8. The Trinitarian Foundation of These Letters

Another essential doctrine for this biblical theology study is that of the Trinity. Just as Christ gave the Great Commission to make disciples of all nations "baptizing them in the name of the Father, and of the Son and of the Holy Spirit," in a similar forthright statement Peter addressed the exiles as being "chosen and destined by God the Father and sanctified by the Spirit for obedience to Jesus Christ" (1 Pet. 1:2). In language just as clear Jude wrote, "Pray in the Holy Spirit; keep yourselves in the love of God; wait for the mercy of our Lord Jesus Christ unto eternal life" (Jude 20, 21). Quite frequently these writers brought together references to God and Christ (1 Pet. 1:3; 2 Pet. 1:2; Jude 1). In none of these cases did either author formally declare the triune being of God. Nevertheless, the verses quoted set forth this truth in clear language. To use modern terminology Peter and Jude made a personal distinction among the Father, the Son, and the Holy Spirit. Alongside this it is equally apparent that they set forth the oneness of the Three. Let us note further that the Three are named in relation to the distinctive work of each person. With the Father, Peter associated the doctrine of election; and Jude, that of God's love. Peter referred to the redemptive work of Christ and Jude to His mercy. Peter directed attention to the sanctifying work of the Holy Spirit, and Jude to our praying in the Holy Spirit. Add to these the distinctive Deity activities mentioned singly throughout these letters, and it will become clear how the work of each Person is distinctly Deity activity.

9. The Written Word

The discipline of biblical theology has a large concern for the nature of the written Word, both of the Old Testament and the New. Peter made about forty quotations or allusions to the Old Testament and Jude about five. Peter's witness to the character of the Old Testament stands forth in the formula, "It is written" (1 Pet. 1:16); also in the words "the living and abiding word of God" (1:24); and "It stands in scripture" (2:6). These expressions lay hold of the accepted tradition of the Jews and the Christians to the effect that the Old Testament was a completed body of writings, authoritative in character, and as being the Word of God.

Peter unfolded the extraordinary character of the written Word in 2 Peter 1:19-21. It is a context in which Peter declared that he was an eyewitness of Christ's majesty and glory. He had heard the voice borne to him as the majestic glory as certain and undeniable as was this experience. Peter declared, "We have the prophetic word made more sure" (1:19). The KJV translates the statement, "We have also a more sure word of prophecy." The majority of scholars interpret this statement according to the RSV and other modern translations. The Berkeley version reads, "So we have the prophetic message reaffirmed."

Jews and Christians alike placed unquestioned confidence in the prophetic Word. They felt no need of questioning its accuracy. What Peter is saying, is that the certainty of Christ's transfiguration based on the testimony of the three apostles, "confirmed the messianic prophecies and made clear the deity of Jesus Christ."[5]

He proceeded to show why this is true. "First of all you must understand this, that no prophecy of scripture is a matter of one's own interpretation, because no prophecy ever came by the impulse of man, but men moved by the Holy Spirit spoke from God" (1 Pet. 1:20, 21). The bearing of this statement on the quality of the written Word should be evident. The Holy Spirit by His power *bore, carried, effected* the dynamic in men so that what they spoke came from God. In other words the Holy Scriptures are the very Word of God.

For Additional Reading and Reference:

Beyschlag, *New Testament Theology*, Vol. I, pp. 377-419; Vol. II, 499-501.
Hunter, *Introducing New Testament Theology*, pp. 111, 116.
Morris, *The Cross in the New Testament*, pp. 316-338.
Newman, *The Meaning of the New Testament*, pp. 274-283, 286-289.
Ryrie, *Biblical Theology of the New Testament*, pp. 265-297.
Sheldon, *New Testament Theology*, pp. 270-299.
Stevens, *The Theology of the New Testament*, pp. 293-324.
Taylor, *The Atonement in the New Testament*, pp. 24-34, 44.
Taylor, *The Person of Christ*, pp. 134-137.
Van Oosterzee, *The Theology of the New Testament*, pp. 198-223.
Weidner, *Biblical Theology of the New Testament*, Vol. I, pp. 151-155, 171-201, 214-219, 227-238.
Weiss, *Biblical Theology of the New Testament*, Vol. I, pp. 163-168, 204-247; Vol. II, pp. 234-248.
See articles on the *Letters of Peter* and of *Jude* in Bible dictionaries and Bible encyclopedias.

1. 1 Pet. 1:3-9, 13, 21; 2:2; 3:5, 15; 5:9; 2 Pet. 1:1, 5; 3:15.
2. Acts 2:23, 24; 3:13-15; 4:12; 5:30, 31; 10:39-43.
3. Ex. 6:6; Deut. 7:8; Is. 43:1; 51:11; 62:12; 63:16; etc.
4. Deut. 4:30; Hos. 3:5; Mic. 4:1; Ezek. 38:16; Dan. 2:28; etc.
5. Robertson, *op. cit.*, p. 157.

CHAPTER I

INTRODUCTION TO PAUL'S THEOLOGY

1. Methods of Approach to Pauline Theology

Among the many works on Pauline theology there are no less than four different patterns of developing Paul's theological teaching. Each approach possesses definite values and at the same time certain limitations. A brief presentation of each method may serve as an orientation to my approach to this subject. I have no interest in drawing hard and fast lines among these several methods of approach. I prefer to utilize the values of each method in the pursuit of my own procedure.

a. Search for the Controlling Thought of Paul and the Manner of Unfolding His Doctrines as They Center in This Theme

Following are some of these themes, including the theological writers who presented Paul's theological thought accordingly: justification by faith (Luther), salvation (Anderson Scott, Archibald Hunter, Dibelius), union with Christ (Stuart, Wahlstrom), eschatology (Schoeps, Vos), liberty (Longenecker), and man (Bultmann). Certainly, if it is possible to discover the controlling idea or doctrine of Paul, the presentation of his theology would assist the reader in gaining a proper perspective of Paul's entire teaching. This is certainly a worthy goal, if it can be achieved. There appear to be at least two serious limitations to this procedure: the first being that it tends to place all Paul's teaching on a common level, and by so doing to miss his developing and unfolding thought. Further, this method of study may oversimplify the breadth of Paul's teachings. One of the most overwhelming challenges confronting the student of Paul's theology is that of gaining a full comprehension of his profound teachings.

b. The Systematic Theology Approach to Paul's Doctrines

In this method the chapter headings would correspond quite closely with those of a systematic theology, such as God, man, sin, Christ's redemptive work, salvation, church, and eschatology. Stevens and Whiteley followed this procedure. This method is most valuable for gaining a true perspective, as well as a comprehension of the logical relationship among the great theological doctrines. Any method which fails to achieve these results suffers severe limitations. However, this method may fail to set forth the unfolding and progressive nature of the revelation through Paul. This limitation jeopardizes the distinctive genius of biblical theology.

c. The Inductive Approach to the Theology of Paul

By this method the doctrinal contents of Paul's letters are gained through a direct study of each book and by tabulating the references relating to each doctrine. This might result in a tabulation such as the following: repentance, faith, salvation, the person of Christ, eternity, biblical inspiration, Christ's return, the resurrection, the judgment, etc. Here the central value is that of discovering truth by direct study. Sometimes the study of a theological text may lead the student to bypass the direct approach to the Scriptures. This method also has its limitations. The student may fail to lay hold of the grand concept of an unfolding revelation. The theological content of the Bible must be gained in the perspective of an unfolding revelation.

d. An Approach by Way of Setting Forth the Central Teachings in Each of the Four Groups of Paul's Letters (Weidner, Weiss, Bruce with some modifications, and my own presentation)

The central teachings of the Thessalonian letters center in Paul's eschatology. Included in this discussion are the eschatological teaching drawn from the three other groups of his letters. The doctrine of salvation appears to be the central teaching of the letters to the Galatians, Corinthians, and Romans. I shall introduce this discussion with the teachings on salvation from the Thessalonian letters, and pursue the study with the teachings on this theme from the prison and pastoral letters. The dominant theological thought of Paul's letters to the Colossians, Ephesians, Philemon, and Philippians is that of Christ's work and also of the church. The teachings on these themes from the first two groups of letters will introduce this discussion, while the teaching gained from Paul's pastoral letters will follow the main discussion. The fourth group of these letters (1 and 2 Timothy and Titus) are concerned chiefly with the organization of the church. It will be introduced by the teachings on this theme drawn from all the earlier letters.

The values which I find in this approach are: first, it relieves one of the problem of attempting to determine the controlling thought of Paul's theology; second, by this method the unfolding and progressive aspects of Paul's theology stand forth most clearly; third, this method seems to preserve best the genius of biblical theology; fourth, it does not exclude an attempt to organize Paul's teaching into a consistent whole; and fifth, it seeks to preserve in the best possible manner the living, dynamic, and growing thought of Paul. Obviously, this pattern of approach presents some difficult problems relating to organization and the presentation of the doctrinal content set forth in Paul's letters. I shall seek also to appropriate the values found in the other methods of approach.

2. Paul's Religious Life Prior to His Conversion[1]

To understand Paul's religious life as a Pharisee is essential to the understanding of his conversion experience and the theological content of his teachings. Paul grew up in a Jewish home. But he was brought up in Jerusalem at the feet of Gamaliel and educated according to the strict manner of the law. He was zealous for God. He was not influenced by the intellectual environment of Tarsus but held to the traditions of his fathers. He had high regard for the entire Old Testament. He adhered rigidly to the beliefs of the Pharisees but he did not share in their hypocrisies. The entire Old Testament and especially the law of Moses were, to use modern terminology, his rule for faith and life. He saw no need for God's saving grace. The sacrificial system of the law carried no spiritual significance for him. Perfect obedience to the Law was the full requirement for being righteous. Sin pertained merely to breaking the law, so that he was unaware of having a sinful nature. He had full confidence that he could keep the law perfectly. Looking back to his life as a Pharisee Paul wrote, "As to righteousness under the law blameless" (Phil. 3:6). All this changed when, on his way to Damascus, the Lord appeared to him. From that time onward he was aware that he had been a slave to sin, and that his sinful nature had wrought all kinds of wickedness within him.

3. Paul's Experience of Conversion[2]

a. Paul's Conversion Experience: Objective and Spiritual in Nature

In the several accounts of what happened on the Damascus road, we learn that suddenly a light from heaven flashed about Paul and he fell to the ground. He saw in the way a light from heaven brighter than the sun shining around him. He heard the voice of Christ speaking to him to which he answered. The Lord appeared to him in a vision. The gospel preached by Paul came to him through a revelation of Jesus Christ. These facts stand as Paul's testimony and witness to his conversion experience.

On the objective side Paul saw the Lord and heard His voice. Its spiritual aspect was the revelation of Jesus Christ to Paul which became the source of Paul's gospel. This experience came to a climax when through the ministry of Ananias, Paul regained his sight and was filled with the Holy Spirit. This marked his conversion, and his being baptized was the seal of his commitment to Jesus Christ as his Savior and Lord. The supreme value of all these incidents for the study of Paul's theology lies in the fact that his gospel came through this revelation of Jesus Christ. From this point of view Paul stands in the class of the Old Testament prophets to whom the Lord had spoken. We may say that Paul ranked above these prophets in view of his personal experience with the Lord Himself, and that he had been set apart by the Lord as an apostle. Therefore, it is proper to conclude that the ministry of Paul whether in preaching the gospel or in writing his letters was prophetic in the highest sense. He was Christ's spokesman of the gospel.

b. Paul's Understanding of Christianity at His Conversion

Paul's understanding of the gospel had its solid foundation in Christ's revelation to him. This revelation showed Paul conclusively that Christ was raised from the dead. His ascension marked His exaltation to kingship at the right hand of God. Thus the Jesus of Nazareth was at once the Messiah, the Son of God, and the Lord from heaven.[3]

Paul's exhaustive comprehension of the Old Testament became completely revolutionized through his experience with the exalted, glorified Christ. His understanding of the law was raised far above the legalistic interpretation of the Pharisees. He had come to realize that righteousness was not attained through perfect obedience to the law, but on the basis of faith in God a believer is accounted righteous by God. The sacrificial system observed by Israel did not possess redemptive values. It was only a symbol and type of the atoning work of Christ on the cross. Through this conversion experience Paul learned that he was sinful by nature and also a slave to sin. He had come to realize how wretched a man he was as a Pharisee. Deliverance from that bondage had come through the work of his Lord and Savior, Jesus Christ. His firm confidence in the merit of good works through keeping the law was completely shattered. When he came to realize that he was saved by the grace of God, the overwhelming truth which he had come to experience was that the gospel "is the power of God for salvation to everyone who has faith" (Rom. 1:16).

4. The Preaching Ministry of Paul as Recorded in the Acts

It is essential to a biblical approach to Paul's theology to observe how his theological understanding of the gospel became crystallized in his preaching. His messages, recorded in Acts 9 to 13, were given before he wrote his earliest letters, and the remaining messages recorded in the book were given after he had written two or more of his letters.

The brief notes to his messages recorded in Acts 9:20, 22, 29 give the first pattern of Paul's gospel message. They centered in a declaration concerning Jesus. He is the Son of God and the Christ. For this reason he preached in the name of Jesus the Lord. These brief statements constituted the foundational teachings of Paul's gospel as set forth in his letters.

Paul's sermon at Antioch of Pisidia (Acts 13:16-47) revealed, first of all, his comprehension of Israel's history. Undoubtedly his hearers had never understood its messianic significance.

While the Jews recognized that they were the chosen people of God and that their history was guided by the Lord, they failed to comprehend the great prophetic significance of David's kingship. While he noted that Jesus was a descendant of David, he did not use the title of King or Messiah. Instead, he used the name *Savior,* and drew attention to the message of John dealing with a baptism of repentance addressed to all the people of Israel. Paul moved forward in his sermon by noting that God had sent the message of His salvation to the descendants of Abraham.

He then related how the Jews of Jerusalem refused to believe in Jesus their Savior and were responsible for His being crucified. But God raised Him from the dead, and He appeared to His followers who then became His witnesses to the people. When this good news which God had promised to the fathers was fulfilled by raising Jesus from the dead, Paul clinched this testimony by quoting Psalm 2:7; Isaiah 55:3; and Psalm 16:10. These quotations served as indisputable evidence that the Old Testament had predicted Christ's resurrection, which made possible the forgiveness of sins through this Holy One. Paul concluded this message by declaring. "Every one that believes is freed from everything from which you could not be freed by the law of Moses" (Acts 13:39).

Let us note some of the distinctive elements which characterized Paul's comprehension of the gospel in this early period of his ministry.

First, Paul had grasped God's leadings in Israel's history. He had comprehended the prediction that a descendant of David would be the Savior, Jesus. This corresponded to Peter's insight expressed in his Pentecostal sermon. It was a profound interpretation of Israel's history. Second, Paul had grasped that the message of salvation had its foundation in Christ's redemptive work, a truth which had been forecast in the Old Testament. Third, Paul had already comprehended the efficacy of Christ's work for the forgiveness of sins appropriated by faith. He was fully aware of the powerlessness of the law of Moses to effect justification. Thus the truth to which Paul devoted the major content of his letters to the Galatians and Romans was already crystal clear in his thinking.

Another insight expressed by Paul in this early period of his ministry becomes evident in his use of the Servant of the Lord passage (Is. 49:6), quoted in support of his turning to the Gentiles when the Jews at Antioch rejected his message. The meaning of this great prophetic Scripture lay beyond the comprehension of the Pharisees. But this experience at Antioch led Paul to comprehend its predictive significance as it voiced the universal mission of the gospel. Luke may have reflected Paul's thought when he mentioned the responsive attitude of the Gentiles by adding, "As many as were ordained to eternal life believed" (Acts 13:48). There is need for guarding against interpreting this statement as expressing unconditional predestination to eternal life. In a slightly different context Paul himself wrote, "There is a remnant chosen by grace" (Rom. 11:5). If this senses properly Paul's thinking at the time of preaching this sermon, then we may conclude that he had grasped the evangelical interrelationship among election, faith, grace, and salvation. This was far removed from Paul's former views as a Pharisee. Paul in an authentic way was preaching the gospel of Christ.

When Paul came to Lystra and had healed the man who had been a cripple from birth, people were ready to regard him and Barnabas as gods. He corrected their thinking by stating that they were also men and had come to bring good news. They should turn from their vain things to a living God who made all things. While God had allowed these nations to walk in their own ways, yet He gave them a witness. He did good by providing them rains and fruitful seasons which satisfied their hearts with food and gladness. By this Christian theistic approach Paul would lead them to believe in the living God (Acts 14:8-18). Thus Paul's view of God as a Pharisee had been greatly enriched as he advanced from the narrow theism of the Pharisees to the full-orbed biblical view of God, the Creator and Preserver of the universe.

Paul pursued a similar way of approach to the people at Athens. His enlarged view of God and the world enabled him to lead the

Athenians to comprehend God, not as one among many others, but as Lord of heaven and earth. In a skillful manner Paul pursued a Christian theistic approach designed to capture the thinking of these intelligent and philosophically minded Athenians. The implications which naturally followed the idea of God as Creator included God as the source of life in human beings, the oneness of the human race, the responsibility of man to seek God, and the possibility of communication with Him. Since mankind is the offspring of God, it is utter folly to represent God by the art and imagination of man. Paul could add that the true God has overlooked this ignorance and is now commanding all men to repent because of the coming day of judgment in which Christ, who was raised from the dead, will judge all mankind in righteousness (Acts 17:16-31).

These two messages addressed to pagans possess special value for the purpose of showing how Paul by way of the natural universe could lead people to a knowledge of the true God and of salvation in Christ. His knowledge of the Creation and of God's direction of history from Abraham to Christ made this approach effective and affirmed the oneness of God's revelation in the universe and through His revealed Word.

The remaining messages of Paul to Jewish hearers repeated a number of the themes already observed in earlier discourses.[4] To the Jews at Thessalonica, Paul went to great lengths to show them from the Scriptures "that it was necessary for the Christ to suffer and to rise from the dead, and saying, 'This Jesus . . . is the Christ' " (17:3). This shows again that the Jews failed to associate the suffering Servant with the Christ. They could think only of Christ as a political king. The idea that Jesus was the Christ made no sense whatever to Paul's hearers.

Paul's conversation with the Ephesian church elders introduces us to his understanding of congregational life and organization (20:17, 28). He used two titles for the church leaders, *elders (presbuteros)* and *guardians (episkopos)*. The former term suggested that the church leaders were composed of older brethren in the church, and the second term expressed the nature of their responsibilities as being overseers or guardians of the congregations. As to his preaching ministry he was testifying to Jews and Greeks "of repentance to God and of faith in our Lord Jesus Christ" (20:21). The doctrinal content of this preaching was essentially foreign to pharisaical-minded Jews. He admonished these church elders in the familiar figure of shepherd-life, to take heed to themselves and to all the flock. Christ through the Holy Spirit had made them guardians in which their chief task was "to feed the church of the Lord which he obtained with his own blood" (v. 28). This perpetuated the shepherd concept of Psalm 23, as well as Jesus' teaching on being a good shepherd.

It was significant that Paul drew attention to the price of redemption through Jesus' blood. He proceeded to warn them concerning the "fierce wolves," which would soon come to devour the flock. He was very realistic about the tribulation which the church would suffer. In most appropriate language Paul could add, "I commend you to God and to the word of his grace, which is able to build you up and to give you the inheritance among all those who are sanctified" (v. 32). Throughout Paul's service for Christ he experienced the genuine dynamics of God's grace. He also directed attention to the practical aspect of Christian service relating to self-support and also of helping the weak (vv. 33-35). Somewhere along the way Paul had learned of Jesus' precious maxim. "It is more blessed to give than to receive."

When Paul gave his testimony to Governor Felix, he expressed a significant confession of his faith in the words, "I worship the God of our fathers, believing everything laid down by the law or written in the prophets, having a hope in God . . . that there will be a resurrection of both the just and the unjust" (24:14, 15). The breadth of Paul's theological thinking became evident when he spoke to Felix about faith in Christ Jesus and included in his conversation some matters related directly to Felix's responsibility. One point had to do with the governor's responsibility of exercising justice in the courts of law. Felix could not escape the moral responsibility of self-control in his own personal life. It was essential for him to think of future judgment from which he himself as a judge could not escape (vv. 24, 25).

Paul testified before King Agrippa that he had lived as a strict Pharisee, and on account of a fundamental belief of the Pharisees, that of hope in the promise made by God to their fathers, he was on trial. The particular point of tension centered in the belief that God would raise the dead. While this was the chief point of tension between Pharisees and Sadducees, it appears that to many of the Pharisees this belief was of little consequence. To Paul, however, the resurrection of the dead had become almost the central tenet of his faith, as is evidenced in 1 Corinthians 15 and in other letters. Paul's closing words in this defense before Agrippa constitute a compact statement of his theological position. He was saying "nothing but what the prophets and Moses said would come to pass; that the Christ must suffer, and that, by being the first to rise from the dead, he would proclaim light both to the people and to the Gentiles" (Acts 26:22, 23). Significant for this study is what Paul found in the Old Testament predictions of Christ's death and resurrection, and also of the universal mission of the gospel.

In a similar message to the Jews at Rome Paul centered his teaching on the kingdom of God. This indicates again the place that the kingdom of God occupied in Paul's gospel. [5] By way of conclusion, note Paul's witness to the nature of the written Word in his declaration, "The Holy Spirit was right in saying to your fathers through Isaiah the prophet" (Acts 28:25). A concept such as this underlay Paul's classic statement of inspiration as found in 2 Timothy 3:15, 16.

For Additional Reading and Reference:

Bernard, *The Progress of Doctrine in the New Testament,* pp. 130-180.
Beyschlag, *New Testament Theology,* Vol. II, pp. 1-27.
Bruce, A. B., *St. Paul's Conception of Christianity,* pp. 26-47.
Longenecker, *Paul, Apostle of Liberty,* pp. 21-42.
Matheson, *Spiritual Development of Paul.*
Schoeps, *Paul,* pp. 13-43, 47-50, 51-87.
Stevens, *The Pauline Theology,* pp. 1-26.
Stewart, *A Man in Christ,* pp. 32-122.
Weidner, *Biblical Theology of the New Testament,* Vol. II, pp. 11-16.
Whiteley, *The Theology of St. Paul,* pp. 1-16.

1. Acts 22:3; 23:6; 26:4, 5, 9-11, 14; Rom. 7:4-25; 1 Cor. 15:9; Gal. 1:13, 14; 3:10; 5:3; Phil. 3:4-7; 1 Tim. 1:13.
2. Acts 9:3-18; 22:6-16; 26:12-18; Rom. 7:24, 25; 1 Cor. 15:8-10; Gal. 1:12-16.
3. Rom. 1:4; 6:4; 8:11; 1 Cor. 15:15; 2 Cor. 1:20; Phil. 2:8 f.; Col. 2:12; 1 Thess. 1:10.
4. Acts 17:2, 3; 22:1-21; 24:10-21; 26:4-23; 28:23-28.
5. Acts 14:22; 19:8; 20:25; 28:23, 31.

CHAPTER II

THE ESCHATOLOGY OF PAUL

1. The Teachings of the Thessalonian Letters

a. The Coming of the Lord

Almost all Paul's letters have an opening paragraph of thanksgiving in which he introduced some of the leading ideas which he developed later in the letter. In 1 Thessalonians he closed the thanksgiving with reference to their having turned to God from idols and of their waiting for His Son from heaven, this coming One to deliver them from the wrath to come (1:9, 10). Paul reminded his readers of the holy, righteous, and blameless behavior which he and Timothy had demonstrated in their midst. This led to his exhortation that they should lead a life worthy of God who calls them into His own kingdom and glory. Paul felt that these Christians were their hope or joy or crown of boasting before the Lord Jesus at His coming. He concluded this exhortation with a benedictory prayer that the Lord would establish their hearts unblamable in holiness before God the Father at the coming of the Lord Jesus with all His saints (1 Thess. 2:19; 3:13).

In these introductory statements concerning the return of Christ, several important ideas stand forth. First, Christians should wait for the return of Christ from heaven. Second, it is He who delivers the righteous from the wrath to come. Third, there is need for leading a life worthy of God who calls us into His kingdom and glory. Fourth, the word *parousia (presence, coming, advent)* stands forth as one of the significant words relating to the return of Christ. Fifth, the *parousia* marks the coming of our Lord Jesus with all His saints.

Paul was aware that the Thessalonian Christians had a concern for the welfare of the fellow believers who had died. At once he encouraged them not to grieve as others did who had no hope. He then proceeded to relate more fully the coming of the Lord in relation to the living and the dead (1 Thess. 4:13-18). He began this account by stating that God through Jesus will bring with Him those who have fallen asleep. They who will be living until the parousia of the Lord will have no advantage or take any precedence over those who had died. He clarified this by noting the order of events relating to the parousia. "The Lord himself will descend from heaven with a cry of command, with the archangel's call, and with the sound of the trumpet of God. And the dead in Christ will rise first; then we who are alive, who are left, shall be caught up together with them in the clouds to meet the Lord in the air; and so we shall always be with the Lord" (1 Thess. 4: 16, 17). What a simple yet most glorious presentation of Christ's parousia!

Paul's closing benediction brought together in true relationship his exhortation to holy living in relation to Christ's return. "May the God of peace himself sanctify you wholly; and may your spirit and soul and body be kept sound and blameless at the coming of our Lord Jesus Christ. He who calls you is faithful, and he will do it" (5:23, 24). Several truths found in this major portion relating to the parousia deserve notice. First, those who will have died before Christ's parousia are regarded as having fallen asleep. Second, those who are living at the time of the parousia will have no advantage whatever over those who had fallen asleep. Third, the parousia of the Lord shines forth with unspeakable glory, power, and kingly authority, never before manifested in its fullness to mankind. Fourth, the dead in Christ will be the first to respond to Christ's parousia, then those who are alive will be caught up together with the risen dead in Christ. Fifth, all the redeemed will meet the Lord in the air and shall always be with Him. While there are some unanswered questions in this first account of the parousia, the clarity of the details predicted was sufficient for those who believed that Jesus died and rose again.

By reason of the severe persecutions which the Thessalonian Christians were enduring, Paul wrote his second letter in which he encouraged them to endure these afflictions. Through this endurance they would be deemed worthy of the kingdom of God. This would become evident at the judgment when God would condemn the wicked and would grant these steadfast and faithful Christians entrance into the unspeakable glories of the eternal kingdom of God. Paul enlarged on this prediction by giving a fuller account of what would take place at the parousia of Christ. God will deem it just to repay with affliction those who afflicted these Christians. He will grant rest to them who were being afflicted along with all other faithful Christians. This will take place at the *revelation (apokalupsis)* of the Lord Jesus. Paul used this word in order to give a fuller view of the parousia. It expresses the full disclosure and manifestation of the Lord in all His glory. Accompanying Him will be His mighty angels appearing in flaming fire. At this moment the Lord Jesus will bring vengeance upon those who do not know God and those who do not obey the gospel of Christ. The awfulness of this judgment is expressed in the language of their suffering "the punishment of eternal destruction and exclusion from the presence of the Lord and from the glory of his might" (2 Thess. 1:9).

One purpose of His coming will be "to be glorified in his saints and to be marveled at in all who have believed" (v. 10). Paul's practical concern for these Thessalonians was that the Lord would make them worthy of His call and that the name of the Lord Jesus would be glorified in them and they in Him. The theological aspects of Paul's presentation include: first, the fuller view of God's kingdom; second, the manifestation of Christ at His revelation; third, the issues of the final judgment at His return; and fourth, the grace of the Lord Jesus Christ manifested in His revelation.

b. The Day of the Lord

After Paul dealt with the concerns of the Thessalonians with regard to those who had passed away, he advanced directly from the *parousia* teaching (1 Thess. 4:13-18) to a closely related theme, the *day of the Lord.* This expression was not new to the apostle, having had its source in the Old Testament (Is. 2:12-31; Joel 2:11 ff.; Amos 5:18-20; etc.). The parousia, according to Paul, would mark the beginning of the day of the Lord. The suddenness of its coming should lead the Thessalonian Christians and all others since that time to a watchfulness and expectancy of the imminent return of the Lord. Paul's exhortation included the words, "Let us be sober, and put on the breastplate of faith and love, and for a helmet the hope of salvation" (1 Thess. 5:8). Paul added to his discussion on the parousia the bearing it would have on the ungodly. God has destined them for wrath, this in sharp contrast to the obtaining of salvation through the parousia of Christ. For this new church of believers this brief explication of the day of the Lord was sufficient.

In the meantime, however, a new situation arose among these Christians. A report had gained wide circulation that the day of the Lord had already come (2 Thess. 2:1, 2). While some scholars interpret the perfect active indicative of the verb *enistemi* as "is just at hand," it seems that the RSV, NEB, Berkeley, and other modern translations express Paul's thought: "the day of the Lord has come." He declared that the apostasy, "the final rebellion against God" (NEB), will come first. Paul identified the leader of this apostasy as the man of lawlessness, evidently making specific reference to the archenemy of God's people predicted in the Book of Daniel (7:25; 8:25; 11:36). The near fulfillment of Daniel's prediction was undoubtedly Antiochus Epiphanes. But Paul's reference to these predictions would lead us to believe that Antiochus Epiphanes typified the archenemy of mankind, the man of lawlessness. In this manner Paul related New Testament eschatology with that of the Old Testament. It demonstrated again that the Old Testament view of the latter days extended beyond the time of Christ, even to the day of the Lord of which the focal point is Christ's parousia. Such is the nature of God's unfolding revelation, which is the genius of biblical theology.

Paul disclosed further the character of this anti-god, man of lawlessness. He will stand as the arch opponent of God. Building on the symbolism of the Old Testament temple, Paul predicted that this coming one would usurp God's place in the holy of holies of the temple. Paul referred to the restraining power to the man of lawlessness. We could wish that he had expanded the idea of this restraining power. Certainly it must be spiritual in nature. If Paul was aware of Jesus' teaching on the work of the Holy Spirit (Jn. 16:7-11), it would be easy to conclude that he was referring to the Holy Spirit's work of convincing "the world of sin and of righteousness and of judgment." The nearest clue to this identification is Jesus' closing words, "of judgment, because of the ruler of this world is judged." Whether or not Paul was consciously alluding to these words of Jesus, I believe that the man of lawlessness is identical with the ruler of this world. Paul clarified to his readers that the mystery of lawlessness was already at work, and that the restraining power of the Holy Spirit will continue until the lawless one will be revealed. Paul assured the Thessalonians that "the Lord Jesus will slay him with the breath of his mouth and destroy him by his appearing and his coming" (2 Thess. 2:8). By bringing together the two words for Christ's return (*epiphaneia* and *parousia)* Paul may actually be expressing some possible impacts of Christ's return upon the lawless one.

It was essential for the Thessalonians to learn that the coming of the lawless one by Satan's activity will be "with all power and with pretended signs and wonders, and with all wicked deception for those who are to perish" (2 Thess. 2:9, 10). The reason for this stern language was to serve as a warning to those who were refusing to love the truth. On this account they would not be saved. The deceptiveness of this lawless one would be all the more real because "God sends upon them a strong delusion, to make them believe what is false, so that all may be condemned who did not believe the truth but had pleasure in unrighteousness" (vv. 11, 12). All this shows Paul's great concern for these Thessalonians who were being shaken in mind and disturbed. Having dealt so forthrightly with the coming day of the Lord and of all the potential involvements with the man of lawlessness Paul closed his exposition of this theme with the words. "So then, brethren, stand firm and hold to the traditions which you were taught by us, either by word of mouth or by letter" (2:15).

2. The Eschatological Teachings of Paul's Other Letters

a. The Coming of the Lord

In view of the great emphasis which Paul gave to Christ's parousia and the day of the Lord in the Thessalonian letters, it seems almost unexplainable why neither of these themes received any attention in the letters to the Romans and to the Ephesians, with exception of the expression "the day of redemption" found in Ephesians 4:30. A possible explanation of this phenomenon may be that in these two letters Paul was dealing with the doctrines of salvation and the church, respectively; and on this account, he did not introduce these eschatological themes, since they related so closely to the problems of Christian living in a situation of persecution.

In 1 Corinthians 1:4-9 and 4:1-5 Paul made two references to the parousia. The former occurred in a context of thanksgiving where he noted that his readers were not lacking in any spiritual gift as they "wait for the revealing of our Lord Jesus Christ . . . guiltless in the day of our Lord Jesus Christ" (1:7, 8). The latter is in a setting where Paul was responding to those who were judging him. He wrote, "It is the Lord who judges me. Therefore do not pronounce judgment before the time, before the Lord comes, who will bring to light the things now hidden in darkness and will disclose the purposes of the heart. Then every man will receive his commendation from God" (4:4, 5). These Christians were waiting for Christ's return. In both cases the imminency of Christ's coming stands forth. They could depend on the sustaining grace of the Lord to the end (*telos*) (1:8). It is evident that the revelation of Christ marks the beginning of the day of our Lord Jesus Christ. This gives a clue as to the order of events at the revelation of Christ. In this day the inner character of all mankind will be evident: the guiltless and the guilty. In Paul's second reference he noted that the coming of the Lord will be the time of judgment which will bring to light all things hidden including the purposes of the heart. It is then that every man will receive his commendation from God. These brief, almost casual references to Christ's return furnish a number of details which have an important bearing on presenting an orderly account of the parousia, including its relation to other related topics such as the day of the Lord, the resurrection, the final judgment, Christ's messianic reign, the tribulation, whether or not there is any distinction between the rapture and the revelation of Christ, and the time when the day of salvation closes.

Leaving the great resurrection chapter (15) for later consideration, let us observe the manner in which Paul introduced this great theme by a reference to the parousia after having noted that Christ was the firstfruits of the resurrection. He added, "Then at his coming those who belong to Christ. Then comes the end, when he delivers the kingdom to God the Father after destroying every rule and every authority and power" (15:23, 24). Note again the interrelation of the several eschatological themes in these verses. Observe also the details in Paul's statement in Colossians 3:4, 6: "When Christ who is our life appears, then you also will appear with him in glory. . . . The wrath of God is coming." To Timothy who was being confronted with severe tests in his ministry, Paul gave the charge, "to keep the commandment unstained and free from reproach until the appearing of our Lord Jesus Christ; and this will be made manifest at the proper time" (1 Tim. 6:14, 15) by the Lord. In Paul's second letter to Timothy he wrote, "I charge you in the presence of God and of Christ Jesus who is to judge the living and the dead, and by his appearing and his kingdom" (2 Tim. 4:1). Looking to his imminent martyrdom Paul wrote, "Henceforth there is laid up for me the crown of righteousness, which the Lord, the righteous judge, will award to me on that Day, and not only to me but also to all who have loved his appearing" (4:8). Observe again the close correlation among the eschatological factors such as Christ judging the living and the dead, His appearing and kingdom, and the crown of righteousness to be awarded on that "Day." Paul's last words on the parousia, written to Titus, encouraged him to await "our blessed hope, the appearing of the glory of our great God and Savior Jesus Christ" (2:13). It was appropriate for Paul to hold forth in this final statement on the Lord's parousia that it is our blessed hope. I have consciously bypassed some of the interpretative problems relating to the parousia, leaving them for consideration under the heading "Summary of Pauline Eschatology."

b. The Resurrection

Paul's teaching on the resurrection in 1 Corinthians 15 came in a different setting from that of 1 Thessalonians. With the Corinthians the problem centered in the possibility of there being a resurrection of the dead. Paul confronted his readers with the assertion that if there is no resurrection of the dead, then Christ Himself had not been raised. If this were true, all his preaching would be in vain and their faith likewise would be in vain. In fact, he would have been misrepresenting God. Paul continued his rebuttal by building on the fact that Christ had been raised from the dead. Since death came by one man, Adam, and as a consequence, all die, so by one man, Christ, shall all be made alive. This sort of logic could not be gainsaid by the Corinthians. Christ was the firstfruits of the resurrection and then at His coming all those who belong to Christ will be raised. Paul then gave some additional teachings which undoubtedly confirmed his claims concerning the resurrection. These additional factors are vital to the entire subject of eschatology. Thus the coming of Christ marks the end (*telos*). At this climactic moment Christ will deliver the kingdom to God the Father, after He destroys every rule, authority, and power; that is, the messianic reign must of necessity continue until He has put all enemies under His feet. The last enemy is death.

Paul continued to wrestle with the Corinthians' problem, now centering in how the dead are raised and with what kind of bodies they come. In genuine frankness Paul declared the questioner a foolish man, and proceeded to answer his question by simple answers from nature. The seed sown must die before it grows up. Nor is all flesh alike. They vary from brute animals to human beings. Also there are terrestrial bodies and celestial bodies, each possessing a degree of glory according to its place in God's creation. These differences in glory find expression also in the resurrection of the dead. It is the difference of glory shown on the one side by what is perishable, weak, and physical, as it stands, in contrast with that which is imperishable, glorious, powerful, and spiritual. This became evident in the contrast between the first Adam, who became a living being and was a man of the dust while the last Adam, Christ, became a life-giving Spirit, and it is He who came from heaven. Expressing his conclusion bluntly to the Corinthians, Paul declared that "flesh and blood cannot inherit the kingdom of God, nor does the perishable inherit the imperishable" (15:50). In this manner he showed how fallacious it was for them to declare that there is no resurrection of the dead. In most dramatic language Paul declared to them a great mystery. He declared that at the last trumpet "the dead will be raised imperishable, and we shall be changed" (v. 52). To buttress this glorious foreview of the resurrection Paul said, "Death is swallowed up in victory" (v. 54; Is. 25:8). Most triumphantly Paul concluded, "But thanks be to God, who gives us the victory through our Lord Jesus Christ" (v. 57).

In Paul's second letter to the Corinthians he also built his teaching on the resurrection. The central burden of his message becomes apparent in the opening paragraph, "Blessed be the God and Father of the Lord Jesus Christ" (1:3). He drew attention to his sharing "abundantly in Christ's sufferings," but with it the sharing "abundantly in comfort" (v. 5) as well. He struck the resurrection note when he advised them "we had received the sentence of death; but that was to make us rely not on ourselves but on God who raises the dead" (v. 9). He developed this theme by noting that God had qualified him and his companions "to be ministers of a new covenant, not in a written code but in the Spirit; for the written code kills, but the Spirit gives life (3:6).

Here the two dispensations stand in sharp contrast; the former, that of death and condemnation; and the latter, that of the Spirit and of righteousness (vv. 8, 9). The contrast was sharpened still further by the fact that Moses had put a veil over his face so that the Israelites could not see his glory (v. 13). Paul noted that "when a man turns to the Lord the veil is removed" (v. 16) and then added, "We all with unveiled face, beholding the glory of the Lord, are being changed into his likeness from one degree of glory to another; for this comes from the Lord who is the Spirit" (v. 18). With this comprehension of Christ's glory, Paul maintained the courage to continue his ministry, adding the significant observation, "always carrying in the body the death of Jesus, so that the life of Jesus may also be manifested in our bodies" (4:10). Paul then struck a genuine resurrection note in the words, "He who raised the Lord Jesus will raise us also with Jesus and bring us with you into his presence" (v. 14). Paul was aware also that his outer nature was wasting away, but he could also triumphantly note that his inner nature was being renewed every day. He added, "For this slight momentary affliction is preparing for us an eternal weight of glory beyond all comparison, because we look not to the things that are seen but to the things that are unseen; for the things that are seen are transient, but the things that are unseen are eternal" (vv. 17, 18).

With this buildup of thought Paul moved forward into a sublime presentation of the resurrection. This approach to the resurrection theme differs sharply from that of 1 Corinthians. Paul's teaching was not merely a doctrinal presentation of this glorious future event, but that it stands as a firm foundation of hope in view of the severe persecutions being experienced by Paul and these Christians. With no desire to delve into controversial matters of interpretation I shall proceed with a positive exegetical approach. The earthly tent, the physical human body, deteriorates, but the believer has a building from God, the resurrection body, which is eternal. Due to our physical weaknesses we groan and long to put on this heavenly dwelling, the resurrection body. While we are in this tent, we sigh with anxiety that we would be further clothed. We yearn that what is mortal may be swallowed up by life. In order to confirm this hope God has given us the Spirit as a guarantee. We know that as long as we are at home in the body we are away from the Lord. Throughout this life in the body, we walk by faith. True indeed, we would rather be away from the body and at home with the Lord; nevertheless, it is our constant aim to please the Lord. "For we must all appear before the judgment seat of Christ, so that each one may receive good or evil, according to what he has done in the body" (5:10). The resurrection truths that stand forth in this passage are: first, that the resurrection body is a building from God; second, that it is eternal in the heavens; third, that life in this resurrection body is that of being at home with the Lord; and fourth, that we must all appear before the judgment seat of Christ.

c. The Day of the Lord

The problem of isolating for discussion purposes the several topics relating to Paul's eschatology is apparent. The manner in which Paul has integrated them shows that they bear a very close interrelation. I am seeking to gain a proper understanding of the fundamental unity among these various topics even though I am treating them separately in this chapter.

Let us note how Paul brought together the revelation of Christ and the day of our Lord Jesus Christ (1 Cor. 1:7, 8). Their interrelation in this context leads to the conclusion that Christ's revelation ushers in the day of our Lord Jesus Christ. It indicates the time of the end (*telos*). At the revelation of Jesus Christ all mankind will be in either one of two classes, guiltless or guilty. This change of expression from the day of the Lord (1 Thess. 5:2; 2 Thess. 2:2) to that of the day of our Lord Jesus Christ may have some significance. But what difference in meaning each may possess seems to lie beyond our comprehension. There is no difficulty in passing from the Old Testament expression *day of the Lord* to the New Testament *day of the Lord Jesus Christ* because many predictions referring to the Lord had their fulfillment in Christ. The strongest evidence in support of their being synonymous in meaning is that both are identified with the judgment of God, and in the New Testament in a very special way, the phrase is directly related to the Lord Jesus Christ.

In the context of building God's building (1 Cor. 3:10-15) Paul noted that if anyone builds on the foundation Jesus Christ, his work will become manifest; and in future time, the day, when it will be revealed of what material, whether destructible by fire, using a natural figure, or of indestructible material, he will be rewarded accordingly. With this grim figure Paul described the judgment to take place on the Day. Thus the effectiveness of Christian builders will be determined at that future time. He noted that some builders will suffer loss, though the building itself will be saved as by fire. This was a soul-searching counsel on the part of Paul, and it should speak to every Christian builder. It is conceivable that the work of many such builders will display great size and grandeur according to human judgment but the day will disclose the durability of their work through Jesus Christ, the Judge. Paul made his point still more decisive when he asked, "Do you not know that you are God's temple and that God's Spirit dwells in you? If any one destroys God's temple, God will destroy him. For God's temple is holy, and that temple you are" (vv. 16, 17). These words intensified the judgment aspect of the day.

Paul counseled the Corinthians relative to a very serious disciplinary problem which confronted them (1 Cor. 5:1-5). With reference to the conduct of a man guilty of a most degrading immorality, Paul said that he had already pronounced judgment upon him in the name of the Lord Jesus. He laid the responsibility upon the assembled church with the power of the Lord Jesus to deliver this man to Satan for the destruction of the flesh. Through this discipline the guilty brother's spirit may be led to repentance to the end that he would be saved in the day of the Lord Jesus. Here again the day of the Lord Jesus predicts the time of judgment in which He will be the Judge. At this judgment men will either be saved or lost. In a later context (2 Cor. 1:9-14) where Paul by reason of his severe persecution was relying on God who raises the dead, he looked forward to the day of the Lord Jesus, as a time when both the Corinthians and he himself could be mutually proud of one another. This suggests that this day will be one of reward for all the faithful.

Paul's words with regard to sowing and reaping (Gal. 6:7-9) seem to fit into the day of the Lord theme even though he did not use this heading. "He who sows to his own flesh will from the flesh reap corruption, but he who sows to the Spirit will from the Spirit reap eternal life" (v. 8). Undoubtedly this time of reaping is the day of the Lord. The expression *reap corruption* is a vivid figure describing the nature of eternal destruction. Just as the sins of the body result in bodily corruption so these sins of the body lead to spiritual corruption and finally to eternal ruin.

Paul's thanksgiving at the opening of his letter to the Philippians gave him the occasion to express the confidence that he who had begun a good work in the Philippians would bring it to completion at the day of Jesus Christ. He added the prayer that they may approve what is excellent and be pure and blameless for the day of Christ (Phil. 1:6). Thus the day of Jesus Christ would mark the completion of God's saving act. On this account he was concerned that on this day of judgment they might be pure and blameless (vv. 6-11). In 2:16 Paul again urged the Philippians to hold fast the Word of life that in the day of Christ he could have the satisfaction of not having run in vain.

He expressed his concern that their "manner of life be worthy of the gospel of Christ" (1:27). In a significant manner he stated that their steadfastness in a situation of severe opposition was a clear omen of their opponents' destruction, but to the Philippians, of their salvation. Here again Paul was referring to two different outcomes issuing from the day of the Lord, namely destruction and salvation. This sharpened still further the judgment aspect of the day of the Lord. In a similar context (3:18-21) Paul spoke of the end of these evil-doers as destruction, but to the faithful he spoke of their commonwealth as being in heaven and then added the resurrection note that the Lord Jesus Christ would change their lowly body to be like His glorious body, which He will bring about by the power which enables Him to subject all things to Himself.

In Paul's final references to this theme there appears to be no change in his view of the day of the Lord. Through his long service as an apostle he could say, "I know whom I have believed and I am sure that he is able to guard until that Day what has been entrusted to me" (2 Tim. 1:12). Paul also had the concern that the Lord would grant the household of Onesiphorus "to find mercy from the Lord on that Day" (2 Tim. 1:18). Paul's sublime valedictory expressed the profoundest truth of "that Day" as related to a faithful Christian. He wrote, "Henceforth there is laid up for me the crown of righteousness, which the Lord, the righteous judge, will award to me on that Day, and not only to me but also to all who have loved his appearing" (4: 8). These last references clearly show that the expressions "the Day of the Lord Jesus," "the Day," "that Day," and "Day of redemption" are synonymous in meaning. It is this judgment day that inaugurates the eternal "kingdom of Christ and of God" (Eph.5:5). There appears to be no differentiation between these expressions and the "Day of the Lord" used in 1 and 2 Thessalonians.

d. The Kingdom of God

The first impression one gains in studying this topic is that Paul definitely gave more attention to this teaching in these letters than in the Thessalonian letters. One objective in making this study is to determine the reason for this difference. This inquiry becomes all the more important when we reflect on the relatively great consideration Paul gave to the parousia, the resurrection, and the day of the Lord in the Thessalonian letters. In addition to the general doctrinal presentation of the kingdom of God, three fundamental questions will receive consideration in this discussion: (1) the present and future aspects of the kingdom; (2) the relation of the present and future ages to the kingdom of God; and

(3) the distinction between the kingdom of Christ and the kingdom of God. From another point of view, since Jesus gave so much teaching on the kingdom of God, the major problem before us is to discover the harmony of Paul's eschatology with that of the teachings of Jesus. (See 4 of this chapter.)

Noting Paul's references to the kingdom in the Book of Acts (14:28; 19:8; 20:25; 28:23, 31) we would think that he would give some exposition of the kingdom of God in his letters. What we do observe, however, are a number of pointed references in which he directs attention to conditions or sins which are antagonistic to the kingdom of God. As an example, "For the kingdom of God does not mean food and drink but righteousness and peace and joy in the Holy Spirit" (Rom. 14:17). To the Corinthians Paul wrote, "For the kingdom of God does not consist in talk but in power" (1 Cor. 4:20). In 6:9, 10 he wrote, "The unrighteous will not inherit the kingdom of God"; and then he specified nine groups of those making up the unrighteous. In Galatians 5:19-21 he listed fifteen works of the flesh, stating that "those who do such things shall not inherit the kingdom of God." In a similar passage (Eph. 5:3-5) he lists eight classes of sinners who do not have any inheritance in the kingdom of Christ and of God. In each of these cases it appears evident that Paul assumed the reader's comprehension of the kingdom.

The positive content of the kingdom stands forth in the language *righteousness, peace, joy in the Holy Spirit,* and *power* (Rom. 14:17; 1 Cor. 4:20). They who produce the fruit of the Spirit shall inherit the kingdom of God (Gal. 5:19-22). They have been delivered from the dominion of darkness and transferred to the kingdom of His beloved Son (Col. 1:13). These passages refer to a present aspect of the kingdom, but Paul clearly presented a future aspect when he noted that the unrighteous will not inherit the kingdom of God (1 Cor. 6:9). Most explicit in this respect is Paul's language, in which he declared that at the end of the age Christ will deliver the kingdom to God the Father after having destroyed every rule and every authority and power (15: 20-50). When this has been accomplished, Christ will also be subjected to the Father. We learn also that flesh and blood cannot inherit the kingdom of God (v. 50). The mode of existence in the eternal future kingdom will be spiritual and not physical. The present aspect of the kingdom stands forth in equal clarity when Paul noted that the saints have been delivered from the kingdom of darkness and transferred to Christ's kingdom (Col. 1:13). Thus Christ's kingdom belongs to the present age, and at its close He will deliver it to the Father (1 Cor. 15:24). Paul described His exaltation in the words, "The blessed and only Sovereign, the King of kings and Lord of lords, who alone has immortality and dwells in unapproachable light" (1 Tim. 6:15, 16).

e. The Apostasy

Judging from what Paul wrote to the Thessalonians concerning a coming rebellion and the revelation of *the man of lawlessness* (2 Thess. 2:3), we would expect that his later letters to other churches would supplement these predictions. While he warned these churches with reference to many specific sins he made no reference to a coming apostasy. This point becomes all the more unexplainable in view of what Paul wrote to Timothy at a still later time. He predicted a departure from the faith in later times (1 Tim. 4:1-5). He gave another prediction to be fulfilled "in the last days" (2 Tim. 3:1-9). Some Bible students hold that this second expression looks to a different time from that of the former. They regard the "later times" as predicting a departure from the faith in some period later than their time, while they place the *last days* as the era just preceding the close of the age at Christ's return. In view of the imminency of our Lord's return it appears to be consistent to regard these two Scriptures as being prophetic of imminent apostasy, as well as of that which will mark the close of this age.

The nature of the departure from the faith bears the mark of Gnostic and dualistic heretical views (1 Tim. 4:1-5). Paul frankly stated that this departure from the faith had its source in the people's giving heed to deceitful spirits and doctrines of demons. It gained recognition through the pretensions of liars whose consciences were seared. They forbad marriage and enjoined "abstinence from foods which God created to be received with thanksgiving by those who believe and know the truth" (v. 3). This shows how the early Christians were being confronted by the pagan religious and philosophical views of the times. Many Christians had not yet grounded their thinking in what we would, today, call the Christian view of God and the world.

The nature of the apostasy predicted in 2 Timothy follows the pattern of people's forsaking Christian standards of holy living (3:1-9). One of the subtle aspects of this prediction is that these people would hold the form of religion but would deny its power. In reality they would oppose the truth. They are men of corrupt minds and counterfeit faith. From the standpoint of church history these evils have confronted the church from earliest times to the present. To what extent this wickedness will yet manifest itself, the Lord alone knows. It is certainly descriptive of the sinfulness of mankind during this seventh decade of the 20th century. Paul enlarged still further on this imminent era of wickedness in the words, "For the time is coming when people will not endure sound teaching, but having itching ears they will accumulate for themselves teachers to suit their own likings, and will turn away from listening to the truth and wander into myths" (4:3, 4). This language is quite picturesque, especially the words "itching ears." With the pretense of being obedient to what they had been taught they were content to choose teachers to their own likings. It had a show of following the truth but in reality it was a complete rejection of sound teaching.

f. The Unfolding of the Old Testament Predictions Concerning the Last Days

In this group of Paul's letters a number of fulfillments of the latter days become apparent. We have already noted two or three of Paul's expressions which directly referred to the Old Testament expression of the latter days (1 Cor. 10:11; 1 Tim. 4:1; 2 Tim. 3:1). He also used the expressions "this age" and "the age to come," the same as used by Christ in His teachings (Mt. 12:32; 13:39; Lk. 18:30; 20:34-36). Undoubtedly Paul had learned of this expression and continued to build on its eschatological structure.[1] He also spoke of this age alone.[2] In this connection he also used the expression *the end* (1 Cor. 1:8; 15: 24). His clearest reference to the latter days is evident in the words, "They were written down for our instruction, upon whom the end of the ages has come" (*ta tele ton aionon*) (10:11). He was referring to some meaningful incidents of Old Testament history which had been written down for the instruction of those who had lived in the era of time predicted by the prophets, the latter days. From their viewpoint it would be the age of the Messiah; and as Paul implied, this would be *the end of the ages*. This era, the end of the ages, would come to a close at "the end" (1:8). Just as Jesus had divided these latter days into two eras, *this age* and *the age to come*, Paul did likewise.

Let us observe the setting of some of these occurrences. As Paul was bringing to a climax the truth that nothing is able "to separate us from the love of God in Christ Jesus our Lord" (Rom. 8:39), he drew in the expression "things present, nor things to come" (*oute enestota oute mellonta*) (v. 38). Definitive of the present era is the expression *the present evil age* (*tou aionos tou enestotos ponerou*) (Gal. 1:4). This stands in sharp contrast with Paul's expression "eternal life" which will receive consideration under the next main heading. As Paul magnified the glory of the exalted Christ (Eph. 1:19-23), he marked its eternal duration in the language "not only in this age *[aioni toutoi]* but also in that which is to come" (*toi mellonti*) (v. 21).

In all ten of Paul's uses of the expression "this age" he was pointing up various forms of sin which characterize the present age. It would appear that the fundamental reason he stressed so frequently the sinfulness of this world was to show his readers how this present evil world stands in sharpest contrast with .the glory of the age to come. These examples intensify the definite qualitative difference between the present age and the age to come. This gave his readers an accurate perspective of these two ages. Careful thought will show the bearing of this distinction upon the entire subject matter of Pauline eschatology.

g. The Eternal State

A study of Paul's eschatology leads naturally to the grand climax of life in the world to come. This theological inquiry should not minimize but rather intensify the experiential aspect of eternal life, as well as eternal death. By way of introduction to what this group of Paul's letters reveals concerning the eternal state, it is worthwhile to repeat the most refreshing words, "So we shall always be with the Lord" (1 Thess. 4:17). Since Paul wrote of eternal death in contexts where he revealed the nature of eternal life, I shall present these two aspects in the manner in which he interrelated them. Although I shall not relate the several teachings on the eternal state to their respective contexts, such a procedure would add definitely to the value of this study.

The first context (Rom. 2:6-11) speaks of two destinies, eternal life and that of wrath and fury. To those who do good there will be glory, honor, and peace. While the expression eternal life may not appear to give much meaning to the state of the righteous, yet the expression does carry great significance. Paul and his readers were well aware of the temporal aspect relating to the life of the Christian. For this life to become eternal it accumulates the content of meaning bound up in Paul's own words, *glory, honor*, and *peace*. In sharp contrast with this is the language describing the state of the wicked as they suffer the wrath and fury of God. It will be tribulation and distress. A study of these words shows how awful the punishment of the wicked will be.

When Paul described the results of being justified by faith, he climaxed his description with the words, "We rejoice in our hope of sharing the glory of God" (Rom. 5:2). Aside from the most meaningful terms setting forth God's holiness and righteousness, the attribute of glory is the most frequently used biblical term to set forth the majesty, sublimity, and splendor of God.

Another approach to the nature of eternal life is that of the perfected sonship. As Paul described the glory that is to be revealed in us, he set it forth in terms of the Christian's exalted state of being sons of God. Being children of God we are "heirs of God and fellow heirs with Christ" (Rom. 8:17). In view of this sonship "we wait for adoption as sons, the redemption of our bodies" (v. 23). Thus as redeemed humanity we are destined to be conformed to the image of His Son. Undoubtedly Paul had in mind the glory of the exalted Lord Jesus Christ who is the likeness of God (2 Cor. 4:4). This perfected sonship becomes evident once more in the words, "When Christ who is our life appears, then you also will appear with him in glory" (Col. 3:4).

Typical of Paul's approach to the Word of God was his quotation from Isaiah, a sublime portion predicting the eternal state of the righteous, "What no eye has seen, nor ear heard, nor the heart of man conceived, what God has prepared for those who love him" (1 Cor. 2:9; Is. 64:4). Paul presented the nature of eternal life in a rather unexpected manner when he wrote, "Now we see in a mirror dimly, but then face to face. Now I know in part; then I shall understand fully, even as I have been fully understood" (1 Cor. 13:12). The expression "face to face" is simple, but in this context it expresses a most intimate fellowship. In conclusion let us note again Paul's valedictory. "Henceforth there is laid up for me the crown of righteousness, which the Lord, the righteous judge, will award to me on that Day, and not only to me but also to all who have loved his appearing" (2 Tim. 4:8).[3]

h. The Future of Israel

Paul's unfolding of God's purpose led inevitably to his explanation of God's election and grace as it related to Israel. He observed how Israel's trespass brought salvation to the Gentiles. This led him to explore the possible bearing of Israel's repentance upon the Gentiles (Rom. 11:5-12). He pressed his point further with the question, "For if their rejection means the reconciliation of the world, what will their acceptance mean but life from the dead?" (v. 15). Bible scholars have wrestled long and hard with the meaning of this question, as well as with Paul's later statement, "And so all Israel shall be saved" (v. 26). I believe that the most satisfactory recent treatment of these statements is that of Franz J. Leenhardt. He interprets this "life from the dead" as foreshadowing "the reawakening of the people of promise, and its spiritual resurrection by the inspiration of the Holy Spirit."[4]

Paul built further on this idea by noting that if the people of Israel did not persist in their unbelief they would be grafted in again. He noted that a hardening, "obtuseness of intellectual discernment, mental dullness,"[5] had come upon part of Israel. This would continue "until the full number of the Gentiles come in, and so all Israel will be saved" (vv. 25, 26). Again Leenhardt seems to interpret this difficult passage by noting that "Paul did not write: *kai tote (and then)* but *kai houtos (and so)*. This is to say that the two events are logically related but the relation should not be understood in a rigid arithmetical fashion."[6] He interprets *all Israel* "as referring to the whole of Israel, as the elect people, in a view of history which is concerned with collectives rather than individuals."[7]

If this interprets Paul's language correctly, he viewed the possibility of Israel's being grafted in providing they do not persist in their unbelief. The declaration of verses 25 and 26 seems to be prophetic. It looks to the time when the full number of Gentiles will have come in, and in this manner all Israel will be saved. I have entertained the idea that Paul may be viewing the full number of the Gentiles as filling the gap made by the people of Israel who turned away from God and thus comprise the branches which are broken off. The all Israel would be spiritual Israel composed of Jews and Gentiles. As Paul wrote elsewhere, "There is no distinction between Jew and Greek; the same Lord is Lord of all and bestows his riches upon all who call upon him" (Rom. 10:12; Gal. 3:26-29; Col. 3:11).

Whether or not this interpretation senses the meaning of Paul's language, this portion of the letter to the Romans presents the eschatological aspect of Israel's future. On this account Paul's eschatology rightfully includes this disclosure of Israel's future. Perhaps the most difficult problem yet to be solved in his eschatology is that of reconciling this disclosure of Israel's future with that of the imminency of Christ's return. By way of an attempted reconciliation we should remember that he did not declare when Christ will return nor did he give guidelines for determining the fulfillment of these predictions concerning Israel.

3. Summary of Pauline Eschatology

A summary of Paul's eschatology should lead to understanding the interrelation of the several elements and factors which make up his view of the future. This should also serve as a perspective for grasping their meaning, as well as their bearing on the aims and purposes of life.

a. The Structure of Pauline Eschatology

(1) The Last Days. This expression, having its origin in the Old Testament, is viewed by Paul as representing the entire era of time from the earthly ministry of Christ until His parousia. It includes Christ's earthly ministry resulting in His death, and continues with His resurrection and exaltation to messianic kingship. He will reign until He delivers the kingdom to the Father at His return.

(2) The Two Ages. Paul regarded the present age as continuing until Christ's return. The age to come will begin with the consummation at Christ's return. It will mark the eternal reign of the Father.

b. The Course of This Age

Through the preaching of the gospel God "desires all men to be saved and to come to the knowledge of the truth" (1 Tim. 2:4). In slightly different language Paul wrote, "For the grace of God has appeared for the salvation of all men . . . awaiting our blessed hope, the appearing of the glory of our great God and Savior Jesus Christ" (Titus 2:11-13). Concurrent with this is the fact of sin and apostasy in this world. This departure from the faith will be headed by the man of sin. This conflict will continue until the parousia. Paul expressed the hope that the people of Israel will not persist in their unbelief but will be grafted in again as God's chosen people. This includes the conviction that Israel's return to God will result in a still greater diffusion of the gospel among the Gentiles. The coming departure from the faith is not incongruent with this hope.

c. The End (telos)

Paul's significant uses of this word (1 Cor. 1:8; 10:11; 15:24) bring into close correlation four great eschatological themes: the parousia, the resurrection, the judgment, and the eternal state. At Christ's coming He will raise the dead, both the righteous and the unrighteous. They will stand before the judgment seat of God, there to give an account of the deeds done in the body, whether good or evil. The ungodly will suffer the punishment of eternal destruction and exclusion from the presence of the Lord, but the righteous will realize the hope of eternal life.

4. The Harmony of Pauline Eschatology with That of Christ

Nowhere throughout Paul's eschatological teaching did he make any reference to the teachings of Jesus on this theme. As we shall note presently, there is a close affinity between the two, and this fact makes a comparison all the more important. This similarity has great bearing on the source of Paul's eschatology, as well as that of all his doctrinal teaching.

a. The Last Days

This expression is absent in the teachings of Jesus, nevertheless we have a very significant statement from His teachings which most certainly reflects the fulfillment of this prediction.[8] Jesus said, "The law and the prophets were until John; since then the good news of the kingdom of God is preached" (Lk. 16:16). Jesus said also, "Elijah does come, and he is to restore all things; but I tell you that Elijah has already come, and they did not know him" (Mt. 17:11, 12).

b. The Two Ages

In language similar to what Paul used Jesus spoke of this age and the age to come (Mt. 12:32; Mk. 10:30; Lk. 20:34, 35). Jesus had also identified the present age as that of the messianic kingdom, and that of the future as the kingdom of the Father (Mt. 13:41-43; 28:18).

c. The Course of This Age

In the same manner as Paul, Jesus gave a twofold view of this age. On the one side: wars, famine, earthquakes, tribulation, persecution, culminating in the desolate sacrilege of the man of sin; while on the other side Jesus declared, "This gospel of the kingdom will be preached throughout the whole world, as a testimony to all nations; and then the end will come" (Mt. 24:14, 15).

d. The Consummation (sunteleia)

Unexpectedly Paul used the term *(telos)* in contexts which were quite similar to Jesus' use of *(sunteleia)*. On the other hand Jesus used this term in a very meaningful way (Mt. 13:39, 40, 49; 24:3; 28:20). It should be recognized, nevertheless, that Paul's teaching concerning the end of this age stressed the same forthcoming events in quite the same manner as Christ had done. An examination of Matthew 16:27; 24:30; and 26:64 will show a veritable likeness between Christ's references to His second coming and those given by Paul. Jesus' teaching on the resurrection (Lk. 20:35-38; Jn. 5:28; 11:25, 26) follows the same pattern as that of Paul in his letters. The same is true concerning Jesus' teaching on the judgment (Mt. 12:36, 37; 25:31-46; Jn. 5:28, 29; 16:8-11). Finally, Jesus' teaching on the eternal state (Mt. 5:8, 12; 13:41-43; 25:46; Jn. 14:2, 3) was matched by similar teachings on the part of Paul, both as to eternal life and eternal death. By way of conclusion this comparison of Paul's eschatology with that of Jesus is most instructive. Since it is not possible to prove that Paul did not have access to the teachings of Jesus, Paul's teaching stands in its own right as to content, manner of presentation, and as a body of revealed truth. It is this fact which gives to Christians the firmest ground of hope for the future.

For Additional Reading and Reference:

Beyschlag, *New Testament Theology,* Vol. II, pp. 254-381.
Bowman, *Prophetic Realism and the Gospel,* pp. 270-273.
Furnish, *Theology and Ethics in Paul,* pp. 115-134.
Hunter, *Interpreting Paul's Gospel,* pp. 121-139.

Kittel, *Bible Key Words,* Vol. II, Book III, Basileia; Vol. V, Book I, Hope; Book II, Life and Death.
Ryrie, *Biblical Theology of the New Testament,* pp. 211-222.
Schoeps, *Paul,* pp. 43-46, 88-125.
Scott, *Christianity According to Paul,* pp. 236-243.
Sheldon, *New Testament Theology,* pp. 258-269.
Stevens, *The Theology of the New Testament,* pp. 470-482.
Stevens, *The Pauline Theology,* pp. 339-367.
Stewart, *A Man in Christ,* pp. 260-272.
Vos, *The Pauline Eschatology;* also I.S.B.E., Art. "Eschatology of the New Testament."
Weidner, *Biblical Theology of the New Testament,* Vol. II, pp. 35-69.
Weiss, *Biblical Theology of the New Testament,* Vol. I, pp. 305-315; Vol. II, pp. 52-74.
Whiteley, *The Theology of St. Paul,* pp. 233-273.

1. Rom. 8:38; 1 Cor. 3:18, 22; Gal. 1:4; Eph. 1:21; 2:7; 1 Tim. 4:8; 6:17-19.
2. Rom. 12:2; 1 Cor. 1:20; 2:6, 8; 7:31; 2 Cor. 4:4; Eph. 6:12; 2 Tim. 4:10; Tit. 2:12.
3. For some additional references to the eternal state note the following: Rom. 6:22, 23; 9:23; Gal. 6:7, 8; Eph. 5:5, 6; Phil. 1:28; 3:19.
4. *The Epistle to the Romans* (Cleveland: The World Publishing Co., 1961), pp. 284-294.
5. Robertson, *op. cit.*, Vol. IV, *The Epistles of Paul*, p. 398.
6. *Ibid.*, pp. 293, 294.
7. *Ibid.*, p. 294.
8. See Jn. 6:39, 40, 44, 54; 11:24; 12:48.

CHAPTER III

THE CHRISTIAN WAY OF LIFE

1. The Christian Way of Life as Taught in the Thessalonian Letters

While the Thessalonian Letters are best known for their eschatological content, there is need for gaining a proper understanding of what Paul wrote concerning the Christian way of life in these letters. In a very real way these two letters constitute a presentation of practical Christian ethics. The Christian way of life becomes evident in the words, "Work of faith and labor of love and steadfastness of hope" (1 Thess. 1:3). Their manner of life "became an example to all the believers" and their faith in God had gone forth everywhere (vv. 7, 8). They had "turned to God from idols, to serve a living and true God" (v. 9). Paul showed how pure and honest motivation is essential to Christian living (2:3-6). He was speaking "not to please men, but to please God who tests our hearts" (v. 4). Paul upheld a number of Christian graces, which should be expressed in their living: gentleness, self-sharing, faith, love, hearts unblamable in holiness, and others (2:7, 8; 3:6, 13). He stressed the matter of personal integrity of character in the terms: holy, righteous, blameless, love of God, and steadfastness of Christ (2:10; 2 Thess. 3:5). Sanctification and holiness (*hagiasmos*) stand forth with richest ethical meaning (1 Thess. 4:3, 4, 7; 2 Thess. 2:13). Paul specified the practical content of sanctification by noting the prevalent sins of immorality and unchaste marriage relations.

In simpler language Paul said, "You learned from us how you ought to live and to please God" (1 Thess. 4:1). He also used the word *uncleanness (akatharsia)* which stands as an emphatic antithesis to sanctification. It signifies moral impurity and viciousness. Since (*hagaismos*) is "an active verbal noun . . . it signifies properly the process (*to hagiazein,* rather than the resultant state *hagiosune*)."[1] It is significant that *hagiosune* occurs in 1 Thessalonians 3:13. Holiness, then, is the resultant state which Paul would have the Thessalonians achieve in their Christian growth.

Paul made it clear that the Christian way of life is achieved through the power of the Holy Spirit (1 Thess. 1:5, 6; 4:8; 5:19; 2 Thess. 2:13). This pattern of associating power (*dunamis)* with the Holy Spirit becomes quite characteristic in his later letters. From a Trinitarian point of view we should note that God gives His Holy Spirit to the believers. On this account Paul exhorted the Thessalonians to stop quenching the

Spirit. As Robertson says, "Some of them were trying to put out the fire of the Holy Spirit, probably the special gifts of the Holy Spirit, as verse 20 means."[2] The relation of the Spirit's work in the life of a Christian stands forth in the words, "God chose you from the beginning to be saved, through sanctification by the Spirit and belief in the truth" (2 Thess. 2:13). The interrelation among the several acts of the Holy Spirit calls for careful interpretation.

Paul used the expression "word of the Lord" in a manner which deserves some attention (1 Thess. 1:8; 2:13; 4:15; 2 Thess. 3:1). As Robertson says, "This phrase, the word of the Lord, may be subjective with the Lord as its author or objective with the Lord as its object. It is both."[3] Paul explains specifically that the Word of God was not the word of men. By this he was declaring the authoritative character of his preaching. On this account his teaching concerning the parousia of Christ declared a certitude which could not be gainsaid. Finally, Paul requested the prayers of the Thessalonians for him "that the word of the Lord may speed on and triumph." Thus the word of the Lord possessed the dynamic of Deity.

2. Paul's Teachings on Salvation

a. The Experiential Approach to the Interpretation of Galatians and Romans

One of the distinctive characteristics of these two letters is the fact that Paul repeatedly built his doctrinal truths on his own spiritual experiences. Obviously this method of presentation would have a special value for his readers. They would be challenged with the idea that the profound teachings of the apostle had their confirmation in his own personal experience. What was real for him could also be real for themselves.

Let us examine some of these teachings in the letter to the Galatians, which had their confirmation in Paul's own religious experience. In Galatians 2:16-21 he speaks of faith in Jesus Christ from the viewpoint of a personal experience. Through believing in Christ he was seeking to be justified by faith in Christ. Through this endeavor he came to realize that he was a sinner. Having come to realize the ineffectiveness of the law, he died to the law that he might live to God. Paul then gave his testimony which is hardly excelled anywhere in the Bible. From his own personal experience with Christ he wrote, "I have been crucified with Christ; it is no longer I who live, but Christ who lives in me; and the life I now live in the flesh I live by faith in the Son of God, who loved me and gave himself for me" (v. 20). It was this expression of most intimate relationship with Christ which should lead his readers to forsake their pharisaical attitude toward the law. What was true in Paul's personal experience, could also become theirs. He confronted them with the questions, "Did you receive the Spirit by the works of the law, or by hearing with faith? . . . Did you experience so many things in vain?" (3:2, 4). Pitifully these Galatians were rejecting the reality of these inner spiritual experiences in order to have the outward satisfaction gained by keeping every detail of the law, but at the same time not facing up to their failures to keep the law according to God's requirement.

Paul pursued this experiential approach on to chapter 5, where most climactically he set forth the inner nature of the Christian life (vv. 16-26). The walk by the Spirit becomes intensely real in the conflict between the desires of the flesh and those of the Spirit. Paul's listing of fifteen works of the flesh as over against the fruit of the Spirit should have been most convincing to these Galatians. In listing these Paul was undoubtedly giving testimony to his own inner struggles against these sins. But he had crucified the flesh with its passions and desires, experiential, indeed; and in a positive manner he was living and walking by the Spirit. Consequently, the fruit of the Spirit had genuine reality in his life. So essential was this entire experience to him that he repeated his testimony in the conclusion to his letter: "Far be it from me to glory except in the cross of our Lord Jesus Christ, by which the world has been crucified to me, and I to the world" (6:14).

The letter to the Romans elaborates this experiential aspect of Christian experience in a most remarkable manner. A number of scholars interpret chapter 7 as being autobiographical. They hold that Paul was interpreting his manner of life before his conversion in the light of his personal experience with Christ. With this interpretation of Romans 7 I am in entire agreement. My own studies of this book have led me to believe that in the large the entire Book of Romans is an autobiography of his spiritual experiences. I desire not to stress this interpretation too much, but yet it is essential to grasp Paul's personal religious experience which is reflected in this book. It needs to be said, nevertheless, that he nowhere stated that this book reflected his own experience.

In 1:18 — 3:20 Paul portrayed most graphically the nature of man's sinfulness. It is not a description made by one who had no experience with sin or who had a sinless nature. Undoubtedly, Paul was personally aware of the wrath of God revealed from heaven against all ungodliness and wickedness of men. He had lived close enough to a sinful world to know that God had given up sinful men to impurity and all kinds of sin. The catalog of sins listed by Paul and the scriptural evidence which he gave that all men are under the power of sin did not stem from his imagination, because it was through the law that he gained a knowledge of sin. In a commendable manner Paul identified his own sinfulness with that of mankind in general (3:5-8). Thus out of actual experience Paul acknowledged the wickedness and falsehood which had been a part of his experience. This leads to the conclusion that this portion of Romans sprang from one who knew sin through personal experience.

The section on justification by faith (3:21 — 5:21) makes still clearer Paul's sharing with all believers the experience of being justified by faith. This becomes very evident in the repeated uses of the first person pronoun. Note the following: "It will be reckoned to us who believe in him . . . who was put to death for our trespasses and raised for our justification" (4:24, 25). "Since we are justified by faith, we have peace with God through our Lord Jesus Christ. Through him we have obtained access to this grace in which we stand, and we rejoice in our hope of sharing the glory of God. . . . God's love has been poured into our hearts through the Holy Spirit which has been given to us" (5:1-5). These precious gems definitely assert that being justified by faith was a personal experience both of himself and of all believers.

The exercise of faith involves one's entire being. It results in the precious experiences of having peace with God, rejoicing in hope of sharing the glory of God, rejoicing in sufferings, testing of character and the producing of hope. This hope has the firm support of God's love which has been poured into our hearts through the Holy Spirit. This is Paul's first reference to the Holy Spirit (Rom. 5:5), and it reveals the profound nature of Christian experience, namely that of the inner working of the Holy Spirit in the life of the Christian. This activity of the Holy Spirit makes Christian experience possible and gives reality to it. This shows that Paul, the author of these words, experienced to the full the reality of these spiritual blessings.

Chapters 6 to 8 unfold most completely the experiential nature of the Christian life. For this reason it is essential to grasp the meaning of the several aspects of the Christian life recorded here. Paul dealt first of all with the radical change which takes place in the believer at the beginning of the Christian life (chapter 6). It involves the crucifixion of the old self and the being raised to a newness of life. Consequently being dead to sin and alive to God is most descriptive of the spiritual change wrought in the believer at the beginning of the Christian life. It is experiential to the core. Fifty first-person pronouns in chapter 7 show clearly that the writer was depicting personal experiences.

These phenomena give the strongest support to the autobiographical character of this chapter, if not of the entire letter to the Romans. Evidently Paul is looking back to his manner of life prior to his conversion. He now sees that it was sin which worked death in him. He was sold under sin. He was experiencing to the full the evident contradiction in his own life of his not doing what he wanted, and of his doing the very thing he hated. He had gained the insight that indwelling sin was the cause of this dilemma in which he could will what is right but was powerless to do it. This strange paradox became evident in the delight his inmost self had in the law of God, but at the same time another law was at work which had made him captive to the law of indwelling sin. This picture of his slavery to sin, in spite of his delight in the law of God, could not have had its origin in his imagination. All that he wrote here had its foundation in his own personal experience. It is all the darker because he was describing it in the light of his new life *in* and *through* the Holy Spirit.

Chapter 8 may well constitute the *summum bonum* of Paul's witness to the experiential nature of the Christian life. There is no condemnation for those who are in Christ Jesus. The law of the Spirit of life had set Paul free from the law of sin and death. The indwelling of the Spirit of God gives the power for the Christian to put to death the deeds of the body. When we cry, "Abba! Father!" we have witness of the Holy Spirit to our spirit that we are children of God. The Holy Spirit "helps us in our weakness; for we do not know how to pray as we ought, but the Spirit himself intercedes for us with sighs too deep for words" (v. 26). This is one of the most precious experiences of the Christian life. On this account, "We know that in everything God works for good with those who love him, who are called according to his purpose" (v. 28). With utmost confidence Paul could ask, "If God is for us, who is against us? . . . Who shall separate us from the love of Christ?" to which he could reply, "In all these things we are more than conquerors through him who loved us" (vv. 31, 37). With fullest assurance he could conclude that nothing "will be able to separate us from the love of God in Christ Jesus our Lord" (v. 39).

The chief reason for my presenting at such length the experiential aspect of Christian life lies in the fact that at heart the Christian religion is experience-centered. The theological content of the Christian faith gains meaning only through the living reality of the life in Christ Jesus. It is to be deeply regretted that some theologians practically ignore the experiential relation of God to man, and of man to God. A cold intellectualism allows no room for spiritual experiences. Nevertheless, Paul's testimony confirmed by all Christians throughout the Christian era completely nullifies such an intellectual approach.

b. The Righteousness of God

This section deals directly with Paul's definitive statement in which he set forth the theme of his letter to the Romans. He wrote, "I am not ashamed of the gospel: it is the power of God for salvation to every one who has faith, to the Jew first and also to the Greek. For in it the righteousness of God is revealed through faith for faith; as is written 'He who through faith is righteous shall live'" (Rom. 1:16, 17). In a word, we have here an explicit statement setting forth the nature of the gospel. Specifically it is the power, the dynamic of God, which is able to effect salvation. Through this power the righteous shall live. This salvation manifests the righteousness of God; that is, God is consistent with His nature in saving mankind from sin. This becomes evident to man through faith, and it leads to growing faith in Him. In support of this, Paul quoted the very meaningful words of the prophet Habakkuk, which declared, "He who through faith is righteous shall live." All this declares the comprehensive meaning of the word *salvation*. Paul's entire letter constitutes the unfolding of this salvation. In the most comprehensive manner, this salvation reveals the righteousness of God.

This leads us to a study of the definitive words *righteousness, righteous,* and *to declare righteous.* These words lead to some of the most important themes of biblical teaching. The scope of materials for study is also extensive. To begin with a splendid orientation would be gained by running down all the uses of these words in a concordance. Extensive treatments of these words are found in Greek lexicons of the New Testament, theological dictionaries, and word studies in the New Testament. All commentaries on Paul's letters give an exegetical approach to these great words. They were used extensively both in classical Greek and in the Septuagint. According to classical usage *dike* means *right.* Its earlier sense was *custom* or *usage*. It developed a strongly moral sense. *Dikaios* means *right. Dikaiosune* had the sense of *rightness*. It was used to characterize the entire being of man.

Of much greater significance for understanding all the uses of these words is their significance in the Septuagint. Here we meet the phenomena that *dikaios* and *dikaiosune* are at times interchanged with *eleemosune (mercy)* and *eleos (kindness)*. The Hebrew word *chesed (kindness)* is usually rendered *eleos,* but is translated nine times by *dikaiosune* and once by *dikaios*. The Hebrew word *tsedaka* is usually translated by *dikaiosune* but nine times by *eleemosune* and three times by *eleos*.

Since the usage of these Hebrew words was so frequent in the Old Testament and their rendering in the Septuagint forms the bridge to their New Testament use, the meaning which Paul gave to them becomes quite clear. Paul used *dikaios* both of God and of men. According to the Greek lexicon, it means *upright, just, righteous, pure in life.* When used of men, it denotes their normal relation to the will and judgment of God. *Dikaiosune* means righteousness. There are some cases in Paul's writing where it may carry the sense of charitableness (2 Cor. 9:9), uprightness (Rom. 9:30; 1 Tim. 6:11; 2 Tim. 3:16), and righteous deeds (Titus 3:5). The verb *dikaioo* also has a number of meanings, especially in Paul's use of the verb, thus, *to justify* (Rom. 2:13; 3:20), *to become free* or *pure* (Rom. 6:7; 1 Cor. 6:11), and *prove to be right* (Rom. 3:4; 1 Tim. 3:16). This range of meanings shows how essential it is to gain the right connotation in a given reference.

This should prepare us to interpret the frequently used expression *righteousness of God.* Two meanings become quite clear: first, righteousness as an attribute of God; and second, as stating God's dealings with man in righteousness. It is not always easy to determine which meaning Paul had in mind. It seems evident that in some cases he was drawing together both connotations. On this account there is no special value gained by interpreting a given example one way or the other. The uses of the word in Romans 3:5 and 25 may be regarded as setting forth *righteousness* as an attribute of God. Its occurrences in Romans 3:21; 2 Corinthians 5:21; and Philippians 3:9 properly express righteousness as an activity of God or as bestowed on man by God. It becomes quite a challenge to study every example of this expression for the purpose of determining its distinctive meaning.

In anticipation of Chapter IV, "Justification Through Redemption," let us give thought to God's righteousness as manifested in justification by faith.[4] Paul asserted this truth directly in the words, "The righteousness of God has been manifested apart from the law . . . the righteousness of God through faith in Jesus Christ for all who believe" (Rom. 3:21, 22). This act of justification on the part of God does not violate His righteousness in view of its basis in the redemption through Christ, "whom God put forward as an expiation by his blood" (v. 25). Further confirmation of this truth is found in the words, "For our sake he made him to be sin who knew no sin, so that in him we might become the righteousness of God" (2 Cor. 5:21).

In Paul's later letters he moves from the doctrinal presentation of God's righteousness to that of its being the standard and pattern for Christian living. He exhorted the Ephesians to put off their old nature which belonged to their former manner of life and then wrote, "Put on the new nature, created after the likeness of God in true righteousness and holiness" (4:24). Apparently there was no need for Paul to give the meaning of God's righteousness but rather to show that His righteousness is the absolute standard of ethics and Christian living. The meaning of righteousness is intensified through its close relation with *holiness*. In like manner Paul wrote to the Philippians, "It is my prayer that your love may abound more and more, with knowledge and all discernment, so that you may approve what is excellent, and may be pure and blameless for the day of Christ, filled with the fruits of righteousness which come through Jesus Christ, to the glory and praise of God" (1:9-11). This entire statement sets forth in a practical way the fruits of righteousness. Fruit of this sort could come only through Jesus Christ. To Timothy, Paul wrote: "Aim at righteousness, godliness, faith, love, steadfastness, gentleness" (1 Tim. 6:11). Note the Christian graces which greatly enrich the meaning of righteousness. Most fitting for my purpose is Paul's final witness to God's righteousness, in the words, "There is laid up for me the crown of righteousness, which the Lord, the righteous judge, will award to me on that Day" (2 Tim. 4:8). At that time God will manifest His righteousness through righteous judgment. This asserts the central aspect of God's nature, that is, God's righteousness will be revealed in His righteous judgment. This crown of righteousness will be the imperishable wreath (1 Cor. 9:25) which he will receive. The genitive case used in 2 Timothy 4:8 may thus express not only the victor's crown, but also that the crown consists in righteousness.

c. Sin and Guilt

Paul's discussion of sin in Romans 1:18 to 2:20 possesses a distinctive character. After declaring his central theme with respect to the gospel being the power of God for salvation, he made the most sobering statement relating to the revelation of God's wrath against all ungodliness and wickedness of men. In this manner Paul based his message of sin on the most central doctrine of divine revelation. On this account his treatment of sin and guilt needs to be interpreted in harmony with the salvation theme of the gospel. This integral relationship of Paul's teaching on sin to the gospel finds further confirmation in 3:21 ff., where he introduced his central doctrine of justification through faith. All that the apostle disclosed as to the nature of sin prepared his readers to understand what needs to be accomplished through Christ in order that man might be saved.

Paul had just written that the righteousness of God is revealed in the gospel, and now he adds that the wrath of God is revealed from heaven against all ungodliness and wickedness of men. He noted that both God's righteousness and His wrath are being revealed. It leads to the idea that what Paul will be saying about ungodliness and wickedness is foundational to what he will be giving later on redemption, justification, faith, the work of the Spirit, and Christian living. On this account this study of sin should be made in the perspective of these later teachings.

The first mark of man's sinfulness is that of suppressing the truth (Rom. 1:18). God's work of creation has revealed to all mankind His eternal power and deity (v. 20). In spite of this they did not honor Him as God and became futile in their thinking. This led to the darkening of their senseless minds (v. 21). Through their pride they claimed to be wise but instead became fools (v. 22). This was most evident in exchanging the immortal God for images resembling mortal man, birds, animals, or reptiles (v. 23). So heinous was this sin that God removed His restraints from mankind, giving them up in a threefold manner: first, in the lusts of their hearts to impurity; second, to dishonorable passions; and third, to a base mind and to improper conduct. In these verses (24-32) the apostle gave the darkest picture of man's sinfulness found in the Scriptures. By reason of this utter depravity man was totally unable to save himself. The twenty-one sins or vices listed here expose the almost unbelievable wide gamut of man's degradation.

Paul was aware that some of his readers, whether Jew or Greek, would be passing severe judgment upon such wicked people (2:1-11). They would be doing so, not realizing that they themselves might become entrapped by these sins also. The Jewish Christians who formerly were Pharisees were likely to be most critical of the sinners described by Paul, but they failed to recognize that when they passed judgment upon others they were condemning themselves because their own lives were not free from these sins. They were presuming upon the riches of God's kindness, forbearance, and patience, and failed to realize that God was also seeking to lead them to repentance. They appeared to be unmindful that by their own hard and impenitent hearts they were storing up wrath for themselves on the day of wrath. Only two groups of people will be evident on this day: the righteous to whom will be given eternal life and the wicked for whom there will be tribulation and distress.

In order to drive home this truth, Paul noted the greater responsibility of the Jew over the Greek by reason of the former having been the chosen people of God to whom He had revealed Himself. In developing this point, the apostle introduced the idea that God has written His law on man's innermost being, the heart (2:15). The consciousness of right and wrong, good and evil, belongs to the nature of man through God's creation. Thus when God put man in the garden where He had caused the tree of the knowledge of good and evil to grow, He had endowed him with the capacity to discern good and evil. In accordance with this aspect of man's nature, God also endowed man with the moral faculty known as the conscience. It is by the conscience that man is able to discern right and wrong, and through this capacity he is prompted to perform right actions. Without the heart, man's conscience would be totally unable to function.

Paul's uses of the words *heart (kardia)* and *conscience (suneidesis)* (2:15) are of such significance that they deserve further study. While this may appear as a digression from the general discussion relating to sin, it is essential to observe the bearing of these words on sin and guilt.

d. Paul's Use of Heart (kardia) *and Conscience* (suneidesis)

(1) Heart *(kardia)*. By bringing together these two words Paul was showing their close relationship and also their distinctive meanings (Rom. 2:15). In 9:1, 2, the apostle centered his sorrow and anguish in his heart, and also gave his testimony to the witness of his conscience that he was speaking the truth. Through this language he was referring to his heart as his innermost being and to his conscience as that faculty of the human mind which perceives the ethical quality of his testimony. This function of the conscience gained highest certitude since it bore witness in the Holy Spirit.

In another experience of tight circumstances Paul gave the same stress and distinction in meaning to these words (2 Cor. 4:2-6). He found it necessary to renounce disgraceful and underhanded ways, in the way of practicing cunning or tampering with God's Word. Instead by the open statement of the truth he and his companions would commend themselves to every man's conscience in the sight of God. He explained further that the gospel is veiled only to those who are perishing. The god of this world was blinding the minds of the unbelievers so that they would not see the light of the gospel of the glory of Christ. It was Christ as the Lord whom Paul preached, and then he concluded that Christ "has shone in our hearts to give the light of the knowledge of the glory of God in the face of Christ" (v. 6). In this manner, Paul was asserting that it was the heart that received this light, and therefore his statements of the truth would commend them to every man's conscience. When Paul counseled Timothy with reference to his task at Ephesus concerning those who were teaching different doctrines and occupying themselves with myths and endless genealogies, he gave the searching advice, "The aim of our charge is love that issues from a pure heart and a good conscience and sincere faith" (1 Tim. 1:5). In this expression Paul moved from the center of one's being, the *heart*, out to the *conscience* and to *faith* which function in harmony with the heart. It is unthinkable that a pure heart would express itself in an evil conscience or in unbelief. This should orient us to a study of these two great Pauline concepts.

While Paul at no point gave a formal definition of the word *heart*, his use of this word is consistent and shows that some of the profoundest teachings of the apostle center in this word. A number of references illustrate most clearly its distinctive meaning. [5]

From these references we gain the following significant ideas. To begin with, the heart is of such a nature that what the law requires is written on it. Things of a spiritual nature pertain to the heart. Genuine obedience to God, prayer, and faith have their source in the heart. One's emotions, concerns, worship, and motives all spring from the heart. All this shows that the heart lies beyond psychological analysis even though it seems to be inseparable from the intellect, feelings, and the will. It is natural then that God should test and search the heart, also direct the heart to the love of God and to the steadfastness of Christ (1 Thess. 2:4; 3:13; 2 Thess. 3:5; Rom. 8:27). This leads to the truth that the Holy Spirit's access to man is through the heart; in fact, He dwells in the heart. This accounts for the love of God being poured into the heart through the Holy Spirit. It is He, who through our hearts cries, "Abba! Father!" (Rom. 8:15, 16). In somewhat different language Paul wrote, God "has put his seal upon us and given us his Spirit in our hearts as a guarantee" (2 Cor. 1:22; 5:5). He also credited the Christians of Corinth as being a letter from Christ written not with ink but with the Spirit of the living God (3:3). Paul's prayer for the Ephesians was that God might grant them to be strengthened with might through His Spirit in the inner man (Eph. 3:16). [6]

Finally, let us notice the effects of sin on the heart. [7] Incidentally, in some of these references, the word *heart* is almost equivalent in meaning to the word *mind* and in several cases the RSV translated *kardia mind*. As Paul pictured the downward course of mankind into sin he noted that their senseless minds (hearts) were darkened and that God gave them up in the lusts of their hearts to impurity (Rom. 1:21, 24). In the refusal of sinful people to repent Paul warned them that by their hard and impenitent hearts they were stirring up wrath for themselves on the day of wrath (2:5).

Writing concerning the people of Israel in the time of Moses Paul declared that their minds *noema* were hardened, and that whenever Moses is read a veil lies over their minds (*kardia*) (2 Cor. 3:14, 15). This is one of the clearest examples of the synonymous use of mind and heart, and it shows the common ground of meaning of these two words. The effect of sin upon the heart is expressed by the verb *poroo* (*petrify, harden, dull*). These people failed to see the glory of Moses by reason of his veil. In metaphorical language, a veil lies over their hearts. Even in Paul's day when the law was read he added, "When a man turns to the Lord the veil is removed" (v. 16). The full meaning and implications of this spiritual change become evident in the words, "Now the Lord is the Spirit, and where the Spirit of the Lord is, there is freedom. And we all, with unveiled face, beholding the glory of the Lord, are being changed into his likeness from one degree of glory to another; for this comes from the Lord who is the Spirit" (vv. 17, 18). This is perhaps the most graphic picture of the impact of sin upon the heart. The apostle described this spiritual tragedy in slightly different language when he wrote, "The god of this world has blinded the minds of the unbelievers, to keep them from seeing the light of the gospel of the glory of Christ, who is the likeness of God" (4:4).

One more description of sin's impact upon the heart is graphically set forth with reference to the Gentiles: "They are darkened in their understanding, alienated from the life of God because of the ignorance that is in them, due to their hardness of heart; they have become callous and have given themselves up to licentiousness, greedy to practice every kind of uncleanness" (Eph. 4:18). Paul gave the remedy which alone would correct this effect of sin upon the heart. He wrote, "Put off your old nature which belongs to your former manner of life and is corrupt through deceitful lusts, and be renewed in the spirit of your minds, and put on the new nature, created after the likeness of God in true righteousness and holiness" (vv. 22, 23). Paul's final words on this sobering theme were written to the young bishop, Timothy, as follows, "So shun youthful passions and aim at righteousness, faith, love, and peace, along with those who call upon the Lord from a pure heart" (2 Tim. 2:22). The description which the aged apostle gave of the sinful world in which Timothy served, and also of the wickedness which would sooner or later overwhelm this world, showed most emphatically the necessity for Timothy to maintain a pure heart.

(2) Conscience *(suneidesis)*. In this major presentation of sin the word *conscience (suneidesis)* used with heart *(kardia)* in Romans 2:15 added another dimension to the sinfulness of the human race. Since man by creation possessed in his innermost being the awareness of things right and wrong, it is natural that this aspect of the heart should be accompanied by a functioning power of the mind for discerning right and wrong. To repeat Paul's words, "What the law requires is written on their hearts, while their conscience also bears witness and their conflicting thoughts accuse or perhaps excuse them" (2:15). The other cases where Paul interwove the heart and the conscience (Rom.

9:1, 2; 2 Cor. 4:2-6; 1 Tim. 1:5) confirm this interrelationship. Thus Paul's conscience bore him witness that he had sorrow and unceasing anguish in his heart on account of the unbelief of the Jews. To the Corinthians, Paul had written that he and his companions had sought to live such lives of honesty and integrity of heart that they would thus commend themselves to every man's conscience in the sight of God. Through their preaching Jesus Christ as Lord, God had shone in their hearts to give the light of the knowledge of the glory of God in the face of Christ. Thus when this light shone in the hearts of the apostles it commended their integrity to the Corinthians who consciously sought the truth. Paul made it clear to Timothy that the aim of their charge is love which issues from one's innermost being, the heart, and finds expression in the discernments of a good conscience. Congruent with a pure heart and a good conscience is that of sincere faith.

Paul repeatedly affirmed that man, through his conscience, is bound to absolute obedience to God.[8] In the tense circumstance of his trial before the Jewish council Paul affirmed, "I have lived before God in all good conscience up to this day" (Acts 23:1). In almost identical language he declared in his defense before Felix, "I always take pains to have a clear conscience toward God and toward men" (24:16). To the Corinthians who were bringing charges against him, Paul said, "I am not aware [*sunoida*] of anything against myself, but I am not thereby acquitted. It is the Lord who judges me" (1 Cor. 4:4). Finally, Paul wrote to Timothy, "I thank God whom I serve with a clear conscience" (2 Tim. 1:3). Obviously Paul could not have had a clear conscience if he had in any way been disobedient to God.

In view of man's responsibility to obey God, conscience stands in close relation to one's character.[9] Paul and Timothy gave splendid testimonies of their consciences: "That we have behaved in the world, and still more toward you, with holiness and godly sincerity, not by earthly wisdom but by the grace of God" (2 Cor. 1:12). A failure to behave with holiness and godly sincerity would nullify the testimony of their consciences. Paul recognized that the achievement of this quality of character was possible alone by the grace of God. In almost identical language he affirmed later that only by the open statement of the truth they could commend themselves to every man's conscience in the sight of God. On this account it was necessary for him and Timothy to denounce disgraceful underhanded ways and to refuse to practice cunning or to tamper with God's Word — all of which would destroy their integrity of character (2 Cor. 4:2). To Timothy he wrote that the aim of their charge was "love that issues from a pure heart and a good conscience and sincere faith" (1 Tim. 1:5). He added that certain people by rejecting conscience had made shipwreck of their faith. To Timothy who was taking over leadership responsibilities of the church, the apostle stated the spiritual requirements of deacons to the effect that they "must be serious, not double tongued, not addicted to much wine, not greedy for gain; they must hold the mystery of the faith with a clear conscience. And let them also be tested first; then if they prove themselves blameless let them serve as deacons" (1 Tim. 3:8-10). Paul was well aware of what impact looseness of conduct would have upon a clear conscience. Blameless character is the absolute prerequisite for a clear conscience.

Paul dealt also with a closely related thought, namely, the effects of sin upon the conscience (1 Cor. 8:7-12; 1 Tim 4:2; Tit. 1:15). When the Christians of Corinth, who formerly had eaten meat as a part of their religion, faced an unusual problem of conscience, they became aware that the only meat which they could purchase in the market had been offered to idols. Being spiritually immature they were not yet able to grasp the idea that the offering of the meat to idols had no effect upon this food. On this account the eating of this meat troubled their consciences. They saw no escape from the meaning attached to this meat which they formerly held. So as Paul writes, "Their conscience, being weak, is defiled" (1 Cor. 8:7). The verb *moluno (to stain, soil, defile)* here carries a symbolic sense quite graphic in nature. Thus when some of these people ate this meat they could not escape from the significance formerly attached to this act. On this account, "Their conscience, being weak, is defiled." In other words, since they were eating this meat, even though their conscience forbade them to do so, they were sinning. They were responsible to their conscience, even though the eating of this meat in itself was not wrong. On this account their conscience was stained and defiled. This is one of the most intricate and perplexing examples of how an act which is not sinful in itself is nevertheless wrong because the weak conscience had discerned it as being wrong.

This is an extreme case of where the conscience needed enlightenment, a matter which will presently receive attention. Paul wrote to Timothy concerning the awful sinfulness which will characterize the later times: "Some will depart from the faith by giving heed to deceitful spirits and doctrines of demons, through the pretensions of liars whose consciences are *seared*" (*kausteriazo, to mark by branding with a hot iron*) (1 Tim. 4:1, 2). The sins mentioned in this context were such that had the most awful effects upon the conscience. In Paul's counsel to Titus with regard to appointing elders he set up the ethical requirements for such responsibility as their being blameless, lover of goodness, master of himself, upright, holy, and self-controlled; and then on the other side, he listed many groups of sinners, giving the observation, "To the pure all things are pure, but to the corrupt and unbelieving nothing is pure; their very minds and consciences *are corrupted*" (*miaino to dye, stain, defile*) (Titus 1:15). This is a forceful expression describing the effects of sin upon the conscience.

Paul also showed the effect of sin upon the *mind (phronema,* thought, way of thinking) and upon thoughts (*noema,* purpose, design). Paul wrote, "To set the mind on the flesh is death, but to set the mind on the Spirit is life and peace. For the mind that is set on the flesh is hostile to God; it does not submit to God's law, indeed it cannot; and those who are in the flesh cannot please God" (Rom. 8:6, 7). Hostility to God is a most heinous sin. Note also: "But I am afraid that as the serpent deceived Eve by his cunning, your thoughts will be led astray from a sincere and pure devotion to Christ" (2 Cor. 11:3). This expression is forceful because of its background in the Garden of Eden story. Just as Eve's thoughts were led astray through the serpent's deception and cunning, so the people of God through all time may be led astray in the same manner. Its seriousness becomes evident in the straying away from a sincere and pure devotion to Christ.

This entire discussion shows the need for the enlightenment of the conscience. In the several settings where Paul was dealing with the problems of conscience, his ultimate aim to enlighten the consciences of his readers so that they would be able to discern right from wrong in every sphere of life, including thoughts, words, deeds, motives, etc. (Rom. 14:1 — 15:6; 1 Cor. 8:1-13; 10:23-32). Perhaps Paul's most expressive statement which has a bearing on the growth of discernment of things right or wrong, together with the enlightenment of conscience, are his words to the Philippians, "It is my prayer that your love may abound more and more, with knowledge and all discernment, so that you may approve what is excellent, and be pure and blameless for the day of Christ, filled with the fruits of righteousness which come through Jesus Christ, to the glory and praise of God" (Phil. 1:9-11).

This digression dealing with the heart and the conscience, springing from Romans 2:15, shows conclusively that all mankind by creation possesses a moral nature and a faculty for discerning right from wrong. Through the conscience man is aware of his responsibility to obey God in all things without any reservation. It prompts right conduct and condemns a breach of conscience, which leads to a sense of guilt.

Paul proceeded to show that the Jew had nothing of which to boast with regard to his conduct. Having been entrusted with the law including the rite of circumcision, the Jews carried greater responsibility for holy living than the Gentiles. Through their pharisaical attitude towards the law, they failed to grasp its spiritual content, as Paul wrote, "Real circumcision is a matter of the heart, spiritual and not literal"(Rom. 2: 29). The apostle's exposition of man's sinfulness and guilt came to a climax through his combining seven quotations from the Psalms and Isaiah (Rom. 3:10-18). These describe man's sinfulness and lead to his emphatic verdict that the whole world is held accountable to God. "For no human being will be justified in his sight by the works of the law since through the law comes the knowledge of sin . . . all have sinned and fall short of the glory of God" (vv. 20, 23).

e. The Effects of Adam's Sin upon the Human Race (Rom. 5:12-19; 1 Cor. 15:21, 22)

Paul proceeded to present the manifestation of God's righteousness in providing for man's being justified by faith through Christ's redemptive work. This great truth will be expanded in Chapter IV, "Justification Through Redemption." Why Paul presented this discussion centering in the effects of Adam's sin upon the human race has confronted Bible students with a difficult problem for interpretation. Without question this teaching is basic to the entire field of theological study. On this account there is need for a Holy Spirit illuminated interpretation of this passage. Perhaps Paul's words in 1 Corinthians 15:20-22 may give an overall understanding of this teaching. Observe the contrast between the one and the all in this passage, "For as by a man came death, by a man has come also the resurrection of the dead. For as in Adam all die, so also in Christ shall all be made alive" (vv. 21, 22). Thus Christ's relationship to those who shall be made alive has a close parallel with Adam's relation with all who die. This suggests that by reason of Adam's sin the entire human race experiences death. Adam's transgression left its impact upon all humanity.

The content of the apostle's thought in Romans 5:12-21 becomes clear in verses 6-11. Here he pointed up the profound truth expressed in Christ's death for the ungodly. For us sinners, Christ died. We are now justified by His blood and much more shall we be saved by Him from the wrath of God. Expressing this thought still more emphatically, Paul continued, "For if while we were enemies we were reconciled to God by the death of his Son, much more, now that we are reconciled, shall we be saved by his life" (v. 10). It is this "much more" gained through Christ which continues as the dominant note of verses 12 through 21.

He continues to expound this idea by setting forth the outworking of Adam's sin upon the human race. But what is the apostle declaring in verse 12? "Therefore as sin came into the world through one man and death through sin, and so death spread to all men because all men sinned." Without question Paul had a clear understanding of the Genesis records of creation. God created Adam and Eve in His own image and likeness, therefore with a sinless nature. When they disobeyed God's command by eating of the tree of knowledge of good and evil, they became sinful by nature. Since they were progenitors of the human race, this depravity, including death, spread to all mankind. Evidence for the universality of sin in the human race has its basis in that the entire human race, from Adam onward, has sinned. No human being possesses a sinless nature such as Adam and Eve had before their Fall. The entire human race is guilty before God on account of their own sins, not on account of the first transgression of Adam and Eve.

Later the positive side of this contrast will be discussed. Observe that Paul varied his vocabulary from *sin (hamartia)* and *transgression (parabasis),* to *trespass (pareptoma),* which he used six times in the remainder of this section. Whether or not he attached to each word a distinctive meaning is not clear. The word *sin* is the general term for wrongdoing and is used most frequently in the New Testament. The words *trespass* and *transgression* are used only a few times in the New Testament and are almost synonymous in meaning. In repeating the account of man's first sin Paul intensified his language by using the words *judgment* and *condemnation,* thus showing God's action with regard to man's first sin (Rom. 5:16). The same intensifying of language occurs in the statement that "death reigned" (v. 17). Man was in no position to overthrow death's power. This heightened language stands forth again when Paul noted that the condemnation extended to all men (v. 18). No one escapes this condemnation.

Still further, Paul labeled this first sin as man's disobedience (v. 9). This stresses the idea that Adam and Eve consciously rejected God's law. This focuses attention on the most serious aspect of man's sin. It is his open rebellion against God's authority. God instituted the law so that men might know the extent and character of sin. By way of illustration, the giving of the Ten Commandments plainly declared that disobedience to them was sin. Thus the people of Israel became aware of so many acts as being sinful of which they may have been ignorant before the giving of the Decalogue. Paul's final explication pertaining to the effects of Adam's sin upon the human race was that "sin reigned in death" (v. 21). While it is almost unthinkable that sin should reign in death, this, nevertheless, is an actual fact of which all human history stands as evidence.

By way of conclusion, no other biblical statement, philosophical appraisal, or scientific investigation sets forth so forthrightly the true explanation of the world's most serious problem. Without this inspired and authoritative message, all humanity would be in a terrible dilemma, for how would sin and death be explained?

f. The Knowledge of Sin Gained Through the Law (Rom. 7)

Having already noted the autobiographical aspect of this chapter let us observe the purpose of the law as expressed by Paul in the words, "If it had not been for the law, I should not have known sin" (Rom. 7: 7). In looking back to their experiences before conversion when they "were living in the flesh" (v. 5), he made a very thought-provoking comment in the words, "Our sinful passions, aroused by the law, were at work in our members to bear fruit for death" (v. 5).

Perhaps one's personal experience leads us to grasp Paul's thought. Before we knew the Ten Commandments, it may not have occurred to us that taking the name of the Lord in vain, or working seven days a week, or dishonoring father and mother, as well as killing, committing adultery, stealing, bearing false witness, and coveting, were wrong. But the Decalogue which we may have known from childhood forbade all these sins.

It was then that our sinful passions began to stir within us, tempting us to disobey these commands and as Paul said, "If it had not been for the law, I should not have known sin. I should not have known what it is to covet if the law had not said, 'You shall not covet' " (v. 7). From his own experience he disclosed, "But sin, finding opportunity in the commandment, wrought in me all kinds of covetousness" (v. 8). This certainly expresses the experience of everyone and shows the inner dynamic of sinful passions. The only escape from these sinful passions was to die to the law, to cease to serve under the old fixed code, and to yield to the new life of the Spirit.

Some of Paul's readers may have concluded that the law possessed no worthy purpose, but this would have misinterpreted the vividness of his language. His initial purpose was to show that God gave the law in order to lead His people away from sin, but a more profound purpose becomes evident when we observe that the law aroused sinful passions over which man has no power to control. Purposeful as was the old written code, the spiritual-minded Israelite finally came to realize that the law could not save him. There was need for the power of the Holy Spirit to bring about a new life in Christ Jesus. The real problem was man's carnality, and in sharp contrast with this inner sinfulness, the law is actually spiritual. Paul expressed the real tragedy of this condition in the words, "I do not understand my own actions. For I do not do what I want, but I do the very thing I hate" (v. 15). This shows the indwelling character of sin. Paul could even say that he delighted in the law of God in his inmost self but he was thoroughly conscious of another law in his members which was at war with the law of his mind. It had made him captive to the indwelling law of sin (vv. 22, 23). This is a picture of utter wretchedness, but it reveals a necessary outcome in one's life gained through the law. It was Paul's privilege to add, "For the law of the Spirit of life in Christ Jesus has set me free from the law of sin and death" (8:2).

g. Paul's Rebukes of Sin Among Fellow Believers

This study of Paul's teachings on sin would not be complete without examining fifteen lists of sins given by Paul throughout his letters.[10] With the exception of the first list, all the others are found in settings where Paul was exhorting fellow brethren to refrain from such vices. In these passages the apostle named about ninety-two different sins which could be grouped into ten or more categories.[11] Wahlstrom listed the words used in these tabulations in both the Greek and the English, together with the references in which they were used. Since he does not accept the Pauline authorship of the pastoral epistles, the additional sins named in these books are lacking. These word lists deserve close study. The reader should study each of them in their respective contexts.

A few general observations may be made of these vices. First, the number of different sins is quite sobering; yet if we check on the different evils named in the Old Testament we will observe that they total some thirty different sins. Second, these different vices show that the believers were confronted with all the sins found in this wicked world. Their being Christians did not isolate them from the wickedness of the world. Third, the apostle was seeking to show how all these forms of wickedness challenged genuine Christians in living. Fourth, the real nature of sin and its culpability become apparent. Fifth, they suggest the kind of remedy and cure required to be liberated from them. Sixth, they expose the kinds of vices found even in a civilized society. Seventh, they show that man through his own ability is absolutely unable to curb sin. Eighth, the contagious nature of sin becomes very apparent.

In a number of these lists the apostle introduced or concluded a tabulation with a positive exhortation. To the Romans he wrote, "Let us conduct ourselves becomingly as in the day . . . put on the Lord Jesus Christ, and make no provision for the flesh, to gratify its desires"

(Rom. 13:13, 14). To the Corinthians he added the words, "You were washed, you were sanctified, you were justified in the name of the Lord Jesus Christ and in the Spirit of our God" (1 Cor. 6:11). To these people he introduced another list with the words, "It is in the sight of God that we have been speaking in Christ, and all for your upbuilding, beloved" (2 Cor. 12:19). He challenged the Galatians by listing the fruit of the Spirit over against the works of the flesh (Gal. 5:19-23). This should have caused his readers to reflect seriously on the bearing of these sins on the life of a Christian. He exhorted the Ephesians to put away certain sins and to "be kind to one another, tenderhearted, forgiving one another, as God in Christ forgave you" (Eph. 4:32). Having admonished the Colossians to put to death and to put away various sins, he commended them for having "put on the new nature, which is being renewed in knowledge after the image of its creator" (Col. 3:10) and later adds some Christian graces among which are compassion, kindness, lowliness, meekness, patience, and love (vv. 12-14). He paid a high tribute to love by noting that "it binds everything together in perfect harmony" (v. 14). These positive notes serve to intensify both the flagrancy of the respective vices, as well as the beauty of a blameless and holy life.

For Additional Reading and Reference:

Beyschlag, *New Testament Theology*, Vol. II, pp. 27-229.
Bowman, *Prophetic Realism and the Gospel*, pp. 236-258.
Bruce, A. B., *St. Paul's Conception of Christianity*, pp. 49-361.
Bultmann, *Theology of the New Testament*, Vol. II, pp. 190-252.
Conzelmann, *An Outline of the Theology of the New Testament*, pp. 171-235, 275-286.
Davies, *Paul and Rabbinical Judaism*.
Ellis, *Paul's Use of the Old Testament* (consult Contents).
Hunter, *Interpreting Paul's Gospel*.
I.S.B.E., Vol. IV, Art. "Sacrifice in New Testament," I; II, 2; III, 4; V, 2; VI, 2; VII, VIII.
Kittel, *Bible Key Words*, Vol. I, Book III, *Sin;* Book IV, *Righteousness;* Vol. III, Book I, *Faith;* Vol. IV, Book II, *Wrath*.
Klassen and Snyder, *Current Issues in New Testament Interpretation*, pp. 143-177.
Lehman, *The Holy Spirit and the Holy Life*, Chapter VI.
Morris, *The Cross in the New Testament*, pp. 180-269.
Morris, *The Apostolic Preaching of the Cross*.
Munck, *Paul and the Salvation of Mankind* (consult Contents and Index of References).
Newman, *The Meaning of the New Testament*, pp. 197-214.

Rall, *According to Paul*, pp. 24-148.
Ryrie, *Biblical Theology of the New Testament*, pp. 167-187, 203-210.
Scott, *Christianity According to St. Paul.*
Stevens, *The Pauline Theology*, pp. 96-198, 227-318.
Stevens, *The Theology of the New Testament*, pp. 338-457.
Stewart, *A Man Named Christ*, pp. 81-260.
Van Oosterzee, *The Theology of the New Testament*, pp. 252-285.
Wahlstrom, *The New Life in Christ.*
Weidner, *Biblical Theology of the New Testament*, Vol. II, pp. 70-112, 131-166, 174-182.
Weiss, *Biblical Theology of the New Testament*, Vol. I, pp. 315-489; Vol. II, pp. 1-52, 75-124.
Whiteley, *The Theology of St. Paul*, pp. 130-185, 205-232.

1. G. Abbott Smith, *op. cit.*, p. 5.
2. *Ibid.*, p. 37.
3. *Ibid.*, p. 12.
4. Gal. 3:6-9, 11-14; Rom. 3:22; 4:3-6, 9-12, 13, 22; 5:17, 21; 2 Cor. 3:9; 5:21.
5. Rom. 2:15, 29; 6:17; 10:1, 6-10; 1 Cor. 4:5; 7:37; 14:25; 2 Cor. 2:4; 6:11; 7:2, 3; 8:16; Eph. 5:19; 6:5, 22; Phil. 1:7; Col. 2:2; 3:15, 16, 22; 1 Thess. 2:17; 2 Thess. 2:17.
6. See Gal. 4:6; Rom. 5:5; 2 Cor. 1:22; 3:2, 3; Eph. 3:16, 17.
7. Rom. 1:21, 24; 2:5; 2 Cor. 3:14-16; 4:4, 6; 9:7; Phil. 4:7; 2 Tim. 2:22.
8. Acts 23:1; 24:16; Rom. 2:15, 16; 13:5; 1 Cor. 4:4; 2 Cor. 5:11; 2 Tim. 1:3.
9. 2 Cor. 1:12-14; 4:2; 1 Tim. 1:5, 19; 3:9, 10; 2 Tim. 1:3.
10. Rom. 1:29-31; 13:13; 1 Cor. 5:9-11; 6:9, 10; 2 Cor. 12:20, 21; Gal. 5:19-21, 26; Eph. 4:31; 5:3, 4; Col. 3:5, 8, 9; 1 Tim. 1:9, 10; 6:4, 5; 2 Tim. 3:2-5; Tit. 1:7, 10, 12; 2:3, 9, 10; 3:2, 3.
11. See Eric H. Wahlstrom, *The New Life in Christ* (Philadelphia: Muhlenberg Press, 1915), pp. 281-287.

CHAPTER IV
JUSTIFICATION THROUGH REDEMPTION

Perhaps the most meaningful statement of the entire Bible stands forth in Paul's words, "The righteousness of God has been manifested . . . the righteousness of God through Jesus Christ for all who believe. For there is no distinction; since all have sinned and fall short of the glory of God, they are justified by his grace as a gift, through the redemption which is in Christ Jesus, whom God put forward as an expiation by his blood, to be received by faith" (Rom. 3:21-25). Observe the correlation of the teachings integral to salvation, such as *justification, grace, redemption, expiation, Christ's blood, faith, God's righteousness,* together with some expressions found elsewhere, such as *adoption, life in Christ, sanctification,* and *forgiveness of sins.* In the brief presentation of these great and unfathomable doctrinal teachings which follows, let us persistently hold to their integral relationship and their oneness bound up in the word *salvation.*

1. The Meaning of Justification

The key word for this discussion is *justified.* The verb *justify (dikaioo)* together with other words with the same root (*dikaiokrisia, dikaios, dikaiōs, dikaiosis*) has the meaning *declare,* or *pronounce righteous, being set right with God,* and *being acquitted.* As a good biblicist, Paul quoted in support of his assertion, the words "Abraham believed God, and it was reckoned to him as righteousness" Rom. 4:3; Gal. 3:6; Gen. 15:6). In Romans and Galatains Paul enlarged on the experience of Abraham. In the former, he also quoted David's words which express the same truth, "Blessed are those whose iniquities are forgiven, and whose sins are covered; blessed is the man against whom the Lord will not reckon his sin" (Rom. 4:7, 8; Ps. 32:1, 2). This is Paul's major step in his exposition of Habakkuk's words, "He who through faith is righteous shall live" (1:17).

2. It Is God Who Justifies the Ungodly

Paul repeatedly stressed the idea that justification is an act of God, a manifestation of His righteousness (Rom. 3:26, 30; 4:5; 8:30, 33; Gal. 3:8). Paul explained further that this act of justification had the purpose of showing "God's righteousness, because in his divine forbearance he had passed over former sins; it was to prove at the present time that he himself is righteous and that he justifies him who has faith in Jesus" (Rom. 3:25, 26). Only Deity possesses the perfection of holiness necessary to reckon sinful man as righteous. Corollary to this, God manifested His righteousness when He accounted men as righteous (v. 21).

3. Justification Through Redemption

The element of redemption is most central to God's act of accounting man as righteous. The Greek word *apolutrosis* conveys the meaning of *a release by ransom, a deliverance*. All of its uses in the New Testament, together with words of similar meaning, deserve careful study.[1] This redemption arises through the efficacy of Christ's shed blood. It will become effective in us through the resurrection of our bodies. The source of this resurrection life is in Christ because God made Him our wisdom, righteousness, sanctification, and redemption (1 Cor. 1:30). It finds expression in the forgiveness of our trespasses (Eph. 1:7). The full realization of this redemption lies in the future. The Holy Spirit has placed His seal upon all believers, thus giving full assurance that this redemption will be completely realized (2 Cor. 1:22). All believers have been delivered from the dominion of darkness and transferred to Christ's kingdom so that in Christ we have redemption even the forgiveness of our sins (Col. 1:13, 14). Paul used the simple verb *lutroo (redeem, release on receipt of ransom)* in a very expressive manner when he wrote of the return of Christ "who gave himself for us to redeem us from all iniquity and to purify for himself a people of his own who are zealous for good deeds" (Titus 2:14). In this statement the verbs *redeem* and *purify* almost merge in meaning. It shows that the impact upon us of Christ's redemption is a cleansing and purifying spiritual renewal.

Three other verbs with closely related meanings to those just considered are: *agorazo*, buy, purchase (1 Cor. 6:20; 7:23, *exagorazo, redeem, ransom* (Gal. 3:13; 4:5), *eleutheroo, make free, set free* (Gal. 5:1). Thus to the Corinthians Paul wrote, "You were bought with a price" (1 Cor. 1:20). These words occur in contexts in which Paul was warning the Corinthians not to become involved in sexual immorality nor to be bound by the pharisaical notion of circumcision. He asked them, "Do you not know that your body is a temple of the Holy Spirit within you, which you have from God?" (v. 19). This sublime experience of being a temple of the Holy Spirit was at the market price of Christ's blood. On this account Paul expressed their ethical responsibility in the words "Glorify God in your body" (v. 20). In a more expressive manner Paul wrote to the Galatians, "Christ redeemed us from the curse of the law, having become a curse for us" (3:13). The compound form of the word used here stresses the idea of redeeming or ransoming in a slavery setting. In this case it was at the price of Christ's having become a curse for us since He had been hung on a tree. Under the law the Jews were slaves but through their being redeemed they could receive adoption as sons. In spiritual language, Christ purchased all mankind from the slavery of sin in order that they might receive the glorious status of being sons, thus making possible their calling the God of heaven "Abba! Father!"

Paul expressed this redemption idea through another family of words centering in the idea of *freedom, liberty (eleutheria).* He presented this positive note of redemption in the words, "For freedom Christ has set us free; stand fast therefore, and do not submit again to a yoke of slavery" (Gal. 5:1). These words stand as the climax to the apostle's allegorical interpretation of the two women, Sarah and Hagar, the former a free woman and the latter a slave. Hagar symbolized the old covenant, which according to the apostle's application bound the people of Israel to a legal slavery, whereas Sarah foreshadowed the new covenant embodying spiritual freedom.

In his letter to the Romans, Paul moved from his major theme of justification on to its application in the Christian life. He was deeply concerned to show to his readers that justification by faith involved a spiritual renewal of being set free from sin (6:18). This involves, however, a new kind of slavery in their becoming "slaves of righteousness." In still more significant language they have "become slaves of God, the return you get is sanctification and its end, eternal life." This eternal life is "in Christ Jesus, our Lord." It is a *free gift (charisma)* of God (vv. 22, 23). This clinches the gift aspect of redemption. No language surpasses these definitive words relating to the outcome of redemption. After the apostle depicted the wretchedness of one enslaved to sin (Rom. 7), he cried out, "Who will deliver (*rhuomai — rescue, save*) me from this body of death?" (v. 24). In this context this verb expresses a fundamental aspect of redemption.

This becomes still more evident when Paul develops his thought in the words, "For the law of the Spirit of life in Christ Jesus *has set me free [eleutheroo]* from the law of sin and death" (8:2). Enlarging still further this new life of freedom, he draws in again the great word *apolutrosis,* which sets forth the climactic stage of salvation, *the redemption* of our bodies. Observe again Paul's words, "He who was called in the Lord as a slave is a freedman of the Lord" (1 Cor. 7:22). The word translated *freedman, apeleutheros,* occurs only once in the New Testament, but as noted earlier, he *was bought (agorazo)* with a price. Gaining the status of a freedman was like the purchase of a slave on the market, in this case, at the price of Christ's blood. One more use of the word freedom *(eleutheria)* confirms still further the truth embodied in the redeeming work of Christ. When Paul referred to Moses "who put a veil over his face," he explained, "When a man turns to the Lord the veil is removed. Now the Lord is the Spirit, and where the Spirit of the Lord is, there is freedom. And we all, with unveiled face, beholding the glory of the Lord, are being changed into his likeness from one degree of glory to another; for this comes from the Lord who is the Spirit" (2 Cor. 3:16-18). Thus in the Spirit of the Lord is the dynamic which brings freedom. Since Paul's other references to the believer's gaining freedom clearly associate this liberating act as a redemption, it may not be overreaching the mark to conclude that he implied this idea in this statement. In closing, let us observe the profound significance which he attaches to the idea of redemption through the blood of Christ.

4. Christ, the Expiation

The stepping-stone to the next topic finds expression in Paul's words "For there is one God, and there is one mediator between God and men, the man Christ Jesus, who gave himself as a *ransom [antilutron]* for all" (1 Tim. 2:5, 6). These words may serve as a guide to the translation of *hilasterion,* whether *propitiation* or *expiation*. Exodus 25:17-22; Leviticus 16:14-16 and 17:11 should serve as a guide to ascertaining its meaning. The Septuagint translation of Exodus 25:17 uses the words *hilasterion epithema* to translate the Hebrew word *kapporeth* (*mercy seat*). The Septuagint may give us a lead — the English translation of which is, "Thou shalt make a propitiatory, a lid of pure gold."[2]

The cherubim with their outstretched wings overshadowed the mercy seat. God said, "There I will meet with you, and from above the mercy seat, from between the two cherubim that are upon the ark of the testimony, I will speak with you of all that I will give you in commandment for the people of Israel" (Ex. 25:22). It was on the mercy seat where the high priest sprinkled the blood of the animal sacrifice on the Day of Atonement. Since the Lord dwelt between the cherubim, and from this dwelling place spoke to the high priest, it seems to be consistent to think of the bloody offering both as a covering of sin which the word *expiation* suggests and as a *propitiation* which relates the sacrifice to its bearing upon God against whom man had sinned.

God had spoken to His people about His own nature in the words, "You shall be holy; for I the Lord your God am holy" (Lev. 19:2). Centuries before this Abraham had already recognized that the Lord is righteous. All the bloody sacrifices offered by God's chosen people served as an expression of penitence to God. The offerers recognized that their sins and transgressions were in all reality against God. Through these sacrifices they sought to gain forgiveness. God had revealed His nature to Moses in the words, "The Lord, a God merciful and gracious, slow to anger, and abounding in steadfast love and faithfulness, keeping steadfast love for thousands, forgiving iniquity and transgression and sin, but who will by no means clear the guilty, visiting the iniquity of the fathers upon the children and the children's children, to the third and the fourth generation" (Ex. 34:6, 7). Since Israel possessed this knowledge of God's nature, it would seem to be clear beyond all question that the blood sprinkled on the mercy seat had for its purpose an appeal to God's steadfast love and faithfulness, on the basis of which they could be assured of God's forgiveness of their sins.

Since the Old Testament sacrificial system supports both the propitiatory and expiatory aspects of the Day of Atonement sacrifices, and that they were typical of Christ's sacrifice, I believe that *hilasterion* in Romans 3:25 embodies the meanings of both *propitiation* and *expiation,* i.e., the former does not negate the latter nor vice versa. The several occurrences of the expression *wrath of God* found in this letter[3] give support to the propitiation aspect of this word. Thus Christ's sacrifice was propitiatory in satisfying God's wrath against sin. Likewise God's having put forward Jesus Christ as the sacrifice for sin, gives support to the expiation sense of the word. On this account *expiation* appears to be the more accurate translation of this word. Paul used the word in very close relationship to God's righteousness, forbearance, and justification. All "are justified by his grace as a gift" (3:24).

5. Expiation by the Blood of Christ

The meaning of this great passage on justification depends on Paul's significant use of prepositions. According to the *Standard Dictionary* a preposition is "the part of speech that denotes the relation of an object to an action or thing." Note the use of prepositions in three very significant passages of Romans: 1:16, 17: *eis, for* salvation; *en, in* it; *ek, through* faith; *eis, for* faith; 3:24, 25: *dia, through* the redemption; *en, in* Christ; *dia, by* faith; *en, by* His blood; *dia, in* His forbearance; 5:1; 2: *ek, by* faith; *pros, with* God; *dia, through* our Lord; *dia, through* him, *eis, to* this grace; *en, in* which; *epi, in* hope. Note the use of prepositions in other crucial Scriptures as Acts 13:38, 39; Galatians 2:20; Titus 3:5-7; and so on.

The foregoing reflection on frequently used prepositions by Paul may serve to make clear the relation between Christ's shed blood and its expiatory value. In this case Paul expressed it in a phrase, "*By [en]* his blood." In very similar language Paul stated that Christ died *for (huper)* the ungodly, and *for (huper)* us (Rom. 5:6-9). In 1 Corinthians 11:24, 25 Paul quoted Christ's words concerning the bread and the wine, using the phrases *for (huper)* you, and *in (en)* my blood. He varied this in Ephesians 1:7, using the expression *through (dia)* His blood; and in 2:13 *in (en)* the blood.

In a number of references Paul wrote of Christ's death in our behalf in language almost identical with the references just given relating to the blood of Christ. Three of them (Rom. 6:10; 8:34; 14:9) give general statements of Christ's death while seven others use the expressive prepositions *huper* or *dia* in order to set forth the close intimate relation of Christ's death to us.[4] These references most specifically set forth the efficacy of Christ's death for man's salvation. Theologically, they give us the firmest ground for the substitutional view of the atonement. On this account we need to probe into the precise meaning of these prepositions. Thus when Paul writes that Christ died *for (huper)* the ungodly and used the clause "for *(dia)* whom Christ died," the specific relation between Christ's death and ourselves is of supreme moment. His repeated use of these expressions asserts the height and depth of their meaning. Greek lexicons give the following meanings to *huper: for, on behalf of,* and *for the sake of.* It is equivalent in meaning to the preposition *anti* which carries the sense: *instead of* and *in the name of.* The preposition *dia* when used with the genitive case carries the meaning *through;* when used with the accusative has the sense *by reason of, because of, for the sake of.*

6. Received by Faith

Here again the force of prepositions, in this case *dia* used with the genitive case, and *ek* used with the dative case, express the relationship of faith through the appropriation of Christ's sacrificial blood. While these two prepositions are practically synonymous, yet Paul used their respective meanings in Romans 3:30, "He [God] will justify the circumcision *on the ground of [ek]* faith and the uncircumcised *because of [dia]* their faith." Commenting on this statement Sanday wrote, "*Ek* denotes 'source,' *dia,* 'attendant circumstances.' "[5] Paul had made a similar interchange of prepositions relating to faith in Galatians 2:16, "A man is not justified *by [ex]* works of the law but *through [dia]* faith in Jesus Christ, even we have believed in Christ Jesus, in order to be justified *by [ek]* faith in Christ, and not *by [ex]* works of the law, because *by [ex]* works of the law shall no one be justified." On this statement Lightfoot commented, "Faith is strictly speaking only the *means*, not the *source* of justification. The one preposition *dia* excludes this latter notion, while the other *ek* might imply it."[6]

Two other illustrations on this interchange of prepositions, but in slightly different settings, follow. "For by grace you have been saved *through [dia]* faith . . . not *because of [ek]* works" (Eph. 2:8, 9). Also, "Not having a righteousness of my own *based on [ek]* law, but that which is *through (dia)* faith in Christ, the righteousness *from [ek]* God that depends on *[epi]* faith" (Eph. 3:9)[7] Paul's frequent uses *of* these phrases served to intensify their significance in setting forth the great doctrine of justification through faith.

7. The Resulting Peace and Reconciliation

In at least three contexts Paul brought together the meaningful words *peace* and *reconciliation* (Rom. 5:1-11; Eph. 2:12-18; Col. 1:20-22). The word *peace (eirene)* carries the meaning *completeness, soundness, wholeness, and well-being*. Since it is used in the Septuagint to translate the Hebrew word *shalom*, the New Testament builds directly on its Old Testament background.[8] Paul added to the connotation of this word the profound thought bound up in the expression "God of peace."[9] Equally significant is the expression "Peace from God,"[10] which occurs in his greetings to the churches.

The word *reconciliation (katallage)* and its derivatives are used less frequently and carry the meaning *of doing away with enmity and restoring peaceful relations*. Second Corinthians 5:18-20 expresses most significantly its meaning, "All this is from God, who through Christ reconciled us to himself and gave us the ministry of reconciliation; that is, God was in Christ reconciling the world to himself, not counting their trespasses against them, and entrusting to us the message of reconciliation. So we are ambassadors for Christ, God making his appeal through us. We beseech you on behalf of Christ, be reconciled to God."

This illustrates both the Godward and manward aspects of reconciliation. It was very natural that Paul would bring together the words *peace* and *reconciliation* to express the results of justification through faith (Rom. 5:1-11; Eph. 2:12-18; Col. 1:20-22). Paul's letter to the Romans most significantly set forth the experiential aspect of justification as it establishes peace and reconciliation. In a fitting manner he wrote, "Since we are justified by faith, we have peace with God through our Lord Jesus Christ" (Rom. 5:1). In my judgment, both the textual evidence and Paul's unfolding thought support the reading *let us have*. Here is an example which calls for a careful weighing of textual evidence, as well as thought content.

After expressing the results of justification Paul developed his thought further by stating, "If while we were enemies we were reconciled to God by the death of his Son, much more, now that we are reconciled, shall we be saved by his life. Not only so, but we also rejoice in God through our Lord Jesus Christ, through whom we have now received our reconciliation" (5:10, 11). Here as in 2 Corinthians 5:18-20 Paul was declaring that God through the death of Christ was seeking to reconcile man to Himself. Thus the love of God, manifested in the giving of His only Son, possessed the dynamic of leading men to repent from sin, believe in Christ as Savior, and to be reconciled to God the Father. In slightly different language Paul was declaring that God did His utmost to win sinful man to Himself. In the context of Ephesians 2:13-18 Paul declared that God is reconciling both Jews and Gentiles to Himself through the cross of Christ. On this account through Christ all have access in one Spirit to the Father.

As Paul was building up the thought of Christ's preeminence (Col. 1:18-22), he was showing that alone through the genuine deity of Christ, the God-Man, could the Father lead mankind to be reconciled to Himself. This reconciliation and making peace were effected through the blood of Christ on the cross. Here Paul brought together again the meaningful relation of peace and reconciliation. They express the terminal effects of God's justification of man.

8. Justified by His Grace as a Gift

God's great act of justifying the penitent sinner springs from His grace bestowed as a gift. The word *grace (charis)* is one of the most significant words used by Paul, occurring 101 times in his letters. This is twice as many as found in all of the remaining New Testament books. *Charis* occurs quite frequently in the Septuagint, used to translate most frequently the Hebrew word *chen (favor).* While the word *chen* does not possess the wealth of meaning as *charis,* yet a number of its occurrences serve as a foundation for the use of *charis* in the New Testament (Gen. 6:8; Ex. 33:12-17; Ps. 45:2). Thus both Noah and Moses "found favor in the eyes of the Lord." With these slender roots of meaning in the Old Testament, the word *charis* nevertheless grew, but chiefly by its own connotation. Quite strangely the word is not found in Matthew and Mark, and its eight occurrences in Luke carry the meaning of *favor* or *credit.* This means that to Paul must be attributed the credit for the extraordinary meaning expressed by the word. While a systematic presentation of *charis* would possess genuine values, there is need for limiting this discussion to Paul's use of this word.

To begin with, Paul availed himself of this word in all the greetings and benedictions of his letters. Its meaning gained greater significance through being associated many times with the words *peace (eirene)* and *mercy (eleos)*. We may properly conclude that the reason Paul used the word *grace* in all the greetings and benedictions lay in the buildup of significance which he gave to it in the doctrinal contents of his letters.

There are two significant occurrences of *charis* in the main body of 2 Thessalonians (1:12; 2:16). Paul was praying for them so that the name of Christ might be glorified in them according to the grace of God and the Lord Jesus Christ; that is, God's grace possessed the dynamic for achieving the goal of their being worthy of His call. Paul also assured them that the eternal comfort and good hope was given to them through grace.

Returning to the Book of Romans let us observe how Paul related grace to the theological structure of this letter. Already in the salutation (1:1-6) Paul gave an abridgment of his gospel in which he declared that on the grounds of the finished work of Christ, he had received grace and apostleship to accomplish the worldwide mission of the gospel. His responsibility of fulfilling his apostolic mission was accompanied by the empowering grace of God. The heading of this subtopic seeks to capture the element of grace as related to one's gaining right standing with God. The gift aspect of this grace becomes profoundly meaningful when seen in relation to Christ's expiatory redemptive work. This gift of grace did not violate God's righteousness by reason of the expiation and propitiation through Christ's blood. Paul illustrated this act of justification by relating the experience of Abraham who lived before the giving of the law. Righteousness was reckoned to Abraham on the basis of his faith. This was proof that the promise to Abraham rested on grace and not on works of the law. Thus Paul exhorted his readers to experientially appropriate the peace which accompanies being justified by faith and to have confidence that through him all believers have had access to this grace in which they stand (Rom. 5:1, 2). The perfect tense used in both of these verbs yields the meaning that our obtaining access to this grace and our standing in it is a continuing experience and not a mere passing event.

As Paul held forth the superlative blessings gained through Christ in contrast with the devastating effects of Adam's sin, he centered his thought on the grace of God and the free gift in the grace of Jesus Christ which abounded for many (Rom. 5:15). He enlarged on this thought a bit by bringing together in parallel statements the abundance of this grace and the free gift of righteousness, thus showing them to be synonymous in the larger context. With the increase of sin in the world, grace abounded all the more so Paul could conclude, "As sin reigned in death, grace also might reign through righteousness to eternal life through Jesus Christ our Lord" (5:21).

Knowing that some legalistic-minded leaders might interpret his exposition of justification by faith with the resulting peace in one's heart as a way of gaining liberty to continue in sin, Paul hastened to declare that one's being justified by faith took place as a result of one's dying to sin. One cannot draw from the inexhaustible supply of abounding grace in order to continue to indulge in sin (6:1-4). For the change wrought in justification was a spiritual renewal involving death to sin, since believers are no longer under the dominion of sin. They are under grace and are able to draw from its ever-abounding resource in Christ (v. 14). This tension between grace and works presented a problem to many of Paul's readers as they reflected on Israel being the chosen people of God. They pondered the problem as to whether election had a higher priority with God than grace or vice versa. Paul showed that the elect who departed from God were sinners and were no longer God's people. But there was a remnant who turned back to God who again became His chosen people through the grace of God (11:5, 6). Further, the dispensing of God's grace is to the elect but they are not the chosen ones of God irrespective of their response to God's love and mercy (11:7).

When Paul turned to the experiential side of his doctrinal treatment, he wrote of the work of grace in his own life, as well as in that of all believers. Through the grace given to him he could exhort them as to the nature of the Christian life. He noted that the different gifts entrusted to them were according to God's grace and should be used according to His leading (12:3-8). In an apologetic manner Paul referred to his boldness in reminding them of some of the exhortations given to them noting that the grace given to him set him apart as a minister of Christ to the Gentiles in the priestly service of the gospel. Thus he recognized that the special responsibility which he exercised had been entrusted to him through the grace of God (15:15, 16).

To the Corinthians, Paul wrote of the grace of God which was given them in Christ Jesus. He noted that in every way they were enriched in Christ with all speech and all knowledge and were not lacking in any spiritual gift. Christ would sustain them to the end so that they would be guiltless in the day of Christ. Here is a splendid example of the empowering grace of Christ in the believers (1 Cor. 1:4-9). Paul witnessed also to the workings of God's grace in himself. His accomplishments as an apostle of Christ were due solely to this grace (15:10). In his second letter he referred also to the testimony of his conscience, "We have behaved in the world, and still more toward you, with holiness and godly sincerity, not by earthly wisdom but by the grace of God" (2 Cor. 1:12), or according to the Berkeley Version they behaved in the world "with devout motives and godly sincerity." Note how Paul intertwined Christian motivation and sincerity with the working of God's grace. Later in the letter he commended the Corinthians for excelling in faith, utterance, knowledge, earnestness, and love, and then urged them to excel in the work of grace such as Titus had bestowed upon them (8:6, 7, 16). With these words Paul was giving a wider spread to the aspects of the Christian life which bore a close relation to their gracious work. And then he declared the superlative example of Christ's gracious work in the words, "You know the grace of our Lord Jesus Christ, that though he was rich, yet for your sake he became poor, so that by his poverty you might become rich" (v. 9). Paul commended the Corinthians for their offerings to those in need which resulted in the yearning of these people for the Corinthians in their worship because of "the surpassing grace of God" in them (9:14). Paul also disclosed to these Corinthians a very personal note relating to the abundance of revelations which were entrusted to him and also of the thorn in his flesh. He interpreted this thorn as "a messenger of Satan," to harass him and to keep him from being too elated. He earnestly prayed to the Lord that this thorn should leave him but the reply he received was, "My grace is sufficient for you, for my power is made perfect in weakness." This expression equated God's grace with His power. On this account Paul could conclude, "For when I am weak, then am I strong" (12:1-10).

In his letter to the Galatians, Paul followed much of the same pattern, but with greater stress on the relation of grace to justification (Gal. 1:15; 2:9, 21; 5:4). Here he noted his being called and set apart to apostleship by the grace of God. He presented in most sublime language some of the profound facets of God's grace in the words, "I have been crucified with Christ; it is no longer I who live, but Christ who lives in me; and the life I now live in the flesh I live by faith in the Son of God, who loved me and gave himself for me. I do not nullify the grace of God; for if justification were through the law, then Christ died to no purpose" (2:20, 21). This leads us to see that the working of grace in the life of Paul involved his identification with Christ in his crucifixion. This results in a new life through Christ's indwelling. It is obtained through personal faith in Christ. All this magnified the grace of God and showed to the Galatians that justification was not gained through the law.

Paul clinched this point by declaring that if his readers returned to the practice of circumcision they were bound to keep the whole law (5:3). But still more seriously they would be separated from Christ and would be falling away from grace (v. 4). With this stern language Paul declared that grace works in the human heart only on the basis of obedience and faith. It is the kind of faith that works through love (vv. 5, 6).

Paul enriched these thoughts still more in his letter to the Ephesians (1:6, 7; 2:5, 7, 8; 3:2, 7, 8; 4:7, 29). As he was disclosing the spiritual blessing gained through Christ, he climaxed the declaration that it is "to the praise of his glorious grace which he freely bestowed on us in the Beloved" (Eph. 1:6). He depicted the new life in Christ in resurrection language and added, "For by grace you have been saved through faith; and this is not your own doing, it is a gift of God" (2:8). Paul added still another facet to this great truth by noting that the stewardship of God's grace was given to him for the Ephesian saints. Specifically, this grace was given to Paul "to preach to the Gentiles the unsearchable riches of Christ" (3:7, 8). In the introduction to the practical exhortations of this letter Paul begged his readers to lead a life worthy of their calling, and closed with the words, "Grace was given to each of us according to the measure of Christ's gift" (4:7). Thus the grace appropriated by each believer is specifically that measured to him by Christ.

Out of the background of his former life as a Pharisee, Paul wrote "But I received mercy because I had acted ignorantly in unbelief, and the grace of our Lord overflowed for me with the faith and love that are in Christ Jesus. . . . And I am the foremost of sinners; but I received mercy for this reason, that in me, as the foremost, Jesus Christ might display his perfect patience for an example to those who were to believe in him for eternal life."[11] These references to the grace of God, which underlie justification, together with others not quoted, reveal most closely the dominance of this theme in Paul's theology.

9. Forgiveness

Paul's doctrine of justification includes still another important facet, the forgiveness of sins. He brought this into the picture when he illustrated this teaching in the lives of Abraham and David (Rom. 4). Abraham trusted God who justifies the ungodly. On this account his faith was reckoned as righteousness. The experience of David was parallel to that of Abraham. He quoted a Davidic psalm setting forth this truth. "Blessed is he whose transgression is forgiven, whose sin is covered. Blessed is the man to whom the Lord imputes no iniquity" (Ps. 32:1, 2). Thus God's justifying the ungodly results in the personal experience of forgiveness of sins, the same as we have already noted with reference to the peace experienced by those who are justified. Paul expressed this same truth very forcibly in a similar setting, "In him we have redemption through his blood, the forgiveness of our trespasses, according to the riches of his grace which he lavished upon us" (Eph. 1:7, 8; Col. 1:14). This interrelation among redemption, forgiveness, and grace shows again the close relationship among the cardinal doctrines of the Christian religion. In Colossians 2:11-15 Paul presented the idea of forgiveness by building on the Old Testament requirement of circumcision, its New Testament fulfillment in the experience of being buried with Christ in baptism, of being raised with Him through faith, in the working of God, and of being forgiven all our trespasses — all accomplished by Christ's suffering on the cross. This is another sample of how Old Testament religious life forecast the far richer Christian experiences described in the New Testament. This becomes still more experiential when those forgiven demonstrate the same forgiving spirit to one another (2 Cor. 2:7-11; Eph. 4:31, 32; Col. 3:12-14).

10. Regeneration and Renewal in the Holy Spirit

This heading stands as Paul's final definitive statement concerning the new life in Christ Jesus commonly called the new birth (Titus 3:5). Galatians 2:20 is Paul's earliest unfolding of this doctrine: "I have been crucified with Christ; it is no longer I who live, but Christ who lives in me; and the life I now live in the flesh I live by faith in the Son of God, who loved me and gave himself for me." With him there was a death experience and also the gaining of a new life in Christ. He labeled this life-giving experience as "a new creation" (Gal. 6:15). In Romans (6:1 — 7:6) Paul enlarged upon this truth as it stood in relation to his teaching on justification. He sought to show that being justified by faith necessitated a change in one's manner of life. Most forcefully he declared that those "who have been baptized into Christ Jesus were baptized into His death" (Rom. 6:3). Consequently, as Christ was raised from the dead, the parallel experience in the believer is a "walk in newness of life" (v. 4). Throughout this section Paul unfolded this truth clearly. Once they were slaves of sin but now have become slaves of righteousness (vv. 17, 18). The yielding of self to righteousness leads to sanctification and the end of this experience is eternal life in Christ Jesus (vv. 19-23). This is the new life of the Spirit.

To the Corinthians, Paul wrote, "If any one is in Christ, he is a new creation [creature]; the old has passed away, behold, the new has come" (2 Cor. 5:17). Paul expounded this teaching most fully to the Ephesians (2:1-10). Here again he built his teaching on the analogy of death and resurrection. He sharpened his comparison by a vivid description of human passions in contrast with the new life of sitting with Christ in the heavenly places in Christ Jesus. In conclusion he wrote, "We are his workmanship, created in Christ Jesus for good works" (v. 10). This expression gives real meaning to the new birth and regeneration. Later in this letter in a different context Paul wrote: "Be renewed in the spirit of your minds, and put on the new nature, created after the likeness of God in true righteousness and holiness" (4:23, 24). This makes still clearer the spiritual nature of the new birth by directing our thoughts to the creation when God made man in His own image.

The language *true righteousness and holiness* is most descriptive of God's nature. In quite similar language Paul wrote to the Colossians, "When Christ who is our life appears, then you also will appear with him in glory" (3:4). This future experience is made possible alone through having died to sin and of possessing a new life "hid with Christ in God." Note also, "Put on the new nature, which is being renewed in knowledge after the image of its creator" (v. 10).

By way of summary this experience of regeneration and renewal in the Spirit is simultaneous with that of being justified by faith. It is a punctiliar spiritual experience, a crisis wrought by the Holy Spirit. It is a spiritual resurrection bringing about a new nature and a new life in Christ. This new creation is "after the likeness of God in true righteousness and holiness" (Eph. 4:24), and results in a newness of life. It marks the initial experience of sanctification in which the individual consecrates himself to God, setting himself apart for holy purposes according to God's direction.

11. Adoption

Paul's unfolding of God's plan of salvation leads quite naturally to the experience of adoption.[12] As he began to disclose the nature of the new life in Christ Jesus, he noted that "all who are led by the Spirit of God are sons of God" (Rom. 8:14). This is not an experience of receiving the spirit of slavery, but rather that of receiving the spirit of *sonship (huiothesia).* They who have been adopted as sons are enabled to address God as "Abba! Father!" The realization of adoption as sons is through the witness of the Holy Spirit with our spirit. This is a present experience but Paul proceeded to show that it leads to the grand and glorious realization of being heirs of God and fellow heirs with Christ. Paul presented the eschatological picture of all creation longing for the revealing of the sons of God. There is the need of being set free from its bondage to decay, after which the redeemed will obtain the glorious liberty of the children of God. Full confidence in the realization of this hope rests on the firstfruits of the Spirit experienced in this life. This adoption as sons will be fully realized in the redemption of our bodies at the return of Christ.

To the Galatians, Paul expounded this truth in a slightly different setting (3:24-29). He noted that the Jewish people were under the custodian of the law from which they were delivered by Christ, and through this deliverance they are now sons of God. They had been slaves to the elemental spirits of the universe, but through Christ they had been reclaimed and thus received adoption as sons. Since they are now sons, they are also heirs of God. On this account Paul warned them not to return to Judaism, which in other words would be returning again to the weak and beggarly elemental spirits. It would be a return to slavery, a loss of sonship (4:1-10).

Paul's profoundest presentation of adoption stands forth in the words, "He destined us in love to be his sons through Jesus Christ, according to the purpose of his will, to the praise of his glorious grace which he freely bestowed on us in the Beloved" (Eph. 1:5, 6). Here Paul related adoption to the purpose of God's will as manifested in predestination or foreordination. But this predetermining act of God is bound up in His love toward man to be realized in their becoming sons through Jesus Christ. This adoption as sons was made possible through the redemption wrought by Christ. It made possible the forgiveness of our sins according to the riches of His grace. The final goal of all this is, "To unite all things in him, things in heaven and things on earth" (vv. 7-10). This relation of adoption to the purpose of God's will is similar to Peter's words: "This Jesus, delivered up according to the definite plan and foreknowledge of God, you crucified and killed by the hands of lawless men" (Acts 2:23). Let us praise God for the outworking of His grace lavished upon us.

In a very appropriate manner Paul broadened his teaching on adoption as it related to the people of Israel. In the survey given above we should observe that Paul's teachings had to do with the personal experience of adoption, but in Romans 9:1-5 he wrote briefly of Israel's involvement in sonship. Overwhelmed with sorrow and anguish in his heart that the Jews of his day were not experiencing the precious truths involved in adoption, he proceeded to set forth Israel's place in the plans and purposes of God. He wrote, "They are Israelites, and to them belong the sonship, the glory, the covenants, the giving of the law, the worship, and the promises; to them belong the patriarchs, and of their race, according to the flesh, is the Christ" (vv. 4, 5). He unfolded this problem by showing that from the time of

Abraham to that of Moses, God was revealing His purpose of *election (ekloge)*. This noun and related verb and adjective forms reveal a profound aspect centering in God's salvation (vv. 6-13). In this context Paul set forth very clearly that God's purpose of election did not have its basis in works but in His call. By reason of His call, sonship and the extraordinary spiritual privileges and blessings belong to Israel.

It is essential to observe the close interrelation among sonship and these attending spiritual blessings. By reason of their adoption as sons a special glory belonged to God's people. To them and them alone God entered into covenant relationship. This is true also with regard to the law. To no other people in the world did God reveal His law. This relation of sonship was climaxed in their worship. Israel alone experienced God's dwelling among them. Their worship was God-centered. Eschatologically, their sonship looked forward to God's special blessings to be given to their descendants and in the most significant manner in Jesus Christ, the Messiah. Thus adoption meant to Israel all the extraordinary blessings from God culminating in the Messiah.

12. Called According to God's Purpose

In the unfolding of Paul's theology this theme naturally follows that of adoption. The classic passage reads, "We know that in everything God works for good with those who love him, who are called according to his purpose. For those whom he foreknew he also predestined to be conformed to the image of his Son, in order that he might be the firstborn among many brethren. And those whom he predestined he also called; and those whom he called he also justified; and those whom he justified he also glorified" (Rom. 8:28-30). In similar language Paul admonished Timothy to take his share of suffering, "For the gospel in the power of God, who saved us and called us with a holy calling, not in virtue of our works but in virtue of his own purpose and the grace which he gave us in Christ Jesus ages ago, and now has manifested through the appearing of our Savior Christ Jesus, who abolished death and brought life and immortality to light through the gospel" (2 Tim. 1:8-10). While the former passage is the more definitive statement relating to being called according to God's purpose, the latter adds essential ideas to this truth. Note the words *gospel, saved, holy calling, grace, life,* and *immortality*. Thus when we probe into the meaning of *calling,* we should note its almost synonymous meaning with *saved*. Similarly the word *holy* attributes a definite spiritual quality to *calling*. God's *grace* expresses itself most fully in His *purpose,* and finally, *life* and *immortality* express sublimely the ultimate goal of God's *purpose*.

In order to grasp the meaning of Paul's language in these passages, the theological significance of his vocabulary, together with the relationship he asserted among these words, calls for most scrutinizing attention. To begin with, Paul was relating this teaching to those who love God. This leads to the clue that his entire declaration makes no reference whatever to those who do not love Him. To be more explicit, those whom he foreknew, whom he predestined, called, justified, and glorified, include those alone who are saved. That is, God predestined no one to be lost. This harmonizes with the larger context of Romans 8. Paul was giving an explication of the hope of those who are in Christ Jesus. He endeavored to show his readers the certainty of their salvation and the resultant new life in the Spirit as sons (8:15). In view of this, their sufferings were not worthy of being compared with the glory that was to be revealed in them. The intercessory work of the Holy Spirit confirmed this assurance. On this account Paul could write, "We know that in everything God works for good with those who love him, who are called according to his purpose" (v. 28). The following verses expressed the solid foundation for the Christian's assurance of salvation.

a. The Meaning of Paul's Terms

Let us now examine this meaningful vocabulary used by Paul. The word *kletos* and the verb form *kaleo* used in this context, as well as *klesis* found in later contexts refer to God's call to salvation. These words express a profound meaning as related to man's salvation.[13] Some of these significant ideas are: (1) the call is according to God's purpose; (2) it is through His grace; (3) it is a call to belong to Jesus Christ, a call to be saints; (4) it is a holy calling, the upward call of God in Christ Jesus; and (5) a call to a worthy walk in life.

The word *prothesis* (purpose) in this context focuses supremely in the salvation of those who are called. This word is perhaps most definitive of God's personality as shown in Romans 9:11; Ephesians 1:11; 3:11; 2 Timothy 1:9. As noted earlier, the profound outworking of God's purpose shows its significance as related to predestination, calling, justification, and glorification (Rom. 8:29, 30). In a similar context we observe that according to God's purpose, He "accomplishes all things according to the counsel of his will, we who first hoped in Christ have been destined and appointed to live for the praise of his glory" (Eph. 1:11, 12). Thus the *counsel (boule)* of God's *will (thelema)* expresses the fulfillment of His *purpose*. Paul brought God's *purpose* into relation with *election (ekloge)* in Romans 9:11. This relationship of *purpose* and *election* enlarges still further the broad scope of meaning bound up in God's purpose. Paul's statement to Timothy, noted earlier, stressed the fact that God's saving work and call are not in virtue of man's works but rather in God's own purpose and the grace which He gave in Christ Jesus. This is a very essential truth because some interpreters of Romans 8:28-30 fail to see the element of grace in this classic passage. Note again topic 8: "Justified by His Grace as a Gift."

Proginosko, occurring only twice in Paul's letters (Rom. 8:29; 11:2), carries the meaning to *foreknow, to perceive beforehand,* to *know previously,* and *to choose beforehand.* A rather technical question with reference to the meaning of this verb centers in whether it means merely to know beforehand or whether it merges with a choosing beforehand. The structure of Paul's sentence leads to a clear distinction between *foreknowing* and *predestining,* yet their being brought together in this sentence denotes a significant relationship between the two.

Perhaps the surest guide to the understanding of this word is to be found in the Hebrew word *yada (to know).* In the Septuagint the verb *ginosko* is used uniformly to translate this word. It would seem that the compound form *proginosko* would build on the same distinctive meaning. A study of a number of references[14] would support the idea that Paul's use of this verb goes far beyond an objective knowledge of something beforehand. As Leenhardt puts it, "In this kind of knowledge the subject is inclined toward the object, encounters it and there are no longer an object and subject face to face with each other; there is set up a relationship, a communion. This knowledge is experiential and presupposes an initiative by the subject; it often carries with it an elective judgment; to know is to choose, to commit oneself, it is already to love, and to choose from motives of love, the 'knowledge' which God has of man is prior to the love of man for God and is the foundation of the latter."[15]

This comprehension of *proginosko,* especially in its experiential aspect, leads to the next great word *predestined (proorizo).* Its various uses in the New Testament (Rom. 8:29, 30; 1 Cor. 2:7; Eph. 1:5, 11) yield the meanings *predestine, foreordain, predetermine, decree, decide,* and *appoint beforehand.* This verb continues to intensify the activity of God as a person. As Paul was expounding the thought of how God "has blessed us in Christ with every spiritual blessing" (Eph. 1:3), he brought together additional expressive words in the language, "He chose us in him before the foundation of the world, that we should be holy and blameless before him. He destined us in love to be his sons through Jesus Christ, according to the purpose of his will, to the praise of his glorious grace which he freely bestowed on us in the Beloved" (vv. 4-6). Here we should note that God's choosing and destining took place before His work of creation. He spoke more explicitly with reference to the goal to be achieved in the words, holy and blameless, two of the most definitive words used in the Bible to express uprightness of character. Here Paul mentions God's love for us manifested in predestination and also its goal in that we should be His sons through Christ Jesus.

Paul also related God's purpose to His will (vv. 11, 12) in the words, "According to the purpose of him who accomplishes all things according to the counsel of his will, we who first hoped in Christ have been destined and appointed to live for the praise of his glory." Here the RSV intensified the more literal rendering, "to the end that we should be" to "have been destined and appointed to live." From this it may be proper to conclude that predestination is implicit in verse 12.

Paul advanced from God's act of predestining to that of calling. The verb *kaleo* carries the meanings: *to call, to summon, to invite.* This verb occurring frequently in common speech obtained distinctive meaning in Paul's letters as well as elsewhere.[16] Its specialized connotation becomes apparent in Romans 8:30. The adjective form *kletos* already noted in verse 28 furnishes the groundwork for the significant uses of the verb in Paul's letters. To begin with, all those *predestined* are *called* and those *called* are *justified.* In Romans 9 Paul took a backward look on Hebrew history and noted its use with reference to the outworking of God's promises. To Abraham, God said, "Through Isaac *shall* your descendants *be named" [kaleo]* (v. 7).

Paul observed that God's purpose of election as illustrated in patriarchal history was not because of works but because of His call. (vv. 11, 12). He illustrated this truth still further by noting that God has called to be vessels of mercy not only from the Jews but also from the Gentiles (v. 24). He substantiated this by quoting from Hosea: "Those who were not my people I will call 'my people,' and her who was not beloved I will call 'my beloved.' And in the very place where it was said to them, 'You are not my people,' they will be called 'sons of the living God' " (vv. 25, 26). Paul testified to the Galatians (1:15) that God *had set him apart (aphorizo)* before his birth and had called him through His grace. Here the apostle drew attention to the aspect of grace involved in God's call. This shows again that God's call has no basis in human merit. Later in the letter Paul warned the Galatians that their yielding to the propaganda of the Judaizers was a departure from God who had called them. He added that they were called to freedom. He noted however that they should not use their freedom as an opportunity for the flesh.

At this point Paul disclosed the ethical aspect of their call. He enlarged upon this idea of showing that obedience to this call issues in a walk by the Spirit and not by yielding to the works of the flesh (Gal. 5:8-24). In the letter to the Ephesians, Paul approached this truth in a similar manner when he advanced from the profound doctrinal teachings of chapters 1 to 3 over to the application of these truths in Christian living. He wrote, "I . . . beg you to live a life worthy of the call to which you have been called." He then proceeded to give the ethical implication of this call by noting some of the cardinal qualities of the Christian life such as "lowliness and meekness, with patience, forbearing one another in love, eager to maintain the unity of the Spirit in the bond of peace" (4:1-3). These traits of Christian character are marks of the body of Christ, the church. Paul added, "You were called to the one hope that belongs to your call, one Lord, one faith, one baptism, one God and Father of us all" (vv. 4-6). With this language Paul related the oneness of God's call to the oneness of Christian hope which has its center in God's salvation and God Himself. This adds immeasurable depths of meaning to the calling to which the redeemed have been called.

In 2 Timothy Paul interwove some additional profound truths related to God's call. He admonished Timothy to take his share of suffering: "For the gospel in the power of God, who saved us and called us with a holy calling, not in virtue of our works but in virtue of his own purpose and the grace which he gave us in Christ Jesus ages ago, and now has manifested through the appearing of our Savior Christ Jesus, who abolished death and brought life and immortality to light through the gospel" (2 Tim. 1:8-10). Observe that Paul brought the verbs *saved* and *called* into an almost synonymous relationship. Further that this call is characterized as being holy, or as the Berkeley Version expresses it, "a call for dedication." This is not a call based on works but rather "in virtue of his own purpose and the grace which he gave us in Christ Jesus ages ago" (v. 9). In passing let us observe again the sequence of Romans 8:30, namely *predestined, called, justified,* and *glorified.* The uses of *kaleo* noted above add immeasurable meaning to Paul's statement, "called according to his purpose."

The relation of the next word in Paul's sequence of thought, namely *justified,* should now be easily discerned. In the outworking of God's *purpose* those who *are called* are also *accounted righteous.* (See Chapter IV, 1, 2.)

The final aspect in the outworking of God's purpose for those who love Him is that of *being glorified.* This word *doxazo* has a variety of meanings all of which contribute to its distinctive significance in this verse. According to the great lexicons *doxazo* means *to praise, magnify, hold in honor, clothe with splendor, exalt to state of glory,* and *glorify.* Let us probe into its meaning as used by Paul. Paul exhorted the Thessalonians "to lead a life worthy of God, who calls you into his own kingdom and glory" (1 Thess. 2:12). This suggests that the chief aspect of God's kingdom is its glory. The present tense of the participle translated *calls* suggests a present aspect of entering into God's kingdom and glory. Paul predicted the eternal punishment of the wicked and their "exclusion from the presence of the Lord and from the glory of his might when he comes on that day to be glorified in his saints" (2 Thess. 1:9, 10). Paul was praying that God would make them worthy of His call so that the name of the Lord Jesus might be glorified in them and they in Him. Here are two directions of glorification, both intimately interrelated. There is that in which the Lord Jesus is glorified in His saints, also that in which His saints are glorified in Him. This certainly points to the exaltation of the saints to the state of heavenly glory.

Paul's use of this word in the letter to the Romans illustrated in a very direct manner its use (8:30). In sharp contrast to the outpouring of God's wrath upon the wicked, Paul could write, "Glory and honor and peace for every one who does good" (2:9, 10). When he begins to expand the experiences accompanying that of being justified by faith, he wrote, "We rejoice in our hope of sharing the glory of God" (5:2). In the context of describing the nature of one's life in the Spirit which comes to its climax in 8:28-30, he notes that the children of God are fellow heirs with Christ and will be glorified with Him. He added, "I consider that the sufferings of this present time are not worth comparing with the glory which is to be revealed in us" (8:17, 18). Paul expounded the eschatological aspect of this glory by noting that the creation had been "subjected to futility" (v. 20). God had done so in the hope that the creation would be set free from its bondage and obtain the glorious liberty of the children of God. This was a masterful way of picturing the future liberty of God's children. They would be clothed with the splendor which characterizes heaven itself and partakes of the nature of God's glory. It is this buildup of meaning which Paul had in mind when he wrote the climactic words, "Those whom he justified he also glorified" (v. 30).

b. God's Call in Relation to Israel

This line of thought became the occasion for Paul to express his great sorrow and unceasing anguish in his heart when he thought of his own people Israel to whom belonged the exalted status of sonship, glory, covenants, and other invaluable blessings and privileges which they were no longer possessing. He proceeded to draw from Israel's history the lessons which disclosed God's purpose of election as it revealed both the justice of God and His mercy. From the angle of His kindness and mercy, God had "endured with much patience the vessels of wrath made for destruction" (9:22) not that these vessels of wrath were unconditionally predestined for destruction, but rather that through their disobedience and sinfulness these vessels brought judgment upon themselves. On the other hand those who yielded themselves to God's love and mercy became the vessels through which God manifested the riches of His glory. They, both Jews and Gentiles, became the recipients of this glory (vv. 23, 24). It was natural then for Paul to close this section of the letters with the doxology "To him be glory forever" (11: 36).[17]

The apostle distinguished clearly between the glory of celestial bodies and that of terrestial bodies. In this contrast he noted that the glory of the terrestrial is *another in kind (heteros),* but when he compared the glory of the sun, moon, and stars, he used the word *allos (another of the same kind).* This distinction gives special meaning to Paul's words, "We all, with unveiled face, beholding the glory of the Lord, are being changed into his likeness from one degree of glory unto another; for this comes from the Lord who is the Spirit" (2 Cor. 3:18). He underscored this idea in the words, "Though our outer nature is wasting away, our inner nature is being renewed every day. For this slight momentary affliction is preparing for us an eternal weight of glory beyond all comparison, because we look not to the things that are seen but to the things that are unseen; for the things that are seen are transient, but the things that are unseen are eternal" (4:16-18). All this adds richness of meaning to God's glorifying those whom He justified. The dominance of this thought in Paul's letters becomes still clearer in the following quotations: "That you may know what is the hope to which he has called you, what are the riches of his glorious inheritance in the saints" (Eph. 1:18). "When Christ who is our life appears, then you also will appear with him in glory" (Col. 3:4). "I endure everything for the sake of the elect, that they also may obtain the salvation which in Christ Jesus goes with eternal glory" (2 Tim. 2:10).

A concluding thought to this section is its solid basis for Christian assurance of salvation. Having given it in a setting of life's varied experiences, Paul could assure his readers, "That in everything God works for good with those who love him," which as we have noted mounts to the immeasurable height of being glorified. Thus the Christian faith becomes genuinely experiential. The exceedingly significant theological presentation in this letter relates more directly to the reality of Christian experience.

For Additional Reading and Reference:

Beyschlag, *New Testament Theology,* Vol. II, pp. 67-88, 133-190.
Bowman, *Prophetic Realism and the Gospel,* pp. 236-258.
Bruce, A.B., *St. Paul's Conception of Christianity,* pp. 49-70, 107-124, 147-186.
Bultmann, *Theology of the New Testament,* Vol. I, pp. 270-330.
Conzelmann, *An Outline of the Theology of the New Testament,* pp. 171-235.
Furnish, *Theology and Ethics in Paul,* pp. 162-181.
Hunter, *Interpreting Paul's Gospel,* pp. 67-93.
I.S.B.E., Vol. IV, Art. "Sacrifice in the New Testament," I; II, 2; III, 4; IV; V, 2; VI, 2; VII, VIII.
Lehman, *The Holy Spirit and the Holy Life,* pp. 77-104.
Morris, *The Apostolic Preaching of the Cross.*
Morris, *The Cross in the New Testament,* pp. 180-269.
Rall, *According to Paul,* pp. 46-67.
Ryrie, *Biblical Theology of the New Testament,* pp. 185-187.
Schoeps, *Paul,* pp. 219-293.
Scott, *Christianity According to Paul,* pp. 26-133, 244-279.
Stevens, *The Theology of the New Testament,* pp. 403-430.
Stevens, *The Pauline Theology,* pp. 227-291.
Stewart, *A Man in Christ,* pp. 204-260.
Taylor, *The Atonement in New Testament Teaching,* pp. 54-101.
Wahlstrom, *The New Life in Christ,* pp. 53-86.
Weidner, *Biblical Theology of the New Testament,* Vol. II, pp. 131-149.
Weiss, *Biblical Theology of the New Testament,* Vol. I, pp. 419-453; Vol. II, pp. 75-90, 105-124.
Whiteley, *The Theology of St. Paul,* pp. 155-165.

1. Rom. 3:24; 8:23; 1 Cor. 1:30; Eph. 1:7, 14; 4:30; Col. 1:14.

2. *The Septuagint Version of the Old Testament with an English Translation* (New York: Harper and Brothers), p. 103.

3. Rom. 1:18; 2:5, 8; 4:15; 5:9; 9:22; 12:9; 13:5.

4. 1 Thess. 5:10; Rom. 5:6-8; 14:15; 1 Cor. 8:11; 2 Cor. 5:14, 15.

5. Sanday and Headlan, *A Critical and Exegetical Commentary on the Epistle to the Romans* (New York: Charles Scribner's Sons, 1915), p. 96.

6. J. B. Lightfoot, *St. Paul's Epistle to the Galatians,* 10th edition (New York: Macmillan and Co., 1890), p. 115. See also his *Notes on the Epistles of Paul* (New York: Macmillan and Co., 1904) for his extensive comment on *ek pisteos* and *dia tes pisteos* (III, 27), p. 274, 275.

7. For other significant uses of the phrase *ek pisteos* see Rom. 9:9, 30, 32; 10:6; 14:23; Gal. 3:8, 11, 22, 24; 5:5, and for other occurrences of *dia pisteos* see Gal. 3:14, 26; Eph. 2:8; 3:12; 3:17; Phil. 3:9; Col. 2:12; 2 Tim. 3:15.

8. Some examples of its significant usage in the New Testament are Mk. 10:34; Lk. 1:79; 2:14; 19:38; Jn. 14:27; 16:33; Acts 10:36; Rom. 8:6; 14:17; Gal. 5:22; Eph. 4:3; Col. 1:20; 2 Thess. 3:16.

9. Rom. 15:33; 16:20; 2 Cor. 13:11; Phil. 4:9; 1 Thess. 5:23.

10. Rom. 1:7, 1 Cor. 1:3; 2 Cor. 1:2; Gal. 1:3; Eph. 1:2; Phil. 1:2; Col. 1:2; 2 Thess. 1:2; 1 Tim. 1:2; 2 Tim. 1:2; Tit. 1:4; Philem. 3.

11. 1 Tim. 1:3-16. See all 2 Tim. 1:9; 2:1; Tit. 2:11; 3:7.

12. Rom. 8:14-23; 9:1-5; Gal. 3:26; 4:1-7; Eph. 5:1, 6.

13. 1 Thess. 2:13; 2 Thess. 2:14; Rom. 1:6, 7; 77; 8:28, 30; 9:11; 1 Cor. 1:9; 7:15-24; Gal. 1:6, 15; 5:8, 13; Eph. 1:18; 4:1, 4; Phil. 3:14; 2 Tim. 1:9.

14. Gen. 4:1; 18:19; Ex. 1:8; 33:12; Is. 42:25; Jer. 1:5; 16:21; Hos. 13:5; Amos 3:2; plus hundreds of others.

15. Franz J. Leenhardt, *The Epistle to the Romans* (Cleveland and New York: The World Publishing Co., 1961), p. 233.

16. Rom. 8:30; 9:7, 11, 24-26; 1 Cor. 7:15-24; Gal. 1:15; 5:8, 13; Eph. 4:1, 4; 2 Tim. 1:9.

17. Note other doxologies in Rom. 16:27; 2 Cor. 1:20; Ga. 1:5; Eph. 3:21; Phil. 1:11; 2:11; 2:11; 4:20; 1 Tim. 1:17; 2 Tim. 4:18.

CHAPTER V

SANCTIFICATION

1. Introduction

A word of explanation may be in order for introducing a study of *sanctification* at this point. At least two references from Paul's writings may show that in the unfolding revelation of the New Testament *sanctification* quite consistently follows the theme, "Called According to God's Purpose," of the preceding chapter, p. 344. The first reference, Romans 6:19, 22, reads, "For just as you once yielded your members to impurity and to greater and greater iniquity, so now yield your members to righteousness for sanctification. . . . But now that you have been set free from sin and have become slaves of God, the return you get is sanctification and its end, eternal life." Ephesians 4:23, 24 reads, "And be renewed in the spirit of your minds, and put on the new nature, created after the likeness of God in true righteousness and holiness." In both settings Paul was giving appropriate exhortations to those who had experienced justification by faith and had begun the Christian life. He was counseling them to "walk in newness of life" (Rom. 6:4) and to lead a life worthy of the calling to which they had been called (Eph. 4:1).

This leads to a very significant vocabulary used by Paul to express the ideas involved in sanctification. The verb *hagiazo* was used in the Septuagint to translate the Hebrew verb *qadesh*. The Hebrew verb and its derivatives are used very often in the Old Testament. They have to do with the setting apart of people and things which relate to worship.[1] This sampling of verb forms, together with hundreds of noun and adjective forms having the same root, determine quite definitely the meaning of the Greek work *hagiazo* together with its noun and adjective forms. With this background of *hagiazo* and its derivatives, let us proceed to study Paul's teaching on this great theme.

2. Meaning, Significance, and Doctrinal Import of Sanctification

Proceeding again with the study of some significant uses of these words in Paul's letters, let us note first of all his own testimony, "You are witnesses, and God also, how holy and righteous and blameless was our behavior to you believers . . . we exhorted each one of you . . . to lead a life worthy of God, who calls you into his own kingdom and glory" (1 Thess. 2:10-12). The apostle brought together three significant ethical terms: *holy, righteous,* and *blameless,* each intensifying tne meaning of the others. Thus *holy (hosios)* is strongly buttressed by *righteous (dikaios)* and *blameless (amemptos).* This adverb is synonymous with the frequently used word *hagios.* Observe how Paul tied in these words *holy, righteous,* and *blameless* with the thought that God was calling them into His own kingdom and glory. This connection serves to justify the consideration of *sanctification* after the topic "Called According to God's Purpose."

Later in this letter Paul repeated his concern in the words, "That he may establish your hearts unblamable in holiness before our God and Father, at the coming of the Lord Jesus with all his saints" (3:13). The word *holiness (hagiosune)* expresses the resultant state of sanctification. The word *unblamable (amemptos)* intensifies this idea of an attained holiness. Paul added the words, "For this is the will of God, your sanctification" *(hagiasmos)* (4:3). This is an active verbal noun which signifies the process of being sanctified, or more specifically, the resultant state. He gave the exhortation, "That each one of you know how to take a wife for himself in *holiness* and honor. . . . For God has not called us for uncleanness, but in *holiness*" (vv. 4, 7). The sequence of thought from 3:13 to 4:7 is quite basic to Paul's teaching on *sanctification.* He first expressed the goal for their achievement, "unblamable in holiness," and then looked to the process of achieving it, in the words *sanctification* and *holiness.* This is a fundamental distinction to be gained from Paul's later teaching on *sanctification.*

In the closing benediction of this letter Paul gave another dimension to this idea of sanctification. He wrote, "May the God of peace himself sanctify you wholly; and may your spirit and soul and body be kept sound and blameless at the coming of our Lord Jesus Christ" (5:23). The aorist optative *hagiasai (sanctify)* expresses the punctiliar aspect of sanctifying as it stands in contrast to the linear or continuous action as expressed by the Greek present and imperfect tenses. This punctiliar action receives further stress in the aorist optative form of the verb *tereo (keep, guard).* Thus Paul wishes the Thessalonians would experience a point or punctiliar action of being sanctified and of being kept sound and blameless.

In contrast with this kind of action Paul implied a process of sanctification through his use of the word *hagiasmos,* noted above, when he wrote, "God chose you from the beginning to be saved, through sanctification by the Spirit and belief in the truth" (2 Thess. 2:13). This process of sanctification receives further support when Paul used two present imperative verbs expressing actions to be continued. He wrote, "So then, brethren, stand firm and hold to the traditions which you were taught by us" (v. 15). These verses give grounds for believing that there are both punctiliar and linear aspects of sanctification. If this is a true observation, we should seek to determine when the respective punctiliar and linear actions take place in Christian experience.[2] I shall return to this point after giving the survey of *hagiazo* and its derivatives.

The adjective *hagios* has a number of significant uses in Paul's letters which contribute rich meaning to the idea of sanctification. It is uniformly translated *holy*, and thus carries the meaning "characteristic of God, separated to God, worthy of veneration."[3] The word has a wide range of uses, its highest application being to God Himself and to things and places set apart for sacred uses such as the temple and also of persons employed of God as angels. It is also applied to persons separated to God's service and so possesses also a moral sense of sharing God's purity. It also characterizes clean sacrifices and offerings.[4]

Pursuing further the noun and verb forms of sanctification, observe Paul's emphasis on the Holy Spirit as being the agent of sanctification when he wrote of himself as being "a minister of Christ Jesus to the Gentiles in the priestly service of the gospel of God, so that the offering of the Gentiles may be acceptable, sanctified by the Holy Spirit." This was accomplished "by the power of the Holy Spirit" (Rom. 15:16, 19). In this manner Paul brought together both the cleansing work of the Spirit and the manifestation of the Spirit's might and power, obviously of a spiritual nature. Paul disclosed to the Corinthians a profound spiritual truth when he wrote, "He is the source of your life in Christ Jesus, whom God made our wisdom, our righteousness and sanctification and redemption" (1 Cor. 1:30). The structure of this sentence leads us to understand that *wisdom* comprehends the remaining terms *righteousness*, *sanctification*, and *redemption*. Obviously *righteousness* and *redemption* refer to the complete work of Christ in these areas, but the word *sanctification (hagiasmos)* gives expression to a continuous work of making the believer holy.

Paul's words in 6:11 call for special attention: first, on account of its significant use of *hagiazo* but supremely because of the profound doctrinal content relating to the general theme of this chapter. It reads, "But you were washed, you were sanctified, you were justified in the name of the Lord Jesus Christ and in the Spirit of our God." The use of the aorist tense in all three of these verbs brings them into close relation as to their respective meanings and suggests that these experiences were simultaneous. This leads to the conclusion that their experiencing "the washing of regeneration" (Tit. 3:5), their being sanctified and being justified (1 Cor. 6:11), had taken place in their experience of "renewal in the Holy Spirit" (Tit. 3:5). According to this interpretation, their being sanctified was a punctiliar act of their being set apart by God and cleansed by the power of the Holy Spirit in their experience of conversion.

That the verb *hagiazo* possesses some latitude of meaning becomes evident in 1 Corinthians 7. Here he notes that "the unbelieving husband is consecrated through his wife, and the unbelieving wife is consecrated through her husband" (v. 14). Undoubtedly Paul used the most appropriate word *consecrate (hagiazo)* to express the influence of a believing husband or wife upon the respective unbelieving companion. As Charles W. Carter says, "Paul means, as we would say today, that her life is a benediction or blessing to him. Her example serves as a constant reminder to him of what is right and wrong in life and of his personal responsibility to God whom he does not yet know; it is a deterrent to evil in his life and perhaps the creation of a secret longing to know personally the God of his believing wife." [5]

In 2 Corinthians 1:12, where Paul was seeking to restore the integrity of his reputation, he wrote, "For our boast is this, the testimony of our conscience that we have behaved in the world, and still more toward you, with holiness and godly sincerity, not by earthly wisdom but by the grace of God." His use of the word *hagiotes* (holiness) in this setting gives it distinctive spiritual and ethical meaning, especially when combined with *eilikrinia tou theou (the sincerity of God,* or better, *the God-kind of sincerity).* This connotation receives further support through Paul's denial of its being carnal or sensual wisdom. Still greater weight obtains for this expression through the apostle's testimony that his behavior marked by holiness and godly sincerity was by the grace of God, not through his own power. These words of the apostle underscore yet again man's inability to achieve this goal. It is accomplished alone through the power of God, bestowed upon us by His grace.

The spiritual nature of sanctification becomes still clearer when Paul comments on the wasting away of his outer nature but then adds, "Our inner nature is being renewed every day" (2 Cor. 4:16). This expresses a continuing inner experience of being made new through the power of God. This is simply another way of presenting the continuing spiritual experience of being sanctified. These comments apply as well to Paul's exhortation in 7:1 which reads, "Let us cleanse ourselves from every defilement of body and spirit, and make holiness perfect in the fear of God." The verb *katharizo (cleanse, make clean)* refers in a literal way to physical cleansing, but it mounts to a forceful ethical sense signifying a moral purging of all that is wrong.

Paul was relating it to every defilement of body and spirit.

According to Zahniser, it expresses "the outward sin and the inward wrong, the sin which arises from our human life and that which arises from our sinful disposition. . . . Our passions must be regulated and our motives must be purified." [6] The present participle, translated *make perfect*, indicates a continuing and progressing effort to accomplish and complete, in this case, *holiness*. ***Hagiosune***, which as we have noted earlier, describes the state in man which results from a process of sanctifying. The motivation which should activate this perfecting process of holiness dare be nothing less than in the fear of God.

In Paul's letter to the Ephesians he probed still deeper into the theme of *sanctification*. This becomes evident in his opening words of praise to God the Father of our Lord Jesus Christ, "who has blessed us in Christ with every spiritual blessing in the heavenly places, even as he chose us in him before the foundation of the world, that we should be holy and blameless before him" (1:3, 4). Here the purpose of God's choosing us stands forth in the words, *holy* and *blameless*. Its purpose is the spiritual goal of purity and faultlessness of the chosen ones of God set apart and destined to be His sons.

Another note expressing the spiritual nature of holiness is evident in the words, "But you are fellow citizens with the saints and members of the household of God, built upon the foundation of the apostles and prophets, Christ Jesus himself being the chief cornerstone, in whom the whole structure is joined together and grows into a holy temple in the Lord; in whom you also are built into it for a dwelling place of God in the Spirit" (2:19-22). Here the *saints* (*hagioi*) noted as belonging to God's family are also a part of a spiritual structure which is growing into a holy temple in which they are being built for a dwelling place of God in the Spirit. The spiritual connotation of *holy* as used here mounts to that of characterizing the dwelling place for God most holy.

In line with this lofty concept of sanctification Paul added a similar exhortation, "Be renewed in the spirit of your minds, and put on the new nature, created after the likeness of God in true righteousness and holiness" (4:23, 24). Thus through a spiritual transformation and a being clothed with a new purpose and life, brought into existence after the likeness of God, they would manifest the genuine reality of righteousness and *holiness* (hosiotes). Here again *holiness* stands forth as that which is most descriptive of God's nature. On this account such grievous sins as immorality, impurity, covetousness, filthiness, and many others dared not be mentioned among these Christians. They stand opposed to what is fitting among the saints (5:3, 4).

This brings us to the climactic depiction presented by the apostle on the theme of *sanctification*. In a context in which he was setting forth to the Ephesians the Christian view of husband-and-wife relationships he fittingly intensified his exhortations by moving to its most glorious analogy, the relation of Christ and the church (5:23-29). Paul could not present any nobler comparison of husband-wife relationship than that of Christ's headship of the church. Paul would have husbands love their wives "as Christ loved the church and gave himself up for her, that he might sanctify her, having cleansed her by the washing of water with the word" (vv. 25, 26). In this setting husbands' love for their wives had its archexample in Christ's love for the church — He gave Himself as a sacrifice for her. In the purpose clause which follows we have the aorist subjunctive form of *hagiazo* and the aorist participle *katharizo*. These two words are brought together in such close relationship that they are practically synonymous in meaning. The second word carries the literal sense of *cleaning* or *cleansing* from physical stains and dirt. It lends itself easily to a spiritual sense of freeing from the defilement of sin and of purifying from wickedness. This spiritual connotation of cleansing leads to the spiritual act of making holy. The aorist tenses used here express a punctiliar act complete in itself as over against repeated actions expressed by the present and imperfect tenses.

Moving from the analogy of Christian marriage to that of Christ's marriage to the church, we gain the idea that this sanctification marks the experience of the church as she enters into the marriage experience to the Lord. Passing by the controversial matters relating to "the washing of water with the word," let us grasp the second purpose clause, "so He may present the church to Himself gloriously, having no spot or wrinkle or any such flaws, but holy and blameless" (Eph. 5:27, *Berkeley Version*). This states Christ as presenting His bride the church to Himself, the bridegroom, in the splendor of her marriage garments. In spiritual terms this bridal attire signifies the spiritual cleansing of the body of Christ. The word *amomos,* as used here, carries the meaning *without blemish, faultless, unblamable,* and shows again how Paul combines meaningful adjectives with *hagios* (holy), so as to enrich its spiritual meaning. In Colossians 1:22 Paul added a third adjective *irreproachable* (anegkletos) *that cannot be called to account, unreprovable, unaccused, blameless*. Thus by combining these significant adjectives with *holy* Paul enriched its meaning to a still greater degree.

3. United with Christ

Another expression used by Paul to describe the nature of *sanctification* is "united with him" (Rom. 6:5). The word *sumphutos* carries a physical sense, *congenital, innate,* and on a higher level, *grown along with, united with.* Thus according to the *Berkeley Version,* Paul was saying, "For if we have grown jointly with Him in experiencing a similar death, then the same must be true of our resurrection with Him." The nature of this experience is that of our old self being crucified with Christ and of our being raised to walk in newness of life. This union with Christ is genuinely experiential in nature.

In a slightly different context Paul likened this union with Christ to that of husband-wife relationship. He quoted from the Creation account the relation of husband and wife in the language, "The two shall become one flesh" (1 Cor. 6:16). To this he added, "But he who is united to the Lord becomes one spirit with him" (v. 17). Paul had already expanded this thought most intensively when he wrote, "I have been crucified with Christ; it is no longer I who live, but Christ who lives in me; and the life I now live in the flesh I live by faith in the Son of God, who loved me and gave himself for me" (Gal. 2:20). We can hardly fathom all that lay back of these words in Paul's own personal experience. Certainly he was describing his death to sin and resurrection to newness of life. But it may also include his own excruciating experiences suffered for the sake of Christ. Most marvelously he envisioned the climactic experience of those who are united with Christ when with reference to God's purpose, he wrote, "Which he set forth in Christ as a plan for the fullness of time, to unite all things in him, things in heaven and things on earth" (Eph. 1:9, 10). This brief presentation of the believers' union with Christ has involved another keynote thought of Paul's letters, namely "*in Christ*" (Rom. 6:11, 23).

4. The New Life "in Christ"

It may not have dawned on the readers of Paul's letters that the expression "*in Christ*" occurring in 1 Thessalonians 2:14; 4:16; 5:18; Romans 6:11, 23; 8:1, 2 is the "most important phrase in which Paul's intimacy with the risen Lord finds expression."[7] Both Stuart and Wahlstrom[8] noted that this expression occurs no less than 164 times in his writings, and that it is not used in the same way in the rest of the New Testament. Variant forms of this expression are "in him," "in the Lord," "in God," and "in the Spirit." With no purpose of classifying the uses of this expression I shall examine a number of them, paying attention to their respective meanings in specific cases.

The wording of this section has its basis in Romans 6:4, 11, 23. The Greek word *kainotes* is built on the adjective *kainos* which carries the meaning *new in respect to form or quality,* and so gives to this word *kainotes* the sense of *freshness, newness,* especially implying *a qualitative superiority of the object* being described. This newness of life possesses the quality of "the new life of the Spirit" (7:6). So then when Paul wrote that we must consider ourselves "dead to sin and alive to God in Christ Jesus" (6:11), he was giving this phrase distinctive meaning.

The preposition *en* is the most frequently used preposition in the New Testament and consequently carries a wide range of meanings including *in, within, on, at, by, upon, with, in the presence of,* etc. It is used "of that in which any person or thing is inherently fixed, implanted, or with which it is intimately connected . . . of a person to whom another is wholly joined and to whose power and influence he is subject, so that the former may be likened to the place in which the latter lives and moves. So used in the writings of Paul and of John particularly of intimate relationship with God or with Christ, and for the most part involving contextually the idea of power and blessing resulting from that union." Thayer explained the phrase "in Christ" in the language "ingrafted as it were in Christ, in fellowship and union with Christ."[9]

The context of Romans 6 to 8 gives special significance to the expression *in Christ* as found in 8:1, 2. Paul declared, "There is therefore now no condemnation to those who are in Christ Jesus. For the law of the Spirit of life in Christ Jesus has set me free from the law of sin and death." First is the negative expression of there being no condemnation for those who are in Christ Jesus, and second is the positive affirmation of their having been set free from the law of sin and death. In this manner Paul gave a definite declaration of the spiritual state of those in Christ Jesus. The agent for setting them free from the law of sin and death was the Holy Spirit, who is at once the Source of life and its Giver. The distinctive nature of this life is that it is *in Christ Jesus.* Thus there is a spiritual unity and affiliation with Christ. This means a spiritual oneness with Christ, manifested by faith in Him, absolute dependence on Him, and fellowship with Him.

In Romans 9:1, where Paul was giving the most positive attestation to his honesty, he linked his affirmation to the truth in Christ. He confirmed this testimony with the witness of his conscience "in the Holy Spirit." By this he was giving a twofold affirmation supporting the truth of his testimony. Here again Paul's oneness with Christ and with the Holy Spirit gave infallible testimony to his honesty. As Paul was dealing with a practical problem relating to the varied functions of the membership, he noted that they are "one body in Christ" (12:5). Though their respective gifts differed according to the grace given to them, yet each member was in Christ and so all the members constituted one body in Christ. There existed a spiritual oneness with Him (vv. 6-8).

In addressing the church at Corinth, Paul wrote to them as being the church of God and as those *sanctified in Christ Jesus* (1 Cor. 1:2). The bringing together of these two expressions enriches the phrase "*in Christ Jesus.*" These saints constitute the church of God. A new dimension of meaning becomes apparent in 2 Corinthians 5:19-21 where Paul was expounding the meaning of Christ's death. He noted that "God was *in Christ* reconciling the world to himself," and that God had made Christ "to be sin" "so that *in him* we might become the righteousness of God." It lies beyond human comprehension to fathom the depths of meaning bound up in these statements. Certainly they set forth the oneness of God and Christ in the work of redemption. So then when Christ was made to be sin for us, a oneness with Christ in the sphere of God's righteousness, is at once apparent. To the Ephesians Paul noted how the Father "has blessed us in Christ with every spiritual blessing in the heavenly places" (1:3). The union of the believers with Christ becomes the channel whereby every spiritual blessing in the heavenly places becomes ours. This blessing bears a close likeness to our being chosen "in him before the foundation of the world." This oneness with Christ finds its realization in our being holy and blameless before God in love. It seems apparent that the phrase *en agapei* (*in love*) has the syntactical use as the phrase *en xristoi (in Christ).*

Six occurrences of this phrase in 2:6 — 3:11 reveal the outworking of God's eternal purpose which He realized in Christ Jesus. In the language of a spiritual resurrection Paul noted that believers had been raised up with Christ and made to "sit with him in the heavenly places in Christ Jesus, that in the coming ages he might show the immeasurable riches of his grace in kindness toward us in Christ Jesus" (2:6, 7). This is possible because "we are his workmanship, created in Christ Jesus for good works" (v. 10).

We begin to measure the length and breadth, height and depth of the mind *in Christ Jesus* when Paul disclosed the steps of Christ's humbling Himself from being in the form of God, taking the form of a servant, being found in human form, and becoming obedient unto death on the cross (Phil. 2:5-8). To be in Christ involves similar steps of humiliation. In a word, to be *in Christ* means to share in His death. Pressing this thought still further, Paul showed that to be found *in Him* is possible alone through appropriating the righteousness from God through faith in Christ (3:9). On this account Paul pressed "on toward the goal for the prize of the upward call of God in Christ Jesus" (v. 14). For the achievement of this goal on the part of the Philippians, Paul wrote, "The peace of God, which passeth all understanding, will keep your hearts and minds in Christ Jesus" (4:7). To this he added, "My God will supply every need of yours according to his riches in glory in Christ Jesus" (v. 19).

These promises establish very clearly the grace element involved in this experience of being in Christ. The apostle recognized his own responsibility to "present every man mature in Christ" (Col. 1:28). He also commended the Colossians for their good order and the firmness of their faith in Christ (2:5). On this account he gave the encouragement, "So live in him, rooted and built up in him and established in the faith" (vv. 6, 7). This exhortation broadened still further the gamut of meaning expressed by being "in Christ."

To Timothy also Paul expressed the spiritual character of being in Christ when he wrote, "Follow the pattern of the sound words which you heard from me, in the faith and love which are in Christ Jesus" (2 Tim. 1:13). To this he added "Be strong in the grace that is in Christ Jesus" (2:1). Nevertheless, Paul added, "All who desire to live a godly life in Christ Jesus will be persecuted" (3:12). In a personal way Paul opened up to Philemon some additional aspects of being in Christ (vv. 6, 8, 20, 23). Paul was praying that the sharing of Philemon's faith "may promote the knowledge of all the good that is ours in Christ" (v. 6). To this he added, "I am bold enough in Christ to command you to do what is required" (v. 8). He gave this request, "I want some benefit from you in the Lord. Refresh my heart in Christ" (v. 20). Through Philemon's response to this request he would buoy up Paul's "deepest feelings in Christ" (v. 20, *Berkeley Version*).

A summary of Paul's use of this expression "in Christ" is hardly necessary. The spiritual nature of this life "in Christ" certainly enriches the meaning of sanctification: being set apart unto God, being transformed by the renewal of the mind, being united with Christ in His death and resurrection, and being found in Christ. Having God's righteousness as His free gift we are enabled to gain and appropriate some of the immeasurable values of being in Christ.

5. The Punctiliar and Linear Aspects of Sanctification

Near the beginning of this study of sanctification I drew attention to two aspects of this subject: the punctiliar (point action) and the linear (continuing action). The former centers in the punctiliar act of one's setting himself apart to God at the beginning of the Christian life. It is simultaneous and closely related to the experience of being born again and of being justified by faith. The latter deals with the linear aspect which is continuous and progressive in nature. This distinction between the punctiliar and linear aspects of sanctification became evident in the study of such portions of Paul's letters dealing with the nature of the Christian life: Romans 6 to 8; Galatians 5; Ephesians 4 and 5; and Colossians 3. In these Scriptures I observed the intertwining of Greek aorist tenses which expressed point action with the Greek present and imperfect tenses which expressed continuous, repeated, or linear action. These phenomena led me to believe that these punctiliar and linear aspects of sanctification have great significance. Notice the two lists of verbs which appeared in my book *The Holy Spirit and the Holy Life.*[10]

a. The Punctiliar Aspect — Action Stated as a Point:

Romans
6:2 — *died* to sin
6:3 — *baptized* into Christ
— *baptized* into his death
6:4 — *were buried* . . . with him
— as Christ *was raised*
— we too *might walk*
6:5 — *have been united* with him (perfect tense)
6:6 — our old self *was crucified*
— sinful body *might be destroyed*
6:7 — he who *has died*
6:8 — we *have died* with Christ
6:13 — *yield* yourselves to God
6:17 — *have become obedient* from the heart
6:18 — *having been set free* from sin
— *have become slaves* of righteousness
6:19 — you once *yielded* your members
— now *yield* your members
6:22 — that you *have been set free*
— *have become slaves* of God
7:4 — you *have died* to the law
— you *may belong* to another
7:6 — *are discharged* from the law
8:2 — has *set* me *free*
8:15 — *have received* the spirit of sonship
12:1 — *present* your bodies
13:14 — *put on* the Lord Jesus

1 Corinthians
15:34 — *awake* to righteousness (KJV)

2 Corinthians
1:21 — *has commissioned* (anointed — ASV, *Berkeley*) us
1:22 — *has put* his *seal* upon us
— *given* us His Spirit
7:1 — *let us cleanse* ourselves

Galatians
5:1 — Christ *has set* us free
5:13— you *were called* to freedom
5:24 — *have crucified* the flesh

Ephesians
1:13 — *have believed* in him
— *were sealed* with the promised Holy Spirit
4:22 — *put off* your old nature
4:24 — *put on* the new nature
4:25 — *putting away* falsehood
5:26 — he *might sanctify* her
— *having cleansed* her
Colossians
3:1 — you *have been raised* with Christ
3:3 — you *have died*
— your life *is hid* with Christ (perfect tense)
3:5 — *put to death*
3:8 — now *put* them all *away*
3:9 — *have put off* the old nature
3:10 — *have put on* the new nature
3:12 — *put on* then as God's chosen
1 Thessalonians
5:23 — sanctify you wholly (be kept sound)

b. The Linear Aspect — Continuous or Repeated Action:

Romans
6:6 — might no longer *be enslaved* to sin
6:8 — *shall* also *live* with him
6:11 — *consider* yourselves *dead* to sin
— *alive* to God
6:13 — *do* not *yield* your members
6:22 — ye have your fruit (ASV) unto sanctification (the process)
7:6 — we *serve* in newness of the Spirit (ASV)
8:13 — *put to death* the deeds of the body
12:2 — *do* not *be conformed* to this world
— *be transformed* by the renewal of your mind
1 Corinthians
15:34 — *sin* not (ASV)
2 Corinthians
1:21 — God who *establishes* us with you in Christ
4:16 — our inner nature *is being renewed*
7:1 — *make* holiness *perfect*
Galatians
5:1 — *stand fast*
— *do* not *submit* again
5:13 — *do* not *use* your freedom
— *be servants* of one another
5:16 — *walk* by the Spirit
5:18 — you *are led* by the Spirit
Ephesians
4:23 — *be renewed* in the spirit of your minds
4:25 — *speak* the truth

Colossians
3:1 — *seek* the things that are above
3:2 — *set* your *minds* on things that are above
3:9 — do not lie to one another
3:10 — *being renewed* in knowledge
3:13 — *forbearing* one another
— *forgiving* each other
3:15 — *let* the peace of Christ *rule*
Hebrews
2:11 — those who *are sanctified*
10:14 — those who *are sanctified*

The former list may be summarized in the following punctiliar experiences relating to sanctification: a death experience, a yielding to God and of becoming obedient to Him, being set free from the slavery to sin, His Spirit being given to us and our being sealed with the Spirit, putting off the old nature and putting on the Lord Jesus, being raised with Christ, being sanctified wholly and of being kept sound, cleansing ourselves, and finally, entering the state of being united (perfect tense) with Christ.

The linear aspect of sanctification may be summarized in the following: living with Christ, one's inner nature being renewed, serving in the new life of the Spirit, making holiness perfect, not letting sin reign in our mortal bodies nor yielding our members to sin, putting to death the deeds of the body, sinning no more, not using our freedom as an opportunity for the flesh, speaking the truth, standing fast in the faith and not submitting again to a yoke of bondage, and finally, forbearing one another, forgiving each other and letting the peace of Christ rule in our hearts.

The theological impact of these two aspects of sanctification at once becomes apparent. Thus the punctiliar aspect leads to a more comprehensive understanding of the conversion experience. It adds profound meaning to the meaning of repentance, faith and the new birth. The linear aspect of sanctification punctuates the lifelong experience of being renewed and transformed into the likeness of Christ. It deals forthrightly with putting to death the deeds of the body and of walking and being led by the Spirit. At no point do we achieve the perfection that is in Christ, noted in the words of Paul, "I press on [present tense of *dioko]* toward the goal for the prize of the upward call of God in Christ Jesus" (Phil. 3:14).

For Additional Reading and Reference:

Beyschlag, *New Testament Theology*, Vol. II, pp. 190-204.
Bruce, A. B., *St. Paul's Conception of Christianity*, pp. 188-292.
Bultmann, *Theology of the New Testament*, Vol. I, pp. 330-352.
Conzelmann, *An Outline of the Theology of the New Testament*, pp. 275-286.
Furnish, *Theology and Ethics in Paul*, pp. 207-241.
Hunter, *Interpreting Paul's Gospel*, pp. 94-120.
Lehman, *The Holy Spirit and the Holy Life*, pp. 105-120.
Rall, *According to Paul*, pp. 68-88.
Richardson, *An Introduction to the Theology of the New Testament*, pp. 242-265.
Scott, *Christianity According to St. Paul*, pp. 134-180.
Sheldon, *New Testament Theology*, pp. 243-252.
Weidner, *Biblical Theology of the New Testament*, Vol. II, pp. 150-166.

1. Note the following: Gen. 2:3; Ex. 13:2; 19:14; 20:8, 11; 29:1, 21; 30:29; Lev. 8:11, 12; Is. 29:23; Jer. 1:5; Ezek. 20:12; 28:25; 36:23; Joel 1:14; 2:15, 16.
2. Chester K. Lehman, *op. cit.*, pp. 108-122.
3. G. Abbott Smith, *op. cit.*, p. 5.
4. 1 Thess. 1:27; Rom. 7:12; 11:16; 12:1; 16:16; 1 Cor. 3:17; 7:13, 34; Eph. 1:4; 2:21; 3:5; 5:27; Col. 1:22; 3:12; 2 Tim. 1:9.
5. *The Wesleyan Commentary* (Grand Rapids: Wm. B. Eerdmans Publishing Co., 1965), Vol. V, p. 168.
6. *Ibid.*, Clarence Howard Zahniser, Vol. V., p. 293.
7. James E. Stuart, *op. cit.*, p. 154.
8. Wahlstrom, *op. cit.*, p. 93.
9. *Thayer's Greek-English Lexicon of the New Testament*, Corrected Edition (New York: American Book Company, 1889), p. 211.
10. Chester K. Lehman, *op. cit.*, pp. 108-120.

CHAPTER VI
THE NEW LIFE IN CHRIST

1. The Bridge Between Sanctification and the Christian Life

It is conceivable that Paul consciously sought to span this possible gap or probably to show the obvious outworking of sanctification in the everyday experiences of the Christian life. The following references may have a bearing on this point. To the Thessalonians, Paul wrote, "How holy and righteous and blameless" was his behavior to these believers. He exhorted, encouraged, and charged each person "to lead a life worthy of God, who calls you into his own kingdom and glory" (1 Thess. 2:10-12). A similar span, in this case, making reference first to a practical aspect of the Christian life followed by a reference to holiness occurs in 3:12, 13. This reads, "And may the Lord make you increase and abound in love to one another and to all men, as we do to you, so that he may establish your hearts unblamable in holiness before our God and Father."

A third possible example occurs in 4:1-8 in which Paul expanded his discussion with some important matters pertaining to Christian living. He exhorted them again on how they ought to live and to please God, saying, "This is the will of God, your sanctification" (4:3a). Following this he gave the most extended teaching in this letter on the Christian life (4:3b-12). Romans 6-8 is another example of Paul's bridge-building between sanctification and the Christian life. Note again the references to sanctification, such as 6:4, 19, 22; 7:4, 6, 12, 25; 8:2-4; and then observe the detailed exhortations relating to Christian living. If this bridge-building interpretation possesses any value, let us proceed to give attention to Paul's teachings on the Christian life. Most certainly, he moves from teachings which are theological in nature over to the common everyday affairs of life. Some of these details of life may on the surface appear to be trivial but a closer study will show that they involve important ethical principles.

2. The Spirit-Led Life

It is quite significant that Paul structured four of his letters on the general pattern of a doctrinal presentation followed by teachings relating to Christian living. Note the practical portions of Galatians 5; 6; Rom. 8:9; 12—15; Eph. 4—6; Col. 3; 4. At the same time the doctrinal portions of these letters include references to Christian living, while the practical portions of these letters include important theological teachings.

a. As Taught in Galatians and Romans

This becomes apparent in Paul's letter to the Galatians, where he develops the Christian ethic of the walk by the Spirit, relating it to the various aspects of the Christian life. As he was seeking to lead the Galatians away from their rigid adherence to the legalism of the law, he explicitly noted the dynamic of the Holy Spirit in effecting the experiences of the Christian life. The Holy Spirit was the Source of their new life. They had appropriated this divine power through faith (Gal. 3:3-5). The indwelling Holy Spirit empowered them to cry, "Abba! Father!" (4:6). This leads us to the *locus classicus* of Paul's teaching on the "walk by the Spirit" (5:16-25). Here he shows the only way of ceasing to gratify the desires of the flesh.

Paul's explication of this point sets forth clearly the depravity of human nature, deliverance from which is possible alone through the power of the Holy Spirit. He faced up, forthrightly, to the antagonism between the desires of the flesh and the desires of the Spirit. Everyone who walks by the Spirit is fully aware that these works of the flesh have their source in man's sinful nature. The Christian graces of love, joy, peace, and so forth cannot spring from this depraved nature. These graces are the fruit of the Spirit. It is the Holy Spirit who gives new life to sinful man, which makes it possible for him to walk by the Spirit. The works of the flesh as they stand opposed to the fruit of the Spirit give heart-searching meaning to the nature of the Christian life.

The Galatians needed to learn that their concept of obeying the law utterly failed to enlighten them; on the one side, with regard to the real nature of all the sins listed; and on the other, of the spiritual nature of these Christian graces. Paul was certainly down-to-earth in listing these sins, as well as naming these noble expressions of Christian living. The Christian, in his own personal life or in relation to his family or society, is well aware of the outcroppings of one's sinful nature, as well as the manner of life made possible through the Holy Spirit's power. He sharpened this truth most forcefully by noting that "those who belong to Christ Jesus have crucified the flesh with its passions and desires" (5:24). Paul supplemented this teaching with additional exhortations relating to one's rising above sinful practices and of giving expression to a distinctive spiritual law in the words, "He who sows to his own flesh will from the flesh reap corruption; but he who sows to the Spirit will from the Spirit reap eternal life" (6:8).

Romans 8:1-27 gives another disclosure of the Spirit-led life. In a setting similar to that of his letter to the Galatians, Paul stressed his thought in the words, "The law of the Spirit of life in Christ Jesus has set me free from the law of sin and death" (v. 2). Here the apostle noted the powerlessness of the flesh as it stands in contrast to the earthly life of Jesus who came "in the likeness of sinful flesh and for sin, he condemned sin in the flesh" (v. 3). In this setting Paul showed that those "who live according to the flesh set their minds on the things of the flesh, but those who live according to the Spirit set their minds on the things of the Spirit" (v. 5). This liberating power of the Holy Spirit becomes still clearer in the words, "If by the Spirit you put to death the deeds of the body you will live. For all who are led by the Spirit of God are sons of God" (vv. 13, 14). Thus the Christians' conflict with sin becomes resolved by the death-dealing blows of the Holy Spirit upon the deeds of the body. This is definitely a death-dealing experience, the explanation of which lies beyond human comprehension. Perhaps the key to its meaning becomes apparent in the Spirit's work of leading (*ago*), which according to the connotation of the Greek verb suggests the ideas of *carrying, guiding,* and *impelling*.

Let us note again the bearing of 8:26 on this experience where Paul speaks of the Spirit's helping us in our weakness. The compound Greek verb *sunantilambanomai* carries the meanings, *take hold with at the side for assistance, help in obtaining,* or *come to the aid of someone.*[1] Paul brought this meaning to the attention of his readers as he exhorted them: "Be transformed by the renewal of your minds. . . . Be aglow with the Spirit, serve the Lord" (12:2, 11). This advice given in the midst of specific instructions relating to the Christian life intensified his teaching on the practical aspects of the Spirit-led life. He brought these teachings to a climax in the benediction, "May the God of hope fill you with all joy and peace in believing, so that by the power of the Holy Spirit you may abound in hope" (15:13). In expanding this thought he referred to what Christ had wrought through him "to win obedience from the Gentiles, by word and deed, by the power of signs and wonders, by the power of the Holy Spirit" (vv. 18, 19).

b. As Taught in 1 and 2 Corinthians

In 1 Corinthians Paul made repeated references to the activities of the Holy Spirit in the lives of the believers. He challenged these believers to holy living by noting that they are God's temple, that God's Spirit dwells in them, and that God's temple is holy (3:16, 17). Later he reminded them of their sinful practices before they became believers in Christ. Then he added, "You were washed, you were sanctified, you were justified in the name of the Lord Jesus Christ and in the Spirit of our God" (6:11). Later in the letter he elaborated on the varieties of gifts, service, and of working (12:4-6). Then he noted, "To each is given the manifestation of the Spirit for the common good" (v. 7). He specified such gifts as the utterance of wisdom, the utterance of knowledge, faith, gifts of healing, the working of miracles, prophecy, the ability to distinguish between spirits, various kinds of tongues, and the interpretation of tongues. He declared, "All these are inspired by one and the same Spirit, who apportions to each one individually as he wills" (v. 11). By giving thought to these varied gifts it becomes apparent that they are impressive evidences of a Spirit-led life. He added later, "Since you are eager for manifestations of the Spirit, strive to excel in building up the church" (14:12).

In 2 Corinthians Paul gave the basis or foundation for a Spirit-led life when he noted that God "has put his seal upon us and given us his Spirit in our hearts as a guarantee" (1:22). Later he strengthened this idea by noting that the new covenant was written in the Spirit and that the Spirit gives life (3:6). Since this is "the dispensation of the Spirit" (v. 8), Paul could add that "where the Spirit of the Lord is, there is freedom" (v. 17). On this account we "with unveiled face, beholding the glory of the Lord, are being changed into his likeness from one degree of glory to another; for this comes from the Lord who is the Spirit" (v. 18). This is a profound way of setting forth the nature of the Spirit-led life. At the heart of this experience is "the fellowship of the Holy Spirit" (13:14).

c. *As Taught in the Prison and Pastoral Letters*

Still another way of setting forth the Spirit-led life becomes evident in the "holy temple in the Lord" in whom we "are built into it for a dwelling place of God in the Spirit" (Eph. 2:21, 22). This is perhaps the most expressive way of showing the Spirit's access to us in the Spirit-led life. Being fully aware of the power that needs to be manifest in this manner of life, Paul prayed for the Ephesians that "he may grant you to be strengthened with might through his Spirit in the inner man" (3:16). In contexts where he was exhorting his readers with reference to the many grievous sins of the day, Paul counseled them not to grieve the Holy Spirit of God and to be filled with the Spirit. This would enable them to address one another in psalms and hymns and spiritual songs (4:25-31; 5:15-20). Knowing that the life in the Spirit involves a spiritual warfare, Paul admonished the Ephesians to use "the sword of the Spirit, which is the word of God," also that they should "pray at all times in the Spirit" (6:17, 18).

Paul in his imprisonment did not lose his trust in God, for he could write, "I know that through your prayers and the help of the Spirit of Jesus Christ this will turn out for my deliverance" (Phil. 1:19). With certainty he could write of his fellowship in the Spirit (2:1). This is one of the richest privileges of a Spirit-led life. Knowing full well the spiritual conflicts which would confront Timothy, Paul wrote, "Guard the truth that has been entrusted to you by the Holy Spirit who dwells within us" (2 Tim. 1:14). His final note on the Spirit-led life centered in the believer's initial experience of the Spirit's work expressed in the words "the washing of regeneration and renewal in the Holy Spirit, which he poured out upon us richly through Jesus Christ our Savior" (Titus 3:5, 6).

This survey of the Spirit-led life repeatedly led us to Paul's teachings on the nature of the Christian life. Turning now to a study of this line of thought, let us continue to associate its deep involvement in the workings of the Holy Spirit in the life of the believer.

3. The Nature of the Christian Life

Paul's teachings on sin, presented in an earlier section, may serve as an orientation to his teaching on the Christian life. It is quite the pattern in all of his letters for him to interweave doctrinal and practical teachings. While it would be consistent and instructive to interrelate the doctrinal and practical aspects of these teachings, space does not permit such an approach. I am leaving it to the reader to observe this interrelationship.

a. As Taught in 1 and 2 Thessalonians

Paul's concern in the area of vital Christian living becomes evident in the opening verses of 1 Thessalonians, where he gave thanks to God for their "work of faith and labor of love and steadfastness of hope in our Lord Jesus Christ" (1:3). This showed the highest motivation lying back of their manner of life. Later he noted how holy, righteous, and blameless their behavior was to the believers, and that he had charged them "to lead a life worthy of God" (2:10, 12). By way of directing their thought to the grievous sin of immorality, or it might have been to his exhortation on how they ought to live and please God, he exposed the lustful passions of heathen marriage practices by noting that they should abstain from immorality, and that each one "know how to take a wife for himself in holiness and honor" (4:1-5).

He then moved on to another area of Christian living by noting that they had been taught by God to love one another, to aspire to live quietly, to mind their own affairs, and to work with their hands, so that they can command the respect of outsiders, and be dependent on nobody (vv. 9-12). After he had presented the glorious picture of our Lord's return and of the judgment to take place in the day of the Lord, the apostle concluded this section with some down-to-earth exhortations in the words, "Be at peace among yourselves. . . . Admonish the idlers, encourage the fainthearted, help the weak, be patient with them all. . . . See that none of you repays evil for evil, but always seek to do good to one another and to all. . . . hold fast what is good, abstain from every form of evil" (5:13-22). Finally, note his benedictory prayer, "May the God of peace himself sanctify you wholly, and may your spirit and soul and body be kept sound and blameless at the coming of our Lord Jesus Christ" (v. 23).

Similar practical teachings are apparent in 2 Thessalonians. Paul observed that their faith was growing abundantly and their love one for another was increasing (1:3). He exhorted them in the words, "Stand firm and hold to the traditions which you were taught by us" (2:15). He gave wholesome advice relating to an unacceptable manner of living when he advised the brethren to "keep away from any brother who is living in idleness and not in accord with the tradition that you received from us. For you yourselves know how you ought to imitate us; we were not idle when we were with you, we did not eat any one's bread without paying, but with toil and labor we worked night and day, that we might not burden any of you. . . . We gave you this command: If anyone will not work, let him not eat. For we hear that some of you are living in idleness, mere busybodies, not doing any work." They were "to do their work in quietness and to earn their own living" (3:6-13). These exhortations interwoven so closely with the great eschatological messages of these letters certainly speak to the close relation between faith and life as taught by the apostle. They cannot be separated into different categories. This expressed to the Thessalonian Christians who were young in their Christian beliefs that their acceptance of the gospel needed to bear fruit in daily Christian living.

b. As Taught in Galatians and Romans

Paul's letter to the Galatians ends in quite sharp contrast with the letters just considered in respect to his teachings on the Christian life. The Jewish legalism with which Paul dealt in this letter shows the need for establishing the truly ethical character of the gospel as it stood in contrast with the legalistic interpretation of the law. This underlay his exposure of the works of the flesh, the sinful nature of which these legalistic Christians had failed to realize. He made this point clear by listing the fruit of the Spirit, which, perhaps, his readers had failed to comprehend (Gal. 5:16-26). Undoubtedly, Paul had hoped that through his enumeration of the works of the flesh, they would begin to see both in themselves and in others examples of such carnality, especially, if they had begun to experience the leading of the Holy Spirit in their lives. Through the illumination of the Spirit they would come to understand that the beautiful graces of love, joy, peace, and so forth should be found in the life of every Christian. They may have been shocked to learn that to achieve these graces would involve crucifying "the flesh with its passions and desires." Paul came still nearer to the problems of Christian living when he advised these Galatians how to deal with anyone overtaken in any trespass. They should be restored in a spirit of gentleness. They would need to bear one another's burdens, but at the same time each one would need to bear his own load.

Another responsibility of which his readers were not aware came in the words, "Let him who is taught the word share all good things with him who teaches" (6:6). His final exhortation with respect to Christian living came in the words, "Do not be deceived; God is not mocked, whatever a man sows, that he will also reap. For he who sows to his own flesh will from the flesh reap corruption; but he who sows to the Spirit will from the Spirit reap eternal life. And let us not grow weary in well-doing, for in due season we shall reap, if we do not lose heart" (vv. 7-9). Thus in these few practical exhortations Paul covered a wide scope relating to Christian living (5:16 — 6:10).

Coming to Paul's masterpiece on salvation, his letter to the Romans, we need to observe again that he interwove teachings on the sinfulness of man with those on justification by faith (Rom. 1:18 — 3:24; 5:12-21; 6: 12-23; 7:4-25). In these contexts he forthrightly laid bare the sinfulness of sin, but in contexts such as these, he had shown how a sinner gains right standing with God through justification by faith. Paul pressed onward to the great truth that the experience of being justified by faith involved being baptized into Christ's death — this to result in the walk in newness of life (6:1-4).

In chapter 8 Paul expounded this new life in Christ Jesus. This becomes the prelude to his practical teachings on the Christian life (12 to 15). Here he revealed the nature of the Spirit-led life in Christ. He laid the foundation for these teachings in the words, "Present your bodies as a living sacrifice, holy and acceptable to God, which is your spiritual worship. Do not be conformed to this world but be transformed by the renewal of your mind, that you may prove what is the will of God, what is good and acceptable and perfect" (12:1, 2). Paul would have his readers know that just as the burnt offerings under the law symbolized total dedication to God on the part of the offerer, so the Christian should present himself as a living sacrifice completely dedicated to God. In a negative manner he exhorted his readers not to be fashioned or configured according to this evil world, but to be transformed, transfigured, and remolded by the renewing of the mind. The Greek verbs lying back of these exhortations express definitely the real nature of Christian living. This becomes clear in the remainder of this section. Note Paul's admonition, "Let love be genuine; hate what is evil, hold fast to what is good; love one another with brotherly affection; outdo one another in showing honor. . . . Contribute to the needs of the saints, practice hospitality. Bless those who persecute you. . . . Live in harmony with one another; do not be haughty, but associate with the lowly; never be conceited. Repay no one evil for evil but take thought for what is noble in the sight of all. . . . 'If your enemy is hungry, feed him; if he is thirsty, give him drink. . . .' Do not be overcome by evil, but overcome evil with good" (vv. 9-21).

Paul probed into another area of Christian living by setting forth the Christian's duty to the state. He wrote, "Let every person be subject to the governing authorities" (13:1). He showed that this includes the paying of taxes and also giving respect to those to whom respect is due. He included the responsibility of obeying the Ten Commandments, especially those dealing with adultery, murder, stealing, and coveting (v. 9). He made clear that the love of neighbor as one's self is the fulfilling of the law.

He brought in still another aspect of Christian living when he dealt with the differences in moral judgment with reference to such nonmoral practices as eating only vegetables, and esteeming one day better than another, noting that "each of us shall give account of himself to God." He set before them a higher level of thought in the words, "For the kingdom of God does not mean food and drink but righteousness and peace and joy in the Holy Spirit; he who thus serves Christ is acceptable to God and approved by men" (14:17, 18). In this manner, Paul showed that "we who are strong ought to bear with the failings of the weak, and not to please ourselves; let each of us please his neighbor for his good, to edify him" (15:1, 2). Through these practical exhortations he again made clear the real nature of the Christian life.

In his closing admonitions and personal greetings, Paul referred to his going to Jerusalem with aid for the saints which the churches of Macedonia and Achaia had contributed. Paul noted its spiritual significance when he wrote, "If the Gentiles have come to share in their spiritual blessings, they ought also to be of service to them in material blessings" (15:27). Paul also included a word of personal concern, "Take note of those who create dissensions and difficulties, in opposition to the doctrine which you have been taught; avoid them. For such persons do not serve our Lord Christ, but their own appetites, and by fair and flattering words they deceive the hearts of the simple-minded" (16:17, 18). This appeal makes it clear again that Paul, the theologian, laid hold also of personal problems and differences found among the believers, evidence again that Christian doctrine relates very definitely to the believer's manner of life.

c. As Taught in 1 and 2 Corinthians

Paul's first letter to the Corinthians has a great deal to say concerning certain problems of Christian living. The church at Corinth was being wrecked by party spirit. There were quarrelings among them; some claiming to belong to Paul, others to Apollos, others to Cephas, and still others to Christ (1:10 — 3:21). There was jealousy and strife among them. Many were claiming to be wise, but Paul showed them that it was the wisdom of this world. Some were misjudging Paul, and on account of this, he was reviled, persecuted, and slandered (4: 11-13). They were arrogant in their attitude toward him.

Immorality was also found among these believers, as well as idolaters, revilers, drunkards, and robbers. Instead of settling their grievances in the brotherhood they took these cases to the courts of law (6:1-8). Paul sought to show them the sanctity of marriage, and in this way, denounced immorality and prostitution. Some had raised the question of the legitimacy of marriage; in which case Paul upheld this God-ordained institution, including the indissolubility of marriage.

These Corinthians also faced up to an ethical problem relating to eating food which had been offered to idols. On account of this weakness of conscience Paul admonished the church to refrain from eating this food in order not to wound the consciences of their weak brethren. This was a detail of Christian living which showed the mutual responsibility of the brotherhood to do all in their power to save their brethren from falling.

Paul mentioned another item pertaining to Christian living regarding the right of their ministers to receive material benefits for their spiritual ministry. This illustrated the brotherhood idea of the church. It was another area of mutual responsibility building on the principle involved in the priests of the temple receiving their share in the sacrificial offerings. Paul wrote, "In the same way, the Lord commanded that those who proclaim the gospel should get their living by the gospel" (9:14). He noted still another aspect of the Christian life, according to which he saw the need of becoming all things to all men: to Jews, to

Gentiles, to the weak, and to all others in order that he might better serve them and through which he might be able to save some. He brought in a unique illustration drawn from the athlete, whether a runner or a boxer, when he wrote, "I pommel my body and subdue it, lest after preaching to others I myself should be disqualified" (vv. 24-27).

In order to bolster these exhortations he directed his reader's attention to the discipline which God brought upon Israel during the wilderness wanderings. He warned them not to desire evil as Israel did. Nor dare they be idolaters, immoral or drunkards. He advised them, "No temptation has overtaken you that is not common to man. God is faithful, and he will not let you be tempted beyond your strength, but with the temptation will also provide the way of escape, that you may be able to endure it" (10:13). In this setting Paul warned again against the worship of idols, showing that in the observance of the Lord's Supper they were participating in the body of Christ.

Paul touched on another ethical problem of husband-wife relationship relating to the Christian life when he wrote of the prayer veil to be worn by the women (11:1-16). He recognized the headship of man in the husband-wife relationship, but at the same time he maintained, "In the Lord woman is not independent of man nor man of woman" (v. 11). This principle relates directly to the nature of the Christian life in the home.

The apostle touched on still another aspect of Christian living as it came into close relationship with worship. The Corinthians were losing out in their observance of the Lord's Supper, making it a time of carnal feasting. Added to this were the many divisions and factions among them which destroyed the spiritual unity required for participation in this sacred meal. Paul drew attention also to an aspect of Christian living which becomes evident in the great variety of spiritual gifts found in the church. At the very center of the apostle's teaching relating to these spiritual gifts, he found it consistent to present the more excellent way of Christian love (ch. 13).

In this setting Paul's description of the way of love as exemplified in the life of a Christian must have been quite sobering to these Corinthians as they misjudged the real nature of these spiritual gifts. Note how beautifully he described the nature of the Christian life, when he wrote, "Love is patient and kind; love is not jealous or boastful; is not arrogant or rude. Love does not insist on its own way; it is not irritable or resentful; it does not rejoice at wrong, but rejoices in the right. Love bears all things, believes all things, hopes all things, endures all things" (vv. 4-7). Paul appropriately concluded this letter with the exhortation, "Be watchful, stand firm in the faith, be courageous, be strong. Let all that you do be done in love" (16:13).

The situation in the church at Corinth was such that necessitated a second letter which dealt forthrightly with their failures in Christian living. Paul's exhortations on these matters make clear a still wider range of the Christian life. As he begins to unburden his heart, he gives the testimony of his conscience that he had behaved himself in the world "with holiness and godly sincerity, not by earthly wisdom but by the grace of God" (2 Cor. 1:12). When someone caused pain to these Corinthians, Paul advised that they should "turn to forgive and comfort him" (2:7) and also to reaffirm their love for him (vv. 8-11).

In defense of his own integrity of character, Paul wrote, "We have renounced disgraceful, underhanded ways; we refuse to practice cunning or to tamper with God's word, but by the open statement of the truth we would commend ourselves to every man's conscience in the sight of God" (4:1, 2). He gave a meaningful statement regarding Christian motivation in one's life when he wrote, "Those who live might live no longer for themselves but for him who for their sakes died and was raised" (5:15). Serious meditation on this expression certainly reveals the far-reaching impact of a Christ-centered life which covers the entire range of Christian living. In Paul's circumstances the only manner in which he could commend himself to the Corinthians was "through great endurance, in afflictions, hardships, calamities, beatings, imprisonments, tumults, labors, watching, hunger; by purity, knowledge, forbearance, kindness, the Holy Spirit, genuine love, truthful speech, and the power of God; with the weapons of righteousness for the right hand and for the left; in honor and dishonor, in ill repute and good repute" (6:4-8). It appeared necessary for the apostle to uphold his own integrity of character as supported by his manner of life through all these persecutions. Note especially the Christian graces which stood forth most clearly throughout his trying experiences. This illustrates clearly the real nature of the Christian life.

Paul probed into another serious aspect of what is involved in Christian living when he wrote, "Do not be mismated with unbelievers" (6:14). This exhortation reflected the prohibition of plowing with an ox and ass together and similar restrictions (Lev. 19:19; Deut. 22:10). In this manner he set forth the sharp antagonism between righteousness and iniquity, light and darkness, Christ and Belial, and finally, a believer and an unbeliever. This command should have led the Christians to see how the Christian life differs radically from that of an unbeliever. He could conclude with the positive counsel, "Make holiness perfect in the fear of God" (7:1).

Throughout the remainder of the letter Paul injected a number of ideas which reflect the nature of the Christian life. Thus he made a clear distinction between godly grief and worldly grief: the former producing repentance that leads to salvation and the latter producing death (7:9, 10). He commended the churches of Macedonia for their giving beyond their means for the relief of the saints, especially in light of their own extreme poverty; "but first they gave themselves to the Lord and to us by the will of God" (8:5). This liberality would find expression in two directions, as Paul wrote, "But that as a matter of equality your abundance at the present time should supply their want, so that their abundance may supply your want, that there may be equality" (v. 14). Here is an example of mutual Christian sharing which has been characteristic of the Christian life all through the pages of church history.

Paul would have his readers gain some lessons on the nature of the Christian life from his own experiences of sufferings and persecutions at the hands of his opponents. At the same time he had been enabled to experience the most glorious privilege of being caught up into paradise and of being given an abundance of revelations. Alongside this a thorn was given to him in the flesh to harass him and to keep him from being too elated. Three times he besought the Lord that this should leave him but instead of being relieved of this thorn, he heard the words, "My grace is sufficient for you, for my power is made perfect in weakness" (12:9). His weaknesses were completely and fully offset by the power of Christ resting upon him. On this account he wrote, "For the sake of Christ, then, I am content with weaknesses, insults, hardships, persecutions, and calamities; for when I am weak, then I am strong" (v. 10).

This otherwise inexplicable situation in Paul's life serves to interpret experiences in the lives of many Christians which lie beyond human understanding. We need to probe earnestly into his experiences which lay back of his words, "I will most gladly spend and be spent for your souls" (v. 15). This was all the more realistic to Paul as he contemplated another visit with the Corinthians when he noted, "That perhaps there may be quarreling, jealousy, anger, selfishness, slander, gossip, conceit, and disorder. I fear that when I come again my God may humble me before you, and I may have to mourn over many of those who sinned before and have not repented of the impurity, immorality, and licentiousness which they have practiced" (vv. 20, 21). From all of this we should see that as Paul was following in the footsteps of Christ, he was suffering many similar experiences to those endured by his Lord.

d. As Taught in Ephesians, Philippians, and Colossians

Paul's letter to the Ephesians follows an entirely different pattern and consequently his teachings on the Christian life have a different mold. This becomes apparent already in his hymn of praise (1:3-10) when he wrote, "He chose us in him before the foundation of the world, that we should be holy and blameless before him" (v. 4). These two words *holy* and *blameless* are the most expressive in the entire Bible for describing the nature of the Christian life. He brought his teaching on the new life in Jesus Christ to a climax in the words, "We are his workmanship, created in Christ Jesus for good works, which God prepared beforehand, that we should walk in them" (2:10). When Paul moved from his doctrinal presentation (1 — 3) to the practical teachings of his letter, he wrote, "I . . . beg you to lead a life worthy of the calling to which you have been called, with all lowliness and meekness, with patience, forbearing one another in love, eager to maintain the unity of the Spirit in the bond of peace" (4:1-3). This is a forthright introduction to what may be thought of as Paul's most profound teaching on the nature of Christian living. He had the concern that "we all attain to the unity of the faith and of the knowledge of the Son of God, to mature manhood, to the measure of the stature of the fulness of Christ" (v. 13).

From this sublime presentation of the Christian life Paul moved on to exhort the Ephesians that they "must no longer live as the Gentiles do, in the futility of their minds . . . alienated from the life of God" (vv. 17, 18). After laying bare some of the heinous sins of the Gentiles, he gave the positive exhortation, "Put on the new nature, created after the likeness of God in true righteousness and holiness" (v. 24). Again he elaborated sinful practices which they should put away, concluding with the positive advice, "Be imitators of God. . . . And walk in love" (5:1). Yet again he laid bare still other forms of wickedness, concluding with the positive counsel, "Understand what the will of the Lord is. . . . Be filled with the Spirit . . . singing and making melody to the Lord with all your heart . . . giving thanks in the name of our Lord Jesus Christ to God the Father" (vv. 17-20).

Having specified so clearly both the positive and negative aspects of Christian ethics Paul advanced to the social aspects of Christian society involving the relationships of husbands and wives, children and parents, and slaves and masters. Most significantly he gave the pattern of husband-wife affiliation in the language of Christ's relationship to the church. This restored the institution of marriage to the Christian level according to that instituted by God at the creation. The Christian home must also embody the biblical standards of children honoring father and mother, as well as parents bringing up their children in the "discipline and instruction of the Lord" (6:1-4).

Living in a society in which slavery was an accepted social practice, Paul naturally applied the principles of Christian living to this social custom (6:5-9). He had already delved into this matter in 1 Corinthians. In a context where he was drawing attention to some ethical aspects of human society, he advised slaves to remain in a state in which they were called. If, however, they could gain their freedom they should avail themselves of the opportunity (7:20, 21). He directed their thought to a higher level of thinking when he noted that in the Lord they were freed men. To this he added the truth that those who were free when called are in all reality slaves of Christ (v. 22). This gave a new perspective for slaves who were Christians. Addressing himself to them he wrote, "Be obedient to those who are your earthly masters, with fear and trembling, in singleness of heart, as to Christ; not in the way of eye-service, as men-pleasers, but as servants of Christ, doing the will of God from the heart, rendering service with a good will as to the Lord and not to men" (vv. 5-7; Col. 3:22-25). He counseled the masters in the words, "Treat your slaves justly and fairly, knowing that you also have a Master in heaven" (Col. 4:1; Eph. 6:9). To Philemon, the master of Onesimus, he advised that he receive him back not as a slave but as a beloved brother (vv. 15-17).

From our twentieth-century viewpoint we may wonder why Paul did not condemn the institution of slavery, but when we examine his counsel to slaves as well as to masters, he was upholding an interrelationship between them which for all practical purposes uprooted the wrongs of this social institution. Most certainly, if slaves would be obedient to their masters in singleness of heart and to Christ, and masters would recognize that Christ was the Master both of themselves as well as of their slaves, a Christian brotherly relationship would exist. Slaves would be beloved brethren of their masters. It is quite clear that Paul made an impact against slavery which through the following centuries led Christians to reject slavery per se and to regard all men as equal. In a word, the walk by the Spirit leads to a pattern of Christian living in which all human beings are on the same level of brotherhood and as servants of Christ.

Paul's final exhortations relating to Christian living (Eph. 6:10-20) present this theme in the language of a spiritual conflict which most profoundly sets forth the most serious involvements of Christian living. The Christian's foe is the devil who uses all of his powers of craftiness and deception in order to entrap and ensnare the servants of Christ. Using the figure of a soldier's armor Paul commended to his readers such defensive protection as truth, righteousness, the gospel of peace, faith, and salvation. His weapon is the Word of God through which the Holy Spirit operates. Praying at all times in the Spirit, with prayer and supplication, these offensive and defensive weapons are appropriated. In order to accomplish this purpose he would have them "keep alert with all perseverance, making supplication for all the saints" (v. 18). The bearing of this upon the daily life of Christians is at once apparent.

Paul's letter to the Philippians was personal and contained many practical exhortations which related to his intimate fellowship with them. This becomes apparent in his opening thanksgiving when he wrote, "It is my prayer that your love may abound more and more, with knowledge and all discernment, so that you may approve what is excellent, and may be pure and blameless for the day of Christ, filled with the fruits of righteousness which come through Jesus Christ" (Phil. 1:9-11). This at once reflects the high level of Christian living to which he would have the Philippians achieve. Paul was aware that he would be released from prison for their "progress and joy in the faith" (v. 25). He added the exhortation, "Only let your manner of life be worthy of the gospel of Christ . . . that you stand firm in one spirit, with one mind striving side by side for the faith of the gospel, and not frightened in anything by your opponents" (vv. 27, 28).

These exhortations also presented the nature of the Christian life from the angle of a Holy Spirit-directed life, in a setting which had its source in the encouragement and consolation centered in Christ, as well as the incentive of love and fellowshiping in the Spirit which resulted in an outflow of affection and sympathy. Paul would have the Philippians complete his joy "by being of the same mind, having the same love, being in full accord and of one mind" (2:2). From this sublime view of the Christian life he added the practical counsel in the words, "Do nothing from selfishness or conceit, but in humility count others better than yourselves. Let each of you look not only to his own interests, but also to the interests of others" (vv. 3, 4). Counsels such as these could be understood only by mature Christians. The strongest appeal possible took the form, "Have this mind among yourselves, which you have in Christ Jesus." Paul would have the Philippians lay hold of the mind of Christ manifested in His humiliation, suffering, and death. He laid hold of this truth in a practical manner by saying, "Work out your own salvation with fear and trembling; for God is at work in you, both to will and to work for his good pleasure" (vv. 12, 13). Then he injects some commonplace advice, "Do all things without grumbling or questioning," with the motive "that you may be blameless and innocent, children of God without blemish in the midst of a crooked and perverse generation, among whom you shine as lights in the world, holding fast the word of life" (vv. 14-16).

As Paul drew his letter to a close he gave two of the women a bit of personal advice, "To agree in the Lord" (4:2). Some additional counsel came in the words, "Let all men know your forbearance. . . . Have no anxiety about anything, but in everything by prayer and supplication with thanksgiving let your requests be made known to God" (vv. 4-6). Finally, he advised them to think and ponder over whatever is true, honorable, just, pure, lovely, and gracious (v. 8). Here again was noble advice given on the level of their spiritual comprehension.

On a similar plane Paul set forth to the Colossians the pattern of Christian living. This becomes evident when he commended them for their faith, love, and hope (Col. 1:4, 5). He added several admonitions which spoke to them on their level of spiritual comprehension. Paul was praying that they "may be filled with the knowledge of his will in all spiritual wisdom and understanding, to lead a life worthy of the Lord, fully pleasing to him, bearing fruit in every good work and increasing in the knowledge of God. May you be strengthened with all power, according to his glorious might, for all endurance and patience with joy, giving thanks to the Father" (vv. 9-12). He found it necessary, nevertheless, to give counsel against certain heretical teachers, likely from the Essenes and others, later called Gnostics. Through these warnings Paul showed how the Spirit-led life encountered false philosophical and religious views which had an appearance of wisdom but in all reality promoted "rigor of devotion and self-abasement and severity to the body," but had "no value in checking the indulgence of the flesh" (2:23). The nature of a Spirit-led life far transcended any legalistic prohibitions such as, "Do not handle, do not taste, do not touch" (v. 21).

In similar pattern to what he had written to the Ephesians, Paul would have them set their minds "on things that are above" (3:2). He spelled this out both by negative and positive ethical exhortations. He listed eleven flagrant sins, such as immorality, covetousness, anger, and foul talk, which they should put away (vv. 5-9) and urged them to put on the new nature which would manifest compassion, meekness, love, and a half-dozen other Christian graces (vv. 10-14). He concluded with the general advice, "Whatever you do, in word or deed, do everything in the name of the Lord Jesus" (v. 17). Through these counsels the Colossians would come to realize that Christian living involved the total manner of life. As noted earlier (3:18 — 4:1) Paul directed admonitions to wives, husbands, children, fathers, slaves, and masters, similar to that given in the letter to the Ephesians. A closing down-to-earth, practical admonition came in the words, "Let your speech always be gracious, seasoned with salt, so that you may know how you ought to answer everyone" (4:6).

e. As Taught in the Letters to Timothy and Titus

Paul's letters to Timothy and Titus are filled to the brim with the kind of practical advice which these young leaders of the church needed for their service in it. From a pastoral point of view these letters show again the many facets of life in which Christian ethics finds application. To Timothy he declared, "The aim of our charge is love that issues from a pure heart and a good conscience and sincere faith" (1 Tim. 1:5). Among the ethical standards for bishops Paul noted that they should be above reproach, temperate, sensible, dignified, gentle, godly, steadfast, blameless, and holy. [2] Instructions for the brethren included such Christian graces as godliness, good deeds, being generous, being steady, enduring suffering, being temperate, sound in faith, showing integrity and gravity, and perfect courtesy toward all men. [3]

For women he gave the instruction that they should adorn themselves modestly and sensibly in seemly apparel. They should continue in faith, love, and holiness. They should be serious, temperate, and faithful in all things. They should devote themselves to doing good in every way. They should be reverent in behavior, sensible, chaste, domestic, kind, and submissive to their husbands. [4] Slaves should be submissive to their masters, give satisfaction in every respect, show entire and true fidelity so that in everything they may adorn the doctrine of God (1 Tim. 6:1, 2; Titus 2:9, 10). Paul drew attention to different classes of sinners: sodomites, kidnappers, perjurers, slanderers, profligates, reckless, lovers of pleasure, deceivers, slaves to various passions, and the factious. [5]

This detailed presentation of the Christian life certainly discloses the almost innumerable phases of practical Christian living involved in the Spirit-led life. Looked at from the perspective of biblical theology, let us observe that the doctrines of salvation as presented by Paul centered ultimately in a manner of life in which every thought, motive, purpose, habit, deed, practice, and so forth were held in view. Paul presented all this data not from a legalistic approach to Christian living, but rather as depicting the life in Christ and the walk by the Spirit.

4. Salvation by Grace

This chapter centering in the doctrines of salvation naturally comes to a climax in the study of this great word as used by Paul. The great doctrinal vocabulary, including redemption, justification, regeneration, sanctification, reconciliation, grace, peace, and the Christian life are all included in this great word *salvation*.

a. Paul's Initial Teaching on Salvation

In his great sermon at Antioch of Pisidia (Acts 13:16-41) Paul developed his message by showing that God had brought to Israel a Savior, Jesus, according to His promise. The message of this salvation brought by Christ centered in His teaching ministry, suffering, death, and resurrection; all foretold in the Old Testament in such passages as Psalms 89:20-27; 107:20; 2:7; 16:10; Isaiah 55:3. On the following Sabbath, Paul continued his gospel message, and when the Jews opposed him, he declared that they were judging themselves unworthy of eternal life. In support of his rebuke he quoted, "I have set you to be a light for the Gentiles, that you may bring salvation to the uttermost parts of the earth" (Acts 13:47; Is. 49:6). Luke made the observation, "As many as were ordained to eternal life believed" (v. 48). These uses of the words *Savior* and *salvation* show that Paul was building his gospel message of salvation directly on the Old Testament. The word *soter* (Savior) was used in the Septuagint to translate the Hebrew word *yasha*. *Soteria* (salvation) was used to translate *yeshuah*, together with other forms built on the same root. The verb *sozo* (to save) was used to translate *yasha*, together with correlate forms. In the Old Testament these words were used with reference to physical actions of salvation (Ex. 14: 13, 30), but soon these words came to express a spiritual aspect which became dominant throughout the Old Testament.[6] The controlling idea in these Old Testament uses are: first, man is helpless in saving himself; second, God alone is the Savior of mankind; third, this salvation is that of being delivered from sin; fourth, salvation is an act of God's grace depending upon man's repentance from sin and turning to God in faith; and fifth, this salvation is provided for both Israel and the Gentiles.

b. Salvation the Central Theme of the Letter to the Romans

After reading Romans 1:16 it soon becomes evident that this masterpiece among Paul's writings centers in the gospel which "is the power of God for salvation for every one who has faith." Paul did not need to orient his readers to his use of this word, *salvation*. It was this doctrinal truth which underlay his being "set apart for the gospel of God which he promised beforehand through his prophets in the holy scriptures, the gospel concerning his Son" (Rom. 1:1-3). In this compact statement of his theme (v. 16) it is apparent that salvation is the central theme of the gospel. Already in verses 2 to 4 Paul had pointed to the Old Testament source of this truth. The verb *euaggelizo (announce glad tidings)* was used in the Septuagint to translate *basar*. Most significant uses giving support to Paul's teachings are Psalm 40:9; 96:2; Isaiah 40:9; 52:7; 60:6; 61:1. So clear is this definition of the gospel (v. 16) that further explanation may seem unnecessary. Give thought, nevertheless, to the essential ideas in this statement. In a definitive way the gospel is the power of God for salvation. The Greek word *dunamis* sets forth the aspects of *power, might,* and *strength,* which the gospel manifests. It was used to express the divine power manifest in a miracle. Since it occurred so frequently in the Gospels, Paul's use of this word captures the central idea of power and energy manifested in the Gospels. In a distinctive way, it is the manifestation of God's might. This stands in sharp contrast to the finiteness of human power. Through this power of God man is saved.

As noted earlier the word salvation used here capitalizes on all the meaning given to it in the Old Testament and was demonstrated in Christ's mighty miracles. This leads us to realize more fully one of the larger purposes revealed in the miracles of the Bible. They not only gave ground for believing in the deity of Jesus but led very directly to the people's grasping the nature of His saving work. In other words, God's act of saving us is in essence, a miracle. It is the giving of spiritual life to those who are dead through trespasses and sins. God grants this salvation to everyone who believes. Obviously the act of believing involves far more than an intellectual recognition. It includes personal faith, trust, dependence, and reliance of one upon another. This idea finds support in the frequent occurrences of the expression "believed in him" (Jn. 2:11; 4:39; 6:40; 7:5, 31, 48; 8:30; etc.). The use of this expression, and those of similar nature, show the projection of the believer's faith in Christ. It was a Christ-centered faith.

Paul went further and said that in this salvation God's righteousness is revealed, that God manifested His righteousness in this provision of salvation for all mankind, that is, He in no way violated the attributes of His nature in any way. This becomes evident when we note the relation of faith to justification and sanctification in the outworking of His righteousness. The expression "through faith for faith" (Rom. 1:17). may become intelligible in some other translations, such as "a way that starts from faith and ends in faith" (NEB), "a process begun and continued by their faith" (Phillips), "resulting from faith and leading on to faith" (Twentieth Century New Testament), "The Way of faith that leads to greater faith" (WMS). Paul supported his statement by quoting from Habakkuk, "He who through faith is righteous shall live" (v. 18; Hab. 2:4). It may be more accurate to follow Habakkuk's own words which read, "The righteous shall live by his faith [faithfulness]" (Hab. 2:4).

These words from the Lord to the prophet solved the latter's problem relating to the wickedness of God's people which to the prophet seemed to go unpunished while at the same time the righteous were suffering at the hands of the wicked. The Lord solved the problem by showing that His people would live by reason of their faithfulness to Him. Thus the central idea of salvation is that of living through faith. Paul expanded this truth by noting that we shall be saved by Christ from the wrath of God, and in a positive way we shall be saved by His life (Rom. 5:9, 10). Those who receive the abundance of grace and the free gift of righteousness shall reign in life through Jesus Christ. Christ's act of righteousness leads to acquittal and life for all men.

On this account grace reigns through righteousness to eternal life through Christ our Lord. (vv. 18-21). This salvation through Christ enables the believer to "walk in newness of life" (6:4). On this account we must consider ourselves "dead to sin and alive to God in Christ Jesus" (v. 11). We need to yield ourselves to God as those "who have been brought from death to life" (v. 13). In a climactic manner Paul added, "The free gift of God is eternal life in Christ Jesus our Lord" (v. 23). This eternal life in Christ gains still larger meaning by noting that it is "the new life of the Spirit" (7:6). These references lead us to see the meaning of salvation in terms of "newness of life" and "the new life of the Spirit." This is a present experience but its future aspect is "eternal life in Christ Jesus." It is indescribably more glorious. Paul proceeded to show the nature of salvation as experienced in this world in terms of the workings "of the Spirit of life in Christ Jesus" as manifested in setting us "free from the law of sin and death" (8:1, 2). In sharp contrast with those who live according to the flesh the apostle declared, "Those who live according to the Spirit set their minds on the things of the Spirit" (v. 5). In doing this "life and peace" (v. 6) become central in Christian experience. The Spirit of God in a very real way dwells in the believer. The Spirit will give eternal life to all who have the Spirit of Christ. To this Paul added, "If by the Spirit you put to death the deeds of the body you will live" (8:13). He brought this thought to a climax when he added, "For all who are led by the Spirit of God are sons of God." (v. 14) They are "heirs of God and fellow heirs with Christ" (v. 17). Speaking for himself, along with fellow believers, Paul added, "We ourselves who have the first fruits of the Spirit, groan inwardly as we wait for adoption as sons, the redemption of our bodies. For in this hope we were saved" (vv. 23, 24).

After this positive presentation of salvation, Paul proceeded to present this teaching in the context of Israel's unbelief. He laid the foundation for this teaching by noting the bearing of works and of grace upon election and in its outworkings in his call. Paul built his case on the story of Pharaoh, who by stubborn unbelief refused to believe in the God of Israel. God's judgment of heart-hardening came upon Pharaoh when he refused to believe in Israel's God. On account of this unbelief and stubbornness of heart God brought judgment upon the Egyptians. Centuries later when Israel rebelled against God, a similar judgment was brought upon His people. On this situation Isaiah wrote, "Though the number of the sons of Israel be as the sand of the sea, only a remnant of them will be saved" (Rom. 9:27; Is. 10:22; 11:11). These references to Israel's history showed pointedly the bearing of faith and obedience upon salvation. In fact Paul's entire presentation in Romans 9 to 11 stands forth plainly in his words, "My heart's desire and prayer to God for them is that they may be saved" (10:1). In order to make this truth clear to his readers he explained the conditions for salvation in verses 9-13. He noted that salvation is dependent on the individual's confession that Jesus is Lord and in believing that God raised Him from the dead. He stressed the thought that belief springs from the heart, not merely from the lips. This heart-based confession of Jesus as Lord and of belief in His resurrection is the condition for being accounted righteous and leads to one's being saved. In support of this conclusion, Paul quoted the words of Joel, "Everyone who calls upon the name of the Lord will be saved" (v. 13; Joel 2:32).

c. Paul' References to Salvation in His Other Letters

We may conclude that Paul's presentation of salvation in the letter to the Romans is full and complete, but he gave a number of comprehensive statements in his other letters. The absence of any reference to salvation in his letters to the Galatians and the Colossians is almost unbelievable. However, he treated the doctrines of justification by faith and of the Spirit-led life in Galatians, and of Christ's preeminence together with the new life in Christ in Colossians. Paul noted the full realization of salvation to be experienced in the day of the Lord Jesus (1 Cor. 5:5). The element of salvation as a continuing experience leading to a final triumph in Christ becomes evident in Paul's pictorial language, "We are the aroma of Christ to God among those who are being saved . . . a fragrance from life to life" (2 Cor. 2:15, 16). In harmony with his usual pattern of treatment, Paul based his teaching of salvation on God's words quoted by Isaiah on which he commented, "Now is the acceptable time; behold now is the day of salvation" (6:2). This quotation is from the great Servant of the Lord passage in Isaiah 49. It was the Lord's plan that His Servant should be a light to the nations in order that His "salvation may reach to the end of the earth" (v. 6). He spoke of a day of salvation in which he had helped his people. Paul interpreted this as being prophetic of the present era. On this account he entreated the Corinthians "not to accept the grace of God in vain" (v. 1). From this context it becomes clear that the entire Christian era is the *day of salvation.* It is that day to which God's revelation throughout the Old Testament looked forward. Thus the idea of *salvation* is the dominant theme of the entire Bible.

As Paul revealed to the Ephesians the profound truth manifested in the outworking of God's purpose, noting that it was to the praise of His glorious grace, he added the explanation, "In him you also, who have heard the word of truth, the gospel of your salvation, and have believed in him, were sealed with the promised Holy Spirit, which is the guarantee of our inheritance until we acquire possession of it, to the praise of his glory" (Eph. 1:13, 14). In a word, Paul's hymn of praise centers in the *gospel of salvation.* When he unfolded the concept of the spiritual resurrection when those who were dead through trespasses and sins were made alive with Christ, he added the momentous parenthetic expression, "By grace you have been saved" (2:5). He stressed the truth that this act of being saved by grace is possible through faith, and it is the gift of God. He enlarged on this concept of salvation in the words, "We are his workmanship, created in Christ Jesus for good works, which God prepared beforehand, that we should walk in them" (v. 10). This saving work of God indicates that the act of making us alive is a work of God, in fact, an act of creation in Christ Jesus. Its purpose finds expression in good works. These elements of being God's workmanship and of being created in Christ Jesus contribute vitally to our understanding of salvation. This becomes still clearer when Paul pictured for us "the whole armor of God" (6:13-17). In this vivid language the interrelation of all truth, righteousness, peace, faith, salvation, and the Word of God, becomes clear. Each part of this armor is integral to the whole armor of God.

In 1 Timothy, Paul wrote of "God our Savior, who desires all men to be saved and to come to the knowledge of the truth. For there is one God, and there is one mediator between God and men, the man Christ Jesus, who gave himself as a ransom for all" (2:4-6). Here we should observe that in Paul's terminology the act of being saved is practically synonymous with one's coming to the knowledge of the truth. The word *truth* expresses a spiritual concept. It centers in Christ. It expresses the heart of the gospel. Truth is an integral part of the whole armor of God. Its profoundest expression stands forth in the oneness of God and in the one Mediator between God and men, Jesus Christ. The price of our Lord's mediatorial work was the giving of Himself as a ransom for all mankind.

In the setting of giving instructions to Timothy with regard to woman's role of silence and submissiveness, Paul added the instruction, "Yet woman will be saved through bearing children, if she continues in faith and love and holiness, with modesty" (2:11-15). In this manner Paul continued to build up the ethical aspects involved in the experience of being saved. Later in the letter he gave additional instructions with regard to Christian living in which he stressed speech, conduct, love, faith, purity, and then concluded with the words, "Take heed to yourself and to your teaching; hold to that, for by so doing you save both yourself and your hearers" (4:12-16). These exhortations relating to the ethical standards accompanying the experience of salvation show clearly that Paul throughout all his writings built up a solid structure of thought relating to the ethical standards for those who are being saved.

In 2 Timothy he repeated another fundamental truth by stating that it is "in the power of God who saved us and called us with a holy calling . . . in virtue of his own purpose and the grace which he gave us in Christ Jesus" (2 Tim. 1:9). These words give confirmation and additional support to what Paul set forth in his letter to the Romans. His last declaration on this theme stands forth in the words, "When the goodness and loving kindness of God our Savior appeared, he saved us . . . in virtue of his own mercy, by the washing of regeneration and renewal in the Holy Spirit, which he poured out upon us richly through Jesus Christ our Savior, so that we might be justified by his grace and become heirs in hope of eternal life" (Titus 3:4-7). Here the saving act of Christ our Savior stands forth in the words *regeneration (palingenesia)* and *renewal (anakainosis)* — two expressive words which enrich the concept of salvation.

Paul's teachings on salvation may be summarized as follows. Sinners are dead in trespasses and sins; hence God's act of saving the lost is that of making them alive in Christ. The Holy Spirit is the agent for this renewal. It is a manifestation of God's grace (Eph. 2:1-10; Titus 3:5). Salvation stands forth both as a present experience, and also as one of the future, extending throughout eternity. Paul viewed the present aspect of salvation as being both punctiliar (1 Thess. 2:16; 2 Thess. 2:13; Eph. 2:5, 6, 10; 2 Tim. 1:9; Titus 3:5) and also as linear (1 Cor. 1:18; 15:2; 2 Cor. 2:15). The future aspect is eternal and most glorious (Rom. 5:9, 10; 9:27; 10:9; 1 Cor. 3:15; 5:15; 1 Thess. 5:8; 2 Tim. 4:18). Both God the Father and Christ stand forth as our Saviors (1 Tim. 1:1, 15; Titus 1:3, 4). The Holy Spirit indwells the believers and empowers them for Christian service, including their warfare against the powers of evil. The experiences of repentance from sin and faith in the Lord Jesus

Christ lead to salvation. [7] God's saving act delivers the sinner from death, destruction, and God's wrath. [8] The experience of salvation possesses definite ethical aspects involved in holy living. [9]

For Additional Reading and Reference:

Beyschlag, *New Testament Theology,* Vol. II, pp. 204-229.
Bruce, A. B., *St. Paul's Conception of Christianity,* pp. 344-361.
Bultmann, *Theology of the New Testament,* Vol. II, pp. 203-236.
Hunter, *Interpreting Paul's Gospel,* pp. 94-120.
Lehman, *The Holy Spirit and the Holy Life,* pp. 199-201.
Rall, *According to Paul,* pp. 89-148.
Ryrie, *Biblical Theology of the New Testament,* pp. 203-210.
Scott, *Christianity According to St. Paul,* pp. 197-235.
Stevens, *Pauline Theology,* pp. 292-318.
Wahlstrom, *The New Life in Christ,* pp. 87-275.
Weiss, *Biblical Theology of the New Testament,* Vol. I, pp. 472-489.
Whiteley, *The Theology of St. Paul,* pp. 205-213.

1. See Greek lexicons for additional significant connotations of this verb.
2. 1 Tim. 3:2-12; 4:12-16; 6:3-16; 2 Tim. 1:13, 14; 2:14-18, 21-26; 3:10; 4:5; Tit. 1:6-9, 13.
3. 1 Tim. 4:7, 8; 5:24, 25; 6:17; 2 Tim. 2:19; 4:3, 4; Tit. 2:2, 6-8, 12, 14; 3:1, 2, 8.
4. 1 Tim. 2:9, 10, 15; 3:11; 5:3-15; Tit. 2:3-5.
5. 1 Tim. 1:8-10; 2 Tim. 3:2-9; Tit. 1:10-12, 14-16; 3:3, 9-11.
6. Deut. 32:15; Ps. 3:8; 62:2; 68:19; Is. 12:2, 3; 25:9; 45:15, 17, 21; etc.
7. Rom. 1:16, 17; 10:9, 13; 1 Cor. 1:21; 2 Cor. 7:10; 2 Tim. 3:15.
8. Rom. 5:9; 1 Cor. 1:18; 2 Cor. 2:15; 7:10; Phil. 1:28; 1 Thess. 5:9.
9. Eph. 2:10; Phil. 2:12-16; 1 Tim. 2:15; Tit. 2:13, 14.

CHAPTER VII

PAUL'S TEACHINGS ON THE PERSON OF CHRIST

1. Introduction

Paul's greetings found at the opening of all his letters follow the common pattern in the words, "Grace to you and peace from God our Father and the Lord Jesus Christ" (Rom. 1:7). This form of greeting makes it clear that Paul's views of the person of Christ were not undergoing a process of development, but rather that his theology was founded on his declarations at the time of his conversion when he proclaimed that Jesus was the Christ, the Son of God, and the Lord (Acts 9:20, 22, 29). These declarations clearly set forth the deity of Christ. This means that there is a unified view of this doctrine in all of his letters. There is, however, an evident enlargement of his presentation in the prison letters. At no point, however, did he set forth the person of Christ in doctrinal form per se. The nearest approaches to such a presentation are found in Philippians 2:5-11; Colossians 1:15-20; and Titus 2:13, 14. It is my purpose to note Paul's teachings on the deity and humanity of Jesus, including His preexistence and incarnation, the oneness of His person, and also the conjunction of Father, Son, and Holy Spirit which underlies the doctrine of the Trinity.

2. Paul's Teachings in the Thessalonian Letters

The repeated expression, "God the Father and the Lord Jesus Christ," is at once a definite assertion of Christ's deity and also of the dominant idea in the doctrine of the Trinity. The references to the Father, the Son, and the Holy Spirit in 1 Thessalonians 1:2-10 confirm the Trinitarian implication of Paul's greeting. Let us note further the significance of the expression "Lord Jesus Christ" as it sets forth His deity. The Greek word for *Lord* (*kurios*) was used in the Septuagint to translate *Adonai,* as well as *Yahweh,* in this manner, expressing clearly the idea of deity. Thus, when Paul wrote of Jesus as being Lord, he was giving the clearest expression of Jesus' deity. Another of Paul's expressions which sets forth the deity of Christ emphatically stands forth in the words, "According to the grace of our God and the Lord Jesus Christ" (2 Thess. 1:12). A similar statement occurs in Titus 2:13, "The glory of our great God and Savior Jesus Christ." According to Robertson, "Strict syntax requires that since there is only one article with *theou* and *kuriou* one person is meant.[1] While scholars differ on the syntactical structure of the former passage there appears to be no difference of opinion with regards to the latter. With some hesitance I believe that the former passage identifies God and Lord. Paul's words to Titus, on the other hand, definitely identify God and Savior Jesus Christ. Peter's expression in his second letter confirms this (2 Pet. 1:1).

Paul made several statements in these letters which indirectly set forth his views of the Trinity (1 Thess. 1:1-10; 5:18, 19, 23; 2 Thess. 1:1, 2; 2:13, 16). The manner in which Paul introduced the work of the Holy Spirit in connection with that of the Father and of Christ supports two fundamental ideas: first, the oneness or unity of the Father, the Son, and the Holy Spirit; and second, the personal distinction among the three. Perhaps the most expressive are the words, "We are bound to give thanks to God always for you, brethren beloved by the Lord, because God chose you from the beginning to be saved, through sanctification by the Spirit" (2 Thess. 2:13). The Father, the Son, and the Holy Spirit all perform deity functions. Thus while Paul gave much additional teaching on the person of Christ and on the Trinity, there is practically no progress of doctrine in these fundamental truths.

It is significant to observe also the distinctive function of each person of the Godhead. While Paul did not follow a fixed pattern in ascribing deity functions of the Father, the Son, and the Holy Spirit, yet, something of value may be gained from these observations. It was God who had chosen them. The work of the Holy Spirit manifests divine power. The Holy Spirit inspired these Thessalonians with joy. Jesus will come from heaven and deliver the believers from the wrath to come. God approved Paul to be entrusted with the gospel. Paul shared the gospel of God with the Thessalonians. God called them into His own kingdom and glory. He referred to the churches of God, but still more significantly to those in Christ Jesus. Paul spoke of Timothy as being God's servant in the gospel of Christ. Paul was concerned that the Thessalonians stand fast in the Lord. He was concerned to render thanksgiving to God for them. He spoke of God as the Father and of Jesus as the Lord. He exhorted them in the Lord Jesus that they should live to please God. He had given them instructions through the Lord Jesus. The will of God centered in their sanctification.

God had called the believers in holiness and He gives His Holy Spirit to the believers. They had been taught by God to love one another. Through Jesus, God will bring with Him those who had fallen asleep. The Lord Himself will descend from heaven with the sound of the trumpet of God. The dead in Christ will rise to meet the Lord in the air. The events will take place in the day of the Lord. God has not destined the believers for wrath but to obtain salvation through our Lord Jesus Christ. It is the will of God in Christ for believers to give thanks in all circumstances. Believers should not quench the Spirit. The God of peace Himself will sanctify the believers wholly. It was Paul's benedictory prayer that the grace of the Lord Jesus Christ be with the Thessalonians (2 Thess. 3:18).

From these details we may gather at least two ideas: first, there are distinctive functions which relate to each person of the Trinity; second, certain activities are common to all three, but more particularly to the Father and to the Son.

3. Teachings Found in Paul's Later Letters

We look to Paul's later letters for some significant statements concerning the person of Christ.[2] Paul forthrightly set forth our Lord's divine-human nature in the words, "God sent forth his Son, born of woman, born under the law" (Gal. 4:4). He made no effort to explain this mystery, but his assertion of Christ's deity and of His humanity are definitely clear. In his explanation of the Lord's Supper to the Corinthians, he combined the deity title *Lord* and the human name *Jesus* and declared that the bread and wine symbolized, respectively, the broken body and shed blood of Jesus. With unquestioned clarity he combined deity and humanity in the expression "The Lord's death until he comes." In like manner he used the divine name, Christ, in referring to Jesus' death and resurrection. In 2 Cor. 4:4 Paul ascribed deity to Jesus in the language, "The glory of Christ, who is the likeness of God." The word *glory* as used here is restricted to that which belongs to Deity. While the Greek word *eikon* usually has the meaning *image* such as an imprint of the emperor's head on a coin, it also possesses the meaning of *likeness* which is the sense Paul undoubtedly intended in this statement; and in this manner ascribed deity to Christ, that is, Paul preached Jesus Christ as Lord.

His message to the Philippians (2:5-11) deserves intensive study. Here the expressions "the form of God" and "equality with God" stand forth as the clearest assertions of Jesus' deity found in Paul and rank with John 1:1-18 and Heb. 1:1-14 as the noblest expressions of Christ's deity and His humanity. The word *morphe* also possesses a wide range of meanings but its connotation in a given context clearly establishes its sense. Robertson says, "*Morphe* means the essential attributes as shown in the form. In His preincarnate state Christ possessed the attributes of God and so appeared to those in heaven who saw Him."[3] The Greek word *isos* means *equal, the same in size, number, quality,* and so on. As used here it stands as another conscious declaration of Jesus' deity. Obviously human speech lacks adequate expressions for ascribing deity to Christ. On this account Paul again sought for meaningful language to express Jesus' incarnation. Jesus "emptied himself, taking the form of a servant, being born in the likeness of men" (Phil. 2:7). Not to enter into the theological controversies centered in these words, it is sufficient to say that Jesus being born in the likeness of men did not assert that He was no longer deity, but emphatically that Christ in utmost humility took upon Himself the likeness of men. This incarnation made possible the experience of being obedient unto death on a cross. Paul did not stagger in the presentation of this mystery but rather challenged the believers to yield themselves to similar experiences of humiliation. The climax to this challenge comes to us in the words "that at the name of Jesus every knee should bow . . . and every tongue confess that Jesus Christ is Lord" (Phil. 2:10, 11).

In 3:8-11 Paul made some additional statements which confirm the deity and humanity of Jesus as expressed in chapter 2. He declared that Jesus Christ is Lord, that Christ's righteousness is identical with that of God, and that the death and resurrection of Christ confirm His divine-human nature. As Paul pictured the preeminence of Christ in his letter to the Colossians he declared again that Jesus, the beloved Son of God, is "the image of the invisible God" (1:15). He added deity activities on the part of Jesus relating to His work of creation and of divine providence. He declared further, "In him all the fulness of God was pleased to dwell" (v. 19). He made additional statements which related to Christ's humanity, referring to His body of flesh and to His death. In another context the apostle declared, "In him the whole fulness of deity dwells bodily" (2:9). To Timothy Paul declared, "There is one mediator between God and men, the man Christ Jesus" (1 Tim. 2:5). Only a divine-human being could serve as mediator between God and man. On this account, the expression "the man Christ Jesus" is most significant for our present inquiry. We already noted Paul's significant words to Titus. It suffices to note that this last expression from his pen relating to the person of Christ is perhaps his most forceful declaration of Christ's deity. Most assuredly "the appearing of the glory of our great God and Savior Jesus Christ" (Titus 2:13) is the blessed hope of all believers. Even in this context he added the words which declare Christ's humanity: "Who gave himself for us to redeem us from all iniquity" (v. 14). Most assuredly Paul's teachings on the person of Christ present an unfathomable mystery which can be received only on the basis of faith. Nevertheless, personal Christian experience unquestionably confirms the divine-human nature of our Lord Jesus Christ.

4. Paul's Trinitarian Perspective

By way of orientation to this discussion it may be well to note that with one possible exception (2 Cor. 13:14) Paul's Trinitarian teaching becomes apparent in contexts where he involves the distinctive work of each Person of the Trinity. Paul made reference in hundreds of contexts to the Father and the Son. These references become basic to our understanding of the Trinity. While it is not my present purpose to give an exhaustive presentation of the distinctive work relating respectively to the Father, to the Son, and to the Holy Spirit, in practically all his references, these distinctive functions are apparent. It is my present purpose, nevertheless, to note three elements: first, the personal distinction of the Father, the Son, and the Holy Spirit; second, the ascription of deity to each of the three; and third, the oneness of the Godhead which underlies monotheism.[4]

Galatians 4:4-7 is a notable example of Paul's bringing each person of the Trinity into personal relationship with the believer. God the Father sent forth His Son to redeem mankind and the Holy Spirit to indwell those who are redeemed. To the Romans, Paul declared (7:4-6) that believers died to the law through the body of Christ. He was raised from the dead in order that we may bear fruit for God. Through this redemptive work, the believer serves God in the new life of the Spirit.

Romans 8:1-17 is perhaps the *locus classicus* among Paul's Trinitarian passages. The work of Christ and of the Holy Spirit has its origin in God. The interrelation of their work stands forth in the words, "Spirit of life in Christ Jesus" (v. 2). The intimacy of the believer's relation to Christ finds most meaningful expression in Paul's phrase "in Christ." This intimate relation of being *in Christ* is the result of the Spirit's work, as expressed in the words "Spirit of life." It is the Spirit who indwells the believer and leads him in holy living. Here we should observe the mystery of God's nature. It becomes manifest through the believer's being in Christ and of being indwelt and led by the Holy Spirit. In the Romans 15:15-20 context the interworking of Christ and the Holy Spirit again becomes apparent in the expressions "sanctified by the Holy Spirit" and "what Christ has wrought through me." This work becomes manifest through the power of the Holy Spirit. All this was possible because of the grace given to Paul by God. Later he shared his burden in the words, "I appeal to you, brethren, by our Lord Jesus Christ and by the love of the Spirit, to strive together with me in your prayers to God" (v. 30).

In 1 Corinthians 3:9-17 Paul involved the Trinity in a profound manner when he wrote of God's field and God's building, the church, the foundation of which is Jesus Christ, and that God's Spirit dwells in this temple of believers. Through probing the depths of meaning in this figure, our understanding of the Trinity becomes more intelligible by noting that the believer is God's temple of which the foundation is Jesus Christ and in whom the Holy Spirit dwells. In this context Paul set forth the interworking of the Father, Son, and Holy Spirit. In another setting of this letter he noted, "No one can say 'Jesus is Lord' except by the Holy Spirit . . . there are varieties of gifts, but the same Spirit; and there are varieties of service, but the same Lord; and there are varieties of working, but it is the same God" (12:3-6). In this context Paul expanded his teaching on the Holy Spirit in a significant manner by showing His distinctive work in the life of God's children.

In 2 Corinthians 3:3-6 Paul gave another meaningful expression in the words, "You show that you are a letter from Christ . . . written . . . with the Spirit of the living God" (2 Cor. 3:3). Paul's benedictory prayer at the close of this letter is perhaps the most compact statement of the Trinity. He wrote, "The grace of the Lord Jesus Christ and the love of God and the fellowship of the Holy Spirit be with you all" (13:14). This closing prayer brings into close relationship three vital elements of Christian experience as they relate to the triune Being, God.

In Ephesians 2:13-22 Paul again used the symbolism of the holy temple of which Christ is the chief cornerstone. It grows into a holy temple in the Lord in whom all the believers are built into it for a dwelling place of God in the Spirit. Through Christ we have access in the Spirit to the Father. While the language of Paul is a bit complicated in this section, its meaning is quite clear, especially as it reveals the activities of the triune God. In 3:14-19 of this letter Paul decribed the inner workings of the triune God which enlarges still further our understanding of the Trinity. He bows in prayer before the Father, requesting that He might grant the Ephesians "to be strengthened with might through his Spirit in the inner man" (v. 16) and that Christ may dwell in their hearts. This also stands as an enlightening statement relating to the distinctive work of the Father, Son, and Holy Spirit.

Perhaps the profoundest Trinitarian statement given by Paul stands forth in 4:4-6 when he wrote, "There is one body and one Spirit . . . one Lord, one faith, one baptism, one God and Father of us all, who is above all and through all and in all." There was hardly a more forceful way in which Paul could make clear the unity of the Spirit than by relating these aspects of the Christian life which are distinctive by their respective onenesses. With these, the one Spirit, one Lord, and one God and Father, are constituted the most holy oneness of divine revelation. From the point of view of this study of the Trinity this truth possesses the most profound significance. The oneness of the Spirit, of the Lord, and of God the Father stands alongside the inevitable truth that these three constitute the one and only Deity. It allows no room for a tri-theistic interpretation nor a rejection of the three Persons constituting the Godhead. The reader should also examine the references which have not been quoted but which contribute significant meaning to this inquiry.

A few concluding remarks may be in order. First, Paul gave no impression of grappling with the profoundest truths of God's revelation to man. Second, he presented these ideas entirely in the context of God's relation to His people through Christ and the Holy Spirit. Third, his approach to these overwhelming truths was supremely experiential.

For Additional Reading and Reference:

Beyschlag, *New Testament Theology,* Vol. II, pp. 63-132.
Bruce, A.B., *St. Paul's Conception of Christianity,* pp. 327-343.
Heim, *Jesus the Lord,* pp. 139-176.
Hunter, *Interpreting Paul's Gospel,* pp. 56-63.
I.S.B.E., Vol. IV, pp. 2338-2341.
Kittel, *Bible Key Words,* Vol. II, Book I, "Lord"; Vol. III, Book II, "Spirit of God."
Lightfoot, *Epistle to Philippians,* pp. 108-113, 125-131.
Mackintosh, *The Doctrine of the Person of Christ,* pp. 49-77.
Rall, *According to Paul,* pp. 113-133.
Rolston, *Consider Paul,* pp. 181-188.
Schoeps, *Paul,* pp. 149-160.
Sheldon, *New Testament Theology,* pp. 219-226.
Stauffer, *New Testament Theology,* pp. 103-152.
Stevens, *The Pauline Theology,* pp. 199-226.
Stevens, *Theology of the New Testament,* pp. 389-402.
Stewart, *A Man in Christ,* pp. 273-319.
Taylor, *The Person of Christ in New Testament Teaching,* pp. 32-79, 129-133, 223-285.
Van Oosterzee, *The Theology of the New Testament,* pp. 261-267.
Warfield, *The Lord of Glory,* pp. 220-261.
Weidner, *Biblical Theology of the New Testament,* Vol. II, pp. 120-130, 183-188.
Weiss, *Biblical Theology of the New Testament.* Vol. I, pp. 390-419.
Whiteley, *The Theology of St. Paul,* pp. 99-129.

1. Robertson, *op. cit.*, Vol. IV, pp. 46, 604.
2. Gal. 4:4; 1 Cor. 11:23-27; 15:3-28; 2 Cor. 4:4-6; Phil. 2:5-11; 3:8-11; Col. 1:15-20; 2:9; 1 Tim. 2:5; Tit. 2:13, 14.
3. Robertson, *op. cit.*, Vol. IV, p. 444.
4. Significant references which set forth the Trinity are: Rom 7:4-6; 8:1-17; 15:15-20, 30; 1 Cor. 2:1-5; 3:9-17; 12:3-12; 2 Cor. 1:18-22; 3:3-6; 5:1-10; 13:14; Gal. 4:4-7; Eph. 2:17-22; 3:14-19; 4:4-6; Col. 1:3-8; Tit. 3:4-6.

CHAPTER VIII

THE NATURE AND FUNCTION OF THE CHURCH

1. Introduction

It is quite essential to discover how the church became crystallized in Paul's thinking, especially in view of his having been brought up in Jerusalem at the feet of Gamaliel, educated according to the strict manner of the law of his fathers and of being zealous for God (Acts 22:3). This change involved a complete revolution in his thinking. We should observe that his concept of the church was at once mature and clear-cut. We do not know what impact Stephen's defense had on Saul who was consenting to Stephen's death, especially on how he reacted to Stephen's words, "This is the Moses who said to the Israelites, 'God will raise up for you a prophet from your brethren as he raised me up.' This is he who was in the congregation [*ekklesia*] in the wilderness with the angel who spoke to him at Mount Sinai" (7:37, 38). Stephen's use of the word *ekklesia* may have struck Paul with fire. He may have reacted with the revulsion, "Does this man, Stephen, mean to say that God has actually raised up the prophet who was in the wilderness congregation, who will be the prophet in a new *ekklesia*"? Without question Paul was one of the "stiff-necked people, uncircumcised in heart and ears" (v. 51).

Stephen's stern rebuke of his hearers undoubtedly angered Saul still more, and especially so when Stephen added that his hearers were those who had betrayed and murdered the Righteous One and by so doing were rejecting the law as delivered by angels. Undoubtedly Saul became still more enraged when Stephen declared, "Behold, I see the heavens opened, and the Son of man standing at the right hand of God" (v. 56). To Saul this was utter blasphemy. Even though he completely rejected Stephen's message and forthwith laid waste the church, he knew what Stephen had said. We may be safe in concluding that Saul knew that the body of believers was recognized as the *church (ekklesia)*. Without question Paul was aware that *ekklesia* occurred in the Septuagint to translate two Hebrew words — *edhah* and *qahal*. According to Richardson, "The translators of the Pentateuch translated both *edhah* and *qahal* by *ekklesia* but later reserved *synagoge* (synagogue) for *edhah* and *ekklesia* for *qahal*. Like *qahal* it is rarely used absolutely in a technical sense but normally with a qualifying genitive 'of the Lord' or 'of Israel,' expressed or understood. The phrase '*ekklesia* of the Lord' acquires the same theological content as Hebrew '*qahal* of Yahweh.'"[1] Saul could not conceive of a new *ekklesia* of which the Son of Man exalted to the right hand of God was the Head in the same way as Yahweh was the Head of the Old Testament *qahal*. To him, the highly educated Pharisee, this was blasphemy. All this accounts for Saul's brutal treatment of these early Christians. Observe Paul's own words in which he described this brutality (Acts 22:3-5; 26:9-11).

It discloses the radical revolution which took place in Saul's mind when the Lord appeared to him on the Damascus road manifesting Himself as the risen and exalted Lord Jesus Christ. When Ananias was sent to Saul, he found him praying. When Ananias laid his hands on Saul, the latter regained his sight and was filled with the Holy Spirit. At once Saul began to testify that Jesus is the Son of God and that He was the Christ and to preach boldly in the name of the Lord (Acts 9:20, 22, 29; 22:6-21; 26:12-21).

When Barnabas became deeply involved in the church at Antioch, he went to Tarsus to enlist Saul in this service. Luke makes the comment, "For a whole year they met with the church, and taught a large company of people; and in Antioch the disciples were for the first time called Christians" (11:25, 26). In a short time the Holy Spirit directed the church at Antioch to set apart Barnabas and Saul (from this point on called Paul) to go out into the Roman Empire on a tour of evangelism.

A study of Paul's sermon at Antioch of Pisidia shows clearly his understanding of the gospel and his comprehension of the church. He had grasped the mission of God's people, Israel, as culminating in the Savior Jesus Christ. Paul declared, "Through this man forgiveness of sins is proclaimed to you, and by him every one that believes is freed from everything from which you could not be freed by the law of Moses" (Acts 13:38, 39). These details of Paul's conversion and the beginning of his Christian ministry serve to show that he did not pass through a long period of development in his comprehension of the church and her mission, but that at once he laid hold of its full meaning. The account of his ministry and public witness in the remainder of the Book of Acts shows that he had become the authoritative spokesman on the church of the Lord Jesus Christ.

2. The Church, the New People of God

With this background relating to Paul's comprehension of the church, it was to be expected that he would instruct these Christian believers concerning the nature of the church and its place under the rule of God. There are at least four contexts in which Paul explicitly set forth these cardinal teachings: 1 Corinthians 3:16, 17; 6:19; 2 Corinthians 6:16-18; Ephesians 2:19-22. He declared that the Christian believers are God's holy temple, and that God's Spirit dwells in them — quoting or reflecting such passages as Leviticus 26:12; Jeremiah 32:38; Ezekiel 37:27; Isaiah 52:11; Ezekiel 20:34, 41; 2 Samuel 7:8, 14; Isaiah 43:6; Jeremiah 31:9; Amos 3:13. Paul set forth the following facets of the church's nature: (1) Believers are the temple of the living God. (2) God will live in them, move among them, and be their God. (3) God declared, "They shall be my people" (Rom. 9:25, 26; 2 Cor. 6:16). Just as Israel were the people of God *(Qahal)* under the old covenant (Lev. 26:12), so the believers have become the new people of God *(ekklesia)* under the new covenant. (4) This covenant relationship with the Lord required a separation from the evil world. To the Ephesians, Paul declared that they were "fellow citizens with the saints and members of the household of God, built upon the foundation of the apostles and prophets" (2:19, 20). Of this structure Christ was the chief cornerstone which, joined together the whole body of believers, and grows into a holy temple in the Lord. In this new holy temple, God dwells in the Spirit (vv. 21, 22). With these foundation truths in mind we are in position to explore further Paul's teachings on the church.

a. Paul's Use of the Word "Church" (ekklesia)

Paul used this word both with reference to the local gathering of God's people[2] and also when referring to the whole body of believers.[3] Undoubtedly this meant a great deal to the scattered groups of believers. In a real way any gathering of believers constituted a church. Thus the entire body of believers throughout the Roman Empire constituted the church of Jesus Christ. All Christian believers constituted one body in Christ. The existence of denominations and sects is a gross violation of this unity.

b. The Close Relation of the Church and the Kingdom of God[4]

Only they who live a life worthy of God are called into His kingdom and glory. Only they who are led by the Spirit will inherit the kingdom of God. On this account Paul instructed the believers to lead lives consistent with their profession. Only faithful believers shall inherit the kingdom of God. In quite definitive language Paul wrote,

"The kingdom of God does not mean food and drink but righteousness and peace and joy in the Holy Spirit; he who thus serves Christ is acceptable to God and approved by men" (Rom. 14:17, 18). When Paul laid bare the sins of the Corinthian Christians, he concluded with the words, "The kingdom of God does not consist in talk but in power" (1 Cor. 4:20). In another setting Paul asked, "Do you not know that the unrighteous will not inherit the kingdom of God? . . . But you were washed, you were sanctified, you were justified in the name of the Lord Jesus Christ and in the Spirit of our God" (6:9-11).

In this manner Paul drew a sharp line between some members of the brotherhood and the righteous. Only those who had the spiritual experience of being washed, sanctified, and justified would inherit the kingdom of God. He brought this truth to a climax in the great resurrection chapter (15) when he noted that those who belong to Christ will share in the resurrection and will be among those of the kingdom which Christ will deliver to the Father (vv. 23, 24). Paul stressed the point that "flesh and blood cannot inherit the kingdom of God, nor does the perishable inherit the imperishable" (v. 50). In this manner the apostle confirmed yet again the idea that membership in the church does not guarantee one's eternal salvation, but being a citizen in the kingdom of God does give assurance of salvation.

To the Ephesians, Paul again stressed the spiritual requirements for sharing in the kingdom in the words, "Be sure of this, that no immoral or impure man, or one who is covetous [that is, an idolator], has any inheritance in the kingdom of Christ and of God" (5:5). He magnified the glory of the church as being the bride of Christ. Just as the husband is the head of the wife so Christ is the Head of the Church, His body. Paul left it to the Ephesians to associate the kingdom of Christ with the church of Christ (5:5, 23, 24).

To the Colossians Paul built up a similar relationship. The present reality of the kingdom stands forth in the words, "He has delivered us from the dominion of darkness and transferred us to the kingdom of his beloved Son" (Col. 1:13). Thus citizenship in Christ's kingdom has its beginning in this world. But since Christ is "the first-born from the dead" (v. 18), all believers have the sure hope of sharing in the eternal kingdom. This most sublimely magnifies the preeminence of Christ. It was worthwhile for him to name those who were his fellow workers for the kingdom of God.

c. Christ, the Head of the Church

Paul's informative note to the Colossians that Christ "has delivered us from the dominion of darkness and transferred us to the kingdom of his beloved Son" (1:13) advanced naturally to his setting forth the preeminence of Christ in the development of this theme. He wrote the significant statement, "He is the head of the body, the church" (v. 18). Expositors have probed into the meaning of this declaration and have given some very helpful explanations. Note the following. Beare wrote that Paul was thinking "of the organism as a whole, deriving its vital powers from the head. . . . For him Christ as head is the unifying principle and the source of life, not only guiding and governing but also vivifying."[5] Bruce wrote, "Christ and His people, that is to say, are viewed together as a living unit; Christ is the head, exercising control and direction; believers are His body, individually His limbs and organs, under His control, obeying His direction, performing His work. And the life which animates the whole is Christ's risen life, which He shares with His people."[6] Taylor wrote, "The name 'the Head' asserts His inseparability from the church, but excludes His identity with it."[7]

Paul himself explained the statement in the words, "The Head, from whom the whole body, nourished and knit together through its joints and ligaments, grows with a growth that is from God" (2:19). In the letter to the Ephesians he made the relationship still clearer in his exhortations to husbands and wives: "For the husband is the head of the wife as Christ is the head of the church, his body, and is himself its Savior" (5:23). Earlier in the letter Paul wrote of Christ's being exalted by the Father, expressed in the words, "He has put all things under his feet and has made him the head over all things for the church, which is his body, the fulness of him who fills all in all" (1:22). Christ's being made the Head of the church bears a close relationship to His being exalted to messianic kingship and His sitting at the right hand of the Father, "far above all rule and authority and power and dominion" (v. 21).

In other contexts Paul centered his thought on the relation of Christ's headship to the church.[8] A study of these references is instructive from the point of view of the church's relation to Christ. Repeatedly, Paul referred to the members of the body in the thought framework of the parts of the physical body. All the members cannot have the same function. Members have different gifts such as prophecy, service, teaching, exhortation, giving aid, and doing acts of mercy (Rom. 12:4-8). In 1 Corinthians 12:4-31 Paul expanded this idea in terms of the varieties of gifts. On the one side, he noted the oneness of the Spirit, the Lord, God, and on the other side, he listed the varieties of gifts of service and of working, all for the common good. He specified further other gifts of the Spirit such as the utterance of wisdom and of knowledge, faith, gifts of healing, working of miracles, prophecy, the ability to distinguish between spirits, various kinds of tongues, and the interpretation of tongues. But then he reminded them, "Just as the body is one and has many members, and all the members of the body, though many, are one body, so it is with Christ" (v. 12). Just as every part of the body is essential to the proper functioning of the body, so it is with the members of the body of Christ. Thus Paul set forth the relation of the church as the body of Christ, and by so doing added to the profound truth of Christ being the Head of the church. No worldly organization begins to have any such dignity as the church. Nor is there any official in human affairs which bears any likeness to Christ, the Head of the church.

d. The Believers Called into the Fellowship of the Son and of the Spirit

It was natural for the apostle to expand the truths centering in the headship of Christ. The keynote to this thought is found in the words, "God is faithful, by whom you were called into the fellowship of his Son, Jesus Christ our Lord" (1 Cor. 1:9). The apostle wrote also of the "participation in the Spirit" (Phil. 2:1). While some difficult problems of syntax are apparent in the uses of *fellowship (koinonia),* I shall pass them by and refer the serious student to Bible dictionaries, lexicons, and commentaries. As used by Paul, the word *koinonia* means the fellowship which Christians experience with Christ, with the Holy Spirit, and with fellow believers. Paul used the word in 1 Corinthians 10:16, "The cup of blessing which we bless, is it not a participation [communion, fellowship, sharing] in the blood of Christ?" On this account Paul could be thankful for the Philippians' "fellowship in furthering the Gospel" (Phil. 1:5, *Berkeley Version).* In the same letter Paul wrote, "That I may know him and the power of his resurrection, and *may share [koinonia]* his sufferings, becoming like him in his death, that if possible I may attain the resurrection from the dead" (3:10, 11). To have fellowship with Christ's sufferings meant to Paul his sharing in Christ's death. This intensified again the intimacy of relation bound up in the word *koinonia.* According to Galatians 2:9, giving the right hand became a symbol of this fellowship. This has become one of the most significant expressions of Christian fellowship.

The ethical aspects of Christian fellowship received significant attention in Paul's stern warning, "Do not be mismated with unbelievers. For what partnership have righteousness and iniquity? Or what *fellowship [koinonia]* has light with darkness? What accord has Christ with Belial? Or what has a believer in common with an unbeliever? What agreement has the temple of God with idols?" (2 Cor. 6:14-16). There are a number of cases where noun or verb forms carry a different sense such as *sharing, contributing, distributing, partaking,* but even in their respective contexts they have the potential of fellowship.[9] In other words, this sharing on the part of Christians with those in need was an expression of this fellowship. Their fellowship with Christ found meaning in their being partakers with others in their needs.

3. Church Life

a. Christian Worship

Paul's contribution to Christian worship built directly on the worship experiences of the body of believers from Pentecost onward. Immediately after Christ's ascension the disciples together with the dedicated women, including the mother of Jesus, and also Jesus' brothers, "with one accord devoted themselves to prayer" (Acts 1:12-14). A few days later Peter stood up among the brethren numbering about 120 and took the initiative to ordain one of their number to take the place of Judas as an apostle. Then at Pentecost when all these believers were together in one place they experienced the outpouring of the Holy Spirit. On this occasion, many devout Jews and proselytes from many parts of the Roman world were present in Jerusalem and heard this body of believers speaking in other tongues. Quite naturally they were bewildered by this experience and then Peter again exercised leadership in explaining to the multitude the meaning of what was taking place.

This great Pentecostal message led the Jewish multitude to a consciousness of a personal spiritual need to which Peter came to their assistance by saying, "Repent, and be baptized every one of you in the name of Jesus Christ for the forgiveness of your sins; and you shall receive the gift of the Holy Spirit" (Acts 2:38). About three thousand Jews responded to this invitation. Luke observed, "They devoted themselves to the apostles' teaching and fellowship, to the breaking of bread and the prayers" (Acts 2:42). All this took place in the precincts of the temple, the center of Jewish worship. These incidents serve as the foundation for the idea that temple worship had come to an end, and that henceforth the true worship of God would center in this body of believers soon to be called the church (Acts 5:11).

This did not mean that the body of Christian believers no longer participated in any activity of temple worship. Rather, Christian worship, that of the church, had no dependence on the temple worship. This new mode of worship centered in Christian fellowship under the guidance of the Holy Spirit (Acts 2:1-13, 37-47; 3:1-16). Their worship and fellowship became evident in the words, "When they had prayed, the place in which they were gathered together was shaken; and they were all filled with the Holy Spirit and spoke the word of God with boldness. Now the company of those who believed were of one heart and soul. . . . And with great power the apostles gave their testimony to the resurrection of the Lord Jesus, and great grace was upon them all" (Acts 4:31-33).

As the number of disciples was constantly increasing, there were widows among them who were in need of support. The twelve apostles summoned the body of disciples and laid before them this problem. The apostles felt that they should not give up preaching the Word of God in order to serve tables. They took the initiative in leading the group in choosing seven of their number and appointing them for this service. This body of disciples assumed the right to guide the church in dealing with specific problems which arose. They performed this service with no consultation with the Jewish authorities. Luke observed, "And the word of God increased; and the number of the disciples multiplied greatly in Jerusalem, and a great many of the priests were obedient to the faith" (Acts 6:7).

It was not long until a sharp schism took place between the church and the Jews. Stephen's defense resulted in this breach. We read, "On that day a great persecution arose against the church in Jerusalem; and they were all scattered throughout the region of Judea and Samaria, except the apostles. . . . But Saul laid waste the church, and entering house after house, he dragged off men and women and committed them to prison" (Acts 8:1-3). This tension gained further stress when Peter in obedience to his heavenly vision led Cornelius a Gentile to faith in Jesus Christ. On Peter's return to Jerusalem, the circumcision party criticised him for not requiring Cornelius to be circumcised (11:1-18). From this it appears that among the Jewish Christians were those who insisted on continuing this practice. Here was a bond between unbelieving Jews and those who had become Christians which was almost impossible to sever. Peter's testimony satisfied them. "And they glorified God, saying, 'Then to the Gentiles also God has granted repentance unto life' " (v. 18).

Paul's first contact with the church after his conversion was with the disciples at Damascus. At once he became an ardent disciple of Christ, and in the synagogue he proclaimed that Jesus is the Son of God. Undoubtedly, Paul gained some concept of the church in his contact with the disciples at Damascus. When he came to Jerusalem, he learned more of the church, even though it was difficult for the disciples to receive him. Perhaps more outstanding in these early contacts with the church was the opposition of the Hellenists to his preaching. Through these experiences he learned what it meant to be a disciple of Christ. With the help of Barnabas, Paul became acquainted with the church at Antioch. Significant to his understanding the nature of the church was his witnessing her concern to send relief to the church in Judea. Accompanying Barnabas on this errand, they went to the church in Jerusalem to deliver this financial aid. This contact with the Jerusalem church undoubtedly enlarged his comprehension of the church and her work. On their return to Antioch they became involved in their worship and fasting. In this atmosphere the Holy Spirit said, "Set apart for me Barnabas and Saul for the work to which I have called them" (Act 13:2). We need to gather that Paul was not merely a learner or observer of the church and her place in the world, but also that the Holy Spirit was illuminating his understanding of Christ's church. I have gone to this length in presenting the foundation of Paul's comprehension of the church so that the teachings in his letters on this theme may become more clearly understood.

Paul's sermon at Antioch of Pisidia showed his comprehension of the gospel as the culmination and climax of God's revelation to His people Israel. He showed how God had directed this history which culminated in bringing to Israel a Savior, Jesus Christ. Through Him has come the message of salvation. This salvation through Christ was the good news which God had promised to the Fathers. Through Christ forgiveness of sins is proclaimed. The writer, Luke, concluded with the words, "As many as were ordained to eternal life believed" (Act 13:48). The writer noted also that "the disciples were filled with joy and with the Holy Spirit" (v. 52). We may conclude that this message had its basis in Paul's mature comprehension of the church.

Another expression which gives further support to this idea becomes evident when Paul and Barnabas returned to Antioch, "strengthening the souls of the disciples, exhorting them to continue in the faith, and saying that through many tribulations we must enter the kingdom of God. And when they had appointed elders for them in every church, with prayer and fasting, they committed them to the Lord in whom they believed" (Acts 14:22, 23). Paul had already learned that the disciples of Christ were suffering tribulations. It becomes evident also that to Paul the church and the kingdom of God sustained a close relationship. Church organization again becomes apparent in the appointment of elders (*presbuteros).* Note also the fundamental element of worship expressed in the words "prayer and fasting" (v. 23).

Paul also shared in enlarging the church functions which became evident in the Jerusalem Council. The Judaizers were continuing their efforts to require circumcision of the Gentile Christians. On this account Paul and Barnabas were sent to Jerusalem to consult with the apostles and elders on this matter. In this council we get a picture of how the church came to grips with vital problems. The question at issue involved much debate. There was the freedom of response on the part of all, but chief among the spokesmen were Peter, Barnabas, Paul, and James. The leadership of the Lord's brother James was evident in his presentation of the solution of the problem. Then the writer, Luke, concluded, "It seemed good to the apostles and the elders, with the whole church, to choose men from among them and send them to Antioch with Paul and Barnabas" (Acts 15:22). With this pattern of church polity, Paul was evidently in perfect harmony. His understanding of this matter received further expression as he and Silas went on their way to the cities where "they delivered to them for observance the decisions which had been reached by the apostles and the elders who were at Jerusalem" (16:4). Thus Paul recognized that the Jerusalem council exercised certain authority over the churches established by Paul on his first missionary journey.

When many of the believers left Jerusalem, they worshiped in the synagogues with the Jews (Acts 9:2, 20; 13:5, 43; 14:1). Naturally they continued to observe the Sabbath day as the day of worship (13:14, 42, 44). The first references to worship on the first day of the week are found in Paul's ministry at Troas (20:7) and in Paul's letter to the Corinthians when he spoke of their making contributions for the saints on the first day of the week (1 Cor. 16:2). These incidents show that the church was gradually coming into its own as a distinct body of worshipers separate from the Jews.

Luke presented another experience of worship at Troas (Acts 20:7-12). As noted above, this worship experience took place on the first day of the week, thus disassociating it from the Jewish day of worship. On this occasion they had come together to break bread. This was likely an observance of the Lord's Supper, but it may have included a full meal. Paul's conversation with the people, lasted all through the night. This lengthy meeting may be quite typical of the early worship services. Likely they were quite informal but evidently they were occasions for spiritual conversation, eating together, observing the Lord's Supper, together with other expressions of Christian fellowship. Undoubtedly, these meetings soon developed into a worship service centering in a message of exhortation or teaching. Paul's message to the elders of the church as recorded in Acts 20:18-35 may give something of a pattern of such exhortation.

Paul used at least four different expressions to set forth the nature of worship. First is *latreuo*, which carries the literal meaning of *work for hire* or *serve*. Naturally, it lent itself to divine service and worship as found in Acts 24:14; 27:23; Romans 1:9; 9:4; 12:1; Philippians 3:3; 2 Timothy 1:3. Thus Paul in his defense before Felix forthrightly declared, "I worship the God of our fathers." To the shipwrecked crew on the way to Rome he declared, "There stood by me an angel of God to whom I belong and whom I worship." This worship was the expression of his faith in God. To the Romans Paul wrote, "For God is my witness, whom I serve with my spirit in the gospel of his Son, that without ceasing I mention you always in my prayers" (Rom. 1:9). Here the verb seems to have the sense of serving, but this act of serving is *en toi pneumati mou* which carries the meaning *with my spirit*, or probably *in my spirit*. This expression appears to reveal the inner character of Christian worship. It was appropriate for Paul to introduce his final appeal to the Romans thus, "Present your bodies as a living sacrifice, holy and acceptable to God, which is your spiritual worship" (Rom. 12:1). Since the expression "spiritual worship" stands in opposition to the purposive infinitive preceding it, the infinitive and its modifiers constitute a meaningful definition of spiritual worship.

Paul used the burnt offering of the Mosaic law as the framework of this statement. Just as an animal in its entirety was burned on the altar, thus symbolizing Israel's being set apart wholly unto God, so Paul exhorted Christian brethren to consecrate themselves as living sacrifices separated (holy) and well pleasing to God. This is the essence of spiritual worship. In similar language Paul described Christian believers, the true circumcision, as those "who worship God in spirit, and glory in Christ Jesus, and put no confidence in the flesh" (Phil. 3:3). The marginal reading, "Worship by the Spirit of God" may express a bit more clearly his thought. In any case the worship of God stands in opposition to the legalistic interpretation of circumcision. Note also that worshiping God in spirit is accompanied by glorying in Christ Jesus. Naturally, this excludes putting any confidence in the flesh. One more example illustrating the meaning of *latreuo* occurs in his second letter to Timothy (1:3). "I thank God whom I serve with a clear conscience, as did my fathers, when I remember you constantly in my prayers." This example may illustrate the serving aspect of *latreuo* but some versions prefer *worship* instead. In this case the relation of the conscience (*suneidesis*) discloses the inner nature of worship. Here the inner consciousness of things right or wrong prompts the individual to do the right, which may be defiled by sin and thus may lead to wrong actions. It is restricted by the term *clear* or perhaps more accurately *pure (katharos.)* In other words Paul was telling Timothy that true worship of

God springs alone from an honest commitment to God. In this way could Paul's prayers for Timothy be efficacious.

The second word used by Paul for worship is the verb *proskuneo*. Since he used this word in the same context as *latreuo* in his defense before Felix, we may gather that the two words are practically synonymous. Paul said, "I went up to worship at Jerusalem" (Acts 24:11). This verb was "used to designate the custom of prostrating one's self before a person and kissing his feet, the hem of his garment, the ground, etc."[10] In Paul's discussion of the various spiritual gifts in 1 Corinthians 14 he noted that through the workings of the Spirit the secrets of an individual's heart are disclosed. "And so falling on his face, he will worship God and declare that God is really among you" (v. 25). Here Paul definitely expressed having seen this thing happen to worshipers, which is practically the literal rendering of *proskuneo*. At this point Paul amplified the essence of this worship by saying, "Each one has a hymn, a lesson, a revelation, a tongue, or an interpretation." Then he adds, "Let all things be done for edification" (or *upbuilding*). From this we would gather that a certain spontaneity characterized Christian worship and yet Paul injected a certain guideline, namely, that all things should contribute to building up the church.

A third insight as to the nature of worship comes to us in Paul's letter to the Philippians in which he referred to the gifts sent to him from this church. He described these gifts as "a fragrant offering, a sacrifice acceptable and pleasing to God" (4:18). Here is a description of worship cast in metaphorical language drawn from the Old Testament in the description of the burnt offerings (Lev. 1:3-9; 3:1-5; Num. 28:16-25). The Lord spoke of the burnt offering as "a pleasing odor to the Lord" (Lev. 1:9). With this background we can understand Paul's explanation of the gifts sent him as an act of worship typified by the Old Testament offerings. The significance of this mode of describing worship ascended to the highest conceivable level of meaning in Paul's words to the Ephesians, "And walk in love, as Christ loved us and gave himself up for us, a fragrant offering and sacrifice to God" (5:2). He drew in yet another Old Testament symbol of worship, "If I am to be poured as a libation upon the sacrificial offering of your faith, I am glad and rejoice with you all" (Phil. 2:17). This being poured out as a *libation (spendomai)* came very near to fulfillment when he wrote, "I am already on the point of being sacrificed" (2 Tim. 4:6). His use of the same verb in this statement confirms his interpretation of his coming martyrdom. His reference to being poured out as a libation builds on the Mosaic sacrificial system.[11] The drink offering or libation regularly followed a bloody sacrifice. All the bloody sacrifices bore some relation to making atonement for sin. The sin and trespass offerings related especially to expiation while burnt offerings symbolized the offerer's setting himself apart or consecration to God. In the case of the peace offering the offerer's sacrifice symbolized the resulting peace and blessedness which he had come to experience. The libation or drink offerings, according to Daniel Steele, were "the joyous emblems of conscious salvation through the atonement. Wine is a symbol of joy."[12] Adding this sacrifice to the bloody offering became "a pleasing odor to the Lord" (Num. 15:7).

According to this Old Testament background Paul was anticipating his coming martyrdom, interpreting it as the culminating act of the Philippians' faith expressed in Old Testament sacrificial terminology. For just as Israel expressed their faith in God through sacrificial offerings, which were completed through drink offerings, so the Philippians' faith in the sacrificial work of Christ could view Paul's martyrdom as a libation which completed Christ's redemptive sacrifice, and so, to paraphrase his words to Timothy, "I am now being poured out [being offered as a libation] through the shedding of his own blood" (2 Tim. 4:6). The contribution of this metaphorical language to Paul's presentation of worship is significant. The faith of the Philippians reached its climax in the joy and satisfaction gained through their personal relation to Christ. To repeat Paul's words, "I am glad and rejoice with you all. Likewise, you also should be glad and rejoice with me" (Phil. 2: 17, 18).

In concluding this discussion on Christian worship let us note some directives for worship given by Paul: "Be filled with the Spirit, addressing one another in psalms and hymns and spiritual songs, singing and making melody to the Lord with all your heart, always and for everything giving thanks in the name of our Lord Jesus Christ, to God the Father" (Eph. 5:18-20). To the Colossians he wrote, "And be thankful. Let the word of Christ dwell in you richly, as you teach and admonish one another in all wisdom, and as you sing psalms and hymns and spiritual songs with thankfulness in your hearts to God. And whatever you do, in word or deed, do everything in the name of the Lord Jesus, giving thanks to God the Father through him" (3:15-17). This leads to other related experiences with prayer, such as, fasting, thanksgiving, supplication, and intercession in prayer.[13] These several facets of worship disclose the intimate, personal relationship of Christians with the Lord Jesus Christ and God the Father. This truth becomes real in some additional statements from the pen of Paul (Rom. 8:26, 27; 12:12; Eph. 6:18; 1 Tim. 5:5). To the Romans, Paul noted the involvement of the Holy Spirit in the Christian's prayer life by using three forceful expressions: "the Spirit helps us" (*sunantilambanomai*), having the literal meaning, *to take hold, with, at the side, for assistance;* "the Spirit himself intercedes for us" (*huperentugxano*), which means *to plead, intercede, make petition*; and "with sighs too deep for words" (*stenagmos*) which means *sigh, groan,* this intensified by *alaletos (inexpressible).* The verbs used above by reason of their compound form possess emphatic and intensified meaning, typically Pauline in style. In his letter to the Ephesians, Paul also expressed in pertinent language the experiential aspect of prayer when he wrote, "Pray at all times in the Spirit, with all prayer and supplication" (6:18). This describes explicitly the involvement of the Spirit in the prayers of Christians. To Timothy, Paul expressed the prayer life of devout widows in the words, "She . . . continues in supplications and prayers night and day" (1 Tim. 5:5).

By reason of this personal aspect of prayer, it was natural for Paul to lay special stress on the meaning, privilege, and responsibility of Christians being involved in intercessory prayer.[14] A study of these examples of intercessory prayer is instructive from a number of points of view. First, the Christian's privilege and responsibility of praying for each other; second, the efficacy of prayer; third, the wide scope of prayer concerns; and fourth, the intimacy of the spiritual relations between the one who prays and God. Also, prayer is a measure of the believer's comprehension of spiritual values. As illustrated in the prayers recorded in the letter to the Ephesians, only a person of Paul's spiritual caliber could utter prayers such as these. In bringing this discussion of prayer to conclusion, let us note also the urgency, priority, and spiritual prerequisites of prayer.[15] Briefly expressed, Paul wrote, "You also must help us by prayer," and "I urge you that supplications, prayers, intercessions, and thankgiving be made for all men."

b. Symbols of Christian Worship

(1) Water Baptism. Perhaps the most significant way in which to introduce Paul's teaching on baptism, the Lord's Supper, the prayer veiling for women, and the holy kiss is to regard them as symbols of Christian worship. With the background of Jesus' teaching on baptism at the Lord's Supper, as well as His recognition of the kiss as an expression of love, it is natural that Paul would unfold further their meaning.

In Luke's report of Paul's conversion experience (Acts 9:17-19), he brought Paul's experience of being filled with the Holy Spirit and his water baptism into close relationship, from which it would appear that Luke understood water baptism as symbolizing Paul's being filled with the Holy Spirit. As Paul recounted this experience he noted the words of Ananias, "Be baptized, and wash away your sins, calling on his name" (22:16). This suggests that the act of being baptized symbolized the washing away of his sins. This leads to the significant teaching of the apostle relating to baptism (Rom. 6:1-11; Col. 2:11-15). In the letter to the Romans, Paul advanced from his teaching on justification by faith to the bearing of this experience on one's manner of life. He asked, "How can we who died to sin still live in it?" He proceeded to show that all who had been baptized into Christ Jesus were baptized in His death. They were buried with Him by baptism into death. In this manner Paul proceeded to set forth the meaning of this symbol. Paul found in Christ's death, burial, and resurrection the archtype of Christian's baptism. He himself who had been baptized into Christ Jesus had experienced a corresponding death to sin and resurrection to a walk in newness of life. He would have his readers understand that they who have been united with Christ in a death like His "shall certainly be united with him in a resurrection like his."

In the letter to the Colossians, Paul presented the same truth in a slightly different setting. He introduced Christian baptism by noting that the Colossians had come to fullness of life in Christ. He then laid hold of the symbolic, as well as the typical meaning of circumcision by noting that in Christ they "were circumcised with a circumcision made without hands, by putting off the body of flesh in the circumcision of Christ" (2:11). By this he was declaring that Christ's literal circumcision was the type of His crucifixion. The spiritual significance of circumcision in the Old Testament stands forth in the words, "And the Lord your God will circumcise your heart and the heart of the offspring, so that you will love the Lord your God and with all your heart and with all your soul, that you may live" (Deut. 30:6).

With this background of Old Testament teaching Paul found in water baptism a symbol of the believer's being buried with Christ and of being raised with Christ through faith in the working of God. To this he added, "You, who were dead in trespasses and the uncircumcision of the flesh, God made alive together with him, having forgiven us all our trespasses, having canceled the bond which stood against us with its legal demands; this he set aside, nailing it to the cross" (Col. 2:13, 14). All this gives great depths of meaning to the significance of water baptism. In a word, he who is being baptized is identifying himself with Christ in His death, burial, and resurrection. For the believer also, by this symbol, is dying to sin and being raised to newness of life.

These contexts may have some bearing on the mode of baptism. While many Bible scholars conclude that Paul's language explicitly sets forth immersion as the mode of baptism, I have come to believe that Paul did not express his thought through the imagery of immersion, but rather that of symbolizing our identification with Christ in His death, burial, and resurrection. This finds support in the references to baptism in the Book of Acts, as well as in Paul's letters.[16] Paul's significant words in 1 Corinthians 6:11 may refer to baptism, "You were washed, you were sanctified, you were justified in the name of the Lord Jesus Christ and in the Spirit of our God." The aorist form of each of these verbs gives grounds for believing that Paul is referring to their conversion experience. It is significant that *apelousasphe (were washed)* is the aorist middle voice in contrast with the aorist passive forms of the other two verbs. Hence it carries the meaning, "You washed yourselves" or "You washed your sins away." Robertson adds the comment, "This was their own voluntary act in baptism which was the outward expression of the previous act of God in cleansing . . . and justified. . . . The outward expression is usually mentioned before the inward change which precedes it. In this passage the Trinity appears as in the baptismal command in Matthew 28:19."[17] This verse bears some relation to the Great Commission (Mt. 28:19), which may add weight to interpreting "were washed" as referring to baptism. It should be further noted that the aorist form of these verbs gives grounds for the acts of being washed, sanctified, and justified, as being simultaneous. On this account the punctiliar acts of being sanctified and justified intensify to a superlative degree the meaning of "were washed."

In 1 Corinthians 10:1-5 Paul used the expression which illuminates the meaning of baptism. He wrote, "Our fathers were all under the cloud, and all passed through the sea, and all were baptized into Moses in the cloud and in the sea." This incident vividly portrays an intimate relation of Israel to Moses as expressed by the words "were baptized into Moses." So closely were the people associated with Moses that no difference could be made between his experiences and theirs. This thought is enriched by noting that they shared with Moses the same supernatural food and drink. The phrase "into [eis] Moses" should help us understand the similar phrase, "baptized into Christ Jesus" (Rom. 6:3).

Paul gave another definitive expression in Galatians 3:26-29, "For in Christ Jesus you are all sons of God, through faith. For as many of you as were baptized into Christ have put on Christ. . . . You are all one in Christ Jesus. And if you are Christ's, then you are Abraham's offspring, heirs according to promise." The verb *enedusasthe (put on)* was commonly used in the sense of clothing one's self or putting on garments. Paul expressed this truth elsewhere in the words, "Let us then cast off the works of darkness and put on the armor of light; let us conduct ourselves becomingly as in the day, not in reveling and drunkenness, not in debauchery and licentiousness, not in quarreling and jealousy. But put on the Lord Jesus Christ, and make no provision for the flesh, to gratify its desires" (Rom. 13:12-14). Walter F. Adeney gave the explanation, "As the garment covers the person and is closely wrapped about him, so Christ is thought of as closely united to His people and giving them their characteristic appearance."[18]

Finally, it is essential to observe that the apostle noted that there is one baptism (Eph. 4:5). The context of this expression (vv. 1-6) is one of the most profound teachings of Paul. Note its setting: "Eager to maintain the unity of the Spirit in the bond of peace. There is one body and one Spirit, just as you were called to the one hope that belongs to your call, one Lord, one faith, one baptism, one God and Father of us all, who is above all and through all and in all" (vv. 3-6). The most essential truths set forth in this context include the definite assertion of monotheism and at the same time of the Trinity. This gives immeasurable significance to the one hope, one faith, and one baptism. Baptism is one because Christ alone instituted it. Paul made it clear to the Corinthians that they were baptized, not in his own name, but in the name of Jesus Christ (1 Cor. 1:12-17). Thus baptism is distinctive of the Christian faith, having been instituted by Christ Himself (Mt. 28:18-20).

(2) The Lord's Supper. The second symbol of Christian worship set forth by Paul was the Lord's Supper (1 Cor. 10:14-22; 11:20-34). In order to comprehend Paul's teaching on the Lord's Supper it is essential to grasp the significance of 10:1-13 which serves as an unusual introduction to this teaching. Without any stated purpose Paul referred to Israel's redemption out of Egypt. "All were baptized into Moses in the cloud and in the sea, and all ate the same supernatural food and all drank the same supernatural drink." Then by way of interpretation he added, "For they drank from the supernatural Rock which followed them, and the Rock was Christ" (vv. 2-4). This rich type of water baptism, noted above, in a typical manner foreshadowed the supernatural food and the supernatural drink and thus the broken body and shed blood of Christ. For our understanding of both water baptism and the Lord's Supper it is pertinent that we grasp Paul's meaningful words. His reference to the food and the drink supplied to Israel was undoubtedly to the manna and the water which came from the rock, both given to Israel as a miraculous demonstration of God's power and care for His people.

Christ's explanation of the supernatural food given to Israel (Jn. 6: 25-59) makes it clear that this food typified Christ Himself, "It was not Moses who gave you the bread from heaven; my Father gives you the true bread from heaven" (v. 32). And at the close of this discourse He added, "I am the living bread which came down from heaven; if any one eats of this bread, he will live forever; and the bread which I shall give for the life of the world is my flesh" (v. 51). To the disputing Jews, Jesus added, "For my flesh is food indeed, and my blood is drink indeed. He who eats my flesh and drinks my blood abides in me, and I in him. . . . This is the bread which came down from heaven, not such as the fathers ate and died; he who eats this bread will live forever" (vv. 55-58).

Paul had noted that Israel's experiences in the wilderness serve as warnings to Christians so that they should not become idolaters by following the ways of Israel. In most emphatic language Paul continued, "Therefore [*dioper on which very account, from which very reason*] . . . shun the worship of idols" (1 Cor. 10:14). Then he asks, "The cup of blessing which we bless, is it not a participation in the blood of Christ? The bread which we break, is it not a participation in the body of Christ? Because there is one loaf, we who are many are one body, for we all partake of the same loaf" (vv. 16, 17). The key word here is *koinonia (fellowship, communion, close relationship)*, a word which deserves very careful study.[19] Thus in a positive way the cup of blessing is a fellowship in the blood of Christ and the bread a participation in the body of Christ. In the deepest spiritual manner the Christian shares in the death of Christ. It is a sharing in Christ's sufferings and a becoming like Him in His death (Phil. 3:10). The partaking of the Lord's Supper becomes the symbol of the Christian's sharing in the suffering and death of Christ.

Paul set forth another central teaching by noting the oneness of the church as one body. Every believer partakes of the loaf and by so doing becomes a partner with Christ. This fellowship at the table of the Lord allows no partnership with demons. The cup of the Lord absolutely excludes the cup of demons. For this reason Paul gave additional warning against the desecration of the Lord's Supper. The divisions among the Corinthians were a disqualification for eating the Lord's Supper. In confirmation of this verdict Paul quoted the words of Jesus, "This is my body which is for you" (1 Cor. 11:24). This was similar to the expression, "This cup is the new covenant in my blood" which is the strongest metaphor conceivable. Since Jesus spoke these words personally with the disciples, it is sound exegesis to conclude that His statement was a metaphor and not a literal identification of Himself with the bread and the wine.

By reason of the fact that the Christian church differs so widely in the interpretation of this passage, it may be in order to give a few additional words of explanation. It is apparent that the verb *to be* is the common verb which identifies the subject and the predicate noun. English syntax also recognizes a meaning less than that of identification by interpreting the verb as asserting the most significant characteristic of its subject. Less significant uses of this verb include mere descriptions or likenesses of the predicate noun with its subject. By reason of the greatest possible significance of Jesus' words, there is the corresponding need to interpret accurately the words of Jesus.

"This cup is the new covenant in my blood. Do this, as often as you drink it, in remembrance of me" (1 Cor. 11:25). These words of Jesus quoted by Paul introduced another central idea of the Lord's Supper but which is closely related to the apostle's teachings already noted. Observe again that Paul found significant meaning in Israel's wilderness experiences under the leadership of Moses, noting especially their being fed with manna and drinking from water supplied to them miraculously. Paul found in these experiences the foreshadowing or type of something of far greater meaning in the Lord's Supper. This becomes apparent in Jesus' words, "the new covenant." In this manner Jesus had declared the relation of the new covenant to that instituted by God with Israel through Moses (Ex. 19:5, 6; 24:3-8). When the Lord drew Israel into a covenant relationship, the people became God's own possession. In all reality they were then a kingdom of priests and a holy nation. This covenant became effective through the blood and peace offerings sacrificed by Moses in behalf of the people. These offerings symbolized the people of Israel setting themselves apart unto the Lord with the accompanying experience of fellowship with God. When Moses read the book of the covenant to the people, they solemnly responded, "All that the Lord has spoken we will do, and we will be obedient" (Ex. 24:7).

On this covenant foundation Jesus structured the idea of the new covenant. The word *new* gave attestation to the qualitatively, infinite superiority of this covenant over that instituted at Mount Sinai. This becomes apparent in the same qualitative difference between Jesus' blood through which the new covenant was instituted and the blood of the oxen through which the covenant at Mount Sinai was established. In the shedding of Jesus' blood alone lies the efficacy for the forgiveness of sins. All this contributes to our understanding of the Lord's Supper, in the words of Paul, "As often as you eat this bread and drink the cup, you proclaim the Lord's death until he comes" (1 Cor. 11:25). Through this declaration, Paul was affirming the abiding and eternal value of the new covenant. All the hope of believers which center in this covenant will come to full realization at the Lord's return. Thus Paul added the strong exhortation to eat the bread and drink the cup of the Lord only in a worthy manner. This calls for self-examination; for otherwise one would be eating and drinking without discerning the meaning of the bread and the wine.

We should now note how closely related baptism and the Lord's Supper become in the total experience of Christian worship: the former standing as the great punctiliar experience of being baptized into Christ and of being raised to newness of life and the latter finding expression in the linear experience of repeatedly eating the bread and drinking the cup through which Christians proclaim the Lord's death until He comes. Through these symbols the new covenant becomes definitely experiental to Christians.

(3) The Holy Kiss. A third symbol of Christian worship becomes apparent in Paul's command, "Greet one another with a holy kiss" (Rom. 16:16; 1 Cor. 16:20; 2 Cor. 13:12; 1 Thess. 5:26). The Old Testament background to the holy kiss shows how a common practice can be sanctified and raised to the high level given to it by Paul.[20] The kiss was used by relatives such as the patriarchs, Moses, Aaron, David, and Elisha;[21] of friendship and affection as between David and Jonathan (1 Sam. 20:41); of love (Song of Solomon 1:2); and other social classes including idolatrous practices. Undoubtedly the most significant example shines forth in the words, "Steadfast love and faithfulness will meet; righteousness and peace will kiss each other" (Ps. 85:10). Significant New Testament uses found in the Gospels and Acts include the case of the woman who kissed the feet of Jesus (Lk. 7:38, 45), the father's greeting the returning prodigal (Lk. 15:20), and the Ephesian Christians' farewell to Paul (Acts 20:37). It was entirely natural that Paul should raise the kiss to the high spiritual level connoted by "*holy* kiss." In this manner *holy kiss* appropriately signifies the fellowship of Christians one with another. It stands in direct antagonism to its erotic use and exalts the relationship of friendship to the highest spiritual level connoted by the word *holy*. All this has a very definite bearing on Christian worship. Only on the basis of Christian love can the body of believers, the church, involve themselves in worship. This thought becomes greatly enriched by observing the setting of Paul's exhortation regarding the *holy kiss*. In Romans 16, twenty times he gave specific requests to the Roman church that they greet twenty or more individuals and households living among them and concluded his requests by stating, "Greet one another with a holy kiss. All the churches of Christ greet you" (v. 16). He also listed eight of his fellow companions and workers who sent their greetings to the Roman church. This is a beautiful picture of Christian fellowship and shows how this intimate relationship enriches worship.

For Additional Reading and Reference:

Beyschlag, *New Testament Theology,* Vol. II, pp. 229-254.
Bowman, *Prophetic Realism and the Gospel,* pp. 258-269.
Bruce, A.B., *St. Paul's Conception of Christianity,* pp. 362-378.
Conzelmann, *An Outline of the Theology of the New Testament,* pp. 254-274.
Hunter, *Interpreting Paul's Gospel,* pp. 99-106.
Newman, *The Meaning of the New Testament,* pp. 214-255.
Rall, *According to Paul,* pp. 149-165.
Richardson, *An Introduction to the Theology of the New Testament,* pp. 266-387.
Robinson, *Biblical Doctrine of the Church,* pp. 55-74.
Ryrie, *Biblical Theology of the Old Testament,* pp. 188-202.
Schweizer, *Church Order in the New Testament.* pp. 89-116.
Scott, *Christianity According to St. Paul,* pp. 181-196.
Sheldon, *New Testament Theology,* pp. 252-258.
Stevens, *The Pauline Theology,* pp. 319-338.
Stevens, *The Theology of the New Testament,* pp. 458-469.
Van Oosterzee, *The Theology of the New Testament,* pp. 286-293.
Wahlstrom, *The New Life in Christ,* pp. 224-257.
Weidner, *Biblical Theology of the New Testament,* Vol. II, pp. 167-173.
Weiss, *Biblical Theology of the New Testament,* Vol. II, pp. 29-52, 125-149.
Whiteley, *The Theology of St. Paul,* pp. 186-204.

1. *A Theological Word Book of the Bible* (New York: The Macmillan Co., 1955), p. 47.
2. 1 Thess. 1:1; 2:14; Rom. 16:5; 1 Cor. 1:2; Gal. 1:2; etc.
3. 1 Cor. 10:32; 12:28; 15:9; Gal. 1:13; Eph. 1:22; 3:10, 21.
4. 1 Thess. 2:12; 2 Thess. 1:4, 5; Gal. 5:21; Rom. 14:17; 1 Cor. 4:17-20; 6:4-11; 15:9, 24, 50; Eph. 5:5, 23-32; Col. 1:13-18; 4:11.
5. *The Interpreter's Bible, Vol. XI, The Epistle to the Colossians* (New York: Abingdon Press, 1952), p. 169.
6. *The New International Commentary on the New Testament. Commentary on the Epistles to the Ephesians and the Colossians* (Grand Rapids: Wm. B. Eerdmans Publishing Co., 1957), p. 201.
7. Quoted by Moule in *Cambridge Greek Testament Commentary, The Epistle of Paul the Apostle to the Colossians and to Philemon* (Cambridge: University Press, 1962), p. 68.
8. Rom. 12:4, 5; 1 Cor. 11:3; 12:12, 13, 27; Eph. 4:11-16; Col. 2:19.
9. Rom. 12:13; 15:27; 2 Cor. 8:4; 9:13; Gal. 6:6; Phil. 4:15; 1 Tim. 5:22.
10. William F. Arndt and F. Wilbur Gingrich, *A Greek-English Lexicon of the New Testament and Other Early Christian Literature* (Chicago: University of Chicago Press, 1957), p. 723.
11. See Ex. 25:29; 29:40, 41; Lev. 23:13, 18, 37; Num. 6:15-17; 15:5-7; 28:7.
12. *Commentary of the Old Testament* (New York: Hunt and Eaton, 1891), Vol. II, p. 312.
13. Acts 13:2, 3; 14:23; 16:25; 27:35; Phil. 4:6; 1 Thess. 1, 2; 5:17, 18; 1 Tim. 2:1, 2.
14. Rom. 1:9; 10:1; 15:30-32; 2 Cor. 9:14; 13:7-9; Eph. 1:16-23; 3:14-19; Phil. 1:4, 5, 9-11; Col. 1:3, 9-18; 4:2-4, 12; 1 Thess. 5:25; 2 Thess. 1:11, 12; 3:1, 2; 1 Tim. 2:1.
15. Acts 9:11; 20:36; 1 Cor. 7:5; 2 Cor. 1:11; 1 Tim. 2:1-8.
16. Acts 9:18; 13:24; 16:15, 33; 18:8; 19:3-5; 22:16; 1 Cor. 1:14-17; 12:13; Gal. 3:27; Eph. 4:5.
17. Robertson, *op. cit.*, "The Epistles of Paul," p. 120.
18. Walter F. Adeney, General Editor, *The Century Bible, Thessalonians and Galatians,* edited by Walter F. Adeney (Edinburgh: T. C. and E. C. Jack), p. 304.
19. Consult the words *fellowship* and *communion* in Bible dictionaries and encyclopedias. For a simple but informative discussion see Wick Broomall, *Baker's Dictionary of Theology,* article, "Fellowship," pp. 218-220. For fuller comments see Anderson Scott, *Christianity According to St. Paul,* pp. 158-169.
20. See W. L. Walker, *The International Bible Encyclopaedia* (Chicago: The Howard-Severance Co., 1930), Vol, III, pp. 1813 D, 1814; article, "Kiss."
21. Gen. 27:26, 27; 45:15; Ex. 4:27; Ruth 1:9, 14; 1 Kings 19:20; etc.

CHAPTER IX

PAUL'S TEACHINGS ON THE HOLY SCRIPTURES

A study of Paul's theology naturally involves his view of the Holy Scriptures. This also leads to a consideration of his attitude toward his preaching ministry and also to his view of the authoritative character of his own writings. This becomes quite basic to the rise of the new body of writings which came to be known as the New Testament. Since the Old Testament had been a completed book for at least four centuries, it becomes apparent that adequate grounds for adding a new body of writings to the completed Old Testament would require adequate proof in support of their being Holy Scriptures. Most fundamental to this discussion is the question as to whether or not Paul visualized a new body of sacred writings, and whether his own letters would possess the authoritative character of the Old Testament.

1. Paul's View of the Old Testament Scriptures

Paul's sermon at Antioch (Acts 13:16-41) gives a splendid introduction to his view of the Scriptures. Being present in the synagogue on the Sabbath day and having heard the reading of the law and the prophets, he was invited by the rulers of the synagogue to give words of edification to the people. Paul responded by giving a brief account of Israel's history from the time of their deliverance from Egypt until the kingship of David. He then declared that God had brought to Israel the Savior, Jesus, who was the descendant of David. Paul's message of salvation centered in the redemptive work of Jesus. He then gave some statements which showed his view of the Scriptures, noting that the Scriptures were the writing of the prophets. He then added that all the prophetic predictions had been fulfilled. Perhaps the most significant among these predictions related to the raising of Jesus as recorded in Psalm 2. He introduced this quotation with the words, "It is written" (v. 33). This is an expression used approximately forty times in Paul's messages and letters.

On this account it is essential to understand the distinctive meaning which it possessed for him. With a concordance in hand one soon discovers that this mode of reference to the Old Testament evaluated this body of writings as being the authoritative Word of God. The perfect passive form of the verb possesses the meaning *it stands written,* and carries the idea that the Old Testament was a complete Book and constituted the body of writings which very properly were to be understood as "the Word of God."[1] Cremer gives the sense of this perfect passive form *(it is written)* as follows, "In the sphere of revelation the written records hold this authoritative position, and *gegraptai* always implies an appeal to the indisputable and normative authority of the passage quoted.[2] In this discussion of Paul's teachings on the Holy Scriptures it is essential to give careful consideration to every teaching for which he gives the support, "It is written." In this message at Antioch Paul also declared the vast superiority and efficacy of Jesus' teachings over that of the law of Moses. He drew attention to lack of dynamic of the law of Moses in that it was not able to make atonement for sin nor to make possible forgiveness of sins. Herein the immeasurable superiority of the gospel stood forth as over that of the Mosaic law in which the Jews trusted. This fact does not nullify the innumerable spiritual values of the Old Testament on which Paul based the great body of his teachings, both in his preaching and in his letters. The pursuit of this inquiry becomes basic to our understanding the relation of the New Testament to the Old, which body of writings had not yet come into existence. The bearing of these facts upon the unfolding revelation, which is the chief motif of biblical theology, calls for intensive study.

Paul's view of the Scriptures became apparent also in his references to both the law and the prophets (Acts 24:14; 26:22; 28:23; Rom. 3:21). These references focalize in a general way on the entire record of the Old Testament.

Paul's view of the Old Testament Scriptures gains greater significance in view of the extended discussions in his letters for which he finds support in the teachings of the Old Testament. As an example, he underlined the legalism of the Galatians by showing that the New Testament teaching on justification by faith had its basis in the Old Testament, specifically in the case of Abraham (Gal. 3:6-18; Rom. 4). Nevertheless, Paul recognized the true function of the law which becomes evident in the words, "We know that whatever the law says it speaks to those who are under the law, so that every mouth may be stopped, and the whole world may be held accountable to God" (Rom. 3:19). He proceeded, however, to declare the inadequacy of mere obedience to the law when he added, "For no human being will be justified in his sight by works of the law, since through the law comes knowledge of sin" (Rom. 3:19, 20). The closing benediction of this letter contributes further to this idea in the words, "Now to him who is able to strengthen you according to my gospel and the preaching of Jesus

Christ, according to the revelation of the mystery which was kept secret for long ages but is now disclosed and through the prophetic writings is made known to all nations, according to the command of the eternal God, to bring about obedience to the faith" (16:25, 26). In a word, Paul viewed the prophetic writings as having revealed beforehand the gospel of Jesus Christ.

Paul's final witness to his view of the Old Testament Scriptures stands forth in the words, "You have been acquainted with the sacred writings which are able to instruct you for salvation through faith in Christ Jesus. All scripture is inspired by God and profitable for teaching, for reproof, for correction, and for training in righteousness, that the man of God may be complete, equipped for every good work" (2 Tim. 3:15-17). The title *the sacred writings* is equivalent to Paul's other expression "*the holy scriptures*" (Rom. 1:2) as used in relation to Israel's religion. *Hagios* means *holy, sacred,* thus Israel was a holy people. Their temple was holy, and supremely, God is holy. So when Paul applied this word to the Scriptures, it at once elevated this body of writings to the highest plane of dignity and authority. The adjective *hieros* also carries the sense *holy*. The noun form *hieron* is translated *sanctuary, temple*. Everything belonging to the temple and its service was holy. Paul gave the foundation for this truth when he wrote, "All scripture is inspired by God." This most definitive language pertaining to the nature of the written Word asserts the fact that God is the Source of the written Word, which includes the idea of deity nature and authority. The expression *theopneustos,* according to Greek lexicons, means *God-breathed, prompted by God,* or *God-inspired*. This meaning becomes accentuated by Paul's additional words quoted above. By adding to this what he said concerning the *sacred writings,* the profound nature of the Holy Scriptures becomes still clearer. Undoubtedly, Paul was writing out of his own comprehension of these distinctive qualities. Supported by his use of these writings in his gospel ministry, as well as in his own writing, it becomes evident that Paul based his authoritative teaching on these inspired Scriptures. These messages and writings also included many distinctive functions of the Scriptures. A presentation of these two aspects of his teaching will now receive consideration.

2. The Scriptures, the Basis of Paul's Authoritative Teaching

It is noteworthy that Paul quoted the Old Testament more than 90 times, and made allusions to it about 120 times.[3] Let us note some of the most significant examples in which Paul based his authoritative teaching on the Old Testament Scriptures. Perhaps the most significant case is that of Romans 1:16, 17, where in most definitive language Paul set forth the meaning of the gospel, which becomes the major theme of this letter. He notes, "It is the power of God for salvation to every one who has faith, to the Jew first and also to the Greek. For in it the righteousness of God is revealed through faith for faith; as it is written, 'He who through faith is righteous shall live.' " Thus the heart of the gospel had already shone forth in the prophetic writing of Habakkuk (2:4). When Habakkuk wrote these words spoken to him by the Lord, he may not have realized their full meaning, but he did close his book with the significant expression, "I will joy in the God of my salvation" (3:18). In Romans 3:9-18 Paul brought the severest indictment against all mankind, both Jews and Greeks, declaring that they "are under the power of sin." In proof of this he gave six quotations from the Psalms and Isaiah. Realistically, Paul would not have dared to declare that all men are under the power of sin, in view of both Jews and Greeks, particularly of the Pharisees. On this account Paul based his declaration on the body of writings regarded by the Jews as the authoritative Holy Scriptures.

In chapter 4, Paul threw another nuclear bomb against the tradition of the Pharisees, which devastated their belief in Abraham's being justified by works. Quoting from Genesis, the great book of the law, Paul wrote, "Abraham believed God, and it was reckoned to him as righteousness" (v. 3). How the pharisaical Jews could bypass this great teaching which declared that their foremost Patriarch, Abraham, experienced the reckoning of his faith to him as righteousness, lies beyond our comprehension. On this account Paul went to the length of devoting chapter 4, and in fact, chapters 5 to 8 to an explication of this great truth.

This led Paul to another apparently inexplicable problem centering in God's purpose of election and calling as related to the Gentiles (Rom. 9—11). He was seeking to solve a difficult problem for his readers. They thought that this doctrine proves injustice on God's part. This was a very complicated problem but Paul sought to explain it on the basis of the Scriptures. In a forthright manner he set forth the scriptural basis of election in the words, "Through Isaac shall your descendants be named" (9:7). He proceeded to show that election did not have its basis in works but in God's call. In support of this Paul gave two quotations "The elder will serve the younger," and "Jacob I loved, but Esau I hated" (vv. 12, 13). As Paul moved step by step in solving this almost unexplainable mystery, he continued to quote Old Testament Scriptures in support of his teaching. He concluded his solution to these problems with the exclamation, "O the depth of the riches and wisdom and knowledge of God! How unsearchable are his judgments and how inscrutable his ways!" Then he added a final quotation, part of which reads, "For who has known the mind of the Lord, or who has been his counselor?" (11:33, 34). Briefly stated, Paul found the solution to the exceedingly intricate problem of election and calling on the basis of the Holy Scriptures. Near the close of his letter he quoted four significant Old Testament passages in support of the truth that Christ became a servant "in order that the Gentiles might glorify God for his mercy" (15:8-12).

In the letter to the Galatians, Paul refuted the legalism of the Galatian Christians in the same manner in which he set forth the Old Testament teaching of justification by faith in his letter to the Romans. In the former letter, however, he was dealing with a highly controversial issue. These Christians had become addicted to the pharisaical teachings to the effect that one obtains right standing with God by keeping the law. But in this letter to the Romans Paul quoted from Genesis the declaration that "Abraham believed God, and it was reckoned to him as righteousness" (Rom. 4:3; Gal. 3:6). On this scriptural basis Paul added, "So you see that it is men of faith who are the sons of Abraham. And the scripture, foreseeing that God would justify the Gentiles by faith, preached the gospel beforehand to Abraham, saying, 'In thee shall all the nations be blessed.' So then, those who are men of faith are blessed with Abraham who had faith" (Gal. 3:7-9). Here was irrefutable biblical support to Paul's doctrine of justification by faith. Then he proceeded to expand this teaching by adding six Old Testament quotations (vv. 10-18).

An almost humorous example of Paul's basing his authoritative teaching on these Scriptures occurs in his first letter to Timothy, where he wrote, "Let the elders who rule well be considered worthy of double honor, especially those who labor in preaching and teaching; for the scripture says, 'You shall not muzzle an ox when it is treading out the grain,' and, 'The laborer deserve his wages' " (5:17, 18). Of course Paul trusted the ability of Timothy to pass from the literal practice of muzzling an ox over to a valid spiritual application of honoring those who labor in preaching and teaching. A careful perusal of Paul's letters will show how frequently he supplied brief references or allusions to the Old Testament in support of his teachings.[4]

3. Some Distinctive Functions of the Scriptures

It is in order to observe some distinctive functions, uses, and purposes of the written Word of God. They become evident in some casual statements of the apostle, especially in instances where he is developing some practical teachings or giving some special exhortations which have their basis in the Scriptures. As Paul was giving some practical instruction relating to Christian freedom, he warned his readers not to use their freedom as an opportunity for the flesh and added the positive note, "Through love be servants of one another" (Gal. 5:13). He confirmed this counsel by adding, "The whole law is fulfilled in one word, 'You shall love your neighbor as yourself' " (v. 14). Here is a very significant use of the Scripture. Paul in this case was noting one of its distinctive functions, namely to set forth the love relationship which should obtain between neighbors.

The opening verses of Paul's letter to the Romans set forth a fundamental purpose of the Word of God. Paul declared that he was "set apart for the gospel of God which he promised beforehand through his prophets in the holy scriptures, the gospel concerning his Son" (1: 1-3). It is tragic that many students of these holy Scriptures utterly fail to grasp this strong affirmation concerning the content and purpose of the Scriptures. Later in the letter when Paul was explaining more fully the work of faith in the life of Abraham, he noted, "But the words, 'It was reckoned to him,' were written not for his sake alone, but for ours also" (4:23). In this context Paul was laying hold of an important aspect of the Scriptures. In a word, divine truths recorded in the first book of the Bible continued to possess their sacred values throughout biblical history, even to the degree of being used in the New Testament as the expression of inspired truth. A careful study of Paul's quotations from the Old Testament confirms the truth. As Paul was grappling with the difficult problem relating to Israel's unbelief, he drew in two quotations which specifically spoke to his point. Note the words, "No one who believes in him will be put to shame"; also, "Every one who calls upon the name of the Lord will be saved" (10:11, 13). Observe that the Scriptures quoted from Isaiah and Joel related to the specific problem with which Paul was dealing. Note another example from the letter to the Romans. Having quoted Psalm 69:9 in support of the fact that Christ did not please Himself, Paul added, "For whatever was written in former days was written for our instruction, that by steadfastness and by the encouragement of the scriptures we might have hope" (15:4).

As Paul was counseling the Corinthians on one of their difficult problems, he added the advice, "That you may learn by us to live according to scripture" (1 Cor. 4:6). Through these words Paul was noting an important practical purpose of the Scriptures, to the effect that they set forth the standard and pattern of godly living. He found it necessary also to explain to them the meaning and significance of Christ's death and resurrection. The foundation stone for his explanation was that these things took place "in accordance with the scriptures" (1 Cor. 15:3, 4). It was consistent for Paul to strengthen his readers' confidence in the written Word by adding the confirmation of eyewitness testimonies to Christ's resurrection.

He was well aware of the spiritual conflicts in which the Ephesian Christians were involved. In a most significant manner he counseled them to "be strong in the Lord." Using the analogy of a soldier's armor, he counseled these Christians to "put on the whole armor of God" (6:11). As he delineated the spiritual function of each part of this armor he urged them to take "the sword of the Spirit, which is the word of God" (v. 17). It may be proper to interpret "the word of God" as the words that came from God, the voice of God, or the message of God. While this expression does not make direct reference to the written Word, the Scriptures, it is certainly applicable to the *sacred writings*, the *Holy Scriptures*. The Holy Spirit uses God's Word as the sword to fight against the wiles of the devil. This has a definite experiential significance to Christians. On this account Paul commanded Timothy, "Attend to the public reading of scripture" (1 Tim. 4:13). Thus Paul was explaining the overall function of the holy Scriptures as they related to the entire body of the church. On this account Scripture reading became the focal point in public as well as private Christian worship.

Another distinctive function of the Word became clear in this letter when Paul counseled Timothy, "Let the elders who rule well be considered worthy of double honor, especially those who labor in preaching and teaching" (1 Tim. 5:17). In support of this rather unexpected kind of advice, Paul gave two quotations of the Scriptures, noted earlier in this discussion, by which Timothy became aware that the Scriptures give directions pertaining to some unexpected practical areas of life. This does not mean that these writings constitute a set of rules and directions for all the facets of life, but rather that the principles embodied in its practical teachings do extend over the entire scope of Christian living.

Paul's letter to Titus contains advice relating to the broad spectrum of scriptural teaching. Concerning the bishop, Paul wrote, "He must hold firm to the sure word as taught, so that he may be able to give instruction in sound doctrine and also to confute those who contradict it" (1:9). Undoubtedly Paul was again referring to the written Word which a bishop used in his manifold services to the church.

By way of conclusion, these functions of the Scriptures noted by Paul prove conclusively that these sacred writings relate to every sphere of faith and life of the Christian.

4. Paul's View of His Own Writings

In view of Paul's claims relating to the distinctive nature of the Holy Scriptures and his assertion, "All scripture is inspired by God," it is pertinent to these studies to gain an understanding of how the apostle regarded his own writings. Throughout his letters he made approximately 25 references to what he had written to the churches as well as to Timothy and Philemon. Specifically did he regard his writings as being on the level of the Old Testament Scriptures? In other words did he believe that his letters were inspired by God? Did he regard them as Holy Scriptures and as sacred writings? The implications of these questions undoubtedly have utmost significance as we evaluate Paul's apostolic authority, but more especially as it bears on the rise of a new body of writing which would also be known as Holy Scriptures. If the letter of James was written as early as AD 45, it was likely the only New Testament book in existence when Paul wrote his letters. Further, since the Old Testament had been a completed body of writings for at least four centuries, Paul's view of his own writing becomes all the more pertinent. With this background in mind let us pursue the inquiry as to how he regarded his own writings.

At the close of 1 Thessalonians, Paul wrote, "I adjure you by the Lord that this letter be read to all the brethren" (5:27). Observe that he made no reference to the circulation of this letter to other churches. In 2 Thessalonians he gave the exhortation, "So then, brethren, stand firm and hold to the traditions which you were taught by us, either by word of mouth or by letter" (2:15). In this manner Paul was exercising his authority as an apostle. He opened his letter to the Galatians with the expression, "Paul, an apostle — not from men nor through man, but through Jesus Christ and God the Father" (1:1). This reference to his apostleship became the pattern of address in all his later letters, excepting the one to Philemon. This statement of his call to apostleship through Jesus Christ and God the Father, at once placed this letter into the category similar to that of the Old Testament Scriptures. While there are a number of personal details in this letter, its authoritative character is clearly evident. This letter was not merely one of social correspondence; rather its message was binding to the Galatians.

The opening verses of the letter to the Romans give a longer presentation of his office as an apostle and of the gospel for which he was set apart. This finds confirmation in the unique and distinctive character of his letters which at once placed them in the rank of the Holy Scriptures written by the prophets. Paul enlarged on his apostolic authority in his personal comments in which he wrote, "On some points I have written to you very boldly by way of reminder, because of the grace given me by God to be a minister of Christ Jesus to the Gentiles in the priestly service of the gospel of God, so that the offering of the Gentiles may be acceptable, sanctified by the Holy Spirit" (Rom. 15:15, 16). First Corinthians presents two aspects which need to be harmonized. On the one side he wrote, "To the married I give charge, not I but the Lord." Then he adds "To the rest I say, not the Lord" (1 Cor. 7: 10, 12). The over-all authoritative character of his letter becomes apparent in the words, "If anyone thinks that he is a prophet, or spiritual, he should acknowledge that what I am writing to you is a commandment of the Lord" (14:37). This claim places his letter on the level of the Holy Scriptures. Second Corinthians gives further light on this issue.[5] These counsels need to be interpreted in the light of his final advice, "Finally, brethren, farewell. Mend your ways, heed my appeal, agree with one another, live in peace, and the God of love and peace will be with you" (13:11).

To the Ephesians, Paul expressed in a profound manner his view of his writings (3:1-7). Here he noted the stewardship of God's grace that was given to him for the Ephesians. It was given to him by revelation. He added, "When you read this you can perceive my insight into the mystery of Christ, which was not made known to the sons of men in other generations as it has now been revealed to his holy apostles and prophets by the Spirit" (vv. 4, 5). In this manner Paul was placing his letters on the same prophetic level as the writings of the Old Testament. At the close of his letter to the Colossians he wrote, "When this letter has been read among you, have it read also in the church of the Laodiceans; and see that you read also the letter from Laodicea" (4:16). This note shows that Paul viewed this letter as possessing the same authoritative value to the Laodiceans as well. To the young bishop Timothy, Paul wrote, "I am writing these instructions to you so that . . . you may know how one ought to behave in the household of God, which is the church of the living God, the pillar and bulwark of the truth" (1 Tim. 3:14, 15). Without question Timothy would recognize the apostolic authority of his spiritual father, Paul. Paul's final expression which set forth the authority of his writings occurs in Philemon 21. It reads, "Confident of your obedience, I write to you, knowing that you will do even more than I say."

5. Did Paul Visualize a New Body of Sacred Writings?

This question obtains great significance especially in view of the new body of writings which arose in the church during the second half of the first century and which came to be regarded as the New Testament. While Paul regarded his letters as being authoritative by reason of his apostleship, at no point did he express his belief that they would constitute a new body of Scriptures. It is essential to observe, nevertheless, that his references to the new covenant instituted by Jesus Christ did become the foundation of a new body of writings just as the old sacred writings centered in the Mount Sinai covenant. It would seem that when Paul penned the lines of Romans 9:1-5 his thought consciously looked forward to a new body of writings centering in the new covenant. For, just as to the Israelites belonged "the sonship, the glory, the covenants, the giving of the law, the worship, and the promises" (v. 4), so to the church belonged the sonship, the glory, the new covenant, the gospel message, the worship, the eschatological promises, and supremely, the Lord Jesus Christ. As Paul found in Isaiah's prophetic message (59:20, 21) a prediction of a new covenant in which God would take away the sins of mankind, he could with little difficulty anticipate a new body of writings centering in the gospel of the new covenant (Rom. 11:25-27). Again as Paul depicted the glory of God manifested in the giving of the law, he could easily visualize the far greater glory to be manifested in the writings built on the new covenant based on the manifestation of Christ in the world and the life-giving work of the Holy Spirit (2 Cor. 3:4-18).

In Ephesians 2:11-22 Paul built up another contrast between the law and the gospel which could culminate in a new body of writings "built upon the foundation of the apostles and prophets, Christ Jesus himself being the chief cornerstone" (v. 20). These comments may be reading too much into the meaning of Paul's reference to the new covenant, but we need to bear in mind, nevertheless, the thought processes lying back of these statements. The remainder of this letter, especially chapters 3 and 4, appear to give support to this idea. In like manner a paragraph such as Philippians 2:1-11 would naturally suggest that Paul conceived of a new body of writings which would set forth the redemptive work of Jesus Christ. A written gospel would certainly be essential to the fulfillment of Paul's words, "At the name of Jesus every knee should bow, in heaven and on earth and under the earth, and every tongue confess that Jesus Christ is Lord, to the glory of God the Father" (vv. 10, 11). Whether or not Paul visualized the rise of the new body of sacred writings, this did become a reality by the close of the first century.

For Additional Reading and Reference:

Beyschlag, *New Testament Theology,* Vol. II, pp. 21-24, 123-132.
Conzelmann, *An Outline of the Theology of the New Testament,* pp. 236-254.
Hunter, *Paul and His Predecessors*, Chap. VII.
Kittel, *Bible Key Words,* Vol. IV, Book I, Law.
Lindars, *New Testament Apologetic,* pp. 222-250.
Rolston, *Consider Paul,* Chaps. IV, VI, VII.
Schoeps, *Paul,* pp. 168-218.
Stevens, *The Pauline Theology,* pp. 362-374.
Weidner, *Biblical Theology of the New Testament,* Vol. I, pp. 375-385; Vol. II, pp. 107-116.

1. Acts 13:44, 48; 15:35, 36; Rom. 9:6; 1 Cor. 14:36; 2 Cor. 3:17; 4:2; etc.
2. *Biblical Theological Lexicon of New Testament Greek,* Fourth English Edition (Edinburgh: T. & T. Clark, 1954), p. 165.
3. See E. Earle Ellis, *Paul's Use of the Old Testament* (Grand Rapids: Wm. B. Eerdmans Publishing Co., 1960), pp. 11, 150-154.
4. 1 Cor. 2:6-10; 3:19-23; 6:16; 9:6-12; 10:25-27; 15:44-46; 2 Cor. 6:16-18; 9:8, 9; Gal. 4:26, 27; Eph. 4:7-10; 5:28-33; etc.
5. Note especially 2 Cor. 1:12-14; 2:3, 4, 9; 3:5-9; 4:1-6; 7:8-12; 9:1, 2; 10:9-11; 13:2, 10.

PART FOUR:
THE THEOLOGY OF THE LETTER TO THE HEBREWS AND OF THE JOHANNINE WRITINGS

CHAPTER I

THE THEOLOGY OF THE LETTER TO THE HEBREWS

1. Introduction

a. The Distinctive Nature of This Letter

In sharp distinction with the epistles of Paul, this letter makes no mention of the author's name. The writer gave no Christian greetings. The closing exhortations of the letter do possess, however, the character of a personal message to those addressed.

The opening words of this message indicate that the letter centers in a profound doctrinal content. This, undoubtedly, led its readers to probe into the unfathomable depths of thought which the letter sets forth. It soon becomes clear that chapters 1 and 2 set forth the doctrinal structure of the letter. God's final and climactic revelation to man came through His Son. Through Him God declared the great salvation for all mankind. It is this central truth which the author unfolds throughout the letter.

b. The Exhortations Addressed to Brethren

Four times in the letter he addressed his readers as *brethren* (3:1, 12; 10:19; 13:22). This suggests that the writer had great concern for the spiritual welfare of his readers. This becomes clear in the seven emphatic exhortations given in the letter.[1] These warnings point up the fundamental doctrinal content of the letter. Their impact will be given some attention throughout this presentation.

c. Keynotes of the Letter

Most obviously the central keynote is the *Son* Himself.[2] The second keynote is *salvation*.[3] The prominence given to this word accentuates its great significance found throughout the Bible, especially in the Psalms, Isaiah, the Gospels, and Paul's letters. This leads to the word *covenant,*[4] which defines the relationship into which God drew His people from the time of Noah onward, and by reason of its central meaning led to the naming of the Holy Scriptures as the old covenant followed by a similar title, the new covenant, canonized during the second century, AD. Its many occurrences throughout the Old Testament give grounds for its centrality in this letter. The author capitalized also on the word *faith,* used many times throughout the New Testament. This word sets forth the proper response of God's people to the mighty works of God and of Jesus Christ.[5] These and other keynote words such as *redemption, perfection, hope,* and others will receive consideration later in this chapter.

d. The Author's Approach to His Message

The unnamed author, probably Apollos, undoubtedly a Christian Jew, seemed to have clearly understood the serious problems confronting his Christian-Jew readers. This becomes evident in his approach by way of a copious use of their Scriptures. In developing his message he gave no less than 100 quotations from the Old Testament in support of his profound teachings. In view of the circumstances which were leading Christian Jews to discard their new Christian faith and to return to a rigid legalism based on the law, the author structured his letter on the Old Testament foreview of Jesus' person and work, focusing his attention on Jesus' service as High Priest, and reaching the climax in His institution of the new covenant. He showed very clearly that these truths which have their solid foundation in the Old Testament had a definite bearing on the Christian's eternal salvation. At strategic places in his doctrinal approach he exhorted his readers to hold to their Christian faith.

Appropriately and consistently he portrayed the nature of Christian faith as found in the God-fearing men and women of the Old Testament, which became the keynote of the Christian's relation to the Son of God. The author's structure of thought was such as to lead his readers to a full comprehension of Israel's religion as it centered in their faith in God.

A biblical theology approach to this letter to the Hebrews can hardly improve on the orderly presentation of God's revelation as set forth in this letter. In a word, the theology of the letter to the Hebrews centers in God's revelation as it culminated in Jesus Christ, the Son of God. Thus the letter to the Hebrews in a real way constitutes a biblical theological approach to God's revelation.

2. God's Final Revelation in His Son

The author launches on his message by giving a profound view of divine revelation; it is God speaking to man. It lies beyond man's power to disclose a revelation of God. While it is true that "in many and various ways God spoke of old to our fathers by the prophets" (Heb. 1:11), these words assert definitely that man is unable to reveal divine truth. It was a most extraordinary privilege entrusted by God to the prophets that they should be His spokesmen to mankind.

a. Revelation Through the Son Superior to That Through the Prophets

The writer advances at once to the supreme level of divine communication to man through His Son. This deity level of God's spokesman, the Son, should arrest the attention of these Hebrew Christians in order that they might grasp the significance of God's revelation in His Son.

b. The Dignity of the Son

The author enlarged on His deity by noting that God appointed Him the heir of all things and that through Him God created the world. The deity of the Son becomes still clearer in that "he reflects the glory of God and bears the very stamp of his nature, upholding the universe by his word of power" (v. 3). At this point the writer flashed before his readers a truth of which they were on the verge of ignoring, namely that the Son "had made purification for sin." These Hebrew Christians had been turning back to the Mosaic sacrificial system for their atonement. They failed to see that the need for repeating those bloody sacrifices was evidence of their inefficacy to expiate their sins. The fact that God had exalted the Son to sit at the right hand of the Majesty on high capped the climax to the finality of Christ's redemptive work. This initial presentation of Christ's atoning work undoubtedly had the design of leading his readers to the most serious contemplation of what it meant to turn back to their obsolete mode of worship.

Then to challenge his readers still further, the writer pointed to the superior position of the Son over that of angels. Throughout the Old Testament, God had communicated to His people through angels. Now the writer confronts his readers with the fact that the Son is God, not merely a messenger of God as were the angels. To bring this truth to his readers, the author quoted eight significant messianic predictions from the Old Testament which declared the deity of the Son. In the words of B. B. Warfield, "To the author of this Epistle our Lord is above all else the Son of God in the most eminent sense of that word;

and it is the divine dignity and majesty belonging to Him from His very nature which forms the fundamental feature of the image of Christ which stands before His mind."[6] While the writer did not in a formal way give a doctrinal presentation of Christ's deity, yet the first chapter comes near to being such. He expressed explicitly Christ's deity in the title *the Son of God.* On this account he added the words, "He reflects the glory of God and bears the very stamp of his nature, upholding the universe by his word of power" (1:3).[7] Other expressions setting forth Christ's deity are *Lord* (1:10; 2:3; 7:14; 13:20); *sitting at God's right hand* (1:3, 13; 8:1; 10:12; 12:2); *crowned with glory and honor* (2:7-9); *eternal* (1:12); and *after the order of Melchizedek* (5:6-10; 7:15-28).

c. Jesus, a Sharer in Flesh and Blood with Man

The classic passage declaring this truth is 2:9-18. The writer did not set forth the humanity of Jesus in theological language but rather in common terminology to express the redemptive reason for Christ's becoming man. Only as a human being could He experience the suffering of death. The writer stressed the element of suffering in that Jesus was made perfect through suffering. But it was through death that He destroyed "him who has the power of death, that is, the devil, and deliver all those who through fear of death were subject to lifelong bondage" (2:14, 15). And further, "He had to be made like his brethren in every respect, so that he might become a merciful and faithful high priest in the service of God, to make expiation for the sins of the people. For because he himself has suffered and been tempted, he is able to help those who are tempted" (2:17, 18). Only through Jesus' death is it possible for man to be saved. He alone is able to help those who are tempted.

d. The Necessary Response of Faith

Thus in chapters 1 and 2 the writer was challenging these Hebrew Christians who were on the verge of casting aside their faith in the divine-human Lord Jesus Christ through whom they had gained salvation. Instructed in the high-priestly work of Israel's priesthood, this presentation suddenly challenged the faith of these Christian Jews to believe that Jesus Christ had made expiation for their sins and was able to help them in their temptations. Throughout the letter the response of faith on the part of these Christians received repeated attention.[8] The author brought these exhortations to a climax by presenting the heroes of faith gleaned from their spiritual fathers, from Abel to the prophets (11).

3. Jesus, the Apostle and High Priest of Our Confession

The writer certainly challenged these Hebrew Christians by referring to Jesus as the apostle and high priest of their confession. The word *apostolos* had a wide and significant usage both in classical and New Testament Greek. In the New Testament an *apostle* was a *delegate, messenger*, or *one sent on a mission*. Christ named His twelve disciples *apostles* (Lk. 6:13). Paul called himself an apostle by reason of his heavenly call (Gal. 1:1). In a broader sense Barnabas, Timothy, and Silvanus were called apostles (Acts 14:14). By bringing together these two terms—*apostle* and *high priest*—a significant intensifying of meaning was declared. The special God-given mission and high-priestly responsibility entrusted to Christ were central to the Hebrew Christians' profession.

Examining further Christ's work as High Priest let us observe that in order to perform this service, it was necessary for Him "to be made like his brethren in every respect, so that he might become a merciful and faithful high priest in the service of God, to make expiation for the sins of the people" (2:17, 18). To these Hebrew Christians this should have carried great meaning. From the time of Moses onward, the service of the high priest was closely bound up with the Israelites' relation to God. His most significant service to Israel was to enter the holy of holies with a bloody offering to make expiation for Israel's sin. Rightly understood, this offering also had a Godward bearing by serving as a propitiation to the wrath of God. On the one side sin was covered and on the other God's righteous judgment was satisfied. This service of the high priest thus stood in very close relationship to every Israelite. His offering of a bloody sacrifice in the holy of holies on behalf of the people gave birth to the idea bound up in the word *intercession*. This becomes evident later in the letter when the author wrote, "He is able for all time to save those who draw near to God through him, since he always lives to make intercession for them" (7:25). The writer implied the same truth in the words, "For Christ has entered, not into a sanctuary made with hands, a copy of the true one, but into heaven itself, now to appear in the presence of God on our behalf" (9:24). It was on this account that Christ had to be made like His brethren, for only through this relationship could He be a merciful and faithful High Priest. He became human that "he might taste death for every one" (2:9), and in this way "make expiation for the sins of the people" (v. 17). Through this sacrifice "he is able to help those who are tempted" (v. 18). The writer drew further attention to Christ's faithfulness as Apostle and High Priest by comparing Him with Moses. The latter "was faithful in all God's house as a servant" but Christ "was faithful over God's house as a son" (3:5, 6). After giving appropriate exhortations the writer concluded with the words, "Let us then with confidence draw near to the throne of grace, that we may receive mercy and find grace to help in time of need" (4:16).

The writer of this letter made yet another comparison relating to Christ as High Priest by drawing in two profound Old Testament quotations: "Thou art my Son, today I have begotten thee"; and "Thou art a priest for ever, after the order of Melchizedek" (5:5, 6). The first quotation declares Christ's eternal sonship to God, and the second ranks Christ as High Priest after the order of Melchizedek, not after the order of Aaron. Assuming that David wrote both of these psalms just quoted (Ps. 2:7; 110:4) contributes a great deal to their significance in this context (See Acts 4:25, 26). As he envisioned the coming Messiah he declared Him to be none less than the Son of God and the One to sit at the Lord's right hand. Great as was Aaron's position as high priest, the coming Messiah would rank far above him. Only one priest, Melchizedek, was great enough to serve as a basis for comparison with the priest predicted by David. On the brief attention given to Melchizedek in Genesis 14:17-30 the author of Hebrews built up a marvelous description of this high priest (7:1-17). The meaning of his name declares him to be the king of righteousness; being the king of Salem, he is the king of peace.

The Genesis narrative gave no record of his parents or genealogy. To this the writer of Hebrews added that he "has neither beginning of days nor end of life, but resembling the Son of God he continues a priest for ever" (v. 3). While it does not appear from the Genesis record that Melchizedek stood higher than a human being, it is remarkable that the author of Genesis did not follow the usual pattern in Hebrew history of supplying genealogical data, including his parents and the record of his death. The apparent reason for this lies in the fact that Melchizedek did not belong to the Hebrew race even though he was a monotheist. On account of the genuine dignity of Melchizedek the author of Hebrews placed our Lord on his rank as high priest. Through this superior high priestly service of the Son of God, he became the source of eternal salvation to all who obey him, being designated by God a high priest after the order of Melchizedek" (5:9, 10). Only through Christ our Lord is perfection attainable. He did not belong to the order of Aaron but He was descended from Judah. On this account He did not become a priest "according to a legal requirement concerning bodily descent but by the power of an indestructible life" (7:16). Herein lies the foundation of a better hope "through which we draw near to God" (7:19). With this presentation of Christ as High Priest forever, the writer concludes, "This makes Jesus the surety of a better covenant . . . he holds his priesthood permanently . . . he is able for all time to save those who draw near to God through him, since he always lives to make intercession for them. For it was fitting that we should have such a high priest, holy, blameless, unstained, separated from sinners, exalted above the heavens. . . . But the word of the oath . . . appoints a Son who hath been made perfect for ever" (7:22-28).

4. Jesus, the Mediator of the New Covenant

Since Jesus is a Priest forever after the order of Melchizedek He has become the *surety (guarantee, surety, pledge)* of a better covenant. Chapter 8 stands as a marvelous buildup of thought in which the author led these Hebrew Christians to see that the Old Testament worship centering in the ministry of the priests serves as a *copy (hupodeigma: example, model, figure, copy, pattern, imitation)*, and *shadow (skia: shade, foreshadowing, sketch, outline, adumbration)* of the heavenly sanctuary. When Moses was about to build the tabernacle, God instructed him to make everything according to the *pattern (tupos: model, example, design, form, type, figure)* which was shown to him on the mountain. Of the several connotations of this word *tupos*, I agree with Bruce's interpretation. "It may have been a model for which the verbal directions served as a commentary; it may have been the heavenly dwelling place of God which Moses was permitted to see."[9] While the word *tupos* has the literal meaning of model or pattern, the description of Moses' experience on the mountain (Ex. 24:15-18) would seem to declare that Moses saw the glory of the Lord in all its splendor. Certainly Moses, in his natural body, could not behold God's glory in its fullness; nevertheless, he saw the dwelling place of God in all the glory which human eye could stand. This certainly enriches the idea expressed by *tupos* and gives support to the interpretation that Moses actually saw the heavenly dwelling place of God. This was the *true (alethinos: real, genuine, dependable)* tent which is set up by the Lord.

With this explanation of the heavenly sanctuary, the true tent, the writer moved forward with his key to showing that the covenant Jesus mediated is better than the old. This conclusion finds support in the fact that the new covenant was enacted on better promises (8:6). The author confirmed this conclusion by quoting the Old Testament prophetic message of Jeremiah through which he declared that the Lord "will make a new covenant with the house of Israel and the house of Judah. . . . I will put my law within them, and I will write it upon their hearts; and I will be their God, and they shall be my people. . . . I will forgive their iniquity, and I will remember their sin no more" (Jer. 31:31-34).

The immeasurable superiority of the new covenant over the old leads to the old becoming obsolete, and to its vanishing away (Heb. 8:13).

The writer proceeded to add further details relating to the old covenant worship, and through this description showed that the Holy Spirit was indicating "that the way into the sanctuary is not yet opened as long as the outer tent is still standing" (9:8). The author interpreted this as being symbolic (*parabole: type, figure, symbol*) for the present age. From the angle of the experiential aspect of biblical religion, the sacrificial system under the old covenant lacked the power to "perfect the conscience of the worshiper" (v. 9). Nevertheless, this form of worship was "imposed until the time of reformation (*piorphosis: new order, improvement, reformation*). This expressive word declares very emphatically the ineffectiveness of the old forms of worship and the necessity for God's establishing the new covenant which would purify the "conscience from dead works to serve the living God" (v. 14). This became possible through "the blood of Christ, who through the eternal Spirit offered himself without blemish to God" (v. 14). On this account Christ "is the mediator of a new covenant" (v. 15). At this point the author builds on another connotation of the word *diatheke* that of *will.* He notes that a will involves the death of the one who makes it (v. 16). It "takes effect only at death" (v. 17). This truth underlies the bloody sacrifices of the old covenant, for "without the shedding of blood there is no forgiveness of sins" (v. 22).

Having laid the foundation for his majestic structure of thought, the writer advanced to a description of the true sanctuary of which the old was a *copy (antitupos: antitype, representation).* In a most glorious manner Christ entered "into heaven itself, now to appear in the presence of God on our behalf" (9:24). Stressing still further Christ's mediatorial work, the author added, "He has appeared once for all at the end of the age to put away sin by the sacrifice of himself" (v. 26). This self-sacrifice of Christ imposes upon sinful mankind the responsibility for repentance and faith in Jesus Christ who will judge all mankind but will save those "who are eagerly waiting for him" (v. 28).

A close examination of the author's carefully structured thought shows that he had three points yet to clarify: (1) The law had "but a shadow of the good things to come"; it did not have "the true form of these realities" neither could it "make perfect those who draw near." There remained a consciousness of sin on the part of the worshipers (10:1, 2). (2) Since God had taken no pleasure in burnt offerings and sin offerings, Christ abolished these sacrifices in order that He might establish the new order of worship through the offering of His own body once for all (Heb. 10:10). (3) "When Christ had offered for all time a single sacrifice for sins, he sat down at the right hand of God. . . . For by a single offering he has perfected for all time those who are sanctified" (10: 12-14). At last the author reached the goal to which he was ascending step by step with irrefutable evidence given in its support. He could triumphantly state, "Where there is forgiveness of these, there is no longer any offering for sin" (10:18). This was possible because Christ the High Priest had mediated the new covenant and had been enthroned at the right hand of God.

5. The Response of Faith

a. The Meaning of Faith

It seems appropriate at this time to note again the author's approach to his entire structure of thought as presented in 1, d. The author, being a Christian Jew, understood the problems confronting his fellow Jewish Christians. His approach was through a careful interpretation of their Scriptures (Old Testament). He drew from these Scriptures the predictions relating to the person and work of the Messiah which centered in His high-priestly work, the institution of the new covenant, culminating in His enthronement at the right hand of God. Repeatedly he had exhorted them to hold fast to the confession of their hope. Thus the entire letter magnifies the nature of Christian faith.

Let us observe how the writer structured the concept and meaning of faith in this letter, giving special attention to his exposition of faith in chapter 11. At crucial junctures of his discussion he injected pertinent exhortations which revealed the many facets of a living faith. Thus in 2:1 he advises his readers to pay closer attention to what they have heard. There was a real danger of drifting away from the truths which had their foundation in faith. Having declared the profound truths bound up in the divine-human nature of Jesus, the author advised them to consider Jesus the Apostle and High Priest of their confession, especially because He was faithful to God who had appointed Him. In 4:1-3 he pointed up the necessity of believing the good news which came to his readers because only those who believe enter into the heaven rest. The author led his readers to understand that faith lays hold of the promises given by God, which will be fulfilled in the future. The author's exposition of Christ's high-priestly work called for a maturity of faith in God which far transcends the initial expressions of repentance and faith at the beginning of the Christian life. There was need for showing earnestness "in realizing the full assurance of hope until the end." Thus genuine faith involves patience (6:11).

After presenting Melchizedek as the king of righteousness and of peace, the writer proceeded to show that Jesus, the Son of God, became the surety of a better covenant, a minister in the true tent. This becomes evident in His single sacrifice for sins, followed by His sitting down at the right hand of God. Through Him there is actual forgiveness of sins. Even though the readers of this letter had a real problem to move from the need of repeated sin offerings to the efficacy of Christ's sacrifice for sins, the author held before them the supreme challenge of faith to believe in this new and living way which Christ opened up for them through His own sacrifice. He exhorted them in a most challenging manner in the words, "Let us draw near with a true heart in full assurance of faith, with our hearts sprinkled clean from an evil conscience and our bodies washed with pure water. Let us hold fast the confession of our hope without wavering, for he who promised is faithful" (10:22, 23). Let us observe the spiritual ingredients of *faith,* such as, *a true heart, a good conscience,* and *the confession of hope*. The author bolsters this idea further with the counsel, "Do not throw away your confidence. . . . For you have need of endurance" (vv. 35, 36).

As a climax, the author quoted from Habakkuk, 'My righteous one shall live by faith, and if he shrinks back, my soul has no pleasure in him' " (v. 38; see Hab. 2:3, 4). They who shrink back are destroyed but those who have faith keep their souls. These words from the prophet Habakkuk should certainly have arrested the attention of these Hebrew Christians, for the prophet was bringing to their attention the most meaningful Old Testament statement relating to the nature of faith which was matched alone by the words spoken concerning Abraham, "he believed the Lord; and he reckoned it to him as righteousness" (Gen. 15:6). By reason of this supremacy of faith in the lives of godly people, the author proceeded to give an extensive elaboration of the work of faith in the lives of their spiritual ancestors.

He began with the familiar words, "Now faith is the assurance of things hoped for, the conviction of things not seen" (11:1). On these words Westcott made a significant comment, "The order (*estin de pistis)* shows that the object of the writer is not to give a formal definition of faith but to bring out characteristics of faith which bear upon his argument. It seems to suggest the affirmation of the reality of faith as well as the nature of faith."[10] With this language the author was probing into one of the fundamental aspects of the Christian's relation to God. Central to this relationship was that of hope. His readers were certainly aware that from the beginning of Hebrew history God was promising His people unspeakable blessings to be realized in their future. The author is now leading his readers to examine the foundations of this hope. He declares that faith is the assurance (*hupostasis*) and the *conviction (elegxos)* of this hope. The former of these words has the literal meaning: *thing put under, substructure, foundation,* and *that which is firm.* This literal meaning easily lends itself to broader concepts such as: *substantial quality, steadfastness of mind, firmness, courage, confidence, firm trust,* and *assurance.* The second word carries the meaning *proof*: that of which a thing is proved or tested.[11] While faith is a common word in nonreligious usage it obtains highest significance in the Bible and the Christian religion. Its meaning lies deeper than an intellectual concept. It springs from man's innermost being and is fundamentally a spiritual reality.

The writer at once proceeds to show how faith manifested itself in the lives of God's chosen people. He begins with one of the most meaningful expressions of faith, that of believing "that the world was created by the word of God, so that what is seen was made out of things which do not appear" (11:3). Undoubtedly the most momentous task confronting the scientific world is that of accounting for the existence of the universe, involving the origin of matter and the millions of heavenly bodies. In exceedingly simple but yet most meaningful language the first verse of the Bible declares, "In the beginning God created the heavens and the earth." The truth of this statement lies beyond the realm of scientific investigation or of reason. Christians lay hold of this statement by faith, faith in God, and in the truth of His written Word. They believe this even though men of science might declare the impossibility of the universe being made "out of things which do not appear" (v. 3).

With this understanding of faith the author proceeds to show how godly men and women throughout biblical history manifested faith in their lives. A study of these examples of faith shows how dominant this grace manifested itself in these people. In almost every instance the men and women of God believed what, from a human point of view, was impossible. How did Abel know what an acceptable sacrifice would be? It was certainly beyond human comprehension that Enoch should not see death. To Noah's contemporaries, his building an ark to save his household from a worldwide flood was utterly ridiculous, especially in view of the time needed to build it and of its necessary size to preserve all living creatures from destruction. Imagine how foolish it was for Abraham to leave his homeland without knowing where he was going, and add to this his immeasurable faith in looking "forward to the city which has foundations, whose builder and maker is God" (11:10). Space would fail me to tell of Sarah, Isaac, Jacob, Joseph, Moses, and all the others who through faith achieved goals possible alone through the manifest power of God. Most certainly faith is the expression of one's personal relation to God. It means trust in God to the extent of absolute self-surrender. All these noble servants of God exemplified the meaning of faith in their lives.

b. Looking to Jesus, the Pioneer and Perfecter of Our Faith

The author introduced his conclusion by using the word *toigaroun*, an inferential particle (*wherefore then, for that very reason then, therefore*) (12:1). With this word he gave special emphasis to his concluding exhortations. Christian believers are surrounded by a great crowd of witnesses. What a wonderful privilege and experience for all Christians! On this account the writer urged, "Let us also lay aside every weight, and sin which clings so closely, and let us run with perseverance the race that is set before us, looking to Jesus the pioneer and perfecter of our faith" (vv. 1, 2). It was He who endured the cross, despised the shame, and endured from sinners such hostility against himself; but is now seated at the right hand of the throne of God. Appropriately, the author interpreted his reader's struggle against sin by quoting Proverbs 3:11, 12, according to which these experiences should be viewed as the Lord's discipline of His children. He loves those whom He disciplines and chastises. On this account the author challenged his readers to regard their experiences in this world of sin as evidence that God was treating them as sons. God disciplines His children for their good, that they may share His holiness. Discipline "yields the peaceable fruit of righteousness to those who have been trained by it" (Heb. 12:11).

With this interpretation of his readers' persecutions he urged further that no one should fail to obtain the grace of God. He gave the exhortation that no "root of bitterness" (v. 5) should spring up and cause trouble. He reminded them of the tragic case of Esau who refused to believe the great promises given to his father and grandfather, and when it was too late, "he found no chance to repent, though he sought it with tears" (vv. 16, 17). The writer brought his appeal to the climax in the words, "You have come to Mount Zion and to the city of the living God, the heavenly Jerusalem, and to innumerable angels in festal gathering, and to the assembly of the first-born who are enrolled in heaven, and to a judge who is God of all, and to the spirits of just men made perfect, and to Jesus, the mediator of a new covenant, and to the sprinkled blood that speaks more graciously than the blood of Abel" (vv. 22-24). His final exhortation was; "Therefore let us be grateful for receiving a kingdom that cannot be shaken, and thus let us offer to God acceptable worship, with reverence and awe; for our God is a consuming fire" (vv. 28, 29). This closing counsel gave the firmest ground for the Christian's response of faith.

The biblical theological approach to this letter to the Hebrews furnishes a true perspective of Christian faith. Let us note again that the ministry of Jesus led His disciples to believe that He was the Christ, the Son of God, and the Savior of the world. The Apostle Paul developed this truth further by noting that "we are justified by faith" (Rom. 5:1). This letter to the Hebrews becomes then the capsheaf to the biblical presentation of faith by showing that faith in the finished work of Christ stands as "the assurance of things hoped for, the conviction of things not seen" (Heb. 11:1). Jesus established a pattern of living for those who believed in Him such as "be perfect, as your heavenly Father is perfect" (Mt. 5:48), and "seek first his kingdom and his righteousness" (6:33). Paul wrote to the churches, "Do not be conformed to this world but be transformed by the renewal of your mind" (Rom. 12:2), and set forth the fruit of the Spirit as "love, joy, peace, patience, kindness, goodness, faithfulness, gentleness, self-control " (Gal. 5:22, 23). So also this author held forth the outworking of faith in Christian living by the admonition, "Let brotherly love continue" (Heb. 13:1) together with other exhortations relating to showing hospitality, holding marriage in honor, keeping one's life free from the love of money, obeying leaders, and other practical exhortations.

6. Other Doctrines Briefly Noted

The author drew into his presentation references to a number of other doctrinal ideas, but in most cases he only mentioned them without giving any doctrinal significance. Nevertheless, their use in this letter carries significance. On this account I shall refer to them, giving a few comments relating to their theological implications.

a. The Holy Spirit

In harmony with Paul's teachings the writer refers to gifts of the Holy Spirit, noting that they are "distributed according to his own will" (Heb. 2:4). Twice the writer introduced quotations from the Old Testament in the language of the Holy Spirit *saying*, or *bearing witness* (3:7; 10:15). In a setting where the author was noting constituent elements of a genuine Christian experience he mentioned the aspect of becoming partakers of the Holy Spirit. It was an effective way of setting forth the inner experience of one who is born again (6:4, 5). Again as the writer was describing Israel's worship on the Day of Atonement (Lev. 16), he gave the explanatory note, "By this the Holy Spirit indicates that the way into the sanctuary is not yet opened as long as the outer tent is still standing" (Heb. 9:6-8). Thus Leviticus 16 is a sample of where the Holy Spirit was setting forth the inadequacy of the Day of Atonement ritual. In another context where the author was giving a most serious warning against Christians sinning deliberately after having received the knowledge of truth, he declared that such apostasy is a case of spurning the Son of God, of profaning the blood of the covenant, and of outraging the Spirit of grace (10:26-29). This reference to the Holy Spirit assumes the inner involvement of the Holy Spirit in the life of a Christian.

b. Angels

The author followed a unique pattern of setting forth the deity of the Son by showing His superiority to the angels. God had never said to an angel what He had said prophetically of the Son. Even when the Lord brought the Firstborn into the world He said, "Let all God's angels worship him" (Heb. 1:6). Their subordinate position as related to the Son became evident in the author's quotation of Psalm 104:4, "Who makes his angels winds, and his servants flames of fire" (v. 7). God had never exalted an angel to sit at His right hand, but they should be "ministering spirits sent forth to serve" (v. 14). Nevertheless, a message declared by angels was valid. Both Stephen and Paul had already testified that the law had been delivered and ordained by angels. Since angels had not sinned, Christ's coming into the world was not for the sake of angels. As to their number the author of the letter declared, "You have come to Mount Zion and to the city of the living God, the heavenly Jerusalem, and to innumerable angels in festal gathering" (12:22). Note the glorious scene of the angels in heaven. In his exhortation to show hospitality to strangers, the author noted how Lot entertained angels unawares (13:2). These several details with reference to angels contribute some significant data setting forth their position as related to both Christ and man, also their work and their number.

c. Sin

The writer made about two dozen references to sin which contribute significantly to the biblical presentation of this subject.

In Hebrews 6:4-6 the writer gave some illuminating expressions descriptive of the Christian life such as being enlightened, tasting the heavenly gift, becoming partakers of the Holy Spirit, tasting the goodness of the Word of God, and the powers of the age to come, and then of their *committing apostasy (parapipto — fall beside, go astray, fall away)*. Thus he probed into one of the most heinous aspects of sin. On the one side were these blessed spiritual experiences of the child of God, and on the other the forceful expression descriptive of their loss. By so doing, their falling away is equivalent to their crucifying the Son of God on their own account, and of holding Him up to contempt (v. 6). Later as the writer was quoting the predictions of Jeremiah with reference to God's making a new covenant with His people, he said, "I will be merciful toward their *iniquities (adikia — wrong doing, unrighteousness, wickedness, injustice*), and I will remember their sins (*hamartia*) no more" (8:12). This quotation from Jeremiah expresses a comprehensive view of sin as found in the Old Testament. Arndt and Gingrich give this significant comment, "In Hebrews (as in Old Testament) sin appears as the power that deceives men and leads them to destruction, whose influence and activity can be ended only by sacrifices."[12] Speaking of Moses, the author noted that he chose "rather to share ill-treatment with the people of God than to enjoy the fleeting pleasures of sin" (11:25). It would appear that Moses had come to realize through his experience in Egypt that the pleasures of sin were fleeting. Only a God-fearing man could come to this understanding of sin without having gone to the depth of sin's pleasures.

The darkest picture of sin stands forth in the words, "See to it . . . that no 'root of bitterness' spring up and cause trouble, and by it many become defiled; that no one be immoral or irreligious like Esau" (Heb. 12:15, 16). This quotation from the Septuagint is worded a bit differently in the Hebrew translation into English, "Beware . . . lest there be among you a root bearing poisonous and bitter fruit, one who, when he heard the words of this sworn covenant, blesses himself in his heart, saying, 'I shall be safe, though I walk in the stubbornness of my heart' " (Deut. 29:18, 19). The readers of this letter were in a position to understand the forcefulness of this Old Testament quotation. Observe that this sinfulness is marked first, by the person's heart turning away from the Lord; second, by serving the gods of the other nations; third, by the presence of a root producing poison and wormwood; and fourth, that of blessing oneself in the heart by saying that he is safe even though he persists in his stubbornness. The writer finally pointed up the nature of Esau's sin by noting that he was *immoral (pornos — fornicator, one who practices sexual immorality)* and *irreligious (bebelos — godless, profane, irreverent, irreligious)*.

Another aspect of sin, that of sinning willfully, is dealt with in Hebrews 10:26-29. The author wrote, "If we sin deliberately after receiving the knowledge of the truth, there no longer remains a sacrifice for sins" (v. 26). He appears to be reflecting on a distinction made in the law between sinning unwittingly and of doing anything with a high hand (Num. 15:27-31). In the case of the former, atonement could be made for his sins leading to his being forgiven, but in the latter case, he was regarded as having reviled the Lord, as having despised His Word, and as having broken His commandment. This person was utterly cut off and his iniquity remained upon him. The obvious statement, that for sinning deliberately there remained no longer a sacrifice for sins, evidently carries the meaning that such a one through his deliberate sinning is rejecting Christ's sacrifice for him. On this account no provision remains for making expiation for sin leading to forgiveness. The author added the forthright statement, "A man who has violated the law of Moses dies without mercy at the testimony of two or three witnesses. How much worse punishment do you think will be deserved by the man who has spurned the Son of God, and profaned the blood of the covenant by which he was sanctified, and outraged the Spirit of grace? . . . It is a fearful thing to fall into the hands of the living God" (Heb. 10:28-31). This is certainly a frank presentation of what it means to willfully disregard God's saving grace manifested through Jesus Christ.

In a forceful manner the author depicted the effects of sin upon the sinner. The first instance was the circumstance in which he exhorted his readers to hold fast their confidence and pride in their hope (3:6). In support of this exhortation he quoted some warnings expressed in Psalm 95, which forcefully probes into this problem. The psalmist had said, "Do not harden your hearts as in the rebellion." He added the words of God, "They always go astray in their hearts; they have not known my ways" (vv. 8, 10). The author used this reference to Israel's wilderness experience as the basis for warning in the words, "Take care, brethren, lest there be in any of you an evil, unbelieving heart, leading you to fall away from the living God . . . that none of you may be hardened by the deceitfulness of sin" (vv. 12, 13). In this manner the author exposed the most serious effect of sin, especially among the children of God. The metaphor of heart-hardening expresses a spiritual tragedy in which they who have experienced a living relation to God, including experiences of discipline and testing, have willfully turned away from God. Such actions make a most serious impact upon an individual's innermost being. Such an individual no longer hears the Word of God nor does he have fellowship with Him. Maintaining one's belief in God is a personal responsibility. There is need to scrupulously recognize the deceitfulness, the deception, and the delusion of sin. The proper attitude toward these effects of sin is that of holding "our first confidence firm to the end" (3:14).

Another context setting forth the effects of sin upon the believer is Hebrew 12:1-17. Observe the exhortation, "Lay aside every weight, and sin which clings so closely" (v. 1). Quoting loosely from Robertson[13] the runners ran in the stadium nearly naked. These weights may refer to such handicaps like doubt, pride, sloth, which may trip the Christian. The author noted how Jesus, in His race endured the cross and despised the shame of suffering death as a criminal. He had endured hostility against Himself. The antidote to this effect of sin was that of not growing weary or fainthearted. They should regard such experiences as the expression of God's discipline to them. Looking again to the case of Esau, the author noted the "root of bitterness," which had the effect of defiling him, resulting in an immoral and irreligious life. These several warnings against the tragic effects of sin upon the Christian serve as a significant contribution to the New Testament doctrine of sin.

This discussion of sin has assumed that the author viewed sin in its relation to God. This becomes evident in 3:16-18, where Israel's rebellion against God *provoked (parapikraino — embitter, make angry)* and *grieved (prosochthizo — be angry, offended, provoked)* Him. The meaning of these words needs to be lifted above the human level to that of God. On account of Israel's rebellion He did not let them enter into His rest. Observe also the author's statement in 12:14-17, where he asserts that failure to strive for peace and for holiness results in one's being denied the glory of seeing the Lord. There were those who by their sins were failing to obtain the grace of God. For his readers, the classic example was that of Esau, who was immoral and irreligious and on this account failed to receive the special blessings of the Lord (12:16).

Nevertheless the writer would have his readers know that God provided a remedy for sin. Already in the introduction to the letter he asserted that Christ "had made purification for sins" (1:3) and this expression undoubtedly led his readers to reflect on the ritual of the Day of Atonement (Lev. 16), when atonement was made for the sins of the people. This Day of Atonement was most significant in teaching Israel that God through these bloody offerings had made provision for the removing of their sins, symbolically expressed by the "sprinkling of blood on the mercy seat" and in this way made expiation for Israel's sins. Since this Day of Atonement was observed every year, the immeasurable superiority of Christ's suffering and death becomes evident in His having made purification for sins through His once-for-all sacrifice. The price of this sacrifice reveals the sinfulness of sin and shows that only through the death of the Son of God could sin be removed. From one point of view the central message of this letter has to do with the efficacious sacrifice of Christ for sin and in this way showed the costly remedy for sin provided by God Himself.

d. Grace

The use of this word is another example of how the author capitalized on the significance of a word without elaborating on its meaning. Jesus had become man "so that by the grace of God he might taste death for every one" (Heb. 2:9). This statement asserts most assuredly that Christ's death on the cross was the supreme expression of God's grace. The source of all grace is God Himself. It is then natural that the throne on which His Son is seated is called "the throne of grace" (4:16). Since our great High Priest experienced temptations just as all human beings do, He is able to sympathize with human weaknesses. Here are the grounds for our coming with confidence to the throne of grace. To apply the term *grace* to this throne is to assert its greatest significance to mankind. On this account the writer says, "Let us then with confidence draw near to the throne of grace, that we may receive mercy and find grace to help in time of need" (4:16). It was entirely consistent then for the author to associate grace with the Holy Spirit (10:29). He encouraged his readers to strive for peace and holiness so "that no one fail to obtain the grace of God" (12:15). To these Christians who were still attributing spiritual values to foods offered on altars, the author noted that the heart is strengthened by grace (13:9). There was real dynamic in God's grace as over against the ritual offering of food on the altar in Mosaic worship. The author appropriately closed his letter with the words, "Grace be with all of you. Amen" (v. 25).

e. Salvation

The author's use of this word is significant. The buildup of its meaning in the Old Testament is the foundation for its use in this letter. When the author was setting forth the subordinate position of angels in relation to the Son, he noted their great work as ministering spirits serving "for the sake of those who are to obtain salvation" (1:14). Undoubtedly this statement flashed before his readers all that the Old Testament had given through Moses, the Psalms, Isaiah, and other prophets concerning God's salvation. Not only was the word descriptive of what Israel experienced in being delivered from Egypt but it was also predictive of the salvation to be revealed in the coming Messiah. Note the great Servant of the Lord passage, "I will give you as a light to the nations, that my salvation may reach to the end of the earth" (Is. 49:6). The author at once grasped this truth as it related to the weakening of faith on the part of his readers. Putting his question bluntly he asked, "How shall we escape if we neglect such a great salvation?" (Heb. 2:3). This salvation in Christ becomes immeasurably more meaningful and spiritual than that experienced by Israel in the Old Testament. Jesus, the Lord, had declared this salvation, and it had been attested to these Christian Jews by the apostles. God also confirmed this witness through signs, wonders, and various miracles, and in the most intimate way by gifts of the Holy Spirit.

The author needed to give the reason for Jesus' incarnation. Only through being a man could He suffer death, and through His being the God-man He tasted death for everyone (2:9). In bringing many sons to glory it was necessary for God to make the Founder, the Author, the Pioneer, the Leader of their salvation perfect through suffering (v. 10). That is, Jesus, the Savior of mankind, could effect this salvation only through His death. The author gave further explication of this truth by noting that absolute obedience to God required His suffering and death. But through this obedience He became the Author, the Source, of eternal salvation (5:8, 9). Through this statement the author was noting that Isaiah's prediction of everlasting salvation through the Lord was now a reality (Is. 45:17). He found it necessary to stress the true meaning of salvation as it stood in contrast with their immature understanding of this truth. They had "tasted the goodness of the word of God and the powers of the age to come" but were returning to a ritualistic concept of the Christian life. The author wanted them "to show the same earnestness in realizing the full assurance of hope until the end" (6:11). In this way they would realize the "better things that belong to salvation" (v. 9). The author sought to build up their hope of salvation through the words "Christ, having been offered once to bear the sins of many, will appear a second time, not to deal with sin but to save those who are eagerly waiting for him" (Heb. 9:28).

f. Repentance

The major theme of this letter did not include a lengthy presentation of repentance; nevertheless, the exhortation of 6:1-6 does make a significant contribution to this doctrine. The readers of this letter with their legalistic background of Judaism were failing to advance in their Christian experience. They were continuing to lay stress on such foundational elements of Christian experience as repentance from dead works and of faith toward God. They were still delving into matters relating to ablutions, the laying on of hands, and other elemental ideas, and were not growing in grace and in knowledge of the truth. In other words there was need for them to move beyond the kind of repentance needed to be experienced by Jews with their ritualistic background of worship on to the realities of the life in Christ. They, who had once been enlightened, had tasted the heavenly gift, had become partakers of the Holy Spirit, had tasted the goodness of the Word of God and the powers of the age to come. If they fall away from the Christian faith it is impossible to restore them again to repentance. In the words of Robertson, "It is a terrible picture and cannot be toned down."[14] The impossibility of their being restored to repentance centered in the gravity and internal nature of their apostasy. They are crucifying the Son of God on their own account and holding Him up to contempt. This is not an unpardonable sin, as some would interpret it, but rather it is descriptive of their hardness of heart which closes them to God's redemptive love and mercy. It is a spiritual condition for which there is no remedy. In modern language it is an incurable disease. For the purpose of this discussion let us observe that there is a state of spiritual degradation in which it is impossible for one to repent.

g. *Sanctification*

A biblical theological approach to the author's teaching of sanctification involves a careful study of its meaning, its Old Testament background, the punctiliar and linear verb forms, and the agent of sanctification. According to the Greek lexicons, the verb *hagiago* means to *make holy, consecrate, sanctify, dedicate, treat as holy, purify,* and so on. The noun form *hagiasmos* means *holiness, consecration, sanctification, purification,* etc. The Hebrew background is *qadash* which means *set apart, consecrate, hallow, dedicate,* and so on. The linear uses of the verb occur in 2:11 (he who sanctifies and those who are sanctified); 9:13 (sanctifies for the purification of the flesh); and 10:14 (those who are sanctified). In 10:10 occurs the periphrastic perfect passive indicative of the verb which emphatically sets forth the state of being sanctified. Aorist forms of the verb occur in 10:29 (by which *he was sanctified)* and 13:12 (in order *to sanctify the people).* Two noun forms occur in 12:10 *hagiotes (share his holiness);* and 12:14 *hagiasmos (strive . . . for the holiness).* The former carries the sense of holiness, while the latter looks to the process, or more frequently, the result of being made holy. It is significant that the author interprets God's discipline as being for the good of Christians, specifically that they may share God's holiness. On this account he stresses the exhortation that they should strive for peace and for holiness. He concluded his thought by noting that without peace and holiness no one will see the Lord.

The keynote truth expressed in the verb forms is that Christ is He who sanctifies. The use of the present participles in this verse sets forth a continuing and repeated work of sanctification. The Old Testament background to this teaching includes both the ceremonial act of setting apart for God and also a continuing process of being holy, even as God is holy. The spiritual aspect of being sanctified receives further support in 9:14, where the writer declares that the blood of Christ purifies the conscience from dead works to serve the living God. The spiritual aspect of cleansing and purifying becomes evident again in 12: 10, 14, where the writer declares, "He disciplines us for our good, that we may share his holiness." His exhortation, "Strive for peace with all men, and for the holiness without which no one will see the Lord," stresses the goal of spiritual growth. The writer gave to sanctification a spiritual connotation which Israel had failed to maintain throughout their history. This accords with the central objective of this letter.

h. Righteousness

As the writer depicted the divine majesty of the Son it was entirely natural that he should draw on Psalm 45:6, 7 for its most descriptive language of the Deity attributes possessed by the Son of God (Heb. 1:8, 9). Perhaps the most central attribute of Deity is *righteousness (dikaiosune)*. On this account it was significant that the writer of Genesis declared, "Noah was a righteous man, blameless in his generation" (Gen. 6:9). From this time onward throughout the Old Testament and the New this term possessed the most significant meaning setting forth the uprightness of character, both of God and of His people. It was entirely natural that the author of this letter should declare how Noah "became an heir of the righteousness which comes by faith" (Heb. 11:7). The author sought to make clear to his readers that they were in need of being taught again "the first principles of God's word" — that is, they were "unskilled in the word of righteousness" (5: 12, 13). Undoubtedly this was a severe blow to these Christian Jews. The author proceeded to set forth the foundations of genuine Christian faith. Available to the author was the most highly respected man of God known to Israel, Melchizedek, whose name declared him to be king of righteousness and king of peace. Through the kingly dignity of Melchizedek, the legalistic Christian Jews could observe the most outstanding human example of godly righteousness.

The writer clarified to his readers that Noah "became an heir of the righteousness which comes by faith" (11:7). Thus righteousness bears a very close relationship to faith in the lives of God's people. The writer stressed this point by naming such outstanding godly characters as Gideon, David, and many others "who through faith conquered kingdoms, enforced justice, received promises" (v. 33), etc. That is, their bringing about justice (*righteousness*) had its source in their faith. The author showed the relation of godly discipline to its outcome. But he wrote that God "disciplines us for our good, that we may share his holiness . . . later it yields the peaceful fruit of righteousness to those who have been trained by it" (12:10, 11). This brings the idea of righteousness into an experiential relation to the children of God.

i. The Conscience (Suneidesis)

The writer used this word in contexts where he was showing the inefficacy of the Old Testament ritual as over against the sacrifice through Christ which possessed redemptive value (9:9, 14; 10:2, 32; 13:18). The author declared, "According to this arrangement, gifts and sacrifices are offered which cannot perfect the conscience of the worshiper" (9: 9). To this he added, "How much more shall the blood of Christ, who through the eternal Spirit offered himself without blemish to God, purify your conscience from dead works to serve the living God" (v. 14). By this he was saying that these bloody sacrifices availed only to make the offerer ceremonially clean. They were ineffective in removing the guilt of sin. The conscience is that part of man's personality which is conscious of moral and ethical values. It commends good conduct and expresses guilt for sinful conduct, whether in thoughts, motives, or acts. The inefficacy of the old sacrifices to perfect the conscience of the worshiper was evident from the continuing sense of guilt on the part of the wrongdoer.

On the other hand, the blood of Christ possessed the dynamic of purifying, purging, and cleansing the conscience from dead or lifeless formality.[15]

In 10:2 the translations of this word vary between *conscience* and *consciousness.* This is evidence of both a nonmoral sense of this word, as well as its ethical significance. That is, in the realm of man's consciousness the integral part of its awareness is that relating to things right and wrong, good and evil. Another aspect of the conscience becomes evident in 10:22: "Let us draw near with a true heart in full assurance of faith, with our hearts sprinkled clean from an evil conscience and our bodies washed with pure water." This is made possible by the new and living way, the blood of Jesus. The conscience centers in the heart. When the heart is cleansed, the conscience no longer has a sense of guilt. The author claimed to have a clean conscience. The adjective *kalos* carries the meaning *good, honorable,* and *clean.* In other words the author had a consciousness of having lived a life of good deeds. These uses of the word *conscience* stand as a valuable supplement to Paul's grasp of this word.

7. The Author's Use of the Old Testament

a. The Old Testament the Fundamental Basis of the Letter

As noted at the beginning of this chapter the writer began his letter with the comprehensive statement, "In many and various ways God spoke of old to our fathers by the prophets" (1:1). In this manner he asserted the prophetic nature of the Old Testament. He proceeded to structure the letter on the Old Testament view of the prophets and their messages. God speaking through the prophets was fundamentally on the same level as His speaking by (*Greek: en*) a Son. The structuring of these opening verses showed that God's speaking *in* a Son was the culmination and climax of God's revelation to man. These opening verses thus serve as a foundation for grasping the author's use of the Old Testament.

b. The Modes of Citation and Their Significance[16]

(1) God, the Speaker (1:5, 7, 13; 4:7; 5:5, 6; 6:14; 8:8-12; 12:26). These quotations are from the Psalms, where God is speaking directly or through a prophet. The significant point, however, is that the author of the letter uniformly ascribes the words to God.

(2) Words attributed to Christ (2:11-13; 10:5-7, 8, 9). In these quotations from the Psalms and Isaiah the respective speakers are the psalmist and the prophet. The author of the letter ascribed all of them to Christ. Whether or not the readers had recognized their messianic significance, the writer of the letter was making the most meaningful advance in the interpretation of the Scriptures. Stating this conclusion in another manner the author was showing his readers that Christ was already speaking in the Old Testament, consequently these words belong on the same level as Jesus' teachings recorded in the Gospels.

(3) The Holy Spirit, the Speaker (3:7-11; 10:15-17; see also 9:8). Here again the Old Testament Scriptures quoted are not ascribed to the Holy Spirit and further the author quoted these passages again in 4:7 and 8:8, referring them to God. From a doctrinal point of view the author's attributing Old Testament Scriptures indiscriminately among God, Christ, and the Holy Spirit, was thus ascribing the Old Testament Scriptures to the triune God.

(4) Undesignated References (1:6; 2:6; 3:15; 7:17, 21; 10:30, 37, 38; and others). In more than a dozen cases the writer quoted Old Testament passages without giving their source. The occurrence of these quotations alongside those attributed to God, Christ, and the Holy Spirit, stands as evidence that to the writer any quotation from the Old Testament is from the authoritative Word of God. In no case did the author at-

tach to the quotation a claim for the unique character of the Old Testament, such as Paul and Peter expressed in their definitive statements setting forth the inspiration of the Old Testament (2 Tim. 3:15, 16; 2 Pet. 1:20, 21).

c. Significance of the Author's Use of the Old Testament for Biblical Theology

(1) God's words to Israel possess value for all mankind throughout human history. Christians, whether Jew or Gentile, need to reassess the Old Testament for its values fulfilled in Christ.

(2) The writer's use of the Old Testament shows its values for understanding the revelation through Christ and the Holy Spirit. This has a definite bearing on the discipline of biblical theology. A basic motif for biblical theology is the recognition of both the Old Testament and the New as being God's revelation through Christ and the Holy Spirit.

(3) There is a need for grasping the author's exposition of the Old Testament as it laid the foundation for interpreting the new revelation. This accounts for the author's building his message on the Old Testament Scriptures, not that he was quoting them to support the revelation through Christ, but rather, that there is a structural unity in both the old and the new covenants. The writer did not use the key expression, "It is written," which other New Testament writers used so frequently. Herein is a profound concept.

(4) In the words of Westcott, "There is a spiritual meaning in the whole record of the Old Testament."[17] A glance at several portions of the letter such as 2:6 ff.; 4:1 ff.; 9:8 ff.; etc., confirm this statement. A thorough study of the entire letter most certainly enlarges our understanding of the Old Testament.

d. Laying Hold of the Author's Use of the Old Testament

This inquiry comes into focus when we observe that the Old Testament's quotations are not given as proof texts, but rather that their meaning becomes clear in the light of what is being realized in Christ and the Holy Spirit. The significance of this statement becomes clearer in view of the total absence of the expression "It is written" or "is fulfilled." This becomes evident throughout the letter as the author presents his respective major teachings. The first *catena* or series of quotations found in 1:5-14 makes this thought clear. Observe that the Scriptures quoted are not in the form of predictions, but the author is drawing from these references their inherent meaning. They all focus attention on the superiority of the Son to the angels. Another significant catena of quotations is found in 5:1-10. In this context the writer is presenting Christ as High Priest. In support of this truth he draws in three different passages from the Old Testament, none of which is used in a predictive sense.

The most significant example of the author's unfolding the meaning of the Old Testament in the light of the New stands forth in chapters 5-7. In this section the author sets forth Christ as "a high priest for ever after the order of Melchizedek." Thus Psalm 110:4 furnishes the Old Testament foundation for the author's explication of Christ as Priest and King. Another example of this structure of thought occurs in 8:1-7. Note the reference to the *true* or *real (alethinos)* tent. Thus the Old Testament tabernacle was not the real tent. Further the sacrifices under the law served as a *copy* (*hupodeigna)* and *shadow (skia)* of the heavenly sanctuary. God had commanded Moses to make everything according to the *pattern (tupos),* which was shown to him in the mountain. In this context the author presented Jeremiah's prediction of God's establishing a new covenant. This in effect makes the first covenant old or obsolete. In this manner the writer was making still clearer the grand concept of how Christ's institution of the new covenant unfolded most profoundly the meaning of the Sinaitic covenant, which had then become outmoded. He wrote of the new covenant, not in terms of the fulfillment of a prediction but rather in that of the infinitely superior quality of the new over that of the old covenant.

Chapter 9 brings to the fore another example of how the author unfolded the meaning of the Old Testament in the light of what was being realized in the New. Verses 6 to 10 bring this point into focus. While there are some exegetical problems in this paragraph, I shall seek to give a positive presentation, trusting that this rightly interprets the thought of the writer. He introduced this discussion by noting the regulations for worship in the tabernacle in accordance with the Sinaitic covenant. The central point of his thought was the once a-year entrance of the high priest into the holy of holies with a bloody offering. Then he states, "By this the Holy Spirit indicates that the way into the sanctuary is not yet opened as long as the outer tent is still standing (which is symbolic for the present age)" (vv. 8, 9). By this he was stating that the old covenant did not provide direct access to God. The writer then gave the parenthetic note that this is a *parabole (symbol, figure, parable, similitude, type).* The meaning of the author's expression, *the present age,* may become evident in the expressions: *the world to come* (2:5); *the age to come* (6:5); *the end of the age* (9:26); and the *good things to come* (10:1).

Perhaps the starting point in solving this problem is the expression "these last days" (1:2), which the writer definitely labels as the time in which God spoke by His Son. Here also is an exegetical problem. Should we translate the phrase literally *in the end of these days* or *in these last days?* According to F. F. Bruce this is an expression from the Septuagint which reflects the Old Testament expression, "In the latter end of the days" as found in numerous Old Testament Scriptures including Isaiah 2:2; Jeremiah 23:20; Ezekiel 38:16; Daniel 10:14; Hosea 3:5; etc.[18] If this gives us the true sense of this expression, then we should understand *these last days* as defining the eschatological era inaugurated by the Son. This would lead us to understand the expression "*the world to come*" (2:5) as referring to the same era of time as that expressed in 1:2. The expression "age to come" of 6:5 would then refer to this same period of time.

The interpretation of 9:8-10 remains to be resolved. Does the expression "the present age" refer to the time when the old sacrificial system was still to be observed or to the time introduced by Christ's sacrifice? The expression "time of *reformation*" *(diorthosis)* in verse 10 would suggest that the "*present age*" of verse 9 comes to an end at the time of *reformation*. According to the lexicons *diorthosis* carries the meaning *making straight, the new order*, and *reconstruction*. From this we would gather that the writer was clarifying to his readers the termination of Israel's sacrificial worship at the coming of Christ. He inaugurated the era of time appropriately labeled the *reformation*. This shows again that the author's use of the Old Testament was not dialectical or rhetorical but interpretative.

Perhaps the most significant illustration of the author's use of the Old Testament is apparent in 10:11-18. In this context he shows from Jeremiah's predictions that Christ's offering for all time, a single sacrifice for sins, instituted the new covenant. On this account the writer could most triumphantly conclude, "Where there is forgiveness of these, there is no longer any offering for sin" (10:18). In a most marvelous way he depicted the nature of faith, making it clear that the faith manifested by God's people in the Old Testament was the same in quality as that of Christian believers. These Christian Jews needed to learn that the pharisaical doctrine of good works misrepresented the Old Testament people of God. The Pharisees had been stressing the necessity of keeping every detail of the law and completely ignored the faith relationship between Israel and the Lord.

A concluding observation has to do with the question as to whether or not the writer of this letter gave any inclination or anticipation of a new body of Holy Scriptures or Sacred Writings. Since the writer gave such a profound interpretation of the Old Testament, we could expect that he would in some verbal manner lay the groundwork for the New Testament. It is conceivable that his sublime benediction might be giving some such suggestion. It reads, "Now may the God of peace who brought again from the dead our Lord Jesus, the great shepherd of the sheep, by the blood of the eternal covenant, equip you with everything good that you may do his will, working in you that which is pleasing in his sight, through Jesus Christ; to whom be glory for ever and ever. Amen."

For Additional Reading and Reference:

Beyschlag, *New Testament Theology*, Vol. II, pp. 282-347.
Bruce, F. F., *New Testament Development of Old Testament Themes*, pp. 51-67.
Hunter, *Introducing New Testament Theology*, pp. 117-124.
Klassen and Snyder, *Current in New Testament Interpretation*, pp. 53-78.
Morris, *The Cross in the New Testament*, pp. 270-308.
Newman, *The Meaning of the New Testament*, pp. 256-268.
Ryrie, *Biblical Theology of the New Testament*, pp. 225-261.
Sheldon, *New Testament Theology*, pp. 270-299.
Stevens, *Theology of the New Testament*, pp. 483-522.
Taylor, *The Atonement in New Testament Teachings*, pp. 101-130.
Taylor, *The Person of Christ*, pp. 89-98.
Van Oosterzee, *The Theology of the New Testament*, pp. 304-323.
Vos, *The Teaching of the Epistle to the Hebrews*.
Weidner, *Biblical Theology of the New Testament*, Vol. II, pp. 204-228.
Weiss, *Biblical Theology of the New Testament*, Vol. II, pp. 150-155, 166-234.

1. Heb. 2:1-4; 3:7-19; 4:1-13; 5:11-14; 6:1-12; 10:19-31; 12:1-17.
2. Heb. 1:2, 5, 8; 2:6; 3:6; 4:14; 5:5, 8; 6:6; 7:3, 28; 10:29; 11:17, 24.
3. Heb. 1:14; 2:3; 5:7-9; 6:9; 7:25; 9:28.
4. Heb. 7:22; 8:6-10, 13; 9:1, 4, 15, 18, 20; 10:16, 29; 12:24; 13:20.
5. Heb. 4:2, 3; 6:1, 12; 10:22, 38, 39; 11:1-39; 12:2; 13:7.
6. *The International Standard Bible Encyclopaedia* (Chicago: The Howard-Severance Co., 1930), Vol. IV, article, "Person of Christ," p. 2341.
7. He supported this claim by quoting Ps. 2:7; 2 Sam. 7:14; Deut. 32:43 (Sept.); Ps. 97:7; 104:4; 45:6, 7; 102:25-27; 110:1. Note other occurrences of this title in 3:6; 4:14; 5:5, 8; 7:28; 10:29.
8. Heb. 3:6-19; 4; 5:11-14; 6:1-12; 10:19-39; 12:1-17.
9. *The New International Commentary on the New Testament, The Epistle to the Hebrews* (Grand Rapids: Wm. B. Eerdmans Publishing Co., 1964), p. 165.
10. *The Epistle to the Hebrews*, Second Edition (London and New York: Macmillan and Co., 1892), p. 349.
11. For more elaborate definitions of these words see Greek lexicons, dictionaries of the Bible, and theological word study books of the Bible.
12. *A Greek-English Lexicon of the New Testament*, p. 43.
13. Robertson, *op. cit.*, Vol. V. pp. 432, 433.
14. *Ibid.*, p. 375.

15. By reason of the importance of these ideas the reader should consult Greek lexicons and the various translations of these verses.

16. For this treatment I am greatly indebted to Brooke Foss Westcott's note, *On the Use of the Old Testament in the Epistle, The Epistle to the Hebrews*, Second Edition (New York: Macmillan and Co., 1892), pp. 469-495.

17. *Ibid.*, p. 480.

18. *Ibid.*, p. 3.

CHAPTER II

THE THEOLOGY OF JOHN

1. Introduction

a. The Reasons for Giving a Unified Treatment of John's Theology

In the first place I believe that sound biblical criticism gives adequate attestation to John's being the author of his Gospel, letters, and the Revelation. Second, there is a common viewpoint even though there are differences of purpose, subject matter, and mode of treatment in these books. Third, the dates of their being written are very close together, thus showing that the author's fundamental viewpoint would be the same in all of them. Fourth, there is much common doctrinal content in these books in that all have a common focus in Christ and in the consciousness of a world conflict bringing tribulation upon the church.

b. John's Gospel in Relation to the Synoptics

Although there are a sizable number of common incidents found in all the Gospels, yet a very limited amount of the material in John is parallel to accounts found among the Synoptics. These factors certainly reflect a distinctive purpose of John's Gospel, which he expressed in the words, "these are written that you may believe that Jesus is the Christ, the Son of God, and that believing you may have life in his name" (20:31). The late Dr. Charles R. Erdman noted that three dominant ideas are set forth in this Gospel: "testimony, faith, and life." He wrote "This Gospel is a record of testimony and shows that faith is belief founded upon evidence." Robertson noted that this Gospel is John's portrait of Christ. [2]

c. The Distinctive Nature of the Revelation

The world situation during the last decade of the first century is definitely reflected in this book. This becomes evident in its opening words "the revelation of Jesus Christ, which God gave him to show to his servants what must soon take place." He expanded this in the words, "I John, your brother, who share with you in Jesus the tribulation and the kingdom, and the patient endurance, was on the island called Patmos on account of the word of God and the testimony of Jesus" (Rev. 1:9). The tribulation announced by Christ in John 16:33

had come upon the church. John was sharing the patient endurance with the fellow believers. The centrality of the motif in this book becomes apparent in 2:2, 3, 9, 10, 19; 3:10; 7:14; 13:10; and 14:12. Four times he refers to those "who had been slain for the word of God and for the witness they had borne" (6:9, 11; 12:11; 20:4). Further, this book is distinctive in being an *apocalypse (revelation).* This title places the book in the same category as Ezekiel and portions of other Old Testament books as Isaiah, Joel, Zechariah, and Daniel. Its language is symbolic, mysterious, and cryptic in character. Thus while this book was a revelation, its structure of thought presents difficult problems for interpretation.

d. Reasons for John's Apocalyptic Presentation

On the one side it is conceivable that John gave this apocalyptic presentation so that the Roman world would not grasp its distinctive purpose of bracing the Christians for their life-and-death struggle with paganism. To the pagan world this form of presentation concealed the real purpose of the book. The church, on the other hand, was in a position to interpret Babylon (14:18; 16:19; 17:5; 18:2, 10, 21) as the archenemy, Rome. This revelation disclosed to the church that their suffering persecution was due to the resistance of the earthly powers against the power of Christ manifested in the church. Involved in this was a warning to the Christians against emperor worship. It interpreted to them the real meaning of Domitian's reign of terror. It manifested his self-deification. In a positive way John sought to build up the hope of the church in Christ's final triumph, but also that they were in a life-and-death struggle with the world, the flesh, and the devil.

e. Structure of the Revelation

One clue to the structure of this book becomes evident in the seven churches, seals, trumpets, and vials. This phenomenon leads to perceiving a telescopic arrangement in which one section develops out of the last part of the preceding section. Thus the seven trumpets are sounded after the opening of the seventh seal. The personages of chapters 12 and 13 appear in the sounding of the seventh trumpet, and the judgments of chapters 17-20 grow out of the seventh vial. In this structure history is carried forward a number of times to the return of Christ and the judgment: 6:12-17; 11:15-19; 14:14-20; 16:12-21; 19:11-21; and 20:7-15. Close study of these sections will show striking similarities, sufficient it seems to confirm their identity. They all describe Christ's return for judgment. The vision of the throne in chapter 4 presents the enthronement of Christ at His ascension. If this interprets correctly the telescopic or spiral arrangement structure of the book, the foundation is laid for the true interpretation of the book.

f. The Contents of the Revelation Grounded in Three Hundred and Forty-eight Allusions or Brief Quotations from the Old Testament

These are among the most remarkable phenomena of the book. This becomes evident by noting the boldface type for these quotations in a Greek New Testament. Most of these quotations come from the Psalms, Isaiah, Ezekiel, and Daniel. The manner in which these quotations occur in the book shows that John was writing from the background of these Scriptures and was weaving them into his book in somewhat the same manner as a minister, more or less, consciously intertwines biblical quotations in a sermon. In other words this book is grounded in the Old Testament. For the study of biblical theology this fact is significant. This becomes evident when we observe that the last book of the New Testament builds on the doctrinal content of the Old Testament. Most significantly in the area of eschatology the Revelation gives final confirmation both to the unity and to the progress of God's revelation in the Scriptures. This becomes most graphically apparent in the fact that the opening chapters of Genesis reveal God's act of creation, while the closing chapters of Revelation predict the creation of the new heavens and the new earth.

2. Jesus, the Christ, the Son of God

This assertion stands out most significantly in John's stated purpose of writing his Gospel, "These are written that you may believe that Jesus is the Christ, the Son of God" (Jn. 20:31). John's presentation of Jesus as the Christ is the most elaborate and profound in the entire New Testament. This is not to lower the distinctive nature of Paul's teachings on the Lord, but rather to grasp this momentous characteristic of John's writings. Paul's approach was more explicitly doctrinal and theological. I have no interest in stressing any contrast between John and Paul with regard to any difference in their respective approaches to the person and work of Christ.

a. Jesus, the Word (logos)

John's presentation of this truth in the prologue of his Gospel is most profound. The Greek word *logos* calls for special study. "The source of John's *logos* doctrine," wrote Andrew S. Walls, "is in the person and work of the historical Christ. 'Jesus is not to be interpreted by *logos; logos* is intelligible only as we think of Jesus.' "[3] The secondary quote is from W. F. Howard, *The Interpreter's Bible* (New York, Abingdon-Cokesbury Press, 1962), Vol. VIII, p. 442. The meaning which John gives to *logos* thus centers in Christ Himself. The Word was in the beginning, the Word was with God, the Word was God. "The Word became flesh . . . "we have beheld his glory, glory as of the only Son from the Father" (1:14).

John did not give any background to his use of *logos*. On this account there is little to be gained by probing into philosophical uses such as by *Philo* or even its use in the Old Testament. Nevertheless, the buildup of meaning of this term must include its literal sense of language *(vox)* on to its more complex connotation referring to what someone has said, a discourse or speech, doctrine (that which is communicated by instruction), anything reported in speech such as a narration, matter under discussion, reason, and finally, the deeply enriched meaning given to it by the Apostle John in his prologue.[4]

With this background of thought we should observe how John was revealing to his readers the dignity of Christ, the Son of God. The Christ is genuine Deity, yet He is a distinct Person just as God is. He shared in God's work of creation. The life manifested by Christ possessed the spiritual quality of being the life of men. Being divine He could take upon Himself human nature so that mankind could behold His divine glory. In this manner these opening verses of John's Gospel led his readers to understand the person and work of Jesus Christ, and would lead them to believe that Jesus was the Word, the Son of God.

Two other expressions of John may relate to this *logos* teaching (1 Jn. 1:1-3; Rev. 19:13). As John introduced his first letter, he set forth the manifestation of Jesus in the flesh, referring to Him as the *Word of life*. In the apocalyptic language of Revelation he disclosed the glorified Christ in the language "*the Word of God*" (Rev. 19:13). A careful study of these references gives grounds for believing that they explicitly contribute to the *logos (Word)* teaching of John 1:1-14.

The author enlarged his affirmation of the Christ being the Word by noting that His followers beheld His glory (1:14). In a significant way John related the signs performed by Jesus as manifestations of His glory. Note John's comment on Jesus' turning the water into wine: "This, the first of his signs, Jesus did at Cana in Galilee, and manifested his glory" (2:11). The words of Nicodemus to Jesus add to this conclusion: "We know that you are a teacher come from God; for no one can do these signs that you do, unless God is with him" (3:2). John concluded his references to these signs in the words, "Now Jesus did many other signs in the presence of the disciples, which are not written in this book" (20:30).[5] (See also: 4:54; 6:2, 14, 26; 7:31; 9:16; 11:47; 12:18, 37).

The word *sign (semeion)* is a significant word used by John with reference to Jesus' miracles and wonders. It is these "by which God authenticates the men sent by Him, or by which men prove that the cause they are pleading is God's."[6] Richardson makes the significant comment, "The miracles of Jesus are *signs:* they are never mere *tereta (wonders),* but *tereta* and *semeia* (signs). But they are signs only to those who have eyes to see, those to whom it is given to understand the mystery of who Jesus is."[7] Of such importance were the signs performed by Jesus that there would be those who would deceive the people by false signs: Revelation 13:13, 14; 16:14; 19:20.

b. The Son of God

This title ascribed to Jesus is the most important of all. It attributes deity to Christ in the most significant language found in the Scriptures. It is basic to the doctrine of the Trinity. According to the Old Testament, as well as the New, sonship to the Father asserts the equality of the two. John's use of this title expresses most emphatically both the deity and trinitarian declaration and affirmation of this fact. Thus the glory manifested by the Son is that of the Father (Jn. 1:14). John declared, "The only Son, who is in the bosom of the Father, he has made him known" (v. 18). Hendriksen gives a significant comment, "The added clause *who lies upon the Father's breast* indicates a relation of abiding closeness between the Father — God and the Son — God. Because Jesus Christ is the Son in the highest sense of the term, He knows the Father thoroughly."[8] Having witnessed the Spirit descend upon Christ, John the Baptist declared, "This is the Son of God" (v. 34). The Baptist was well aware that he could not make this declaration without such a witness from heaven. If Jesus spoke the words of 3:16-18, which are the most treasured words of the Bible, they express Jesus' affirmation of being the Son of God. When Jesus called God His Father, the Jews properly understood that He was "making himself equal with God" (5:18). Jesus expanded this Father-Son relationship in the words, "The Son can do nothing of his own accord, but only what he sees the Father doing" (v. 19). In this manner Jesus asserted the Father-Son relationship which characterized His entire earthly ministry. In Jesus' final conversation with the disciples, He said, "Whatever you ask in my name, I will do it, that the Father may be glorified in the Son" (14:13). In His great high-priestly prayer, Jesus said, "Father . . . glorify thy Son that the Son may glorify thee" (17:1). These and other statements in this Gospel lay at the foundation of John's purpose, expressed in the words, "These are written that you may believe that Jesus is the Christ, the Son of God" (20:31).

The author, John, made a number of significant uses of this title in his letters, plus one in the Revelation. The apostle opened his first letter with a profound presentation of the Son who was made manifest in human form. He noted, "Our fellowship is with the Father and with his Son Jesus Christ" (1:3). Throughout the letter John declared the equality of the Son with the Father. Emphatically he stated, "No one who denies the Son has the Father. He who confesses the Son has the Father also. . . . If what you heard from the beginning abides in you, then you will abide in the Son and in the Father" (2:22-24). Later he added, "The reason the Son of God appeared was to destroy the works of the devil" (3:8). John brought into clear focus the necessity of confessing "that Jesus is the Son of God" (4:15). John underscored this thought in the words, "This is the testimony of God that he has borne witness to his Son. He who believes in the Son of God has the testimony in himself. He who does not believe God, has made him a liar, because he has not believed in the testimony that God has borne to his Son. And this is the testimony, that God gave us eternal life, and this life is in his Son. He who has the Son has life; he who has not the Son has not life" (5:9-12). In his second letter John wrote, "Any one who . . . does not abide in the doctrine of Christ does not have God; he who abides in the doctrine of Christ has both the Father and the Son" (2 Jn. 9). The only but significant use of this title in the Revelation is: "The words of the Son of God, who has eyes like a flame of fire, and whose feet are like burnished bronze" (2:18). From these uses of this title it becomes evident that John attached highest meaning to it, especially as it set forth Christ's deity and oneness with the Father. The theological import of this truth becomes evident when we note again John's first reference to the title when he declared that the Word had become flesh and that His manifested glory revealed Him as the only Son from the Father (1:14).

c. The Son of Man

In John's earliest recorded words of Jesus He declared to Nathanael, "You will see heaven opened, and the angels of God ascending and descending upon the Son of man" (1:51). Thus at the very beginning of His ministry Christ identified Himself with the "Son of man," whom Daniel had seen in his night vision (Dan. 7:13, 14). Thus at the beginning of His ministry Christ declared Himself as being the One to whom "was given dominion and glory and kingdom, that all peoples, nations, and languages should serve him; his dominion is an everlasting dominion, which shall not pass away, and his kingdom one that shall not be destroyed" (v. 14). John's twelve references to Jesus' use of this title serve as the sure foundation for his purpose in writing this Gospel. Thus Jesus made clear to Nicodemus that He was qualified to tell him of "heavenly things" in proof of which Jesus said that the Son of Man would be lifted up "that whoever believes in him may have eternal life" (Jn. 3:14-15).

Jesus brought together in one context both the titles Son of God and Son of Man (5:25-29). When the Jews persecuted Jesus because of His miracle-working on the Sabbath, He declared, "My Father is working still, and I am working" (v. 17). The Jews became enraged at the Lord because He was "making himself equal with God" (v. 18). As Jesus gave further answer to His opponents, He declared, "The hour is coming, and now is, when the dead will hear the voice of the Son of God, and those who hear will live. For as the Father has life in himself, so he has granted the Son also to have life in himself, and has given him authority to execute judgment, because he is the Son of man" (vv. 25-27). In bringing together these two titles Jesus was asserting the deity significance of the latter. Thus the title *the Son of Man* asserted Christ's deity as plainly as the title *the Son of God.* Jesus' claim that God the Father had set His seal upon Him as the Son of Man may carry the significance that God had marked Him with a seal (certified, attested) to show that God was working through Him. The feeding of the five thousand, together with Jesus' other signs, were evidences of God's seal.

Other uses of this title are significant for the manner with which they set forth the divine-human nature of Christ. Note the words, "Unless you eat the flesh of the Son of man and drink his blood, you have no life in you; he who eats my flesh and drinks my blood has eternal life, and I will raise him up at the last day. For my flesh is food indeed, and my blood is drink indeed" (6:53-55). In this manner Jesus passed from the miraculous feeding of the five thousand to its almost unfathomable spiritual significance. The Son of Man who was at once divine and human needed to be appropriated spiritually just as natural food is eaten. If on the grounds of implicit faith we believe that the Son of Man suffered and died for our sins, we will live forever. There was hardly a more instructive way in which our Lord could set forth Himself as the Son of Man than through this discourse on the bread of life.

The deity significance of this title becomes all the more meaningful when Jesus asserted, "When you have lifted up the Son of man, then you will know that I am he, and that I do nothing on my own authority but speak thus as the Father taught me" (8:28). Here again those who heard Jesus' words could easily believe in His genuine humanity. But their laying hold of His deity remained an incomprehensible mystery. In response to the request on the part of some Greeks to see Jesus, He replied, "The hour has come for the Son of man to be glorified" (12:23). Here again Jesus asserted that His being the Son of Man involved His suffering and death. When Judas left the upper room at the Last Supper, Jesus declared, "Now is the Son of man glorified, and in him God is glorified" (13:31). In this incident Jesus repeated the declaration made in the preceding passage. Climactically John declared the actual enthronement of the Son of Man as noted in the Revelation.[9]

d. The Word Became Flesh

Having noted the deity of Christ as set forth in the title *Son of Man,* we should note His humanity as declared in the words, "The Word became flesh" (Jn. 1:14). Repeatedly throughout his writings John related incidents which set forth the genuine humanity of Jesus. Note the following: Jesus' conversation with His first disciples (vv. 35-51); Jesus going down to Capernaum with His mother and His brothers (2:12); Jesus persecuted by the Jews who tried to kill Him (5:18); Jesus following His brothers to the Feast of Tabernacles, where the Jews recognized Him as a man (7:1-15); Mary anointing the feet of Jesus (12:1-8); Jesus washing the disciples' feet (13:1-20); Jesus under trial before Caiaphas and Pilate (18:1-38); after His resurrection Jesus speaking to Mary and the disciples showing them His hands and His side (20:11-29); John bearing witness to the human Jesus whom he heard, saw, and touched with his hands (1 Jn. 1:1-4); and many other incidents which confirm His humanity often in contexts which also assert His deity.

John gave adequate grounds for believing that Jesus was at once divine and human, but one person. This establishes the unfathomable mystery of the incarnate Son of God. In view of the total message of the author we have adequate grounds for believing in the unity of His person, as well as His genuine deity and humanity. There is absolutely no uncertainty as to what the writer, John, believed and declared concerning Jesus, the Son of God. In plain language he declared Christ's deity, "The Word was God," and at the same time making clear distinction between Him and God; and also asserting, "The Word became flesh." The author's Gospel, letters, and the Revelation gave fullest confirmation of these unfathomable truths.

e. Jesus Christ, the Messiah

After Jesus ascended to heaven, He became known as Jesus Christ. This becomes evident in the Acts and in the letters of Paul, Peter, and

John. In other words, Jesus Christ became the name of our Lord.[10] It is significant, then, that we observe the transition from such expressions as Jesus, the Christ, to that of Jesus Christ. In other words, there was the transition from identifying Jesus as the Christ to that of being named Jesus Christ.

The Old Testament background to Jesus' title, the Christ, becomes evident in Psalms 2:2; 18:50; 84:9; 89:38, 51; 132:10, 17. The prophets seemed to lay hold of these psalms, giving them a more distinctive significance of referring to One to come to be known as the Messiah. Jacob had given a sense of direction to this thought in the words, "The scepter shall not depart from Judah, nor the ruler's staff from between his feet, until he comes to whom it belongs; and to him shall be the obedience of the peoples" (Gen. 49:10). Balaam gave further direction to this prediction in the words, "I see him, but not now; I behold him, but not nigh: a star shall come forth out of Jacob and a scepter shall arise out of Israel" (Num. 24:17). A significant statement made by Moses to Israel undoubtedly helped to crystallize the concept of a coming Anointed One. He said, "The Lord your God will raise up for you a prophet like me from among you, from your brethren — him you shall heed. . . . I will put my words in his mouth, and he shall speak to them all that I command him" (Deut. 18:15-18).

Several of the Psalms gave a still clearer picture of God's Anointed One.[11] This One stands out as the Lord's Anointed One. His divine throne endures forever. He loves righteousness and hates wickedness. He shall be made highest of the kings of the earth. His throne shall continue as the days of the heavens. He will sit at the Lord's right hand. He shall be a priest forever after the order of Melchizedek. He shall be a descendant of David. The latter prophets predicted still more specifically concerning the Anointed One.[12] The One to come shall be born of a virgin and shall be called Immanuel. The government shall be upon His shoulders and He will have the majestic names: Wonderful Counselor, Mighty God, Everlasting Father, and Prince of Peace. "Of the increase of his government and of peace there will be no end, upon the throne of David, and over his kingdom, to establish it, and to uphold it with justice and with righteousness from this time forth and forever more" (Is. 9:6, 7). Through this One the Lord will make a new covenant with the house of Israel and with the house of Judah. Like David He will be a shepherd and He will make a covenant of peace with His people. In the language of Daniel's apocalyptic vision, the time of the coming of the Anointed One will be sixty-nine weeks after the word to restore and build Jerusalem (Dan. 9:25).

These and other predictions crystallized the concept of the coming

Anointed One. When Andrew had his first conversation with Jesus he told Peter, "We have found the Messiah" (Jn. 1:41). In similar language Philip said to Nathanael, "We have found him of whom Moses in the law and also the prophets wrote, Jesus of Nazareth, the son of Joseph" (1:45). The concept of the Messiah of those who had not met Jesus was quite indefinite (Jn. 4:25-29; 7:26, 27, 31; 12:34). Nevertheless, those who believed in Jesus had no problem in recognizing Him as the Christ. Throughout John's writings Jesus, the Christ, was called the Son of God (Jn. 11:27; 1 Jn. 1:3; 3:23; 5:20; 2 Jn. 3), and also the Son of Man (Jn. 12:34). In the Revelation the Christ and God are practically identified (11:15; 12:10). In Jesus' prayer He recognized that God had sent Him into the world. In response to Pilate's question Jesus answered, "My kingship is not of this world" (Jn. 18:36). So clearly had Jesus been attested as the Christ that His name became Jesus Christ (Jn. 1:17; 1 Jn. 2:1; Rev. 1:1, 2, 5). It is well to note the buildup which these several titles of our Lord gained in John's writings. Jesus was at once the Son of God, the Son of Man, the incarnate Word, the Messiah. The following subtopic gives still further significance to these titles.

f. The Light of the World

John set forth in his prologue yet another declaration concerning Jesus Christ. It stands forth in the words, "In him was life, and the life was the light of men. The light shines in the darkness, and the darkness has not overcome it" (1:4, 5). The setting of these words gives John's perspective of their significance. The literal use of light and darkness throughout the Bible prepares the way for its most meaningful significance as a spiritual concept, the identification of life with light. Thus the light possesses the dynamic of life. John noted the opposition of darkness to light, a warfare in which the darkness is not succeeding. The author noted that the Word was the true light. The Greek word *alephinos* has the meanings *dependable, true, genuine,* and *real.* They stand opposed to what is imperfect or defective.[13] In other words, there is no other light which is comparable to the Word. This true light came into the world to enlighten every man. The writer's further presentation of the Word in the prologue is properly understood as an unfolding of the great truth bound up in Jesus, the light of the world. The opposition of the world to the true light becomes more apparent in 3:16-21. In this setting Jesus set forth the condemnation of those who did not believe in Him. He declared, "And this is the judgment, that the light has come into the world, and men loved darkness better than light, because their deeds were evil. For every one who does evil hates the light, and does not come to the light, lest his deeds should be exposed. But he who does what is true comes to the light, that it may be clearly seen that his deeds have been wrought in God" (vv. 19-21). This language exposes the tragedy involved in hating the light. In this manner our Lord declared the ethical nature of the light.

Jesus stressed this truth repeatedly throughout His ministry. He declared, "I am the light of the world" (9:5). Those who follow Him will have the light of life" (8:12). In Jesus' closing message of His public ministry, He said, "While you have the light, believe in the light, that you may become sons of light" (12:36). "I have come as light into the world, that whoever believes in me may not remain in darkness" (v. 46). John added to the doctrinal content of this theme when he wrote, "God is light and in him is no darkness at all . . . if we walk in the light, as he is in the light, we have fellowship with one another, and the blood of Jesus his Son cleanses us from all sin" (1 Jn. 1:5-7). In this manner John was declaring the fellowship of those who walk in the light, together with the redemptive aspects of this manner of life. He expressed this truth more explicitly in the words, "The darkness is passing away and the true light is already shining. He who says he is in the light and hates his brother is in the darkness still. He who loves his brother abides in the light, and in it there is no cause for stumbling" (2:8-10). As a grand climax to this theme John gave a description of the heavenly temple, in the words, "And the city has no need of sun or moon to shine upon it, for the glory of God is its light, and its lamp is the Lamb. By its light shall the nations walk . . . and there shall be no night there" (Rev. 21:23-25). To this he added, "And night shall be no more; they need no light of the lamp or sun, for the Lord God will be their light" (22:5). Thus the glorious and majestic light of Jesus our Lord will shine forth through the ceaseless ages of eternity.

g. The Lamb of God

Undoubtedly John the Baptist amazed his disciples when on seeing Jesus, he declared, "Behold, the Lamb of God, who takes away the sin of the world!" (Jn. 1:29). At once we ponder the meaning of John's statement; especially since a number of different interpretations have been given to the Baptist's words. I am inclined to believe that a number of Old Testament references to a lamb contribute to the meaning of this title. First, in order of time, was the Passover lamb (Ex. 12: 3-11). This was a lamb without any blemish. The use of its blood was distinctive in setting forth the expiatory aspect of the sacrifice through which the firstborn of every Israelite family was spared from the destruction of the last plague upon the Egyptians. Since the Passover had become Israel's most significant sacrificial service, we have grounds for believing that the Baptist was identifying the Lamb of God as the fulfillment of this foremost typical sacrifice. It is possible that the Baptist was referring to the lamb sacrifices in Israel's worship (Ex. 29:38-42; Num. 28:3-13), which by reason of the frequency of these offerings occupied an important place in Israel's worship. By reason of the outstanding Servant of the Lord passage of Isaiah 52:7 — 53:12, it is perhaps most likely that the Baptist's words reflected this context, most specifically the portion, "He was oppressed, and he was afflicted, yet he opened not his mouth; like a lamb that is led to the slaughter, and like a sheep that before its shearers is dumb, so he opened not his mouth. . . . Yet it was the will of the Lord to bruise him; he has put him to grief; when he makes himself an offering for sin" (53:7-10). It may be that the Baptist was identifying Jesus with the words of Jeremiah, "I was like a gentle lamb led to the slaughter" (Jer. 11:19). In view of the fact that repeated predictions of certain messianic events characterize the Old Testament, it is possible that a similar relationship exists among these Lamb of God statements. It is possible that the writer, John, confirmed the Baptist's reference to the Paschal lamb when he noted, "For these things took place that the scripture might be fulfilled, 'Not a bone of him shall be broken' " (Jn. 19:36).

The Apostle John made twenty-nine references to the "Lamb" in the Revelation. A factor of major interest centers in the meaning and significance of the uniform use of this title to set forth the reigning Lord and Christ. It becomes a question of major importance as to why he did not use the kingly titles Messiah and Lord. Did the apostle seek to magnify the grounds for Jesus' messiahship by noting that it was He who had been slain and through His shed blood had ransomed men for God (Rev. 5:6-13)? The great multitude of the redeemed in heaven "standing before the throne and before the Lamb, clothed in white robes, with palm branches in their hands," cried with a loud voice, "Salvation belongs to our God who sits upon the throne, and to the Lamb" (7:9, 10). One of the elders added the words, "These are they who have come out of the great tribulation; they have washed their robes and made them white in the blood of the Lamb" (v. 14). Here again the redemptive work of Christ receives special mention. In contrast with the statements concerning the Lamb stand forth the words, "Now the salvation and power and the kingdom of our God and the authority of his Christ have come" (12:10). The brethren have conquered their accusers by the blood of the Lamb and by the word of their testimony. Their names were written "before the foundation of the world in the book of life of the Lamb that was slain" (13:8).

John also had the grand view of Mount Zion on which "stood the Lamb and with him a hundred and forty-four thousand who had his name and his Father's name written on their foreheads" (14:1). Observe the grandeur of those who sing the song of Moses and the song of the Lamb (15:3). The author noted also the conflict between the forces of evil and the Lamb in the words, "They will make war on the Lamb, and the Lamb will conquer them, for he is Lord of lords and King of kings, and those with him are called and chosen and faithful" (17:14). This graphic revelation of the enthroned Lamb's conflict and overthrow of Satan's power, centering in the Roman Empire and symbolized by Babylon, sets forth His authority as Judge of this world.

This portion, compared with the reverent worship of the Lamb set forth in 5:6-14, discloses the enthroned Lamb's relation to the wickedness of this world as compared with His relation with those who had been ransomed by His blood. The most sublime picture of the enthroned Lamb depicts the marriage of the Lamb to His bride, the church, "Blessed are those who are invited to the marriage supper of the Lamb" (19:9). Without a doubt this marriage scene served as the greatest encouragement to the church in tribulation. Undoubtedly it led them to patient endurance. The glory of this scene becomes still greater as the angel disclosed the bride, the wife of the Lamb, set forth in the image of the Holy City, Jerusalem, which had twelve foundations on which the twelve names of the twelve apostles stood forth (21:9-14). There was no temple in this city: "For its temple is the Lord God the Almighty and the Lamb. . . . The glory of God is its light, and its lamp is the Lamb. . . . But only those who are written in the Lamb's book of life" (vv. 22-27) shall enter the city. "Then he showed me the river of the water of life, bright as crystal, flowing from the throne of God and of the Lamb. . . . The throne of God and of the Lamb shall be in it, and his servants shall worship him; they shall see his face, and his name shall be on their foreheads. . . . They shall reign for ever and ever" (22:1-5). Observe again how the author structured his thought, beginning with the Baptist's declaration, "Behold the Lamb of God" on through the Gospel and the Revelation where the Lamb is enthroned forever with God, the Father.

h. Jesus, the Savior of the World

This topic deals with Jesus' work as Savior in a manner almost parallel to the preceding discussion. The saving work of Christ comes into the limelight when Jesus was disclosing to Nicodemus His own work of salvation. Reflecting on the work of Moses Jesus said, "As Moses lifted up the serpent in the wilderness, so must the Son of man be lifted up, that whoever believes in him may have eternal life" (Jn. 3:14, 15). This led naturally to the heart of biblical revelation. Whether this portion records the words of Jesus or of the author has little significance. Those who believe in Christ have eternal life; those who do not believe will perish. They are already condemned. The reason for this condemnation is that they "loved darkness rather than light, because their deeds were evil" (v. 19). When the Samaritans spoke with Jesus, they became convinced that "this is indeed the Savior of the world" (4:42). It would appear that these people had come to grasp the meaning of Jesus' saving work just as Nicodemus had. In the context of Jesus healing a multitude of invalids, blind, lame, and paralyzed, He spoke of His life-giving work to be climaxed in the resurrection. He declared that He was performing all these signs in order that they may be saved (5:2-34). In the sublime Good Shepherd context Jesus declared, "I am the door; if anyone enters by me, he will be saved. . . . I came that they may have life, and have it abundantly. . . . The good shepherd lays down his life for the sheep" (10:9-11).

It is significant that John unfolded the meaning of Christ's saving work in his first letter. In a word, the apostle set forth Christ's work of redemption through His blood. He wrote, "The blood of Jesus his Son cleanses us from all sin. . . . If we confess our sins, he is faithful and just, and will forgive our sins and cleanse us from all unrighteousness" (1 Jn. 1:7, 9). The verb *katharizo (cleanse)* has the literal meaning of cleaning from physical stain and dirt. This literal sense leads to an ethical meaning of freeing from defilement of sin and purifying from wickedness. John's use of the word in this context expresses explicitly the freeing from the guilt of sin and of purifying. The present tense views this as a continuing process. Thus the cleansing work of Jesus' blood continues throughout one's life. Observe also that the forgiveness of sins accompanies the cleansing from unrighteousness. The author unfolds further Jesus' saving work by noting that He through His death "is the expiation *[hilasmos]* for our sins, and not for ours only but also for the sins of the whole world" (2:2). The word *hilasmos (a means of appeasing,* expiation), together with its cognate forms *hilaskomai* and *hilasterios* possesses a profound buildup of meaning extending from the time of Israel's building the tabernacle, the center of which was the ark of the covenant. On its mercy seat the high priest sprinkled blood on the Day of Atonement. By this act he made expiation, atonement, and propitiation for the sins of the people. In this framework of thought John declared that Christ laid down His life for us and by so doing He was the expiation for our sins. Through this self-sacrifice Christ became the Savior of the world. John made yet another statement, the meaning of which is quite perplexing. He wrote, "This is he who came by water and blood, Jesus Christ, not with the water only but with the water and the blood. . . . There are three witnesses, the Spirit, the water, and the blood; and these three agree" (1 Jn. 5:6, 8). Undoubtedly John's readers understood these words. There are several interpretations of this passage. The words of John R. W. Stott are challenging.[14] His interpretation: "takes *water* as referring to the baptism of Jesus, at which he was declared the Son and commissioned and empowered for His work, and *blood* to His death, in which His work was finished." The *Twentieth Century New Testament* confirms this interpretation, "He it is whose Coming was attested by means of Water and Blood." Through these significant references John intensified his teaching that Jesus was the Savior of the world.

John's message in the Revelation gave the occasion for his adding several other references to Jesus' saving work. This becomes apparent in his introduction to the Revelation in which he declared that Christ "has freed us from our sins by his blood" (1:5). Later in the book he recorded the new song of the glorified saints, "Worthy art thou to take the scroll and to open its seals, for thou wast slain and by thy blood didst ransom men for God" (5:9; 14:3, 4). To John, Christ's saving work was expressed in the most meaningful language of His being the ransom price paid for man's salvation. See also 7:10, 14; 12:10; 19:1, where the apostle drew attention to the salvation wrought by our Lord. All these references give profound meaning to John's closing words in which the Spirit and the Bride invite the thirsty to "take the water of life without price" (22:17). These redeemed people would also have their share "in the tree of life" (v. 19). In my judgment John's presentation of Jesus as the Savior of the world is the focal point of his theology. All the other subtopics of this section contribute to its significance.

i. Jesus, the Teacher

One of the most important services performed by John the Baptist was to identify Jesus not only as the Lamb of God, but also as a rabbi, which means teacher. This placed Jesus on a high rank among the Jews, which became evident in Nicodemus' approach to Jesus. "Rabbi, we know that you are a teacher come from God; for no one can do these signs that you do, unless God is with him" (Jn. 3:2). While the Apostle John's uses of this title for Jesus were not nearly as frequent as found in the Synoptic Gospels, nevertheless, there is an important buildup of meaning in his Gospel. When Nicodemus addressed Jesus as a teacher come from God, this at once raised the dignity of our Lord to a plane far above the Jewish rabbis. This ruler of the Jews was giving proper recognition to the signs performed by Jesus as adequate grounds for his assertion. John's portrayal of Jesus at the Feast of Tabernacles becomes significant from this point of view (7:14-31). John noted that Jesus went up into the temple and taught. The Jews marveled at Jesus' learning, knowing that He had not pursued rabbinical studies.

In response to this attitude Jesus declared, "My teaching is not mine, but his who sent me; if any man's will is to do his will, he shall know whether the teaching is from God or whether I am speaking on my own authority. He who speaks on his own authority seeks his own glory; but he who seeks the glory of him who sent him is true, and in him there is no falsehood" (vv. 16-18). Giving further support to His authoritative teaching, Jesus added, "I have not come of my own accord; he who sent me is true. . . . I know him, for I come from him, and he sent me" (vv. 28, 29). In this manner John set forth the deity level of Jesus, the Teacher. He was giving undeniable grounds for recognizing the highest levels of truth and authority in Jesus' teachings. This fact is fundamental to the whole concept of God's revelation to man as recorded in the Scriptures. Jesus heightened this concept of His being the Teacher when He combined it with the title *Lord* in His conversation with the disciples. He said, "You call me Teacher and Lord; and you are right, for so I am" (13:13). Jesus' involvement in teaching becomes evident in His words, "I have spoken openly to the world; I have always taught in synagogues and in the temple . . . I have said nothing secretly" (18:20).

j. Jesus, the Truth

Jesus made the definite declaration, "I am the way, and the truth, and the life; no one comes to the Father, but by me" (14:6). In this statement Jesus brought the words: *way, truth,* and *life* into close relationship. The center of His thought lay in the believer's access to the Father alone through Himself. These common words — *way, truth,* and *life* — became loaded with immeasurable meaning through this statement. There is no other road to the Father than this road. There is no other truth possessing this dimensional meaning than that personalized in Christ. No life is comparable to that manifest in Jesus. In view of this it was pertinent that John in his prologue identified the true light with the Word (*logos*). The incarnation of the *logos* manifested His grace and truth (1:14). This leads us to understand that the concept of grace enriches the meaning of truth. In other words, truth is not a mere abstract idea, for it becomes manifest through His grace. In sharp contrast with the law given to Moses stand *grace* and *truth* which came through Jesus Christ. To the woman of Samaria, Jesus disclosed the bearing of truth on worship when He declared, "The true worshipers will worship the Father in spirit and truth" (4:23). To the Jews, Jesus declared that the Baptist "has borne witness to the truth" (5:33). The use of the perfect tense in Jesus' statement shows the "permanent and abiding value of John's testimony to Christ."[15] As the Lord Jesus Christ is the eternal being, so the truth abides forever. Our Lord made another meaningful statement concerning the truth in the words, "If you continue in my word, you are truly my disciples, and you will know the truth, and the truth will make you free" (8:31, 32). In this manner Jesus set forth the irrevocable condition for knowing the truth. The dynamic of truth is equally expressive. Jesus added, "If the Son makes you free you will be free indeed" (v. 36).

In his letters and also in the Revelation John used the words *truth* and *true* in a manner which reflected clearly on Jesus as the truth. He consistently declared that "the Spirit is the truth" (1 Jn. 5:7). Finally John saw heaven opened — "and behold, a white horse! He who sat upon it is called Faithful and True" (Rev. 19:11).

The bearing of this theme on the discipline of biblical theology should not escape careful attention. It confirms yet again the unique character of the Scriptures as they center in Him who is the truth and disclose the truth revealed by Him.

k. The Holy Spirit, the Spirit of Truth

Since Jesus declared that He is the truth, we should anticipate that the Counselor whom Jesus would send to His followers would be the Spirit of truth. This is central to Jesus' declaration concerning the Spirit. It enlarges still further the depth of meaning possessed by truth in relation to the Father, Son, and the Holy Spirit. Jesus declared, "When the Spirit of truth comes, he will guide you into all truth" (16:13). From an experiential point of view this promise of Christ is of untold significance. Thus the Holy Spirit continues the mission of Christ in the world. Christ reveals the truth through the Holy Spirit. This has a profound bearing on the Christian's interpretation of God's revealed Word of truth. The extent of truth into which the Holy Spirit leads is unlimited in breadth and depth. John intensified Jesus' teachings in his first letter, "This is he who came by water and blood, Jesus Christ, not with the water only but with the water and the blood. And the Spirit is the witness, because the Spirit is the truth. There are three witnesses, the Spirit, the water, and the blood; and these three agree" (1 Jn. 5:6-8). These uses of the Spirit of truth show "that for John the divine truth is always that which works in revelation, so that the function of the *parakletos* who works as the *pneuma tes aletheias* is described as the revelation which continues to work in the community, and in 1 John 5: 7 the witnessing *pneuma* is simply equated with the aletheia. In the same sense there is reference in 1 John 4:6 to the *pneuma tes aletheias* in contrast to the *pneuma tes planes*."[16]

1. The Truth as the Way of Life

The profound meaning of the truth involves the way of life. This becomes apparent in what may be regarded as the most significant paragraph of the Bible (Jn. 3:16-21). In this context the words *life, light,* and *truth* stand forth in vital relation and with pertinent meaning. He concluded with the words, "He who does what is true comes to the light, that it may be clearly seen that his deeds have been wrought in God" (v. 21). In other words the light manifests the ethical nature of man's conduct. The guidelines for doing the truth have their basis in that which has been wrought in union with God. Jesus expressed this truth in different language by noting that the devil "has nothing to do with the truth, because there is no truth in him. When he lies, he speaks according to his own nature, for he is a liar and the father of lies. . . . I tell the truth. . . . He who is of God hears the word ot God" (8:44-47). John developed this truth still further in his letters. He wrote, "If we say we have fellowship with him while we walk in darkness, we lie and do not live according to the truth; but if we walk in the light, as he is in the light, we have fellowship with one another. . . . If we say we have no sin, we deceive ourselves, and the truth is not in us."[17]

3. The Response of Faith and Life

This topic takes us to the heart of John's Gospel, "These are written that you may believe that Jesus is the Christ . . . and that believing you may have life in his name" (20:31). As noted above (2) a vast amount of material sets forth the truth that Jesus is the Christ, the Son of God. Correlated to this central theme is the response of faith to which Jesus' life and teachings led. John leads us to the heart of this theme when he commented on Jesus' miracle at the marriage feast: "This, the first of his signs, Jesus did at Cana in Galilee, and manifested his glory; and his disciples believed in him" (2:11). John noted also that at the Passover Feast "many believed in his name when they saw his signs which he did" It is clear that Jesus who was God manifest in the flesh needed to give adequate grounds for the people to believe in His deity. The most conclusive evidence for this truth lay in His performing supernatural acts, such as no human being could perform. This becomes evident in the variety of miracles performed by Jesus, such as turning water into wine, giving sight to the blind, feeding the five thousand, healing the sick, raising the dead, and most climactically His own resurrection. John used the word *sign (semeion)* to describe these miraculous deeds. This stands in contrast with the words *dunamis* and *teras*, which express the power and terrifying aspects, respectively, of Jesus' miracles. Note again Peter's words at Pentecost: "Jesus . . . a man attested to you by God with mighty works and wonders and signs" (Acts 2:22). Here we should observe the buildup of thought relating to the miracles performed by Jesus. Peter's words moved from the mighty power manifested in miracles to the impact these miracles had upon those who witnessed them, and to their significance and purpose.

Let us observe some of the significant responses of faith on the part of those who witnessed Jesus' signs. John noted "the second sign that Jesus did" in the healing of the official's son. When Jesus told him that his son will live, John commented, "The man believed the word that Jesus spoke to him and went his way" (Jn. 4:50). Later he learned that the fever had left his son at the very hour that Jesus had spoken to the official. After Jesus had fed the five thousand, He said to the people, "I am the bread of life; he who comes to me shall not hunger, and he who believes in me shall never thirst. . . . For this is the will of my Father, that every one who sees the Son and believes in him should have eternal life" (6:35-40). Jesus' miraculous act of feeding the five thousand gave the grounds for His saying that He is the bread of life. It required faith on the part of the people to believe that the man, Jesus, was the Son of God, but there were those present who refused to believe the meaning of Jesus' sign and consequently did not have eternal life. Even many of Jesus' disciples drew back from following Him, but Peter gave his testimony, "We have believed, and have come to know, that you are the Holy One of God" (v. 69).

In the case of the healing of the man who was born blind we have another significant example of the response of faith as it stood in opposition to those who refused to believe. On this occasion Jesus said, "For judgment I came into this world, that those who do not see may see, and that those who see may become blind" (9:39). The spiritually blind Pharisees had guilt because they claimed to see but refused to believe that Jesus was the Son of Man. The interaction of faith and unbelief comes vividly into view in the story of the raising of Lazarus. On the one side is the overwhelming faith of Mary, Martha, and many of the Jews, but there were some who refused to believe in Jesus, even though this miracle possessed deepest meaning as it related to the deity of

Christ. This came into focus when the chief priests and scribes gathered the council and said, "What are we to do? For this man performs many signs" (11:45-48). This incident showed that the performing of signs by Jesus did not compel the witnesses to believe in the Christ.

At the close of Jesus' public ministry John made some significant observations relating to Jesus' signs and their impact upon the people. He wrote, "Though he had done so many signs for them, yet they did not believe in him" (Jn. 12:37). In the following paragraph he quoted Jesus' words, "He who believes in me, believes not in me but in him who sent me. And he who sees me sees him who sent me. I have come as light into the world, that whoever believes in me may not remain in darkness. . . . He who rejects me and does not receive my sayings has a judge; the word that I have spoken will be his judge on the last day" (vv. 44-48). All these incidents give overwhelming support to John's expressive statement quoted above, which sets forth the profound purpose of this Gospel.

First John and the Revelation give some additional teachings on the response of faith and life. Among many other meaningful declarations of the apostle are the words, "And this is the commandment, that we should believe in the name of his Son Jesus Christ and love one another" (1 Jn. 3:23). Later in the letter he wrote, "Every one who believes that Jesus is the Christ is a child of God, and every one who loves the parent loves the child. By this we know that we love the children of God, when we love God and obey his commandments" (5:1, 2). In this manner John set forth the bearing of genuine faith on obedience. He intensified this truth in the words, "He who believes in the Son of God has the testimony in himself. He who does not believe God has made him a liar, because he has not believed in the testimony that God has borne to his Son. . . . I write this to you who believe in the name of the Son of God, that you may know that you have eternal life" (vv. 10, 13). In this manner John expanded the purpose of this letter in which he had expressed the words, "That which we have seen and heard we proclaim also to you, so that you may have fellowship with us; and our fellowship is with the Father and with his Son Jesus Christ" (1:3).

The Revelation to John presents this theme in the setting of the Domitian persecution experienced by the church. To the church in Smyrna, Christ declared, "Be faithful unto death, and I will give you the crown of life" (Rev. 2:10). To the church in Pergamum Jesus declared, "You hold fast my name and you did not deny my faith even in the days of Antipas my witness, my faithful one" (v. 13). To the church of Thyatira he wrote, "I know your works, your love and faith and service and patient endurance" (v. 19). Here we should observe the oneness of *works, love, faith, service,* and *patient endurance.* All these characterize the response of faith in a true manner of life. This same truth stands forth in the words, "Here is a call for the endurance of the saints, those who keep the commandments of God and the faith of Jesus" (14:12). Note another enlightening statement, "He is Lord of lords and King of kings, and those with him are called and chosen and faithful" (17:14). The doctrinal significance of these words is the unity of these expressions: *called, chosen,* and *faithful*—quite Pauline in meaning. The sequence of these words expresses the genuine response of faith in godly living.

4. The Outworking of Faith in Christian Living

As John stressed the response of faith throughout his writings, he did so with purpose. He was concerned to show that believing in Jesus Christ leads to a manner of life such as was exemplified in the Lord Jesus Christ. This became evident when Jesus said to Philip, "Follow me" (Jn. 1:43). The disciples soon learned that following Christ involved absolute commitment to Him as Lord, both in the realm of faith and way of life. To Nicodemus, Jesus declared, "Unless one is born anew, he cannot see the kingdom of God . . . Unless one is born of water and the Spirit, he cannot enter the kingdom of God" (3:3-5). In this manner Jesus would have Nicodemus learn that that which is born of the flesh leads to sinful living. Only by being born of the Spirit can one live a godly life. Jesus made it clear that "every one who does evil hates the light, and does not come to the light, lest his deeds should be exposed. But he who does what is true comes to the light, that it may be clearly seen that his deeds have been wrought in God" (3:20, 21). Repeatedly throughout the Gospel, John showed that faith in Jesus manifested itself in holy living. Later Jesus declared, "I am the light of the world; he who follows me will not walk in darkness, but will have the light of life" (8:12). Jesus made it clear to the Jews that everyone who commits sin is a slave to sin. The Son of Man alone can make one free from sin (vv. 31-38). In the context of Jesus' giving sight to a man born blind He declared, "For judgment I came into this world, that those who do not see may see, and those who see may become blind. . . . If you were blind, you would have no guilt; but now that you say 'We see,' your guilt remains" (9:39-41). In this way our Lord made it clear that refusal to believe in Jesus involved guilt.

Judas Iscariot stood forth as a pitiful example of one who was a committed disciple of Christ, who failed, nevertheless, to conform his life to real discipleship. He was a thief and a hypocrite. He utterly failed to see the ethical quality of faith as it should manifest itself in following Jesus. In the upper room Jesus said to His disciples, "A new commandment I give to you, that you love one another; even as I have loved you, that you also love one another. By this all men will know that you are my disciples, if you have love for one another" (13:34, 35). In this manner Jesus made it clear to His disciples that the outworking of their faith in Him would be the manifestation of love for each other as He loved them. In harmony with these words Jesus also said, "If you love me, you will keep my commandments" (14:15). This sampling of verses from John's Gospel shows how explicitly Jesus taught the outworking of faith in Christian living.

The apostle stressed this point in his letters and also in the Revelation. In fact, his first letter builds on this truth in a very definite manner. This becomes evident in the words, "This is the message we have heard from him and proclaim to you, that God is light and in him is no darkness at all. If we say we have fellowship with him while we walk in darkness, we lie and do not live according to the truth; but if we walk in the light, as he is in the light, we have fellowship with one another, and the blood of Jesus his Son cleanses us from all sin" (1 Jn. 1:5-7). He stated his purpose specifically in the words, "I am writing this to you so that you may not sin; but if anyone does sin, we have an advocate with the Father Jesus Christ the righteous" (2:1).

John showed great concern for maintaining the love relationship one for the other. He stressed this in the words, "He who loves his brother abides in the light . . . But he who hates his brother is in the darkness and walks in the darkness, and does not know where he is going, because the darkness has blinded his eyes" (2:10, 11). John stressed the point that Christian love excludes any affection for worldly pleasures. He wrote, "Do not love the world or the things in the world. If any one loves the world, love for the Father is not in him. For all that is in the world, the lust of the flesh and the lust of the eyes and the pride of life, is not of the Father but is of the world" (vv. 15, 16). He also touched on a vital matter relating to the definitive nature of Christian faith. He asked, "Who is the liar but he who denies that Jesus is the Christ? This is the antichrist, he who denies the Father and the Son. No one who denies the Son has the Father. He who confesses the Son has the Father also" (vv. 22, 23). This declaration sets forth a serious tragedy that existed already in the early church. In other words, being a Christian involved the honest profession that Jesus is the Christ. This fact should speak to the many so-called Christian scholars who reject the deity of Christ.

This outworking of faith in Christian living has a definite bearing on Christian hope. John wrote, "Beloved, we are God's children now; it does not yet appear what we shall be, but we know that when he appears we shall be like him, for we shall see him as he is. And every one who thus hopes in him purifies himself as he is pure" (1 Jn. 3:2, 3). The apostle punctuated still further the nature of the Christian life in the words, "No one born of God commits sin; for God's nature abides in him, and he cannot sin because he is born of God. By this it may be seen who are the children of God, and who are the children of the devil; whoever does not do right is not of God, nor he who does not love his brother" (vv. 9, 10).

John stressed yet again the nature of Christian belief by referring to the blasphemous sin of denying Jesus' incarnation. Note the words, "Every spirit which confesses that Jesus Christ has come in the flesh is of God, and every spirit which does not confess Jesus is not of God" (1 Jn. 4:2, 3). The strategic importance of Christian love stands forth again in the words, "Let us love one another; for love is of God, and he who loves is born of God and knows God. He who does not love does not know God; for God is love" (vv. 7, 8). John's emphasis on Christian love stands forth again in the words, "By this we know that we love the children of God when we love God and obey his commandments. For this is the love of God, that we keep his commandments" (5:2, 3). He added, "We know that any one born of God does not sin, but He who was born of God keeps him, and the evil one does not touch him" (v. 18).

The pertinence of this teaching becomes evident in 2 John 5-9 and 3 John 9-11. Note his last statement, "Beloved, do not imitate evil but imitate good. He who does good is of God; he who does evil has not seen God" (v. 11).

In the Revelation to John the author set forth these truths in the setting of persecution being experienced by the church. Some significant exhortations deserve attention. To the church in Ephesus Jesus directed John to write, "I know your works, your toil and your patient endurance, and how you cannot bear evil men. . . . But I have this against you, that you have abandoned the love you had at first. Remember then from what you have fallen, repent and do the works you did at first" (Rev. 2:2-5). He commended the church in Pergamum in the words, "You hold fast my name and you did not deny my faith." He added a rebuke, "You have some there who hold the teaching of Balaam who taught Balak to put a stumbling block before the sons of Israel. . . . Repent then. . . . To him who conquers I will give some of the hidden manna" (vv. 13-17). To the church in Thyatira He gave the commendation, "I know your works, your love and faith and service and patient endurance, and that your latter works exceed the first" (v. 19). But they were tolerating the woman, Jezebel, who was teaching and beguiling the Lord's servants "to practice immorality and to eat food sacrificed to idols. . . . She refuses to repent of her immorality" (vv. 19-21). Exhortations to the church at Sardis include, "I know your works; you have the name of being alive, and you are dead. . . . Repent" (3:1-3). A pitiful condition existed in the church in Laodicea, "You are neither cold nor hot. . . . You are wretched, pitiable, poor, blind, and naked. . . . Be zealous and repent. . . . He who conquers, I will grant him to sit with me on my throne, as I myself conquered and sat down with my Father on his throne" (vv. 15-21).

These warnings, given in their apocalyptic settings, reveal clearly the encounters of the early church with the sins of the world. This shows again the responsibility of Christians to translate their faith into genuine Christian living. As John depicted the wickedness that would be found in the world he declared, "The rest of mankind . . . did not repent of the works of their hands nor give up worshiping demons and idols of gold and silver and bronze and stone and wood . . . nor did they repent of their murders or their sorceries or their immorality or their thefts" (9:20, 21). This is the most tragic description of the depths of sin into which mankind, even many professed Christians, have descended. Featuring the sublime picture of heaven where the redeemed were playing on their harps, John declared, "It is these who have not defiled themselves with women, for they are chaste . . . and in their mouth no lie was found, for they are spotless" (14:4, 5). This description closes with the observation, "Here is a call for the endurance of the saints, those who keep the commandments of God and the faith of Jesus" (v. 12). This realistic picture should add the greatest incentive to faithful Christian living. In the majestic description of the heavenly scene picturing the marriage of the Lamb with His bride, we read, "It was granted her to be clothed with fine linen, bright and pure." And then he explains, "The fine linen is the righteous deeds of the saints" (19:8).

The glorious picture of the new heavens and the new earth includes the forthright statement, "He who conquers shall have this heritage, and I will be his God and he shall be my son. But as for the cowardly, the faithless, the polluted, as for murderers, fornicators, sorcerers, idolaters, and all liars, their lot shall be in the lake that burns with fire and brimstone, which is the second death" (21:7, 8). This declaration sets forth again the eternal destiny, both of the faithful and of the unfaithful. A similar statement occurs in verse 27, "But nothing unclean shall enter it, nor any one who practices abomination or falsehood, but only those who are written in the Lamb's book of life." The closing statement on this theme stands forth in the words, "Blessed are those who wash their robes, that they may have the right to the tree of life and that they may enter the city by the gates. Outside are the dogs and sorcerers and fornicators and murderers and idolators, and every one who loves and practices falsehood" (22:14, 15).

By way of conclusion, quite central to John's burden is his disclosure of how genuine faith issues in a life of holiness. The special stress of his Gospel is that real Christian faith has its counterpart in a life that conforms to this faith. Since Jesus was the sinless Son of God, His disciples seek to live a life in harmony with the Word who became flesh. A slightly different emphasis becomes apparent in his letters in which he shows that fellowship with Christ is possible alone to those who walk in the light. The Book of Revelation discloses a slightly different point of emphasis in the way of giving encouragement to patient endurance for those suffering tribulation in a wicked world. Thus John's writings which are so profoundly doctrinal in content possess, nevertheless, the practical objectives of leading the church to holy Christian living.

5. The Enthroned Messiah

a. Jesus' Kingship Not of This World

John's Gospel and the Revelation give two aspects of Jesus' messiahship. The former deals with the earthly ministry of our Lord while the latter presents Him as the enthroned Messiah. At the beginning of Jesus' earthly ministry, Andrew declared to his brother Peter, "We have found the Messiah" (Jn. 1:41). To the Samaritan woman Jesus declared that He is the Messiah (4:25, 26). The signs performed by Jesus led the people to believe that He was the Christ (7:25-52). At the raising of Lazarus, Martha testified, "I believe that you are the Christ, the Son of God, he who is coming into the world" (11:27). On the occasion of Jesus' final entry into Jerusalem He said, "The hour has come for the Son of man to be glorified" (12:23). On this occasion John noted the prophetic words of Isaiah, who spoke of this crisis in the life of the Messiah (Is. 53:1), and John wrote the comment, "Isaiah said this because he saw his glory and spoke of him" (Jn. 12:41). In His great prayer Jesus prayed, "Father, the hour has come; glorify thy Son that the Son may glorify thee. . . . I glorified thee on earth, having accomplished the work which thou gavest me to do; and now, Father, glorify thou me in thine own presence with the glory which I had with thee before the world was made" (17:1-5). Most significant were Jesus' words to Pilate, "My kingship is not of this world; if my kingship were of this world, my servants would fight, that I might not be handed over to the Jews; but my kingship is not from the world" (18:36). These and other incidents show that Jesus, the Messiah, did not exercise His kingship during His earthly ministry even though the Father glorified Him as the Messiah.

The Revelation to John revealed the enthroned Christ. Note the comprehensive language written by John: "Grace to you and peace from him who is and who was and who is to come, and from the seven spirits who are before his throne, and from Jesus Christ the faithful witness, the first-born of the dead, and the ruler of kings on earth" (Rev. 1:4, 5). In this manner John set forth Jesus as the eternal Being who is the supreme Ruler of the world. This becomes evident repeatedly throughout this book. Jesus declared, "He who conquers, I will grant him to sit with me on my throne, as I myself conquered and sat down with my Father on his throne" (3:21). By implication the resurrection and ascension of Jesus marked His enthronement with the Father. When John was caught up to heaven he saw the Lord God Almighty sitting on His throne and one of the elders said to him, "Lo, the Lion of the tribe of Judah, the Root of David, has conquered, so that he can open the scroll and its seven seals" (5:5). This was a majestic way of revealing the enthroned Messiah to John. In this setting John heard a loud voice saying, "Worthy is the Lamb who was slain, to receive power and wealth and wisdom and might and honor and glory and blessing!" (v. 12). Here was His kingship without any rival. When the Lamb opened the fifth seal, the souls of the martyred saints cried, "O Sovereign Lord, holy and true, how long before thou wilt judge and avenge our blood on those who dwell upon the earth?" (6:10).

At the opening of the sixth seal the wicked people of the earth called to the mountains and rocks saying, "Fall on us and hide us from the face of him who is seated on the throne, and from the wrath of the Lamb; for the great day of their wrath has come, and who can stand before it?" (6:16, 17). This introduces the judgment aspect of the enthroned Messiah, which includes the pouring out of God's wrath upon the wicked. A majestic view of heaven pictures an innumerable multitude of humanity who cry out with a loud voice, "Salvation belongs to our God who sits upon the throne, and to the Lamb!" (7:10). Another glimpse of this heavenly scene stands forth in the words, "For the Lamb in the midst of the throne will be their shepherd" (v. 17). The opening of the seven seals was a profound way of setting forth the kingship of the enthroned Messiah. It revealed the bearing of His kingship, not only upon the redeemed in heaven but also upon the wicked world. Just as God's rule of the world as depicted in the Old Testament became manifest in the rise and fall of the nations, so the opening of the seals showed how the enthroned Messiah is guiding the affairs of this world throughout His reign. All things are under His control. In similar language, the blowing of the seven trumpets depicts the course of world affairs. Again the confirmation of all things comes into view at the sounding of the seventh trumpet, when loud voices say, "The kingdom of the world has become the kingdom of our Lord and of his Christ, and he shall reign for ever and ever" (11:15). The attitude of the wicked world became evident in the words, "The nations raged, but thy wrath came, and the time for the dead to be judged . . . and for destroying the destroyers of the earth" (v. 18).

While the next scene presents some problems of interpretation, it pictures, nevertheless, the conflict between Satan and the fallen angels, and Michael and his angels (12:7-12). It may be correct to interpret this scene as being cast in the framework of Satan's encounter with Adam and Eve in the Garden of Eden, which forecast the conflict between Christ and Satan leading to the crucifixion of our Lord. This may find support in the words, "Now the salvation and the power and the kingdom of our God and the authority of his Christ have come, for the accuser of our brethren has been thrown down, who accuses them day and night before our God. And they have conquered him by the blood of the Lamb and by the word of their testimony, for they loved not their lives even unto death" (12:10, 11). Undoubtedly this vision depicted the conflict of the throned Messiah with the archenemy of God and man, the devil. This conflict comes into view again in 17:1-14. The context of this scene is the judgment that would come upon the nations of the world centering at that time in the Roman Empire under Domitian. John described this conflict in the words, "They will make war on the Lamb, and the Lamb will conquer them, for he is Lord of lords and King of kings" (v. 14).

In still more graphic language John disclosed the conflict between the enthroned Messiah and Satan. He "saw heaven opened, and behold, a white horse! He who sat upon it is called Faithful and True, and in righteousness he judges and makes war. . . . And the name by which he is called is The Word of God. . . . From his mouth issues a sharp sword with which to smite the nations, and he will rule them with a rod of iron; he will tread the wine press of the fury of the wrath of God the Almighty. On his robe and on his thigh he has a name inscribed, King of kings and Lord of lords" (19:11-16). Parallel to this and also climactic is the vision in 20:7-10, where Satan gathers together the nation for the battle of Gog and Magog but "fire came down from heaven and consumed them. . . . Then I saw a great white throne and him who sat upon it. . . . And I saw the dead, great and small, standing before the throne" (vv. 9-12). Undoubtedly one of the main objectives of John's presenting these scenes of judgment and the pouring out of God's wrath was to brace these persecuted Christians for their life-and-death struggle with the forces of evil. They had unquestionable assurance for believing that even though they would be martyred for their faith, they would be received into the glories of heaven, there to dwell forever with the enthroned Messiah.

b. This World of Tribulation

The foregoing description of the enthroned Christ gives a true perspective of Jesus' words, "In the world you have tribulation; but be of good cheer, I have overcome the world" (Jn. 16:33). In the foregoing discussion the conflict of the church with the wicked world came into view. It would appear that John's overall purpose of writing the Revelation was to expose the reality of this tribulation. Undoubtedly, the bloody persecutions which the early church experienced tested their faith. Under the kingship of their Lord they may have asked: If Christ is King of kings, and Lord of lords, why should we suffer the bloody persecutions of Nero and Domitian? Let us note how Christ revealed to John the real nature of this tribulation. John introduced this difficult subject with the words, "I, John, your brother, who share with you in Jesus the tribulation and the kingdom and the patient endurance, was on the island called Patmos on account of the word of God and the testimony of Jesus" (Rev. 1:9). From this John's readers could gather that he and they were sharing in the common experience of tribulation, the center of which was Jesus Himself. John's structuring of the words *tribulation, kingdom,* and *patient endurance,* as they centered in Christ, becomes the key to understanding this tribulation. As our Lord suffered tribulation as He exercised sovereignty, and patiently endured suffering even unto death, so the followers of Christ share in these same experiences.

Thus John passed unto the church in Smyrna the words, "I know your tribulation and your poverty (but you are rich). . . . Do not fear what you are about to suffer. Behold, the devil is about to throw some of you into prison, that you may be tested, and for ten days you will have tribulation. Be faithful unto death, and I will give you the crown of life" (2:9, 10). As the Lord commended the church in Ephesus for their patient endurance (v. 2), so to the church in Philadelphia he wrote, "Because you have kept my word of patient endurance, I will keep you from the hour of trial which is coming on the whole world, to try those who dwell upon the earth. I am coming soon; hold fast what you have, so that no one may seize your crown. He who conquers, I will make him a pillar in the temple of my God; never shall he go out of it, and I will write on him the name of my God, and the name of the city of my God, the new Jerusalem which comes down from my God out of heaven, and my own new name" (3:10-12).

At the opening of the fifth seal John declared, "I saw under the altar the souls of those who had been slain for the word of God. . . . Then they were each given a white robe and told to rest a little longer, until the number of their fellow servants and their brethren should be complete, who were to be killed as they themselves had been" (6:9-11). One of the elders told John that they who are clothed in white robes, "are they who have come out of the great tribulation" (7:14). A definite word of encouragement to those suffering persecution stands forth in the words, "Blessed are the dead who die in the Lord henceforth . . . that they may rest from their labors, for their deeds follow them!" (14:13). A final note of encouragement to those in tribulation finds expression in the words, "I saw the souls of those who had been beheaded for their testimony to Jesus and for the word of God, and who had not worshiped the beast or its image and had not received its mark on their foreheads or their hands. They came to life again, and reigned with Christ a thousand years" (20:4). This sampling of references to those suffering tribulation sets forth an aspect of the messianic reign which needed to be understood by those experiencing bloody persecution. The kingship of Christ does not compel allegiance to Him. This is entirely voluntary on the part of all mankind. But alongside this fact is the sober truth that those who refuse to yield themselves to the enthroned Lord will suffer the outpouring of God's wrath in eternal damnation.

c. *The Return of Christ*

In view of the frequent references in the synoptic Gospels to the return of Christ and of the significant description of His coming given in these Gospels, a question of some importance confronts us when we observe that John's Gospel refers only twice to Christ's return. On the other hand the larger number of references to His return in the Revelation is in line with its general content. When Jesus' disciples became overwhelmed with sorrow when they learned that Jesus was about to leave them, He gave them the following words of comfort, "In my Father's house are many rooms; if it were not so, would I have told you that I go to prepare a place for you? And when I go and prepare a place for you, I will come again and I will take you to myself, that where I am you may be also" (Jn. 14:2, 3). He gave no details setting forth the glory of His return. Jesus' second comment in 21:22, 23 also gave no details of this great coming event. A study of Jesus' kingdom parables in Matthew 13 and also of the Olivet discourse in Matthew 24, 25 leads us to wonder why John by-passed these messages of Jesus, especially in view of the lengthy discourse which he did record. A possible answer to this problem may be that John had access to the synoptic Gospels and avoided repetition of these messages.

We should observe, however, that the author made two significant references to Christ's return in his first letter. He wrote, "Abide in him, so that when he appears we may have confidence and not shrink from him in shame at his coming" (1 Jn. 2:28). In a new context centering in the next paragraph he wrote, "Beloved, we are God's children now; it does not yet appear what we shall be, but we know that when he appears we shall be like him, for we shall see him as he is. And every one who thus hopes in him purifies himself as he is pure" (3:2, 3). The author made no reference to the resurrection in this setting. This observation brings to mind the author's presentation of Jesus' teaching on the resurrection (Jn. 5:25-29) in which he did not relate the resurrection to Christ's return. Whether or not these details possess any significance may be an open question. Let us observe, nevertheless, John's use of the verb *phaneroo* (1 Jn. 2:28; 3:2), which carries the meanings: *make visible, reveal, make known, show, manifest,* and others. On this account, whether or not these details possess any significance, may be an open question. Let us observe, nevertheless, John's use of the verb *phaneroo*. He noted that "when he appears . . . we shall see him as he is" (3:2). John included a hortatory note, "Abide in him, so that when he appears, we may have confidence and not shrink from him in shame at his coming" (2:28). He concluded with the note that "everyone who thus hopes in him purifies himself as he is pure" (3:3). How wonderful, how marvelous, how glorious is this hope!

John's references to the Lord's return in the Revelation are equally significant, especially in their apocalyptic setting. John closed his words of greeting with the declaration, "Behold, he is coming with the clouds, and every eye will see him, every one who pierced him; and all the tribes of the earth will wail on account of him" (Rev. 1:7). In this manner the author declared that the glorified Christ will be seen by the entire human race: past, present, and future. Significantly, those who pierced Him, who would on this account completely reject the idea of the living glorified Jesus, will also see Him. This will be a time of wailing on the part of all mankind who did not believe in Him. He urged the church in Thyatira, "Hold fast what you have, until I come" (2:25). Those who are faithful until the end will receive extraordinary blessings from the Lord. In language similar to that of Peter (2 Pet. 3:10), John quoted Christ, "If you will not awake, I will come like a thief, and you will not know at what hour I will come upon you" (3:3). To the church in Philadelphia Jesus declared, "I am coming soon; hold fast what you have, so that no one may seize your crown" (v. 11). In the context centering in the battle of Armageddon, John quoted Christ in the words, "Lo, I am coming like a thief! Blessed is he who is awake, keeping his garments that he may not go naked and be seen exposed!" (16:15). This voices again the imminence of Christ's return as well as the exhortation to prepare for His coming. These words show also the time relation of Armageddon and the Lord's return.

The closing statements of this great book hold forth three statements by the Lord, each asserting the imminence of His return (22:7, 12, 20). The Lord declared, "Behold, I am coming soon," to which He added, "Blessed is he who keeps the word of the prophecy of this book" (v. 7), which shows in a climactic manner the exhortation to faithful living. To the second statement the Lord added, "bringing my recompense, to repay every one for what he has done" (v. 12), which reveals the judgment aspect of His return. In response to the last statement the author added, "Amen. Come, Lord Jesus!" (v. 20). How significant it is that these words should stand forth at the close of this book climaxed by the benediction, "The grace of the Lord Jesus be with all the saints. Amen" (v. 21).

d. Jesus — The Resurrection and the Life

On the occasion of Jesus giving words of comfort to Martha at the death of Lazarus, He declared, "I am the resurrection and the life; he who believes in me, though he die, yet shall he live, and whoever lives and believes in me shall never die" (Jn. 11:25, 26). With these words Jesus brought to a focus one of the most fundamental truths relating to His self-revelation. It is noteworthy that throughout His earthly ministry Jesus drew attention to this. It led John to declare concerning the *logos*, Jesus, "In him was life, and the life was the light of men" (1:4). This revelation came to a climax in the author's statement of his purpose in his concluding words, "that believing you may have life in his name" (20:31). Jesus' closing words with Nicodemus showed the relation of faith to receiving this eternal life: "whoever believes in him may have eternal life" (3:15). John intensified this thought in what stands forth as the dominant theme of his Gospel (v. 6). The experience of having eternal life is so momentous and lies so far beyond human comprehension that the element of faith stands forth as the grand prerequisite for possessing eternal life. This truth becomes still richer when we note that eternal life became possible through God's love for the world. Jesus' conversation with the Samaritan woman at Jacob's well provided a very fitting setting for Him to unfold this grand truth. In the land of Palestine, wells and springs were few in number. The fresh water from these was far more satisfying than the water from cisterns or tanks. Jesus reminded her, "Every one who drinks of this water will thirst again, but whoever drinks of the water that I shall give him will never thirst; the water that I shall give him will become in him a spring of water welling up to eternal life" (4:13, 14). Her failure to understand this metaphor led Jesus to unfold to her the grand truth that believing in Him leads to eternal life. Just as natural water sustains natural life, in like manner the spiritual water which Christ gives wells up in eternal life. This claim on the part of Jesus revealed His deity in that He was the Source of eternal life.

When Jesus healed the lame man at the pool of Beth-zatha, He gave the explanation that He as the Son does "only what he sees the Father doing" (Jn. 5:19). He noted, "As the Father raises the dead and gives them life, so also the Son gives life to whom he will. . . . He who hears my word and believes him who sent me, has eternal life; he does not come into judgment, but has passed from death to life. . . . The hour is coming, and now is, when the dead will hear the voice of the Son of God, and those who hear will live. For as the Father has life in himself, so he has granted the Son also to have life in himself. . . . The hour is coming when all who are in the tombs will hear his voice and come forth, those who have done good, to the resurrection of life, and those who have done evil, to the resurrection of judgment" (5:21-29). This establishes the integral relation of *life* and the *resurrection.* This truth lies at the basis of Jesus' affirmation of being the resurrection and the life.

Another example of where Jesus built a bridge between the natural life and spiritual life came to the fore in His discourse on the bread of life. Here He declared, "I am the bread of life; he who comes to me shall not hunger, and he who believes in me shall never thirst. . . . This is the will of my Father, that every one who sees the Son and believes in him should have eternal life; and I will raise him up at the last day" (6:35-40). Jesus added the faith element in the words, "He who believes has eternal life. I am the bread of life. . . . I am the living bread which came down from heaven; if any one eats of this bread he will live for ever; and the bread which I shall give for the life of the world is my flesh" (vv. 47-51). It is remarkable that Jesus used both water and bread as metaphors depicting His relation to the spiritual life of the believers, which attains its consummation in the resurrection. To the perplexed Jews, Jesus said, "Unless you eat the flesh of the Son of man and drink his blood, you have no life in you; he who eats my flesh and drinks my blood has eternal life, and I will raise him up at the last day. . . . He who eats me shall live because of me. This is the bread which came down from heaven, not such as the fathers ate and died; he who eats this bread will live for ever" (vv. 53-58). In these statements Jesus was showing that He was the heavenly manna coming down from heaven, and those who eat of this bread will live forever. Even the disciples became perplexed at Jesus' words, and on this account He added, "It is the spirit that gives life, the flesh is of no avail; the words that I have spoken to you are spirit and life" (v. 63). In this setting Peter made his noble confession in the words, "You have the words of eternal life; and we have believed, and have come to know, that you are the Holy One of God" (6:68, 69).

Another significant approach to this theme stands forth in the Good Shepherd context. Noting that the thief comes to kill and destroy, Jesus said, "I came that they may have life, and have it abundantly. I am the good shepherd. The good shepherd lays down his life for the sheep. . . . I lay down my life for the sheep. . . . For this reason the Father loves me, because I lay down my life, that I may take it again. . . . I have power to lay it down, and I have power to take it again" (10:10-18). In this manner Jesus set forth His self-sacrifice, as well as His power to rise from the dead. In this message Jesus again reflected His relationship to the Father — a truth which has a definite bearing on His being the resurrection and the life. This brings us again to the story of Lazarus. Martha was aware that Lazarus would rise again in the resurrection at the last day. To this Jesus replied, "I am the resurrection and the life; he who believes in me, though he die, yet shall he live, and whoever lives and believes in me shall never die" (11:23-26).

A helpful approach to understanding Jesus' claim becomes evident in noting the great "I am" assertions of Jesus as recorded in this Gospel. Jesus declared: "I am the bread of life" (6:35). "I am the light of the world" (8:12). "I am the door" (10:9). "I am the good shepherd" (v. 11). "I am the resurrection and the life" (11:25). "I am the way, and the truth, and the life" (14:6). "I am the vine" (15:5). Only He who is Deity could utter these statements. The use of the definite article in each of these quotations establishes the fact that no other one could make the claim.

Several of these statements set forth Deity activity as related to the Creation. Most certainly, He who created life could restore life to the dead. The Word who activated this act of God is the resurrection. Thus the resurrection and the life most appropriately set forth the deity of our Lord. Jesus' statement in 14:6 sets forth the vital relation of *the way, the truth,* and *the life.* Each involves the others. In this same conversation Jesus added, "Because I live, you will live also. . . . I am in my Father, and you in me, and I in you" (vv. 19, 20). This statement finds its support in the resurrection of Christ. Jesus expressed in His prayer a profound statement relating to eternal life. He prayed, "Glorify thy Son that the Son may glorify thee, since thou hast given him power over all flesh, to give eternal life to all whom thou hast given him. And this is eternal life, that they know thee the only true God, and Jesus Christ whom thou hast sent" (17:1-3). The author's declaration of his purpose in writing this Gospel also punctuates the element of faith expressed in the words "that believing you may have life in his name" (20:31).

John reflected on this theme repeatedly in his first letter. This becomes apparent in the opening verses in which he gave testimony to his personal experience with the incarnate Word of life. This Word of life is "the eternal life which was with the Father and was made manifest to us" (1 Jn. 1:2). In another context he wrote, "He who confesses the Son has the Father also. . . . If what you heard from the beginning abides in you, then you will abide in the Son and in the Father. And this is what he has promised us, eternal life" (2:23-25). In another setting he wrote, "We know that we have passed out of death into life, because we love the brethren. . . . You know that no murderer has eternal life abiding in him" (3:14, 15). Most meaningful are his words, "God gave us eternal life, and this life is in his Son. He who has the Son has life; he who has not the Son has not life. I write this to you who believe in the name of the Son of God, that you may know that you have eternal life" (5:11-13). He closed his letter with these significant words, "We are in him who is true, in his Son Jesus Christ. This is the true God and eternal life" (v. 20). This in a most emphatic manner identifies Jesus as the resurrection and the life.

The Book of Revelation supports this great theme, even though there is no specific declaration that Jesus is the resurrection and the life. To the church at Ephesus, Christ declared, "To him who conquers I will grant to eat of the tree of life, which is in the paradise of God" (Rev. 2:7). He spoke similar words to the church in Smyrna. "Be faithful unto death, and I will give you the crown of life" (v. 10). Only the Lord could give such promises to the church in Sardis. He wrote, "He who conquers shall be clad thus in white garments, and I will not blot his name out of the book of life" (3:5). The book of life is most certainly in the hands of Him who is the life. In 13:8 we read, "Every one whose name has not been written before the foundation of the world in the book of life of the Lamb that was slain." It is most natural that He who is the life would possess the book of life which would contain the names of all who had been redeemed by the Lamb of God. Revelation 20:4, 5 discloses the grand truth that those who had suffered martyrdom "came to life, and reigned with Christ a thousand years. . . . This is the first resurrection. Blessed and holy is he who shares in the first resurrection! Over such the second death has no power, but they shall be priests of God and Christ." These words bring to a climax the resurrecting power of Him who is the resurrection and the life. This brings to fulfillment the final consummation of Christ's work of redemption.

The scenes of heaven disclosed in Revelation 21, 22 are climactic in their revelation of Christ who is the resurrection and the life. Christ declared, "I am the Alpha and the Omega, the beginning and the end" (21:6). Thus He is the Creator and the One who brings about the consummation. He alone could give the promise, "To the thirsty I will give water without price from the fountain of the water of life" (v. 6). As John pictured the holy city he declared, "Only those who are written in the Lamb's book of life" (v. 27) shall enter. The angel revealed to John "the river of the water of life, bright as crystal, flowing from the throne of God and of the Lamb . . . also, on either side of the river, the tree of life . . . the throne of God and of the Lamb shall be in it, and his servants shall worship him; they shall see his face . . . and they shall reign for ever and ever" (22:1-5). John exclaimed, "Blessed are those who wash their robes, that they may have the right to the tree of life and that they may enter the city by the gates" (v. 14). John adds the invitation, "Let him who is thirsty come, let him who desires take the water of life without price" (v. 17). It was the Lord who revealed to John the glories of heaven. His last words to His beloved disciple were, "Surely I am coming soon," to which John responded, "Amen. Come, Lord Jesus!" (v. 20).

In closing this section let us note how remarkable it is that Christ's revelation to John in this book should disclose the fulfillment of His prophetic declaration that He is the resurrection.

e. The Son of Man Is the Judge

It is significant that Jesus used the title *Son of Man* when speaking of Himself as the Judge (Jn. 5:21-29). Our Lord brought together in the same context His being the resurrection and the life, and of His being the Judge. As we examine these references to the Son of Man as being the Judge, we should note how they unfold further Daniel's vision of the Son of Man (Dan. 7:13, 14). Jesus declared that the Father had "given all judgment to the Son" (Jn. 5:22). "He who hears my word and believes him who sent me, has eternal life; he does not come into judgment, but has passed from death to life" (v. 24). This underscores the necessity of believing in the Son of Man. Only through this faith can one escape coming into judgment. Jesus declared further that the Father had "given him authority to execute judgment, because he is the Son of man" (v. 27). On this account the resurrection leads to two different destinies: "Those who have done good, to the resurrection of life, and those who have done evil, to the resurrection of judgment" (v. 29).

The *anarthrous* nouns — *son,* and *man* (5:27) — pose a problem of exegesis which is of considerable importance for the study of this title. On the one side are those exegetes who observe that official titles are often used without the article. On this account English versions are divided between "the Son of man" and "son of man." Either translation possesses significant meaning. On this account we need to probe into the meaning of Jesus' statement. If "the Son of man" translates Jesus' words correctly, then our Lord is saying that God has vested authority in Him to execute judgment in view of the deity connotation bound up in this title. On the other hand, if "son of man" translates Jesus' words correctly, then He is saying that God has given Him authority to execute judgment in view of His being a human person. If the latter is the correct rendering of these words, then Jesus is saying that since He is a human being, God has given Him the authority to execute judgment. Some theologians hold that only a human being is qualified to judge mankind. Personally, I am inclined to believe that the latter interpretation expresses Jesus' thought.

The next context in which Jesus used this title is John 6:26-64. Here Jesus spoke of the food which endured to eternal life which the Son of Man would give to His followers, "For on him has God the Father set his seal." By these statements Jesus was declaring that He as the Son of Man would give them eternal life. God the Father had set His seal on the Son. These words likely carry the meaning that God had given clear attestation that Jesus was the Son of Man. Jesus had just referred to the signs *(semeion)* which He had performed, the most recent of which was the feeding of the five thousand. If this interprets Jesus' words correctly, then His miracles served as the grounds for believing that He was the Son of Man. Jesus intensified the meaning of His signs when He declared, "Unless you eat the flesh of the Son of man and drink his blood, you have no life in you." By this profound metaphor

Jesus was declaring the necessity of believing that He the Son of Man was manifest in human form. They who take this step of faith have eternal life.

Another use of this title which deserves attention occurs in 12:32-34. The people said to Jesus, "We have heard from the law that the Christ remains for ever. How can you say that the Son of man must be lifted up? Who is this Son of man?" This is the only case where the titles Messiah and Son of Man occur in the same context. It would appear that the people were not able to reconcile the lifting up of the Son of Man with the Christ, who remains forever. Evidently they identified the titles the Son of Man and the Messiah. If this is correct, then it would appear that when Daniel wrote "son of man" (Dan. 7:13, 14), his readers identified this person with the Messiah spoken of earlier by the prophets.

Jesus' last use of this title also calls for study. He said, "Now is the Son of man glorified, and in him God is glorified; if God is glorified in him, God will also glorify him in himself, and glorify him at once" (Jn. 13:31, 32). It is significant that Jesus did not use the terms *Son,* and *the Father*. We may inquire what difference in meaning the use of these titles would have carried. For Him to have used the titles *the Son* and *the Father* would have given this statement a distinctive Trinitarian connotation. As the statement stands, Jesus' words may carry the meaning that Jesus, the Son of Man, bears a close relation to God, over and beyond the relationship of the Father, the Son, and the Holy Spirit. That is, the Son of Man fulfills His deity work in spheres beyond that of time. This distinctive work centers in the redemption wrought by the Son of Man.

The Book of Revelation makes no reference to *Son of Man*. There are, nevertheless, several references to a *son of man,* some of which may be Christ Himself. For instance John saw one like *a son of man* in the midst of the lampstands (Rev. 1:13). This one declared, "I am the first and the last, and the living one; I died, and behold I am alive for evermore, and I have the keys of Death and Hades" (1:17, 18). These words certainly identify "a son of man" with the glorified Christ. In 14:14 we read, "Then I looked, and lo, a white cloud, and seated on the cloud one like *a son of man* with a golden crown on his head, and a sharp sickle in his hand." This is certainly a description of the enthroned Messiah. If this is a correct interpretation of John's vision, we may properly inquire why he used the expression *a son of man,* as he did in 1:13. It is possible that John was led to use this expression in order to identify this judgment scene with that of John 5:27-29, and in this way to confirm the authority of Christ to execute judgment because

He is "a son of man." This appears to be one of the unfathomable mysteries centering in the person of Christ.

This study of the title *the Son of Man* certainly builds up unquestionable grounds for believing in the deity of Christ. Every use of this title in John's Gospel stands as a positive assertion of His deity.

f. The New Creation

One of the most remarkable characteristics of the Bible is that it begins with an account of the Creation and concludes with a vision of a new creation. John wrote, "Then I saw a new heaven and a new earth; for the first heaven and the first earth had passed away" (Rev. 21:1). This reflects God's words recorded in Isaiah 65:17, "For behold, I create new heavens and a new earth; and the former things shall not be remembered or come into mind." Observe also that just as God added the words, "I create Jerusalem a rejoicing, and her people a joy" (v. 18), in like manner John saw "the holy city, new Jerusalem, coming down out of heaven from God" (Rev. 21:2). Peter had already laid hold of this prediction when he wrote of fellow believers, "Waiting for and hastening the coming of the day of God, because of which the heavens will be kindled and dissolved, and the elements will melt with fire! But according to his promise we wait for new heavens and a new earth in which righteousness dwells" (2 Pet. 3:12, 13).

The Lord unfolded further to John some profound aspects of this new creation. God declared, "Behold, I make all things new" (Rev. 21:5). The adjective *new (kainos)* carries the meaning *made new* and consequently superior to what it succeeds. This becomes still more apparent when the speaker says, "I am the Alpha and the Omega, the beginning and the end. To the thirsty I will give water without price from the fountain of the water of life" (v. 6). John was also shown the bride, the wife of the Lamb, also the holy city Jerusalem which had the glory of God. Unlike the old Jerusalem, the new Jerusalem had no temple. "For its temple is the Lord God the Almighty and the Lamb. And the city has no need of sun or moon to shine upon it, for the glory of God is its light, and its lamp is the Lamb" (vv. 22, 23). John was also shown "the river of the water of life, bright as crystal, flowing from the throne of God and of the Lamb" (22:1). Marvelous to behold was the tree of life which at the time of the Creation was not accessible to man, but now the redeemed could eat of its fruit and live forever. The most sublime anticipation of redeemed mankind is that "they shall see his face, and his name shall be on their foreheads . . . and they shall reign for ever and ever" (22:4, 5). The Lord said to John, "Behold, I am coming soon, bringing my recompense, to repay every one for what he has done. I am the Alpha and the Omega, the first and the last, the beginning and the end" (vv. 12, 13). In view of this hope John wrote, "Blessed are those who wash their robes, that they may have the right to the tree of life and that they may enter the city by the gates" (v. 14).

g. The Book of Life

Several times in the Revelation reference is made to the book of life. This becomes quite significant when we observe the settings in which reference is made to the book of life. Note the words, "He who conquers shall be clad thus in white garments, and I will not blot his name out of the book of life; I will confess his name before my Father and before his angels" (3:5). Of great meaning is the reference to "every one whose name has not been written before the foundation of the world in the book of life of the Lamb that was slain" (13:8). This establishes the great truth that the book of life was in existence before the foundation of the world and that in it were written the names of those who will be redeemed from this world. This has an important bearing on the great theological doctrines centering in God's purpose, foreknowledge, predestination, and calling (Rom. 8:28-30). In a different setting this expression is repeated in 17:8. The significance of the book of life becomes more evident in the words, "Another book was opened, which is the book of life. And the dead were judged by what was written in the books, by what they had done. . . . If any one's name was not found written in the book of life, he was thrown into the lake of fire" (20: 12-15). Finally, "Only those who are written in the Lamb's book of life" (21:27) will enter the heavenly Jerusalem.

By way of conclusion of this major section, the book of life stands as a grand climax to the salvation wrought by the enthroned Messiah. He, through His work of redemption sat down at the right hand of God, and through the exercise of His kingly power and authority has brought all the redeemed to eat of the tree of life, and so to live eternally with their glorified Lord. They whose names are written in the book of life shall see His face (22:4).

6. God the Father

John in his writings refers to God, the Father. This becomes clear as we observe such significant statements as, "Our fellowship is with the Father and with his Son Jesus Christ" (1 Jn. 1:3). "You know the Father" (2:13). "I rejoice greatly to find some of your children following the truth, just as we have been commanded by the Father" (2 Jn. 4). Turning to the prologue of John's Gospel note the words, "The Word became flesh and dwelt among us, full of grace and truth; we have beheld his glory, glory as of the only Son from the Father. . . . No one has ever seen God; the only Son, who is in the bosom of the Father, he has made him known" (Jn. 1:14-18). This at once suggests the dominance of the Father in John's writings. Whether John 3:35 are the words of the author or of Christ Himself, they significantly set forth the leading truth of this Gospel, "The Father loves the Son, and has given all things into His hand." This leads us to the focal point of John's presentation, Jesus' relation to the Father. Space does not permit a detailed presentation of the approximately 150 references to the Father in John's writings, yet there are values to the leading ideas which stand forth in these references. I shall list a few references under each subheading.

a. Jesus' Relation to the Father

(1) The Father's witness to Christ (Jn. 5:36, 37; 6:27, 37-40; 8:18, 19).

(2) Christ honors the Father and the Father glorifies the Son (Jn. 8:49, 54; 12:27, 28).

(3) The Father's love for the Son and Christ's love and obedience to the Father (Jn. 10:15-18; 15:8-10; 17:21-26).

(4) Christ and the Father are One (Jn. 10:25-30; 14:6-16; 17:21-26).

(5) The Father and the Son, each has life in Himself (Jn. 5:19-26; 1 Jn. 1:1-3).

(6) Both the Father and Christ are working (Jn. 5:17; 10:32; 1 Jn. 2:21).

(7) Jesus Christ, our Advocate with the Father (Jn. 14:15, 16; 16:23-28; 1 Jn. 2:1).

(8) The Father's love for those who love Christ (Jn. 14:21-24; 16:27; 1 Jn. 3:1; 4:10, 11, 19).

(9) Those who hate Christ also hate the Father (Jn. 15:23-25; 1 Jn. 2:22-24).

(10) Christ prays to the Father (Jn. 14:16; 16:26; 17).

(11) Jesus returns to the Father (Jn. 13:1, 3; 14:38; 16:10, 17, 28).

(12) The Holy Spirit sent by Christ from the Father (Jn. 14:16, 17; 15:26).

b. Worship of the Father

In Jesus' conversation with the woman of Samaria He set forth the nature of true worship in the words, "The true worshipers will worship the Father in spirit and truth, for such the Father seeks to worship him. God is spirit, and those who worship him must worship in spirit and truth" (Jn. 4:23, 24). In this manner Christ drew a sharp line between true and false worshipers. Perhaps He was referring to the hypocritical worship on the part of the Pharisees. Genuine worship centers in the spirit. It requires absolute honesty and integrity of heart. Outward forms have very little significance in worship. John recorded the witness of the man born blind to those who refused to believe in Christ in the words, "If any one is a worshiper of God and does his will, God listens to him" (Jn. 9:31). He certainly sensed the absolute requirement for the worship of God. There is need for doing God's will. God does not listen to sinners.

Several sublime visions of worship in heaven stand forth in the Revelation. Here the heavenly host fall on their faces before the throne and worship God, saying, "Amen! Blessing and glory and wisdom and thanksgiving and honor and power and might be to our God for ever and ever! Amen" (Rev. 7:11, 12). Note the ingredients of worship found in this paean of praise. God alone is worthy of such adoration. Another sublime scene of worship stands forth in 11:16-18. Here the 24 elders who sit on their thrones before God, also fell on their faces and worshiped Him saying, "We give thanks to thee, Lord God Almighty, who art and who wast, that thou hast taken thy great power and begun to reign" (v. 17). This vision portrays the elements of thanksgiving and adoration which are integral to worship. The remaining instances of worship (19: 4, 10; 22:9) stress the first responsibility of all created beings, "Worship God." So obvious is this responsibility that no other comment is necessary except to stress the truth that worship belongs alone to Deity. Writing in the time when the Roman emperors required worship on the part of all their subjects, John stressed the worship of the Father in all his writings.

c. Love and Obedience to the Father

John did not neglect to make known to his readers that they should manifest their love and obedience to the Father. This becomes evident in a setting in which he was counseling them not to love the world nor the things of the world. He stated very frankly, "If any one loves the world, love for the Father is not in him" (1 Jn. 2:15). He strengthened this admonition in the words, "We love, because he first loved us. . . . He who does not love his brother whom he has seen, cannot love God whom he has not seen. And this commandment we have from him, that he who loves God should love his brother also. . . . By this we know that we love the children of God, when we love God and obey his commandments. For this is the love of God, that we keep his commandments" (4:19 — 5:3). John's final note on this theme stands forth in the words, "Grace, mercy, and peace will be with us, from God the Father and from Jesus Christ the Father's Son, in truth and love. I rejoiced greatly to find some of your children following the truth, just as we have been commanded by the Father" (2 Jn. 3, 4).

7. The Nature of God the Father

John did not give a systematic presentation of God's nature, but he did set forth a number of simple but meaningful statements which are distinctive of John's theology. With little effort to give a systematic discussion of this profound biblical truth, let us ponder the meaning of such statements as "God is spirit" (Jn. 4:24); "The Father has life in himself" (Jn. 5:26; 6:57); "He . . . is true" (Jn. 7:28; 1 Jn. 5:20); "God is love" (1 Jn. 4:8, 16); God is holy (Jn. 17:11; Rev. 4:8; 6:10); "God is light" (1 Jn. 1:5-7); God is righteous (Jn. 17:25; Jn. 1:9; 3:7; Rev. 15:3; 19:2); God "knows everything" (1 Jn. 3:20); He is "Lord God the Almighty" (Rev. 1:8; 4:8; 11:17; 15:3; 16:7, 14; 19:6, 15; 21:22); and He is God "the Father" (1 Jn. 1:2; 2:1; 3:1; 2 Jn. 3, 4).

Let us also give thought to some precious gems. "Worthy art thou, our Lord and God, to receive glory and honor and power, for thou didst create all things, and by thy will they existed and were created" (Rev. 4:11). "Great and wonderful are thy deeds, O Lord God the Almighty! Just and true are thy ways, O King of the ages! Who shall not fear and glorify thy name, O Lord? For thou alone art holy. All nations shall come and worship thee, for thy judgments have been revealed" (Rev. 15:3, 4). "Hallelujah! Salvation and glory and power belong to our God, for his judgments are true and just. . . . Hallelujah! For the Lord our God the Almighty reigns. Let us rejoice and exult and give him the glory, for the marriage of the Lamb has come, and his Bride has made herself ready; it was granted her to be clothed with fine linen, bright and pure" (Rev. 19:1, 2, 6-8).

It is remarkable that John sets forth so many aspects of God's nature. Nevertheless, in hardly any context did he explain in detail the theological significance of these statements. It is obvious that the groundwork of the apostle's presentations were the Old Testament Scriptures and also Jesus' teachings of which he had first-hand knowledge. Perhaps the most instructive way of evaluating John's writing on this theme is to bring together into one setting these simple but profound statements and to view them as components of a masterpiece of art, in this case of God the Father.

a. He Is the Lord God Almighty

The Greek word *pantokrator*, translated *almighty*, has the meanings: *the all-powerful, the omnipotent One, the Ruler of all.* This word was used many times in the Septuagint to translate *shaddai*, the most significant example of which occurs in the Lord's word to Abraham, "I am God Almighty" (Gen. 17:1). The frequent occurrences of the word in the Book of Job reaches a climax in the words of the Lord, "Shall a faultfinder contend with the Almighty? He who argues with God, let him answer it" (Job 40:1,.2). Most sublime are the words of the psalmist, "He who dwells in the shelter of the Most High, who abides in the shadow of the Almighty, will say to the Lord, 'My refuge and my fortress; my God, in whom I trust' " (Ps. 91:1, 2). With this Old Testament background of the title *Almighty,* let us note the buildup of meaning as found in Revelation. Note the expression, " 'I am the Alpha and the Omega,' says the Lord God, who is and who was and who is to come, the Almighty " (Rev. 1:8; see also 4:8). A look at the state of the world at the close of the first century AD shows how significant these statements were for that time, especially to the early Christians. Their experiences of persecution and martyrdom tested them most severely. The patient endurance of these Christians was most significant. These words from the Lord God Almighty served to brace these early Christians for their excruciating sufferings. Since the Lord God is the Almighty One, they could trust Him even though their tribulation led them to death. In spite of the world conditions, they could believe that the Lord God Almighty had taken His "great power and begun to reign" (11:17). When the Lord brought severe punishment upon those who shed the blood of the saints and the prophets, an angel cried, "Yea, Lord God the Almighty, true and just are thy judgments!" (16: 5-7). Another vision of the awful judgment brought by the Lord upon the wickedness of this world stands forth in the words, "From his mouth issues a sharp sword with which to smite the nations, and he will rule them with a rod of iron; he will tread the wine press of the fury of the wrath of God the Almighty" (19:15). Most glorious was the scene depicted by John in the words, "I saw no temple in the city, for its temple is the Lord God the Almighty and the Lamb" (21:22). This sampling of the appearances of God Almighty in the Revelation sets forth most forcibly their special significance. These Christians could most confidently place their trust in the Almighty God.

b. God the Father

In order to grasp the meaning of the title *God the Father,* it is necessary to observe that both John and Jesus used this title in the recorded words of Jesus. *God the Father* occurs more than one hundred times. John, himself, used it more than a dozen times throughout his writings. This phenomenon prepares the way for grasping the profound meaning of this title. It becomes quite a challenge to lay hold of the buildup of meaning from the common concept of an earthly father to that of the heavenly Father, God, Himself.

(1) John's references to God the Father. Since John referred to God the Father in the prologue of his Gospel it seems appropriate to search for the significance of these references before a study is made of Christ's use of this name. Referring to the Word, John wrote, "We have beheld his glory, glory as of the only Son from the Father." At the close of this paragraph, he added, "No one has ever seen God; the only Son, who is in the bosom of the Father, he has made him known" (Jn. 1:14, 18). Note also John's references to the Father in his letters and the Revelation. Quoting briefly from these books, observe: "the eternal life which was with the Father"; "our fellowship is with the Father"; "we have an Advocate with the Father"; "you know the Father"; "love for the Father"; "he who confesses the Son has the Father also"; "you will abide in the Son and in the Father"; "see what love the Father has given us"; "the Father has sent his Son"; "grace, mercy, and peace will be with us, from God the Father and from Jesus Christ the Father's Son"; "he who abides in the doctrine of Christ has both the Father and the Son"; and "made us a kingdom, priests to his God and Father" (Jn. 1:14, 18; 1 Jn. 1:2, 3; 2:1, 13, 15, 16, 22-24; 3:1; 4:14; 2 Jn. 3, 4, 9; Rev. 1:6).

Some distinctive ideas which stand forth in John's references to God the Father are worthy of notice. Through the Word becoming flesh we have beheld the glory of the Father. This truth becomes evident in the personal relationship of the Father and the revealed Son. What more intimate knowledge of the Father could mankind receive than through the Son who is in the bosom of the Father? The real nature of Christian fellowship becomes evident when we note that this fellowship is at heart our relationship to the Father and to His Son. Man's sin breaks this fellowship with the Father, but the righteous Jesus Christ is our *parakletos (advocate, mediator, intercessor, helper*, or *one who appears in another's behalf)*. Through this Mediator we come to know the Father. The requisite for the believer's fellowship with the Father is to hold fast to what we have heard from the beginning. To reject Christ is the same as denying the Father also. John gave a strong testimony to the love which the Father has given us. It stands forth in the reality of being called children of God. Our personal experience with the Son as our Savior leads us to testify that the Father actually sent His Son into the world. It is a most treasured experience that grace, mercy, and peace, bestowed upon us by God the Father, have actually been given in truth and love. Finally, they who abide in the doctrine of Christ have both the Father and the Son. It is evident that what the author set forth concerning the Father had its foundation in his own personal experience with the Father.

(2) Jesus' references to the Father. The more than one hundred instances in which Jesus referred to the Father as recorded in John's Gospel challenges careful study in order to grasp the nature and content of Jesus' teaching concerning the Father. An effort to classify the statements on the part of Jesus also presents some problems. More important than merely to group them according to subject matter is to understand the distinctive ideas reflected in each reference.

(a) Jesus' revelation of the Father. In this group let us reflect on what Jesus revealed concerning the nature and attributes of the Father. Jesus said, "For as the Father has life in himself, so he has granted the Son also to have life in himself" (5:26). This statement made in a resurrection context reveals explicitly that the source of all life is in the Father. In a similar context Jesus noted, "All that the Father gives me will come to me. . . . For this is the will of my Father, that every one who sees the Son and believes in him should have eternal life" (6:37-40). Thus Jesus revealed the will of the Father. He told the Jews that sin enslaves a person, and then He added, "If the Son makes you free, you will be free indeed. . . . I speak of what I have seen with my Father" (8:36, 38). In this manner Jesus showed that the Father was the great Liberator of mankind from sin. Later Jesus added, "If God were your Father, you would love me, for I proceeded and came forth from God; I came not of my own accord, but he sent me" (v. 42). Thus the Father had taken the initiative to send Christ into this world.

As the unbelieving Jews were about to stone Him for blasphemy, Jesus declared, "I have shown you many good works from the Father" (10:32). By this statement Jesus was declaring that He was doing these works in His Father's name. The Father had consecrated Christ and sent Him into the world (v. 36). Jesus reaffirmed His claims that He was doing the works of His Father through these mighty works, and through this they could know and understand that the Father was in Him and He in the Father (vv. 37, 38). Herein was a profound mystery. It declares the oneness of the Father and the Son and at the same time affirms the personal distinction between the Father and the Son. Even the disciples, who associated with Jesus every day, needed to learn this Father-Son relationship.

In response to Philip's question Jesus asked, "Do you not believe that I am in the Father and the Father in me?. . . The Father who dwells in me does his works. Believe me that I am in the Father and the Father in me" (14:10, 11). Thus the disciples were also confronted with the profound mystery of Christ's being in the Father and the Father being in Christ. This was the most meaningful way in which Jesus declared that He was the revelation of the Father. Jesus revealed the Father still more intimately in His prayer (17). Here we learn that Jesus and the Father shared divine glory before the world was made. He addressed God as holy Father and also as righteous Father. He closed the prayer by asking that the love which the Father had for Him might also be found in all mankind.

(b) The Father-Son relationship. Since Jesus revealed the Father, it becomes essential to understand what Jesus taught concerning the Father's relation to the Son. Three times Jesus declared that the Father loves the Son (3:35; 5:20; 10:17). In each case He added a significant statement which declared the nature of this relationship. First, the Father had given all things into Christ's hands. The perfect tense of the verb declares the continuing state of all things being in the hands of the Son. Second, the Father was showing Christ all that He Himself was doing. The present tense of these verbs indicated the continuing acts of God throughout Christ's earthly ministry. Third, the Father loves the Son because He was laying down His life for the sheep.

Jesus also declared, "I can do nothing on my own authority. . . . The works which the Father has granted me to accomplish, these very works which I am doing, bear me witness that the Father has sent me. . . . I have come in my Father's name" (5:30-43). Then as Jesus gave real significance to the feeding of the five thousand, He declared that the Father had set His seal on Him, by which He evidently was saying that the descent of the Holy Spirit upon Him at His baptism was the seal of the Father that He was the Son of God. Throughout Jesus' earthly ministry the Father was giving adequate grounds for the people to believe that Jesus was the Son of Man, the Son of God. This became evident in all of Jesus' teachings and also through His miracles which John called *signs*. In the framework of human father-son relationships, Jesus declared, "All that the Father gives me will come to me" (6:37). In this manner Jesus was declaring another Father-Son relationship. He was recognizing that the Father had given Him the disciples. This becomes very evident in later references (6:39, 65; 10:29; 17:2, 6, 9, 12, 24; 18:9). It gives a profound insight to all that was involved in Jesus' choosing the twelve disciples. They were granted to Him by the Father. It includes all of His sheep. He was enabled to give eternal life to all those given to Him by the Father. It was His desire that they might be with Him to behold His glory which the Father had given Him in His love before the foundation of the world. In this bread of life discourse Jesus asserted another intimate relationship, in that all who had heard and learned from the Father come to Him. He alone has seen the

Father (6:45, 46). Jesus asserted another vital relationship in the words, "As the living Father sent me, and I live because of the Father, so he who eats me will live because of me" (v. 57). In another setting Jesus said, "The Father who sent me bears witness to me" (8:18). When this statement was challenged Jesus added, "If you knew me, you would know my Father also" (v. 19). In response to another challenge Jesus answered, "I do nothing on my own authority but speak thus as the Father taught me" (v. 28). As the debate continued Jesus declared, "I honor my Father" (v. 49), to which He added, "It is my Father who glorifies me" (v. 54).

In His good shepherd message Jesus said, "The Father knows me and I know the Father" (10:15). With reference to His coming death He added, "This charge I have received from my Father" (v. 18). He expanded this truth in the words, "The works that I do in my Father's name, they bear witness to me. . . . My Father, who has given them to me, is greater than all. . . . I and the Father are one" (vv. 25-30). At the tomb of Lazarus, Jesus declared, "Father, I thank thee that thou hast heard me. I knew that thou hearest me always, but I have said this on account of the people standing by, that they may believe that thou didst send me" (11:41, 42). When He entered Jerusalem, just prior to His arrest, condemnation, and crucifixion, He prayed, "And what shall I say, 'Father, save me from this hour'? . . . Father, glorify thy name." God responded in the words, "I have glorified it, and I will glorify it again" (12:27, 28). One must observe the increasing intimacy of the Father's relation to the Son as He was nearing His death on the cross. Our Lord's closing words, as He was entering Jerusalem serve as a final testimony to the Jews of His relation to the Father, "For I have not spoken on my own authority; the Father who sent me has himself given me commandment what to say and what to speak. And I know that his commandment is eternal life. What I say, therefore, I say as the Father has bidden me" (vv. 49, 50)

Of the tense moments during the Last Supper John made the observation, "Jesus, knowing that the Father had given all things into his hands, and that he had come from God and was going to God" (13:3). This stands as John's understanding of Jesus' relation to the Father. Jesus gave a new dimension to prayer when He said,"Whatever you ask in my name, I will do it, that the Father may be glorified in the Son; if you ask anything in my name, I will do it. . . . And I will pray the Father, and he will give you another Counselor, to be with you for ever, even the Spirit of truth" (14:13-15). As a faithful Son Jesus had to be concerned that His Father may be glorified in Himself. Thus Jesus had sought to center all glory in the Father — the most noble response of a Son to His Father. As Jesus looked forward to His resurrection, He declared, "Because I live, you will live also. In that day you will know that I am in my Father, and you in me, and I in you. . . . And he who loves me will be loved by my Father (vv. 19-21). Through these words Jesus was declaring that His followers will share in the same intimate relation with the Father as He the glorified Son would share. In a word, it would be a love relationship. It is the Christian's privilege to recognize that the Holy Spirit sent to us by the Father, in Christ's name, perpetuates this love relationship among the Father, Son, and His followers.

The climactic approach to the Father-Son relationship came in Jesus' use of the expressive metaphor of the vine and the branches. Jesus said, "I am the true vine, and my Father is the vinedresser . . . and every branch that does bear fruit he prunes, that it may bear more fruit. . . . I am the vine, you are the branches. He who abides in me, and I in him, he it is that bears much fruit, for apart from me you can do nothing. . . . If you abide in me, and my words abide in you, ask whatever you will, and it shall be done for you. By this my Father is glorified, that you bear much fruit, and so prove to be my disciples. As the Father has loved me, so have I loved you; abide in my love. If you keep my commandments, you will abide in my love, just as I have kept my Father's commandments and abide in his love" (15:1-10). Later in this message Jesus added, "If you ask anything of the Father, he will give it to you in my name. . . . In that day you will ask in my name; and I do not say to you that I shall pray the Father for you; for the Father himself loves you, because you have loved me and have believed that I came from the Father. I came from the Father and have come into the world; again, I am leaving the world and am going to the Father" (16:23-28).

The Lord's prayer (17) brings this Father-Son relationship to a most sublime culmination. Most precious are the words, "Father, the hour has come; glorify thy Son that the Son may glorify thee, since thou hast given him power over all flesh, to give eternal life to all whom thou hast given him. And this is eternal life, that they know thee the only true God., and Jesus Christ whom thou hast sent. I glorified thee on earth, having accomplished the work which thou gavest me to do; and now, Father, glorify thou me in thy own presence with the glory which I had with thee before the world was made" (vv. 1-5). Near the close of His prayer He said, "Father, I desire that they also, whom thou hast given me, may be with me where I am, to behold my glory which thou hast given me in thy love for me before the foundation of the world. O righteous Father, the world has not known thee, but I have known thee. . . . I made known to them thy name, and I will make it known, that the love with which thou hast loved me may be in them, and I in them" (vv. 24-26).

When Peter sought to defend Christ against those who were about to arrest Him, Jesus asked the question, "Shall I not drink the cup which the Father has given me?" (18:11). This question brought Christ's relation to the Father to its crucial test. But we can rejoice exceedingly that Jesus could say to Mary after His resurrection, "I am ascending to my Father and your Father, to my God and your God" (20:17). This showed that the love relationship between the Father and the Son will continue throughout eternity.

This lengthy presentation of Father-Son relationship possesses highest value because it sets forth clearly Jesus' own declaration of this relationship.

c. The Father's Relation to Man

Jesus made a number of statements setting forth the Father's relation to man. When Jesus came to the temple and found the Jews desecrating this holy place, He declared, "Take these things away; you shall not make my Father's house a house of trade" (2:16). The Father had directed Solomon to build the temple for worship. In this way His people could come into the presence of the Father for worship, the climax of which was the fellowship they experienced with the Father. The entrance of the high priest into the holy of holies once a year was the highest point of Israel's access to God the Father.

Jesus' conversation with the woman of Samaria unfolded further the Father's relation to man. He told the woman that the Father would not continue to require His people to come to the temple for worship. He established a high standard for those who would worship the Father. He said, "But the hour is coming, and now is, when the true worshipers will worship the Father in spirit and truth, for such the Father seeks to worship him. God is spirit, and those who worship him must worship in spirit and truth" (4:23, 24). In this language Jesus was telling the woman that God the Father, the Creator of man, requires of His children integrity of purpose and motive in worship. Only in this way can man experience the Father-Son relationship desired by God.

The Father's relation to man becomes evident in Jesus' words, "For as the Father raises the dead and gives them life, so also the Son gives life to whom he will. The Father judges no one, but has given all judgment to the Son, that all may honor the Son, even as they honor the Father" (5:21-23). Thus Jesus expressed in a most intimate way the Father's relation to man. Even though the human race fell into sin, the Father did not cast away mankind who bear the image of God. Those who repent from sin will experience the resurrection unto life. God the Father continues to deal with man who possesses the dignity of bearing the image of God the Father.

By way of the rich analogy between natural bread and the bread from heaven, Jesus declared that the Father gives the true bread to redeemed mankind. The glory of God the Father ever becomes greater when seen in the Father's provision of the true bread, Jesus Christ, provided to all who believe in the Son. God's compassion for sinful mankind stands forth again in Jesus' words, "No one can come to me unless the Father who sent me draws him; and I will raise him up at the last day. It is written in the prophets, 'And they shall all be taught by God.' Every one who has heard and learned from the Father comes to me" (6:44, 45). The Father's compassion upon mankind is shown by His drawing ungodly men to Him.

Jesus' good shepherd message closes with the significant words, "My sheep hear my voice, and I know them, and they follow me; and I give them eternal life, and they shall never perish, and no one shall snatch them out of my hand. My Father, who has given them to me, is greater than all, and no one is able to snatch them out of the Father's hand. I and the Father are one" (10:27-30). In this setting the Father's relation to man stands forth in a significant manner. In the metaphor of the Father giving sheep to the Son, and by reason of the Father's omnipotence, no one is able to snatch these sheep out of the Father's hand. By reason of the Father's watchful care the followers of Jesus are safe and secure.

The Father's relation to man becomes evident again in Jesus' words, "If anyone serves me, the Father will honor him" (12:26). Just as an earthly father will honor a faithful and obedient son, so the heavenly Father will bestow favor on obedient human beings. One of the most glorious aspects of Christian hope is the heavenly Father's house of many rooms in which redeemed mankind will live forever (14:2). As Jesus unfolded the meaning of being His friends He included the words, "I have called you friends, for all that I have heard from my Father I have made known to you. . . . Whatever you ask the Father in my name, he may give it to you" (15:15, 16). Here the followers of Jesus are called friends, which raises them from the status of being *servants* to that of being *friends*. All friends are on the same level. On this account all that our Lord heard from the Father has been made known to His friends. At the close of the upper room message our Lord gave these precious words, "The Father himself loves you, because you have loved me and have believed that I came from the Father" (16:27). This stands as the climax to the heavenly Father's relation to man. How wonderful it is for our heavenly Father to love human beings in the same manner and degree that He loves the Son. While the discussion of this section brought into view a number of the references quoted in the previous subdivision, my concern has been to emphasize the precious truths bound up in the heavenly Father's relation to mankind.

d. Worship, the Proper Response of Man to God

I noted in the previous section that God provided the temple, the Father's house, as the place of worship for His people. Throughout biblical history, man's relation to God centered in worship. The altar, the tabernacle, and the temple symbolized this relationship. This is what intensified the desecration of the temple when the Jews made it a house of trade. To the woman of Samaria, Jesus gave a forthright definition of worship in the words, "The true worshipers will worship the Father in spirit and truth, for such the Father seeks to worship him. God is spirit and those who worship him must worship in spirit and truth" (4:23, 24). Thus man's relation to God in worship involves his innermost being. This is a spiritual experience and it must be genuine and real, not hypocritical. We are not aware that Jesus was consciously exposing the hypocrisy of pharisaical worship, but obviously, their worship was not in spirit and truth. From a homiletic point of view, we need to grasp Jesus' forthright explication of worship.

e. The Father's Work as Deity

A couple statements stand out in Jesus' teaching which may refer to the activity of the Father on the level of His supernatural power and wisdom. Note Jesus' words, "My Father is working still, and I am working" (5:17). Jesus' healing of the lame man required supernatural power such as that exercised by the Father. Jesus' statement then carries the meaning that He was performing a work on the same level as His Father's works (5:8-10). At the close of His prayer (chap. 17) we have the words, "Father, I desire that they also, whom thou hast given me, may be with me where I am, to behold my glory which thou hast given me in thy love for me before the foundation of the world" (v. 24). In this statement Jesus is looking back to God's creation of the world, a work possible only to Deity.

A review of Jesus' references to the Father deserves reverent attention. In a word, we may say that the profoundest teachings of Jesus center in the Father. Of such primacy is this teaching in John's Gospel that we may safely conclude that Jesus' revelation of the Father stands second only to the stated purpose of John, "These are written that you may believe that Jesus is the Christ, the Son of God, and that believing you may have life in his name" (20:31).

8. The Holy Spirit

The writings of the Apostle John offer distinctive teaching concerning the Holy Spirit. Just as his record of Christ as the Son of God and of God the Father holds primacy, so the person and work of the Holy Spirit stand forth in his writings in similar perspective. Let us probe into these teachings with the special objective of gaining an understanding of the person and work of the Holy Spirit in the same manner as we studied John's presentation of God the Father and God the Son.

a. The Holy Spirit's Work in Jesus

John the Baptist experienced an extraordinary revelation which he expressed in the words, "I saw the Spirit descend as a dove from heaven, and it remained on him. I myself did not know him; but he who sent me to baptize with water said to me, 'He on whom you see the Spirit descend and remain, this is he who baptizes with the Holy Spirit.' And I have seen and have borne witness that this is the Son of God" (Jn. 1:32-34). This leads us to the unfathomable mystery centering in the triune God. Note especially the descent of the Spirit upon Christ. Through this mode of revelation the personality of the Spirit becomes evident. His nature is such that He could come upon our Lord and dwell in Him. This descent of the Spirit upon Christ as recorded by John lies at the foundation of all that he recorded concerning the Spirit's activity during Christ's earthly ministry. Assuming that 3:31-36 are John's own statements, he is expressing a significant truth in the words, "He whom God has sent utters the words of God, for it is not by measure that he gives the Spirit" (v. 34). This leads us to believe that John is drawing a contrast between the unlimited operation of the Spirit in Christ as it stands in contrast with His limited work in the believers. This becomes evident as John presented the matchless teachings and marvelous works of Jesus.

b. The Holy Spirit, Another Counselor

Jesus' final discourse to His disciples included a special announcement concerning the Holy Spirit. He declared, "I will pray the Father, and he will give you another Counselor, to be with you for ever, even the Spirit of truth, whom the world cannot receive, because it neither sees him nor knows him; you know him, for he dwells with you, and will be in you. . . . But the Counselor, the Holy Spirit, whom the Father will send in my name, he will teach you all things, and bring to your remembrance all that I have said to you" (14:16-26). Later in the message Jesus said, "When the Counselor comes, whom I shall send to you from the Father, even the Spirit of truth, who proceeds from the Father, he will bear witness to me" (15:26). The Holy Spirit is another *Counselor (allon parakleton)*. Jesus was saying that the Holy Spirit would be a Counselor of the same rank that He is. The Greek word *parakletos* is rich in meaning. It can be translated *one who appears in another's behalf, mediator, intercessor, helper, advocate, consoler*, and *comforter*. It has the literal sense *called to one's aid*. What more appropriate name could our Lord ascribe to the Holy Spirit! While Jesus' earthly ministry continued until His ascension, the Counselor will be with His people for ever. Undoubtedly many Christians have desired that the Lord Jesus Christ would have remained in this world. But His life as the incarnate Son of God naturally led to His exaltation to the right hand of God the Father.

On the other hand, the Holy Spirit, the other Counselor, has been sent by the Father to be with His people until the end of time. His presence with the children of God is as meaningful as that of Christ during His earthly ministry. Our Lord declared, "He will teach you all things, and bring to your remembrance all that I have said to you" (14: 26). Jesus gave additional testimony in the words, "When the Counselor comes, whom I shall send to you from the Father, even the Spirit of truth, who proceeds from the Father, he will bear witness to me" (15:26). Westcott's comment on the Spirit of truth reads, "The Spirit by whom the Truth finds expression and is brought to man's spirit. The Truth is that which the Spirit interprets and enforces."[18] This stands in sharp contrast with what our Lord said concerning the devil: "He . . . has nothing to do with the truth, because there is no truth in him" (8:44). Jesus spoke further on the work of the Holy Spirit when He said, "If I do not go away, the Counselor will not come to you; but if I go, I will send him to you. And when he comes, he will convince the world of sin and of righteousness and of judgment: of sin, because they do not believe in me; of righteousness, because I go to the Father, and you will see me no more; of judgment, because the ruler of this world is judged" (16:7-11).

John gave his own testimony in the words, "And the Spirit is the witness, because the Spirit is the truth. There are three witnesses, the Spirit, the water, and the blood; and these three agree" (1 Jn. 5:7, 8). A lead to understanding John's statement, "The Spirit is the truth," may be found in Christ's words "the Spirit of truth" as found in John 14:17; 15:26; and 16:13. Robertson gives the comment, "The Holy Spirit is marked by it (genitive case), gives it, defends it (cf. 1:17), in contrast to the spirit of error (1 Jn. 4:6)."[19] Just as Jesus declared, "I am the way, and the truth, and the life," John could properly write, "The Spirit is the truth" (1 Jn. 5:7). Since the Holy Spirit is another Counselor, it reveals His close identity with our Lord as the Counselor.

c. The Work of the Spirit in the Believer

Christ's words to Nicodemus are instructive on this point when He overwhelmed Nicodemus by saying, "Unless one is born anew, he cannot see the kingdom of God." Jesus explained further, "Unless one is born of water and the Spirit he cannot enter the kingdom of God. That which is born of the flesh is flesh, and that which is born of the Spirit is spirit. . . . The wind blows where it will, and you hear the sound of it, but you do not know whence it comes or whither it goes; so it is with every one who is born of the Spirit" (Jn. 3:3-8). With this analogy between natural birth and the spiritual birth, Jesus sought to lead this teacher of Israel to understand the nature of the Christian life. It has its beginning in the work of the Holy Spirit which effects an inner spiritual new birth whereby he is enabled not only to see the kingdom of God but also to enter it. There are no physical aspects to this spiritual experience. We do not know how we are born again, but we do know that we have the new life in us.

On the last day of the Feast of Tabernacles, Jesus gave further explication of the Spirit's work. On this occasion He said, " 'If any one thirst, let him come to me and drink. He who believes in me, as the scripture has said, 'Out of his heart shall flow rivers of living water.' Now this he said about the Spirit, which those who believed in him were to receive; for as yet the Spirit had not been given, because Jesus was not yet glorified" (7:37-39). With no desire to enter into the exegetical difficulty centering in these verses, let us seek to lay hold of Jesus' teaching as it relates to the work of the Spirit in the believer. Here He was offering spiritual drink to those who were spiritually thirsty. They who believed in Him could appropriate this promise. Jesus was the source of the living water which flowed from His heart. By way of explanation, John declared that Jesus was speaking about the Holy Spirit which those who believed in Him were to receive. Just as natural water gushed out from the rock after Moses had struck it (Num. 20:11), so from Christ would flow forth the Holy Spirit after His resurrection and ascension. The truth to be gained from this incident is the outpouring of the Holy Spirit upon those who believe in Jesus Christ as Lord and Savior.

The work of the Spirit in the disciples of Christ gained still greater significance when, after His resurrection He told them, " 'As the Father has sent me, even so I send you.' And when he had said this, he breathed on them, and said to them, 'Receive the Holy Spirit. If you forgive the sins of any, they are forgiven; if you retain the sins of any, they are retained' " (Jn. 20:21-23). The interpretation of this passage as it bears on the work of the Spirit involves problems which lie beyond this study. Most pertinent for this discussion is the relation between this gift of the Holy Spirit and that at Pentecost. Jesus' words, "Even so I send you," seem to express a special mission entrusted to the disciples. It is probable that this command did not include all that was expressed in the Great Commission (Mt. 28:19, 20). Christ's breathing on them the Holy Spirit would suggest a special empowering of the disciples for their apostolic responsibilities.

The office of the apostles was restricted to the twelve chosen by Jesus. It was not a responsibility to be perpetuated in the Christian church. This would lead us to believe that Jesus' breathing on them the Holy Spirit was to enable them to fulfill the special apostolic mission entrusted to them. Their apostolic responsibility included that of forgiving the sins of those who repented and turned in faith to Jesus Christ. Those who refused to repent would remain guilty before God. The meaning of Jesus' words dare not be carried too far. God alone forgives sins. On this account, the apostles were entrusted with this responsibility only on the basis of the authority given to them by the risen Lord. Alone through the authority of the Holy Spirit could the apostles exercise this responsibility which related so closely to the authority of God.

The Apostle John made three references to the Holy Spirit in his first letter, each of which sets forth a distinctive relation of the Holy Spirit to the believer. John was dealing with the practical problem of Christian assurance. He wrote, "All who keep his commandments abide in him, and he in them. And by this we know that he abides in us, by the Spirit which he has given us" (1 Jn. 3:24). By these words John was declaring that the basis for this assurance rested on the foundation of the individual's keeping the commandments of our Lord. Through this obedience an individual knows that Christ dwells in him. This inner assurance has its basis in the witness of the Holy Spirit who indwells the believer. The risen and glorified Lord Jesus bears witness to the believer through the person of the Holy Spirit. In similar language John wrote, "Beloved, do not believe every spirit, but test the spirits to see whether they are of God; for many false prophets have gone out into the world. By this you know the Spirit of God: every spirit which confesses that Jesus Christ has come in the flesh is of God, and every spirit which does not confess Jesus is not of God" (4:1-3). Through these words John established the way of discerning the Spirit of God. Only the Holy Spirit asserts that Jesus Christ has come in the flesh. This was a simple but sure ground for discerning the Holy Spirit in opposition to the spirit of Antichrist. The apostle gave further confirmation of this truth in the words, "By this we know that we abide in him and he in us, because he has given us of his own Spirit" (4:13).

John's final confirmation of the Spirit's work in the believer stands forth in the words, "This is he who came by water and blood, Jesus Christ, not with the water only but with the water and the blood. And the Spirit is the witness, because the Spirit is the truth. There are three witnesses, the Spirit, the water, and the blood; and these three agree" (5:6-8). The Holy Spirit's descent upon Christ at His baptism gave witness to Jesus as the Son of God. The Father confirmed this witness when Jesus was hanging on the cross. Thus the Spirit who is the truth confirmed the deity of Christ. His witness ranks with that of the Father. This gives additional ground for believing that the Spirit is the truth. This bears similarity to Christ's own words, "I am the way, and the truth, and the life; no one comes to the Father, but by me" (Jn. 14:6).

The Book of Revelation gives further witness to the work of the Spirit in the believers. Twice John declared, "I was in the Spirit" (Rev. 1:10; 4:2). The Greek expression *egenomen en pneumati* carries the literal meaning *I became in the Spirit.* Swete says that this "denotes the exaltation of the prophet under inspiration."[20] This was a spiritual experience through which God gave him a revelation. It was this ecstatic experience through which the entire Book of Revelation was disclosed to John. The letters to the seven churches were the written record of what John saw. When the voice from heaven invited him to come up to the glory world, he declared, "At once I was in the Spirit" (4:2). This accounts for John's experience throughout the remainder of the book, which he saw when he was in the Spirit. His experience of being in the Spirit transcends the nature of the experiences in which Christians in general participate. John's experience was similar to that of the Old Testament prophets who revealed the words of God through the power of the Spirit. His experience contributes to our understanding of the Spirit's work in us. It is the privilege of every Christian to be in the Spirit, not on the level of receiving divine revelation but of receiving guidance and direction in all the affairs of life. The exhortation given by John in his first letter finds application here. Christians need to discern the spirit of truth as it stands opposed to the spirit of error.

As John wrote to the seven churches, he gave the exhortation to each, "He who hath an ear, let him hear what the Spirit says to the churches" (2:7, 11, 17, 29; 3:6, 13, 22). From a homiletic point of view, let me urge that we take to heart this same exhortation. The

Spirit is still speaking to the churches.

Several other references to the Spirit deserve notice. Revelation 17:3 reads, "And he carried me away in the Spirit into a wilderness" where he saw a wicked woman, drunk with the blood of the saints and of the martyrs of Jesus. But John was granted a most glorious vision when he declared, "In the Spirit he carried me away to a great, high mountain, and showed me the holy city Jerusalem coming down out of heaven from God" (21:10). Both of these visions were possible alone through the Holy Spirit. John also heard a voice from heaven saying, " 'Write this; Blessed are the dead who die in the Lord henceforth.' 'Blessed indeed,' says the Spirit, 'that they may rest from their labors, for their deeds follow them!' " (14:13). It was John's supreme privilege to give this message to the churches with whom he was suffering tribulation and experiencing patient endurance. It is most thrilling to observe that the last message of the Spirit to the churches stands forth in the words, "The Spirit and the Bride say, 'Come.' And let him who hears say, 'Come.' And let him who is thirsty come, let him who desires take the water of life without price" (22:17). Through these words we learn that the climactic work of the Spirit in the believers stands forth in this sublime invitation to take the water of life without price.

9. Angelology

a. John's References to Angels

John's references to angels present some problems of interpretation, especially those in the Book of Revelation. Significant were Jesus' words to the early disciples, when He said, "Truly, truly, I say to you, you will see heaven opened, and the angels of God ascending and descending upon the Son of man" (Jn. 1:51). This at once reminds us of Jacob's dream, "And he dreamed that there was a ladder set up on the earth, and the top of it reached to heaven; and behold, the angels of God were ascending and descending on it!" (Gen. 28:12). Evidently there was an inner consciousness on the part of Jacob for having wronged his brother and the Lord was revealing to him the spiritual needs of his soul. Only through the ascending and descending angels of God could these needs be supplied. The ascending angels were communicating to God Jacob's needs and the descending angels brought to him God's response to his needs. In Jesus' reference to this incident He set forth the profound truth that *through (epi, upon)* the Son of Man, the angels of God were ascending to heaven with the needs of man and were descending upon the Son of Man with God's response. In other words, through Jesus Christ the needs of man were laid before God and God's response of love, mercy, and grace were revealed through the Son of Man, the angels being the messengers of God performing this service. Since Jesus was God manifest in the flesh, He could not ascend and descend to and from God in human form. On this account the heavenly beings, angels, served as His messengers to and from heaven. For the purpose of biblical theology, Jesus' statements disclosed angels as personal beings, spiritual in nature, and messengers of God to mankind.

On the occasion of Jesus' entry into Jerusalem when His soul was troubled because of His imminent crucifixion, a voice came from heaven declaring that the Father had glorified His name and would do so again. With their Old Testament background, some of the Jews believed that an angel had spoken to Christ (Jn. 12:27-30). John also recorded a touching incident which involved angels. "But Mary stood weeping outside the tomb, and as she wept she stooped to look into the tomb; and she saw two angels in white, sitting where the body of Jesus had lain, one at the head and one at the feet. They said to her, 'Woman, why are you weeping?' She said to them, 'Because they have taken away my Lord, and I do not know where they have laid him' " (Jn. 20:11-13). Here was a visible appearance of angels. They spoke to Mary. Their being clothed in white showed that they were heavenly beings in human form. From the nature of this narrative we may safely conclude that a literal interpretation is entirely consistent. These angels performed the special work of revealing to Mary that the body of Jesus had not been stolen from the tomb but that He had risen from the dead. Evidently these angels did not remain in the tomb. After having performed their mission of informing Mary concerning the Lord, they disappeared from human view. This angel activity harmonized with what the Old Testament revealed concerning angels.

The Revelation to John contains many references to angels, some of which pose difficult problems for interpretation. The first verse of the book sets forth a significant task assigned to an angel, "The revelation of Jesus Christ, which God gave him to show to his servants what must soon take place; and he made it known by sending his angel to his servant John, who bore witness to the word of God and to the testimony of Jesus Christ, even to all that he saw" (1:1, 2). Here an angel was our Lord's message bearer to the author, John. This statement comprehends the entire Book of Revelation. The Lord revealed Himself to John and explained the vision he had seen: "As for the mystery of the seven stars which you saw in my right hand, and the seven golden lampstands, the seven stars are the angels of the seven churches and the seven lampstands are the seven churches" (Rev. 1:20). The simplest declaration of this statement, together with the references to the angels in chapters 2 and 3, seems to be that God had appointed an angel to each of the churches for the purpose of giving them guidance in their bloody persecutions which they were experiencing.

Let us note then what some of these references contribute to the person and work of the angels. John saw a strong angel giving a proclamation with a loud voice (5:2). This suggests differences of strength among angels, which become evident throughout the book. John saw four angels who had power over the earth and its elements (7:1). Another angel was in position to give direction to these four angels (v. 2). One of their responsibilities was to seal the servants of God upon their foreheads so that they would be spared from the imminent judgments coming upon the world (v. 3). John beheld a great multitude of redeemed people from the world who were singing praises to God and to the Lamb. In this setting all the angels stood around the throne and worshiped God (vv. 11, 12). When the Lamb opened the seventh seal, John saw the seven angels who stand before God (8:2). On this occasion another angel came and stood at the altar with a golden censor and he was given much incense to mingle with the prayers of all the saints upon the golden altar before the throne (vv. 3-5). In this manner angels share in bringing the prayers of the saints to God. John then noted that each of the seven angels blew his trumpet which brought about so many different judgments of God upon the earth and all the heavenly bodies (8:7 — 10:7). To the fifth of these angels was given the key of the shaft of the bottomless pit and when he opened this shaft, smoke like that of a great furnace rose up. From this smoke came locusts on the earth, and they were given power like that of scorpions. They were forbidden to harm those who had the seal of God upon their foreheads. When the sixth angel blew his trumpet, a voice commanded him to release the four angels who were bound at the great river Euphrates. These four angels had the charge to kill a third of mankind. This did not lead the rest of mankind to repent from their many sins or to stop worshiping demons, Satan, and all the diabolical and sinister forces of evil. The names Satan and the devil, as well as Antichrist, call for careful study.

b. Jesus' References to Satan

In response to Peter's confession that Jesus is the Holy One of God, Jesus said, "Did I not choose you, the twelve, and one of you is a devil?" (Jn. 6:70). He was thinking of Judas one of the Twelve who later betrayed Him. This statement implies the existence of many devils. The term *diabolos* means *slanderer, false accuser*. This exposed most pointedly the sinful character of Judas. To the Jews who refused to believe Jesus' teachings, Jesus declared, "You are of your father, the devil, and your will is to do your father's desires. He was a murderer from the beginning, and had nothing to do with the truth, because there is no truth in him. When he lies he speaks according to his own nature, for he is a liar and the father of lies" (Jn. 8:44). Just as believers in God are sons of God, in the same respect, they who refuse to believe in Jesus are sons of the devil. As Jesus was entering Jerusalem His soul was troubled by reason of the imminency of His death on the cross. The voice from heaven startled the crowd. In this setting Jesus said, "Now is the judgment of this world, now shall the ruler of this world be cast out; and I, when I am lifted up from the earth, will draw all men to myself" (12: 28-31). Most certainly, "the ruler of this world" is the devil. These words express the effect of Jesus' death and resurrection upon Satan. This leads us to reflect on the words of God to the serpent after Adam and Eve disobeyed Him when He said, "I will put enmity between you and the woman, and between your seed and her seed; she shall bruise your head, and you shall bruise his heel" (Gen. 3:15).

The manner of Satan's attack on mankind becomes evident in John's narrative in the words, "And during supper, when the devil had already put it into the heart of Judas Iscariot . . . to betray him" (Jn. 13:2). Later in the narrative John wrote that Satan entered into Judas. This confirms the personality of Satan, as well as his power to enter into a human being. In Jesus' upper-room conversation with the disciples He said, "The ruler of this world is coming. He has no power over me" (14:30). Jesus' last reference to Satan recorded in John's Gospel is most significant. Setting forth the work of the Holy Spirit, Jesus said that He would "convince the world of sin and of righteousness and of judgment . . . of judgment, because the ruler of this world is judged" (16:8-11). The use of the perfect tense (*is judged*) declares that Satan was already in a state of being judged. In this manner Jesus was declaring the effect of His death and resurrection upon the ruler of this world. This also implies the fulfillment of God's prediction to the serpent in Genesis 3:15. From the viewpoint of biblical theology we should note the fulfillment of God's prediction, especially as it relates to man's salvation in Christ Jesus.

c. John's References to Satan

In the First Letter of John the writer unfolds still further the references to Satan. He observes that it is the last hour and that his readers "have heard that antichrist is coming, so now many antichrists have come" (1 Jn. 2:18). He raises the question, "Who is the liar but he who denies that Jesus is the Christ?" At once John makes clear who this liar is: "This is the antichrist, he who denies the Father and the Son" (2:22). From this letter we gain the idea that the church was passing through a crisis centering in the rejection of Jesus' messiahship. Many had become lax in their manner of living. This led John to write, "He who commits sin is of the devil; for the devil has sinned from the beginning. The reason the Son of God appeared was to destroy the works of the devil. No one born of God commits sin; for God's nature abides in him, and he cannot sin because he is born of God. By this it may be seen who are the children of God, and who are the children of the devil" (3:8-10). Observe that John had laid hold of the reason for the appearance of the Son of God: "to destroy the works of the devil." The author made another observation in the words, "No one born of God commits sin; for God's nature abides in him, and he cannot sin because he is born of God. By this it may be seen who are the children of God, and who are the children of the devil . . . We should love one another, and not be like Cain who was of the evil one and murdered his brother" (vv. 9-12). John made still another comment which set forth the awful truth, "The whole world is in the power of the evil one" (5: 19). Still another observation stands forth in John's second letter: "For many deceivers have gone out into the world, men who do not acknowledge the coming of Jesus Christ in the flesh; such a one is the deceiver and the antichrist" (2 Jn. 7). Thus the forces of evil centering in the Antichrist brought on a real crisis in the church. It was on this account that John wrote so bluntly about the deceivers and the Antichrist.

d. The Revelation of Satan

While the last book of the New Testament is most assuredly the revelation of Jesus Christ, it is essential to observe that it is in a real way the revelation of Satan. To the angel of the church in Smyrna, Jesus Christ said, "I know your tribulation and your poverty (but you are rich) and the slander of those who say that they are Jews and are not, but are a synagogue of Satan. . . . The devil is about to throw some of you into prison, that you may be tested, and for ten days you will have tribulation" (Rev. 2:9, 10). Thus the unbelieving Jews by their rejection of Christ were in a most tragic manner a synagogue of Satan. Satan had taken over the sacred place of worship of the Jews. This became a real hazard to the church in Smyrna. It was the devil who was about to throw some of these Christians into prison. Thus the devil in a real way was a *slanderer* and a *false accuser*. The Lord Jesus spoke to the angel of the church in Pergamum in the words, "I know where you dwell, where Satan's throne is . . . where Satan dwells" (v. 13). While this verse presents some difficult problems of interpretation, definite reference is made to Satan's throne where he dwells. This church needed to be aware of this awful reality. Undoubtedly Satan has many thrones throughout the world. While our Lord Jesus Christ is in all truth the reigning Messiah, the slanderer and false accuser is doing all in his power to take over the kingship of this world.

Another key passage for this study is Revelation 12:7-9: "Now war arose in heaven, Michael and his angels fighting against the dragon; and the dragon and his angels fought, but they were defeated and there was no longer any place for them in heaven. And the great dragon was thrown down, that ancient serpent, who is called the Devil and Satan, the deceiver of the whole world — he was thrown down to the earth, and his angels were thrown down with him." With no desire to get into the difficult exegetical problems of these verses, it would seem that here we have a description of the conflict in heaven when the dragon, the ancient serpent, was thrown down from heaven and became the deceiver of the whole world. The temptation scene in the Garden of Eden appears to be reflected here, giving grounds for believing that the serpent who tempted our first parents was none less than the devil, Satan. From this we may gather that the devil was the angel who was thrown down out of heaven. This leads us to believe that all the forces of evil are under Satan's control.

Alone through the power of God can His people withstand the attacks of Satan and his forces. From a homiletic point of view this fact has had great significance for the children of God all through human history. The final reference to the devil stands forth in 20:1-10. Since this is a climactic portion near the close of this book, let us note that an angel coming down from heaven seized the dragon, the ancient serpent, who is the devil and Satan, and bound him. He was thrown into the pit for a thousand-year period, after which he was loosed from his prison and was allowed to gather all mankind for battle, "but fire came down from heaven and consumed them, and the devil who had deceived them was thrown into the lake of fire and brimstone where the beast and the false prophet were, and they will be tormented day and night for ever and ever" (vv. 8-10). Thus one of the profoundest truths of divine revelation predicts the final judgment and punishment of Satan and all who have served him. It should be observed that this archenemy of mankind is known as "the dragon, that ancient serpent, who is the devil and Satan." Let us gain from this discussion the most meaningful conclusion that Satan is under the power of the glorified Lord Jesus, who will in His own time throw him into the lake of fire and brimstone where he will be tormented day and night forever and ever.

10. Sin

John's presentation of Satan and the forces of evil naturally leads to his teachings on sin. Central to this study is what our Lord revealed concerning the nature of sin and His work of redemption from sin.

a. Jesus Affirmed His Sinlessness

This becomes evident not by direct assertions on the part of Jesus but rather through the undeniable implications of His statements. When the Jews were marveling at the words of Jesus, He said, "My teaching is not mine, but his who sent me; if any man's will is to do his will, he shall know whether the teaching is from God or whether I am speaking on my own authority" (Jn. 7:16, 17). In rebuttal to the Jews' attack on His integrity of character, Jesus said, "Because I tell the truth, you do not believe me. Which of you convicts me of sin? If I tell the truth, why do you not believe me?" (8:45, 46). On the occasion of Jesus' giving sight to a blind man on a Sabbath day some of the Pharisees gave the charge that Jesus was not from God because He did not keep the Sabbath. There were others who said, "How can a man who is a sinner do such signs?" (9:16). In this manner Jesus was giving grounds for believing in His own integrity of character. As the Pharisees continued to bring charges against Jesus for this miracle, the man with restored eyesight said, "We know that God does not listen to sinners, but if anyone is a worshiper of God and does his will, God listens to him. . . . If this man were not from God, he could do nothing" (vv. 31-33). Before Pilate, Jesus demonstrated His sinlessness which led the procurator to tell the Jews, "I find no crime in him" (18:38).

b. The Nature of Sin

As the opposition to Jesus became still more serious, He told the Jews, "Every one who commits sin is a slave to sin" (Jn. 8:34). As the Jews continued to accuse Jesus He added, "You are of your father, the devil, and your will is to do your father's desire. He was a murderer from the beginning, and has nothing to do with the truth, because there is no truth in him. When he lies, he speaks according to his own nature, for he is a liar and the father of lies" (v. 44). In these two statements Jesus was laying bare the real nature of sin. Thus a sinner does not have the inner power to free himself from sin. Only the Son is able to make a sinner free. The Jews were not willing to accept this explanation. In a real way the devil was their father. The real nature of sin becomes evident in its opposition to the truth. On this account every liar is a son of the devil. These words of Jesus certainly expose the gross error of the Pharisees' view of sin. To them, sin was simply the act of breaking the law.

Jesus gave another exposure of sin in His upper-room discourse (15:22-25). He said, "If I had not come and spoken to them, they would not have sin; but now they have no excuse for their sin. He who hates me hates my Father also. If I had not done among them the works no one else did, they would not have sin; but now they have seen and hated both me and my Father. It is to fulfill the word that is written in their law, 'They hated me without a cause.' " Jesus was teaching that the center of sin lies in a hatred of our Lord and of the Father.

In the First Letter of John, the apostle also made some significant statements as to the nature of sin. He wrote, "Every one who commits sin is guilty of lawlessness; sin is lawlessness" (1 Jn. 3:4). He added the explanation, "He who commits sin is of the devil; for the devil has sinned from the beginning. . . . No one born of God commits sin; for God's nature abides in him, and he cannot sin because he is born of God. By this it may be seen who are the children of God, and who are the children of the devil: whoever does not do right is not of God, nor he who does not love his brother" (vv. 8-10). These words give another aspect of sin's nature. It is a refusal to obey God's laws. God had revealed to Israel the antagonism between the sins of murder, adultery, stealing, bearing false witness, and covetousness as they stood opposed to His positive command, "Ye shall be holy; for I the Lord your God am holy" (Lev. 19:2). On this account all humanity is divided into two groups; children of God and children of the devil. In 5:16, 17 John made another distinction in which he set forth the nature of sin. He wrote, "If any one sees his brother committing what is not a mortal sin, he will ask, and God will give him life for those whose sin is not mortal. There is sin which is mortal; I do not say that one is to pray for that. All wrongdoing is sin, but there is sin which is not mortal." This statement presents a difficult exegetical problem centering in a distinction between a mortal sin and a sin which is not mortal. It may be that the Phillips translation leads to the correct understanding of John's statement, "If any of you should see his brother committing a sin (I don't mean deliberately turning his back on God and embracing evil), he should pray to God for him and secure fresh life for the sinner. It is possible to commit sin that is a deliberate embracing of evil and that leads to spiritual death — that is not the sort of sin I have in mind when I recommend prayer for the sinner. Every failure to obey God's laws is sin, of course, but there is sin that does not preclude repentance and forgiveness."

From the Book of Revelation we may gain a few additional insights as to the nature of sin. An angel said, "Fallen, fallen is Babylon the great, she who made all nations drink the wine of her impure passion" (14:8). The expression "impure passion" or as Phillips expresses it, "passionate unfaithfulness" sets forth in expressive language another aspect of sin's nature. This picture of sinfulness is enlarged in 18:1-8 where the sins of Babylon stand forth in the expression, "For her sins are heaped high as heaven." This statement is perhaps most climactic in setting forth the nature of sin.

c. All Have Sinned

In a portion of John's Gospel (7:53 — 8:11) not found in some of the oldest manuscripts we have these words, "And as they continued to ask him, he stood up and said to them, 'Let him who is without sin among you be the first to throw a stone at her.' " In this manner Jesus asserted that all mankind have sinned. John faced this issue definitely when he wrote, "If we say we have no sin, we deceive ourselves, and the truth is not in us. . . . If we say we have not sinned, we make him a liar, and his word is not in us" (1 Jn. 1:8, 10). This statement from the aged Apostle John is in direct harmony with all the Scriptures. From a certain point of view we may say that this is a conclusion he has drawn from the entire body of "the holy scriptures" (Rom. 1:2).

d. Sin Leads to Death

As Jesus continued to speak to the scribes and Pharisees He said, "I go away, and you will seek me and die in your sin. . . . I told you that you would die in your sins, for you will die in your sins unless you believe that I am he" (Jn. 8:21-24). This is in perfect harmony with the Garden of Eden scene where Adam and Eve were driven from the garden because they rejected God's command, "But of the tree of knowledge of good and evil you shall not eat, for in the day that you eat of it you shall die" (Gen. 2:17). All through human history mankind has sinned and on this account experienced death.

e. Deformity of the Body, Not the Result of Sin

It was a common belief among the Jews that sin was a cause of deformity of the body. This led Jesus' disciples to ask, "Who sinned, this man or his parents, that he was born blind?" Jesus answered, "It was not that this man sinned, or his parents, but that the works of God might be made manifest in him" (Jn. 9:2, 3). While it is certainly true that certain acts of sin may bring bodily deformity, the cause of this condition was not limited to some form of sin. In the above case and in many others the cause of such deformity was that "the works of God might be made manifest."

f. The Holy Spirit's Work in Relation to Sin

In explicit language Jesus declared, "It is to your advantage that I go away, for if I do not go away, the Counselor will not come to you; but if I go, I will send him to you. And when he comes, he will convince the world of sin and of righteousness and of judgment: of sin, because they do not believe in me; of righteousness, because I go to the Father, and you will see me no more; of judgment, because the ruler of this world is judged" (Jn. 16:7-11). Perhaps the most meaningful example of this took place on the day of Pentecost in which Peter explained the outpouring of the Holy Spirit upon the body of believers. When they heard Peter's message "they were cut to the heart, and said to Peter and the rest of the apostles, 'Brethren, what shall we do?' Peter said to them,'Repent, and be baptized every one of you in the name of Jesus Christ for the forgiveness of your sins; and you shall receive the gift of the Holy Spirit' " (Acts 2:37, 38). Peter had certainly laid hold of Jesus' teaching on the Holy Spirit's work in relation to sin.

g. Need for Forgiveness and Cleansing from Sin

When Jesus commissioned His disciples, He said to them, "Receive the Holy Spirit. If you forgive the sins of any, they are forgiven; if you retain the sins of any, they are retained" (Jn. 20:22, 23). In this manner Jesus asserted the need for forgiveness of sins. Given in the setting of the disciples being sent out on their mission of evangelism, this command shows how central to their commission was the proclamation involving the need for forgiveness of sins. John built on this theme in his first letter when he wrote, "The blood of Jesus, his Son cleanses us from all sin. . . . If we confess our sins he is faithful and just, and will forgive our sins and cleanse us from all unrighteousness" (1 Jn. 1:7-9). The author also noted, "Every one who thus hopes in him purifies himself as he is pure" (3:3). These words given in a setting describing our Lord's return become significant. Without question the greatest incentive for purifying oneself is the hope of seeing our Lord as He is.

h. Jesus' Expiation for Sin

John asserted this momentous truth in the words, "If any one does sin, we have an advocate with the Father, Jesus Christ the righteous; and he is the expiation for our sins, and not for ours only but also for the sins of the whole world" (1 Jn. 2:1, 2). Here John is speaking of Christ as our *Advocate (parakletos),* the title which Jesus had applied to the Holy Spirit. In this manner John is setting forth the present work of our Lord in His being our Advocate with the Father. John specifically declares that our Lord is the *expiation (hilasmos),* the most expressive word setting forth the meaning of Christ's death on the cross. John expressed this truth again in the words, "He appeared to take away sins" (3:5). All this manifested God's love for us in that He "sent his Son to be the expiation for our sins" (4:10). The Revelation to John also reflects this truth in the words, "Jesus Christ the faithful witness, the first-born of the dead" (Rev. 1:5).

i. Overcoming the Evil One

It is essential for Christians to realize the truth expressed in 1 John 2:13: "I am writing to you, young men . . . for you have overcome the evil one." This expression becomes all the more meaningful in view of another statement near the end of this letter where the author asserted, "The whole world is in the power of the evil one" (5:19). Second, it is alone by the power of God whereby we have overcome the evil one.

j. "No One Who Abides in Him Sins" (1 Jn. 3:6)

John intensified this truth in the words, "No one born of God commits sin; for God's nature abides in him, and he cannot sin because he is born of God" (v. 9). At first thought these words seem to contradict what John had expressed in 1:8, 10 referred to in my comments under letter "c." John's thought becomes clear when we observe his uses of the present tense in verses 6 and 9. John is saying that everyone who is abiding in Christ is not sinning, he does not sin habitually. Every one who is born of God is not committing sin. That is, the present tenses used in these verses express continuing acts of sinning or committing sin. The same truth stands out in 5:18 where John declares, "We know that any one born of God does not sin" that is, he is not living a life of sin.

k. One Who Commits Sin Is of the Devil (1 Jn. 3:8)

The use of the present participle *(poion)* expresses present and continuing acts of sin. John is reflecting on the words of Jesus when He spoke to the unbelieving Jews, the words, "You are of your father, the devil. . . . He was a murderer from the beginning, and has nothing to do with the truth, because there is no truth in him" (Jn. 8:44). It is significant that our Lord expressed so pointedly that sin has its source in the devil and that all who commit sin are actually of the devil. Thus there are two groups of human beings: those who are children of God and those who are children of the devil. It is alone by the power of God that mankind can be saved from a life of sin and from the power of the devil.

11. The Church

Since John wrote his Gospel near the end of the first century, the sections making general reference to the church may be a bit unexpected; nevertheless, his stated purpose of writing this book (20:31) gives sufficient grounds for the absence of any specific reference to the church. Numerous statements in his Gospel reflect or assume its existence. When John the Baptist spoke of Jesus as "the Lamb of God, who takes away the sin of the world" (1:29), we may assume that they whose sins would be taken away would become a body of believers separate from the Jews. This becomes clear when the Baptist was told that this person "is he who baptizes with the Holy Spirit" (v. 33). The apostle's reference to the first group of believers who responded to Jesus' invitation, "Follow me" (v. 43) reveals Jesus' objective of building up a great body of disciples. Naturally such a group would foster a spiritual fellowship centering in the Messiah. Jesus' activity in cleansing the temple during the Passover feast led many to believe in His name (2: 23). Jesus' conversation with Nicodemus unfolded the profound concept "of the kingdom of God" (3:3). They who enter the kingdom of God become members of this kingdom. Thus the body of believers constitutes all those who are under the rule of God. Only they who are born anew enter this kingdom. Jesus' discourse on the bread of life makes definite reference to those who believe in Christ in that they have eternal life. They "eat the flesh of the Son of man and drink his blood" (6:53). The Lord will raise them up the last day. All these statements and many more to which John draws attention, crystallize the concept of the church as the body of believers in Jesus Christ. This thought gains momentum in Jesus' good shepherd message in which He declared, "I am the good shepherd" (10:11), to which He adds, "My sheep hear my voice and I know them, and they follow me; and I give them eternal life" (vv. 27, 28). Thus the shepherd life of many of the Israelites served to lay the foundation for the concept of the church as being made up of the sheep of which Jesus is the Good Shepherd. The upper room discourses also contribute to the crystallizing of the church as composed of all who believe in Jesus Christ as Lord. Perhaps the most significant is Jesus' promise of giving His disciples another Counselor. This visualizes a continuing body of believers in whom the Holy Spirit will dwell. Since this Counselor will be with the body of believers forever, they had grounds for believing that the Old Testament predictions concerning God's outpouring of the Holy Spirit had begun to be fulfilled.

The First Letter of John was addressed to the believers with whom John was associated. From a spiritual point of view they were his little children (1 Jn. 2:1, 12, 18). While he did not use the term *church,* they composed the body of believers with whom he had fellowship, which included a close relationship "with the Father and with his Son Jesus Christ" (1:3). John wrote, "See what love the Father has given us, that we should be called the children of God; and so we are" (3:1). In this manner John expressed the oneness of these believers centering in their fellowship as children of God. Near the close of the letter John added the significant words, "And we know that the Son of God has come and has given us understanding, to know him who is true; and we are in him who is true, in his Son Jesus Christ" (5:20).

John directed his Second Letter to the "elect lady and her children" (v. 1). It appears evident that this is a figurative expression in which the author is addressing the church and her members. This interpretation gains support by observing that the Greek word for *church* is *ekklesia.* If this expresses the meaning of *elect lady,* the author is contributing definitely to the connotation of the *church.* The *elect lady* and her children constitute a family of believers which from the human point of view increases in numbers in geometric progression. Thus the church in the second half of the first century which numbered many thousands of believers has now grown to millions of God's children throughout the world.

We may infer that John's use of the word *elect (eklektos)* carries the same meaning given to it by Paul. I am not aware that John had any access to Paul's use of this word, but since it occurred in the Septuagint, we may infer that John attached the same meaning to it that Paul did. Thus the elect are the chosen people of God, and after Pentecost this was used with reference to all Christians.

In view of the absence of the word *church (ekklesia)* in John's Gospel and in his first and second letters, and also of its frequent occurrences in the Revelation, the author's uses of this word in his third letter is quite significant. John was commending Gaius for his service to the church, especially to strangers. These strangers gave witness to his love in the presence of the church. This suggests that the members of the church involved themselves in brotherly relations with strangers. The church was nevertheless facing some problems as they centered in Diotrephes who refused to acknowledge the authority of John the elder. He also refused to welcome the brethren and blocked those who did show this Christian hospitality. He even put them out of the church. From these references we should gather that the church in John's day was facing some real problems. The sinful nature of some professed Christians was continuing to manifest itself.

The Book of Revelation gives a graphic picture of the church near the close of the first century. While the interpretation of this Book presents some difficult problems, a great deal can be gleaned from it which for biblical theology purposes is instructive. They were experiencing the tribulation which the Lord Jesus had predicted. By reason of the God-fearing lives of these Christians, they were experiencing the opposition of the sinful world. This tribulation gave witness to the antagonism of the sinful world to the righteous and holy living of these Christians. From a biblical theology point of view this conflict of the church with the world possesses immeasurable value to the church until the return of our Lord for final judgment.

It is significant that an angel was given responsibility related to each of the churches. From a practical point of view the church of the twentieth century needs to recognize this truth. Every church could with profit face the question, What would the angels write to the churches of the twentieth century?

Reflecting on Psalm 41:2 John wrote of the heavenly beings who "fell down before the Lamb, each holding a harp, and with golden bowls full of incense, which are the prayers of the saints" (Rev. 5:8). In this manner the author was addressing the churches which were suffering under the severe persecution imposed by Domitian. Their prayers were as golden bowls full of incense which when burned gave a sweet odor unto the Lord. Christ had ransomed them for God and had "made them a kingdom and priests to our God, and they shall reign on earth" (vv. 9, 10). Just as Israel through the institution of the Sinaitic covenant became a kingdom of priests and a holy nation (Ex. 19:6) in like manner the church through the institution of the new covenant through the blood of Christ also became a kingdom and priests to God. Added to this declaration was the promise that "they shall reign on earth." These words of encouragement come to their climax in 20:6, "Blessed and holy is he who shares in the first resurrection! Over such the second death has no power, but they shall be priests of God and of Christ, and they shall reign with him a thousand years." These words of encouragement also come to a climax in the last chapter of the Revelation where the redeemed of this world will eat of the tree of life, shall see His face, and shall reign for ever and ever. Jesus had sent His angel with this testimony to the churches. These climactic words concerning the church are most inspiring. They show the significant place the church occupied in John's thinking. While he had not mentioned the church per se in his Gospel, he did write specifically, "that you may believe that Jesus is the Christ, the Son of God, and that believing you may have life in his name" (20:31).

John, to whom this revelation was given, brought its message to the saints in order that they might understand all that was involved in their persecutions. He noted that the beast "was allowed to make war on the saints and conquer them." After giving some additional comments on this war John concluded, "Here is a call for the endurance and faith of the saints" (13:7-10). Another note of encouragement to these saints stands forth in the words, "These are they who have come out of the great tribulation; they have washed their robes and made them white in the blood of the Lamb. Therefore are they before the throne of God. . . . They shall hunger no more, neither thirst any more. . . . For the Lamb in the midst of the throne will be their shepherd, and he will guide them to springs of living water; and God will wipe away every tear from their eyes" (7:14-17). The saints had the indescribable joy of hearing the words, " 'Hallelujah! For the Lord our God the Almighty reigns. Let us rejoice and exult and give him the glory, for the marriage of the Lamb has come, and his Bride has made herself ready; it was granted her to be clothed with fine linen, bright and pure' — for the fine linen is the righteous deeds of the saints" (19:6-8). In a most fitting manner John closed his message with the words, "The grace of the Lord Jesus be with all the saints. Amen" (22:21).

12. The Eternal Destiny of Man

It is remarkable the extent of details in which John set forth the eternal destiny of man. By reason of their significance I am presenting this theme under six headings.

a. The Conditions for Eternal Life

In a context where Jesus was speaking of the resurrection He said, "For as the Father raises the dead and gives them life, so also the Son gives life to whom he will. . . . I say to you, he who hears my word and believes him who sent me, has eternal life. . . . The hour is coming when all who are in the tombs will hear his voice and come forth, those who have done good, to the resurrection of life, and those who have done evil, to the resurrection of judgment" (Jn. 5:21-29). In a word, the condition for eternal life is believing in the Son of God. They who have done good will come forth to the resurrection of life. These words underlie John's major purpose in writing his Gospel (5:21-29; 20:30, 31). In a setting where the Jews were charging Jesus of having a demon, He responded, "I say to you, if any one keeps my word, he will never see death" (8:51). John himself expressed this truth in the words, "We know that we have passed out of death into life, because we love the brethren" (1 Jn. 3:14). Here our passing out of death into life has its basis in our love for the brethren — simple but expressive. Observe again the words to the angel of the church in Smyrna, "Be faithful unto death, and I will give you the crown of life. . . . He who conquers shall not be hurt by the second death" (Rev. 2: 10, 11). These simple and expressive statements set forth the condition for eternal life in language every Bible reader can understand.

b. The Resurrection

The Scripture underlying this truth has been noted above. Obviously all people are subject to death, but they who believe that God sent Christ into this world have eternal life. Only those who hear the voice of the Son of God will live. They alone will experience the resurrection of life. This great truth shines forth from Revelation 20 where John wrote, "I saw the souls of those who had been beheaded for their testimony to Jesus and for the word of God, and who had not worshiped the beast or its image and had not received its mark on their foreheads or their hands. They came to life, and reigned with Christ a thousand years. . . . This is the first resurrection. Blessed and holy is he who shares in the first resurrection! . . . Another book was opened, which is the book of life. And the dead were judged by what was written in the books, by what they had done.. . . All were judged by what they had done" (20:4-13). The entire human race is subject to death in view of the sins of all mankind. On this account the attainment of life eternal necessitates the resurrection and glorification of the body.

c. Jesus Has the Keys of Death and Hades

When Mary and Martha informed Jesus of Lazarus' illness, He said, "This illness is not unto death; it is for the glory of God, so that the Son of God may be glorified by means of it" (Jn. 11:4). To Martha He said, "I am the resurrection and the life; he who believes in me, though he die, yet shall he live, and whoever lives and believes in me shall never die" (vv. 25, 26). To John the glorified Lord Jesus said, "I am the first and the last, and the living one; I died, and behold I am alive forever more, and I have the keys of death and Hades" (Rev. 1:18). When Jesus raised Lazarus to life, He gave adequate proof that He has the keys of death and Hades. This grand truth stands forth in Paul's letters with inexpressible grandeur. (See 1 Thes. 4:13-18; 1 Cor. 15:12-57; and others.) Thus the eternal destiny of man is in the hands of the Lord Jesus Christ.

d. The Harvest at the End of the World

In his first letter John wrote these words of encouragement to the church, "God is love, and he who abides in love abides in God, and

God abides in him. In this is love perfected with us, that we may have confidence for the day of judgment, because as he is so are we in this world. There is no fear in love, but perfect love casts out fear. For fear has to do with punishment, and he who fears is not perfected in love" (1 Jn. 4:16-18). In this message the apostle was giving assurance to his readers that perfect love casts out fear which centers in the day of judgment. To John was revealed the judgment of the world. Repeatedly this awful judgment is described in Revelation.[21] Descriptive language of this final judgment stands forth in such statements as, "For the great day of their wrath has come, and who can stand before it?" "The nations raged, but thy wrath came, and the time for the dead to be judged, for rewarding thy servants, the prophets and saints, and those who fear thy name, both small and great, and for destroying the destroyers of the earth." "The angel swung his sickle on the earth and gathered the vintage of the earth, and threw it into the great wine press of the wrath of God." "I saw the dead, great and small, standing before the throne, and books were opened. Also another book was opened, which is the book of life. And the dead were judged by what was written in the books, by what they had done. . . . Then Death and Hades were thrown into the lake of fire. This is the second death, the lake of fire; and if any one's name was not found written in the book of life, he was thrown into the lake of fire." These quotations selected from the references above certainly depict the awful judgment of the wicked who are doomed to be thrown into the lake of fire, but the righteous "shall see his face." They shall eat of the tree of life and live forever in the glories of heaven.

e. The Eternal State of the Righteous

This blessed hope already introduced in the preceding section envisions the most soul thrilling anticipation in the Revelation.[22] Observe some of the precious gems from these pictures of heaven: "The Lamb in the midst of the throne will be their shepherd, and will guide them to springs of living water." "The voice I heard was like the sound of harpers playing on their harps, and they sing a new song before the throne." "They sing the song of Moses, the servant of God, and the song of the Lamb, saying, 'Great and wonderful are thy deeds, O Lord God the Almighty! Just and true are thy ways, O King of the ages!' " "I heard what seemed to be the voice of a great multitude, like the sound of many waters and like the sound of many thunderpeals, crying, 'Hallelujah! For the Lord our God the Almighty reigns. Let us rejoice and exult and give him the glory, for the marriage of the Lamb has come, and his Bride has made herself ready; it was granted her to be clothed with fine linen, bright and pure.' " "Behold, the dwelling of God is with men. He will dwell with them, and they shall be his people, and God himself will be with them; he will wipe away every tear from their eyes, and death shall be no more, neither shall there be mourning nor crying nor pain any more, for the former things have passed away." "He showed me the river of the water of life, bright as crystal, flowing from the throne of God and of the Lamb . . . the tree of life. . . . They shall see his face, and his name shall be on their foreheads." "Blessed are those who wash their robes, that they may have the right to the tree of life and that they may enter the city by the gates." What more sublime pictures of heaven and the redeemed could be revealed to us!

13. John's Use of the Scriptures

a. John's Testimony to His Own Writings

The prologue to his Gospel (1:1-18) gives the foundation for his Gospel. This prologue leads us to grasp the central message which he presented. Without question it gives John's testimony to the Word who "became flesh and dwelt among us full of grace and truth; we have beheld his glory, glory as of the only Son from the Father" (v. 14). As we read his Gospel it becomes increasingly evident that this prologue is the foundation of his entire book. His final testimony to this becomes evident in the words, "These are written that you may believe that Jesus is the Christ, the Son of God, and that believing you may have life in his name" (20:31).

His letters in a general way give a similar testimony. Observe some of his statements: "We are writing this that our joy may be complete" (1 Jn. 1:4). Repeatedly throughout his first letter he introduces his reasons for writing in such language as: "That you may not sin." "Because your sins are forgiven for his sake." "That you may know that you have eternal life." In his third letter he declares that he has written something to the church but that Diotrephes does not acknowledge his authority.

In the Revelation to John we may observe a different pattern of structure. This becomes evident in the opening verses where the content of the book is set forth as "the revelation of Jesus Christ, which God gave him to show to his servants what must soon take place." The recording in chapters 4-22 of things shown and seen follows a different literary pattern from that of words spoken and heard in the messages to the angels of the seven churches, chapters 1-3. From this point of view chapters 4-22 are not the product of John's thinking. It is clear, nevertheless, that John states what he saw and heard. In pursuing this inquiry let us note the words, "And he who sat upon the throne said, 'Behold, I make all things new.' Also he said, 'Write this, for these words are trustworthy and true' " (21:5). In the last chapter of the revelation we have these words, "Blessed is he who keeps the words of the prophecy of this book. I John am he who heard and saw these things" (22:7, 8). A final pertinent exhortation stands forth in the words, "I warn every one who hears the words of the prophecy of this book: if any one adds to them, God will add to him the plagues described in this book, and if any one takes away from the words of the book of this prophecy, God will take away his share in the tree of life and in the holy city, which are described in this book" (22:18, 19). All of this testimony is foundational to our understanding John's attitude toward his writing, especially from his viewpoint of its bearing on the rise of a new body of writings which soon became known as the New Testament. As I have noted repeatedly throughout this book, it is essential for us to grasp the grounds for believing that there is a new covenant body of writings which from the point of view of origin and authority constitute Holy Scriptures on the same level as the Old Testament.

b. John's Use of the Old Testament in His Gospel

John records the answer of John the Baptist to the priests and the Levites who asked him who he is. He said, "I am the voice of one crying in the wilderness, 'Make straight the way of the Lord' as the prophet Isaiah said" (Jn. 1:23). This quotation from Isaiah 40:3 illustrates the use of the Old Testament during the time of the Baptist and later. When Jesus drove from the temple those who were offering animals for sacrifice, His disciples remembered that it was written, "Zeal for thy house will consume me" (2:17). The perfect passive form of the verb *it was written* was the common way of referring to some portion of the Old Testament which had come to be regarded as the Holy Scriptures. When the Jews were questioning Jesus with regard to a sign or a work which would prove that God had sent Him, they added, "Our fathers ate the manna in the wilderness; as it is written 'He gave them bread from heaven to eat' " (6:30, 31). This expresses again the common connotation of the perfect passive tense of the verb used here. On the occasion of Jesus' triumphal entry into Jerusalem, He found a young ass and sat upon it. John added, "As it is written," and in this manner linking a detail of Jesus' life with the Old Testament (Zech. 9:9). Later John noted also that the disciples remembered that Zechariah had written this concerning the Messiah. John made another comment which shows his use of the Old Testament: "Though he had done so many signs before them, yet they did not believe in him; it was that the word spoken by the prophet Isaiah might be fulfilled: 'Lord, who has believed our report, and to whom has the arm of the Lord been revealed?' Therefore they could not believe. For Isaiah again said, 'He has blinded their eyes and hardened their heart, lest they should see with their eyes and perceive with their heart, and turn for me to heal them.' Isaiah said this because he saw his glory and spoke of him" (Jn. 12:37-41). Certainly the Old Testament was John's Bible. Note also his references to the Old Testament in 19:24, 28, 36, 37.

Let us observe also how John refers to Jesus' quotations from the Old Testament. Jesus told Nicodemus, "Truly, truly, I say to you, you will see heaven opened, and the angels of God ascending and descending upon the Son of man" (1:51). By implication Jesus was asserting that He would have an experience similar to that of Jacob in the Old Testament (Gen. 28:12). It was significant that Jesus should link His experiences with similar ones found in the Old Testament. By implication Jesus was asserting that the Old Testament record was authentic, even predictive. On the occasion of Jesus feeding the five thousand He responded to the murmuring Jews in the words, "No one can come to me unless the Father who sent me draw him; and I will raise him up at the last day. It is written in the prophets, 'They shall all be taught by God, Every one who has heard and learned from the Father comes to me" (6:44, 45). In this manner Jesus gave support to His profound teaching. The prophetic books of the Old Testament predicted the work of the Messiah, but Jesus' hearers could not withstand these quotations from the Old Testament which supported His mission.

John listed several other quotations of Jesus, all of which deserve careful study (10:34, 35; 12:27; 13:18; 15:25; 16:22). While several of these references do not specifically state that Jesus is quoting the Old Testament, a careful study of them will confirm the Old Testament basis of Jesus' teaching. For my present purpose, perhaps, the most significant statement in these passages is found in 10:35 where Jesus made the parenthetic statement, "And Scripture cannot be broken." The late B. B. Warfield discussed this passage at length in order to show how far the supreme trustworthiness of Scripture extends.[23] Significant for my purpose are his words, "What we have here is, therefore, the strongest possible assertion of the indefectible authority of Scripture; precisely what is true of Scripture is that it "cannot be broken.' Now, what is the particular thing in Scripture, for the confirmation of which the indefectible authority of Scripture is thus invoked? It is one of its most casual clauses — more than that, the very form of its expression in one of its most casual clauses. This means, of course, that in the Savior's view the indefectible authority of Scripture attaches to the very form of expression of its most casual clauses. It belongs to Scripture through and through, down to its most minute particulars, that it is of indefectible authority."

c. The Use of the Old Testament by the Author of the Revelation

The apocalyptic nature of the Revelation presents some data which have a vital bearing on the author's use of the Old Testament. On the one side there is the absence of any direct quotation from the Old Testament but on the other side there are no less than 348 allusions to or citations from the Old Testament. It soon becomes evident that none of these allusions to the Old Testament are given as proof texts of what is unfolded in this book. This fact has some bearing on integrating the New Testament with the Old. In the large, this factor ties the New and the Old Testaments into one prophetic system.[24]

The use of Old Testament quotations in the Revelation may be summarized as follows:

(1) The Revelation to John marks the capsheaf of God's revelation to man. There are no areas of prediction which remain to be disclosed. Our Lord said, "Surely I am coming soon" (22:20).

(2) In the most unique and profound manner this book demonstrates the grand unity of God's revelation in the Bible. If this were not true, the hundreds of allusions to or citations from the Old Testament would stand as evidence that such unity does not exist.

(3) Central to this unity is the revelation of God and the enthroned Jesus Christ. This aspect of unity stands at the very center of Christian theism and also of Christian faith.

(4) God through the Lord Jesus Christ is directing the course of history in the present age in the same manner as He did throughout Old Testament history. The Revelation to John sets forth God's revelation in history in the most graphic manner.

(5) Just as the Old Testament history moved forward to the day of the Lord, in like manner the Revelation maps the course of history to the final day of judgment. In a word, these five points give support to the grand unity of the entire Bible. The roots of the Revelation to John are grounded in the Old Testament.

For Additional Reading and Reference:

Bernard, *The Progress of Doctrine in the New Testament*, pp. 181-208.
Beyschlag, *New Testament Theology*, Vol. II, pp. 347-473.
Bruce, F. F., *New Testament Development of Old Testament Themes*, pp. 40-50.
Bultmann, *The Theology of the New Testament*, Vol. II, pp. 3-92.

Hunter, *Introducing New Testament Theology*, pp. 125-151.
Morris, *The Cross in the New Testament*, pp. 144-179, 338-363.
Newman, *The Meaning of the New Testament*, pp. 283-286, 290-297.
Ryrie, *Biblical Theology of the New Testament*, pp. 301-363.
Sheldon, *New Testament Theology*, pp. 300-360.
Stevens, *The Theology of the New Testament*, pp. 167-244, 527-592.
Stevens, *The Johannine Theology*.
Taylor, *The Atonement in New Testament Teaching*, pp. 34-43, 130-161.
Taylor, *The Person of Christ*, pp. 17-21, 99-128, 138-142.
Van Oosterzee, *The Theology of the New Testament*, pp. 112-153, 328-356.
Weidner, *Biblical Theology of the New Testament*, Vol. I, pp. 124-146; Vol. II, pp. 231-331.
Weiss, *Biblical Theology of the New Testament*, Vol. II, pp. 248-283, 311-421.

1. Charles R. Erdman, *The Gospel of John* (Philadelphia: Westminster Press, 1920), p. 15.
2. Robertson, *op. cit.*, Vol. V. pp. XXI, XXII.
3. *Baker's Dictionary of Theology* (Grand Rapids: Baker Book House, 1960), article, "Logos." p. 328.
4. See comprehensive Greek lexicons such as Thayers, Moulton & Milligan, Arndt & Gingrich, and theological dictionaries.
5. See also Jn. 4:54; 6:2, 14, 26; 7:31; 9:16; 11:47; 12:18, 37.
6. *Thayer's Greek-English Lexicon*, p. 573.
7. *A Theological Word Book of the Bible* (New York: The Macmillan Co., 1965), p. 153.
8. *New Testament Commentary* (Grand Rapids: Baker Book House, 1963), Vol. I, p. 90.
9. Rev. 1:13; 14:14; See also 3:14; 4:2, 3; 5:1, 7, 13.
10. Jn. 1:17; 1 Jn. 1:3; 2:1; 3:23; 4:2; 5:6, 20; 2 Jn. 3, 7; Rev. 1:2, 5.
11. Ps. 2:2-7; 45:3-7; 89:24-34; 110:1-5; 132:11, 12.
12. Is. 7:14; 9:6, 7; 11:1-10; 32:1-8; Jer. 23:5, 6; 31:31-34; Ezek. 34:23-25; Dan. 9:25, 26; Hab. 3:13.
13. See Greek lexicons and theological word books. Note especially Richardson's work, *op. cit.*, pp. 269, 270.
14. John R. W. Stott, *The Epistles of John, The Tyndale New Testament Commentaries* (Grand Rapids: Wm. B. Eerdmans Publishing Co., 1964), Vol. 19, pp. 176-179.
15. Robertson, *op. cit.*, Vol. 5, p. 89.
16. Rudolf Bultmann, *Theological Dictionary of the New Testament*. Edited by Gerhard Kittel (Grand Rapids: Wm. B. Eerdmans Publishing Co., 1964) Vol. 1, p. 247.
17. See also 1 Jn. 1:4, 21, 22; 3:18, 19; 4:6; 2 Jn. 1:4; 3 Jn. 1, 3, 8.
18. Westcott, *The Gospel According to St. John* (Grand Rapids: Wm. B. Eerdmans Publishing Co., 1954), Vol. II, p. 177.
19. Robertson, *op. cit.*, Vol. V, p. 252.
20. Swete, *The Apocalypse of St. John* (Grand Rapids: Wm. B. Eerdmans Publishing Co., 1908), p. 13. See also p. 67.
21. Rev. 6:16, 17; 11:18; 14:14-20; 15:1, 5-8; 16:1-21; 17:1-18; 18:1-24; 19:11-21; 20:11-15.
22. Rev. 6:9-11; 7:14-17; 12:10-12; 14:1-5, 13; 15:2-4; 19:4-9; 21:3, 4; 22.
23. *The Inspiration and Authority of the Bible* (Philadelphia: The Presbyterian and Reformed Publishing Co., 1948), pp. 138-166.
24. For a splendid presentation of the Old Testament background of Revelation see *Interpreting Revelation* by Merrill C. Tenney, Chapter 11; also *The Apocalypse of Saint John* by Henry Barclay Swete, Chapter 13.

EPILOGUE

A number of concluding thoughts may have value for this treatment of biblical theology.

1. I trust that the genius of biblical theology has been made clear in this treatment.

2. What a marvelous divine Revelation is embodied in both the Old and New Testaments!

3. The preeminence of eschatology stands forth in great clarity, having its beginning in Genesis and unfolding throughout the Bible to the last chapter of Revelation.

4. The organic unity, growth, and progress of divine Revelation should now be evident.

5. The unfolding Revelation centers in Jesus Christ, the Son of God.

6. The disclosure of the triune God is most marvelous.

7. This unfolding Revelation of God leads the reader to comprehend the truths bound up in the inspired Word of God. Most certainly men moved by the Holy Spirit spoke from God.

8. The practical emphases centering in salvation, holy living, and the Christian life are very apparent.

9. The profound truths embodied in grace, love, peace, mercy, and truth are everywhere apparent.

10. Truly the Bible constitutes the Sacred Writings and the Holy Scriptures.

11. Alone in the Holy Scriptures do we find predictive prophecy.

12. The letter to the Hebrews exemplifies the legitimate use of the Old Testament not only in terms of the fulfillment in the New but also as giving the foundation for interpreting the New Testament.

13. The quotation of Hebrews 1:1, with which I began my treatment of *Old Testament Biblical Theology*, Vol. I, may well be used in bringing this biblical theology of the New Testament to a close.

"In many and various ways God spoke of old to our fathers by the prophets; but in these last days he has spoken to us by a Son, whom he appointed the heir of all things, through whom also he created the world" (Heb. 1:1).

SELECTED BIBLIOGRAPHY

I. GENERAL WORKS

Allmen, J. J. von, *A Companion to the Bible* (New York: Oxford University Press, 1958).

Bernard, Thomas Dehany, *The Progress of Doctrine in the New Testament* (New York: The Macmillan Co., 1900) I, II.

Beyschlag, Dr. Willibald, *New Testament Theology* (Edinburgh: T. & T. Clark, 38 George Street, 1895).

Bowman, John Wick, *Prophetic Realism and the Gospel* (Philadelphia: Westminster Press, 1955).

Bultmann, Rudolf, *Theology of the New Testament,* I, II (Charles Scribner's Sons, 1951).

Burrows, Millar, *An Outline of Biblical Theology* (Philadelphia: The Westminster Press, 1946).

Conzelmann, Hans, *An Outline of the Theology of the New Testament* (New York and Evanston: Harper & Row, Publishers, 1968).

————, *The Theology of St. Luke* (New York: Harper & Brothers, 1960).

Hunter, Archibald M., *Introducing New Testament Theology* (Philadelphia: Westminster Press, 1957).

Jeremias, Joachim, *New Testament Theology* (New York: Charles Scribner's Sons, 1971).

Richardson, Alan, *An Introduction to the Theology of the New Testament* (New York: Harper & Brothers, 1958).

Ridderbos, Herman N., *When the Time Had Fully Come* (Grand Rapids: Wm. B. Eerdmans Publishing Co., 1957).

Ryrie, Charles Caldwell, *Biblical Theology of the New Testament* (Chicago: Moody Press, 1959).

Sheldon, Henry C., *New Testament Theology* (New York: The Macmillan Company, 1911).

Stagg, Frank, *New Testament Theology* (Nashville: Broadman Press, 1962).

Stauffer, Ethelbert, *New Testament Theology* (New York: The Macmillan Company, 1956).

Stevens, George Barker, *The Theology of the New Testament* (Edinburgh: T. & T. Clark, 38 George Street, 1901).

Van Oosterzee, J. J., The Theology of the New Testament (London: Hodder and Stroughton, 1867).

Vos, Geerhardus, *Biblical Theology — Old and New Testaments* (Grand Rapids: Wm. B. Eerdmans Publishing Co., 1948).

Weidner, Revere Franklin, *Biblical Theology of the New Testament,* I, II (New York, Chicago: Fleming H. Revell Company, 1891).

Weiss, Bernhard, *Biblical Theology of the New Testament,* I, II (Edinburgh: T. & T. Clark, 38 George Street, 1885).

Studies in Biblical Theology, 1-34 (Naperville, Ill: Alec R. Allenson, Inc., 1962).

II. JESUS AS CHRIST AND LORD

Barclay, William, *Jesus As They Saw Him* (New York: Harper and Row, 1962).

———, *The Mind of Jesus* (New York: Harper & Row, 1961).

Braaten, Carl E., and Roy A. Harrisville, *The Historical Jesus and the Kerygmatic Christ* (Nashville: Abingdon Press, 1964).

Bornkamm, Gunther, *Jesus of Nazareth* (New York and Evanston: (Harper & Row, 1817, Translated, 3rd. edition, 1959).

Bultmann, Rudolf, *Jesus Christ and Mythology* (New York: Charles Scribner's Sons, 1958).

Cullman, Oscar, *The Christology of the New Testament* (Philadelphia: Westminster Press, 1959).

Dibelius, Martin, *Jesus* (Philadelphia: Westminster Press, 1949).

Filson, Floyd V., *Jesus Christ the Risen Lord* (New York and Nashville: Abingdon Press, 1946).

Heim, Karl, *Jesus the Lord* (Philadelphia: Muhlenberg Press, 1961).

Henry, Carl F. H., *Jesus of Nazareth: Saviour and Lord* (Grand Rapids: William B. Eerdmans Publishing Co., 1966).

Hunter, Archibald M., *The Work and Words of Jesus* (Philadelphia: Westminster Press, 1950).

Künneth, Walter, *The Theology of the Resurrection* (St. Louis: Concordia Publishing House, 1951).

III. THE TEACHINGS OF JESUS

Baird, J. Arthur, *The Justice of God in the Teachings of Jesus* (Philadelphia: Westminster Press, 1963).

Morgan, G. Campbell, *The Teaching of Christ* (New York: Fleming H. Revell Company, 1913).

Morris, Leon, *The Cross in the New Testament* (Grand Rapids: William B. Eerdmans Publishing Co., 1965).

Paul, Leslie, *Son of Man* (New York: E. P. Dutton & Co., Inc., 1961).

Perrin, Norman, *Rediscovering the Teaching of Jesus* (New York and Evanston: Harper & Row, 1967)

Stonehouse, Ned Bernard, *The Witness of Matthew and Mark to Christ* (Philadelphia: The Presbyterian Guardian, 1944).

Strawson, William, *Jesus and the Future Life* (Philadelphia: Westminster Press, 1959).

Taylor, Vincent, *The Person of Christ in New Testament Teaching* (New York: St. Martin's Press, Macmillan & Co., Ltd., 1958).

Tenney, Merrill C., *The Genius of the Gospels* (Grand Rapids: Wm. B. Eerdmans Publishing Co., 1951).

Todt, Heinz Eduard, *The Son of Man in the Synoptic Tradition* (Philadelphia: Westminster Press, 1965).

Vos, Geerhardus, *The Self-Disclosure of Jesus* (Grand Rapids: Wm. B. Eerdmans Publishing Co., 1954).

IV. THE KINGDOM OF GOD

Bright, John, *The Kingdom of God* (New York and Nashville: Abingdon-Cokesbury Press, 1953).

Bruce, Alexander Balmain, *The Kingdom of God* (New York: Charles Scribner's Sons, 1896).

Hunter, Archibald M., *Interpreting the Parables* Philadelphia: Westminster Press, 1960).

Ladd, George E., *Crucial Questions about the Kingdom of God* (Grand Rapids: Wm. B. Eerdmans Publishing Co., 1952).

Ladd, George Eldon, *Jesus and the Kingdom* (New York: Harper and Row, 1952).

Lundstrom, Costa, *The Kingdom of God in the Teaching of Jesus* (Richmond: John Knox Press, 1963).

Perrin, Norman, *The Kingdom of God in the Teaching of Jesus* (Philadelphia: Westminster Press, 1963).

Ridderbos, Herman, *The Coming of the Kingdom* (Philadelphia: The Presbyterian and Reformed Publishing House, 1962).

Robertson, Archibald, *Regnum Dei* (London: Methuen & Co., 1901).

Vos, Geerhardus, *The Kingdom and the Church* (Grand Rapids: Wm. B. Eerdmans Publishing Co., 1951).

V. THE THEOLOGY OF PAUL

Bruce, Alexander Balmain, *St. Paul's Conception of Christianity* (New York: Charles Scribner's Sons, 1894).

Ellis, E. Earle, *Paul's Use of the Old Testament* (Grand Rapids: Wm. B. Eerdmans Publishing Co., 1957).

Furnish, Victor Paul, *Theology and Ethics in Paul* (Nashville and New York: Abingdon Press, 1968).

Hunter, Archibald M., *Interpreting Paul's Gospel* (Philadelphia: Westminster Press, 1954).

Longenecker, Richard N., *Paul: Apostle of Liberty* (New York, Evanston, and London: Harper & Row, 1964).

Matheson, George, *Spiritual Development of St. Paul* (New York: Anson D. F. Randolph and Co., 1894).

Rall, Harris Franklin, *According to Paul* (New York: Charles Scribner's Sons, 1954).

Schoeps, H. J., *Paul* (Philadelphia: Westminster Press, 1961).

Scott, Charles A. Anderson, *Christianity According to St. Paul* (Cambridge: University Press, 1961).

Stevens, George B., *The Pauline Theology* (New York: Charles Scribner's Sons, 1897).

Stewart, James S., *A Man in Christ* (New York and London: Harper and Brothers).

Vos, Geerhardus, *The Pauline Eschatology* (Princeton: University Press, 1930).

Wahlstrom, Eric H., *The New Life in Christ* (Philadelphia: Muhlenberg Press, 1950).

Whiteley, D. E. H., *The Theology of St. Paul* (Philadelphia: Fortress Press, 1964).

VI. THE THEOLOGY OF THE LETTER TO THE HEBREWS AND OF JOHN

Stevens, George B., *The Johannine Theology* (London: Richard D. Dickinson, 1894).
Vos, Geerhardus, *The Teaching of the Epistle to the Hebrews* (Grand Rapids: Wm. B. Eerdmans Publishing Co., 1956).

VII. MONOGRAPHS

Barr, James, *Old and New in Interpretation* (New York: Harper and Row, 1966).
Bruce, F. F., *The New Testament Development of Old Testament Themes* (Grand Rapids: Wm. B. Eerdmans Co., 1968).
Cullman, Oscar, *Studies in Early Christian History and Theology* (Philadelphia: Westminster Press, 1956).
Dodd, C. H., *According to the Scriptures* (London: Nisbit & Co., Ltd., 22 Berners Street, W. 1, 1953).
Filson, Floyd V., *Christ and Time* (Philadelphia: Westminster Press, 1950).
Hunter, Archibald M., *Paul and His Predecessors* (Philadelphia: Westminster Press, 1961).
Lindars, Barnabas, *New Testament Apologetic* (Philadelphia: Westminster Press, 1961).
Moody, Dale, *Spirit of the Living God* (Philadelphia: Westminster Press, 1968).
Newman, Barclay M., *The Meaning of the New Testament* (Nashville: Broadman Press, 1966).
Ogden, Schubert M., *Christ Without Myth* (New York: Harper & Bros., 1961).
Smart, James D., *The Interpretation of Scripture* (Philadelphia: Westminster Press, 1961).
Taylor, Vincent, *The Atonement in New Testament Teaching* (London: Epworth Press, 1954).
Throckmorton, Jr., Burton H., *The New Testament and Mythology*, Philadelphia: Westminster Press, 1959).
Wahlstrom, Eric H., *God Who Redeems* (Philadelphia: Muhlenberg Press, 1962).
Wright, G. Ernest, *The Rule of God* (Garden City, New York: Doubleday & Company, Inc., 1960).

VIII. BIBLE DICTIONARIES AND ENCYCLOPEDIAS

A Dictionary of the Bible, James Hastings, Ed. (New York: Charles Scribner's Sons, 1905).
Dictionary of the Bible, James Hastings, Ed.; Frederick C. Grant and H. H. Rowley; Rev. Ed. (New York: Charles Scribner's Sons, 1963).
Miller, Madeline S. and J. Lane, *Harper's Bbile Dictionary*, Haprer and Row, New York, Evanston, San Francisco, London.

The International Standard Bible Encyclopaedia, James Orr, Gen. Ed., Melvin Grove Kyle; Rev. Ed. (Chicago: The Howard-Severance Company, 1930).

The Interpreter's Dictionary of the Bible, George Arthur Buttrick, Ed. (New York: Abingdon Press, 1962).

The New Bible Dictionary, J. D. Douglas, Ed. (Grand Rapids: Wm. B. Eerdmans Publishing Co., 1962).

The Westminster Dictionary of the Bible, John D. Davis and Henry Snyder Gehman (Philadelphia: Westminster Press, 1944).

IX. THEOLOGICAL WORD STUDIES

A Companion to the Bible, J. J. von Allmen, (New York: Oxford University Press, 1958).

Baker's Dictionary of Theology, Everett F. Harrison, Ed., (Grand Rapids: Baker Book House, 1960).

Biblico Theological Lexicon of New Testament Greek, Hermann Cremer (Edinburgh: T. & T. Clark, 1954).

Theological Dictionary of the New Testament, I-VIII, Gerhard Kittel and Gerhard Friedrich, Editors (Grand Rapids: Wm. B. Eerdmans Publishing Co., 1963-1972).

X. BIBLE COMMENTARIES

Anchor Bible, The, William Foxwell Albright and David Noel Freedman, Gen. Editors (Garden City: Doubleday Company, Inc., 1971).

Harper's New Testament Commentary, C. F. D. Moule (New York and Evanston: Harper & Row, 1962).

Interpreter's Bible VII-XII, The, George Arthur Buttrick, Commentary Editor; Walter Russell Bowie, Association Editor of Exposition; Paul Scherer, Associate Editor of Exposition; John Knox, Associate Editor of New Testament Introduction and Exegesis; Nolan B. Harmon, Ed. See general articles on the New Testament and each of its books for articles or sections dealing with theological content (New York: Abingdon-Cokesbury Press, 1952).

Interpretation of Matthew-Revelation, 11 vols., R. C. H. Lenski (Columbus: Wartburg Press, 1943).

New International Commentary on the New Testament, The, F. F. Bruce, Editor (Grand Rapids: Wm. B. Eerdmans Publishing Co., 1971).

Tyndale Bible Commentaries, 1-20, R. V. G. Tasker, General Editor (Grand Rapids: Wm. B. Eerdmans Publishing Co., 1961).

Wesleyan Bible Commentary, The, IV-VI, Charles W. Carter, General Editor; Ralph Earle, New Testament Editor. (Grand Rapids: Wm. B. Eerdmans Publishing Co., 1964).

INDEX OF BIBLICAL PASSAGES

GALATIANS

EPHESIANS

PHILIPPIANS

COLOSSIANS

JAMES

1 PETER

INDEX OF SUBJECTS